Time Out

Moscow
& St Petersburg

Penguin Books

PENGUIN BOOKS

Published by the Penguin Group
Penguin Books Ltd, 27 Wrights Lane, London W8 5TZ, England
Penguin Putnam Inc., 375 Hudson Street, New York, New York 10014, USA
Penguin Books Australia Ltd, Ringwood, Victoria, Australia
Penguin Books Canada Ltd, 10 Alcorn Avenue, Toronto, Ontario, Canada M4V 3B2
Penguin Books (NZ) Ltd, 182-190 Wairau Road, Auckland 10, New Zealand

Penguin Books Ltd, Registered Offices: Harmondsworth, Middlesex, England

First published 1999
10 9 8 7 6 5 4 3 2 1

Colour reprographics by Precise Litho, 34-35 Great Sutton Street, London EC1
Printed and bound by William Clowes Ltd, Beccles, Suffolk NR34 9QE

Edited and designed by

Time Out Guides Limited
Universal House
251 Tottenham Court Road
London W1P 0AB
Tel +44 (0) 171 813 3000
Fax +44 (0) 171 813 6001
E-mail guides@timeout.com
http://www.timeout.com

Editorial

Editorial Director Peter Fiennes
Editor John O'Mahony
Deputy Editor Angela Jameson
Project Co-ordinator Ruth Jarvis
Consultant Editor Leonid Ragozin
Listings Researcher Lena Levoshitz
Proofreader Tamsin Shelton
Indexer Douglas Matthews

Design

Art Director John Oakey
Art Editor Mandy Martin
Designers Benjamin de Lotz, Lucy Grant, Scott Moore
Scanner Operator Chris Quinn
Advertisement Make-up Paul Mansfield
Picture Editor Kerri Miles
Picture Researcher Kit Burnet

Advertising

Group Advertisement Director Lesley Gill
Sales Director Mark Phillips
Advertisement Sales Masha Mombelli
Advertising Assistant Ingrid Sigerson

Administration

Publisher Tony Elliott
Managing Director Mike Hardwick
Financial Director Kevin Ellis
Marketing Director Gillian Auld
General Manager Nichola Coulthard
Production Manager Mark Lamond
Production Controller Matthew Forrester
Accountant Catherine Bowen

Features in this guide were written and researched by:

MOSCOW Introduction Owen Matthews. **Moscow by Season** Ben Aris. **History** John O'Mahony. **Moscow Today** David Filipov. **Literary Moscow** Michael Kazmarak. **Architecture** Bay Brown. **Sightseeing** Annika Karlsson, John Kenyon, John O'Mahony, Helen Womack. **Museums & Galleries** Yana Dlugy, Rosalind Gray, Annika Karlsson, Andrei Kovalyov, Masha Makeyeva. **Accommodation** Kevin McElwee. **Restaurants & Cafés** Katya Akimova, Ben Aris, Kevin O'Flynn, Yulia Solovyova, Greg Thain. **Pubs & Bars** Kevin McElwee. **Shopping & Services** Anika Karlsson, Mary McVean, Mitchell McVean. **Banyas** Frank Brown. **Children** Melissa Bloom. **Film** Anya Ardayeva, John O'Mahony. **Gay & Lesbian** Lisa Dickey. **Media** John O'Mahony, Yulia Solovyova. **Music: Classical & Opera** Louise Gray, Lygia O'Riordan. **Music: Rock, Roots & Jazz** Louise Gray, Artyom Troitsky. **Nightlife** Owen Matthews. **Sport & Fitness** Kevin O'Flynn. **Theatre & Dance** John Freedman, Margaret Henry, Yulia Solovyova. **Trips Out of Moscow** Ben Aris, Frank Brown, Frank Brown.
ST PETERSBURG Introduction John O'Mahony. **History** John O'Mahony. **Architecture** John O'Mahony. **Literary St Petersburg** John O'Mahony. **White Nights** John O'Mahony. **Sightseeing** John O'Mahony. **Museums & Galleries** Rosalind Gray, John Nicholson, Barnaby Thompson, Alice Lagnado. **The Hermitage** Rosalind Gray. **Entertainment:** *Ballet* Michelle Welton; *Banyas* Barnaby Thompson; *Children* Elizabeth Williamson; *Film* John O'Mahony; *Gay & Lesbian* Valera Katsuba. *Media* John O'Mahony; *Music: Classical & Opera* Barnaby Thompson; *Music: Rock, Roots & Jazz* Sergei Chernov; *Nightlife* John O'Mahony; *Theatre* Barnaby Thompson. **Accommodation** Alice Lagnado. **Eating & Drinking** Elizabeth Williamson, Gaytri Singh, John O'Mahony, Brett Young. **Shopping & Services** John O'Mahony. **Trips Out of St Petersburg** Peter Kozyrev, Frank Brown.
DIRECTORY Leonid Ragozin, Ruth Jarvis, Ben Hoosen, John O'Mahony.

The editors would like to thank the following:

Masha Mombelli, Brenda Gray, Marc Champion, Frank Brown, Leonid Shutov, Natasha Blumenthal, Lawrence McDowell, Genya Yevdokimov, Lev Lurie, Natalya Belek at the Nevsky Palace Hotel, Yulia Kovalyova, Nelli Leboshitz, Angela, Kristina and Manne.

Maps by JS Graphics, Hill View Cottage, 17 Beadles Lane, Old Oxted, Surrey RH8 9JG.

Photography by Arnhel de Serra except for: pages 5, 11, 127 Society for Cooperation in Russian & Soviet Studies; page 124 British Film Institute; page 129, 187 Associated Press; page 139 Rex Features; pages 156 to 158 Mikhail Guterman; pages 163, 167 Jim Holmes/Axiom; page 161, 165 N & J Wiseman/Trip; page 171 Panos Pictures; pages 182 and 183 David Toase/Travel Ink; pages 130, 185, 204 AKG Photo; page 205 Eitan Simanor/Axiom; page 211 W Jacob/Trip; The following photographs were supplied by the featured establishments: page 126.

Contents

About the Guide

This is the first edition of the *Time Out Guide to Moscow & St Petersburg*, joining our ever-expanding series of guides to cities throughout the world. It has been put together by a team of resident writers who have immersed themselves in the post-Soviet urban experience in order to bring you all the information necessary to tackle these exciting but often chaotic cities. As the difficult transition to a capitalist free-market continues, we've given you the sharpest possible picture of an urban landscape that is still in the process of defining itself.

CRISIS, WHAT CRISIS?

All listings information and other factual details have been thoroughly checked. However, as this guide was going to print in the autumn of 1998, the Russian economy, which had been teetering on the brink for much of that year, finally collapsed. This means that some of the venues listed – particularly shops, restaurants and clubs – may have been forced to close down, either temporarily or permanently, though we hope that most of our selections are strong enough to survive. If you plan on visiting a specific venue, ask staff at your hotel to call ahead to check it's still open. Prices quoted may also change. While some, such as those for accommodation and imported goods, will recover to the dollar equivalent we have listed, others, such as museum admission prices and train tickets, may not. For this reason, you may be pleasantly surprised to find that Russia is less costly than you expected.

While every effort and care has been made to ensure the accuracy of the information contained in this guide, the publishers cannot accept responsibility for any errors it may contain.

NAMES & ADDRESSES

When somewhere is best or most usefully known by its English name – usually tourist sites and institutions – we have given that first, with the Russian name bracketed afterwards or as the first line of the address. Otherwise – usually for commercial concerns – we have given the Russian name with an English translation bracketed afterwards or at the start of the address where relevant.

Russian street numbering can be complicated: *see chapter* **Getting Around Moscow** for details. Map references refer to the street plans on pages 277-282 (Moscow) and 286-289 (St Petersburg). Where no reference is given, the entry falls outside the area covered.

All telephone numbers are given as dialled within that city. The area code for Moscow is **812**, for St Petersburg it's **273**.

MONEY TALK

All prices quoted are in US dollars and can only be approximate. Note that some attractions have different ticket prices for Russians and foreigners. We have given the (higher) price for foreigners.

Major credit and charge cards are now widely accepted, and the financial crisis of 1998 will have minimal impact on this. Be warned, however, that the specific cards taken by each establishment may change. The following abbreviations have been used: **AmEx**, American Express; **DC**, Diners' Club; **JCB**, Japanese credit cards; **MC**, Mastercard; **V**, Visa. Travellers' cheques are very rarely accepted as a means of payment and have not been listed.

PRICES

Because of the threat of inflation in the wake of the devaluation of August 1998, many restaurants and upmarket shops may now quote prices in units (sometimes marked y) each of which will be the equivalent of one US dollar.

RIGHT TO REPLY

It should be stressed that all the information we give is impartial. No organisation has been included because it has advertised in any of Time Out's publications, and all opinions given are wholly independent.

We hope you enjoy the *Time Out Guide to Moscow & St Petersburg*, but we'd also like to know if you don't. We welcome tips from readers – feedback on current entries and suggestions for new ones. There's a reader's reply card for your comments at the back of the book.

TRANSLITERATION

In translating Cyrillic into Latin letters, we have adopted a straightforward system that combines ease of pronunciation with simplicity on the page. In general, we have made exceptions for the names of famous people when a different spelling has gained common currency.

There is an online version of this guide, as well as weekly events listings for several international cities, at **www.timeout.com**

Introduction

By GUM, it's Moscow's biggest department store.

You'll get the general idea driving in from the airport – the soulless tower blocks of the suburbs, the wide boulevard of Leningradsky Prospekt crammed with matchbox Ladas and flashy Mercs, the smart hotels and hookers of Tverskaya. Moscow is not a subtle city. It hits you over the head with its surreal contrasts, its megalomania and monumentalism, its vulgar new wealth and, for all its European aspirations, its overwhelming Russian-ness. From the Kalashnikov-toting policemen patrolling outside the Starlite Diner (transplanted from Detroit) to the leggy and indisputably Slavic kept women who stalk around the Versace and Valentino boutiques, Moscow has the feel of a far-flung colonial outpost apeing the ways of European masters but never quite succeeding. Change, for Moscow, has always been convulsive, flamboyant and almost always imposed from above, which gives it its distinctive, monumental coldness. It has none of the quaint eccentricity of London, or the stateliness of Paris. Every Russian and Soviet leader worth his place in the Kremlin wall has laid a heavy hand on the city, transforming the skyline into a high-rise history of vanity, from St Basil's Cathedral to the spectacular Stalin-era skyscrapers to the superlatively ugly Brezhnev-era monstrosity of the New Arbat. The latest Russian revolution has been no exception, with Moscow's energetic and prolifically tasteless mayor Yury Luzhkov putting his own, unmistakable stamp on the capital. The newly rebuilt Cathedral of Christ the Saviour, the ultra-kitsch underground Manezh shopping mall and the bizarre statue of Peter the Great are all testaments to the hubristic celebration of Moscow's newly found capitalist prosperity.

But despite Moscow's ostentatious new veneer the Soviet past pokes through at every turn, providing endless snapshot moments of historical irony. At VVTs (VDNKh), the All Russia Exhibition Centre, traders sell Korean TVs in the shadow of old Soviet spacecraft. In the former Palace of Communist Youth hundreds of strung-out kids in Day-Glo miniskirts rave till mid-morning.

Moscow is not romantic, relaxing or even particularly friendly. But it has an energy, an extraordinary vibrancy born of inborn exuberance long repressed that's unique among European capitals. It's decadent, flamboyantly vulgar and, for those who have lost out, unspeakably cruel. The conspicuous consumption runs on the high-octane fuel of ephemerality – everywhere, you get the impression that nobody quite believes that the good times are going to last. It's flooded with easy sex, drugs and money, but also has brutal police, totalitarian residency laws and grinding poverty. Think Berlin in the '20s or Shanghai in the '30s and you may catch something of the louche, post-Imperial flavour of '90s Moscow. And as Russia finds itself in another period of political and economic turbulence, Moscow looks set to exceed itself yet again as it prepares for a final round of pre-apocalyptic partying.

Moscow in Context

Moscow by Season

Moscow's festivals are sporadic but frenetic. If the party's on – party on.

As part of its 1990s image change, Russia – and Moscow – has revamped its hitherto worthy events calendar to include such glossy fixtures as a techno music festival and a Paris-like fashion season. However, with change comes unpredictability: an annual car show and several classical music festivals appear to be here to stay, but other events remain irregular (the international twin festival – featuring 2,000 sets of twins – is unlikely to happen a second time).

The longest running festivals celebrate theatre and classical music. A few of the communist days off have survived, of which International Women's Day is the most popular, but some others, like May Day, have become non-events and are little more than a chance to take the family out to the dacha for the weekend.

Russians need little excuse to party and although there are few large festivals there is usually something going on, especially during the summer months. (Outdoor events don't thrive on sub-zero temperatures.) We've listed the main dates on the calendar, but keep an eye on the local listings papers, such as the *Moscow Times*'s Friday supplement *MT Out*, for an up-to-date selection and to check that an event is indeed taking place – festivals are subject to disappearance without trace.

Spring

Orthodox Easter

Date varies.
The irrepressibly religious Russians make as much of Easter as the rest of us make of Christmas. Because of the calendar confusion, Orthodox Easter is usually about two weeks after Catholic Easter. The main Easter midnight mass, led by Russian Patriarch Alexy II, is held in the Epiphany Cathedral. Make your way to a church before midnight. Priests in the gaudy Orthodox robes bless the public in a standing-room-only service (women should wear a scarf on their head) and then the whole troop does a circuit around the outside of the church. Babushki will wander up to you and tell you that 'Christ has risen' in case you'd forgotten. Despite the repression of religion under communism the Party never managed to do more to the faith than knock down a few churches. Russians are fervently religious and this is the holiest day of the year. Look out for the *kulichy*, a traditional cake that tastes like brioche.

International Women's Day

Date 8 March.
A word of warning: don't drive on 7 March. Police stop nearly every car on the road to extract a bribe so they can afford a bunch of flowers for their wife or girlfriend. Originally a communist holiday to celebrate an 1857 demonstration by women textile workers in New York City, this is now the Russian version of St Valentine's Day. In the evening there are any number of parties and restaurants need to be booked well in advance.

Founding of the Russian Republic

Date 1 April.
The 'Rus', or Slavic nation, was confusingly founded in Kiev in today's Ukraine. This day celebrates the beginning of the Slavic people as a people, but festivities are limited to a few traditional costumes on old Arbat and the rest of the population leaves for the dacha.

Chekhov International Theatre Festival

Information *International Confederation of Theatre Unions, Leontyevsky Pereulok 21/1, 103009 (929 7070).*
Date Apr-June every 3 years; next 2001.
An international festival – troupes from around the world turn up to show off their versions of the classic Russian writer's work in venues throughout the city, but it is dominated by local productions (in Russian, of course).

Lenin's Birthday

Date 22 April.
A good chance to see some living communists as they go down to Red Square (Krasnaya Ploshchad) to mourn at Lenin's tomb – if the heavy police contingent lets them through. There's a lot of flag waving and shouting and not much else. There is talk of reinstating Lenin's birthday as a national holiday – odd, since in the days of the Soviet Union it was a *subbotnik*, a day of voluntary unpaid work, when ordinary citizens went around cleaning up the city.

> ## PUBLIC HOLIDAYS
> **1 January** New Year's Day
> **7 January** Orthodox Christmas
> **8 March** International Women's Day
> **April/May** Orthodox Easter (date and day vary)
> **1 May** International Labour Day
> **2 May** Spring Day
> **9 May** Victory Day
> **12 June** Independence Day
> **7 November** Revolution Day
> **12 December** Constitution Day

The first snow of winter transforms Izmailovsky Park into a cross-country ski resort.

Photography Festival
Information *Manezh Exhibition Centre, Manezhnaya Ploshchad 1, 121019 (202 8976/8252/fax 202 8252).* **Date** *late Apr-mid May.*
A city-wide exhibition of photography from both domestic and international artists. The main event is housed in the Manezh Exhibition Centre and features world class and rare foreign prints, as well as contemporary domestic fashion and art photography.

International Labour Day
Date 1 May.
The biggest day of the old Soviet calendar, when the Red Army would parade through Red Square in front of the Politburo. There is no more parading, but events are still organised around the city, in the parks and on Red Square. A jolly holiday with free outdoor concerts and fireworks in the evening.

Victory Day
Date 9 May.
Commemorates the defeat of Nazi Germany in World War II. The city is decked in big communist banners in the 'social realist' style, festivals and shows are held in the parks and cannons are fired.

Festival of Contemporary Music
Date mid-May-mid-June.
Of Moscow's three annual music festivals this is probably the most interesting, celebrating everything from St Hildegard to Hendrix in venues around the city. The brainchild of Moscow Conservatory professor Vladimir Tarnopolsky, it has grown into an exchange between Russian and European contemporary musicians and leans towards the avant-garde.

The Cosmopolitan Show
Information *Independent Media, Vyborgskaya Ulitsa 16, 125212 (232 9272/fax 232 9270).* **Date** mid-May.
Cosmo was the first of the glossy magazines to arrive in Russia and promote Western concepts of fashion and beauty. The high point of this over-commercial show is a modelling

competition. Girls fly in from across the country to compete and the winner gets a contract with Red Stars Model agency. There are also fashion shows, a chance to have a makeover and various silly corporate-sponsored races. Check press for the venue – it varies.

Maxidrome Rock Festival
Information *Radio Maximum, Tverskaya Ulitsa 16/2, 103829 (200 1088/4648/fax 956 3279).* **Date** last Sat in May.
This monster rock concert held in the Olimpiisky Sports Centre plays host to all Russia's rock bands in one go. Crowds of more than 17,000 turn up to see each of the previous year's stars perform their biggest hits and the whole thing runs for more than 12 hours.

Summer

Learning to Swim
Information *FEELEE Promotion, DK Gorbunov Club, Novozadovskaya Ulitsa 27 (145 9670) or Radio Maximum, Tverskaya Ulitsa 16/2, 103829 (200 1088/4648/fax 956 3279).* **No fixed date.**
The annual get-together of Moscow's small but active alternative rock fraternity takes its name from the radio show of Alexander Sklar. The venue is often – but not always – the R-Club, and the gigs last several days.

Maxidance
Information *Radio Maximum, Tverskaya Ulitsa 16/2, 103829 (200 1088/4648/fax 956 3279).* **No fixed date.**
The hip hop equivalent of the Maxidrome rock and pop festival, this one-nighter draws a crowd of 13,000 be-sunglassed teenagers. Of all the music styles, it was techno that was fastest into Russia and opened the country up to the idea of clubbing. After five years the Russian DJs are increasingly being replaced with artists (most of whom earn their living as DJs) and this is their bash. In addition to dance music there are foreign DJs, bands and dance groups, as well as various wacky rave-fashion shows. Check press for venue.

Moscow-St Petersburg Festival of Punk & Ska

Information *FEELEE Promotion, DK Gorbunov Club, Novozadovskaya Ulitsa 27 (145 9670).* **Date** usually early June.

If you are into punk then check out the DK Gorbunov Club. This festival is its annual get-together with manky Russian punk bands and even mankier Russian punks. Heavy police presence hassling the partygoers can be a bit of a downer.

Experimental Film Festival

Information *Cine-Fantom Club, Ulitsa Bolshaya Lubyanka 13 (928 0590).* **Date** from approx 9 June.

A two-week festival of experimental cinema, video and computer art organised by (and held at) the Cine-Fantom Club, one of the principal movers in the new-tech avant-garde to emerge from the underground. The festival is a forum for non-commercial artists to show off the work they have done since the curtain came down.

Russian Independence Day

Date 12 June.

Independent from what, you might ask? A public holiday to commemorate the first democratic presidential elections in 1996, which Yeltsin won. People leave town in droves, but for those left, the parks are the place: in 1998 a disco competition was held in Gorky Park by a local radio station and Coke organised another, enigmatically entitled 'You Answer to the Sun'. Check the *Moscow Times* for concerts and parties.

Tchaikovsky Festival

Information *Tchaikovsky Concert Hall, Triumfalnaya Ploshchad 4/31, 103050 (299 0378).* **Date** late June.

A one-night concert to pick the winner of the Slava/Gloria Lifetime Achievement Award. Set up by Unexim bank, the first one was held in 1997, when Russia's darling cellist and conductor Mstislav Rostropovich walked off with the $250,000 first prize. The size of the prizes should ensure a regular turn-out of big stars. If you are a classical buff then this is one to ring.

Exotica International Car Festival

Date third week of June.

Cars are *the* status symbol for the New Russian about town, and you'll see a sprinkling of VIP rides such as the Nikita Khrushchev ZiL limo. But much of the show is taken up with Russian cars and their owners, who swap tips on how to keep them going. The show is held in the field next to Tushinsky Airport and gets lots of press coverage.

Moscow International Film Festival

Information *Interfest, Khokholski Pereulok 10, 109028 (917 9154/fax 916 0107).* **Date** mid-July.

Controversy dogs the Moscow Film Festival. The first big one in 1997 was a huge success, with the likes of Sophia Loren, Robert DeNiro and Richard Gere showing up for the gala performances. But there was outrage at the $6 million it cost to put on. The following year it was cancelled. (Some critics said that the money would be better spent on sausages for old people.) However, it is bound to resurface – though in 1997 of the 48 films shown only one was Russian. Russians are making good films, but they are mostly working abroad, leaving the festival bereft of creditable home-grown stars. 1997's event lasted two weeks and took place at various cinemas around town.

Kazantip

Information *Radio Station 106.8, Ulitsa Kazakov 16, 103064 (261 0449/9749/fax 265 1356).* **Date** month of August.

Strictly speaking not a Moscow festival, but as most of the Muscovites leave the city during the summer, this is one of the places you're going to find the Bright Young Things. The

Russian equivalent of Glastonbury, Kazantip is held in a small town in the Crimea (the Ukrainian Costa del Sol) of the same name. During the three or four weeks that it runs there are several raves, attracting as many as 5,000 people, and gigs by many of the top Russian bands. The format and line-up change unpredictably and you need to take absolutely everything with you (including food – and a Ukrainian visa).

Autumn

Moscow Food Festival

Information & venue *Manezh Exhibition Hall, Manezhnaya Ploshchad 1, 121019 (202 8976/8252/fax 202 5242).* **Date** 3-7 Sept.

Sponsored by the vodka producers, who give away samples of their wares to eager punters, this festival was inaugurated for the 850th birthday celebrations of the city in 1997 and will probably happen again – if for no other reason than the Russians need very little excuse to drink vodka.

Moscow City Day

Date early Sept.

Moscow's all-powerful mayor, Yury Luzhkov, is attempting to put Moscow on the tourist map with this weekend event. The first was held in 1997 to commemorate the 850th anniversary of the founding of Moscow. More than a million people arrived to hear Pavarotti sing in Red Square and see Jean Michelle Jarre's spectacular light and music show in front of the Moscow State University. Most of the visitors were from the CIS and the whole event was overshadowed by the death of Princess Diana, but it was the biggest public event of the year by far. Given the amount of arm twisting Luzhkov had to do to raise the millions of dollars needed to pay for it, subsequent city days are unlikely to be on such a lavish scale, but Luzhkov usually gets his way so don't count on it.

Moscow International Jazz Festival

Information *Jazz Art Club, Begovaya Ulitsa 5, 125284 (191 8320).* **Date** late Sept-early Oct.

Under communism jazz was considered bourgeois, so its exponents gave up playing or risked getting shot. Since 1991 there has been a quiet revival, but it lacks a die-hard core of 60-somethings to push it along. However, there have been three of these small but lively festivals, which attract both fresh blood and some thorny old heroes, such as the Oleg Lundstrem Jazz Orchestra – in its 63rd year of existence it made the *Guinness Book of World Records* as the world's longest serving ensemble. It takes place in various venues.

Fight for the White House

Date 2-4 Oct.

An unofficial day of remembrance for those killed during fighting outside the White House in October 1993, after communist deputies barricaded themselves inside for a week. Violence erupted in earnest on Sunday 2 October and by midnight tanks were rumbling over the bridge to pound the deputies into submission. Hundreds of people were killed and their mothers, relations and hard-line communists gather in the street beside the White House to mourn the fallen in a service. The wall fencing the White House is hung with photos of the dead and it is a sombre occasion – a reminder of the real pain of transition.

Baltic-Russia Jazz Festival

Information *Jazz Art Club, Begovaya Ulitsa 5, Moscow 125284 (191 8320).* **Date** mid-Oct-early Nov.

Culturally, the Baltics had it better during the communist days, and produced a lot of experimental art of all forms. Relations are pretty icy these days, but this festival brings together jazz aficionados from Russia, the Baltic states and Finland. After all, musos are not well known for their concern with trade relations. At venues around town.

Hallowe'en
Date 31 October.
Not traditionally a Russian holiday, but of all the Western holidays it is the one that Russians have most taken to heart, with nearly any club or bar worth its salt holding a party. Check the *Moscow Times* for recommendations.

Anniversary of the October Revolution
Date 7 Nov.
The October Revolution actually took place in November – calendar confusion strikes again. As communism is generally out of fashion these days, not much happens apart from angry groups of old *babushki* waving their red flags and carrying pictures of Stalin around Red Square telling anyone who will listen that things were better 'earlier'. In the last few years the *tusovshchiki* (the small group of young people at the centre of all that's cool in modern Russia) have been organising 'Rave-a-loution', a huge rave that changes venue each year. Check the *Moscow Times* for details.

Winter

Early November is one of the best times to visit Moscow: the worst of the biting cold is a few weeks off, and the first snow shows Moscow off to its best effect. The city administration ices the paths in Gorky Park, which becomes an enormous ice rink. There is cross-country skiing near Izmailovsky Park, but one of the most popular pastimes is ice fishing in the middle of the frozen Volga

Celtic Music Festival
Information *Caledonian Club, Ulitsa Gastello 37, apt 17, 107014 (268 2629/fax 925 5972)*. **No fixed date**.
There is a sizeable Scottish community in Russia, and the newly formed Caledonian Club has managed to organise this bash for two years in a row. A three-day celebration of Scottish music, food and culture, it is timed to coincide with Robbie Burns's birthday. The festival usually takes place in one of the Irish pubs.

December Nights Festival
Date second half of Dec-early Jan.
A top-line musical orgy in which the cream of Russian and foreign conductors and musicians play in the most beautiful locations. The best places to go (if you can get tickets) are the Pushkin Museum and the Kremlin Palace, but all the theatres and halls will be holding concerts. There are also exhibitions of related classical art as each festival usually revolves around a particular composer or motif. At the Pushkin Museum there is a veritable culture-fest of paintings and music with an exhibition of related paintings from the composer's period and country.

New Year's Day
Date 1 Jan.
Ten minutes before midnight on New Year's Eve, Red Square fills up with revellers who stick about long enough to drink a glass of champagne and listen to the Kremlin chime in the New Year before leaving. Remember, it is the middle of winter – and about -12°C (10°F).

Russian Winter Festival
Date 1-5 Jan.
By St Basil's on Red Square and in the small park on Pushkin's Square fabulous ice sculptures spring up as part of this winter festival, some of them several metres high. Artists clamber about on top with chisels, axes and blow torches, adding the finishing touches to everything from full-sized tanks to dying swans, and children stick coins to the ice to bring them good luck.

Solomon Mikhoels International Festival of Arts
Information *Jewish Music Theatre, Taganskaya Ploshchad 12/4, 109172 (912 5651/fax 912 5698)*. **Date** 5-13 Jan.
In the early morning of 13 January 1948 the NVKD (the predecessor of the KGB) ran Solomon Mikhoels, the 'father of Jewish theatre', down with a car on the personal orders of Stalin. The Russians consider his death one of the greatest tragedies their embattled country suffered during the years of oppression. During the festival week, a number of theatres show Russian classics and foreign productions on Jewish themes.

Orthodox Christmas
Date 7 Jan.
Easter is the big holiday – Christmas is a small stay-at-home affair with a visit to church, with none of the gluttonous feasting of the West. In fact, the opposite: in the 40 days leading up to Christmas, devotees fast, excluding meat, eggs and dairy products from their diets. On the last day they can't eat anything at all until the first star rises over the horizon (a deadline made difficult by the fact that Moscow is often cloaked in cloud at this time of the year).

Old New Year
Date 14 Jan.
It gets very confusing. Religious holidays and Revolution Day are both celebrated according to the old calendar, but New Year's Eve and some other, newer, events are celebrated according to the new. Young Russians use the confusion to have another New Year's party anyway.

Funny House Dance Awards
Information *Radio Maximum, Tverskaya Ulitsa 16/2, 103829 (200 1088/4648/fax 956 3279)*. **Date** 25 Jan.
Russia's answer to the MTV music awards and a get-together for all Moscow's techno glitterazzi. The three main radio stations run a competition for the punters to vote on such categories as best DJ, best club, best party and best remix. All the stars (all Russian) turn up as well as some 4,000 screaming teenies. Venue varies: check press.

International Festival of Orthodox Church Music
Date late Jan-late Feb.
Now a decade old, this is a rambling festival of liturgical and religious music. Gigs are held in the numerous churches and cover the gamut of the genre: from the schism of Rome to the compositions of guerrilla carol writers of the twentieth century working underground during the communist era.

Maslenitsa (Butter Week)
Date week of 23 Feb.
Originally an old pagan rites-of-spring holiday to honour Yarila the Sun God, Maslenitsa was Christianised and is the equivalent of Shrove Tuesday in the UK – the last big feed before the denial of Lent. The food of choice is blini, which, being round and golden, are supposed to represent the sun. Maslenitsa, the fertility goddess, masquerades for a week as a big straw doll, and each day has a different theme. On the Monday, new brides are taught how to cook perfect blini, and on the last day the straw doll is burned and her ashes sprinkled over the fields. Not much more than the blini eating survives today, but celebrations are organised where some of the rites are performed.

Golden Mask Festival
Information *International Confederation of Theater Unions, Leontyevsky Pereulok 21/1, 103009 (929 7070)*. **Date** last week of Feb and first week of March.
The Golden Mask honours the top theatre achievements – the best in opera, dance, drama and puppetry – of the previous year, with nominations coming from throughout Russia. There are dozens of shows all over town during the two weeks (virtually all in Russian), with a gala prize-giving ceremony to cap it off.

History

Moscow's struggles to keep up with the times.

THE ORIGINS OF MOSCOW

The first mention of Moscow in Russia's earliest written historical record is, perhaps fittingly, an invitation to a party. 'Come to me, brother, to Moscow,' Yury Dolgoruky, Grand Prince of Suzdal, asks the Prince of Novgorod in 1147, promising him a 'mighty banquet' to celebrate the forging of their new alliance. Though the invitation implies that there were already at least a couple of wooden shacks on the site, the very minimum needed to accommodate a raucous medieval knees-up, this is the generally accepted date of the foundation of Moscow. Dolgoruky, whose name means 'long of arm', is now taken to be the city's founder.

A load of old Cossacks

Though they may now be known primarily for that strange squatting, whooping dance, the influence of the Cossacks in Russian life and history extends well beyond the area of folk show choreography. The first bands of Cossacks – a name that derives from the Turkish word *kazak*, meaning 'freeman' – appeared on the southern borders of the expanding Russian Empire around the fourteenth and fifteenth centuries. Mostly renegade peasants and assorted bandits, they wandered around the steppes plundering, marauding and generally having a good time. Later, when they had been tamed by the Tsars and organised into their own special cavalry brigades, the Cossacks helped overcome the Mongol hordes, colonise Siberia and, eventually, put down the 1905 Revolution. This, and anti-Bolshevik participation in the civil war, earned the opprobrium of the commies, who did what they could to completely wipe out the Cossacks. Since Perestroika, however, there has been a resurgence of Cossack culture (including dancing), and a decree signed by Boris Yeltsin in 1992 rehabilitated the Cossacks and gave them the status of a separate ethnic group.

The origins of the Russian people can be traced back to the eastern Slavic tribes, who renounced their nomadic ways some time around the sixth century and settled into a life of trade and agriculture on the fertile Russian steppes. Previously these wide open plains in the south of the country had been populated by numerous unruly, roaming peoples, beginning in the seventh century BC with the Scythians, who were famous for drinking the blood of their enemies, flaying them alive and sewing the scalps together into cloaks and other fashion accessories. Later came the Goths, the Huns, the Magyars, the Khazars and finally the Slavs, who, with the help of some Nordic princes, built up the mini-trading empire known as Kievan Rus, centred around present-day Kiev. When Kievan Rus began to disintegrate due to succession squabbles between the eleventh and the thirteenth centuries, the Slavs moved eastwards to the town of Vladimir, with a second power base to the north located in Novgorod.

THE GOLDEN HORDE & THE RISE OF MUSCOVY

Not even the writers of the *Chronicles*, Russia's first written historical record, could fully understand the rise to prominence of the tiny outpost on the banks of the Moskva River that would one day become the hub of the Russian Empire. Its location, right at the junction between two trade routes, was certainly a great advantage. But it was Moscow's wily and somewhat cynical exploitation of Mongol domination that really tipped the balance.

In 1223, the Mongol hordes of Ghengis Khan suddenly materialised to the south-east, routing Russian forces at the Battle of the Kalka River. The Mongols then vanished, only to reappear 12 years later, this time under the direction of Ghengis's grandson Batu Khan, whose ornate silken tent earned his forces the nickname of the Golden Horde. On their way to the conquest of the whole of Europe, the horde laid waste to all Russia's major cities, kicking off two and a half centuries of almost total Russian subjugation. The effect of the invasion was devastating. The Mongol yoke completely cut Russia off from Western influences, editing out the Renaissance and leaving it in a state of medieval suspended animation, perhaps as much as two centuries behind the rest of Europe.

As favourite of the Mongol Khans, Daniel, one of the first Princes of Muscovy, was allowed to subdue and then annex surrounding lands, soon

The long, long arm of Moscow's founder, Prince Yury Dolgoruky.

Was Stalin a Tsarist spy?

It has long been rumoured that during his long career as a Bolshevik terrorist, Joe Stalin was actually leading the double life of a Tsarist spy. Suspicions have been raised in particular by his ability to repeatedly escape from exile and wander freely around St Petersburg while under police surveillance. However, even the great iconoclast Nikita Khrushchev balked at finding out the truth. When shown the proof, he blurted out: 'It's impossible. It would mean that our country was ruled for 30 years by an agent of the Tsarist Secret Police.'

Now that the archives have been thrown open and these materials made freely available, attention has shifted to the significance of Stalin's double-agent activity. It seems that many Bolsheviks played similar roles in Lenin's great chess game with the authorities. Double agents could move more freely and were less likely to be arrested. Lenin himself received money from German sources and has often been branded a German spy. Almost anything, as we would see later, could be justified in the name of the Revolution.

raising Moscow to the level of a principality. Then, in 1328, Prince Ivan, whose very appropriate nickname was Kalita, or Moneybag, obtained permission from the Mongols to collect tributes on their behalf, allowing Moscow to extend its influence even further. At the same time it became the seat of the Orthodox Metropolitan, the leader of the Russian Orthodox Church, a status that gave the ambitious Princes of Moscow the opportunity to consider themselves the rulers 'of all the Russians'.

Ironically, it was the growing confidence of their Muscovite lackeys that first signalled the end of the rule of the Mongol Khans. In 1380, Prince Dmitry of Moscow triumphed over the horde at the Battle of Kulikovo on the River Don, earning himself the sobriquet of Donskoi. Though they came surging across the steppe again two years later, sacking Moscow and burning the remainder of the princedom of Muscovy, by the end of the century the Mongols had split irrevocably into a collection of warring factions.

IVAN THE GREAT & THE THIRD ROME
In 1453, Constantinople, the wellspring of Orthodox Christianity, fell to the Ottoman Turks. This meant that the Russian branch was now the only free Orthodox Church, giving rise to the legend of Moscow as the 'third Rome'. The phrase was coined when a monk from Pskov wrote to Moscow's next great ruler, Ivan the Great, proclaiming: 'Thou art the sole Emperor of all the Christians in the universe… two Romes have fallen, the third stands and there shall be no fourth.'

Ivan quite liked the idea of being the supreme ruler of the Orthodox world, and to bolster his position married Sophie Paleologue, the orphan niece of the last Byzantine emperor, and adopted the Byzantine imperial double-headed eagle as his official coat of arms. Ivan also built the great cathedrals that would give Moscow an architectural claim to the exalted position of being the new Rome. During his reign, the present Kremlin walls were built around the brand new Assumption Cathedral, transforming Moscow from a village into a glorious capital.

Soon Ivan, an autocrat by nature, began to believe his own propaganda and to regard himself as Tsar (a word deriving from Caesar and, incidentally, what the Russians had always called the Khan), the autocratic sovereign, rather than just the head of the nobility. With this overarching self-belief to prop him up and with God securely on his side, Ivan set about zealously expanding the territories of Muscovy, which swelled to an area three times their original size over the 43 years of his reign (1462-1505).

IVAN THE TERRIBLE
The next ruler of note was Ivan IV (1530-84), later known for very good reasons as 'The Terrible', who became ruler at the age of three with his mother Princess Helen as regent. After her death in 1538, the young Ivan fell victim to the squabbling *boyars* (nobles) and was generally ignored, insulted, threatened and often inadequately fed and clothed. This 'difficult childhood' was to leave a profound mark on the boy and perhaps motivated his later excesses. At the age of 14, Ivan finally began to exert himself, executing the most offensive and powerful of the *boyars*, Prince Andrei Shuisky. At 17 he became the first Russian ruler to be crowned Tsar, at an official ceremony in Uspensky Cathedral. In the same year he married Anastasia, a member of the Romanov family, whom he had chosen from a line-up of hundreds of eligible virgins.

The first part of Ivan's reign was anything but terrible as he set about instituting a number of much-needed reforms. In 1549, he called the first Zemsky Sobor, an irregular national assembly representing all classes of Russian society except the peasants. Later, he introduced military service for the gentry and formed a permanent army, which included the highly trained and disciplined *Streltsy* or 'Sharp-shooters'. Ivan's military victories included the capture of the Mongol stronghold of

Kazan, during which the Khan was taken prisoner and baptised as a Christian. It was in commemoration of this victory that Ivan then built St Basil's Cathedral on Red Square.

In 1560, Ivan's beloved wife Anastasia died – poisoned, he suspected, by disgruntled *boyars*. In a theatrical preamble to the reign of terror he was about to unleash, Ivan suddenly disappeared, only to resurface at the Trinity Monastery of St Sergius, announcing that he intended to abdicate because of the double-dealing of the Church and the noblemen. Only after the establishment of his own private police force – the *Oprichnina* – was he convinced to reconsider.

Clothed in black, mounted on black horses and carrying a severed dog's head as a mascot, the *Oprichnina* roamed the country looting, torturing and massacring at the Tsar's behest. Often Ivan would join in, alternating bouts of fervent prayer with sessions of vicious torture. For failing to show sufficient loyalty, the Archbishop of Novgorod was stitched into a bearskin and hunted down by the Tsar's dogs. In Novgorod itself, 60,000 were slain in a five-week orgy of killing. Another victim of Ivan's wrath was his eldest son, struck down by his father in a fit of rage.

THE TIME OF TROUBLES

On Ivan's death in 1585 the tsardom passed first to his sickly, feeble-minded second son Fyodor, and then to Fyodor's uncle Boris Godunov. The death of Boris in 1605 ushered in what has become known as *Smutnoye Vremya* or the 'Time of Troubles'. General discontent had already led to the rise – under the protection of the King of Poland – of an imposter claiming to be Dmitry, a son of Ivan the Terrible who had been murdered, probably on Tsar Boris's orders. This 'False Dmitry' marched on Moscow and was actually authenticated by Dmitry's own mother, in whose arms the child had died.

The pseudo-Dmitry managed to reign for just over 12 months before being murdered by a mob, which then burned his body and blasted his ashes from a canon in the general direction of Poland, whence he came. At this point a Moscow prince, Vasily Shuisky, had himself proclaimed Tsar, only to be challenged by a new pretender, the 'Second False Dmitry', otherwise known as the Thief of Tushino. At the same time, King Sigismund of Poland was eyeing up the Russian throne and attacked from the west. However, it was the people of Moscow who finally deposed Vasily, leaving the throne empty. In the anarchy that followed, another pretender appeared in Pskov, sometimes referred to as the 'Third False Dmitry'. This insanity finally ended with the help of Kuzma Minin, a butcher from Nizhny Novgorod who raised an army in the north-east. Minin, who was then joined by Prince Dmitry Pozharsky and a band of Cossacks, succeeded in ejecting the Poles from Moscow and in 1613 established the 16-year-old Mikhail Romanov on the throne, the first of the Romanov dynasty.

What you need, boy, is a good stabbing: Ivan the Terrible killing his son, by Ilya Repin.

THE FIRST ROMANOVS

Rather shy and retiring, Mikhail Romanov turned out to be something of a disappointment and showed little interest in regaining the losses incurred during the Time of Troubles. However, during his reign the Empire expanded of its own accord as Cossack pioneers surged across the wastelands of Siberia, reaching the Pacific in 1639 and founding the harbour of Okhotsk in 1648.

One thing that Mikhail did manage to do, however, was to enact a series of laws further restricting the freedoms of peasants. Under his son Alexis the Gentle, a law of 1649 practically made serfdom a national institution.

At the same time the Russian Orthodox Church underwent the greatest schism in its history, the result of reforms spearheaded by Patriarch Nikon, a peasant turned monk who had inveigled his way into the affections of the Tsar. It all came down to petty stuff like the spelling of Jesus (the Russian Church Slavonic Isus or the Greek variant Isius) and the manner of blessing oneself (with the traditional Russian two fingers or the new-fangled Greek three), trivialities that resulted in a three-century split between the reformers and the stubborn, oft-persecuted Old Believers.

PETER & THE MOVE NORTH

In 1682, Peter I assumed the Russian throne in tandem with his half-witted, half-brother Ivan, with his devious half-sister Sophia as regent, and by the decade's end had taken full control of the country.

Peter the Great would build up Russia into a great European power and open it up to Western influences. But his decision in 1712 to move the country's capital north to St Petersburg was devastating for Moscow. The 1714 ban on the erection of all stone buildings in the city completely stifled its development. Peter's plan was to keep Moscow ticking over by assigning to it the status of 'Second Capital' and keeping branches of many major state institutions in Moscow, but for the next two centuries the spotlight would be firmly on Peter's shining new city in the north.

PROVINCIAL INTERLUDE & INVASION

Over the next century Moscow was forced to acclimatise itself to the drab reality of life in the Russian provinces. A devastating fire struck in 1737, followed by the last visit to Russia of the bubonic plague in 1771, necessitating the relocation of the city's cemeteries. In between these two cataclysmic events Moscow University was founded under the auspices of the poet, scientist and philologist Mikhail Lomonosov. By 1785, the population of the city had grown to 180,000. Despite its reduced status, it is an oblique tribute to the symbolic power of the old medieval centre that when Napoleon invaded in 1812 he chose not to head towards the Imperial capital St Petersburg but to first capture Moscow.

In June 1812, the French emperor's great army, numbering over 160,000, crossed the River Niemen and entered Russian-dominated Lithuania. However, Napoleon's hunger for battle was left unsatisfied by the fleeing Russians, who relinquished city after city as part of an esoteric strategy that no one could quite work out at the time. Only when the obese and ageing Marshal Mikhail Kutuzov was put in overall charge of the army did it eventually stand and fight at Borodino. It turned out to be a desperate, vicious, unrelenting battle in which 43,000 Russians and 34,000 Frenchmen died in an engagement so indecisive that both sides claimed victory. Borodino convinced Kutuzov that it was impossible to engage directly with the French and shortly afterwards he resolved to switch tactics once more: 'Napoleon is a torrent which as yet we are unable to stem,' he said, famously. 'Moscow will be the sponge that will suck him dry.'

Under the masterplan of Kutuzov, Moscow was entirely abandoned to the French emperor and then deliberately torched. Only a third of the city centre survived the flames – of 9,158 private houses, 6,532 were extensively damaged. Napoleon was forced to flee the city, only to be met by Russia's most able commander, Field-Marshal Winter. In sub-zero temperatures, the flimsily dressed French died by the cartload. Napoleon's fate was sealed.

Moscow's burning

Until the twentieth century, Moscow, a settlement of primarily wooden buildings, was prone to regular, devastating fires. One of the first was in 1343, a conflagration that consumed 20 churches. Two more, in 1547 during the reign of Ivan the Terrible and then again in 1626 again transformed the city into a smouldering wasteland. However, the most famous of all was the Great Fire of 1812, which raged for four days and drove Napoleon out of Moscow. Though he would later deny it, this fire was probably started in Kitai-Gorod by Moscow's eccentric governor, Count Theodore Rostopchin, or 'Crazy Theo' as he was known, who also made sure that all fire-fighting equipment had been removed from the city. Twelve days later, his pyromaniac zeal got out of hand when he needlessly torched his own estate outside Moscow while a group of astonished house guests looked on.

After the fire, the resulting reconstruction plan was an attempt to redraw the chaotic map of Moscow along more ordered, European lines, a scheme that was only partially successful. The second half of the nineteenth century saw Moscow undergo an unprecedented economic boom. Between 1862 and 1897, industrial production leaped by 300 per cent and the population more than doubled to around a million. Moscow had become an industrial city with accompanying industrial problems: overcrowded sweatshops, stinking tanneries, smokestacks fouling the air.

REVOLUTION & REANIMATION

Though Russia's great twentieth-century revolutions all originated in St Petersburg (*see page 175*), Moscow usually joined in wholeheartedly. In 1905 Moscow's outer Garden Ring road was transformed into a battlefield, with government troops holding the main squares and rebels controlling the streets between. The Presnya district practically became a workers' republic, with its own police and revolutionary council. More than a thousand people had been killed before the rebellion was finally crushed. In February 1917, Nicholas II's abdication brought rapturous crowds on to the streets of Moscow, all waving red flags. And in October, the struggle for Moscow was much fiercer than the bloodless coup of the Winter Palace. The battle raged for ten days, with the heaviest fighting taking place around the Kremlin, causing damage to many buildings including the Cathedral of the Assumption.

In March 1918, fearing that the Germans were about to overrun Petrograd, Lenin uprooted the capital once again and brought it back to Moscow, a move that signalled that the country was turning east again and that the Bolshevik court would be as convoluted, cynical and Byzantine as that of the early Moscow princes. Shortly after Lenin arrived in the old medieval capital, the 'shameful' peace treaty of Brest-Litovsk was concluded with the Germans. Under its terms, the new Soviet Republic gave up most of its territories in Poland, Finland, Estonia and Lithuania. It lost 34 per cent of its population, 32 per cent of agricultural land and 54 per cent of its industry. The new Russian state had been hurled back to the position occupied by seventeenth-century Muscovy. However, by the end of the year, at the conclusion of World War I, Russia regained much of this territory.

CIVIL WAR & THE DEATH OF LENIN

In late 1918, Lenin unleashed the first wave of the Red Terror, with just a little help from the *Cheka*, the Bolshevik security organ that would later evolve into *Komitet Gosudarstvennoi Bezopasnosti*, the KGB. Many thousands of 'counter-revolutionary' elements and political opponents were imprisoned or executed. 'How can you have a revolution without shooting people?' ran Lenin's logic.

Counter-revolution on a much grander scale, however, was breaking out on Soviet borders as aristocratic Russia made its final attempt in early 1919 to topple the Bolsheviks. Advancing from his base in the Caucasus, the 'White' General Denikin pushed the 'Red' Bolshevik right out of southern Russia and progressed as far as Orel, a town just 400 kilometres (250 miles) south of Moscow. Admiral Kolchak's troops trampled the Reds in Siberia, leading indirectly to the murder of the Imperial Family in Yekaterinburg on 18 July, a preventative measure by the Bolsheviks against the former monarch falling into the hands of the Whites. To the north, General Yudenich reached the outskirts of Petrograd.

However, the Whites were thwarted by the very forces that had produced the Revolution. Basically a bunch of regressive monarchists, they could never inspire the support of the people. Eventually, the Reds repulsed them on all fronts, and the civil war had been won out by April 1920. In 1921, Lenin instigated the New Economic Policy (NEP), a little blast of capitalism and free enterprise to kick-start an economy decimated by revolution and civil war. As a result Moscow became a hive of commerce and its population began to reach pre-Revolutionary levels. A little later, Lenin was struck down by the first of the series of strokes that would finally kill him in 1924. Apparently, his veins were so calcified by this time that they tinkled like cracked porcelain during his autopsy.

THE COBBLER'S REVENGE

During his period of incapacitation, Lenin tried vainly to warn the Party about his former trusty sidekick Joseph Stalin in a document that became known as Lenin's Testament. A Georgian by birth and the son of a drunken shoemaker, Stalin had originally intended to become a priest. Instead, he embraced the Revolutionary doctrine of socialism and rose up through the ranks of the Party on the strength of his most prominent characteristics: loyalty, tenaciousness and cunning. Dismissing Lenin's Testament before the Party faithful as the delusions of a sick man, Stalin went on to display the same guile in triumphing over his other living political opponents. The mercurial Trotsky, who had played such a prominent role in the Revolution and the civil war was so marginalised by 1925 that he spent Politburo meetings reading French novels. After Trotsky's expulsion in 1926, Stalin went on to crush other potential rivals: Grigory Zinoviev, Lev Kamenev, Nikolai Bukharin and Alexei Rykov, all of whom would star in the spectacular show-trials of the 1930s.

Once his power had been consolidated, Stalin renounced the NEP and set about building a great Soviet socialist utopia, initially with the help of the first five-year plan of 1928, which sacrificed everything, including the wellbeing and living

The myth of benevolent Lenin

It is still a generally held misconception, particularly among the last resilient socialists clinging to their ideals in various corners of the world, that Lenin's great egalitarian dream was perverted by the evil tyrant Joseph Stalin. However, archive material now shows that Lenin assiduously paved the way for Stalin's crimes. As early as June 1918, at the beginning of the civil war, he ordered subordinates to 'prepare everything to burn [the Azerbaijan capital] Baku to the ground, in the event of an attack'. Then, in August of the same year, he commanded communist divisions to 'Hang (hang without fail so the people can see) no fewer than one hundred known Kulaks, rich men, bloodsuckers.'

But the document that is most likely to leave the most devastating impression on Lenin's reputation is his advice to Politburo members on how to crush religious dissent during the worst famine in Russian history. 'It is precisely now and only now,' he wrote in 1922, 'when in the starving regions people are eating human flesh, and hundreds if not thousands of corpses are littering the roads that we can (and therefore must) carry out the confiscation of church valuables with the most savage and merciless energy.'

standards of most Soviet citizens, to rapid industrialisation. A year later, he initiated a campaign of forced 'collectivisation', which herded peasants into vast, mechanised collective farms, triggering a man-made famine that claimed millions of lives.

As the '30s progressed, the Stalinist police state began to tighten its grip on every area of life in the USSR. Whatever artistic freedoms still persisted were resolutely stamped out in 1932, when socialist realism, the optimistic, classical expression of Party ideals, became the accepted dogma. A war was waged on religion that saw the mass razing of churches in Moscow and elsewhere; only one in 40 was functioning by the decade's end.

Then in December 1934, the murder of the popular Leningrad Communist Party chief Sergei Kirov, almost certainly killed on the orders of Stalin himself, signalled the beginning of a reign of terror unknown on Russian soil since the time of Ivan the Terrible. The trial and exile of Zinoviev and Kamenev, who confessed their 'moral and

political responsibility' for Kirov's death, was just the beginning. Over the next few years, the Great Purge decimated the Party ranks, almost completely wiping out the first generation of revolutionaries. More than half the delegates who attended the 17th Party Congress of 1934 would be arrested as 'enemies of the people', many of them to be deported or shot. The élite of industry, science, academia, the civil service, the military and even the security organs were savagely cleansed. This was Stalin's 'Revolution from above', a brutal and obscenely literal way of cutting out society's dead wood. In the bloody years of 1937 and 1938, the terror became more indiscriminate and spilled over into the general public. Over the entire period of the Great Terror, around a million people were killed, while a further two million died in the camps.

THE GREAT PATRIOTIC WAR

In 1939, Stalin caused general global outrage, particularly among communist nations and supporters, by signing a non-aggression pact with Nazi Germany. Then, as the Nazi forces overpowered the nations of Europe, the USSR exploited the situation to gobble up the Baltic states unnoticed. In 1941, believing that Hitler, who was still struggling against Britain, would not want to fight a war on two fronts, Stalin ignored the troop movements along the frontier. When Operation Barbarossa, the German code word for the invasion, got under way at 3.15am on 22 June 1941, Soviet soldiers were unprepared, and perversely under strict orders not to reply to 'provocation'. With its leadership crippled by the purges, the Red Army immediately crumbled, and by October that year the Nazis were already laying siege to Leningrad. In November, the Battle of Moscow got under way. By 1942, Stalingrad on the Volga was also under siege.

In an effort to stem the relentless German advance, many of the best military officers were immediately fetched back from the camps, but even then there were terror-related problems and distortions: the generals were still too afraid to tell Stalin quite how badly it was going; all decisions were taken on the basis of misinformation. However, as had been the case with Napoleon, the Soviets did have one important element on their side: the weather. It is no coincidence that the epic Battle of Stalingrad was won in the bitterly cold, blizzard conditions of January 1943. The battle proved to be a vital turning point after which the Germans were gradually pushed out of Ukraine and the Baltic states. By August 1944, the Red Army had advanced as far as Poland and Romania and on 24 April 1945 Berlin was finally encircled. At last, on 9 May, a date that was set to

The **Lenin Monument** *on Oktyabrskaya.*

become one of the pinnacles of the Russian commemorative calendar, the Germans surrendered.

During the war, the Soviet Union suffered far greater losses than any other nation, with the most recent estimates putting the total casualties at a staggering 26 million soldiers and civilians. Even during the final battles, when the outcome was a foregone conclusion, hundreds of thousands of soldiers were needlessly sacrificed in Stalin's dash to capture Berlin.

At the conference of Yalta in February 1945, which was later dubbed the 'treason of Yalta', the Western allies acknowledged that Russia's enormous sacrifices and its vital role in winning the war entitled it to a prominent role in Eastern Europe. Stalin's heavy-handed socialist restructuring of the Eastern European states soon resulted in tensions, causing Winston Churchill to warn that an 'iron curtain' was descending across Europe. The nuclear arms race and Russian suspicions about the Marshall Plan soon led to outright hostility between Russia and the allies and eventually to the Cold War.

The death of Stalin on 5 March 1953 (the same day, incidentally, that Sergei Prokofiev died) caused a national outpouring of grief. Among Stalin's henchmen, the mood was rather different. Police chief Lavrenty Beria, who may have withheld medication from his boss in the final hours, is reported to have danced beside the tyrant's coffin.

KHRUSHCHEV & THE NUCLEAR AGE

After a brief but rather nasty succession struggle, the unpredictable Nikita Khrushchev emerged as the new Soviet leader. While the Soviet Union remained a totalitarian police state throughout his rule, its attitude and outlook softened somewhat, leading to what became known as the period of 'the thaw'. At the 20th Party conference in 1956, Khrushchev denounced Stalin for promoting his own 'cult of personality' above the interests of the country at large and identified certain crimes, including 'mass arrests and deportations' and 'execution without trial'. A campaign of de-Stalinisation was begun that erased the former leader's name from cities, towns, roads and institutions and expunged his unfeasibly heroic deeds from textbooks. In 1961, Stalin's pickled body was removed from the mausoleum and buried in front of the Kremlin wall.

Khrushchev's erratic behaviour – he once, famously, banged his shoe on the podium at the United Nations to accentuate a point he was making – and his dangerous bravado during the Cuban missile crisis of 1962 (during which he recklessly attempted to set up a nuclear missile base on the US's doorstep but was forced to back down after an ultimatum from President John F Kennedy) caused widespread discontent among his associates. Khrushchev was removed from office in 1964 after which the staid, dependable and none too bright Leonid Brezhnev took over.

BREZHNEV & THE ERA OF STAGNATION

Stagnation (referred to at the time as stability) was the byword of Leonid Brezhnev's 18-year rule as this unimaginative leader slowly clawed back Khrushchev's cultural reforms and steered the country on a dependable, conservative course. This period is generally known for chronic inefficiency in industry, endemic corruption and a burgeoning black market. The scandalous exploits of Brezhnev's own family became legendary. His son Yury went on frequent big-game hunting expeditions to Africa and was often spotted lounging around Parisian casinos and topless bars. His daughter Galina, who was the wife of the deputy interior minister, became a circus groupie and conducted a high-profile affair with a big-top star named Boris the Gypsy. Brezhnev himself, who clung on to power through years of debilitating ill health, contributed to the aura of terminal decline by often skipping pages during his public speeches. But with the onset of painful reforms in the '90s, the Russian people would increasingly look back on the era of stagnation with a sense of fondness and nostalgia.

PERESTROIKA & THE GORBY PHENOMENON

After the brief tenures of ex-KGB chief Yuri Andropov and the Brezhnev lackey Konstantin Chernenko, the Soviet Union's top job passed to the relatively young and dynamic Mikhail Gorbachev, who immediately launched a crackdown on corruption and initiated a (hugely unpopular) campaign against alcoholism. The lack of success of his early efforts, combined with the profound sense of shock that swept the nation in the wake of the Chernobyl nuclear disaster in 1986, led Gorbachev to a more radical attempt to revitalise the Soviet socialist system. His new approach was based on the twin pillars of *glasnost* (openness), which he hoped would revitalise cultural life and inject society with a little initiative and *perestroika* (restructuring), which would bring limited democracy and very limited market reforms. Though this resulted in a cultural and artistic renaissance and a publishing boom fuelled by previously banned material, Gorbachev's tentative economic tinkering just meant that the state system was undermined while nothing effective was put in its place, leading to food shortages and, for the first time since the war, the introduction of ration cards.

Eastern Europe saw the opportunity of escape and grasped it in the tumultuous year of 1989. Incensed by Gorby's moderate reform policies and blaming him for the loss of Eastern Europe, a conspiratorial hardline group of Gorbachev's own cabinet decided to reimpose old-fashioned Soviet authority. They declared a state of emergency in August 1991 while Gorbachev was resting at his dacha in the Crimea. The hero of the hour was Boris Yeltsin, a former Gorbachev opponent who had become president of the Russian republic, a post created by the new democratic reforms. Yeltsin barricaded himself into the White House (the parliament building) and stood defiantly on the approaching tanks. The shambolic coup then petered out and Gorbachev was returned, albeit briefly, to office.

REFORM & HYPERINFLATION

After being reinstated as President of the Soviet Union, Gorbachev's refusal to join the radical reformers weakened his position. In contrast, Boris Yeltsin, a builder by trade and the product of a poor provincial family, had enough energy and disdain for communism and its failings to complete the task of transformation. He had already been elected president of the Russian Federation in the first free elections ever to take place in the USSR, and used his popular mandate to undermine Gorbachev's position. He banned the Communist Party from the Russian workplace. He engineered the dissolution of the Soviet Union, which ceased to exist on 25 December 1991. And after ignominiously ordering Gorbachev to clear his office as the year drew to a close, Yeltsin was ready to deploy the unthinkably radical programme of economic reform, designed to transform the command economy into a free market, that became known as 'shock therapy'.

Yeltsin's team of Young Turk economists – led by Yegor Gaidar, then in his thirties – came up with a 'cure' for the Russian economy that had worked in Bolivia and Poland. It consisted of freeing price controls, scrapping state subsidies to industry and a sweeping programme of privatisation. But 75 years of communism had completely wiped out the legal or financial infrastructure that might facilitate the changeover. The result was a free fall of the ruble, hyperinflation, a precipitous drop (by almost 40 per cent in 1992) in Gross Domestic Product and unthinkable hardship for the Russian people.

TSAR BORIS

Yeltsin weathered the storm, but by the end of 1992 economic hardships were fostering significant discontent. In December, Gaidar was dumped as prime minister in favour of the more dependable Viktor Chernomyrdin. By the middle of 1993, opposition to Yeltsin in the Congress of Peoples' Deputies, a Soviet parliamentary body, was producing political paralysis. Yeltsin dissolved parliament on 21 September – an action that was not allowed for in the Russian constitution at the time – and set a date in December for new elections. When deputies barricaded themselves in the White House and threatened to impeach the president, all electricity, gas and heating supplies to the building were cut off. The stalemate went on for three nervous weeks until the deputies made a misguided assault on the main TV station. Yeltsin persuaded the army to shell the White House and, within 12 hours of destruction, the rogue parliament surrendered. New elections in December under a

new constitution led to an even less co-operative assembly, dominated by communists and ultranationalists led by Vladimir Zhirinovsky, then dubbed 'the Russian Hitler.'

Throughout 1994, Yeltsin's own increasingly hardline, militant stance led to the debacle of the Chechen war. When the tiny Caucasian republic declared its independence in December of that year, Defence Minister Grachev boasted that the problem could be solved 'in 24 hours with just two battalions'. Instead the war continued for 18 months and cost as many as 40,000 Russian lives.

As Yeltsin's popularity sank throughout 1995, so did his health. After suffering a heart attack in December, his chances of winning Russia's first ever post Soviet presidential elections, in May and June 1996, looked bleak. But he bounced back, even dancing at one stage of the campaign, to beat the grey communist challenger Gennady Zyuganov. Even another heart attack on the eve of the second round of the election – explained away as a cold – didn't stop him gleaning 54 per cent of the vote, against the communist showing of 41 per cent.

The last phase of Yeltsin's rule has been characterised by illness and economic uncertainty. Despite a heart bypass in September 1996, he continues to give the impression of a man not quite in control – dazed and punch-drunk. The collapse of the Asian 'tiger' economies in 1997 wiped away any hope of even a modest Russian recovery and, by 1998, the economy was in a similar condition to the president. In April that year, Yeltsin suddenly fired his entire government and his prime minister of five years Viktor Chernomyrdin and installed a little-known, politically untried young technocrat named Sergei Kiriyenko as the head of his new government. Though he proved able and energetic in his attempts to impose fiscal order, even going so far as to attempt to collect taxes from large corporations, Kiriyenko couldn't prevent the collapse of the ruble in August, combined with nationwide debt default. The Russian state was, to all intents and purposes, bankrupt.

Yeltsin instantly transformed an economic crisis into a potentially more dangerous political one by firing Kiriyenko and attempting, on the advice of the financial oligarchs who had been threatened with compliance with tax laws, to reappoint Chernomyrdin. In the end, a compromise candidate was found in Yevgeny Primakov, former Soviet spymaster and foreign minister. Though it contained reformers, Primakov's new 'pink' government seemed set to implement pseudo socialist measures to deal with Russia's deepening crisis: bigger government, more administration, more bureaucracy. This approach had failed before (the USSR being one striking example) and seemed destined to fail once again. The situation in Russia will probably get much worse before it gets better. As usual, the fate of this wild, unruly and always unpredictable country hangs in the balance.

Moscow Today

From drabness to self-styled fabness, post-communist Moscow has packed a century's worth of change into a decade.

A monument to New Russian excess: the **Golden Palace** *casino. See page 148.*

One spring day in 1989, just before the annual May Day military parade, the Soviet army sent a column of tanks on a brisk practice run around the Garden Ring Road, which rings central Moscow. The distinctive low-frequency roar of the oncoming motorised division brought a small crowd of Muscovites out to watch the tanks rumble by from the side of the road, and to wave and cheer at the armoured vehicles' stone-faced crews.

When the last tank had passed and the crowd was about to go back inside, they were halted by a strange, urgent, electronic bleating noise, like a wounded steel nightingale abandoned by its flock. It was coming from one of the few cars parked on the side of the road.

'Car alarm,' one of the bystanders said, although no one had ever heard one before. A car alarm was a sign not only of a private automobile owner, which was rare enough those days, but also a symbol of jealous ownership that was altogether new for the capital of a nominally classless and property-less society.

Noise. Lots of noise. That's the biggest difference between the Moscow of yesterday and the Moscow of today. It isn't just car alarms, although

the auto boom, as well as the auto-theft boom, are articulate indicators of how this city has changed. The incessant hammering and drilling of a hundred construction sites – upmarket shopping malls, glistening office skyscrapers, towering apartment high-rises. The incessant wail of car horns stuck in traffic jams. Tinny pop music thumping from boom boxes in summer cafés. The constant chatter of mobile phones ringing. Beepers, pagers everywhere.

Save for the odd growling of the tanks, Soviet Moscow was a strangely quiet place, especially for a city of over eight million. Now, the city that barely peeps has become the city that beeps. In the process, a xenophobic city that was a drab, grey and forlorn collection of concrete monoliths and barracks-like eyesores has transformed itself into a boisterous, booming capital of world-class ambitions (and picked up an estimated four million new residents). A city that was a stark commentary on the failures of one system – and no denunciation of Soviet power spoke as authoritatively as a Moscow bread line – has become a scorecard for the joys and excesses of the new Russian capitalism.

High-rent apartments and glitzy disco-casinos, shiny black Mercedes and shimmering bank offices, Gucci and Armani, sushi and Dom Perignon. All that, plus homelessness, joblessness, crime rates like those of any big Western city, urban decay and the rot of corruption to the core – to say nothing of the vicious extortion, racketeering, narcotics and prostitution gangs whose violent reign of terror over Moscow, and seeming invulnerability to prosecution, has earned them the nickname 'mafiya'.

ISLAND CITY

'But Moscow is not Russia,' they say. In one way, that is very true, as a drive to cities located even an hour away will prove. Save perhaps St Petersburg, no other Russian city comes even close to the level of prosperity, modern infrastructure and comfort of the capital. In most places outside Moscow, there are few signs that communism ever collapsed. In most rural areas, it looks like the twentieth century is about to begin, not end. Even Moscow's powerful, ambitious mayor, Yury

Luzhkov, has said, 'It is probably proper to view Moscow as a [separate] state.'

But in other ways, Moscow is very much Russia, and not just because it is the seat of federal power that sets the agenda for the rest of the country. Eighty per cent of the country's wealth is located here, but most of it comes from remote and blighted mining towns and oil fields in uninhabitable places. That's too bad for the people who live out there, who enjoy little benefit from their hard work. But for anyone who comes here – and especially for tourists and the ever-growing community of expatriates from the West – that translates to all the boomtown goodies that have sprung up in Moscow: first-rate hotels and supermarkets, well-stocked department stores and fashion boutiques, decent restaurants and plenty of nightlife for all tastes.

Companies such as Gazprom, the huge gas monopoly, whose workers in subsidiaries in far northern Siberia go months without pay, have set up huge, modern offices in Moscow, populated by directors and managers who enjoy the fruits of the labour done thousands of miles away.

New Russians

By their gold chains, leather Gucci T shirts, $2,000 pairs of shoes and Cherokee jeeps will ye know them. They shall go on jet-fuelled shopping sprees to Harrods and Bloomingdales. Their favourite colours shall be maroon and pistachio. And they shall be called the New Russians.

The plague of crass, flashy, ostentatious nouveaux riches that has descended upon Moscow since the collapse of communism must count as the defining social phenomenon of the post-Soviet era. It wasn't just that these people were so breathtakingly rich, but that the backdrop of Moscow in the early 1990s was so bleak and grey and the rest of its population so uniformly impoverished. The mini convoys of BMWs, Mercs and jeeps roaring down Tverskaya couldn't have been in more glaring contrast to the vast sea of dingy Ladas that surrounded them. Their owners – wearing their regulation maroon or pistachio jackets, and always with a primped-up designer moll in tow – came across as a separate, privileged breed. The old élite had been reborn as the new élite – though now with far greater wealth and infinitely more opportunity to display it.

And because money had come too easily (usually by ripping off the State during privatisation) and too quickly (before any consumerist etiquette could develop), New Russians spent with abandon, equating quantity with quality. They bade for the most expensive paintings at

Sotheby's simply because they were the most expensive, bought up half of Corfu, invaded Europe's most exclusive holiday resorts and snapped up townhouses in Hampstead, paying with briefcases stuffed full of cash. In one of Moscow's prime New Russian hangouts, the ludicrously titled Up and Down Club, punters would run up tabs totalling tens of thousands of dollars. Another New Russian club would auction a rose every night, which sometimes fetched three or four thousand dollars. Added to tawdry glitz and wealth was the element of danger. The bodyguards who trailed their masters in riot gear carrying Uzi submachine guns were living testament to the fact that making money in Russia was a very dangerous business.

Though New Russians have generally tended to contribute little to society and usually end up paying no taxes, they have at least given the nation one very valuable commodity: the New Russian joke. Russians have a tradition of dealing with the injustices of their society by laughing them off with jokes, and the New Russian's image as heartless, soulless, big-spenders has spawned a whole rash of them. For example, there's the one about the New Russian who gets an offer from the devil. The businessman responds, dumbfounded: 'You want my soul? And in return I get $1 million? What's the catch?'.

CAPITALIST GAINS?

The inequities of Moscow's relationship to the outlying provinces is a metaphor for the imbalance of Russia's capitalist system, which has extracted six years of pain from ordinary citizens and rewarded well-connected insiders with unheard-of riches.

Presiding over Moscow's transformation is Luzhkov, who is widely expected to be planning a run for the Russian presidency in 2000. As one recent commentator put it, 'He has decreed that Moscow shall be a city of tourism and light like Paris, a financial centre like London, a mighty car-producing centre like Detroit, and, of course, a daunting imperial capital. In the best traditions of Soviet propaganda all this will be on show for the world to admire.'

Shortly after becoming mayor in June 1992, Luzhkov won exemption for his city from Russia's privatisation programme. In Moscow, the city kept ownership over public property. Using this control as leverage, he has transformed the city government into a multibillion dollar property and industrial empire, with its own television station, newspapers, an oil refinery and a controlling share in over 180 other enterprises. And what the city does not own in Moscow, it controls, thanks to its firm grip on all municipal land.

Critics say that the city's dual role as regulator and entrepreneur has encouraged cronyism, discouraged competition, and contributed to the inflation that has made Moscow the world's third most expensive city after Tokyo and Hong Kong. Business people tell dark tales of visits by tax police and fire safety inspectors to those who buck

the mayor. But few people dare to come out and say it: Luzhkov has a 20-0 record in libel cases. And the mayor is popular, because he gets things done.

Under Luzhkov's direction, buildings have been scrubbed and painted, roads have been paved and dozens of sweeping architectural projects have been completed. Among these are the $360-million reconstruction of the Church of Christ the Saviour, which was demolished by Stalin, and a cavernous $350-million underground shopping mall next to the Kremlin, under the square where those Soviet tanks once paraded.

Luzhkov has embellished his can-do image with populist touches, such as personally touring construction sites and leading his City Hall team in soccer matches. He has peppered the calendar with holidays that put his city on display to the world: a gala birthday celebration in 1997 that had to be the most ballyhooed 850th anniversary of anything in the history of mankind; and the 1998 World Youth Games, a youth Olympics created at Luzhkov's behest by the International Olympic Committee.

Luzhkov has also overseen the re-implementation of draconian, Soviet-era rules and practices to keep homeless people off the streets – such as having police lock them up or ship them out of town on trains.

This approach has earned criticism from human rights groups, although most Muscovites seem to approve: Luzhkov won 90 per cent of the vote in his June 1996 re-election. He might not do so well in a presidential election in the provinces, where people have no money, and where Moscow's big-spending policies are seen as the reason.

There's a difference at McLenin's you'll enjoy.

Architecture

The power to build has its users and abusers: Moscow's landscape tells the tales.

Moscow's architecture tells the city's story, writ large in stone, stucco, concrete, steel and russet brick. Each successive period in the city's 850-plus-year history has left its mark. With every new regime came new styles and new ideals, overlaid in an often haphazard fashion, creating the accretive, discordant character of today's Moscow. Moreover, it is a city where politicos and patriarchs have known the propaganda value of architecture. For those who relish the convergence of art and power, it doesn't get any sexier than this.
● More information on buildings picked out in **bold** is given elsewhere in the Guide; see **Index**.

URBAN ORIGINS

When founded in the twelfth century, Moscow lay at the intersection of a number of trading routes and to this day its radial structure reflects its early origins. But it is the successive rings that grew around the original **Kremlin** centre that give it its distinctive urban plan. As the city expanded, new fortifications and boundaries were built beyond the Kremlin. Many of these boundaries were later transformed into main thoroughfares, as with the Boulevard Ring and the Garden Ring. Still later, the circuit railway and, in the 1960s, the Moscow Ring Road widened the circle yet further.

In the mid-sixteenth century, new walls were constructed around the Kremlin and nearby Kitai-Gorod, then a bustling trading area. The newly cordoned area formed the present-day **Red Square** (Krasnaya Ploshchad), where soon after the infamous Ivan the Terrible erected the polychromatic icon of Russian architecture, the Cathedral of St Basil the Blessed.

THE KREMLIN

The Kremlin, the symbol of the Evil Empire for Cold War Western eyes, was first built on its site at Borovinsky Hill during the eleventh and twelfth centuries. In this early incarnation, the citadel was made of earthen ramparts surrounded by wooden walls and moats. The edifice went through a number of rebuilding campaigns, including the reconstruction begun in 1485 that gave the red-brick walls and towers the appearance they have today. The project was overseen by Italian architects, thus its likeness to such structures as Milan's Sforza Castle is no accident. The walls were reinforced with 20 towers designed in a variety of shapes. They were capped by wooden roofs until the seventeenth century, when a number were decorated with the pyramidal roofs and spires we see today. Catherine the Great intended to completely knock

We have lift-off! Moscow's new booster-rocket architecture.

down the Kremlin and replace it with a colonnaded classical monstrosity, courtesy of the hapless Russian architect Vasily Bazhenov. Catherine seems to have enjoyed taunting him with thwarted commissions, and she thankfully cancelled the project just as the first of the Kremlin's walls and towers were in the sights of the wrecker's ball. In Soviet times, red stars made of precious rubies were installed at the pinnacle of the spires.

PIOUS MOSCOW

While often called the third Rome (Constantinople being the second), Moscow doesn't boast the same pagan ruins, but it does have a plethora of Russian Orthodox churches. Before the massive destruction of churches in the Soviet era, Moscow was aptly called the 'City of 500 Churches'. Perhaps because of its former wealth, the city still has a significant number of spectacular churches, many of which are currently in one stage of reconstruction or another. For those interested in ecclesiastic architecture outside of the Kremlin, with its own bounty of late medieval cathedrals, Varvarka Ulitsa in Kitai-Gorod and the area eastwards have a wealth of churches that were spared the bulldozer. Likewise, near the Tretyakov Gallery, Bolshaya Ordynka Ulitsa boasts an enfilade of them. Of the ten extant monasteries and convents, the most noteworthy are the **Donskoi** Monastery and the **Novodevichy** Convent, which date back to the sixteenth century, and the Novospassky Monastery, erected in the seventeenth century.

The most conspicuous and daring ecclesiastical building in Moscow is the red-brick **Cathedral of St Basil the Blessed** on the southern end of Red Square. Construction started in 1555 to commemorate the Russian victory over the Tartars. After Tsar Ivan's death, the remains of one of his more outspoken adversaries, the holy fool Basil the Blessed, were reinterred in a special chapel and bell tower built nearby. The cathedral's ten asymmetrically arranged roofs and onion domes hark back to medieval Russian wooden construction. The fantastic colours were added in 1670 to make it the indelible landmark it is today.

While it was not novel for Russian churches to be capped by helmet-shaped domes or by ten towers (most notably at the Church of the Ascension at Kolemenskoye outside Moscow), St Basil's may have been the first instance of the *lukovitsa*, literally, the onion dome. The current domes were constructed after a fire in 1583, and are among some of the earliest onion domes chronicled in Russian masonry architecture. It is still debated whether the ultimate origins ofr this style came from the Church of the Holy Sepulchre in Jerusalem or Indian sources, or whether they were just an extrapolation of old wooden churches, then still the most pervasive church type. In any case, old domes and tent towers were replaced or capped

with this new model. In contrast to the more open plans of many Russian churches, St Basil's has a number of individual chapels intended to honour the various saints on whose name days particular battles were won against the Tartars. Legend has it that during the Napoleonic invasion the cathedral was used as a stable. After the Revolution it was opened as a museum, whose exhibitions chronicle its own history.

WESTWARD HO!

When Peter the Great relocated Russia's capital to St Petersburg, Moscow felt the reverberations from the new Imperial seat. As St Petersburg evolved into a grand city with hopes of rivalling its occidental counterparts, Moscow, too, adopted the neo-classicism of the West. It was under the reign of Catherine the Great that grand country estates were erected on a scale intended to rival the Sun King's Versailles. A triad of estates on the periphery of the city are open as museums: **Ostankino, Kuskovo** and **Tsaritsyno**.

Both Ostankino and Kuskovo were constructed in the latter half of the eighteenth century for the noble Sheremetyev family, whose name also graces the international airport. The two were designed in the neo-classical style with generous grounds and outbuildings. With its grotto, orangery and formal garden, Kuskovo's opulence vied with its French models, affording it the nickname the 'Moscow Versailles'. Ostankino even boasted Italian architects, including Giacomo Quarenghi, who had worked extensively in St Petersburg.

During Napoleon's invasion of Moscow in 1812 much of the city was set ablaze by Muscovites themselves in an attempt to keep the French at bay. When the city was rebuilt, its noblemen embraced the same empire style that was concurrently lining Paris's *grandes rues*. Today the neighbourhood around Ulitsa Prechistenka has some of the best examples of the Empire style. If you catch one of these old mansions under reconstruction today, you might be in for a surprise. While typically clad in pastel stuccos with a white trim, lurking below is a simple wooden frame. Essentially, they are giant log cabins clothed in confectionery colours.

In Soviet times, many of these homes became embassies as they were clearly inappropriate for single-family use. The Danish embassy (Prechistinsky Pereulok 9) now resides in a butter-yellow mansion that has grown over the years, but, with its low silhouette, maintains its Empire elegance. Now banks and other commercial concerns are moving into the neighbourhood, having discovered its proximity to central Moscow. In the centre, the shell-pink **Bolshoi Theatre**, with its eight-column portico and impressive bronze quadriga, was built in the 1820s to an Empire-style design by the prolific Osip Bove. The building has seen a number of reconstructions after fires and

The elevation of the proletariat

While the Palace of the Soviets, the gigantic, utopian monstrosity that Stalin planned to build on the site of the demolished Church of Christ the Saviour, was thankfully aborted, the seeds of its conception as a rival to anything the West could produce did ultimately bear fruit in the early 1950s. In its stead came the seven more modest skyscrapers that ring Moscow today with their tall spires. With their wedding cake silhouettes, these buildings variously house the prestigious Moscow State University and the Ministry of Foreign Affairs or serve as tourist hotels or luxury housing for the Party elite and today's new Russians.

While the awesome height of the bombastic capital may have been unrealistic, the collective impact of this group of more modest skyscrapers was intended to surpass New York's coveted skyline. Khrushchev quoted Stalin's argument for their erection: 'We've won the war and are recognised the world over as the glorious victors. We must be ready for an influx of foreign visitors. What will happen if they walk around Moscow and find no skyscrapers? They will make unfavourable comparisons with capitalist cities.' Originally, eight buildings were planned. The eighth – intended to be a 38-storey office block near the site of the current Hotel Rossiya across from the Kremlin – was never built because it would have dwarfed the Kremlin. Today, the radial siting of the buildings visually unifies the city. One of them is visible from as far away as Warsaw – a gift to the Poles from the Soviet Union.

The model for these buildings was the 1920s Manhattan skyscraper. One of the architects, Vyacheslav Oltarzhevsky, had worked in New York during that decade and, upon his return in the 1930s, was sent to the gulag. Once released he was able to share his knowledge – especially the technical expertise he had acquired – with the construction team. (Ironically, if it had not been for the intervention of the US embassy, Oltarzhevsky would have remained in the prison camps.)

Today these Soviet beacons are adapting to the new Russia. The mammoth skyscraper

located on Kudrinskaya Ploshchad still houses former Party bigwigs, but also the New Russians who can afford to live there. But it is the transformation of the food shops on the first floor that is most remarkable.

In the early 1950s, under the ultimate direction of Stalin, architect Yakov Zhislin worked on the design of these shops in each of the skyscrapers' four corners. Each would sell something different: fish, meat, bread, dairy products. The design took its cue from the elegant turn-of-the-century Yeliseyev store on Tverskaya Ulitsa. Today, this former fish store has been dusted off and converted into an upscale restaurant, **Le Gastronome**. Instead of seeing a line of babushkas queuing for a kilo of fish, you'll hear the sonorous cellphone bleep of well-polished Muscovites and expats resounding under crystal chandeliers and original stained glass. And after dinner you can relax in the casino located just below, the Beverly Hills Club, owned by none other than Chuck Norris. Ah, progress.

damage incurred during World War II, but has retained its classical character.

MOSCOW MODERNE

In the late nineteenth century, Moscow grew as an urban hub in an increasingly industrialised society and accordingly saw the introduction of new types of building, such as railway stations, department stores, banks, museums and factories. Simultaneously, new technologies like reinforced concrete construction came on the scene, allowing for unsupported and thus unobstructed, open spaces and larger window expanses. Eventually, a new style evolved, the *style moderne*.

The Zuyev Club: *Constructivism's finest and funkiest. See page 25.*

Just as the area around Ulitsa Prechistenka had become the stomping ground for Moscow's nobility, with the rise of commerce, the neighbourhood surrounding Patriarch's Pond (Patriarshy Prudy – best known for its depiction in Bulgakov's *The Master and Margarita)* became home to the city's burgeoning merchant class – the greatest patrons of the *style moderne* – at the end of the nineteenth century. For all their flamboyance, these predecessors of Moscow's present-day nouveaux riches were not entirely without culture nor passion for their country. With fortunes made in everything from textiles to motor

manufacturing, these men were generous patrons of the arts as well as architecture.

As in the West, *fin de siècle* Moscow – on the cusp of the modern movement – saw a quick succession of varied architectural styles in a restless search for something new. The entrepreneurial elite were at the forefront of this attempt to make an original statement. Architects designed sentimental medieval revival buildings in the late nineteenth century, but by 1900 the *style moderne* – not dissimilar from the art nouveau of the West – had hit its stride. While it is often thought that this movement was simply derivative of Western trends, it had a distinctly Russian flavour in its connection to traditional artisanry and craftmanship. Nowhere is this more apparent than in the Abramtsevo artists' colony just outside the city.

The doyen of Moscow's *style moderne* was the prolific architect Fyodor Shekhtel, whose 1903 **Ryabushinsky** house is so spectacular that it has often been ranked before the Kremlin as a must-see. Along with a brood of brothers, Ryabushinsky had founded the first car company in Russia, but with the Revolution his 'Detroit on the Moskva' was appropriated and now stands as the ZiL factory. Other modern gems are fellow architect Leo Kekushev's house, the **Metropol** hotel, the Derozhinskaya house (that is now home to the Australian embassy) and, most publicly, Shekhtel's magnificent Yaroslavsky railway station and the **Moscow Art Theatre**. Other more eclectic buildings of interest built around that time include Savva Morozov's Gothic mansion and the Perlov teashop built in the Chinese style and still open today.

CUTTING EDGE

After the Revolution, Moscow's architects – by their profession an idealistically predisposed bunch – rode the wave of the new zeitgeist with verve. While all the arts rallied around the notion of a new order, architecture brought the most public contributions. Young architects formed new schools and design studios. One avant-garde group, the constructivists, argued that only pure, unadorned geometric forms should be used in a building's plans, which should in any case be flexible, the final form following the function. For these young iconoclasts, economy of form reflected the newly embraced Marxism Leninism. To that end, they put forth manifestos that were condemned by adversaries as esoteric. However, their radical designs would influence modern architecture internationally.

Not only were the constructivists' sleek forms new but so was the type of building they were applied to, notably the workers' club. Known both as a 'palace of labour' and a 'palace of culture', these were expressly ideological in their conception. Workers' clubs were to serve as meeting and recreational spaces for industrial enterprises and trade unions, sometimes for entire urban districts.

In his 1929 Zuyev Club (Lesnaya Ulitsa 18), designed for the Department of Municipal Economy, architect Ilya Golosov designed a building emblematic of the avant-garde constructivist movement. He fronted a rectangular building with a multistorey, transparent glass cylinder that in turn intersects with a horizontal, masonry plane projecting from the convex glass wall. The building as a whole has a sense of movement, representative to Golosov of the spirit of the Revolution and the emerging machine age. For the constructivists, the success of the Soviet experiment was synonymous with the modernisation of society.

One building that shares an aesthetic likeness to the work of the constructivists is the Melnikov house and studio (Krivoarbatsky Pereulok 10), designed by architect Konstantin Melnikov for his family. While Melnikov's penchant for elementary geometries was not dissimilar from the work of the other avant-gardes, Melnikov was a maverick who did not abide by any set rules. At a time when other architects were consumed with designing communal housing for the good of the people, Melnikov was putting up the most bourgeois of buildings, a single-family house. Located just off the Old Arbat on a small site crammed between buildings that dwarf it today, it comprises two intersecting white cylinders punctured by hexagonal windows. It was designated a historic monument in 1987 and has since undergone significant renovations. Melnikov's Rusavov Club, the Narkomfin apartment building and Alexei Shchusev's Ministry of Agriculture building are likewise avant-garde staples. And it would be remiss to exclude modern giant Le Corbusier's one Soviet work, the Tsentrosoyuz building (Myasnitskaya Ulitsa 39). Sadly, most of these modern masterpieces are now badly in need of attention.

SOCIALIST REALISM

By the mid-1930s, the ultra modern architecture of the constructivists had been summarily dismissed as too bourgeois and unsuitable for the ascendant Capital of World Communism. In its place came socialist realism, the aesthetic ideology of the Stalin era, was emerging. Stalinist architects borrowed classical models and modified them as they saw fit in their attempt to appropriate associations of a classical past while simultaneously creating something stamped with the imprimatur of the USSR. It was seldom a successful hybrid.

The **Hotel Moskva** is a typical example of the follies that were produced at the hands of Stalin's architectural darlings. The prestigious building, a stone's throw from the Kremlin, was earmarked as a base for visiting Party elite and, as such, needed to be far more obviously impressive than the original 1932 design. The Moskva's resulting deformity – its asymmetrical façade – is nonetheless a monument to the fear Stalin inspired. As the story goes, Stalin had two design options given to him on one piece of paper; instead of indicating a preference, he simply signed the sheet. Rather than risk incurring the volatile First Comrade's wrath, architect Alexei Shchusev incorporated both variants in the one building, which reinterpreted classicism to dubious effect. As far as his neck was concerned, Shchusev – who had dabbled in constructivism with the Ministry of Agriculture building – probably did the right thing. He was given the honorific title of academician and had an architectural museum named after him.

Upon the hotel's completion in 1937, US architect Frank Lloyd Wright was given a tour by Shchusev himself. When asked through an interpreter what he thought of the massive ensemble, Wright is said to have replied, 'It is the ugliest thing I have ever seen!', which was graciously translated as, 'I am very impressed!'

While much of Stalin's architectural handiwork appears risible, the Moscow underground metro system was an impressive feat. It still vies with the world's best, both architecturally and in terms of its efficiency and cleanliness. The bulk of the system was constructed in two building campaigns: the first launched in 1935 and the second in the 1950s, after an interruption during World War II.

Under Stalin, the metro was not merely a means of transportation for the masses but a political statement. The stations were presented as 'Palaces of the People' and designed with the gilt opulence once reserved for nobility. Stalin's socialist realism found didactic expression in mosaics, murals and sculptures that depicted the glory of the Soviet state: smiling workers toiling arm in arm or the friezes found at Izmailovsky Park station, where AK-47 machine guns are used as abstract ornamentation in traditional floral bas reliefs. One of the most impressive stations is Mayakovsky, where ceiling mosaics depict Soviet aviation triumphs and sleek stainless steel arches create an art deco look. So proud of this station were the authorities that they had a replica constructed for the Soviet pavilion at the 1939 World's Fair in New York.

SHOCK OF THE NEW: MOSCOW TODAY

Today, despite Moscow's wholehearted embrace of the free market, architectural style is still dictated from above by the current Moscow mayor, Yuri Luzhkov. He has adopted numerous pet projects including the reconstruction of the **Cathedral of Christ the Saviour** and the **Okhotny Ryad** underground mega-mall. Luzhkov – who is reported to have his eye on Boris Yeltsin's job – has attempted to redraw Moscow with a laughable brand of the postmodernism that peaked in the West in the mid-1980s. For his architectural autocracy the diminutive politician has gained the moniker the 'Great Architect of Capitalism', a clear reference to Stalin – the 'Great Architect of Socialism' – who also had a penchant for using architecture for political ends.

In general, Luzhkov is trying to decorate the city in postmodern versions of the classical and medieval styles that he feels reflect Russia's architectural history. Though what the mayor himself has dubbed the 'Moscow style' has never been concretely defined, to judge by completed projects it must involve the extensive use of towers and turrets, columns and capitals – the architectural vocabulary of a forward-looking world city

anchored in a rich history. Luzhkov has vociferously declared this Moscow style appropriate for new construction in Moscow.

As Russia embraces capitalism, it seems its buildings have likewise adopted the neon-sign mentality in all its crassest aspects. In Luzhkov's Moscow, this is done with a unique flair. Just steps from Red Square in the new $350-million Okhotny Ryad mall, shoppers can experience a different century in Moscow's architectural history on each of three levels as they make their way to the food court at the bottom. Designer Zurab Tsereteli, known as Luzhkov's court artist for the incredible number of city commissions he receives, attempts to nod to the city's history by simulating marble in sheet metal and covering nearly every surface in glistening gilt.

Despite the mayor's dominance, there are, in fact, a number of contemporary architects both conceiving and actually building provocative alternatives to the Disneyland Moscow style. The International Moscow Bank, prominently sited on the Moscow River a stone's throw from the newly minted cathedral, topped the list of favourite buildings in a recent survey of architects and critics and has won the prestigious Russian State Prize conferred by President Yeltsin. The six-storey bank faced in pink granite, designed by the new private firm Ostozhenka, acknowledges Moscow's architectural history without resorting to appliquéd motifs. With its stainless steel roof and a generous use of industrial glass block, the building's high-tech design flies in the face of the Moscow style and, accordingly, has met with the mayor's disapproval.

Another building that reflects this philosophy is the **Andrei Sakharov Museum** for Peace, Progress and Human Rights, designed by leading architect Eugene Asse in collaboration with a number of young architects and completed in 1996. One of Asse's young collaborators, Ilya Voznesensky, similarly finds the mayor's obsession with historical styles absurd. He has already felt the reach of Luzhkov's long arm on one of his projects: a large mall and multiplex cinema slated to be constructed just off the Garden Ring. After viewing the drawings, Luzhkov said that classical arches and historical towers must be added so that it conformed to the Moscow style. 'I don't know if Luzhkov himself even likes this Moscow style any more, but I think he wants to finish what he has started,' explained Voznesensky recently. 'He wants the 1990s to be remembered as the Luzhkov period in architecture. Russia is trying to catch a train that has already departed. We need to catch our own train.'

Voznesensky's sentiments mark the barometer of change, not only as the words of the new generation of architects, but also because he is Stalin's great-grandson.

Literary Moscow

A guided tour of Moscow's literary landmarks.

The original statue of satirist **Nikolai Gogol**.

Believe it or not, Russians are fond of quoting the nineteenth-century poet Fyodor Tyutchev's dictum: 'Russia cannot be understood with the mind.' But if Russia is an enigma, as Winston Churchill once remarked, then the pleasures of discovering its secrets are all the greater. And there's possibly no better way than through the written word. Russia boasts more literary museums and monuments than any other country and Moscow, as its major city, looms large in many of them.

But, just as Russia is a literary culture, so too is its past. Russian history is shot through with dissent and censorship, suppression and insurrection, and this is reflected in its books. In one of the most famous episodes in Russian literary lore, poet **Alexander Pushkin** (1799-1837) – author of *Eugene Onegin*, who is thought of as the Russian Shakespeare – was summoned to the Winter Palace by Nicholas I, after a period of exile. Questioned by the Tsar about his attitude to the failed plot of

December 14, 1825, intended to institute a constitutional monarchy, Pushkin said 'I could not but have taken part in it. Only my absence saved me, for which I thank God.' He lived to tell the tale.

Two of the places in Moscow most associated with Pushkin are the **Church of the Great Ascension** (Ulitsa Bolshaya Nikitskaya 31), where the poet married the beautiful 18-year-old Natalya Goncherova in 1831, and the turquoise house at Ulitsa Arbat 53, where they spent their first months of married life. It was in defence of Goncherova's honour that Pushkin died tragically in a duel outside St Petersburg.

No walk through the city would be complete without a stop at Moscow's most popular meeting place, the Alexander Pushkin statue, built on Tverskoi Bulvar in 1880 and moved to its present place on Pushkin Square in 1950. After many years of raising money, kopek by kopek, from the people, this was the first monument to be built in Moscow dedicated not to a military hero, but to a writer.

With the arrival of the Soviets after 1917, the state was to erect many more literary monuments. The government renamed streets after writers who had not fallen out of favour, and made those who were banned or persecuted martyrs in the eyes of the intelligentsia. Both the authorities and much of the reading public accorded writers an almost idol-like status. In many ways, it was a reflection of the cult of personality that surrounded Stalin.

There is perhaps no clearer way of gauging the Soviet state's hypocritical attitude toward literature than by comparing the two monuments dedicated to the brilliant satirist **Nikolai Gogol** (1809-52). The sanguine statue of him at the end of Gogolevsky Bulvar is 'a gift from the Soviet government', and portrays him in military uniform, showing how uneasily such an acute critic of political corruption fitted into official Soviet culture. The real monument to Gogol, built by the sculptor Nikolai Andreyev in 1909, was moved to Nikitsky Bulvar in 1951 to make way for the present statue. Nearby, on Malaya Nikitskaya Ulitsa 6/2, is **Maxim Gorky's** (1868-1936) former residence (chosen for him by Stalin), now a museum. The prolific Gorky was an early Bolshevik and a pivotal figure during the Revolution and the early years of the Soviet Union. To the south, at Ulitsa Lva Tolstogo 21, lies the Moscow home, now a museum, of **Leo Tolstoy** (1828-1910). The author of *War and Peace, Anna Karenina, The Cossacks* and many more, Tolstoy's impact on Russian literary culture is impossible to overestimate. His vitriolic attacks on Tsarist policies brought him into contact with pre-Revolutionary elements, but also the enmity of the establishment: in 1901, he was excommunicated from the Russian Orthodox Church.

In 1959, the original monument to Gogol was installed in the courtyard of Nikitsky Bulvar 7, where the author burned the second volume of his masterpiece *Dead Souls,* nine days before his suicide in 1852. It was in this house that Gogol first read his play *The Government Inspector* to actors and such writers as **Ivan Turgenev** (1818-83) and **Sergei Aksakov** (1791-1859).

On the other side of the boulevard at No.8A (now the House of Journalists) is the site of the Left Front of Art, or Lef, a literary group formed in 1922 and made up of former members of the pre-war futurist movement. One of the Lef members, the poet **Vladimir Mayakovsky** (1893-1930), viewed it as an aesthetic enterprise that would transform everyday life through art. Among those who contributed to the organisation's journals were such pioneering artists as the photographer Alexander Rodchenko, film directors Sergei Eisenstein and Dziga Vertov, theatre director Vsevolod Meyerhold and writer **Isaac Babel** (1894-1940).

It was in this building that the Soviet 'poet of the countryside' **Sergei Yesenin** (1895-1925) gave his last reading in October 1922, and here, two months later, that Moscow paid its last respects to him after his suicide in the Angleterre Hotel in what was then Leningrad. Blessed with good looks and behavioural problems in equal measure, Yesenin left a last poem, written in blood, although the laconic plaque on the façade of the hotel ('A great Russian poet has died') doesn't tell you that.

His happiest moments in Moscow were spent, on his return from Petrograd in 1919, in the impressive, eclectic house at Vozdvizheka 16, the Proletkult ('proletarian culture') centre, where he lived on the second floor. The building now rejoices under the felicitous sobriquet the House of Friendship of Peoples. During his marriage to the American-born pioneer of modern dance **Isadora Duncan** (1878-1927), who had come to the USSR at the invitation of the Soviet government, they lived at Prechistenka 20, where Duncan held her dancing school. The couple met at the studio of the avant-garde artist Georgy Yakulov at Bolshaya Sadovaya 10. Duncan spoke little Russian and Yesenin no English. Undeterred, the dancer is reputed to have stroked the poet's blond locks and said in Russian, 'golden head,' thus beginning their tempestuous romance.

This apartment house, built in the Moscow art nouveau style, is also the best-known residence of **Mikhail Bulgakov** (1891-1940), who lived in two communal flats here in the early 1920s. The house is described as No.302-b in his philosophical novel *The Master and Margarita*. He describes one apartment as 'long having enjoyed if not a bad, then in any case a strange reputation'. It has become a mecca for young Bulgakov fans, who, much to the dismay of the building's current residents, have covered the stairwell with graffiti relating to his works. So much of the city was described or hinted at by the writer in his novels that Muscovites sometimes refer to parts of the city as Bulgakov's Moscow.

Bulgakov famously wrote that 'manuscripts don't burn'. This phrase could well be used to sum up his life as a writer. Widely known as a playwright, his plays were closed down again and again, often before they were staged publicly. Until the 1960s, when his four novels were published in the USSR, his reputation rested largely on plays that had passed the censors such as *The Days of the Turbins* and an adaptation of Gogol's *Dead Souls*.

The Moscow Arts Theatre (MKhAT), was of particular importance to Bulgakov. The theatre, designed by Russia's leading art nouveau architect, Fyodor Shekhtel, is closely associated with **Anton Chekhov** (1860-1904), whose last play, *The Cherry Orchard*, premièred here. After all Bulgakov's plays had been banned, the playwright wrote to Stalin in 1930, begging the dictator to make him a director, an extra or even a stage hand at the theatre. In his famous phone call to the playwright's home, when told by Bulgakov that the theatre had refused to take him on, Stalin is reported to have said, 'You make an application there, and I have the feeling they will accept it.' It is possible that Stalin had been motivated to favour the writer by the recent news of Mayakovsky's suicide, which had dealt a blow to the regime's reputation.

Bulgakov's Moscow is vast and all the places mentioned in it too numerous to be listed here. Perhaps the most famous is Patriarch's Ponds, the setting for the opening scene of *The Master and Margarita*. Among the other well-known addresses is Tverskoi Bulvar 25, the Literary Institute, which was created on Maxim Gorky's initiative and which housed such writers as **Osip Mandelstam** (1891-1938) and **Andrei Platonov** (1899-1951). *Doctor Zhivago's* author, **Boris Pasternak** (1890-1960), also lived here briefly in 1932. This is the birthplace of the nineteenth-century writer and liberal journalist **Alexander Herzen** (1812-70). It is also a possible model for the literary club Mosolit, referred to as Griboyedov in *The Master and Margarita*. Another such place mentioned at the end of that novel is Sparrow Hills, where Woland has a panoramic view of the chaos he unleashes on the entire city.

Like scores of other Russian writers, Bulgakov was buried at Novodevichy Monastery, in 1940. Appropriately, his gravestone once stood above the tomb of Gogol, the source of inspiration for many of Bulgakov's works, before Gogol's grave was moved from the Danilov Cemetery to Novodevichy. Inscribed on the stone are the words, 'I shall make fun with bitter words'.

Sightseeing

Sightseeing

It may be ugly on the face of it, but Moscow is a city with hidden charms.

For most visitors, sightseeing in Moscow means the Kremlin, Red Square (Krasnaya Ploshchad), Teatralnaya Ploshchad, the Arbat and, if you're really feeling brave, a jaunt halfway up Tverskaya Ulitsa. The rest of the city remains a grotesque, grey mystery flashing across the windscreen on the taxi-ride between the hotel and the airport, an Orwellian cityscape punctuated by occasional landmarks – the White House, perhaps, or Lubyanka – and encircled by Stalin's famous Gothic skyscrapers. Communist urban planning seems to have been designed to set nerves jangling, eyeballs bulging, necks cricking and to send the average sense of direction into a tailspin. As a consequence, Moscow is not one of the world's most tourist-friendly cities.

But all this bleakness just serves to throw into relief the magnificence of the heart of the city. Rearing up on the horizon as you wander from Teatralnaya (the theatre district) or travel by car across Bolshoi Kamenny Most, the gleaming red walls of the Kremlin never fail to trigger a gasp, either figurative or real. And while the $45 price tag (including the cathedrals and the Armoury) may rank it among the world's most expensive tourist attractions, the only problem visitors may encounter is finding the capacity to soak up so many stunningly beautiful sights over the course of a couple of hours. Red Square is also a doddle.

For those who are determined to venture that little bit further, Moscow conceals some true and often bizarre wonders. If you're not concerned about over-dosing on cupolas and apses, the city is scattered with more churches than the communists had dynamite, as well as quite a few monasteries: the Novodevichy, Danilov and Donskoi, all hidden away in anonymous suburbs. Aristocratic town estates such as Ostankino, Kolomenskoye and Tsaritsyno are terrific attractions as well. Even Stalinism has bequeathed some essential sights to the city, such as the **VVTs,** (often known by its old acronym **VDNKh**) the All Russia Exhibition Centre, which was constructed as a communist showpiece with a massive, inhuman and fantastic allure. Whether you want to take the timid minimalist or the brash maximalist tack, this chapter should help you to plan how best to approach Moscow.

● Sights marked in **bold** are covered in more detail elsewhere in the Guide; refer to the **Index**. For Moscow street maps, *see pages 277-282*

The Heart of the City

The Kremlin

Hunched on the top of Borovitsky Hill, its jagged, ruddy outline simultaneously sullen, suspicious, glittering and majestic, the **Kremlin** is the architectural and psychological nucleus of Moscow. It exerts a gravitational pull not only on the cars scooting along the Kremlevskaya Naberezhnaya, but also on those districts out of sight of its soaring towers, turrets and gilded cupolas. The city of Moscow sprouted from the Kremlin, spreading itself in concentric circles as it grew in stature and its population soared.

Despite various attempts to tame and civilise the city – most recently in a plan formulated by the communists in the 1930s – Moscow still maintains the medieval imprint of the Kremlin walls. While some form of settlement probably existed on the site earlier in the form of earthen, moated ramparts, the date usually quoted for the establishment of the first Kremlin is 1156, when Prince Yury Dolgoruky built oak walls to shelter the clusters of wooden workshops and 'trading rows' that pretty much comprised the whole of Moscow at that time. The name 'Kremlin' first appeared around 1340 and is thought by some to derive from the Greek word *kremn* or *kremnos*, meaning 'a steep hill over a ravine', though it is more likely that it comes from *kremnik*, an economical Slavic word meaning 'thick coniferous woods in a swampy place'.

Visitors now enter the Kremlin either via Troitsky Most (Trinity Bridge) and through the gates of the Troitskaya Tower, or from the far end of the Kremlin via the Borovitskaya Tower. Tickets for foreigners are bought at a kiosk to the left of the Troitsky Most. Entrance to the Kremlin is only about 30¢ (two rubles) for both foreigners and Russians, but that just gets you inside the walls. If you actually want to see any of the cathedrals or visit the museums inside the Kremlin, prices are exorbitant. For foreigners, admission to each of the cathedrals or to the **Patriarch's Palace** costs $6.50 a pop, with an $11 charge for the **Armoury**, so you're looking at an unbelievably costly $45 to see the lot. You'll also have to check your bags in a little nook under the

Kutafya Tower at a cost of 35¢.

To avoid some of this expense, it might be an idea to join the Russian tour that departs hourly from the back of the **State Historical Museum** and covers everything, except the Armoury, for just $3.50. Inside, expect to be brusquely ushered along by whistle-blowing guards, whose job it is to prevent tourists from wandering into the restricted zones, which make up most of the Kremlin. What visitors are actually allowed to see comes to about a third of the total area. For the Patriarch's Palace and the Armoury, *see chapter* **Museums & Galleries**.

Unfortunately, the first building you are confronted with is the Palace of Congresses, now re-christened the **State Kremlin Palace**, a hangar-like monstrosity erected on Khrushchev's behest in a record 18 months in 1960-1. A huge complex featuring the largest indoor auditorium in Russia, where 6,000 seated spectators are addressed through 7,000 concealed speakers, this oversized, marble-clad kennel seems to have been specifically designed to destroy the harmony of the rest of the Kremlin ensemble.

On the left is the Arsenal, built on the orders of Peter I in 1701 as an arms storehouse and military museum, but not finished until 1736 due to the financial exigencies of the war with Sweden and the earlier collapse of its gilded roof. A year later, a fire gutted the building, meaning that by the time it was fully operational almost two decades later, its military storage facilities were entirely outdated. On the pedestal outside are 749 trophy cannons captured from Napoleon's fleeing armies in 1812.

To the right of the Arsenal is the neo-classical Senate, constructed between 1776 and 1788 by Matvei Kazakov to house the advisory body set up by Peter I. When the building was finished, Kremlin officials doubted if its gigantic dome was stable, so Kazakov himself climbed on top and stuck it out up there for more than an hour to demonstrate its safety. The Senate once housed a museum entitled the Kremlin Office and Apartment of Lenin, which paid homage to Lenin's spartan study-cum-bedroom that was located inside. Boris Yeltsin recently had the curious display ripped out and shipped off to the **Lenin Museum** in Gorki, about 30 kilometres (19 miles) outside Moscow (*see chapter* **Trips Out of Moscow**). The Senate, which has mutely accommodated a succession of Russian rulers and witnessed some of the most momentous events in twentieth-century history, found itself serving as office space for President Yeltsin. Further down, towards Sobornaya Ploshchad (Cathedral Square) on the right is the Patriarch's Palace, built for Patriarch Nikon in 1653-6. While Nikon was against the custom of decorating churches in the

*The **Ivan the Great Bell Tower** (p33) shines above the Kremlin's Cathedral Square.*

Those towers again...

It seems supremely ironic that the walls of the **Kremlin**, one of the most potent symbols of the Russian state, was actually built by a bunch of Italians. Between 1485 and 1516, Pietro Antonio Solario, Marco Ruffo, Alviz Novy and Marco Bono da Caracano, were involved in the construction of the distinctive 'swallow-tail' fortifications as well as most of the present batch of 20 towers (*bashnye*), the jagged regalia that gives the Kremlin its character. The most famous and grandest of all the towers is the Spasskaya Bashnya (Saviour Tower), visible to the left of the **Mausoleum** if you are standing on Red Square, was used by Tsars and foreign ambassadors to make their entrances and exits. In the sixteenth century it bore Moscow's first ever clock, which was replaced a century later with the surviving chiming one, which, after 70 years of being subjected to the *Internationale*, now plays the Russian national anthem.

To the left of the Spasskaya Bashnya is the miniature Tsarskaya Bashnya (Tsar's Tower), where the slavering young Ivan the Terrible would watch executions taking place on the slope behind **St Basil's**. The two other most notable towers on the Red Square side face the **State Historical Museum** – the slim, tent-roofed Nikolskaya Bashnya, named after the St Nicholas Monastery that was once located opposite, and the hefty Uglovaya Arsenalnaya Bashnya (Corner Arsenal Tower), with walls up to four metres (13 feet) thick and its own indoor well.

The most striking tower along the **Alexander Garden** side and, at 80 metres (262 feet), the tallest of all, is the Troitskaya Bashnya (Trinity Tower), now the main tourist entrance to the Kremlin. It was through here that Napoleon triumphantly entered the Kremlin in 1812 and, not long after, beat a hasty retreat. On the other end of the Troitsky Most, by the ticket office, you'll find the Kutafya Bashnya (Low Tower, *pictured*), which was built in 1516, though its balustrade of open windows was added in 1685. In the corner, right at the end of the garden, stands the Borovitskaya Bashnya, named for the pine wood, or *bor*, that once stood here. Along the river side of the Kremlin is a flurry of smaller towers, the most interesting of which is the Tainitskaya Bashnya (third from the Borovitskaya corner), named after a secret (*tainyi*) passage for conveying water in case of siege. Built in 1485, this is the Kremlin's oldest tower.

The last thing to note are the Red Stars that crown five of the major towers, and that replaced the earlier Russian emblems after the Revolution. While they look rather plastic and artificial, they are actually made entirely of rubies.

'patterned' style, he seems to have had nothing against the fabulous extravagance of the interiors of this little pad, with its daintily frescoed Cross Chamber, which at 20 metres by 14 (65 feet by 45) was the first hall of its size in Russia without a supporting pillar. The palace now houses the **Museum of Seventeenth-Century Life**, with its entrance at the back of the building.

The epicentre of the Kremlin is Cathedral Square (Sobornaya Ploshchad), the spot where coronation festivities were held and through which processions passed on church holidays. All four cathedrals on the square are open to the public, and unless you have an all-encompassing Kremlin ticket, charge about $6.50 admission.

The oldest of the four cathedrals is the five-domed **Cathedral of the Assumption** (built from 1475 to 1479), which pre-dates the current Kremlin walls. Its solemn simplicity and lightness come courtesy of the Bolognese architect, Aristotele Fioravanti. Tucked away in the corner is the modest, compact **Church of the Deposition of the Robe** (*see page 33*). Peeking over its roof, are the many tiny gilded cupolas (and cute ornate drums) of the seventeenth-century

Terem Churches behind it. These were rather like en suite chapels serving the Kremlin's oldest building, the former residences of the pre-Petrine Tsars, the Terem Palace (or the Palace of the Upper Chamber). It was in this haphazard collection of rooms, connected by corridors in the manner of wooden architecture, that Ivan the Terrible chose each of his seven brides, in the time-honoured Tsarist fashion, from a line-up of eligible virgins. The Terem Palace is not open to the public.

Also closed to all but visiting presidents is the adjacent Faceted Palace, which was built between 1487 and 1491 by the Italians Marco Ruffo and Pietro Antonio Solario. It is named after the diamond-patterned stone carving on the exterior walls. From its famous Red Staircase on the left (actually white) – destroyed in the 1930s, replaced by a canteen and now restored – the newly crowned Peter the Great watched the massacre of his immediate family during the revolt of the armed mercenaries (*streltsy*).

Next is the **Cathedral of the Annunciation** (*see below*), an effusion of sparkling gold, built on the foundation of an earlier church between 1484 and 1489, but much altered since. Across the

Down the hill to the left, towards the Borovitsky Gate, is the confectionery yellow and white Great Kremlin Palace, a lugubrious mélange of styles from Byzantine to late classical, designed by Konstantin Ton, creator of the Church of Christ the Saviour. It was built for Nicholas I as a royal residence and incorporates both the Terem and the Facetted Palaces. Further down the hill is the baroque **Armoury**, also by Ton.

Cathedral of the Annunciation

The breathtaking luminescence of the cupolas on the Cathedral of the Annunciation is achieved by applying gilt to a bronze base. The flight of stairs and porch on the left were only added in 1572, so that Ivan the Terrible could attend mass from behind a grille, as he had been banned from the church because of his lascivious appetite for wives. From here, in 1584, Ivan saw the vision of a 'cross-shaped comet' portending his death. He died a couple of days later.

Cathedral of the Assumption

It's reckoned that this cathedral allowed Russia to leapfrog 100 years of building evolution. In 1472, while local architects were just putting the finishing touches to the cathedral's predecessor, the structure suddenly collapsed. Ivan the Great drafted in the Italian architect Aristotele Fioravanti. It took the Italian only four years to create a cathedral on the Russian Orthodox model that was infinitely lighter and more airy than the dark, skulking cubes of many Russian churches.

Most original frescoes in the interior were painted by a team led by the icon painter Dionysus, though the ones we see today date from the 1640s, based on themes from the original work. The 16-metre- (52-foot-) high, five-tiered iconostasis is of gilt silver and dates from 1652, though some of the icons like the fifteenth-century copy of the Virgin of Vladimir, predate it. Interesting, too, are the works of applied art: the intricately carved Tsar's seat of Ivan the Terrible, the legendary Throne of Monomakh and the huge central Harvest Chandelier, which was made from silver plundered from the cathedral by the French in 1812 and later recovered by Cossacks as Napoleon retreated.

The Cathedral of the Assumption has long been considered Russia's main church. It was used for coronations as well as the inauguration and burial of patriarchs throughout the Tsarist period. Though perhaps the greatest tribute to its power and status was the fact that Stalin secretly ordered that a service be held here in the winter of 1941, when the Nazis were trampling down the gates of Moscow.

square is the **Cathedral of the Archangel Michael** (*see below*), and beside it, the famous **Ivan the Great Bell Tower** (1505-8) which, for a long time, was the tallest structure in Moscow. Originally, it was built for the Cathedrals of the Assumption and the Annunciation, which had no bell towers of their own. Raised by an additional 21 metres (68 feet) in 1600, during the reign of Boris Godunov, it rests on brick walls five metres (16 feet) thick at the base, a factor that has helped it survive fire, French explosives and the Revolution. The tower now hosts temporary exhibitions. Behind Ivan the Great Bell Tower, on the opposite side of the street from the Senate, are the Kremlin's two most famous trinkets: the Tsar's Cannon and the Tsar's Bell. The cannon, which has never been fired, has the largest calibre (890 millimetres/2 feet 11 inches) of any in the world and weighs 40 tons, with each decorative cannon-ball clocking up a ton. The Tsar's Bell, which has never been rung, was cooling off in the foundry casting pit in 1737 when water that was being sprayed on one of Moscow's regular fires came into contact with the bell and caused an 11-ton chunk to crack away.

The Cathedral of the Archangel Michael

The cathedral was built by the Italian Alviz Novy at the beginning of the sixteenth century and displays the most overtly Italianate features of all the Kremlin cathedrals: gable whorls and pilasters. Up to the time of Peter the Great, this is where all of Russia's rulers were buried, with the exception of Boris Godunov, who is interred at the Trinity Monastery of St Sergei. In this tiny space, there is a grand total of 53 tombs, the earliest being that of Ivan Kalita, one of the first Moscow Princes, through to Peter the Great's half-wit brother Ivan V. Unfortunately, the tombs of Ivan the Terrible and his sons are hidden from view behind the iconostasis.

Church of the Deposition of the Robe

This once served as the domestic chapel of the Tsars and Patriarchs. Inside, it's cosy and intimate, if a little musty, with frescoes completed in 1644 by some of the same masters who worked on the Cathedral of the Assumption.

Red Square

Red Square was created at the same moment when the city of Moscow was born, sandwiched between Yury Dolgoruky's new Kremlin walls and the medieval shopping precinct that later became the upper trading rows. Surprisingly, everything is pretty much the same now as it was then, with the new Kremlin just a little bigger than its old wooden ancestor, and **GUM**, the state department store, just a little further back than the tangle of stalls and traders from which it evolved. The square was not always as wide and manicured as it is today. Until Ivan III ordered them dismantled to reduce the threat of fire, squat little wooden houses clung like lichen to the walls for safety. In the sixteenth century a large moat, fed by the Neglinnaya River, was dug through the spot where Lenin's Mausoleum now stands. But a medieval Muscovite wouldn't have much difficulty recognising the modern variant. Red Square remains one of the city's great constants.

It was only in the mid-seventeenth century that it finally became Krasnaya Ploshchad (Red Square), though while the word *krasnaya* now means 'red', in old Russian it translated simply as 'beautiful'. Throughout its history, the square was a place for gatherings, for proclamations, for demonstrations. It was here that the royal will was dispersed verbally among the masses by town criers armed with the sovereign's latest decrees. In Soviet times, the square took naturally to its role as a springboard for the military might of the USSR, a stage on which to showcase the glorious achievements of communism. One of Red Square's most famous and notable moments is still the October Revolution Parade in 1941, when the columns of soldiers marched by

Lenin's Mausoleum and then straight out to the Front to battle with the approaching Germans. These days, the most action that Red Square gets are pop concerts and the occasional tired communist demonstration.

Enter Red Square from almost any one of the roads flowing into it, and the eye is almost immediately drawn to that bulbous clot of cupolas known as **St Basil's Cathedral** It seems only fitting that it was Ivan the Terrible who commissioned this imposing conflagration of anarchical forms and clashing colours. Like no other landmark in the country, not even the walls of the Kremlin, this cathedral is a concrete symbol of the enigmatic spirit of the Russian people. Both are balanced precariously between beauty and chaos, equilibrium and pandemonium, harmony and outright violence. In front of St Basil's is the statue of Minin and Pozharsky, the butcher and the prince, who helped drive the Poles out of the Kremlin during the Time of Troubles. Originally, it stood in the centre of the square, but was dumped to this awkward spot in 1936 because it was getting in the way of military parades.

Flanking the north-westerly side of the square, opposite the Kremlin walls, is **GUM** (pronounced 'GOOM' in Russian), the once austere and largely empty state department store, which now hosts an array of foreign fashion shops including Calvin Klein, Galeries Lafayette, Bosco Di Ciliegi and Benetton. Built between 1890 and 1893 in a pseudo-Russian revival style, the main feature of the building is its arched glass and metal-framed roof, which was, at that time, an impressive engineering feat. There's a fairly decent café on the second floor (imaginatively called Snack Bar) with a view of the square.

The Church of Christ the Saviour

No site in Moscow chronicles the successive changing of the guard more than the site of the recently rebuilt Church of Christ the Saviour.

The completion of the $360-million cathedral was planned to coincide with the September 1997 celebration of Moscow's 850th birthday. Sited a stone's throw from the Kremlin, the hulking, 15-storey, white marble monolith, with its glistening gold domes that can be seen from across town, has infiltrated the Russian psyche. From vodka bottles to souvenir plates bearing its likeness, the church has a powerful presence.

The original cathedral was commissioned by Tsar Alexander I in honour of Napoleon's expulsion in 1812. It took 40 million bricks and 45 years to build, but only one day to destroy. Designed by Konstantin Ton in an eclectic style that combined both traditional Russian ecclesiastic construction with a nod to the neo-classicism of the West. Despite its largesse, the church was never admired by aesthetes as a great beauty, but its symbolic importance was on a par with its scale.

In 1931, the monument was imploded on Stalin's directives, in order to make way for his grandiose new projects, the Palace of the Soviets – an eclectic monstrosity surmounted by a 92-metre (300-foot) statue of Lenin in his famous pose hailing the masses. His index finger alone was to be almost six meters (20 feet)

long. His head would be hidden on cloudy days. Reaching over 130 storeys, it was not lost on its designers that the Palace would surpass New York's recently built Empire State Building as the tallest building in the world and that the Lenin statue would be twice as tall as the Statue of Liberty.

The Palace of the Soviets never really got off the ground and by the late 1950s – during the Great Thaw that the tamer Khrushchev ushered in – the foundation pit had become one of the biggest swimming pools in the world. Today, with history coming full circle, it is the site of the rebuilt Church of Christ the Saviour.

The rebuilding of the church was financed by the Fund for the Reconstruction of the Church of Christ the Saviour; every *babushka* and schoolchild was solicited in a variety of ways, through imploring television ads to berobed Orthodox priests collecting in metro stations. The original design of the nineteenth-century cathedral was reconstructed as closely as possible, although this time concrete was used and a huge car park – a late twentieth century staple – was added.

The Church of Christ the Saviour

Ulitsa Volkhonka 4 (no phone). Metro Kropotkinskaya. **Open** *crypt* 10am-6pm daily. Decoration of the main church is underway but will not be completed for a number of years. **Admission** free. **Map p280 B4**

On the other side of Nikolskaya Ulitsa is the tiny Cathedral of the Mother of God of Kazan, which was knocked down in 1936, on its 300th anniversary, to be replaced by a pavement café and later a public toilet. The cathedral was originally named after the Virgin of Kazan icon, which was accredited with Tsar Mikhail Romanov's defeat of the Poles in 1612. The cathedral has been magnificently restored from blueprints made by the architect Baranovsky, who was given the task of restoring it in the 1930s, before its demolition.

Also making a recent reappearance in the square are the Ascension Gates and the tiny Iverskaya Chapel, where for centuries travellers and Tsars would take their leave of Moscow or pay their respects on arrival. The chapel was knocked down in 1929 to make way for a statue of a worker thrusting his arm skywards – the new socialist

Gatekeeper. The gates themselves, which had been around since 1680, were demolished in 1931 to allow parades better access to Red Square. Both were reconstructed between 1994 and '95 and the chapel once again attracts a steady flow of worshippers. The huge red-brick State Historical Museum, designed by Vladimir Shervud to complement the walls of the Kremlin, looks like a russified doily. Fussy and cluttered, it is another testimony to the excesses of eclecticism in the latter half of the nineteenth century. The same is true of the adjacent building, formerly the Lenin Museum, and once home of the pre-Revolutionary city Duma (council).

The last notable building on Red Square is the Lenin Mausoleum, a low-lying pyramid structure designed by Aleksei Shchusev using the cube elements that originated with the suprematism of the artist Kazimir Malevich.

NB Red Square is closed 10am-1pm Mon-Fri – the hours that Lenin's Mausoleum is open. Closed means you can enter from one of the sides, but you can't get to the middle, or cross it.

*A GUM with a view: looking over **Red Square** from the State Department Store.*

Blading down Novy Arbat. See page 45.

St Basil's Cathedral

Krasnaya Ploshchad 2 (Red Square) (298 3304). Metro Ploshchad Revolutsii. **Open** 10am-4.30pm Mon, Wed-Sun. Closed 1st Mon of month. **Admission** $4.50; $2.50 students. **Map p278 D3**

Confusion still exists as to who actually built the cathedral at the intercession of the Mother of God at the Moat (as St Basil's is formally known), whether it was a duo of architects named Postnik and Barma Yakovlev or a guy called Postnik whose nickname was Barma ('the mumbler' in Russian). In any case, the legend that Ivan the Terrible, who commissioned the cathedral to celebrate a victory over the Golden Horde, put out the eyes of either or both so that they could never again create anything so devastatingly beautiful is probably apocryphal. Later churches also claim the same confused credits. Work began in 1555, with Ivan stipulating that a central chapel be surrounded by seven, and later eight, domed mini-chapels, a schema that gives St Basil's its distinctive anarchic profile. Napoleon was so taken with the cathedral that he considered dismantling it and bringing it back, stone by stone, to Paris. Stalin considered it an impediment to parades, but was prevented from demolishing it by the architect Baranovsky, who threatened to cut his throat on the steps here if it went. Now, it seems, the cathedral is leaving Red Square of its own volition; recent reports have suggested that it is so poorly maintained that it is in danger of slipping into the Moskva River.

Lenin's Mausoleum

Krasnaya Ploshchad (Red Square). Metro Ploshchad Revolutsii. **Open** 10am-1pm Mon-Fri. **Admission** free. **Map p278 D3**

The mausoleum was originally erected in wood, when embalmers were still unsure whether the process being applied to Lenin's body would actually work. The current structure, built in 1924 of red granite and black labradorite, plays host daily to one of the greatest grotesqueries of communism: the display of Lenin's body. Guards usher you into the sacristy, forbidding anything so sacreligious as talking or scribbling in a notepad. Luminous, under a bank of lights, a waxy-looking Lenin, with wretched withered little ears, sleeps off the post-Soviet hangover. The whole thing is both nauseating and thrilling – the weirdest experience on the Moscow tourist trail. Now that the Last Tsar has been buried, however, Lenin's days in the display case are numbered. *See also p37,* **Lenin's waxworks**.

Behind the Mausoleum are the resting places of other communist luminaries: Stalin, Brezhnev, Andropov, Chernenko, all of whom get their own busts. Shut away in the Kremlin wall is John Reed, author of *Ten Days that Shook the World*, as well as Lenin's lover, Inessa Armand, and the world's first astronaut, Yury Gagarin.

Manezhnaya Ploshchad

Manezhnaya Ploshchad, once just a dusty wasteland where tanks would gather on their way to Red Square parades, has now been transformed by the will of the Moscow mayor, Yury Luzhkov (with the help of $350 million) into the labyrinthine underground Okhotny Ryad shopping mall, which makes its presence known in the square with a series of half-domes, rather like postmodernist drumlins, and balustrades, all of which are popular with rollerbladers. There is also a network of fountains and graceless sculptures, courtesy of Luzhkov's favourite artist, the truly egregious Zurab Tseriteli. The Neglinnaya River, which had been hidden away in underground pipes since the beginning of the nineteenth century, was opened up again and rechannelled to facilitate this new watercomplex. The subterranean centre itself, weighed down with tacky gilt and an excess of marble, hosts a variety of 'luxury' shops: Tiffany's, Gucci, Geiger, as well as places like Guess, Next, Benetton and Speedo. The café right down in the bowels of the centre is terrifically expensive – expect to pay around $4 for a cappuccino. On the north-east side of the square is the indescribably hideous **Hotel Moskva**, whose grey, looming, angular form seems to dominate the whole area, as if someone had dumped a gigantic electricity substation right in the centre of Moscow. Its façade is famous for its asymmetric design, which, legend has it, was due to Joe Stalin mistakenly approving two alternative designs. Across Okhotny Ryad from the Hotel Moskva is the Duma (short for Gosudarstvennaya Duma, the state governing body), where the elected lower house of the Russian parliament gathers. This is the scene of much in-chamber brawling by day (courtesy of ultranationalist Vladimir Zhirinovsky) and an apparent den of iniquity by night, if newspaper reports are to be believed. The stories of all-night orgies and an endless stream of prostitutes are backed up by the constantly burning lights in the building. What else could they be doing in there?

Beside Tverskaya Ulitsa to the north-west is the swish **Hotel National**, and a little further down Mokhovaya Ulitsa (No.13) is the totally useless Intourist Tourist Information Centre, where no one knows anything and posters advertising 'Leningrad' adorn the walls. A little further along is the Old University, founded in 1755. This brilliant yellow building by the master of Moscow neoclassicism, Matvei Kazakov, was built between 1786 and 1793, but almost completely burnt down during the great fire of 1812. It was reconstructed from scratch by the architect Zhilyardi.

Flanking Manezhnaya to the south is the **Manezh**, from which the square gets its name. The pared-down Empire-style building was originally used for military training and cavalry manœuvres (Tolstoy had his first riding lessons here), though by the end of the nineteenth century it was being used as a classical music venue where both Berlioz and Saint-Saëns conducted concerts. Now it's more likely to host trade and art exhibitions. Finally, we have the **Alexander Garden** (Aleksandrinsky Sad, *see below*), which stretch all the way along the west side of the Kremlin wall.

Alexander Garden

Manezhnaya Ulitsa. Metro Aleksandrinsky Sad or Biblioteka Lenina. **Open** 8am-10.30pm daily. **Admission** free. **Map p278 C3**
The Alexander Garden were created in 1821, when the Neglinnaya River, which once ran the length of what is now Manezhnaya Ulitsa before draining into the Moskva by the Kremlin's Borovitskaya Tower, was channelled into an underground pipe in 1819. On the dry riverbed, the architect Osip Bove fashioned Moscow's first public garden. The main feature of the gardens is the tomb of the unknown soldier, which commemorates the Russian victory over the Nazis in World War II. While the soldier's remains were placed here directly after the war, the eternal flame actually dates from about 20 years later, when, on 8 May 1967, it was carried here from the Memorial to the Revolutionary Dead in Field of Mars in St Petersburg (*see p197*). Running down the length of the gardens are granite obelisks bearing the names of the former Soviet Union cities that were forced to defend themselves from the Nazi onslaught. Inside the obelisks are handfuls of earth that have been soaked with the blood of Soviet soldiers who died in these cities.

Teatralnaya Ploshchad to Lubyanka

Until the middle of the eighteenth century, Teatralnaya Ploshchad (Theatre Square) was a grubby, squalid marsh on the banks of the Neglinnaya River. After the river was safely stored away underground, the English entrepreneur Michael Maddox founded a theatre here that later became known as the Petrovsky Theatre. When it burned down in 1805, it was replaced in 1821-4 with the **Bolshoi Theatre**, built under the supervision of Osip Bove. However, another fire in 1853, which raged for days and cost a number of lives, means that, though the grand Ionic portico and the fetching statue of Apollo taking a spin in his quadriga is as first intended, the original light and modest interior has been replaced with stodgy pseudo-riches in the neo-baroque style.

The small square and fountain in front of the theatre was Soviet Moscow's premiere gay cruising area, and still retains some of its popularity. On the corner of Ulitsa Petrovka, to the left as you face the Bolshoi, is the luminescent yellow **Maly Theatre** built by Bove in 1818 for a wealthy merchant, who was so captivated by the theatre of the Palais-Royale in Paris that he wanted one for himself in Moscow. The left side of the Bolshoi ensemble is taken up by

Molodyozhny Akademichesky Teatr Rossii (the Academic Youth Theatre). A little way up Petrovka but still very much part of Teatralnaya Ploshchad is **TsUM**, the expansive central state department store that used to be known as Muir & Mirrielees before it was nationalised after the Revolution. The Scotsmen Andrew Muir and Archibald Mirrielees arrived in Russia in the nineteenth century and established Russia's first true department store of the middle classes here in 1909. Chekhov bought his writing paper here and named

Lenin's waxworks

It has long been rumoured that the recumbent, socialist godhead on display in the Mausoleum is not really one Vladimir Ilych Lenin, but a wax dummy secretly substituted long ago for the mouldering, rotting father of Russian communism. Other sceptics estimate that the percentage of authentic Lenin in what we see today could be as low as ten or even five per cent, the difference being made up of putty and embalming fluid.

However, none of these rumours seems to have reached the ten strong team in charge of the monumental job of caring for the hallowed corpse. Twice weekly, they pay a visit to the Mausoleum from their base in the Research Institute for Biological Structures to check for signs of decay – a missing ear or dropped nostril, perhaps. Then, for two months every year, Lenin undergoes major refurbishment. He is removed from the display case, stripped of his natty suit and dropped into a vat of special preservation fluid for a whole month. Once adequately refreshed, the body is placed back in the Mausoleum, where the temperature (exactly 16°C, 60°F) and humidity (no higher than 70 per cent) are strictly controlled. Before 1991, all Lenin maintenance was carried out in a special lab situated under the Mausoleum, but it was axed due to funding cuts. The men who keep Lenin fresh have even been known to rent out their unique expertise for the benefit of other deceased despots the world over. When North Korea's Kim Il-Sung passed away, this is were he came for a shot of immortality. Apparently the waiting list includes Michael Jackson, Saddam Hussein and Baroness Thatcher.

his two dogs after the proprietors. The building was something of an innovation for the time – a modern reinforced-concrete structure, overlaid with neo-Gothic flourishes; inside, it's an airless maze.

The **Metropol** hotel, built between 1899 and 1905, is another groundbreaking building, one of the first in Moscow in the *style moderne*, Russia's indigenous version of art nouveau. The elegant, kinetic bays and intersecting wrought-iron balconies are offset by a ceramic mural, *The Princess of Dreams*, designed by the artist Mikhail Vrubel. There used to be a Nietzsche quote inscribed on the wall on the third storey of the hotel: 'Again, the same story: when you build a house, you notice that you have learned something.' It was replaced in communist times with a quote from Lenin: 'Only the dictatorship of the proletariat can liberate mankind from the oppression of capitalism.' After a refit at the end of the 1980s, the hotel now bears five stars, and if you can afford the overpriced coffee, it's a good place to stop and read the overpriced papers sold at the hotel's extensive newsstand.

In the patch of the square outside Ploshchad Revolutsii metro station, rollerbladers swish by acrobatically in summer for the benefit of the sedentary audience in the nearby street café, part of a curious, arched-bunker shopping arcade whose ancestors were all kiosks.

Teatralny Proyezd, which leads up the hill towards Lubyanka, takes us past a complex of superkiosks on the right, offering everything from food to hi-fi to shoes. On the left is Neglinnaya Ulitsa, which runs along the former basin of the culverted Neglinnaya River. It might be a little excessive to walk its length just to see the *beaux arts*-style building of the Sandunovskaya Banya, but it's worth taking a detour up Neglinnaya to stroll along what was Tolstoy's favourite Moscow street, Ulitsa Kuznitsky Most, which it intersects.

Named after the 'blacksmiths' bridge' that once stood at the intersection, this was the main shopping street of the eighteenth century and home to many French shops. During the Great Fire of 1812, Napoleon's soldiers fought off the flames to protect their compatriots and so it escaped damage. Now, with its Versace and Louvre stores, the street is once again a fashionable haven of the rich. Returning now to Teatralny Proyezd: in early 1998, a devastating fire raged through the Russian Sea Fleet building on the corner of Ulitsa Rozhdestvenka, though firefighters were more worried that the ice forming from the water used to extinguish the fire would simply drag the structure to the ground.

The first building we find on the infamous Lubyanskaya Ploshchad is **Detsky Mir**, the city's largest toy store, built in this unlikely spot as a tribute to the successful efforts of Felix Dzerzhinksy, founder of Cheka (the first incarnation of the KGB), in clearing Moscow's streets of urchins after the Revolution. The building that is most associated with 'Iron Felix' is the massive, rusticated, caramel-coloured building that dominates the square: the Lubyanka. Originally owned by Rossiya Insurance company, it was commandeered after the Revolution and expanded to its current inhuman proportions between 1939 and 1940, a move presumably designed to better accommodate the many thousands being shot in its basements. The statue of Dzerzhinsky that once stood in the centre of the square was pulled down by jubilant crowds in the wake of the failed *putsch* in 1991 and now stands behind the **Tsentralny Dom Khudozhnikov** (Central House of Artists) in the **Graveyard of Fallen Monuments**.

Kitai-Gorod

Kitai-Gorod is the city's third oldest area, after the Kremlin and Red Square. Although the name looks as if it should be directly translated as China (Kitai) Town (gorod), 'kitai', in fact, has nothing to do with the country, but means 'enclosed,' and refers to the old city wall that formerly surrounded the neighbourhood. The wall has been largely destroyed now, mostly by Soviet-era construction projects, but portions can still be seen bordering the east side of the Hotel Rossia and behind the **Metropol** hotel along Ploshchad Revolutsii. Today, Kitai-Gorod is crammed with government buildings. Square metre for square metre, the neighbourhood is probably as dense a bureaucratic nest as one is liable to find anywhere in the world.

It is also the site, in the form of the **Hotel Rossia**, of one of the greatest crimes against aesthetics ever perpetrated by the Soviet state – which is saying a lot. In building this Brezhnev-era monstrosity between 1964 and '69, the Soviets managed to significantly reduce the impact of the Kremlin and Red Square, which, taken together, form an impressive and powerful architectural ensemble.

Dwarfed and given a slightly ridiculous appearance by the presence of the hotel, is a row of some of the city's most historic structures outside the Kremlin walls. Walking from Red Square east along Ulitsa Varvarka, the first building of interest is the one the street was named after: the late eighteenth-century Church of St Barbara. This pink and white church was constructed on the site of an older church built at the beginning of the sixteenth century. Next is the reconstructed **English House (Angliskoye Podvore**, *see below*), one of the oldest dwellings left in the city. This sixteenth-century house was given by Ivan the Terrible to the merchants who were the first emissaries

*The brutalist charm of the **Hotel Intourist**.*

Walk on by... **Alexander Pushkin** *and friends.*

from England to Russia. Next door to the English House is the late seventeenth-century Church of St Maxim the Blessed, which, it is thought, includes parts of a sixteenth-century church that originally stood on the spot. The nearby bell tower dates from 1829. Just past the sweeping ramp up to the entrance to the hotel is the Znamensky Monastery and Church. Founded in 1631, the monastery was built following the death of the mother of the first Romanov Tsar, Mikhail, on the estate of the old family home, and just next to it is the **House of the Romanov Boyars** (*see below*). The church was constructed a little later (finished 1684) than the monastery. The somewhat awkward-looking bell tower top, however, was added a century later.

The last in this row of buildings is the Church of St George, which was originally built in the mid-seventeenth century, but was significantly altered during reconstruction in 1838. The semi-Gothic-style bell tower dates from 1818. Inside, you can see wall paintings from the seventeenth to the nineteenth centuries. Across from the Church of St George, up Ipatyevsky Pereulok, is the lovely Church of the Trinity in Nikitsky, which is decorated with seventeenth-century frescoes.

Just across the street, on the north side of the Rossia, is Gostiny Dvor, one of the city's traditional centres for trade. Built in the late eighteenth and early nineteenth centuries, the building has roughly the same general layout as St Petersburg's Gostiny Dvor. At the time of writing, the building was undergoing restoration (for the umpteenth year), but was starting to see real progress and stores were

even beginning to open up for business along its north side. Its giant courtyard should eventually be an ideal spot for restaurants and cafés.

Further down Ulitsa Varvarka is a Russkoye Bistro restaurant on the south side of the street just before you get to Metro Kitai-Gorod. When you get to the stairs leading down into the metro, go down the first set but then take a right on to Kitaigorodsky Proyezd, which runs along the east side of the Rossia. The most interesting things here are the section of mid-sixteenth-century city wall (restored in the 1960s) and the seventeenth-century Church of St Anne near the river.

Running north from the far side of the Rossia is Staraya Ploshchad (Old Square). In the past the small, elongated park in the middle of the square was, along with the fountain in front of the **Bolshoi Theatre**, one of the traditional meeting places for the city's gays. More recently, the gay scene has shifted to clubs and bars that have opened up as Moscow becomes more progressive.

Further north is the **Polytechnical Museum**, an intricately decorated, oblong structure built simultaneously with the Historical Museum on Red Square, with which it shares an architectural affinity. Just north of the Polytechnical Museum, on the south side of Lubyanskaya Ploshchad, is a monument to the millions who suffered in the gulags of the Soviet Union. The monument is a single large stone taken from the Solovki Islands in the far north, where one of the first gulags was created out of a converted monastery. If you look at the 500-ruble note you'll see the monastery depicted on the back.

To the left from the square is the fashionable Nikolskaya Ulitsa with its cafés, clubs and shops. The Republika (Nikolskaya 17) is a club worth checking out and the Staraya Ploshchad Bar is not far from here either, at Bolshoi Cherkassky Pereulok 8.

At the end of Nikolskaya Ulitsa, across from the entrance to GUM, is a passageway that cuts through to Ploshchad Revolutsii.

The English House

Ulitsa Varvarka 4 (298 3961). Metro Kitai-Gorod.
Open 10am-6pm Tue, Thur, Sat, Sun; 11am-7pm Wed, Fri. **Admission** $1.50; *guided tour* $1.50; 50¢ foreign students. **Map p278 D3**
One of the oldest dwellings remaining in the city, this building (Angliskoye Podvore) offers a glimpse into early Moscow life. The lower storey of the structure dates from the beginning of the sixteenth century, when the house belonged to a private owner. In the middle of that century the house was given by Ivan the Terrible to English merchants sent to Russia by Queen Elizabeth I, to whom he also gave special trading privileges. In 1571, the building was burned during an attack on the city by the Mongol Hordes. It was restored and a second storey was added, only to have the whole thing burn again during an attack by the Poles at the beginning of the 1600s. In 1612, it was rebuilt and expanded for the last time (until restoration in the 1960s). *See also chapter* **Museums & Galleries**.

House of the Romanov Boyars/ Zaryadye Chambers

Ulitsa Varvarka 10 (298 3706). Metro Kitai-Gorod.
Open 11am-6pm Wed; 10am-5pm Mon, Thur-Sun. Closed 1st Mon of each month. **Admission** $4.50, $3 students. **Map p278 D3**
The reason for this rather interesting house-museum now having two names is that it once belonged to the parents of the first Russian Tsar of the Romanov dynasty, Mikhail. Since the Tsar's relatives weren't the most popular people during the Soviet period, the place was given the vague title of Zaryadye Chambers, so that it would have no nostalgic or historical connotations. Both names are currently in use. Fortunately, everything has been left just as it was in the seventeenth century: even the windows have not been replaced with glass, but are still in their original mica.

Central Moscow

Tverskaya Ulitsa

Tverskaya Ulitsa (Tver Street) is to Moscow what the Champs Elysées are to Paris or Oxford Street is to London. It is every (wealthy) shopaholic's must-see. Here you can buy perfumes by Christian Dior and couture dresses by Vivienne Westwood, purchase a Volvo or a Chevrolet or take your pick from the many ethnic restaurants and fast-food joints. But the beggars with their grubby children and performing animals, icons and beseeching palms add a disturbing, almost medieval element to remind you that this is the main street of a city still in the social agony of transition from communism to capitalism.

Running north from directly beneath the Kremlin, Tverskaya Ulitsa ultimately leads to the city of Tver, from which it took its name. In the Soviet period, it was called Ulitsa Gorkogo (Gorky Street) after the Revolutionary writer Maxim Gorky, but in 1994, a year when much of Russia's rewritten history reverted to the original, it recovered its historic name. Hip Muscovites call Tverskaya simply 'Strit' (the street). Tverskaya Ulitsa, or Tsarskaya Ulitsa (Tsar's Street), as it was also called, was always a mixture of luxury and squalor. When, in the sixteenth century, Moscow began to expand beyond the walls of the Kremlin, 'suburban' mansions were built on this street, which today could not be more central. The mansions lacked chimneys, however, so the inhabitants risked being smoked like kippers if not burnt to death, and in order to visit each other in their 'palaces', the *boyars* had to wade through rivers of mud and rotting dog corpses.

Of old Tverskaya, almost nothing remains, of course, apart from the descriptions in the history books. You can still see the legacy of a more elegant nineteenth century in buildings such as the **Yeliseyevsky** food hall (don't miss its glorious chandeliers) and the 100-year-old **Chekhov MKhAT** (Moscow Art Theatre). But the Tverskaya of today is largely the joint creation of dictator Joseph Stalin and Moscow's dynamic modern mayor, Yuri Luzhkov.

The first section of Tverskaya is dominated by the grim tower-block outline of the **Hotel Intourist**, now with a Patio Pizza restaurant grafted on to the first floor. On the street outside, souvenir sellers offer overpriced fur hats, military caps and gas masks. A little further down on the same side you will find a green building, in which, as well as housing shops and the Mexican bar La Cantina, you will see the theatre named after the famous Russian actress Maria Yermolova. At Gazetny Pereulok, where the university press was situated from the eighteenth century and newspapers were always on sale, you will find the Tsentralny Telegraf (**Central Telegraph**), built by Rerberg in 1925-7. These days, it not only has direct-dial international telephones, which are open to the public, but Internet access as well.

The first section of the right or east side of Tverskaya is taken up with shops, shops and more shops: Dior, Danone, **Dieta** as well as a **Kombi's** sandwich bar, which is good for a bite if you're stuck. Off to the right is Kamergersky Pereulok with the famous Chekhov Moscow Art Theatre, once home to Stanislavsky and Nemirovich-Danchenko, the originators of 'the method'. The theatre was built in 1880 and given a significant art nouveau refit by Shekhtel in 1902, which included the unusually modest and simple auditorium. A little further up and to the right, Tverskaya Ploshchad opens out with a statue of Moscow's twelfth-century founder, Prince Yuri Dolgoruky on horseback, directly opposite the Meriya (**City Hall**, *see below*) on the other side of the street. At the back of the square is the Aragvi Restaurant, which has a room decorated with Georgian legendary tigers, where Stalin and his secret police chief Beria used to dine. If that does not put you off, sample the traditional *lobio* (beans) and *khachapuri* (cheese bread). From the back of the square, Stoleshnikov Pereulok leads down to Ulitsa Bolshaya Dmitrovka, where you will find the Federal Archive Service in a forbidding block with the images of Marx, Engels and Lenin in relief on the wall.

The square faces the building often thought of as the centrepiece of the avenue, Tverskaya 13, City Hall, headquarters of Moscow's *khozyain* (master), Mayor Luzhkov.

Through the next arch on the same side of the street as the City Hall you will find Leontyevsky Pereulok; No.7 houses the Museum of Folk Art. On the other side of the street, No.8, former home of Marshal Pavel Rotmistrov, commander of the Soviet tank forces, and Demian Bedny, poet, now houses the Moskva bookshop, which stocks an excellent selection of art and history books. After a browse inside, cross over Glinishchevsky Pereulok, where once there were *glina* (clay) pits, past Pizza Hut, the Sladky Put (Sweet Way) tooth-rot shop and Yeliseyevsky's, Moscow's answer to Harrods food hall, until finally you come to Pushkinskaya Ploshchad (**Pushkin Square**, *see below*) with its fountains and gardens. The centrepiece of the square is Alexander Opekushin's statue of Pushkin in Napoleonic nipple-scratching pose, moved here from the other side of Tverskaya in 1950.

One of the more interesting buildings on the square is the constructivist *Izvestya* Editorial Office to the left of Pushkin. Such was the prevailing spirit when it was built in 1925-7 that its terrazzo plaster façades imitate the fashionable material of the day: concrete.

Dining options here are a little limited: you might like to chomp on cabbage pie washed down with a glass of *kvas* in Russkoye Bistro, a fast-food chain set up by Mayor Luzhkov as a patriotic alternative to McDonald's, or you could always pass between the invidious golden arches themselves, of which there's a set on the other side of the street. One of Moscow's better bars, the **Garazh**, is located right by the **Galleria Aktyor** shopping complex and marked out by the ass-end of a pink Cadillac sticking out from the wall. Further eastwards, set into one corner of the grotesque Rossiya cinema, opposite the beautiful lacy white Church of the Nativity in Putinky, is the rather pricey but very nice U Lukomorya Café.

If you've walked this far, it's well worth continuing east down Strastnoi Bulvar to the intersection with Ulitsa Petrovka and Ulitsa Karetny Ryad,

where you'll find the slightly eerie Upper Monastery of St Peter (Vysoko-Petrovsky Monastyr) with its distinctive Moscow baroque bell tower. Up Karetny Ryad is the huge, sinister-looking Russian police headquarters (confusingly known as Petrovka 38 because this was once a continuation of Ulitsa Petrovka), which features prominently in umpteen Russian detective novels. Further on to the right are the glorious Hermitage Gardens, recently renovated and endowed with some *style moderne* gloss. Inside is the ship-like 'New Opera', the **Hermitage Theatre** and a dinky little café-restaurant called Parizhkaya Zhizn (Parisian Life).

Back at Pushkinskaya Ploshchad, descend into the underpass (where there is another metro station); it's lively with kiosks, but beware the pickpockets who prowl here, waiting to catch you off your guard as you gape at the cosmetics and computer games. It is perhaps wiser and, in clement weather, pleasanter to remain above ground. To continue down Tverskaya Ulitsa, you have to cross Tverskoi Bulvar, the first section of Moscow's beautiful Boulevard Ring to be laid out in 1796. The shop on the corner, **Armenia**, sells real Armenian brandy (as opposed to the paint stripper sold by the kiosks) and has an interesting Stalin-era mosaic of the grape harvest.

To continue down Tverskoi Bulvar brings you to Bolshaya Nikitskaya Ulitsa (Ulitsa Gertsena in Soviet times), noteworthy for the **Moscow Tchaikovsky Conservatoire**, which was founded in 1866 by Nikolai Rubenstein. Pyotr Tchaikovsky, arguably Russia's greatest composer, taught here and there is a statue of him in the front garden, which is especially beautiful in late May when the lilacs are in bloom.

Continuing down the west side of Tverskaya, just beyond the Scandinavia Restaurant, you come across a salmon-pink classical building, with stone lions atop the gatehouses and an old armoured car in the yard; this is the **Central Museum of the Revolution**. A little further up the street is the **Stanislavsky Drama Theatre**, named after Konstantin Stanislavsky.

At the end of Tverskaya is Triumfalnaya Ploshchad, formerly called Mayakovskaya. At the lower end of the square is the **Pekin Hotel**, a wedding cake of a building that testifies to Chinese-Soviet friendship, still intact at the time of the hotel's construction in the late 1940s. In the centre, the statue of the proletarian poet Vladimir Mayakovsky still stands, despite the fact that the square itself ceased to be named after him and reverted to its triumphant historic name in 1994. Mayakovsky, who committed suicide in 1930, is famous for the lines:

'I take from the pocket of my baggy trousers
My red-coated passport.
Read it, envy me,
I am a citizen of the Soviet Union.'

Citizens nostalgic for Soviet rule sometimes meet in the shadow of his craggy bronze figure, which also gives shelter to teenagers engaged in the eternal business of the *tusovka* (hanging out). The metro station at least is still called Mayakovskaya and it's an excellent place to buy cheap cut flowers from *babushki* in summer. The building on the corner of Triumfalnaya Ploshchad and Tverskaya Ulitsa is the mid-twentieth-century **Tchaikovsky Hall**, where you can buy concert tickets for later or stop for a croissant and coffee in the **Delifrance Café**. If you're in need of something more substantial, the American Bar and Grill is nearby, as is the **Starlite Diner**, a full-scale neon and chrome American diner that appears to have been airlifted into the Aquarium Gardens.

At this point, you have no choice but to continue along the Garden Ring, past Bulgakov's house at Bolshaya Sadovaya 10, before turning left down Malaya Bronnaya to the Patriarch's Ponds, once one of three reserves that supplied fish to Patriarch Nikon's table, but better known as the venue for the opening scene of Bulgakov's *The Master and Margarita*. It's one of the best places in the city for relaxing with a good book, people-watching or just gazing into space.

Just around the corner on Spiridonovka is the neo-Gothic Savva Morozov Mansion built by Fyodor Shekhtel at the end of the nineteenth century for the son of a textiles magnate. Further down this street, at the junction with Malaya Nikitskaya Ulitsa, is another Shekhtel creation, the Ryabushinsky house, now the **Gorky Museum**. This superb *style moderne* building, where the writer Maxim Gorky lived until his death in 1936, boasts some of the most beautiful interior décor in the city. The flowing composite marble staircase alone, which cascades from the upper floor to the ground, would rank the house as one of the wonders of Moscow.

Pushkin Square

'Long will I be honoured by the people
For awaking with my lyre kind impulses,
For praising, in this cruel age, freedom
And advocating mercy to the fallen.'
Pushkin, on a par with Shakespeare and Goethe, was too great ever to be affected by changes in political fashion and was respected in communist and non-communist times alike. These lines, carved on the plinth of his statue, are as universally relevant today as they were in the nineteenth century. In the dying days of Soviet rule, the pro-democracy movement met under Pushkin's statue. Now many Russians have come to realise that the new age of freedom is not without cruelty and injustice and other banners are sometimes unfurled here. But most of all, Russians come to Pushkin to relax. The square is as popular with young lovers as with tourists needing to rest their tired feet.

City Hall

Tverskaya Ulitsa 13 (229 4681/290 8687). Metro Okhotny Ryad or Pushkinskaya. **Map p278 C2**
The red classical building, formerly known as 'Mossoviet' and housing the Moscow Soviet of Workers' and Soldiers' deputies after the Revolution, was the headquarters of the

Getting your back up: **St Basil's Cathedral.**

Welcome to Russia!

AEROFLOT
Russian International Airlines

Dome infestation: the gilded cupolas of the Kremlin's **Cathedral Square**. *See page 32.*

armed uprising in Moscow in 1917 and from its balcony Lenin made numerous fiery speeches, but the present-day occupant (Mayor Luzhkov) prefers practical improvement to ideology, which is why long-suffering Muscovites overwhelmingly returned him at the last city elections. During the radical Soviet reconstruction of Tverskaya (then Gorky Street) in the 1930s, this building was created from the old eighteenth-century Governor's Mansion by lopping off the wings and portico and, amazingly, moving the building back 13.6 metres (44 feet), so that it didn't interrupt the flow of the new street. Two more storeys were added in 1944-6 to complete this vicious Stalinist disfigurement. There's nothing much to see inside, and anyway, only diplomats, politicians and journalists have the privilege of access.

The Arbat

'Ach Arbat, my Arbat
You are my religion,
You are all my joy
And all my sorrow...'

With these words, Russia's best-loved bard, Bulat Okudzhava, celebrated the street that is so close to the hearts of all Muscovites. The surface sleaze of the street's tourist industry belies a depth of history and visitors who wish to understand Russia and her long struggle for freedom should make it a priority to walk the Arbat. We know that the Arbat existed as early as 1493, because records speaking of a terrible fire in Moscow that year say it began when a candle fell over in the street's Church of St Nikolai on the Sands (then sited on the corner of Arbat and what is now

called Bolshoi Nikolopeskovsky Pereulok). There are various theories about the derivation of the street's name. Some say Arbat comes from the Russian word *gorbaty* meaning 'humped' (incidentally, Gorbachev's name shares the same root). Others believe Arbat derives from *arba* meaning 'cart' in the Tartar language, while yet others think it is from *rabad arbad* or 'suburb' in Arabic, and that trade links with the Middle East would explain this linguistic borrowing.

During the reign of Ivan the Terrible, the Arbat was the headquarters of the dreaded *oprichnina* or sixteenth-century secret police. By the seventeenth century, it had become the place where aristocrats chose to live – 'the nest of nobles' as poorer Russians called it. Naturally, the nobility attracted artists and by the nineteenth century, the Arbat was a major cultural centre; Russia's greatest poet, Pushkin, lived here for a while. The Arbat took on its current appearance at the turn of the last century when elegant two-, three- and four-storey private apartment buildings went up. After the Bolshevik Revolution in 1917, these were turned into communal flats, each occupied by several working-class families, where previously one bourgeois family had lived. Because the intelligentsia all congregated on the Arbat, it was easy for Stalin to round them up and send them to their deaths or to labour camps in Siberia. Anatoly Rybakov writes about these purges in his famous book, *Children of the Arbat*.

In less than three years, more than 65 Russian families of children with Down's Syndrome have been given the chance for brighter futures.

Downside Up Ltd.
a UK charity, recently opened a centre in Moscow for children with Down's Syndrome to provide the specialised programming they need for a better life.

❖

The charity is pioneering education, integration and normalisation for Russian children with Down's Syndrome.

❖

Downside Up is apolitical.
Funding for Downside Up programmes is raised through sponsored events, corporate giving, individual patronage and the Sponsor A Child programme.

❖

Downside Up needs your help to provide essential services these children require to reach their potentials.

To sponsor a child, or request a newsletter and brochure, please contact us:

Downside Up Ltd.
www.downsideup.org
e-mail:downsideup@bizonline.co.uk
38 Great Windmill Street, London W1V 7PA
Tel: 0171 437 7199 Fax: 0171 437 2062

or the Downside Up
Children's Centre in Moscow:
Tel/Fax: 7 095 256 4525
e-mail: downsideup@matrix.ru

Dissidents gravitated to the Arbat again during the rule of Leonid Brezhnev. They had a concept of 'Arbathood', which implied quiet resistance to totalitarianism, and eventually the Arbat was to become one of the cradles of Perestroika.

Getting to the Arbat from the centre (if you don't simply jump on the oldest line of the metro to Arbatskaya station) involves travelling west along Mokhovaya Ulitsa past the Old University towards the brutal, imposing edifice of the **Russian State Library** (or Lenin Library) – one of the opening shots of Stalinist architecture built between 1927 and 1929. Continuing along Mokhovaya would bring you to the gracious neo-classical Pashkov House, a commission that the hapless architect Vasily Bazhenov was actually allowed to finish. After the junction with Ulitsa Znamenka, on which lies **Rosie O'Grady's**, the best Irish pub in town, comes Ulitsa Volkhonka, which runs past the **Pushkin Museum of Fine Arts** (once the site of a transit prison), all the way to the miraculously recreated **Church of Christ the Saviour** (*see page 35*).

Turning instead at the Lenin Library up the mansion-lined Ulitsa Vozdvizhenka brings you right to the Arbat. The most interesting house on this stretch is the Morozov Mansion (No.14), a Moorish-Gothic castle built in 1886, whose sumptuous interiors are definitely worth a look if you can slip through the cordon of *babushka* security. At the clearing, by Khudozhestvenny (Artistic) Cinema, the first electric cinema in Moscow, you could choose to walk up Novy Arbat (New Arbat), an avenue of grim concrete skyscrapers built during the era of de-Stalinisation (1964-9). The gap-toothed appearance of the street has led to it being nicknamed 'The Dentures' by Muscovites. Along this street is the **Irish House** supermarket, expensive but well stocked, and the **Shamrock Irish Bar**. On the right side of the street is the **Sports Bar**. However, this street, which was supposed to show Moscow off as a cosmopolitan and modern capital, offers very few delights.

Stary Arbat (Old Arbat), one of the oldest streets in the city and mentioned in the *Chronicles* of 1493, is much more of a draw. To get there, veer right after the cluttered underpass crossing beneath the Boulevard Ring. The first thing you will see is a yellow building that looks like a cruise liner with its tower and white balustrades. This is the famous Prague Restaurant, often chosen by wealthy Russians for their wedding parties. After this are turn-of-the-century apartment houses in different pastel colours. Look above the shopfronts to the beautiful architectural features of these houses; most are now used for business rather than residential purposes since property prices on the Arbat are high (it's the most expensive street in the Russian version of Monopoly).

Christ the Saviour's golden dome. See p35.

Official transport at the **Duma**. *See page 36.*

Further up Arbat, on the right, is a wall covered with tiles painted by children; this is the Peace Wall made when America and the Soviet Union were discovering the joys of détente. Beyond is the Vakhtangov Theatre. The delightful little gold statue in the fountain outside is of Princess Turandot, heroine of the eponymous play, which was the theatre's first production in 1921. Immediately after the theatre, turn right up Bolshoi Nikolopeskovsky Pereulok (here stood the church where the great fire started in 1493) and you will find the **Scriabin Museum** (No.11), where the Russian composer Alexander Scriabin once lived. Back on the Arbat, check out No.30: it's a *zoo magazin* (pet shop), which sells racing cockroaches. The apartment block itself was home to Sergei Ivanov (1864-1910), whose paintings can be seen in the **Tretyakov Gallery**, and to Pyotr Kozlov (1863-1935), who explored Central Asia and wrote classic works on Tibet.

The next side lane to the right, Spasopeskovsky Pereulok, will take you to the Spaso House, more formally recognised as the US Ambassador's Residence, an interesting mansion that has been a home to the American ambassador to Moscow since 1933. Returning to the Arbat and continuing upward, you will come to the Georgian Cultural Centre in the house formerly occupied by Princess Zubova (daughter of Alexander Suvorov, Russia's famous eighteenth-century military commander). Unfortunately, there is little culture left in the Georgian Centre apart from a restaurant with traditional food from the Caucasus and a wax museum. The pale blue building at No.44 was home to the drunken poet Nikolai Glazkov, who played Ikarus in Tarkovsky's film *Andrei Rublev*.

'All dissolves and leads to oblivion,
The years, turbulent like water,
Save only the poet –
Eternal slave of his own freedom.'

Glazkov's lines could equally apply to the symbolist poet Andrei Bely, who lived across the street at No.55, another blue house. Or to great Pushkin himself, one-time occupant of No.53, newly painted in bright turquoise.

The top or western end of the Arbat is crowned on one side by McDonald's and on the other by the Stalin-era Foreign Ministry building. It was said of the late Foreign Minister Andrei Gromyko, Moscow's 'Mr Nyet' in the Cold War years, that his feet never touched the pavement as he went straight from his Zil limousine and into the lift, up to the top of this Gothic gateau of a building. But when Mikhail Gorbachev came to power and made Gromyko prime minister, he forced him to go out and meet the people and learn that for most ordinary Soviet citizens, life was one long food queue.

Your walk back down to the eastern end of Arbat will take you past more shops and apartment houses. Take note of No.35: built like a castle with battlements and a décor of knights for the rich who first occupied it in 1912, it now houses the jewellery and souvenir shop **Samotsvety**. Just before it, at Krivoarbatsky Pereulok (Crooked Arbat Lane), there is a wall covered with graffiti in memory of Russian rock idol Viktor Tsoi, who died in a car crash. Krivoarbatsky Pereulok leads to the front door of the **Melnikov House** (Dom Melnikova, *see below*), a curious piece of twentieth-century Russian architecture. A better view can be gained from the yard of Novy Arbat 43, a grey building that was once the home of the bard Bulat Okudzhava, who turned the Arbat into a legend. When he died in 1997, hundreds of thousands of Muscovites filed down the street for hours to say farewell to the author of their favourite song: 'Ach Arbat, my Arbat, you are my religion…'

Melnikov House

Dom Melnikova, Krivoarbatsky Pereulok 10. Metro Smolenskaya. **Map p280 A4**
The Melnikov House was built in 1929 by the architect Konstantin Melnikov in a style so original that it is known as the Melnikov style. Using the limited materials that were available to him at that time, he built a white tower with windows in different geometrical shapes that made economic use of space and cut down to a minimum the number of crude 90° angles. Melnikov escaped the repressions that affected so many other talented Russians: he taught architecture and was allowed to live in his house, which was his own property even during Soviet times, until his death in 1974. At present the building is a private residence and not open to the public.

Zamoskvorechye

The area south of the Moskva River, known as Zamoskvorechye or 'beyond the river', was historically an area of immigrant settlements. During the sixteenth century, Ivan the Terrible ordered the *Streltsy*, the armed mercenary corps he had founded, to be settled in what was then a swampy hinterland. By the end of the seventeenth century their numbers had grown to 22,000, most of whom lived here. Later the settlements expanded to include employees of various monasteries and royal palaces, each of which had a separate settlement with a separate church. As most of the architecture in the locale was built of wood, it was completely transformed during the fire of 1812 into a smouldering, post-apocalyptic vista, after which the nobility moved in en masse, bringing with them their stone mansions.

The Zamoskvorechye has a lot to offer in the way of churches, so for enthusiasts it's quite a treat. Others can content themselves with a visit to the **Tretyakov Gallery** or to one of the clubs or bars in this area, which is unlike any other area in this booming town, in that it has a genuinely relaxed, grungy feel.

Like, psychedelic, man… the **Church of St Gregory of Neocaesarea**. *See page 52.*

Moscow metropolitan

The Moscow metro system is one of the few truly worthwhile legacies of Stalinist architecture. Begun in 1935 with a 13-station line running from Sokolniki to Park Kultury, the metro was viewed as an instrument of propaganda, an underground socialist paradise where each station was another sampler of the Elysium of the new social order. To achieve this, no expense was spared, either in terms of manpower or materials. Apart from the effusion of mosaics, mouldings and sculptures, the metro is clad with acres of bronze, mahogany, granite and marble. In perhaps another inheritance of the Stalinist ethic, where the poor unfortunates who were late for work could be promptly shipped off to the gulag, the metro is one of the few aspects of Moscow life that is totally dependable – it runs on time, all the time.

Stations on the metro fall into two main categories: those that accentuate the cavernous, vault-like characteristics of the underground sites (Krasnye-Vorota, Okhotny Ryad and Teatralnaya Ploshchad) and those that try to create an airy, spacious underground expanse (Mayakovkskaya, Kropotkinskaya, Aeroport). Some of the stations are decorated almost to the point of absurdity – Ploshchad Revolutsii is almost cluttered with statuary, with every pillar flanked by gleaming, muscular soldiers and workers clutching jackhammers and drills. Komsomolskaya is constructed in the baroque style to mimic the nearby Leningradsky train station and features below a near-replica of a church iconostasis. But some of the stations approach perfection. One of the most impressive is Mayakovskaya on the Gorkovsko-Zamoskvoretskaya line. A huge, wide, sweeping underground canyon with pillars that have an art deco feel to them, it's also notable for the Revolutionary mosaics – based on designs by Deineka along the ceiling, which always offer diversion while waiting for the next train. During the Great Patriotic War, this station, one of the biggest in the whole system, was used as an air-raid shelter. Another station to watch out for is Novokuznetskaya, whose marble benches were filched from the demolished Church of Christ the Saviour.

In the 1960s, the insane indulgence of metro construction gave way to the rationalism of simple concrete and steel structures.

Crossing over Bolshoi Moskvoretsky Most, you first come to the luxury **Hotel Kempinski Baltschug Moscau**, with its Luzhkovian spire. The hotel gets its name from Ulitsa Balchug, which in turn derives from the Tartar word *balchyk*, meaning 'mud'. That's pretty much what this whole area was in the Middle Ages, requiring people to wade knee-deep in gloop. To the left of the hotel, in the little nook of 1-ya Raushsky Pereulok, are three fairly good clubs: **Chetyre Komnaty** (Four Rooms), **Cabana** and **Vermel**. Walk along Sofiiskaya Naberezhnaya towards Bolshoi Kamenny Most, and you come to the infamous Government House, known colloquially as the **House on the Embankment** (Dom Na Naberezhnoi, *see below*), a stunning eyesore built between 1927 and 1932 by the same architect who designed the aborted Palace of Soviets. Continue along the embankment and you'll soon see, rearing up in front of you, the gargantuan statue of Peter the Great by Zurab Tsereteli, one of the newest and ugliest features of

Stalin's great wedding cake in the sky: the apartment buildings on Naberezhnaya Kotelnicheskaya.

Moscow's skyline. Next to Government House is the Udarnik Cinema, and across the road is **Sally O'Brien's**, another of the city's Irish bars.

Then, on the corner of Pyatnitskaya Ulitsa and Chernigovsky Pereulok is the lurid green, baroque bell tower of the Church of St John the Baptist, with the church itself positioned halfway up the lane. Inside, it's rather sparse, as if God is in the process of moving in (or out). Notice the curious, flagella-like chandeliers that betray the church's recent Soviet history, when it became a museum of glass ornamentation. By the church at Pyatnitskaya Ulitsa 4 is **Trety Put** (Third Way), a funky hangout that developed from a local squat.

Continuing down Chernigovsky Pereulok and across Ulitsa Bolshaya Ordynka brings you to the Church of the Resurrection on Kadeshevsky, a crumbling baroque edifice named after the coopers' settlement on this spot, and now a restorers' workshop. Further along Ulitsa Bolshaya Ordynka, by Tretyakovskaya metro, is the Church of the Consolation of All Sorrows built by Bazhenov and Bove. A few metres along, on the right, protected by railings, is the curious yet charming Church of the Intercession of the Mother of God in the **Martha and Mary Cloisters** (Marfo-Mariinskaya Obitel, *see below*); and even further down Ordinka, we find the Church of St Catherine at Vspolye, named after the patron saint of pregnant women. You might also want to check out the Church of St Gregory of Neocaesarea round the corner on Ulitsa Bolshaya Polyanka, across the road from Polyanka metro, if only for its nifty psychedelic colour scheme.

This area also hosts two of the town's more popular bars: the cellar dive **Bedniye Lyudi** and the **Canadian Moosehead Bar**, a popular expatriate place. The main sight in the central Zamoskvorechye, located on Bolshoi Tolmachevsky Pereulok a stone's throw from Tretyakovskaya metro, is Moscow's most important repository of Russian art: the **Tretyakov Gallery**. Even if you don't bother going in, the neo-Russian façade of the red-brick building, designed by Viktor Vasnetsov, will reward the journey. Closed for 15 years for an amazingly sluggish reconstruction, the gallery opened again in 1994 with a pristine interior to rival that of any gallery in the world.

House on the Embankment

Dom Na Naberezhnoi, Ulitsa Serafimovicha 2 (959 0317). Metro Borovitskaya. **Open** 5-8pm Wed; 2-5pm Sat. **Map p281 C4/5**
Intended as a luxury block for Party hacks, the House on the Embankment soon became a concrete tomb as the purges got in gear. Vans marked 'bread' or 'fruit' would arrive by night and drag whole families off to be shot or to the gulags. The sinister intruders didn't even have to knock, as service lifts had been thoughtfully installed for the purpose. The apartments, which are now highly coveted, also have an extensive network of false walls and partitions; it is said that residents often hear sneezes coming from nowhere. One of the apartments now houses a museum, which can be visited by appointment only. *See also chapter* **Museums & Galleries**.

Martha & Mary Cloisters

Marfo-Mariinskaya Obitel, Ulitsa Bolshaya Ordynka 36. Map p281 D5
Built by the ever-resourceful Shchusev, who was also responsible for Lenin's Mausoleum and the grotesque Hotel Moskva, the Cathedral of the Intercession, located in these cloisters is a charming conglomeration of cylinders, created between 1908 and 1912. The cloisters were founded by the Grand Duchess Yelizaveta Fyodorovna, elder sister to Nicholas II's wife, who became a nun when her husband was murdered by socialist Revolutionaries in the Kremlin's Senate Square. In July 1918, two days after the royal family was murdered in Yekaterinburg, the nun Varvara, as she was now known, was arrested, then taken to a remote mine, blinded and thrust down a shaft with a handful of grenades. Getting into the cloisters involves much argy-bargying to obtain permission from an office down the street; it's not really worth the effort.

Beyond Lubyanka

The area bordering on Myasnitskaya Ulitsa just up the road from Lubyanskaya Ploshchad is home to several run-of-the-mill cafés and restaurants, including a McDonald's, but the best of the bunch is the friendly Johnny Fat Boy. Its sign (and name) may be a rip-off of the American chain, Bob's Big Boy, but the place has a personality all its own. Downstairs is Papa John's, one of the better bars in town.

The age of Zurab Tsereteli

They call it Luzhkov's folly: the gargantuan weird boat thing, with a mammoth Peter the Great propped on top of it, situated on the southern bank of the Moskva River not far from the **Church of Christ the Saviour**. However, ultimate aesthetic responsibility for this grossly ugly Leviathan should be laid at the feet of Zurab Tsereteli, a Soviet-era sculptor and Luzhkov's favourite courtesan; a man whose influence on the character of New Moscow has been immense. Tsereteli monuments, which retain much of the bombast of socialist realism, are dotted all around the city. There's a fantastically gloomy and repulsive column devoted to Russian-Georgian friendship at Bolshaya Gruzinskaya Ulitsa, close to Belorussky Vokzal, the bloated monument to the 1945 victory at **Park Pobedy** (Victory Park) and the garden-gnome-like sculptures at the Okhotny Ryad shopping centre. But the most infamous and appalling of Tsereteli's works is the 60-metre (196-foot) statue of Peter the Great, unveiled in 1998 on the banks of the Moskva, a grandiose work which reputedly cost Russia's supposedly cash-strapped government $17.5 million. Pressure-groups of artists and intellectuals campaigned to have the statue dismantled, some going as far as to try to blow it up with plastic explosive. Even Yeltsin has been moved by the Tsereteli to chip in a comment: 'Moscow's backing of Tsereteli is a vain thing,' he said in 1997, 'Don't we have other sculptors and artists?'

For a time, it looked as if the critics were winning the argument and that the sculpture would have to be packed up and dispatched to a less obtrusive spot. Deptford in South London, where Peter the Great learned the art of shipbuilding at the end of the sixteenth century, offered to give it pride of place on the banks of the Thames. But, in the end, Luzhkov and his pet sculptor won out, leading to what Alexander Solzhenitsyn has appositely called 'a case of Moscow being recklessly disfigured'.

Further up the street, past Dunkin' Donuts, is by far the most interesting building on the street within the Boulevard Ring: **Chai-Kofe** (also known as the Terlov Tea House) at No.19. This late nineteenth-century structure, part shop, part city dwelling, is the only one in Moscow built in an eclectic Chinese style. Unfortunately, at the time of writing, the façade was undergoing restoration work, so hopefully it will be returned to its original glory soon.

On Ploshchad Myasnitskiye Vorota, across from Metro Chistye Prudy, is a landmark of the new Russia, the worthy-of-Brezhnev-ugly LUKoil building, which has a tasteful, working (or at least moving) Dallas-style oil well in front. The rest of Myasnitskaya past the Boulevard Ring features a number of city estates, including those of Baryshnikov (No.42) and of Lobanov-Rostovsky (No.43).

Perhaps the most interesting building, though, is the Tsentrosoyuz building (No.39). Originally the headquarters for the Central Union of Consumer Co operatives, this building has the distinction of being the only one in Russia designed by Le Corbusier. The great French architect visited Moscow numerous times in the 1920s and 1930s, a period of radical reconstruction in the capital, and called it 'the focus of architecture and city planning of the world'. Le Corbusier and Russian architect Nikolai Kolli won the commission to design Tsentrosoyuz in 1928, but work was not completed until 1935.

While the beauty of Moscow's metro stations is often commented upon, the actual entrances are for the most part fairly boring. Usually they are just doors in buildings or stairs leading into the ground. One of the major exceptions to this, however, is the Krasnye-Vorota vestibule, where Myasnitskaya crosses the Garden Ring. The entrance was designed by the architect Nikolai Ladovsky, who was also famous for coming up with a plan for the future capital that looked a lot like a rocket blasting off for Leningrad. It is a perfect example of the constructivist style: the building employs a series of concentric arcs to draw the viewer into the ground.

Chistye Prudy & Krasnye-Vorota

This section encompasses some of the most pleasant areas in the city. If you fancy a good walk, start at the Bolshoi Ustinsky Most (bridge), and head north up Ustinsky Proyezd along the Boulevard Ring until you get to Metro Chistye Prudy. This will take a while, but you'll get to see parts of the city often neglected by tourists only interested in major sights. Alternatively, allow yourself to get lost in the warren of winding streets within the Boulevard Ring or among the green back-streets between the Boulevard

and Garden Rings. The relatively well-preserved area just inside the Boulevard Ring gives some idea of just how many churches must once have dotted the whole of the city: the fairly small area bordered by Pokrovka and the Boulevard contains at least ten churches.

Some of the more interesting of these are: the early twentieth-century Lutheran Church of Saints Peter and Paul (Starosadsky Pereulok 7); the Ivanovsky Convent (Ulitsa Zabelina 4), which was founded in the 1500s, but the structure that stands there today dates from the nineteenth century; and the late seventeenth-century Church of St Vladimir (Starosadsky Pereulok 9).

Also worth seeing is one of Moscow's main (of the few remaining) synagogues, the nineteenth-century eclectic-style **Choral Synagogue** (Bolshoi Spasoglinishchevsky Pereulok 10).

Ulitsa Pokrovka (Ulitsa Maroseika)

This street runs from Kitai-Gorod, where it is called Ulitsa Maroseika, and it then becomes Ulitsa Pokrovka before it crosses the Boulevard Ring. At Ulitsa Maroseika 5 is the mid-eighteenth-century Church of St Nicholas the Miracleworker, which was built on the site of a church dating from the 1650s. The church's interior, which had been destroyed by the mid-nineteenth century, was restored in 1927.

Just around the corner from here, at Bolshoi Zlatoustinsky Pereulok 7, is **Propaganda**, one of the best clubs to visit on a Friday or Saturday night.

Up the street, at Ulitsa Maroseika 11, is the eighteenth-century, Imperial style Naryshkin-Raguzinsky House with the just pre-Revolutionary Triangle rubber factory across the street (No.12). The impressive city house of the merchant Grachev (No.17) is an elaborately decorated building, which currently houses the Belorussian Embassy. Just across the street (No.14/2) is the early nineteenth-century Church of Sts Kosma and Damian, which is juxtaposed with an ugly Brezhnev-era office building behind it. Just down that cross-street (across from the office building) is **Maharaja**, one of the better Indian places in town. On the corner of Pokrovka and the Boulevard Ring is **Coffee Bean**, a long-overdue authentic American coffeeshop, where you can actually sit down and have a good cup of coffee.

Not far from there, at Ulitsa Pokrovka 19 (again, just around the corner a little), is **Tibet**, the only Tibetan place in town and one of the best options for East Asian cuisine. Finally, on the corner of Pokrovka and the Garden Ring, is the **Country Bar**, whose menu offers an unusual mixture of Ethiopian dishes and West Coast hamburgers and steaks.

Beyond the Garden Ring

Sightseeing on the outer fringes of Moscow requires surgical precision. Ambling, roaming, wandering or any of that kind of leisurely stuff should be entirely avoided. You just want to get to that sight and back, avoiding, as much as possible, contact with the grubby, uniform, nightmarish suburbs that increasingly characterise Moscow as you travel further away from the centre. Carefully planned sightseeing is also advisable because of the distances involved. The sheer vastness of Moscow, where public space was one of the few luxuries available to all in communist times, is capable of exhausting even your best sightseeing intentions. On the whole, one location a day is more than enough for comfort. And some, like the Exhibition of Economic Achievements at **VVTs** (*see below*), are gigantic enough in themselves to transform a jaunt into an odyssey.

All the sights in this section lie outside the Garden Ring, the boundary that separates Moscow from its suburbs. Before you set off, remember to call and check that your destination is actually open that day. Museums and palaces often close for arbitrary reasons: high humidity, low humidity, heatwaves or blizzards – the staff of Russian tourist establishments seem to shut down and go home for the day for the slightest reason.

North

In general, the northern suburbs of Moscow are not inviting; a couple of years ago, the **Titanic** club might have dragged you out to mingle with the beautiful young things in the designer recesses of **Dinamo Stadium**, but the beautiful set has since moved on. There are a couple of half-decent bars out this way, but they're no better than anything in the centre, and certainly no reason to make a special trip as far as Sokol or Rechnoi Voksal.

However, the freakish magnificence of the Stalinist Park of Economic Achievements, now known as the **VVTs** (All Russia Exhibition Centre, *see below*), but still generally referred to by its old acronym VDNKh, more than makes up for this.

Outside VDNKh metro station, three stops north of Prospekt Mira on the Ryzhkaya line, a metropolis of kiosks has sprung up, some of which stock an impressive selection of clubwear as well as Doc Marten's, Shelleys, Grinders and Buffalo footwear. On the other side of Prospekt Mira is the great wedge of elliptical glass and concrete known as the **Cosmos Hotel**. The **Space Museum**, marked out by the 100-metre-high Space Obelisk, a comic-strip titanium rocket propelled into the stratosphere by a great stylised soaring titanium column of smoke, has become a summer assembly point

Upholding the law at **Petrovka 38**. *See p42.*

for Moscow's hippies, all wearing Bob Marley or Beatles T-shirts and twanging on guitars.

As soon as the kiosks begin to thin out, the mammoth triumphal gateway to the Park of Economic Achievements comes into view, bearing a jubilant, striding statue of a tractor driver and farm girl offering to the ether a luxurious sheaf of wheat. Such obscene cereal wealth, however, is a tiny foretaste of what is to come. Most of the 80 pavilions are overflowing with proletarian decoration, though their original exhibitions have been stripped to make way for Japanese hi-fis, Taiwanese computers and German and American cars.

Just to the right, facing the VVTs entrance, is another great Soviet public art icon, also on a gargantuan scale. Vera Mukhina's Worker and Collective Farm Girl is perhaps one of socialist realism's greatest achievements, a dynamic fusion of classicism and ideology, as the hammer and sickle unite in a flash of stainless steel musculature. VVTs melds into the Botanical Gardens to the north. To the west, you can find **Ostankino Palace** and **TV Tower** (*see below*) and the TV centre that played an important role in the White House conflict of 1993.

VVTs (VDNKh)

All Russia Exhibition Centre. VDNKh Metro. **Open** 9am-8pm Mon-Fri; 9am-9pm Sat, Sun, public holidays. **Admission** free.

Established in 1937, at the height of the purges, as the All-Union Agricultural Exhibition, construction work on the more than 80 pavilions of what eventually became the Exhibition of Economic Achievements went on right into the 1980s. Each monstrous structure was devoted to one aspect of the great economic, industrial and technical miracle otherwise known as communism. The Space Pavilion, right at the end, is an astonishing parabolic webbed metal and glass arch that ends in a futuristic orb-like dome. The Forestry Pavilion, a neo-classical temple carved out of wood, displays a peasant logging scene on its frieze, complete with carved wooden chainsaw. Nothing quite approaches the bombast and empty decorativeness of the Fountain of the Friendship of Peoples, a cascade of fresh gilded crops from communist pastures featuring gilded statues of female representatives of the USSR's 16 Soviet republics.

Miniature toy trains ferry shoppers around the huge complex. And, in case you're in need of a diversion, there's a sad floppy-humped camel to be photographed with as long as you're willing to dress up as a sheik.

Ostankino Palace

1-ya Ostankinskaya Ulitsa 5 (283 4645/286 6288). Metro VDNKh. **Open** *18 May-1 Oct* 10am-5pm Tue-Sun. Closed when raining; when humidity is over 80%. **Admission** $1; 40¢ under-17s, students; *guided tour* $3.50; $1.25 students.

Across from the TV Tower is the pink, neo-classical Ostankino Palace, built from 1792 to 1798. This Palladian mansion, commissioned by Count Nikolai Sheremetyev and built by his serfs, gives the impression of being a solid stone building, but it was actually built of wood and given a stucco makeover. The central part of the building was, at the time of writing, under restoration but was set to reopen in September 1998. The interior is generally a little overdone: richly adorned ceilings and walls and a marine and red colour scheme create an almost oriental atmosphere in the main hall. The entrance to the theatre is located on the back of the house, facing the park. Concerts are held here during the summer months. Also facing the park is the exhibition hall for temporary displays, located in the east wing.

Ostankino TV Tower

(282 2293). Metro VDNKh, then bus 85 or 24. **Open** 9am-8.30pm Tue-Sun. **Admission** $2.50; $1.50 children. **No credit cards.**

The Moscow TV Tower at Ostankino, built in 1967, provides visitors with probably the best view in Moscow. The lift takes you 337 metres (1,105 feet) above ground to the viewing platform, which also has a fairly decent restaurant, Sedmoye Nebo (Seventh Heaven). It is best to visit the tower on clear days, as any kind of cloud cover will leave you with a visibility level of a couple of metres. Tickets are for sale in the square, grey building near the tower. Visitors must fill out a form and show their passports and be prepared to have their bags checked.

West

Hugging the Garden Ring to the west are some truly worthwhile and relatively accessible sights, not least of which is the White House, the headquarters of the Russian government. This dull, officious-looking building was made famous by the siege of 1993, when Yeltsin opened fire on deputies barricaded inside, killing a handful and transforming the building overnight into the Black and White House. The gigantic SEV building, which was once the headquarters the Socialist-trading bloc known in the west as Comecon, stands to the left, casting a shadow all the way down Kutuzovsky Prospekt. A little further up the embankment is the World Trade Centre, a building that also houses the **Mezhdunarodnaya Hotel** (International Hotel). Opposite are two interesting restaurants: the Russian Bochka (Barrel) and **Shinok**, a Ukrainian eaterie featuring a real ox and attendant peasant woman. Further down the embankment is **Sadko** shopping arcade, a haunt of New Russians looking to spend as much money as possible in the shortest possible time. Venturing past the skyscraping **Hotel Ukraina** along Kutuzovsky Prospekt, with its luxury apartments built for Party dignitaries and diplomats, you come to the Triumphal Arch and **Park Pobedy** (*see below*), another favourite rollerblading spot. Court sculptor Tsereteli has left his mark here, too, with an ugly charcoal monument to the Russian victory in the Patriotic War of 1945.

Park Pobedy

Victory Park, Kutuzovsky Prospekt. Metro Kutuzovskaya, then trolley or bus to Park Pobedy. **Open** 24 hours.

Park Pobedy, or Victory Park, at Poklonnye Gora, is a vast establishment finished in 1995 for the celebration of the 50th anniversary of the Soviet Union's World War II victory. It is worth noting that it was built on the spot where Napoleon stood as he watched Moscow burning. On Victory Day, 9 May, Muscovites gather here to celebrate the defeat over Nazi Germany. The monumental obelisk in the centre of the park has a symbolic sculpture representing St George and the Dragon at its foot. The white crescent building contains the Great Patriotic War Museum (open 10am-6pm Tue-Sun).

This area, south-west of the Metro station Park Kultury, begins with the upmarket residential area along Komsomolsky Prospekt (much of which was built by German prisoners of war) and then tapers into the Sparrow Hills, before finally reaching Moscow State University (MGU), the biggest and most terrifying of Stalin's Gothic skyscrapers.

On the retail side of things, Komsomolsky is totally moribund and its most notable sight is the massive block of concrete by Frunzenskaya metro – the Moskovsky Dvorets Molodyozhi (Palace of Youth, otherwise known as **MDM**), which serves as a disco and concert venue. Once you reach the untidy parklands around **Luzhniki Stadium**, everything gets much more exciting. The stadium, which was enlarged to its present massive size for the 1980 Olympics, turns into a high-security jail for local Spartak matches, when skinhead fans are escorted to the metro through a corridor of baton-wielding riot troops.

Around the corner, by Bolshaya Pirogovskaya Ulitsa, is the **Novodevichy Monastery** (*see below*), one of the most beautiful in the city. Far more interesting, however, is the adjacent **Novodevichy Cemetery** (*see below*), where you will find the graves of Chekhov, Mayakovsky, Khrushchev and a host of others. No expense or florid excess has been spared on the Soviet-era gravestones. Although it is possible to walk, the easiest way to get to the MGU from here is to get on the metro at Sportivnaya and ride one stop to Universitet. Once there, join the stream of students turning left down Lomonosovsky Prospekt.

The university building, Moscow's biggest when it was built (1949-53), is another Moscow edifice that makes its impression by sheer size and brute scale. Walk around its base and feel yourself shrinking slowly to the size of a cockroach. If you can blag your way in – a special student card is usually required – the marble vestibules are astonishing. From the university, travel the groomed thoroughfare leading to Sparrow Hills. From this red granite-trimmed platform – a traditional spot in Soviet Moscow for the bride and groom to assemble after a wedding ceremony – the whole city shimmers below.

Novodevichy Monastery

Novodevichy Proyezd 1 (246 8526). Metro Sportivnaya. **Open** 8am-7pm daily (exhibitions are closed Sat, Sun). **Admission** $1.50; *exhibition* $1.50; *cemetery* $1.50.
Established in 1524 to commemorate the recapture of Smolensk by Russian forces, the Novodevichy (New Convent of the Maidens) is one of the most beautiful in the city, with its striking baroque bell tower (a later addition) and swallow-tail fortifications. Its main cathedral is named after the icon of the Virgin of Smolensk, which it houses. But almost more interesting are the tombs in the Smolensk Cathedral, which include most of Peter the Great's sisters, including the regent Sofia, who was banished here when Peter came of age. During the Streltsy Revolt of 1698, Peter's suspicions fell on Sofia and he had the conspirators interrogated in the monastery and then hanged outside Sofia's cell.

Novodevichy Cemetery

Bolshaya Pirogovksaya Ulitsa. Metro Sportivnaya. **Open** 8am-7pm daily. **Admission** $1.50.
While the monastery may be beautiful, the Novodevichy Cemetery is one of the most fascinating spots in Moscow. Before the Revolution, this was the place where all the artistic luminaries spent eternity. In the communist era, they were joined by generals and politicians who didn't quite make it into the Kremlin wall, as well as by Soviet scientists and scholars. In the first section of the graveyard are a combination of Soviet generals, scientists, scholars. As you venture further down towards the grave of Khrushchev, the tomb-art gets more wacky until, a couple of rows before the end, on the right, is the headstone of a nuclear scientist with a rack of missiles shooting off into the air. Khrushchev's grave is marked by a morose bust by Ernst Neizvestny, the artist whose work was once described by the splenetic Soviet leader as 'dogshit'.

Through the central arch in the next section of the cemetery, you will find Nikolai Gogol, Anton Chekhov, Stanislavksy, Shostakovich, the poet Vladimir Mayakovsky, Mikhail Bulgakov, Sergei Eisenstein, Fyodor Chaliapin and Alexander Scriabin. If you can't find a grave, ask one of the *babushki* wandering around.

South

South of the Garden Ring is generally a blank expanse with no character whatsoever. At certain points, however, the tower blocks suddenly swing back to reveal something as startling as the **Donskoi Monastery** (*see below*), which rears up at the end of Donskaya Ulitsa, en route from Shabolovkaya metro station. A little less interesting and more formal is the Danilov Monastery, the town residence of the Patriarch, which is next to Tulskaya metro. Beyond that, the only draws are the two superb imperial estates, **Kolomenskoye** (*see below*) and **Tsaritsyno** (*see below*), both of which are popular day-trip destinations with Muscovites. And, though it's not worth a special trip in itself, if you're driving along Leninsky Prospekt, take a moment at Ploshchad Gagarina to strain your neck to gape at the titanium statue of Yuri Gagarin, the first man in space, a monument of cartoon superhero proportions.

Donskoi Monastery

Donskaya Ploshchad 1 (952 1646). Metro Shabolovskaya. **Open** 7am-4.30pm daily. **Admission** free. Cameras forbidden.
Founded in 1591 by Tsar Fyodor Ioannovich to house the Donskaya Icon of the Mother of God as a mark of gratitude for victories over Crimean warlords, the Donskoi Monastery has been plundered three times over – the Time of Troubles, Napoleon and the Revolution – after which it became a museum to atheism. Once inside (the entrance is on the far right), it's a haven of peace and tranquillity, which attracts a steady flow of worshippers. At the time of writing, the Donskoi was undergoing extensive restoration work but the old cathedral with its bold, simple frescoes was still open to the public. Visitors are asked to behave with respect, as it is a working monastery (women should wear a dress or a skirt and long sleeves). If you understand Russian, it is worth asking the monk at the entrance about having a guided tour. A tour is extremely rewarding, but is only granted at the discretion of the chief monk; it is free, but contributions toward the cost of the restoration work are welcomed.

Tsaritsyno

Dolskaya Ulitsa 1 (321 0743). Metro Tsaritsyno. **Open**
10am-5pm Wed-Fri; 10am-6pm Sat, Sun. Closed last Wed
of each month. **Admission** 70¢; 50¢ students; *guided
tour* $40. **No credit cards.**
Moscow's most famous ruins were commissioned by Catherine
the Great, as an out-of-town palace for herself and her son Paul.
Vasily Bazhenov was ordered to build the curious Moorish-
Gothic structure we see today, with its arcane squiggles, stars
and creepy masonic symbols. He also built a decorative ruin at
the back of the garden, now an ironic comment on the entire
escapade. After ten years, Catherine arrived to survey the work,
hated it, and the whole project was simply abandoned. In 1997,
a number of restored buildings were open to the public, most
notably the Opera House, which now hosts concerts and maintains a museum of tapestries, carved bones and various uten-
sils from the time of Catherine the Great, as well as a rather
half-hearted display of Russian crystal. After two centuries of
dereliction, Mayor Luzhkov is now talking about restoring the
whole place. In the meantime, the grounds are perfect for picnicking and generally lazing around in the grass. From the
metro, turn right under the bridge and bear right up the hill

Kolomenskoye

*Metro Kolomenskaya, exit at the front of the train, turn left
in the underpass, then right and walk straight ahead up the
hill.* **Open** *grounds* 10am-8pm Tue-Sun; *museum* 11am-5pm
Tue-Sun; *summer* 11am-5pm Tue, Fri-Sun; 1-8pm Wed,
Thur. **Admission** $6; group tours, call in advance.
Kolomenskoye began life with the Wooden Palace that Tsar
Alexei erected on this spot in 1667, probably the last of its
kind to be built in Russia. A haphazard arrangement of connecting corridors and bulbous domes, it became derelict after
the capital was moved to St Petersburg and was pulled down
in the time of Catherine the Great, though not before she
ordered architects to make an exact model (which is now on
display in the museum). Later, the estate became the stomping ground of the young Peter the Great, who drilled his 'toy'
regiments in the grounds. Now, part of the complex is taken
up by the Museum of Wooden Architecture, an eclectic collection of icons, bells, carving and wooden buildings such as
the cabin where Peter the Great lived while supervising the
building of the northern fleet. Most of all, however,
Kolomenskoye is simply a wonderful expansive park that
attracts hordes of trippers but never gets crowded. Along the
banks of the Moskva are a number of bubbling springs that,
it's claimed, can cure barrenness. You might even try swimming in the somewhat slimy outdoor pool. Or just sit and
drink *medovukha* (a traditional Russian drink made from
honey) in the eighteenth-century mead brewery.

South-east

In the south-eastern suburbs for much of
Moscow's history, just by the Yauza River, was
the infamous Nemetskaya Sloboda, the foreigner's
settlement where Peter the Great developed his
European tastes and lost his virginity during
drunken orgies with 'Lutheran Whores'. Again, it's
a vast region and completely without cohesion,
but, as ever, there are some gems hidden away in
far-flung corners of the district. The **Andronikov
Monastery** (*see below*), the **Novospassky
Monastery** (*see below*) and the **Kuskovo Estate**
(*see below*) are all worth a visit. You might also like
to take the metro to Izmailovsky Park to haggle in
the famous Vernisazh souvenir market with its
unsurpassable selection of icons, *matrioshki*, and
lacquer boxes. Nearby, on an island, is the

Izmailovo Royal Estate, the first of the European-
style royal palaces with adjacent landscaped parklands, that now make up the huge Ismailovo Park.

Andronikov Monastery

*Andronevskaya Ploshchad 10 (278 1467). Metro Ploshchad
Ilicha.* **Open** 11am-6pm Mon, Tue, Thur-Sun. Closed last
Fri of month. **Admission** $3 foreigners; $1.50 Russians;
student discounts available. **No credit cards.**
In somewhat better condition than the Novospassky
Monastery, the Andronikov Monastery is mostly famous for
the **Andrei Rublyov Museum** that it houses. Rublyov was
a famous Russian icon painter who was a resident monk here
in the fifteenth century and is said to be buried in the
grounds. Aside from the museum, there is the cute, wedding-
cake Saviour's Cathedral (Spassky Sabor), which, dating
from 1427, is the oldest stone building in Moscow. The white
Church of the Archangel Michael is also based here.

Kuskovo Estate

*Ryazansky Proyezd 2 (370 0160). Metro Perovo, then 10-
minute walk or Metro Ryazansky Prospekt, then bus 133
or 208.* **Open** 10am-6pm (last entry 4pm) Wed-Sun.
Closed last Wed of month. **Map p279 F1**
Set in parkland landscaped along classical eighteenth-century
lines with marble sculptures imported from Italy, the
Sheremetyev Palace at Kuskovo is the only building of its kind
to have survived to the present day. This pink, neo-classical
building, overlooking the lake, was built of wood in the 1770s
by the serfs of Count Sheremetyev, one of the richest landown-
ers in Russia, also responsible for Ostankino. Its interior decorations – the intricate wooden parquet floors, painted ceilings,
tiled stoves and handwoven tapestries – were recently restored.
Behind the main building you'll find a well-kept French
garden. In the yellow orangery (*Bolshaya kamennaya oranzher-
aya*) opposite the palace is a collection of Russian and European
porcelain dating from the seventeenth to the twentieth centuries, the display of 'Revolutionary Porcelain' is especially
interesting with its cups and plates hand-decorated with
Bolshevik slogans and portraits of the great leaders. Located
at the east end of the park is the green Italian house, built in
1754 as combination of a palazzo and an Italian villa. The main
building closes during humid weather, so it is best to call in
advance, to avoid disappointment.

Novospassky Monastery

*Krestyanskaya Ploshchad 10 (276 9570). Metro
Proletarskaya.* **Open** 7am-5pm daily. **Admission** free,
with permission.
The Novospassky Monastery is oddly surrounded by busy
highways. Its signature is a yellow, fairytale bell tower built
in the eighteenth century, which is now in a very sad condition, as are many of the other monastery buildings. The
monastery was founded in the thirteenth century by Prince
Daniil Moskovsky. After being moved in 1330 from its first
location to a spot inside the Kremlin, it was relocated a second time, when the construction of the three cathedrals of
the Kremlin began in the fifteenth century. The complex was
closed after the Revolution and used as a prison by the Cheka
secret police until World War II. In 1991, it became a working monastery again, and today about 40 monks live here.
The centrepiece of the monastery is the whitewashed Sobor
Spasa Preobrazheniya (Transfiguration Cathedral), built in
1645 by the Romanov family. The cathedral, partly destroyed
during the communist era, is now under reconstruction. The
apse, resembling the Kremlin's Assumption Cathedral, is dominated by an impressive iconostasis, flanked by two shrines
for relics from Kiev, including a piece of clothing from the
Virgin Mary. Women visitors are expected to wear a dress or
skirt rather than trousers and are required to cover their heads
while inside; permission for entrance must be obtained from
the guard in the booth to the right of the entrance gates.
Guided tours in English are available.

Museums & Galleries

Nice art, shame about the space.

Of all Moscow's cultural institutions, its museums have been most battered and brutalised by the changes of recent years. Once the great repositories of communist ideology, almost overnight they became little more than large, expensive, dusty liabilities with spiralling fuel bills and an ever dwindling trickle of visitors. Even world-renowned institutions like the **Tretyakov** and the **Pushkin State** have consistently been regarded by politicians as soft targets for budget cutbacks. Both spent a good deal of the 1990s appealing, protesting, threatening and cajoling in a concerted effort to survive.

Apart from the demise of ideological behemoths such as the Central Lenin Museum and the Karl Marx and Friedrich Engels Museum, however, there have been surprisingly few casualties. Many have managed to hunt down the holy grail of cultural capitalism: private sponsorship, mostly from commercial banks. Second-tier museums have survived entirely through the devotion of their staff, the famed *museychiki* of communist times – saintly folk boasting miniscule salaries, boundless dedication and a predisposition to nervous collapse or alcoholism. These museum heroes, many of them septuagenarian *babushki* who watch vigilantly from the corner of every hall, can tell you more about the exhibits than any scholar or expert, if you have the inclination, or the language skills, to ask.

Overall, there is still something bracing, unpredictable and fantastically eccentric about Moscow's museums. Some exotic examples (such as the **Museum of Wood**) turn out to be prospering, innovative enterprises utilising the latest digital technology, while traditional safe bets (such as the **Literary Museum**) are run-down, dilapidated disappointments. And while St Petersburg museums look west for inspiration, many of the best Moscow examples have an eastern or Byzantine flavour (the **Andrei Rublyov Museum** or the **Oriental Art Museum**, for example), reflecting the Russian temperament before Peter the Great threw the country open to European influences. And nowhere can you see the rapid changes that have ripped through Russia over the past decade better than in the **State Historical Museum**, the **Museum of Revolution** and even in Luzhkov's new creation, the **Cathedral of Christ the Saviour Museum**. Moscow's museums are the most tangible, graphic record of the development of the new Russia and – in what must be the supreme irony of the current situation – the greatest testament to the forces that almost brought about their own destruction.

SOME PRACTICALITIES

The cynical practice of dual pricing (charging foreigners several times more than the indigenous population) is still widespread in Moscow's museums. And as staff are well trained in the art of sniffing out foreigners, you may just have to resign yourself to paying between two and four times as much as the Russian standing next to you in the queue. (We have listed prices for foreigners only.)

Charges for photographing or video-recording in museums generally apply and are usually exorbitant. Expect to pay between $1.60 and $15 for the privilege of taking a couple of snaps and anywhere between $5 and $50 for shooting video. Professional photographers, differentiated by a little drawing of a tripod on price lists, may be charged even more. If you don't want to be watched like a fieldmouse by the hawk-like *babushki*, leave your equipment discreetly in the cloakroom; these are always available, are almost always free and generally safe.

Another quirk of Russia's tourist trail is the fact that so many landmarks are classed as museums, a category that the communists slapped on to any monument that they didn't have the courage to tear down but that would still be an eyesore in the socialist utopia. So, while St Basil's, the Kremlin cathedrals and many of the aristocratic estates are technically classed as museums, we have treated them as sights; *see chapter* **Sightseeing**.

Finally, it is always a good idea to ring ahead to check that your museum is actually open, regardless of what it says in the listings. All Russian institutions close at will and without explanation. And then there are the arcane regulations: buildings over 200 years old don't open when the humidity is over 80 per cent.

Museums of the Moscow Kremlin

The Armoury

Kremlin, Troitsky Most (202 3776/4256/2808). Metro Okhotny Ryad. **Open** 10am-4.30pm Mon-Wed, Fri-Sun; tours 10am, noon, 2.30pm, 4.30pm. **Admission** $14; $7 students, under-17s; $45 tours. **Map p278 C3, p281 C4**

This is the principal Kremlin museum, an unimaginably rich collection that evolved from the royal weaponry and armour workshops once located here. Among the more stunning pieces are the fabulous court carriages – including kiddie-carts for the royal children – that fill an entire chamber on the ground (Russian first) floor. Most of the more lavish examples belonged to Peter the Great's daughter, the Empress Elizabeth, including the sleigh in which she travelled from St Petersburg to Moscow for her coronation, as well as a couple of sumptuous Viennese numbers dripping in gilt. Nearby is a display of the Tsars' thrones and crowns, including the fur-trimmed Cap of Monomachus, first worn by the earliest Kievan princes and subsequently used to crown all of the Tsars up to Peter the Great. Of the thrones, the most striking are Ivan the Great's ivory job, the tandem throne of Peter the Great and his half-wit brother Ivan (which has a 'prompt-box' from where the Regent Sophia fed lines to the boy-tsars) and Elizabeth's unusually wide throne, extended to accommodate her double-decker buttocks. On the first floor is an endless (and sometimes tiringly lavish) collection of foreign ambassadorial gifts to the Russian kings, including a unique collection of seventeenth-century English silverware (look out for the metre high silver leopard), stuff you won't even find now in England, as most of it was melted down to make coins during the Revolution. However, the stars of the Armoury collection are undoubtedly the Fabergé eggs (in the second room on the upper floor): ten of the 50 dazzling Easter presents made by the St Petersburg jeweller for the royal family between 1885 and 1916. The most beautiful are probably the 'rock-crystal' egg containing a scale model of Peter the Great's yacht, the *Shtandart* and the trans-Siberian egg bearing a scale model of the train in gold. Also in the Armoury building is the Diamond Fund, whose exhibits include Catherine the Great's coronation regalia and the massive Orlov and Shakh diamonds.

Tours in English.

Pushkin Museum of Fine Arts

Ulitsa Volkhonka 12 (203 9578/7798). Metro Kropotkinskaya. **Open** 10am-6pm Tue-Sun. **Admission** $9; $4.50 students, under-17s; temporary exhibition prices vary. **Map p280 B4, p281 C4**

This is to Moscow what the Hermitage is to St Petersburg – the city's major collection of Western art and antiquities. The museum was founded in 1898 by Ivan Tsvetayev, art historian, linguist and father of the poet Marina. Originally called the Alexander III Museum of Fine Arts, it was given a ceremonial opening in its present location in 1912, with Tsar Nicholas II presiding. The Pushkin was planned as an educational establishment where the Russian public could see both original works and copies of antique and Renaissance treasures. Tsvetayev not only bought paintings and antiquities for his new museum, but also commissioned plaster casts of famous statues in European museums. The result is one of the most idiosyncratic features of the museum – rooms full of works of art you know you've seen somewhere else. The paintings are originals, however. Don't miss the idyllic landscapes by Poussin and Lorraine, or Canaletto's views of Venice. Leave plenty of time to explore the first floor, as it holds an unrivalled collection of French art from the nineteenth and twentieth centuries. Paintings acquired by Sergei Tretyakov, brother of the Tretyakov Gallery's founder, are on show, including his superb Barbizon School collection. However, it is the works by later French artists for which the Pushkin Museum is famous. These read like a roll call of the most influential impressionist and post-impressionist painters, including Monet, Renoir, Cezanne, Gauguin, Van Gogh, Matisse and Picasso.

In 1995, the Pushkin Museum made international headlines when, along with the Hermitage, it confessed to owning hundreds of works of art taken from Germany by the Red Army during and after World War II. These revelations fuelled worldwide debate about the question of restitution. Russians see the so-called trophy art as small compensation for what their country suffered during the war and, in 1997, against Yeltsin's wishes, the Russian parliament passed a bill that made it the property of the Russian state. However, Germany continues to contest ownership and the scandal has seriously affected diplomatic relations between the two countries. The trophy art in the Pushkin includes masterpieces by El Greco, Goya and Daumier brazenly incorporated into the display.

*Cavalry couture at the **Kremlin Armoury**.*

Central Museum of the Revolution *(p62)*.

State Historical Museum

Krasnaya Ploshchad 1 (Red Square) (924 4529). Metro Ploshchad Revolutsii, Teatralnaya or Okhotny Ryad. **Open** 11am-7pm (last admission 6pm) Mon, Wed-Sun. Closed 1st Mon of month. **Admission** $5; $2.50 students. **Map p278 D3**

After an 11-year renovation, the State Historical Museum reopened in late 1997. However, by the following summer, only 13 halls, just under a third of the total of 40, had actually managed to reopen. The museum traces the development of Russian civilisation, stretching from the first stirrings of the Neanderthals to the formation of Kievan Rus. Exhibits include skeletons of prehistoric rhinos as well as Scythian jewellery and death masks that give a good idea of what one of the first and most ferocious tribes to roam the Russian plains actually looked like.

One of the more interesting new additions is a mini-exhibition that includes portraits of the Tsars, the throne of Alexander the Great and Peter the Great's death mask, cast by Carlo Rastrelli, father of the famous St Petersburg architect. Another new development is the historical cinema, where Western and Russian films are shown at 1pm.

Tretyakov Gallery

Lavrushinsky Pereulok 10-12 (238 1378/230 7788). Metro Tretyakovskaya. **Open** 10am-8pm Tue-Sun (last entry 6pm). **Tickets** $8; $4.50 students, under-17s. **Map p281 C5**

The core of the Tretyakov remains in the pseudo-Russian brick building designed by Victor Vasnetsov and constructed in 1872, but it is now dwarfed by a huge extension, the product of a ten-year renovation. The gallery's layout is not visitor-friendly, and floor plans have yet to be provided. Visitors walk up the main staircase to the first floor, where they follow a chronological progression through the eighteenth and nineteenth centuries. They then descend to the

ground floor to the twentieth-century galleries and, confusingly, rooms full of icons. This jump is not easy, nor is there the option of skipping realms of neo-classical portraits and dipping in where you please. If you want to see Malevich's *Black Square*, for example, it will take a brisk 15-minute walk through acres of art before you get there. Chances are you'll be saturated by that time and have forgotten what you wanted to see. There are masterpieces at every step, the majority of them unjustly neglected and excluded from the canon of Western art history. These include Alexander Ivanov's *Appearance of Christ to the People* and Vasily Perov's *Village Religious Procession*. The huge hall at the end of the first floor is devoted to the outstanding Russian symbolist Mikhail Vrubel, whose tortured works reveal the artist's incipient insanity. The Russian impressionist paintings offer a more restful visual experience before the onslaught of avant-garde paintings, which culminate in the work of Vasily Kandinsky.

Tretyakovka Gallery

Ulitsa Krymsky Val 10/14 (230 7788). Metro Park Kultury or Oktyabrskaya. **Open** 10am-8pm Tue-Sun (last entry 6pm). **Tickets** $8; $4.50 students, under-17s. **Map p280 B6, p281 C6**

Located opposite the entrance to Gorky Park, this branch of the main Tretyakov Gallery is in a square, grey building that it shares with the Tsentralny Dom Khudozhnikov (*see below* **Exhibition centres**). The museum contains a permanent collection of art from the 1920s and 1930s, including many famous works by the cubo-futurists. Closed at the time of writing, it was due to reopen shortly. It often hosts excellent temporary exhibitions of modern art.

Art

Andrei Rublyov Museum

Andronyevskaya Ploshchad 10 (278 1467). Metro Ploshchad Ilicha. **Open** 11am-6pm Mon, Tue, Thur-Sun. Closed last Fri of month. **Admission** $3; student discounts available.

Located inside the Andronikov Monastery near Ploshchad Ilicha (*see chapter* **Sightseeing**), this museum is named after the monastery's most celebrated monk – the world-famous Russian icon painter, who lived here in the fifteenth century. Weirdly enough, the museum does not actually contain any icons by Rublyov, but is nevertheless worth a visit for the collection of works from the Moscow, Rostov and Novgorod schools of painting from the fourteenth to the sixteenth centuries. There are also five impressive seventeenth-century icons from Suzdal and, from the collection of the Greek collector Koostaki, some fragments of the earliest twelfth-century icons.

Museum of Decorative & Applied Art

Delegatskaya Ulitsa 3 (923 1741/consultations 921 0139). Metro Novoslobodskaya. **Open** 10am-6pm (last admission 5pm) Mon-Thur, Sat, Sun; *consultations* 2-5pm Tue. Closed last Thur of month. **Admission** $2.50; $1 students. **Map p278 C1**

The collection includes folk crafts, porcelain (from the beginning of the eighteenth century to the 1920s) and furniture, as well as some unusual artefacts like a special prosthetic for tying your shoelaces without bending down (from the nineteenth century) and *kopoushki*, decorative items for picking the wax out of your ears.

State Museum of Oriental Art

Nikitsky Bulvar 12A (291 9614). Metro Arbatskaya. **Open** 11am-8pm (last entry 7pm) Tue-Sun. **Admission** $5; 35¢ students. **Map p277 A3**

While there is plenty of art from Korea, China, Vietnam, the Caucasus and Japan (including Russia's largest hoard of *netsuke* – more than 500 examples of ivory purse toggles), the real pearl of this museum is the room devoted to the work of Nikolai Rerikh, the prominent philosopher, artist and follower of the ideas of Leo Tolstoy and Ghandi.

Museum of Private Collections

Ulitsa Volkhonka 14 (203 9578/7798). Metro Kropotkinskaya. **Open** 10am-5pm Wed-Sun. **Admission** $5. **Map** p280 B4, p281 C4

Private collecting was rather a clandestine affair under communism, but the tradition of artistic patronage, which had flourished under Tsarist rule, continued throughout the Soviet era. This has been recognised in post-Soviet times with the opening of the Museum of Private Collections, an affiliate of the Pushkin Museum of Fine Arts, in its own building next door. The museum easily outshines Moscow's other museums in terms of organisation and comfort. The building's logical plan means that you find your way without thinking, via the efficient cloakrooms (and Moscow's cleanest public loos), to the ticket office and ceremonial staircase. This leads to two floors of paintings and sculptures organised by collection. Look out for the collections of Alexander Rodchenko, his wife Varvara Stepanova and that of Ilia Zilbershtein, the guiding light behind the establishment of the museum.

Art & culture

English House Museum

Ulitsa Varvarka 4 (298 3961) Metro Kitai-Gorod. **Open** 10am-6pm Tue, Thur, Sat, Sun; 11am-7pm Wed, Fri. **Admission** $1.50; 50¢ students; *guided tour* $1.50. **Map** p278 D3

At various times, this building has served as a store for goods imported by the English in the times of Ivan the Terrible, a chamber of commerce and the first English embassy on Russian soil. Nominally, the exhibition here is devoted to the history of the building itself, but recently the museum seems to have been invaded by none other than the

Queen of England. In 1994, her Highness dropped in for a walkabout during a trip to Moscow and the largest part of the exhibition is now devoted to pictures and documents commemorating that momentous event.

History

Cathedral of Christ the Saviour Museum

Ulitsa Volkhonka 4 (no phone). Metro Kropotkinskaya. **Open** 10am-6pm Tue-Sat. **Admission** *observation ground* $1.50. **Map** p280 B4, p281 C4

This ad hoc museum in an annexe of the new cathedral is dedicated to various buildings that stood (or were supposed to have stood) on this site. These include the original resident of the site, the Alexeyevsky Monastery; the old Cathedral of Jesus Christ the Saviour, which was blown up by Stalin in 1931; the aborted Palace of Soviets, which was to be topped by a monstrous statue of Lenin twice the size of the Statue of Liberty; the 'cursed' Moskva swimming pool, whose currents were said to have dragged swimmers to their deaths and, finally, the new cathedral, masterwork of Moscow mayor Yury Luzhkov. The exhibits include various relics from the older buildings, photos of drunk-looking JCB drivers and mannequins in construction gear with authentic hard hats.

Central Museum of the Great Patriotic War

Ploshchad Pobedy (449 8044). Metro Kutuzovskaya. **Open** 10am-6pm Tue-Sun. **Admission** free.

With the rest of the Victory Square historical complex, this was the first of Mayor Luzhkov's hugely ambitious building projects. The interior of the museum looks very much like the Okhotny Ryad shopping mall: expansive, marble clad, faux-gilt trimmings. The exhibition includes an impressive collection of photos, documents, uniforms, weapons and soldiers' personal belongings. There is also a huge memorial hall with the names of the many thousands who received Hero of the Soviet Union awards engraved on the walls.

*A repository of Russia's past: the **State Historical Museum**. See page 60.*

Central Museum of the Revolution

Tverskaya Ulitsa 21 (299 6724). Metro Tverskaya, Pushkinskaya or Chekhovskaya. **Open** 10am-6pm Mon-Sat 10am-5pm Sun. **Admission** $1.50; *tours* $36 per group of max 25. **Map p278 C2**

Despite the off-putting ideological title, this is the best twentieth-century history museum in Moscow. Where else will you find the actual stones thrown at policemen by workers during the 1905 Revolution? Also of interest is the mock-up of the typical Soviet flat of the 1970s, as good as any Ilya Kabakov installation. The 1980s are represented by documents on the Afghan War as well as chains and rings worn by the fans of a bourgeois cultural aberration known as Heavy Metal. On a more serious note, the museum gives a very level-headed and complete account of the revolutions and coups of the early 1990s.

House on the Embankment Museum

Dom Na Naberezhnoi, Ulitsa Serafimovicha 2 (959 0317). Metro Borovitskaya. **Open** 5-8pm Wed; 2-5pm Sat. **Admission** free. **Map p281C4/5**

This is a private museum dedicated to the victims of Stalin's purges, many of whom lived in this infamous residential complex, built to house the party's esteemed writers, workers, composers and military officials. The display consists of the personal belongings and detailed histories of those who perished. There are even items relating to Stalin's son Vasily, who, despite his impressive family connections, was sent to one of his father's camps at the end of World War II. To enter, ask for Tamara Andreyevna, the 90-year-old founder of the museum. *See also chapter* **Sightseeing**.

Military

Central Museum of Armed Forces

Ulitsa Sovetskoi Armii 2 (281 4877). Metro Novoslobodskaya or Tsvetnoi Bulvar. **Open** 10am-4.30pm Wed-Sun. **Admission** $3.50; $1.50 students, under-17s.

A veritable gunfest that includes rifles, rockets, missile launchers and bullets for every imaginable weapon. Also on display is the tail of a German bomber shot down over Moscow during World War II, a clutch of small planes located in the garden at the back, Dzerzhinksy's leather briefcase and the very latest uniforms. Military buffs will love it.

Panorama Museum of Borodino Battle

Kutuzovsky Prospekt 38 (148 1967). Metro Kutuzovskaya. **Open** 10am-4.45pm Mon-Thur, Sat, Sun (10am-3pm organised tours only). Closed last Thur of month. **Admission** $2.50; $75 groups of max 25.

The main attraction of the museum is a gigantic panel depicting the Battle of Borodino, where the Russians engaged Napoleon's troops in 1812, presented here as a great Russian victory, but actually a vicious tussle that produced no clear winner. The 115-metre (420ft) long panel is credited here to nineteenth-century artist Franz Roubaud, but it's really a mosaic of disparate fragments from different periods. To give the whole thing a unique 3-D effect, real guns, cannons, carts and stuffed horses have been strategically placed all along the length of the picture.

Literature

Ex Libris Museum

Pushechnaya Ulitsa 7/5 (928 2998). Metro Lubyanka or Kuznetsky Most. **Open** 10am-6pm Mon-Fri. **Admission** free. **Map p278 D2**

A cross between a humanities professor's office and a library reading room, this museum is dedicated to ex libris (literally meaning 'from the library of'), the bookplates that

announce a book's owner. There are more than 60,000 bookplate examples here, two thirds of which came from the personal collection of Vladimir Loburev, founder of the museum and its current director. In addition to rifling through folders of various bookplates, visitors can see the permanent display of miniature books, or one of a number of rotating exhibitions. You can also get books bound here, as well as have a personal ex libris made.

Literary Museum

Ulitsa Petrovka 28 (921 7395). Metro Pushkinskaya. **Open** 2-6pm Wed, Fri; 11am-6pm Thur; noon-6pm Sat, Sun. Closed Sun in summer. **Admission** $1; 50¢ students. **Map p278 C2**

While the Dostoyevsky Museum is closed for refurbishment, a process that generally takes between five and 20 years in Russia, all the exhibits have been moved here to the Literary Museum. Unfortunately, the whole affair is pretty bleak and tawdry. The only half-presentable room is the Teatralny (theatrical) Hall where a video about Dostoyevsky is meant to be on continuous play. However, since the VCR and the tapes went missing, visitors find themselves confronted with a blank screen.

Music

Museum of Folk Musical Instruments

Ulitsa Fadeyeva 4 (972 3237). Metro Mayakovskaya. **Open** 11am-6.30pm Tue-Sun. Closed last day of month. **Admission** $1; 35¢ under-17s. **Map p277 B2**

Who'd ever have thought that the balalaika, Russia's three-stringed national instrument, could come in so many varieties? Some of the ones displayed here are miniscule and could only be played by stick insects or people with spindles instead of fingers. Others are gigantic and practically require the player to be strapped on like a mountain climber. Impressive collections of more conventional instruments – violins, pianos, horns – are also on display, along with the instrumental specialities of various ex-Soviet satellite countries – Tartar drums and delicate Dagestani flutes.

House-apartment museums

Gorky Museum

Malaya Nikitskaya Ulitsa 6/2 (290 0535). Metro Arbatskaya. **Open** noon-7pm Wed, Fri; 10am-5pm Thur, Sat, Sun. Closed last Fri of month. **Admission** free. **Map p277 B3**

After emigrating in the early 1920s and settling in Sorrento in southern Italy, the writer Maxim Gorky was persuaded by Stalin to return to the Soviet Union in 1928. Among the many perks that Gorky was to eventually receive was this spectacular *style moderne* house, clad in ceramic tiling and glazed brick and featuring a spectacular ground marble staircase that seems to cascade from the upper storeys to the floor. Originally built by the Russian Gaudi, Fyodor Shekhtel, for the art patron Ryabushinsky, it was Gorky's home from 1931 until his death in 1936, when he was allegedly poisoned by Stalin's henchman, Yagoda. Though the house is definitely the main attraction, the museum proper consists of Gorky's study and library and various of his truly personal belongings.

Marina Tsvetayeva Museum

Borisoglebovsky Pereulok 6 (202 3543). Metro Barrikadnaya or Arbatskaya. **Open** noon-5pm Mon, Fri-Sun; *pre-booked tours* noon-5pm Tue-Thur. **Admission** free. **Map p277 A2**

It was in flat No.3 of this yellow, two-storey house that Marina Tsvetayeva, one of Russia's greatest twentieth-century poets, lived from 1914 until she emigrated in 1922, in order to live in Paris and Prague with her husband, who became a Soviet spy. After returning to

Russia some years later, she lived in desperate poverty and killed herself in the early years of World War II. The museum, which opened in 1992 to mark the centenary of her birth, carefully recreates Tsvetayeva's study, where she wrote some of her most famous poems, as well as her dining room and drawing room.

Mayakovsky Museum

Lubyansky Proyezd 3/6 (921 9560). Metro Lubyanka.
Open 10am-6pm Mon, Tue, Fri-Sun; 1-9pm Thur.
Admission $1; $34 guided tour. **Map p278 D3**
The celebrated futurist poet Vladimir Mayakovsky moved into a modest room in a communal apartment at this address in 1919 and lived here intermittently until 1930, when he committed suicide. One part of the museum consists of the tiny room where Mayakovsky shot himself, complete with the original furniture. The rest, which occupies the four floors of the building, quickly descends into futuristic chaos. Strewn everywhere are comics drawn by the poet, first editions of his poems and love letters to Lila Brik, with whom the poet lived for a time.

Memorial Museum of KI Stanislavsky

Leontyevsky Pereulok 6 (229 2442/2885). Metro Tverskaya or Pushkinskaya. **Open** 11am-8pm Wed, Fri; 11am-6pm Thur, Sat, Sun. **Admission** $2.50. **Map p277 B3**
The legendary creator of the Method approach to acting and co-founder of the Moscow Art Theatre moved here in 1922 after being evicted from his spacious house by the Bolsheviks. One section of the museum consists of his flat on the upper floor, with much of the original furniture and personal belongings in place. On the first floor, there's an exhibition of theatre designs and sketches for various Art Theatre productions.

Memorial Museum of VI Nemirovich-Danchenko

Glinishchevsky Pereulok 5/7 (209 5391). Metro Tverskaya or Pushkinskaya. **Open** 11am-4pm Tue-Fri.
Admission $2.50. **Map p278 C2**
Devoted to Stanislavsky's closest friend and co-founder of Moscow Art Theatre, this museum houses Nemirovich-Danchenko's personal belongings, including various photos, books and authentic furniture, all meticulously preserved from the time he moved here in 1938.

Memorial Flat of V Meyerhold

Bryusov Pereulok 12 (229 5322). Metro Okhotny Ryad.
Open noon-6pm Wed, Thur, Sat, Sun. **Admission** $1; 40¢ under-17s. **Map p278 C3**
The flat of this famous producer of avant-garde theatre, who, it would seem, turned out to be far too revolutionary for even the communists to tolerate, is located in this building, a remarkable, angular constructivist creation, specially built for actors and theatre producers. Part of the museum consists simply of the rooms where Meyerhold lived, while the rest is devoted to pictures and designs of his productions.

Tolstoy Museum, Hamovniki

Ulitsa Lva Tolstogo 21 (246 0944). Metro Park Kultury.
Open *summer* 10am-6pm (cashier until 5pm); *winter* 10am-4pm. Closed last Fri of month. **Admission** $3.50; $1.50 students. **Map p280 A6**
Everything about this little farmstead, where the great writer spent the winter months from 1882 to 1901 while his children attended school in Moscow, has been kept in exactly the same state as it would have been in Tolstoy's day, including the stables, the park and the lack of electricity. Among the fascinating exhibits are the writer's racoon coat, hanging forlornly in the wardrobe, and his exercise dumb-bells.

Elegance moderne: the **Gorky Museum** *(p62).*

Science & technology

Darwin Museum

Ulitsa Vavilova 57 (135 6124). Metro Akademicheskaya.
Open 10am-6pm Tue-Sun. Closed last Fri of month.
Admission $1.50, 50¢ students, under-17s.
Unfortunately, many of the exhibits will be fully appreciated only by Russian speakers, but there is plenty of accessible stuff, like reconstructions of a typical alchemist's laboratory and of Darwin's cabin on the *Beagle*. The modern part of the exhibit demonstrates the effects a city can have on the ecosystem. A superb collection of various types of foxes lies in wait on the third floor, along with wolves, bears, tigers and dogs, among others.

Geological Museum

Mokhovaya Ulitsa 11/2 (203 5287). Metro Okhotny Ryad. **Open** 11am-5pm Tue, Thur, Sat.
Admission $1; 30¢ students, under-17s; $10 tours.
Map p278 C3
Along with the usual crop of old fossils, you'll find chunks of meteorites that landed in Russia, a mammoth's tusk found in Siberia and a pine trunk unearthed a few years ago on Manezhnaya Ploshchad during the construction of the underground mall. Two rooms trace the city's geological history from the time Moscow was nothing more than a sea floor littered with shells (over 300 million

It's life, Jim, but not as we know it: Moscow's enterprising **Space Museum**.

years ago) to a sprawling metropolis with chronic eco-logical problems (now). The displays outlining the city's pollution ills are a sobering stop in anyone's visit.

Museum of Wood

3-y Monetchikovsky Pereulok 4 (956 1561). Metro Paveletskaya. **Open** call for details. **Map p281 D6**
Despite the weird premise, this is probably the best science museum in Moscow – exquisitely modern and featuring an actual river, which runs down a granite riverbed along the entire first floor of the museum. Exhibits include a model of a nineteenth-century *izba* (Russian log cabin), the bows of a ship, real live trees and a mock-up of a forest featuring stuffed animals and authentic sound effects. At the time of writing, the museum was undergoing reconstruction; it is scheduled to reopen in September 1998.

Palaeontology Museum

Profsoyuznaya Ulitsa 123 (339 1500/tour bookings 339 4544). Metro Tyoply Stan, then any bus or trolleybus one stop towards town. **Open** several weeks in summer. **Admission** $1.50; $1 under-17s.
The pride of this museum is its hugely impressive collection of fossilised skeletons, which were found close to the Severnaya Dvina River at the end of the nineteenth century. They include a full example of the skeleton of the Tardosaurus, nicknamed the Russian Godzilla and a relative of the Tyrannosaurus Rex. *Café.*

Polytechnical Museum

Novaya Ploshchad 3/4 (923 0756). Metro Kitai-Gorod. **Open** 10am-5pm Tue, Wed, Fri-Sun. **Admission** $1. **Map p278 D3**
This place really is a techno-boffin's wet dream. The exhibits in the main section of the Polytechnical Museums include miniature cross-sectional diagrams of mines and a range of authentic automobiles all the way from classic

pre-Revolutionary to Soviet-made Volga; a physics exhibition that encompasses the history of the microscope and the development of photo-technology; as well as radio technology, chemistry and space. The whole experience is given a fascinating edge simply by merit of its alluring crudity. Particularly enjoyable is the inclusion of stuff like the first Soviet TV set and a pathetic, Soviet 1980s reproduction ghettoblaster masquerading as great techno-logical strides forward.

Space Museum

Prospekt Mira 111 (283 7914). Metro VDNKh. **Open** 10am-7pm Tue-Sun. Closed last Fri of month. **Admission** $1.50 adults; 30¢ children. **Map P278 D1**
This has to be the easiest museum to find in Moscow – just keep your eyes open for a titanium sculpture of a space rocket jutting hundreds of feet into the air. Walking into its exhibition hall is a bit like stepping on to the set of *Star Trek*: garish, 1960s-style yellow and red neon lights create that perfect *Enterprise* ambience. The Space Museum's collection includes the original space suit of the first cosmonaut Yuri Gagarin and samples of food people eat on space stations: borscht, pelmeni and cran-berries – all from a tube. For $2, you can even have your picture taken wearing Gagarin's space suit.

Zoological Museum

Bolshaya Nikitskaya Ulitsa 6 (203 8923). Metro Okhotny Ryad. **Open** 10am-5pm Tue-Sun. Closed last Tue of month. **Admission** $1; 60¢ students, under-17s. **Map p277 B3**
Moscow's Zoological Museu boasts more than ten thousand kinds of animals, extinct and otherwise. Unfortunately, at the time of writing, the museum was undergoing one of its sporadic periods of closure; staff promised that it would be open again in autumn 1998.

Galleries

The past decade has been something of a roller-coaster for contemporary Russian art. At the height of the post-Perestroika boom, demand soared to unprecedented levels. Artists who had previously only seen their work displayed in clandestine, makeshift apartment galleries were suddenly jetting around Europe and the US, exhibiting in prestigious spaces and fighting off foreign buyers. At the beginning of the '90s, when the craze for Russian exotica was at its height, it seemed as if any bearded, brush-wielding shyster who claimed to have been an underground artist could raise thousands of dollars with his scrawls.

Given the capriciousness of the art world in general, this situation was never going to last. Interest in the Russian art phenomenon began to wane around 1994 and by the following year a general worldwide slump in the art market dumped the Russians back where they were when the Soviet Empire was at its height: unable to exhibit, unable to sell and, for many who had entirely lost their bearings, unable even to work or paint.

Since then, Russian art has been slowly cultivating a domestic market, a process that is only now starting to bear fruit. Many Russian businesses and banks are building up significant collections of contemporary art and, in the process, keeping artists clothed and fed. Whereas the scene was once just a jumble of squats, Moscow has a limited number of presentable, relatively professional galleries. This glossy finish, however, seems to have taken much of the fun out of Russian contemporary art and sapped the energy of the more interesting artists. High-profile scandalmongers such as Alexander Brener and Oleg Kulik, who constituted the last 'big thing', have now moved abroad, where foreigners pay far more to be shocked than Russians can afford. Younger artists have been sucked into the world of graphic design, where dividends are higher. Russian contemporary art has been put on hold until the arrival of the Next Generation.

Actionist antics

In January 1997, a young Russian artist named Alexander Brener slipped into Amsterdam's Stedelijk Museum, pulled out a can of spray paint and set about decorating a work by Kazimir Malevich with a wonderful, lurid green dollar sign.

Immediately afterwards Brener gave himself up to security guards, evoking aesthetic immunity with the immortal words 'I am an artist', and claiming vehemently that his attack on Malevich's $13-million painting, *Suprematism – White Cross*, should be seen as a protest against the increasing and insidious power of money over art. 'My action is for the people,' he insisted during the ensuing court case, referring to what he was now calling his 'dialogue with Malevich'. 'It is a cri-de-cœur about what happens in culture when there is no human voice any more. Malevich wanted to change the world by his art, but nowadays his stature is measured in dollars.'

Brener is one of the leading figures of Moscow's most controversial contemporary movement: the 'actionists'. Other Brener 'works' include appearing on Red Square during the Chechen war dressed as a boxer to challenge Yeltsin to a fight; masturbating on the tower of the old Moskva swimming pool; and arriving at a Moscow Van Gogh exhibition yelling out 'Vincent, Vincent' and then crapping in his pants. His partner in crime and fellow actionist, Oleg Kulik, has photographed himself copulating with farm animals and was once arrested at the opening of a Stockholm exhibition for chaining himself naked to a kennel and mauling passing gallery-goers while snarling like a mad dog. The rationale behind all of this is dressed in woolly theory. One eminent critic has identified it as 'the intelligentsia's revenge on a society which has betrayed it'. Kulik himself has claimed to be 'exorcising the brutal spirit motivating contemporary Russia through the vehicle of the self' (hmmm...). At other times, he just poses as an animal lover: 'To place the worth of our culture, our civilisation, our art, and our spirituality above the culture, art, and spirituality of animals, insects, birds is an unforgivable weakness,' says Kulik – who is a meat-eater.

Many critics, however, feel that the whole thing is just an exercise in crude self-promotion engineered by wimpy, white, middle-class Russian boys. To back up this position, they note Brener's choice of the Stedelijk as a venue for his 'art terrorism'. The subsequent wrath of the liberal Dutch judicial system meant less than a year in prison conditions far better than most Russians could afford in their daily lives. If he had just defaced one of the many Malevich paintings in the Tretyakov or the Russian Museum, he would likely have faced a 15-year sentence in the hellish medieval torture chambers that make up Russia's prison system. Now, that would have been truly radical, man.

Exhibition centres

Maly Manezh
Georgiyevsky Pereulok 3/3 (292 4459). Metro Okhotny Ryad.
Open call for details. **Map p278 C3**
Saturated with the spirit and the conservative taste of Mayor Luzhkov, its patron and protector, Maly Manezh hosts exhibitions of '60s era artists or contemporary neo-socialist realists. Some exhibitions are really worth seeing.

Manezh
Manezhnaya Ploshchad 2 (202 8976/8252/fax 202 5242). Metro Oknotny Ryad. **Open** 11am-7pm daily. **Map p278 C3**
Originally built as a stable, this is now one of the city's main trade fair and exhibition centres. Squeezed between promotions of Italian clothes and German cars, the organisers often come up with a modern art exhibition. Some of these are downright eccentric, like the Sunday painting of pop-stars or politicians. But a few, like the Art Manezh exhibition every February (one of the biggest showcases of contemporary Russian art in the country), are well worth seeing.

Tsentralny Dom Khudozhnikov (TsDKh)
Central House of Artists, Ulitsa Krymsky Val 10/14 (238 9843/9634). Metro Park Kultury or Oktyabrskaya. **Open** 11am-8pm Tue-Sun. **Admission** $2; $1 students. **Map p280 B6**
A modern art exhibition venue that shares a building with the Tretyakov Gallery's collection of twentieth-century art. Sometimes the exhibitions are commercial dross, sometimes really outstanding modern art. The first floor is usually given over to socialist realism, the second is taken up by whatever exhibition the gallery is hosting and the third is devoted to the most radical and experimental art. A number of low-key commercial galleries are located here, as well as some furniture salesrooms. Don't be too offended if the art you are assiduously following suddenly bleeds into the latest divans or bedside lockers. At the back of the gallery, you'll find the Graveyard of Fallen Monuments, the last resting place of the various statues of Lenin, Stalin and Dzerzhinsky that were once dotted around the city.

Galleries

Aidan Gallery
Novopeschanaya Ulitsa 23/7 (943 5348). Metro Sokol or Polezhayevskaya, then trolleybus 43, 65. **Open** by appointment only. **Admission** free.
This gallery was founded in 1992 by artist Aidan Salakhova, who was the co-owner of the first private gallery in Moscow. Unfortunately, this venture is one of the most mundane places on the Moscow art map. It mainly supports the work of figures from the Russian 'Middle' generation, such as Sergei Schutov, Timur Novokov and Anatoly Shuravlev, as well as a few newer names. Although the place has a high profile and is among Moscow's more prominent, it avoids radicalism of any kind.
English spoken.

Gelman Gallery
Ulitsa Malaya Polyanka 7/7 (238 8492/2783/guilman@ russ.ru). Metro Polyanka or Oktyabrskaya. **Open** noon-6pm Mon-Sat. **Admission** free. **Map p281 C6**
This is the most famous Moscow gallery in the world, which unfortunately isn't really saying much. Nearly all the best-known Russian artists have exhibited here, from Komar & Melamid to Oleg Kulik and Alexander Brener. Exhibitions in the gallery are usually incorporated into some kind of 'happening' or provocative performance.
English spoken.
Website *http://www.guilman.ru*

M'ARS
Malaya Filevskaya Ulitsa 32 (144 8426/146 6331). Metro Pionerskaya. **Admission** free. **Credit** V.
An eclectic gallery promoting various outmoded versions of surrealism. However, in the back you might be able to dig out some interesting pieces of art.

SpiderMouse
Leningradsky Prospekt 58 (287 1360/spider@ica.msk.ru). Metro Aeroport. **Open** 5-8pm Thur-Sat. **Admission** free.
One of the most radical galleries, appropriately located deep in a dingy basement. It shows mainly sophisticated installations or live art and performance-based work.

XL Gallery
Bolshaya Sadovaya Ulitsa 6 (299 3724/arizine@chal.ru). Metro Mayakovskaya. **Open** by appointment only. **Admission** free. **Map p277 B1**
A microscopic little space that has somehow managed to become the centre of the visual arts scene in Moscow. The curator regularly publishes a catalogue in English containing info on forthcoming events. The artists supported here include the drag queen performance artist Vladislav Mamyshev-Monro and Pavel Pepperstein, leader of the once influential Medical Hermeneutics group.
Websites *http://www.xlgallery.home.nil.org; http://www.geocities.com/'So Ho/'8070*

Adonisky at the **Pushkin Museum.** *See p59.*

Consumer Moscow

Accommodation

If you have neither the ingenuity nor the time to fuss, expect to pay deluxe-style prices for budget-style beds.

Moscow routinely comes close to topping those mysterious 'World's Most Expensive Cities' charts that appear on a six-monthly basis, and one of the main reasons why is the astronomical rates charged by the city's ever-expanding pack of luxury hotels. Often foreign-run and located in renovated turn-of-the-century buildings, these hotels typically offer all the services a business person with an expense account could possibly want or need, amid settings of Imperial grandeur in various guises. At the other end of the scale are the usually unrenovated, grey, Soviet-era monoliths, which have far less to offer by way of comfort or services at rather more modest prices.

Moscow may be a relatively large city, but almost everything is oriented toward the centre. As a result, unless you have a specific reason for seeking accommodation on the outskirts, this is where you will probably want to stay. In addition to the seriously overpriced properties, the centre has a wide range of cheaper (and usually less comfortable) options. If you do end up staying at some distance from the centre, close proximity to a metro station is a must.

PRICES & SERVICES

Expect to pay (for a double room, per night) $30-$90 in a budget hotel; $80-$200 in a mid-range hotel; and $200 and up (all the way to about $2,000 for luxury suites) in the first-class hotels. At most of the exorbitantly priced, centrally located hotels you're paying more for prestigious location and services than world-class luxury; at some of the higher-priced, Soviet-era places you'll be wondering what you're paying for at all. At all but a few hotels, the quoted rates are subject to a tax of 20 per cent.

Unless otherwise stated, all rooms include a TV and telephone. Parking, when available, is not usually included in the price of the room and non-smoking rooms are usually only available in the Western-run establishments. Most of the hotels listed below offer prospective guests visa support and have on-site bars and restaurants. In the more old-school places, the restaurants may be closed or operating on greatly curtailed schedules; often these places will have less formal cafeterias or snack bars available instead.

CHEAP SLEEPS

The absolutely cheapest option in town is a room in a private flat. Although less common than in other large former Soviet cities, this is still a viable option, especially if you are arriving by train. The average price for a bed is $5-$15; typically, this type of accommodation can be found in the morning or early afternoon by looking for a grandmotherly woman standing outside one of the main rail stations holding a sign that reads *komnata* (room) or *kvartira* (flat). If you're interested, remember to keep your wits about you and, if possible, find out where the flat is located before leaving – it's not uncommon for a flat located 'near the centre' to be way out at the end of a metro line. In addition to being inexpensive, this alternative is also an excellent way to see how the average Muscovite lives. Both agencies listed in our **Hostels & B&Bs** section can generally arrange a short-term stay in a private flat, with or without a host. For longer-term stays, by far the best resource in town is the advertisement newspaper *Iz Ruk v Ruki* (From Hand to Hand), published every weekday. For non-Russian speakers, the classifieds section of the *Moscow Times* also has a small selection of flats. However, most of these ads come from the smaller rental agencies, which generally charge a finder's fee. A few of the more respected agencies are:

Penny Lane Realty *954 0041/London 0171 233 4444/New York 212 695 5353/penny@dol.ru www.pennylane.ru.*
Blackwood Real Estate *915 4000/black@blackw.msk.ru www.blackwood.ru.*
Realcom *737 0258/0259/realcom@mail.infotel.ru www.rusinter.ru/realcom*

First-class

Aerostar Hotel

Leningradsky Prospekt 37/9, 125167 (213 9000/fax 213 9001/aerostar@sovcust.sprint.com). Metro Aeroport or Dinamo. **Rates** *single $282; double $330; suite $325 $375.* **Credit** AmEx, DC, JCB, MC, V.

This Canadian-run establishment, located a couple of kilometres north of the city centre, is popular with both foreign and Russian businessmen. The atmosphere is typically soulless, but the 415 rooms are extremely comfortable, some offering attractive views of the historic Petrovsky Palace just across the road. The in-house food (watched over closely by a gamut of foreign chefs) has been among the most reliable in Moscow's hotels for several years, with the Café Taiga's lunch buffet tending to be a pretty good (and tasty) bargain. The hotel is a 15-minute walk from the closest metro stations, but if you're staying here you're probably not relying on public transport anyway.

Hotel services *Air-conditioning. Bars. Buffet breakfast. Business services. Casino. Concert hall. Conference facilities. Currency exchange. Disabled: access. Fitness*

Stalinist chic on the cheap: the **Leningradskaya**. *See page 79.*

facilities (gym, massage, sauna, solarium). Interpreting services. Laundry. Limo service. Multilingual staff. Non-smoking rooms. Parking. Restaurants. Safe. Shops. Tennis court. Theatre & travel desks. **Room services** *Cable TV. Hairdryer. Minibar. Modem line. Room service (24 hours). VCR for hire.*
Website: www.aerostar.ru

Art Hotel

3-ya Peshchanaya Ulitsa 2, 125252 (955 2300/fax 955 2310/725 0904/artsport@glasnet.ru). Metro Polezhayevskaya. **Rates** *single $210; double $250; suite $365.* **Credit** AmEx, DC, JCB, MC, V.

A fairly new, overpriced hotel that looks (and feels) more middle-of-the-road than its pricetag might suggest. It's a bit of a hike to the metro, but the relatively quiet residential neighbourhood can make for a pleasant stay. It's also situated on the edge of the massive CSKA sports complex, so copious athletic facilities (including a great tennis centre) are nearby.

Hotel services *Air-conditioning. Bar. Continental breakfast. Conference facilties Currency exchange. Multilingual staff. Parking (paid). Restaurants.*
Room services *Minibar (suites only). Room service. Satellite TV.*

Hotel Kempinsky Baltschug

Ulitsa Balchug 1, 113035 (230 6500/9502/fax 230 6502/reservation.mos@kempinski.com). Metro Tretyakovskaya. **Rates** *single $350; double $350; suite $600-$1,650.* **Credit** AmEx, DC, JCB, MC, V.
Map p281 D4

State of the art facilities, top-notch restaurants and breathtaking views of the Kremlin and St Basil's are just a few of the things that have made this German-run hotel the destination of choice among visiting entertainers such as Michael Jackson, Tina Turner, David Bowie and Chuck Norris (to name but a few) since it opened in 1992. The ten-floor Balchug is the result of a complete reconstruction of a hotel originally built at the turn of the century, and its 202 rooms featuring such extras as antique furnishings and hand-crafted wood are considered by many to be the most luxurious in town. Besides being located just across the river from the very heart of the capital, the hotel is also an easy walk from a number of Moscow's most popular nightspots.

Hotel services *Air-conditioning. Currency exchange. Disabled: access. Fitness facilities (gym, Jacuzzi, sauna, massage, solarium). Limo service. Medical service. Non-smoking rooms. Nursery. Parking. Shops. Swimming pool. Theatre desk.* **Room services** *Cable/satellite TV. Hairdryer. Minibar. Refrigerator. Room service (24 hours). Safe. VCR (suites only).*
Website: www.kempinski-moscow.com

Marriott Grand Hotel

Tverskaya Ulitsa 26, 105030 (935 8500/fax 935 8501). Metro Pushkinskaya. **Rates** *single/double $315 $345.* **Credit** AmEx, DC, MC, V. **Map p278 C2**

Marriott's recently opened entry into the local luxury-hotel scene is a modern nine-storey affair with 368 comfortable, well-equipped rooms and tremendous views down Tverskaya toward the Kremlin. The hotel has less in the way of amenities than many of its rivals, but its state-of-the-art business and communications facilities and relatively modest rates have earned it a niche among the Moscow business class. The French and Russian cuisine in the main restaurant has been earning rave reviews, both for its taste and affordable price.

Hotel services *Air-conditioning. Bar. Business services. Concierge. Conference facilities. Interpreting services. Laundry. Multilingual staff. Restaurants. Shops.* **Room services** *Cable/satellite TV. Hairdryer. Minibar. Modem line. Refrigerator. Room service (24 hours). Safe.*
Website: www.marriott.com/MOWGR

Metropol

Teatralny Proyezd 1/4, 103012 (927 6000/fax 927 6010/moscow@interconti.com). Metro Teatralnaya. **Rates** *single/double* $360. **Credit** AmEx, DC, JCB, MC, V. **Map p278 C3/D3**

Like the National just around the corner! (*see below*), this pre-Revolutionary art nouveau structure was restored to its former grandeur during the early 1990s and is now considered one of the finest hotels in Moscow. Although the lobby is every bit as opulent as that of its neighbour and the exterior mosaics are truly beautiful, the views are rather less impressive and the 436 rooms and suites, while certainly comfortable, are not quite as luxurious. Still, the location is top-notch, and included among the Metropol's huge assortment of fine restaurants and cafés is probably the best place for fresh seafood in town.

Hotel services *Air-conditioning. Babysitting. Bars. Beauty salon. Business services. Car rental desk. Computers. Conference facilities. Concierge. Currency exchange. Disabled: access. Fitness facilities (gym, massage, pool, sauna, solarium). Interpreting services. Laundry (valet). Multilingual staff. Parking. Restaurants. Travel desk.* **Room services** *Cable TV. Hairdryer. Minibar. Modem line. Radio. VCR for hire.* **Website:** *www.interconti.com/pages/m/mosmeta.html*

Mezhdunarodnaya Hotel

International Hotel, Krasnopresnenskaya Naberezhnaya 12, 123610 (253 1391/2103/1071/fax 253 2051/2400). Metro Ulitsa 1905 Goda. **Rates** *single* $228; *double* $264. **Credit** AmEx, DC, MC, V.

Designed by Armand Hammer and perched at a particularly unattractive point on the Moskva River, the 'Mezh' is ugly on the outside, but intriguingly quirky on the inside. Originally intended as a self-contained unit of capitalism for resident foreigners, today its copious food shops, boutiques and restaurants tend to resemble a ghost town, although the 13-floor hotel does still attract its share of business travellers. The smallish, sterile rooms combine with the shopping mall ornamentation of the lobby to give the place the feel of a loony bin for the extremely wealthy. The connecting Mezh-2 to the north, which has more expensive apartments, takes the sterile institution thing a step further: it looks like an old hospital. The complex is attached to the International Trade Centre and near Mayor Luzhkov's ridiculous pedestrian bridge to nowhere, but rather distant from the metro and any real sights.

Hotel services *Air-conditioning. Babysitting. Bars. Beauty salon. Business services. Computers. Concierge. Conference facilities. Currency exchange. Laundry (valet). Multilingual staff. Nightclub. Non-smoking rooms. Parking. Restaurants. Shops. Swimming pool.* **Room services** *Cable TV. Hairdryer. Minibar. Modem line. Room service. Safe.*

Hotel National

Mokhovaya Ulitsa 15/1, 103009 (258 7000/fax 258 7100/hotel@national.ru). Metro Okhotny Ryad. **Rates** *single* $320-$380; *double* $360-$430; *suite* $500-$1,400. **Credit** AmEx, DC, JCB, MC, V. **Map p278 3C, p281 C4**

Built in 1903 and reopened in 1995 after a painstaking four-year restoration, the seven-storey National has probably the most enviable location of any hotel in Moscow, literally across the street from the Kremlin. Past guests have included HG Wells, John Reed and even Lenin himself. The art nouveau landmark is now run by the city of Moscow with the assistance of consultants from Forte Hotels, which might explain why the staff are so friendly and helpful. The standard rooms are nothing special, but the Kremlin-facing doubles combine impressive grandeur with stunning views. Among the hotel's four restaurants is a Maxim's, though it's generally considered to be far inferior to the Paris branch.

Hotel services *Air-conditioning. Babysitting. Bars.*

Business services. Computers. Concierge. Conference facilities. Currency exchange. Interpreting services. Laundry. Multilingual staff. Parking. Pool. Restaurants. Safe. Travel & theatre desks. **Room services** *Hairdryer. Minibar. Modem line. Radio. Room service. Telephone. TV.* **Website:** *www.national.ru*

Novotel Sheremetyevo 2

Sheremetyevo II Airport, 103339 (926 5900/fax 926 5903). Metro Rechnoi Vokzal then bus. **Rates** *single* $230; *double* $253. **Credit** AmEx, DC, MC, V.

A great Mexican restaurant and easy access to the West in case of armed uprising are the only identifiable benefits of staying at this lifeless monstrosity located just across the access ramp from the main international airport. There's a free shuttle bus to the city centre, but it's nearly an hour's ride (even more during rush hours). The bar area has its share of prostitutes to prey on the unsuspecting foreign businessmen who will sure as hell be booking themselves into one of the more centrally located luxury hotels the next time they do business in Moscow.

Hotel services *Air-conditioning. Bar. Beauty salon. Business services. Conference facilities. Currency exchange. Disabled: access. Fitness facilities (gym, sauna). Multilingual staff. Nightclub. Parking. Restaurants. Swimming pool. Theatre & travel desks.* **Room services** *Hairdryer. Minibar. Radio. Room service.*

Radisson Slavjanskaya Hotel

Berezhkovskaya Naberezhnaya 2, 121059 (941 8020/fax 240 6915). Metro Kievskaya. **Rates** *single* $185-$295; *double* $185-$310; *suite* $450-$595. **Credit** AmEx, DC, JCB, MC, V.

A joint venture between Radisson and the Moscow city government, this bland, off-white box of a hotel on the banks of the Moskva River and 3km from the city centre is popular with

Throwing some light on the Metropol.

US government officials all the way up to the president and, for some reason, rock bands like the Smashing Pumpkins. The spacious rooms are pretty middle of the road, and the lounges are a bit like *The Shining* on valium. There's a Western-standard health club, a 24-hour business centre and a gallery full of stratospherically priced fashion boutiques frequented by leggy blondes wearing skimpy clothing – whether you call them New Russians, molls or prostitutes is largely a matter of semantics. The overpriced restaurants serve pretty respectable fare, but not including the 20 per cent tax in the menu prices is pretty sneaky. Also, in the very back is the better-equipped of Moscow's two English-language cinemas.

Hotel services *Air-conditioning. Bar. Beauty salon. Business services. Computers. Casino. Concierge. Conference/banquet facilities. Currency exchange. Cinema (English-language). Fitness facilities (sauna, massage, solarium). Interpreting services. Laundry (valet). Multilingual staff. Non-smoking rooms. Parking ($1.20 per hour). Restaurants (3). Swimming pool.* **Room services** *Cable TV. Hairdryer. Minibar. Modem line. Refrigerator. Room service (24 hours). VCR (suites only). Website: www.radisson.com/rr*

Renaissance Moscow Hotel

Olimpiisky Prospekt 18/1, 129110 (931 9000/fax 931 9077/223 9076). Metro Prospekt Mira or Rizhskaya. **Rates** *single $255-$315; double $295-$355; suite $650-$680.* **Credit** AmEx, DC, JCB, MC, V.

Originally built for the 1980 Olympics and upgraded in 1990, this 472-room glass monster is home to the less expensive of Moscow's two English-language cinemas. The lobby and rooms (including 11 luxury suites) are spacious, modern and mostly devoid of style; the restaurants reliable but bland. The state-of-the-art gym, which includes a 22-metre pool, is one of the best in town and nestled among the expensive shops is a tiny bakery specialising in a wide variety of delectable German breads and pastries. The ritzy banquet hall in the futuristic silver dome just across the driveway (where the cinema is located) is an extremely popular spot for New Russian weddings.

Hotel services *Air-conditioning. Babysitting. Bar. Beauty salon. Business services. Cinema (English-language). Conference facilities. Currency exchange. Fitness facilities (sauna, massage, pool, solarium). Laundry. Multilingual staff. Non-smoking rooms. Parking. Restaurants. Safe. Shops.* **Room services** *Hairdryer. Minibar. Modem. Room service (24 hours). Satellite TV. Voicemail. Website: www.renaissancehotels.com/MOWRN*

Hotel Savoy

Ulitsa Rozhdestvenka 3, 103012 (929 8500/8558/fax 230 2186/929 7571). Metro Kuznetsky Most. **Rates** *single $360-$425; double $390-$470; suite $595-$890.* **Credit** AmEx, DC, JCB, MC, V. **Map p278 D2**

Originally opened as a luxury hotel in 1912, the Hotel Savoy operated under the name Hotel Berlin from 1958 to 1987 and was reopened as Hotel Savoy in 1989 after a massive renovation. Inconspicuously housed in an opulent five-storey Victorian building on a side street just minutes from Red Square, the hotel has 66 superbly outfitted standard rooms and 17 suites (including four super-deluxe executive suites). Although more low-key and generally considered to be less prestigious than the other centrally located luxury hotels, the Savoy's impeccable Finnish management has earned a steady clientele that includes actor Ralph Fiennes. The main restaurant offers exquisite French and Scandinavian cuisine in a grand turn-of-the-century setting; the two bars feature equally tasty, less expensive meals in more modest surroundings.

Hotel services *Air-conditioning. Banquet hall. Bars. Beauty salon. Buffet breakfast. Business services. Casino. Catering services. Concierge. Conference facilities. Currency exchange. Disabled: access. Multilingual staff. Parking. Restaurant. Sauna.* **Room services** *Cable TV.*

Hairdryer. Minibar. Modem line. Radio. Room service. Safe. Satellite telephone. Trouser press.

Sheraton Palace Hotel

1-ya Tverskaya-Yamskaya Ulitsa 19, 125047 (931 9700/256 3000/fax 931 9704/256 3008/ palacehotel.sales@ns.co.ru/). Metro Belorusskaya. **Rates** *single $374; double $418.* **Credit** AmEx, DC, JCB, MC, V. **Map p277 B2**

With 221 tastefully modern rooms and suites, the Palace Hotel has a steel and glass façade that would look much more at home in mid-town Manhattan than central Moscow. Originally opened in the late 1980s by the Marco Polo group, it has since been taken over by Sheraton, but the clientele – primarily foreign business people with fat expense accounts – has largely remained unchanged thanks to its location near many major banks and law firms as well as superlative business facilities and restaurants. The major drawback is the numerous surrounding buildings that seem to have been under construction for years now – hence it can be rather noisy during working hours.

Hotel services *Air conditioning. Babysitting. Bars. Business services. Conference facilities. Disabled: access, rooms. Florist. Fitness facilities (Jacuzzi, massage, pool, sauna). Non-smoking rooms. Restaurants.* **Room services** *Hairdryer. Minibar. Room service. Website: www.sheraton.com/destinations/ properties/hr_137.html*

Mid-range

Arbat Hotel

Plotnikov Pereulok 12, 121002 (244 7635/fax 244 0093). Metro Smolenskaya. **Rates** *single $148; double $178 (luxury rooms $20 extra).* **Credit** AmEx, DC, JCB, MC, V.* **Map p280 A4**

The comfortable rooms in this concrete edifice located just off the historic old Arbat offer a bit of faded Soviet grandeur on a more modest scale than places like the Ukraina (*see below*). The staff here are extremely friendly and the location is excellent.

Hotel services *Air-conditioning. Bar. Business services. Conference facilities. Currency exchange. Multilingual staff. Parking (paid). Restaurant.* **Room services** *Minibar (luxury rooms only). Safe. Satellite TV. Telephone.*

Hotel Belgrade

Smolenskaya Ulitsa 8, 121099 (248 2841/fax 248 2814). Metro Smolenskaya. **Rates** *single $90; double $100.* **Credit** MC, V. **Map p280 A4**

The somewhat dingy rooms in this 1970s-era hotel are offset by the top-notch location at the end of the Arbat and relatively low prices.

Hotel services *Air-conditioning. Bar. Currency exchange. Restaurant.* **Room services** *Refrigerator. TV.*

Hotel Budapest

Ulitsa Petrovskiye Linii 2/18, 103051 (921 1060/924 8820/fax 921 1266/5290). Metro Kuznetsky Most. **Rates** *single $120-$150; double $160-$200.* **Credit** AmEx, DC, JCB, MC, V. **Map p278 C2**

Located unassumingly on a quiet alley in one of central Moscow's most attractive districts, the Budapest is a medium-sized establishment with 125 comfortable rooms that offer a bit of old-fashioned splendour at a decidedly reasonable price. The staff speak only limited English, but tend to be pretty helpful nonetheless.

Hotel services *Air-conditioning. Bar. Parking.* **Room services** *Minibar. Radio. Safe.*

Bugs...

During Soviet times, it was generally assumed that any hotel frequented by foreigners was loaded with clandestine listening devices, each of which was monitored for suspect activity by some low-level KGB agent. Of course, no one knows for sure just how extensive the bugging was, and given the extremely foggy nature of the activity of the Federal Security Service (the KGB's successor), it is anyone's guess how many of these devices remain. Although most press coverage of the new rash of bugging in recent years has rightly identified newly wealthy business people as the likely targets, there are still plenty of rumours floating around concerning what, if anything, ever happened to all those leftover bugs. The **Intourist** (*see page 72*) and **Mezhdunarodnaya** (*page 70*) are both likely spots, but perhaps because its ominous form is so reminiscent of Stalin himself, the massive Hotel Moskva is one of the sites most frequently cited as a potential treasure trove of miniature listening devices. Needless to say, such rumours are more the product of idle minds than actual fact; even if these bugs are still around (and, even less likely, are still operational), the chances that anyone is still listening in are slim to none.

Cosmos Hotel

Prospekt Mira 150, 129366 (215 6791/fax 215 8880). Metro VDNKh. **Rates** *single* $95; *double* $118. **Credit** AmEx, MC, V. **Map p278 D1**
This grey Soviet monolith 10km (6 miles) north of the city centre has long been a hotbed of prostitution, with the multi-level lobby looking like a cross between a fashion show and a zoo in the evening. A recent renovation sought to remake the place as more of a Western-style establishment, but so far the Cosmos's image has withstood the attempt at being cleaned up. The rooms are comfortable enough, but the dreary atmosphere and outdated fixtures make the price seem a bit steep. The remote location isn't convenient to much of anything, but the west-facing rooms do at least offer intriguing views of the space obelisk and the Worker and Collective Farm-Girl monument in the Exhibition Centre across the street. The nightclub and casino are great places to catch a glimpse of lowlifes in ill-fitting suits dancing the night away or dropping thousands of bucks at the roulette tables. **Hotel services** *Air-conditioning. Bars. Beauty salon. Buffet breakfast. Casino. Concert hall. Conference facilities. Currency exchange. Dry-cleaning service. Nightclub. Parking. Restaurants. Sauna. Swimming pool.* **Room services** *Cable TV. Minibar. Radio. Safe.*

Holiday Inn Vinogradovo

Dmitrovskoye Shosse 171, 127204 (937 0670/fax 937 0671). Shuttle bus between city centre and Sheremetyevo Airport. **Rates** *single* $150; *double* $170; *suite* $190-$300. **Credit** AmEx, DC, MC, V.

This 154-room piece of pure Americana was set to open in late 1998. Located on an attractive lakefront in a small suburb just barely within the city limits, this Holiday Inn promises to be a bit more upscale than the roadside lodges of the US. Offering a full range of business services and 16 well-equipped executive suites, it should become a haven for business people and tourists who expect a little fresh air (or at least whatever qualifies as fresh air in Moscow) from their surroundings. **Hotel services** *Air-conditioning. Bar. Beauty salon. Business services. Conference facilities. Currency exchange. Fitness facilities. Laundry. Nightclub. Non-smoking rooms. Restaurant. Sauna. Shops. Swimming pool.* **Room services** *Minibar. Room service. Satellite TV. VCR for hire.*
Website: www.holiday-inn.com

Hotel Intourist

Tverskaya Ulitsa 3/5, 103009 (956 8400/8426/ 8430/8304/fax 956 8450). Metro Okhotny Ryad. **Rates** *single* $130; *double* $138. **Credit** DC, JCB, MC, V. **Map p278 C2**
This 20-storey slab, which single-handedly mucks up one of the city's most impressive streets, was once the primary destination of foreign tourists. The place is now controlled by Marriott and rumours of a demolition and complete reconstruction have been circulating for several years now, but so far the concrete and metal eyesore remains. The rates may seem a bit steep for the Econo-Lodge-style accommodation, but the views are tremendous and the prime location, within shouting distance of the Kremlin walls, can only be topped by the nearby (and much more expensive) National or Metropol. The comfortable café in the rear atrium is the only bright spot in an otherwise dark and dreary lobby that's full to bursting with tacky, overpriced souvenirs. There's an expensive but very good Mexican restaurant on the top floor with panoramic views of the Kremlin and beyond. **Hotel services** *Air-conditioning. Bar. Conference facilities. Continental breakfast. Currency exchange. Hairdresser. Laundry service. Multilingual staff. Restaurants. Radio. Theatre & travel desk.* **Room services** *Minibar. Telephone. TV.*

Hotel Mir

Bolshoi Devyatinsky Pereulok 9, 121099 (290 9150/9504/fax 252 0141/5241). Metro Krasnopresnenskaya. **Rates** *single* $127; *double* $240. **Credit** MC, V. **Map p277 A3**
Dwarfed by the nearby White House and former COMECON building, this vaguely futuristic-looking 1970s structure has large comfortable rooms and a decidedly non-Soviet atmosphere. Unfortunately, the prices are a bit steep for what you get, and it's a bit of a hike to the nearest metro. **Hotel services** *Air-conditioning. Bar. Café. Conference facilities. Currency exchange. Dry-cleaning & laundry service. Restaurant. Safe. Sauna.* **Room services** *Minibar. Radio. Telephone. TV.*

Hotel Moskva

Okhotny Ryad 2, 103009 (960 2020/fax 928 5938). Metro Okhotny Ryad. **Rates** *single* $60; *double* $70; *suite* $120.* **Credit** AmEx, MC, V. **Map p278 C3**
This sombre concrete edifice, looking like a giant Greek tomb, dominates nearby Manezh Square and was once the realm of visiting Communist Party bigwigs. There's still a certain amount of Soviet customer-service hostility at the front doors, but once you get inside the staff tend to be fairly helpful and the rooms are reasonably comfortable, at least considering the price and the prime location. West-facing rooms overlook the Kremlin, while the south-facing rooms with balconies were prime real estate when Prodigy played on Manezh Square in autumn 1997. The east-facing rooms, meanwhile, overlook Moscow's busiest avenue of prostitution, which business tends to overflow into the hotel lobby most days

after about four in the afternoon. Discount rates of under $50 for singles/doubles are available for groups of ten or more. **Hotel services** *Air-conditioning. Bars. Beauty salon. Business services. Cocktail lounge. Conference facilities. Currency exchange. Laundry service. Parking. Restaurants. Safe. Theatre & travel desk.* **Room services** *Radio. Refrigerator. Telephone. TV.*

Pekin Hotel

Bolshaya Sadovaya Ulitsa 5/1, 103001 (209 2442/3323/3425/fax 200 1420). Metro Mayakovskaya. **Rates** *single* $85-$95; *double* $105. **Credit** AmEx, EC, MC, V. **Map p277 A2/B1/2**

Built as a monument to the communist friendship between the Soviet Union and the People's Republic of China, this imposing Stalin skyscraper has faded considerably on the inside since its heyday, even if the exterior is looking all spic and span after it was cleaned up for the Moscow 850 celebration. The views are decent and the rooms on the large side for the price but somewhat lacking in comfort. The Hong Kong restaurant downstairs serves up some awfully dubious 'Chinese' cuisine against the backdrop of a strictly Russian floorshow, while the neighbouring casino/nightclub draws a crowd of prostitutes, sketchy *biznesmeny*, and their automatic-weapon-toting bodyguards. The Pekin's east façade put in an unlikely guest appearance as the US embassy in the recent movie version of *The Saint* starring Val Kilmer.

Hotel services *Air-conditioning. Bar. Casino. Currency exchange. Dry-cleaning & laundry service. Nightclub. Parking. Restaurant. Theatre desk.* **Room services** *Cable TV. Hairdryer. Radio. Refrigerator. Safe.*

Hotel Rossia

Ulitsa Varvarka 6, 103495 (232 5000/fax 232 6262/6248). Metro Kitai Gorod. **Rates** *single/double* $84; *suite* $180; *apartment* $230. **Credit** DC, MC, V. **Map p278 D3**

This 3,000-room rectangular monument to the ugliness of Soviet aesthetics has been under partial renovation since the sanitary authorities threatened to close it down in 1994 due to rat and cockroach infestations, but so far the critters seem to be holding strong. One of the hotel's main attractions, the maddening main reception area worthy of Terry Gilliam's *Brazil*, has been closed since late 1997 in connection with the refurbishment, but hopefully they won't meddle too much with this unique Soviet artefact. Vermin and bureaucracy aside, the smallish rooms are the cheapest you're likely to find with unobstructed views of the Kremlin and St. Basil's. The Rossia is also home to Manhattan Express, Moscow's first 'American' nightclub; it's not nearly as happening as it used to be, but it's still worth a peek, if only for the respectable Italian menu. The world's largest hotel when it was opened in 1967, it is still the largest in Europe (at least as far as single structures go; the six-unit Izmailovo – *see below* **Budget** – is even larger).

Hotel services *Air-conditioning. Bars. Beauty salon. Business services. Cinema. Conference facilities. Currency exchange. Dry-cleaning service. Hairdresser. Kitchenette. Parking. Nightclub. Several restaurants and snack bars. Sauna. Solarium. Swimming pool. Theatre & travel desks.* **Room services** *Radio. Telephone. TV.*

Sovietskaya Hotel

Leningradsky Prospekt 32/2, 125040 (250 7253/960 2000/fax 960 2006/250 8003/hotsov@orc.ru). Metro Dinamo. **Rates** *single* $150; *double* $170; *suite* $300; *apartment* $350. **Credit** AmEx, MC, V.

This attractively designed, medium-sized hotel located just 5km (3 miles) north of the city centre is popular with business people without limitless expense accounts. The 100 rooms are well-appointed, modern without being completely soulless. The Sovietskaya has also attracted a significant crowd among New Russians with its resurrected version of the Yar restaurant, originally a grand pre-Revolutionary

eatery in the centre of town frequented by such leading cultural figures as Leo Tolstoy and Anton Chekhov. The atmosphere today may be less majestic, but the food is some of the best old-style Russian cuisine you'll find.

Hotel services *Bar. Beauty salon. Business services. Conference/banquet facilities. Currency exchange. Dry-cleaning and laundry service. Restaurants. Multilingual staff. Parking. Shops.* **Room services** *Cable TV. Hairdryer. Minibar. Modem line. Room service.*

Hotel Ukraina

Kutuzovsky Prospekt 2/1, 121249 (243 2598/3030/fax 956 2078). Metro Kievskaya. **Rates** *single* $90; *double* $120; *suite* $150; *apartment* $350. **Credit** AmEx, DC, MC, V.

The height of Soviet classicism, the Ukraina opened in 1957, and its 1,013 spacious, somewhat modernised rooms

...and other critters

If your hotel room *is* infested, it is much more likely that the culprits will be cockroaches. When left unchecked, these and other vermin (most commonly rats) will run rampant over any building in town. Of course, you probably won't come across such creatures in a $300 room in the Metropol, but there are plenty of other places where less vigilant anti-pest regimes are in effect. You can almost bank on running into some non-paying guests in the dirty corners of run-down places like the **Kievskaya** (*see page 73*) or the unrenovated places outside the centre, but the most notorious rat-trap of them all is located in the very heart of the city. With 3,000 rooms full of nooks and crannies in which little things can hide and scurry, it's no wonder the **Rossia** (*page 73*) has had such problems with critters over the years. In fact, even the recent refurbishment carried out in part to rid the hotel of its pests once and for all seems to have met with little success. Perhaps this is just nature's way of laughing at the folly of erecting such a hideous structure so near to one of the world's most historic squares.

offer unrivalled views of the White House, the Moskva River and the city centre (10km/6 miles away), as well as a taste of the overblown pomp of a largely bygone era. The above-average facilities and in-room amenities make this the best of the old-style Soviet hotels, especially considering the price and location. That said, some of the holdovers from the past – such as being forced to pay for all telephone calls (even local ones) in advance – are less than welcome. In addition to the grand-scale restaurants, there are numerous smaller cafeterias located on various floors.
Hotel services *Bars. Beauty salon. Business services (24 hours). Casino. Conference facilities. Currency exchange. Kitchenette. Non-smoking rooms. Nursery. Parking. Post office. Restaurants (3). Sauna. Supermarket.* **Room services** *Cable TV. Minibar. Radio. Refrigerator. Room service. Safe. Telephone.*

Hotel Varshava

Leninsky Prospekt 2/1, 117049 (reservations/front desk 238 4101/fax 238 9639). Metro Oktyabrskaya. **Rates** *single $65; double $95 (25% surcharge for advance reservations).* **No credit cards.**

With a convenient central location that's right above a ring-line metro station and cosy, spacious rooms, the Varshava is a pretty good deal for the money. Be warned: the hot water supply can be unreliable.
Hotel services *Air-conditioning. Bar. Currency exchange. Restaurant.* **Room services** *Refrigerator. Telephone. TV.*

Budget

Aeroflot Hotel

Leningradsky Prospekt 37/5, 125167 (151 0442/fax 151 7543). Metro Aeroport or Dinamo. **Rates** *single $85; double $75 and up.* **Credit** DC, JCB, MC, V.
Not to be confused with its similarly named neighbour, the much more expensive Aerostar, the Aeroflot offers pretty much the grey atmosphere and surly staff you'd expect from an $80-a-night hotel just outside the centre.
Hotel services *Air-conditioning. Bar. Continental breakfast. Conference facilities. Currency exchange. Parking (paid). Restaurants.*

Success with a bullet?

In a city where business-related murders are practically an everyday occurrence, it is hardly surprising that Moscow's hotels have occasionally found themselves caught in the crossfire. Since late 1997, at least two hotel directors have been murdered near their homes in apparent contract killings connected with struggles for control of their respective businesses. In November 1997, Boris Gryaznov, director of the Sovincentre complex, of which the **Mezhdunarodnaya Hotel** (*see page 70*) is a part, was gunned down in a gangland-style shooting just outside his apartment building. Many saw his murder as an attempt by mafia groups to establish control over the hotel and conference centre. A little over a month later, Yevgeny Tsimbalistov, director of the **Hotel Rossia** (*page 73*), was shot in similar circumstances. Adding weight to the argument that the murder was mafia-related was the fact that Tsimbalistov's predecessor had left after being wounded by an attacker wielding an axe. So far, no arrests have been made in either case.

On a few occasions, shots have even rung out in or near the hotels themselves. In spring 1997, a local businessman was murdered in the parking lot of the **Aerostar Hotel** (*page 69*). Although there has been a well-publicised dispute between the hotel's Canadian and Russian partners, the murder victim was apparently just a regular guest. But the most notorious of Moscow's hotel-related murders occurred in November 1996, when US businessman Paul Tatum was shot 11 times with a Kalashnikov assault rifle in the entrance to a metro station

just outside the **Radisson Slavjanskaya** (*page 70*). Tatum's death came in the midst of a long and bitter tug-of-war for ownership of the $50-million joint-venture hotel between its three partners – Tatum's Americom Business Centres, the US-based Radisson Hotel Corporation and the Moscow City Property Committee. The dispute between Tatum and the Property Committee was being heard in a Swedish arbitration court at the time, and was decided in favour of the city several months later. Naturally, there was much speculation that the city of Moscow was behind the murder, or that it was related to the dubious loans that Tatum had allegedly been taking out to cover his legal costs. Regardless of who was behind the shooting, it came as a chilling shock to all foreign business people working in Russia, most of whom had previously thought themselves immune to the dangers faced by their Russian counterparts.

Always something of a local legend among Moscow's close-knit foreign community for his often bizarre antics (such as barricading himself inside his office or placing full-page ads for so-called 'Freedom Bonds', actually loans to cover his legal costs, in the *Moscow Times*) during the ownership dispute, Tatum became something of a martyr after his murder, which led many who had previously viewed him as a jingoistic jerk or a reckless cowboy to label him a pioneer in the fight for fair business practice in Russia. To this day, Tatum's memory haunts any foreigner involved in business in Russia, and, as usual, there have been no arrests made in the case.

The heights of Soviet-era luxury: the **Hotel Ukraina**. *See page 73.*

http://www.timeout.co.uk

Hotel Orlyonok

Ulitsa Kosygina 15, 117334 (reservations/front desk 939 8884/fax 938 2200). Metro Leninsky Prospekt. **Rates** *single/double* $65. **No credit cards**.

Formerly destination No.1 for the Soviet youth travel agency, the Orlyonok is now just another greying monolith with passable rooms. On the plus side, there's a cheap, respectable Chinese restaurant and good views, and the surrounding neighbourhood is quite attractive (and green).

Hotel services *Air-conditioning. Bar. Currency exchange. Restaurants.* **Room services** *Refrigerator. Telephone. TV.*

Hotel Sputnik

Leninsky Prospekt 38, 117526 (938 7106/fax 938 7096). Metro Leninsky Prospekt. **Rates** *single* $35; *double* $45. **Credit** MC, V.

A fairly hideous 1970s skyscraper with unrenovated rooms, shifty staff and occasionally frightening security guards. However, it's dirt cheap, and the outstanding Indian restaurant in the lobby is one of Moscow's most affordable.

Hotel services *Air-conditioning. Bar. Conference facilities. Currency exchange. Parking (paid). Restaurants.*

Tsentralny Dom Turista

Central Tourist House, Leninsky Prospekt 146, 117526 (434 9467/fax 434 3197). Metro Yugo-Zapadnaya. **Rates** *single* $75; *double* $90. **Credit** MC, V.

Nondescript 22-storey behemoth with clean, functional rooms and extremely helpful staff. The location might be distant from both the nearest metro and the city centre, but the nearby People's Friendship University makes this Moscow's best neighbourhood for budget-priced ethnic (Indian, Middle Eastern, Asian, African) cuisine.

Hotel services *Air-conditioning. Bars. Conference facilities. Currency exchange. Parking (paid). Restaurants.* **Room services** *Refrigerator.*

Izmailovo Tourist Complex

Izmailovskoye Shosse 71, 105613 (166 2763/0254/fax 166 2180/hunter@aha.ru). Metro Izmailovsky Park. **Rates** *single* $36-$45; *double* $44-$62; *suite* $80-$120. **Credit** AmEx, DC, JCB, MC, V.

This gargantuan complex of six 28-floor towers, built for the 1980 Olympics and 15km (10 miles) from the city centre, has a combined total of 8,000 beds, making it Moscow's (and Europe's) largest hotel. The complex is actually comprised of five separate hotels (the sixth tower houses entertainment facilities) with identical layouts but slightly differing prices due to variations in fixtures and amenities. The contact numbers given above are for Relax, a company within the complex that represents and handles reservations for all five units. The atmosphere is generally pretty upbeat, and the location, although remote from the centre, is near the popular **Izmailovsky** market in the beautiful Izmailovsky Park.

Hotel services *Air-conditioning. Bars. Beauty salon. Bowling. Business services. Casino. Conference/banquet facilities. Currency exchange. Fitness facilities (massage, sauna). Parking. Restaurants. Safe. Tennis court. Swimming pool.* **Room services** *Minibar. Room service. Safe. Telephone. TV.*
Website: www.moscow-guide.ru/Travel/Relax

Kievskaya

Kievskaya Ulitsa 2, 121059 (240 1444/fax 240 5388). Metro Kievskaya. **Rates** *single* $26 (shared bath); *double* $33-50 (bath in room). **No credit cards**.

A charming little dump of a place across the street from Kiev rail station that's generally packed with all sorts of unsavoury-looking shuttle traders and the thugs who shake them down. The unsmiling staff will likely do their best to warn foreigners off, but those on a limited budget and carrying nothing worthy of theft will like the fairly central location and easy access to the metro. Needless to say, don't

*Dome from home: Moscow's **Radisson** (p70).*

expect much in the way of extras. However, all rooms do have phone and TV, which is very out of character for this kind of establishment.

Hotel services *Conference hall.* **Room services** *Refrigerator. Telephone. TV.*

Leningradskaya Hotel

Kalanchevskaya Ulitsa 21/40, 107245 (reservations/front desk 975 3032/fax 975 1802/4943). Metro Komsomolskaya. **Rates** *single* $50-$85; *double* $65. **Credit** AmEx, MC, V. **Map p279 F1**

Occupying the least impressive of the seven Stalin sky-scrapers, the Leningradskaya overlooks Komsomolskaya Square and its three rail stations, but this apparent plus is generally a minus after dark when the area is teeming with all kinds of undesirables and equally threatening police officers. Fairly cheap for the almost-central location, but you basically get what you pay for.

Hotel services *Air conditioning. Bar. Beauty salon. Conference facilities. Currency exchange. Nightclub. Restaurant.*

Hotel Minsk

Tverskaya Ulitsa 22, 103050 (299 1213/1349/fax 299 0362). Metro Pushkinskaya. **Rates** *single* $38-$50; *double* $50-$75. **Credit** AmEx, DC, MC, V. **Map p278 C2**

Perhaps the most aptly named hotel in town, this grey 1960s structure looks like it could have been transplanted in its entirety from the stodgy Belarussian capital. There's very little in the way of facilities, the service varies from non-existent to hostile and the spartan rooms are hardly what you'd call comfortable, but the central location close to the metro is just about the best you'll find for the price. Unfortunately, the high concentration of guests from the Caucasus region sometimes increases the level of police harassment, especially at night.

Hotel services *Air conditioning. Bar/café. Currency exchange. Restaurant.* **Room services** *Fridge. Radio. TV.*

Sport Hotel

Leninsky Prospekt 90/2, 117415 (reservations/front desk 737 6700/fax 737 6720). Metro Prospekt Vernadskogo. **Rates** *single* $36; *double* $50. **No credit cards.**

This concrete and glass skyscraper seems to sit all alone in the midst of the vast expanse of Leninsky Prospekt, halfway between the city centre and the middle of nowhere. The location is pretty dismal (unless you're shopping for furniture), but the smallish rooms are matched by the low rates.

Hotel services *Air-conditioning. Bar. Continental breakfast. Currency exchange. Parking (paid). Restaurant.* **Room services** *Refrigerator. Telephone. TV.*

Tsentralnaya Hotel

Tverskaya Ulitsa 10, 103009 (229 8957/8589/0607/fax 292-1221). Metro Pushkinskaya. **Rates** *single* $40, *double* $66. **No credit cards.** **Map p278 C2**

The aptly named Central Hotel may be ugly and gloomy, but it's definitely the cheapest option available in the very centre of town. There's precious little in the way of facilities, with shared toilets and bathrooms, but the rooms are spacious enough and with a bit of imagination you could even call them cosy. It's a toss-up who is more gruff, though: the grim staff or the shady folks with whom you'll be sharing a toilet.

Room services *Telephone. TV.*

Hotel Yunost

Khamovnichesky Val Ulitsa 34, 119048 (reservations/front desk 242 4861/fax 242 0284). Metro Sportivnaya. **Rates** *single* $40; *double* $60. **Credit** V.

A run-down but utilitarian place just outside the city centre that is convenient for the metro, Novodevichy Convent and Luzhniki sports complex. Friendly staff and affordable rates.

Hotel services *Air-conditioning. Bar. Continental breakfast. Currency exchange. Parking (paid). Restaurants.* **Room services** *Refrigerator. Telephone. TV.*

Hostels & B&Bs

It is important to note if you are staying in bed and breakfast accommodation or in a private apartment (or one of the lower-class hotels) that the local authorities always shut off the hot water for a month in summer for maintenance. If the idea of washing yourself using a bucket of tepid water or going to the banya every day (as most Russians do) turns you off, then ring ahead to find out about the hot water situation in that district. Or stay somewhere pricier with its own heating system.

B&B Agency

Reservations 252 4451/fax 205 7683. **Rates** *two-room apartment* $60. **No credit cards.**

This small agency has a dozen or so spacious apartments available for short- or long-term rent in the vicinity of Belarus rail station. Discounts are typically available for stays of one week or more. The staff don't speak much English, but are generally very helpful.

Moscow Bed & Breakfast

Reservations (US numbers) 603 585 3347/fax 585 6534/jkates@top.monad.net. **Rates** *single* $35; *double* $52. **No credit cards.**

This New Hampshire-based US agency specialises in arranging Moscow homestays with English-speaking hosts. The agency has an extensive network of contacts both within and beyond the city centre, and can also book apartments without hosts accommodating up to four people. Visa support and guide/interpretation services are also available. Dinner weighs in at $15 extra.

Hotel services *Airport transfers. English-speaking staff.*

Prakash Guest House

Profsoyuznaya Ulitsa 83/1, entrance 2 (phone/fax 334 2598). Metro Belyayevo. **Rates** *single* $30-$40; *double* $45. **No credit cards.**

This Indian-run guesthouse about 20 minutes south of the city centre has space for about 70 travellers in clean, comfortable rooms. It also provides visa support, can arrange for tours and guides and offers in-room meal service that includes some outstanding Indian vegetarian options. All rooms have private bath, and it's just a couple of minutes' walk from the metro.

Hotel services *Air-conditioning. Airport transfers. English-speaking staff.* **Room services** *Room service.*

Traveller's Guest House

Bolshaya Pereyaslavskaya Ulitsa 50, 10th floor, 129041 (971 4059/280 8562/fax 280 7686/tgh@glasnet.ru/). Metro Prospekt Mira. **Rates** *single* $45 (with bath); $30 (shared bath); *double* $40 (shared bath); *dormitory* $15. **Credit** AmEx, MC, V.

Established in 1993, Traveller's Guest House is still the only genuine hostel-type experience in Moscow. Its central location and the different types of inexpensive accommodation options it offers – from dormitories through private rooms with shared bath to en-suite – make it popular with a wide variety of budget travellers, which in turn makes it a good place to meet people if you're travelling alone. The extremely helpful English-speaking staff are available 24 hours every day and can arrange airport transfer and city tours, as well as accommodation in one of St Petersburg's hostels should you be heading in that direction. Advance reservations are highly recommended, and are virtually essential during the summer months.

Hotel services *Air-conditioning. Airport transfers. English-speaking staff.*
Website: www.iro.ru/link5.html

Restaurants & Cafés

It's not all borsch and tears: Moscow has embraced international cuisine and some international standards.

Not long ago, a guide to restaurants in Moscow would have been one of the world's most redundant volumes. It would also have been one of the shortest. During communist times, there were barely 20 restaurants in the city and just as few cafés. Restaurants were only open until 10 or 11pm at the latest and cafés shut at 7pm prompt. And, unless you had access to élite party establishments, most of them were dreadful anyway.

The situation has changed radically. Moscow now has several thousand restaurants, with new ones opening every week. The choice of cuisine ranges from Chinese to Mexican, Indian, American and, of course, Russian. One particular highlight is the amount of good Caucasian restaurants, where the food is often excellent and moderately priced.

In general, dining in Moscow probably doesn't cost a lot more than in other European capitals: while prices are definitely higher than in, say, Prague or Budapest, they don't quite match Paris or Geneva. In mid-range joints expect to pay between $30 and $50 per person; at the luxury end of the scale, about $200. Whether you'll be getting the same value for money as elsewhere is another matter. The deluge of new establishments has pushed up the demand for chefs to unprecedented levels, which has had a huge impact on consistency, with restaurants starting off well but sliding into oblivion once the original chef has earned his accolades and moved on to greener pastures and higher wage packets.

Levels of service have improved immensely over recent years, but you may still experience surliness or unexplained delays. Stomach bugs can sometimes lurk in low- to mid-range restaurants. Use your common sense and check for basic cleanliness. Russian cuisine is also very meaty – lumps of dead animal lurk at the bottom of many stews and stews including borsch and shchi. Vegetarians are not generally well served here outside Indian restaurants.

The average prices given are for three courses, starter, entrée and dessert. They do not include the cost of drinks. Note that restaurants do not accept travellers' cheques in payment. It is normal to leave a tip of about ten per cent, but check that it has not been not included in the bill.

Restaurants

The top spots

Arkadia
Teatralny Proyezd 3 (926 9008). Metro Lubyanka or Teatralnaya. **Open** noon-2am daily. **Average** $125. **Credit** AmEx, MC, V. **Map p278 C3/D3**
A sumptuous *style moderne* haven of excellent traditional cuisine. Try the Merchant's Sterlet, a miniature sturgeon smothered in cream cheese sauce and served with potatoes, the *ukha makarievskaya*, a Russian speciality soup made from three kinds of fish, or the *blini poshekhoskiye*, ultra-thin blinis served with caviar. The immaculate service is in line with the eye-popping prices, and everything is astonishingly well presented on Bohemian porcelain plates and in dazzling crystal goblets.

Borodino
Aerostar Hotel, Leningradsky Prospekt 37/9 (213 9000). Metro Aeroport or Dinamo. **Open** 6pm-midnight daily. **Average** $100. **Credit** AmEx, DC, V.
Named after the hotly disputed battle against Napoleon's forces in 1812. Russian cuisine wins hands down on the menu. Sample the selection of black and red caviar with *alushkami* (fat Russian blini) and a platter of spring vegetables. For the more adventurous and unburdened of conscience, there's a wide selection of deer, moose and wild bear dishes, several of them oozing with luscious port-wine sauces.

Dorian Gray
Kadashevskaya Naberezhnaya 6/1 (237 6313/6342). Metro Tretyakovskaya. **Open** noon-midnight daily. **Average** $65. **Credit** AmEx, MC, V. **Map p281 C5/D4**
One of the better Italian restaurants in Moscow, located just south of the Kremlin on the riverbank. Among the more interesting starters are smoked salmon with olives and the vongole alla marinara (clams with garlic, olive oil and herbs). For the main course, try the lasagne al crostacei or the ostrich. Finish off with the rather excellent tiramisu. The restaurant is known as the site of a famous shoot-out in 1996, but things have been relatively calm since.

Fuji
Ulitsa Bolshaya Dmitrovka 32 (200 0717). Metro Pushkinskaya. **Open** 1-11pm daily. **Average** $115. **Credit** AmEx, DC, JCB, MC, V. **Map p278 C2**
The speciality of this cute little restaurant, the interior of which is cluttered with Japanese knick-knacks, is *nabe*, which translates roughly as 'pot', a DIY affair in which you are expected to take part in the preparation of your meal.

The Russian menu

Most of the restaurants listed in this section will have menus written in English, often with adequate explanations of what the dishes contain. A number of restaurants, particularly ethnic ones, will just give literal translations. Below you will find a list of most of the dishes you are likely to encounter on a trip to Russia.

Starters/first courses (zakuski/perviyeblyuda)

borsch
Ukrainian beetroot soup with cabbage and meat, served with sour cream (*smetna*)
(**postny borsch** – borsch without meat)

forshmak
Jewish hors d'œuvre made of sliced herring

kharcho
A rich Georgian beef soup with rice

khash
An ancient Armenian rich soup (known as an emergency hangover cure)

klyotski
Belorussian soup with dumplings

kvashennaya kapusta
Sauerkraut with carrot

lobio
Georgian bean dish

okroshka
cold *kvas* soup with chopped vegetables and meat

rassolnik
meat or fish soup with pickled cucumbers

salo
Ukrainian dish of salty bacon fat

satsivi
Cold Georgian dish of chicken, garlic and walnuts

selyodka pod shuboi
Literally 'herring in a fur coat'; herring with beet, vegetables and mayonnaise

shchi
sauerkraut and meat soup
(**postny shchi** – shchi without meat)

studen, kholodets
Cold jelly with meat

solyanka
Sharp-tasting thick soup of vegetables and meat or fish. Can also be a second course (stewed meat and cabbage with spices)

turiya
Soup made with bread and water or *kvas*

ukha
Fish soup

Entrées/second courses (vtoriyeblyuda)

blini
Thin pancakes with a filling, known since pagan times

brynza
Salty cheese

chakhokhbili
Georgian chicken and vegetable stew

galushki
Ukrainian dumplings

kalach
Traditional Russian loaf (horseshoe shaped)

khachapuri
Cheese-filled pastry

kulebyaka
Pie filled with meat, fish or cabbage

pampushki
kind of fritter

pelmeni
Siberian meat dumplings

pirog
Pie or tart with a sweet or savoury filling

pirozhki
Small pies

plov
Equivalent of pilau – Asian dish of rice and mutton
(**ovoschnoy plov** – with vegetables instead of meat)

rastegai
Open-topped pastry

shashlik
Pieces of mutton roasted on a spit

tolma/dolma
Asian dish: mutton and rice wrapped in vine leaves

vareniki
Curd or fruit dumplings

The waiters serve up a mini-cooker and pan plus your raw ingredients: chrysanthemum leaves, mushrooms, bamboo shoots, tofu, two kinds of noodles and a fistful of spices. A chef is on hand in case you get stuck. If you prefer less audience participation, try the excellent and reasonably priced sushi or the teppanyaki.

Incognito

Renaissance Moscow Hotel, Olimpiisky Prospekt 18/1 (931 9000). Metro Prospekt Mira. **Open** 6-11pm Mon-Sat. **Average** $150 (minimum order $60). **Credit** AmEx, DC, MC, V.
An intimate culinary hideaway that seats only 26. The atmosphere is intoxicating: a permanent grainy twilight punctuated only by twinkling tabletop candles. The menu is packed with terrific and exotic meat dishes, highlights being the veal sweetbreads in a burgundy sauce and the

superlative foie gras. This is not a place for the weak of wallet; bills can be as high as $2,500, depending on which champagne you choose.

Praga

Prague, Ulitsa Arbat 2 (290 6171). Metro Arbatskaya. **Open** noon-midnight daily. **Average** $150. **Credit** AmEx, DC, MC, V. **Map p280 B4**
The décor at Prague is a mélange of palatial interiors of different styles and eras; each of its nine halls takes a slightly different approach to overwrought glam décor. In the Brazilian Room you'll find an imposing white statue of Jesus Christ; in the Oriental Hall there's a Caucasian menu, and it's pasta all round in the Italian Room. The other halls are devoted to Russian cuisine. The most lavish by far is the Tsar's Hall, where, if you book three days before, waiters in seventeenth-century costumes will serve you roast pheasant on a silver platter.

Serebryanny Vek

Silver Age, Teatralny Proyezd 3, building 3 (926 1352).
Metro Teatralnaya. **Open** 6pm-1am daily. **Average**
$200. **No credit cards. Map p278 C3/D3**
In the nineteenth century, this mansion belonged to a
family of wealthy merchants. Once the Revolution had
disposed of them, it became the central bathhouse. Now the
building has been restored to its pre-Revolutionary
condition – sparkling chandeliers, griffins and gilt garlands
abound – and houses one of Moscow's most lavish
restaurants. The menu lists more than 300 traditional
Russian dishes, though the *boyar ukha*, a traditional soup
made with sterlet (a small sturgeon) and served with
rastegai (Russian pies) or the excellent pike perch should
suffice for one visit.

Sloboda

Bolshaya Kommunisticheskaya Ulitsa 2A (956 2862).
Metro Taganskaya. **Open** noon-midnight daily.
Average $180. **Credit** AmEx, DC, MC, V. **Map
p282 F5**
This is one of the most expensive places in town and one of
the most gigantic. There are 11 dining halls in total, many
of them named after Russian folk arts. The cuisine is Russian
and almost uniformly excellent. Try the stuffed carp in ruby
jelly, fillet of deer or the pork brisket with mushrooms. You
won't find better anywhere else.

Tsarskaya Okhota

The Tsar's Hunt, Rublyovo-Uspenskoye Shosse 186A,
Zhukovka, Odintsovsky (418 7983/7982). No public
transport. **Open** noon-midnight daily. **Average** $100.
Credit AmEx, MC, V.
Located out in the sticks in an *izba* (log hut), Tsarskaya
Okhota is about as traditional Russian as cuisine gets. The
chairs are upholstered with bearskins, carved wood
panelling stretches off into the distance, and a large Russian
stove, where the cooking takes place in front of your eyes,
sits proudly in the centre of the dining room. A good choice
to kick off proceedings is the Russian buffet, which includes
all manner of vegetables à la Russe, including gherkins and
cabbage. Then move on to grilled deer served with wild
berries or the wild duck with baked apples in a cherry sauce.
This is one of Boris Yeltsin's favourite restaurants, and it's
easy to see why. If you want to go, get your hotel to call a
cab (street taxis will probably get lost). It'll cost – but not
as much as the meal.

TsDL

Central House of Writers, Povarskaya Ulitsa 50
(291 1515/290 1589). **Open**
noon-midnight daily. **Average** $175 Oak Room, $50
Brasserie Room. **Credit** AmEx, DC, V. **Map p277
A3/B3**
This place has always been something of a legend,
featuring in the works of Tolstoy and, most famously, in
Mikhail Bulgakov's novel *The Master and Margarita*
when the devil drops by for dinner with his cat. In Soviet
times, it was a favourite of party functionaries (the chandelier in the Dubrovy Room was a gift from Joseph Stalin).
Now it's a haunt of the super-rich, who come not only for
the cuisine but also for the unsurpassable décor. The walls
of the Brasserie Room (which serves up a traditional Soviet
selection with some innovations) are decorated with writer-
ly memorabilia. The Dubrovy Room (where the cuisine
veers towards French) is like a grand Imperial library from
the last century. In the Brasserie, you can't go wrong with
any of the zakuski (a selection of traditional entrées), then
caviar and smoked salmon followed by sturgeon or rack
of lamb. Only for the very brave are eggs stuffed with
anchovies, or tongue in aspic. In the Dubrovy, go for fried
eel with beet or the deer fillet with ground cedar nuts
and pistachio. If you get the choice right, this can be a
pre-Revolutionary dining classic.

American/Latin

Azteca

Tverskaya Ulitsa 3/5 (956 8467/8359). Metro Okhotny
Ryad. **Open** noon-6am daily. **Average** dinner $35.
Credit MC, V. **Map p278 C2**
On top of Hotel Intourist, this was one of the first foreign-
managed restaurants to open in Moscow. The story goes that
two American students, who were living in the Intourist, persuaded the management to let them knock two rooms together and put in a bar and restaurant. The quality of food has
been up and down since then as chefs (mainly Cubans) come
and go, but now seems to be on the ascent. The fajitas and
nachos with meat sauce are good and the frozen Margaritas
terrific. But best of all is the view – one side of the room is
little more than plate glass window looking down on western Moscow and all the way up to the university.

Cali's

Leningradsky Prospekt 31/9 (212 2273). Metro Dinamo.
Open 11am-late daily. **Average** $30. **No credit cards.**
This Californian oasis is situated in one of the castles that
Russian Tsars used to drop in at on their way from Moscow
to St Petersburg. For homesick beach-bums, views of the lazy
American western shoreline decorate the walls. Half a
Californian chicken with garlic will set you back $17, or a
quarter $14.50. All the steaks are marinated before being
grilled on an open fire on slabs of wood with potatoes stuffed
with tomatoes and other veggies. Portions are big. You can
wash them down with beer or Californian semi-dry wines.

U Dyadi Gilyaya

Uncle Guilly's, Stoleshnikov Pereulok 6 (229 2050).
Metro Chekhovskaya. **Open** 11am-midnight daily.
Average dinner $60. **Credit** AmEx, MC, V. **Map
p278 C2**
This place is named after the famous turn-of-the-century
Russian journalist and writer Vladimir Gilyarovsky. In the
first four years of its existence the cuisine slowly mutated
from Russian to American, and it is now pretty much a fully
fledged steak restaurant, with a couple of meat-free dishes
thrown in for good measure. A hefty T-bone will cost you
$45. Vegetarians have the option of mushrooms in sour
cream, and Russophiles can go for traditional pelmeni.

Gambrinus

Tverskoi Bulvar 3/4 (203 0149). Metro Pushkinskaya.
Open noon-midnight daily. **Average** $50. **Credit**
AmEx, DC, MC, V. **Map p277 B2**
A funky, smart place that is growing in popularity with the
inner-city business set. It also boasts one of Moscow's
longest bars, decked out with an impressive array of
bottles. The cuisine is mainly Tex-Mex but makes curious
forays into French and Italian. You can't go wrong here with
any of the usual Tex-Mex favourites: the burritos or the
terrific fajitas. The French onion soup with croûtons is
generous and tasty. And to wash it all down, there's a wide
selection of Mexican and European beers.

Planet Hollywood

Krasnaya Presnaya Ulitsa 23B (255 0539/9191/fax 255
9190). Metro Ulitsa 1905 Goda. **Open** 11am-2pm daily.
Average dinner $30. **Credit** AmEx, MC, V.
Glitzy, huge and very American, this Planet Hollywood is
no different from any other Planet Hollywood anywhere else
in the world. Offers all the usual staples: burgers, steaks, buffalo wings and pretty good Margaritas.

Santa Fe

Mantulinskaya Ulitsa 5/1 (256 1487/fax 256 2126).
Metro Ulitsa 1905 Goda. **Open** noon-2am daily.
Average dinner $50. **Credit** AmEx, DC, JCB, MC, V.
Santa Fe was one of the first purpose-built restaurants
in Moscow. In the style of a ranch house and located on

the edge of a park, it has a green and airy atmosphere that pervades its large dining area, comfortable bar and covered summer patio. The Tex-Mex food is good but overpriced owing to the fact that Santa Fe has become a New Russian favourite – a criticism that can be levelled at most decent places in Moscow. The fajitas and enchiladas are great, and the BBQ rack of ribs huge and dripping with tasty sauce.

Starlite Diner
Ulitsa Korovy Val 9 (tel/fax 959 8919). Metro Oktyabraskaya or Dobryninskaya. **Open** 24 hours daily. **Average** dinner $20. **Credit** AmEx, MC, V. **Map 281 C6**
The Starlite Diners rank among the most striking of all the anachronisms of modern Moscow – completely authentic, completely intact chrome-plated American diners that have landed like alien spacecraft among the city's Stalinist buildings. The newer of the two in Korovy Val is slightly bigger (with 250 seats), but the one on Bolshaya Sadovaya Ulitsa (Mayakovskaya metro) is busier and far easier to get to. The food is traditional American, ranging from sweet waffles through eggs Benedict to a selection of burgers. The breakfasts, served until 11am, make it a good post-clubbing option.
Branch: Bolshaya Sadovaya Ulitsa 16 (290 9638).

TGI Fridays
Tverskaya Ulitsa 18/2 (209 3601). Metro Pushkinskaya. **Open** 11am-1.30am daily. **Average** $30. **Credit** AmEx, DC, MC, V. **Map p278 C2**
Another international chain sticking faithfully to a formula that works the world over. The food is the same full-on combination of burgers and pasta that you get in other countries and you get the trademark juggling barmen here, too – though they're notorious for dropping their bottles. A good place to grab a drink before going to the cinema (at Pushkinskaya) and a favourite with the emerging middle class.

Best for...

Observing the foibles of the nouveau riche
Maxim's, TsDL (the Oak Room), Grand Opera, Kabanchik, Incognito

Mixing with the powerbrokers
Fuji, Tsarskaya Okhota

Playing the bohemian
Shinok, Elegance, Khlestakov Traktir, Dorian Gray

Fabulous views
Dorian Gray (the Kremlin cupolas), Azteka (the Kremlin cupolas), Sidmoya Neba (the whole damn city), Praga (Arbatskiye Vorota Ploshchad)

Great service
Petrovich Club, Tibet

Spiffy interiors
Petrovich Club, Serebryanny Vek, Grand Opera, Zamok Mephisto, TsDL

Caucasian

Elegance
Maly Ivanovsky Pereulok 9 (917 0717). Metro Kitai-Gorod. **Open** noon-midnight daily. **Average** $50. **Credit** DC, MC, V. **Map p279 E3**
The chef here is the famous Anatoly Davtian, who is a whizz with such Armenian specialities as *basturma*, a dish of dried beef and peppers, and *spas*, a variety of sweet and sour soup. However, this restaurant's pride and joy is *kuftu*, a dish made from beef that has been tenderised by burly Armenian *babushki* who place it on an authentic Armenian rock and then beat the hell out of it with hammers. This special meat is pre-prepared for Elegance in Armenia and delivered to Moscow daily by air. Every visitor gets a free glass of Armenian Cognac.

Guriya
Komsomolsky Prospekt 7/3 (246 0378). Metro Park Kultury. **Open** 11am-11pm daily. **Average** $20. **No credit cards. Map p280 A6/B6**
Serves some of the best and cheapest Georgian food in town. Centrally located in a courtyard across the street from a colourful church, it's extremely popular with expats and backpackers. Queues, especially at weekends, can be annoying, so book ahead. The cuisine is the usual hearty and spicy Caucasian, with arguably the best khachapuris in town. Don't let the abundance of plastic flowers or the eclectic Soviet interior with cheap, pseudo-wooden panelling and fans like helicopter propellers put you off.

Iberia
Ulitsa Rozhdestvenka 5/7 (928 2672). Metro Kuznetsky Most. **Open** noon-midnight daily. **Average** $35. **Credit** AmEx, MC, V. **Map p279 D2**
Georgian and international cuisine. Start off with onion soup then proceed to *satsivi*, a chicken dish with nut sauce. In between courses you can enjoy an exhibition of Georgian paintings. Live music in the evenings.

Kabanchik
Ulitsa Krasina 27/1 (tel/fax 254 9664). Metro Belorusskaya. **Open** noon-midnight daily. **Average** $75. **Credit** MC, V. **Map p277 A1/2**
The best Georgian place in town. You'll be greeted by two doormen dressed in costumes that could well be on loan from the Tower of London. The food is superb. Begin by choosing from starters such as red and green beans, cheeses, salad, aubergine and walnuts with khachapuri. Follow this with soup and a kebab.

Moosh
Oktyabrskaya Ulitsa 2/4 (284 3670). Metro Novoslobodskaya. **Open** *summer* 11am midnight, *winter* 9am-midnight, daily. **Average** $30. **Credit** MC, V.
A small Armenian eatery decorated with pictures of rifle brandishing national Armenian heroes and indoor fountains. Try the *dolma*, meatballs made from beef and rice, wrapped in vine leaves and served with sour cream. Also recommended is the *spanakh* – fried spinach with eggs.

Ne Goryui!
Arena Hotel, Ulitsa Desyat-letya Oktyabrya 11 (245 6856). Metro Sportivnaya. **Open** 9am-11pm daily. **Admission** non-members $9 after 7pm. **Average** $70. **Credit** MC, V.
This restaurant, whose upbeat name means 'Don't be sad!' or 'Cheer up!', is owned by a famous Soviet actor and singer of Georgian origin, Vakhtang Kikabidze. The house speciality is kebab made with meat marinated in tea, and the khachapuri with home-made Suluguni cheese is delicious. Kikabidze's pop celebrity buddies often sing here. Attached to it is a shockingly cheap bistro that lacks atmosphere but serves the same tasty food as the slightly overpriced restaurant.

Pirosmani

Novodevichy Proyezd 4 (247 1926). Metro Sportivnaya.
Open 1-10.30pm daily. **Average** $50. **Credit** V.
Named after the Georgian artist Pirosmani, some of whose original paintings hang on the walls. It has a good reputation that extends to the US – Bill Clinton has dined here – and a superlative shashlik. Georgian wine is served in big earthenware jugs.

Tiflis

Ulitsa Ostozhenka 32 (tel/fax 290 2897). Metro Park Kultury. **Open** noon-midnight daily. **Average** dinner $30. **Credit** MC, V. **Map p280 B5**
Inside this mock Tblisi townhouse are several pleasant dining rooms decorated with traditional Georgian costumes and puppets. The food is good – they do the best khachapuri and aubergines – and reasonably priced.

French

Aktyor

Actor, Mosfilmovskaya Ulitsa 1 (143 9400/9308). Metro Kievskaya, then tram 17 or 34, or taxi to Mosfilm. **Open** 2-11pm daily. **Average** $150. **Credit** AmEx, DC, JCB, MC, V.
Housed in Russia's premier film studios, Aktyor is the best French restaurant in town (with prices to match). The classy and subdued atmosphere aids digestion far better than the supercilious décor of the other top restaurants. And this is one of the few places to have kept their chef, who gets sent to France from time to time for training. Konstantin Grimoshin's touch is light and delicate compared to the cream-sauce heavy hand of Dmitry Spirin at Club T (*see below*), the other contender for the title of best French restaurant. Highly recommended are the home-made foie gras and the asparagus in hollandaise sauce, lightly flavoured with a little orange zest. Both the perch in lemon and white wine sauce and the veal medallions in goose liver sauce are a dream. And finish with the best chocolate mousse in the former Soviet Union. All the ingredients are flown in direct from France and the wine selection is formidable.

Le Chalet

Korobeinikov Pereulok 1/2, 2nd floor Chaika Club (202 0106). Metro Park Kultury. **Open** noon-midnight daily. **Average** $55. **Credit** AmEx, DC, JCB, MC, V. **Map p280 B5**
A combination of French and Swiss cuisine. Try the delightful Swiss fondue, which gurgles away in the corner on a warm stove. The restaurant has stained-glass windows and a magnificent view of the Moskva River.

Club T

Ulitsa Krasina 21 (232 2778/6520). Metro Belorusskaya or Mayakovskaya. **Open** noon-11pm daily. **Average** $125. **Credit** AmEx, DC, MC, V. **Map p277 A1/A2**
Excellent traditional French food – rich, expensive and presented in an exclusive atmosphere. If you've forgotten to pack your Armani suit and tie, don't even try to get in. This is where rich, cultured Russians celebrate the birthdays of their wives and daughters or, alternatively, deals over $5 million. To start, the Forest Salad, with slices of white and black pudding, is a dream and the caviar is the best. Frogs' legs, burgundy snails and foie gras complete the choice. Then move on to small stuffed cabbage with scampi on a butter caviar sauce or pheasant supreme, stuffed with foie gras. To finish: apple cinnamon tart with honey sauce.

From Dusk Till Dawn

Sredny Tishinsky Pereulok 5/7 (253 2323). Metro Belorusskaya. **Open** noon-midnight daily. **Average** $50. **Credit** AmEx, MC, V. **Map p277 A1**
This place has precious little to do with the Tarantino film of the same name – there are no vampire strippers, no crazed outlaws. It's not even a saloon, just a pretty standard restaurant in a nightclub, with average modern décor and a cosy fireplace in the centre. The cuisine is French but swerves occasionally in the direction of Italian. Menu highlights include foie gras with grape sauce, goose liver with grape sauce and frogs' legs. Cognac and cigars are available in the bar if you want to do a little puffing and posing after dinner.

Where east meets east: an Indian junket at **Moscow Bombay**. *See page 86.*

*For the best Cyrillic antipasti in town, go to **Stelle del Pescatore**. See page 86.*

Le Gastronome

Kudrinskaya Ploshchad 1 (255 4433). Metro Barrikadnaya. **Open** noon-11pm daily. **Average** $80. **Credit** AmEx, DC, MC, V.

Located in the former landmark Stalinist food shop of the same name, this is one of the most impressively decorated restaurants in Moscow – on the ground floor of one of Stalin's famous skyscrapers, it has marble columns, dazzling chandeliers and a wasteful expanse of space. The food is equally impressive: giant T-bone steaks, lobsters fresh from the aquarium, duck served on a silver platter. Try the house speciality, foie gras with papaya and raspberry. Other options include frogs' legs, and snails on brioche, washed down with the most exclusive Dom Perignon Rosé 1985, a snip at $695.

Maxim's

Hotel National, Mokhovaya Ulitsa 15/1 (258 7000/7148). Metro Okhotny Ryad. **Open** noon-5pm, 6.30-11pm, daily, **business lunch** noon-3pm Mon-Fri. **Average** $110. **Credit** AmEx, DC, V. **Map p278 C3/P280 C4**

A prestigious restaurant that keeps bucking the general Moscow trend by continually reducing its prices. You'll get a very nice French onion soup now for about $6.50 and a salad 'Maxim' (beans, celery, duck liver terrine, foie gras with nut sauce) for about $30. Other favourites include lobster charlotte with aubergine and fresh basil, duck liver escalope and foie gras with mango and ginger sauce.

Nostalgie

Chistoprudny Bulvar 12A (916 9478). Metro Chistye Prudy. **Open** noon-midnight daily. **Average** $110. **Credit** AmEx, DC, JCB, MC, V. **Map p279 E2**

Nostalgie has the best wine list in Moscow, the highlight of which has got to be the 1900 Château Margaux, which will set you back a mean $12,000. It also does ten types of foie gras, a wonderful plaice with caviar sauce and fillet of deer with juniper sauce. Plus there's a never-ending supply of superb and always fresh oysters costing around $35 for six.

Vinso Grand

Taganskaya Ploshchad 12 (912 5726). Metro Taganskaya. **Open** 24 hours daily. **Average** $65. **Credit** AmEx, DC, JCB, MC, V. **Map p282 F5**

The interior of this classy joint is luxurious but manages not to be pompous, while its moderate size makes it cosy and private. The pricing is similarly balanced: decent prices for decent food. Particularly good is the rabbit stewed in wine and the baked quails stuffed with mushrooms and herbs.

Indian

Darbar

Hotel Sputnik, Leninsky Prospekt 38 (930 2925/2365). Metro Leninsky Prospekt. **Open** noon until last customer leaves daily. **Average** $40. **Credit** MC, V.

When it first opened this was the best Indian restaurant in town. However, once the Indian chefs left and the Russians took over, the cream factor shot up and the spice factor plunged. Tandoori chicken is still good and the butter chicken excellent, but avoid the kormas and mild dishes. The menus are annoying cloth scrolls. Darbar offers the most extensive vegetarian selection in town.

Maharaja

Ulitsa Pokrovka 2/1 (921 9844/fax 928 1661). Metro Kitai-Gorod. **Open** noon-10.30pm daily. **Average** $55. **Credit** AmEx, DC, MC, V. **Map p279 E3/F3**

The excellent Maharaja opened its doors in 1994 and has maintained impeccably high standards ever since. To begin, go for the Maharaja kebab platter, a serious selection of skewered meats and fish tikka. Then, for frontier cooking at its best, try the whole leg of lamb marinated in spiced yoghurt with vegetable biryani and dahl. The murg makhani (tandoori chicken in tomato cream sauce) and the bhuna gosh are well above the norm. There is a good meat-free selection, plus an extensive choice of paratha, naan, roti and kulcha breads.

Moscow Bombay

*Glinishchevsky Pereulok 3 (292 9731). Metro
Pushkinskaya.* **Open** noon-midnight daily.
Average $35. **Credit** AmEx, DC, MC, V. **Map
p278 C2**
Similar to Tandoor (*see below*), but the food is not quite as
good and the clientele more Russian. The chicken and lamb
come on the bone unless you stipulate otherwise, but the
butter chicken and sturgeon curry are great.

Talk of the Town

*Leninsky Prospekt 131 (956 5999/fax 956 5998). Metro
Yugo Zapadnaya.* **Open** 12.30-11.30pm daily. **Average**
$45. **Credit** AmEx, DC, MC, V.
Housed in one of the original expat complexes, built
in 1992-3, Talk of the Town offers an interesting mixture
of Asian dishes. For starters try the ribs or chilli chicken,
then Peking duck. Then you could either go for the
Singapore noodles with double-cooked pork in honey or
Rainbow Lobster Cantonese. If you prefer straight Indian
all the tandoori dishes are tasty and the choice extensive.
Branch: Tryokhprudny Pereulok 9 (299 5771).

Tandoor

*Tverskaya Ulitsa 30/2 (299 5925/4593/fax 209 9949).
Metro Mayakovskaya.* **Open** 11am-midnight daily.
Average $25. **Credit** AmEx, V. **Map p278 C2**
The very first Indian restaurant to open in Moscow still
combines excellent value for money with good service. If
you are looking for beer and curry, this has got to be the
place. The seekh kebab is good, as are the rogan josh and
prawn masala. The dahl makhani (with black lentils) is one
of the best in the city and the mushrooms with peas wonderfully tasty. The only real problems are that the spicing
is mild unless you ask nicely, and the chicken served is
brown meat only.

Italian

Amarcord

Ulitsa Pokrovka 6 (923 0932). Metro Chistye Prudy.
Open noon-midnight daily. **Average** $32. **Credit**
AmEx, MC, DC, V. **Map p279 E3/F2**
An Italian restaurant whose greatest attraction is economy
rather than ambience. The business lunch at $12 is one of
the best-value offers in town, and parties of over five get a
five per cent discount after 9pm and at weekends to further
lighten the financial burden. Foodwise, good fresh pastas
are prepared daily and there's a wide range of antipasti,
too. You shouldn't leave without trying the Amarcord specialities – garish green and yellow pasta with mushroom
sauce and berry-stuffed blini.

Mario

*Klimashkina Ulitsa 17 (253 6505/fax 253 6398).
Metro Ulitsa 1905 Goda.* **Open** 1pm-midnight
daily. **Average** $85. **Credit** DC, MC, V. **Map
p278 A1**
Mario is without a doubt the best restaurant in Moscow –
real Italian food with the taste of sunshine. As at all the
good places in Moscow, the ingredients are flown in, but
at Mario they are attended to by two excellent Italian
chiefs – all the pasta and gnocchi are freshly made. For a
sampling of the extensive antipasti, go for the antipasto
misti, which includes carpaccio of salmon, tuna and beef
and frutti de mare that tastes as if it only emerged from
the Mediterranean half an hour beforehand. This is the
only place in the city to serve liver, cooked Venetian style
with onions and served with spinach and creamed potatoes. There are also lamb, veal, beef and rabbit dishes, but
best of all is the quail. To finish, go for the unbelievable
panna cotta or the tiramisu, accompanied by one of the
many grappas on offer.

Il Pomodoro

*Bolshoi Golovin Pereulok 5/2 (924 2931). Metro
Sukharevskaya or Tsvetnoi Bulvar.* **Open** noon-11pm
daily. **Average** $40. **Credit** AmEx, DC, MC, V. **Map
p278 D1**
Il Pomodoro is the closest Moscow comes to an Italian-style
trattoria, and a favourite with the young business set.
The food is consistently excellent. Any of the pasta
dishes is a good bet and the salads are fresh and generous.
Unfortunately, however, popularity has brought with it a
steep incline in prices.

Patio Pasta

*1-ya Tverskaya-Yamskaya Ulitsa, off Triumfalnaya
Ploshchad (251 5626). Metro Mayakovskaya.* **Open**
noon-midnight daily. **Average** $20. **Credit** JCB, MC, V.
Map p277 B2
Patio Pasta is the sister of the more widespread Patio Pizza
chain. It's a cool, Doric-columned room with a pleasant enough
atmosphere. The food is average; the main selling point is value
for money, especially at the salad bar, where $8 allows you as
many trips to the bar as you can stomach (provided the waitress doesn't whip your plate away when you're not looking).

San Carlo

*Ploshchad Pobedy 2/1 (148 7556/fax 148 6208). Metro
Kutuzovskaya.* **Open** noon-11pm daily. **Average** $55.
Credit V.
A high-quality Italian restaurant opposite the Kutuzovsky victory arch. It was originally opened by Jan Carlo, previously of
Dorian Gray (*see above*), and his high standards have been
maintained since his departure. For starters try the carpaccio
of salmon or beef or the shrimp cocktail with avocado. The
spaghetti vongole is absolutely wonderful and there's a full
selection of seafood, including a terrific brazino (a small bass)
in mushroom and tomato sauce.

Spago

*Bolshoi Zlatoustinsky Pereulok 1 (921 3797). Metro
Kitai-Gorod.* **Open** noon-midnight daily. **Average** $55.
Credit AmEx, DC, V. **Map p278 D3**
A small, cosy restaurant daubed in uplifting tones: solar yellow walls and bright blue ceiling. To further elevate your
mood, try the beef fillet with rucola salad and Parmesan or
the swordfish. The tiramisu is excellent. No relation, by the
way, to Wolfgang Puck's Spago.

Stelle del Pescatore

*Pushechnaya Ulitsa 7/5 (924 2058). Metro Kuznetsky
Most.* **Open** noon-12.30am daily. **Average** $100.
Credit AmEx, DC, MC, V. **Map p278 D2**
A cosy two-room restaurant with regulation wooden beams
and scattered with wrought iron pots and jugs. It serves a
wide selection of seafood, from sturgeon to swordfish to
salmon. Particularly unusual and tasty is the mussel and
baby octopus soup.

Mongolian

Tamerlan

*Ulitsa Prechistenka 30 (202 5649). Metro
Kropotkinskaya or Park Kultury.* **Open** noon-midnight,
lunch noon-2pm, daily. **Average** $65; lunch $12.
Credit MC, V. **Map p280 A5/B5**
At last, real Mongolian stir-fry arrives in Moscow in this
soothing, elegant restaurant that wouldn't be out of place in
Paris or New York. Invent your own dish from a selection
of meats, vegetables and herbs or follow the suggested
recipes. The chefs do the rest, slamming the ingredients
down on the giant circular hot plate and conjuring up your
meal in about a minute and a half. There's also a wonderfully piquant pickled salad and home-made bread to complement an unbeatable 'as much as you can eat' stir-fry deal.

Heil Ronald! Impeccable service at Moscow's **McDonald's.** *See page 89.* **Snack Attack**

Oriental

China Tang

Ulitsa Panfilova 18/2 (158 6338/fax 158 6088). Metro Sokol/tram 23 to Aviatsionny Institut. **Average** $40. **Open** noon-midnight daily. **Credit** MC, V.

Difficult to find (on a back road a longish walk from Sokol metro), China Tang is the best-kept secret in Moscow. Go through the courtyard and up the stairs to the second floor for easily the best Chinese food in Russia, if not the entire former Soviet Union. Entertainment is a Las Vegas-style floorshow, complete with girls in feather boas, strippers and a sword-swallowing woman. The spicy snake and the pork in peanuts are both delicious, but the pièce de résistance is 'flaming dragon fish' – a crispy skinned sea bass in a pool of sweet and sour sauce that arrives in a cloud of blue flames. Eat your fill and leave paying not more than $40.

Dinastiya

Zubovsky Bulvar 29 (246 5017/7071). Metro Park Kultury. **Open** 11.30am-10.30pm daily. **Average** $65. **Credit** AmEx, DC, MC, V. **Map p280 A5**

Make an entrance at **Praga.** *See page 81.*

More expensive than your average Chinese restaurant, but good spring rolls, a great selection of traditional Chinese soups (chicken, shark fins, crab, etc) and an interesting Peking-style pelmeni.

Dzhonka

Junk Boat, in MKhAT Theatre, Tverskoi Bulvar 22 (203 9420). Metro Pushkinskaya. **Open** noon-midnight daily. **Average** $25. **Credit** DC, JCB, MC, V. **Map p277 B2**

This dimly lit establishment with red lamps and a pool table looks a bit dilapidated but remains popular thanks to its central location and decent, reasonably priced Chinese food. Good value meals include the $38 Peking duck and the $19 carp with cucumbers and bamboo shoots in a sweet sauce. Dumplings taste more like Russian pelmeni than their Chinese counterparts, but the aubergine and cashew chicken are excellent. The Russian waitresses in satin dresses can be slow, but the biggest flaw is the floral plastic kitchenware.

Hong Kong

Bolshaya Sadovaya Ulitsa 1/5 (209 2456). Metro Mayakovskaya. **Open** noon until last customer leaves daily. **Average** $40. **Credit** MC, V. **Map p277 B1/B2**

A band of painters and decorators was shipped in from Hong Kong to ensure this place looked authentic. In the kitchen, the same principle applies: indigenous chefs prepare such favourites as Hong Kong duck, fried eel in garlic and those lovely Chinese black eggs (two for $5). Wash it all down with rice vodka.

Khram Luny

Temple of the Moon, Bolshoi Kislovsky Pereulok 1/12 (291 0401). Metro Arbatskaya. **Open** 1.30-11pm daily. **Average** $50. **No credit cards. Map p278 C3**

The perfect place for culinary adventures. To begin, go for marinated scorpion accompanied by a salad of Chinese wood mushrooms, followed by Chinese black eggs, which are cooked in sand, soil or sawdust over a period of a month. Another tasty entrée is snake soaked in Chinese vodka, with

Snack attack

Finding a quick snack in Moscow if you're sightseeing and on the hoof can be an extremely frustrating business. Unlike almost any other major city in the world you could wander for miles without finding anywhere offering a straightforward sandwich and a mineral water. In desperation, you may find yourself resorting to McDonald's (which has branches at the far end of Ulitsa Arbat, No.50/52, just off the Manezhnaya Ploshchad end of Tverskaya at Gazetny Pereulok 17/9 and right by Pushkinskaya at Bolshaya Bronnaya 29) or the Russian fast-food alternative Russkoye Bistro (branches at Varvarka 14 right by Kitai-Gorod Metro, on Tverskaya at Nos.19A and 23 and at Bolshoi Gnezhnikovsky Pereulok 10.) A half-decent submarine sandwich option is the chain Kombi, with branches at Tverskaya 4 at the Manezh Ploshchad end and at 1-ya Tverskaya-Yamskaya 2, by Triumfalnaya (Mayakovskaya) Ploshchad. In Moscow's snack-desert you may also be glad to find Dunkin' Donuts (together with Baskin Robbins) at Myasnitskaya 24/1, between Lubyanka and Chistye Prudy metros.

Johnny-Tolstyak

Johnny Fat Boy, Myasnitskaya Ulitsa 22 (923 4961). Metro Lubyanka. **Open** 8am-midnight daily. **Credit** DC, MC, V. **Map p278 D2, p279 E2.**
Offers ten varieties of pizza, chips with hot Mexican salsa and draft beer. The place is thoroughly decent and the staff approachable and friendly.

Manhattan

Ulitsa Rozhdestvenka 5/7 (921 2006). Metro Kuznetsky Most. **Open** 11am-11pm daily. **No credit cards. Map p278 D2**
A fairly decent salad bar and cheap food sold by weight; 100g (4oz) of any hot or cold dish costs the same – just under $3. Don't expect luxury.

Okhotny Ryad shopping mall

Manezhnaya Ploshchad. Metro Okhotny Ryad. **Open** 11am-10pm daily. **No credit cards. Map p278 C3**
Unsurprisingly, the snack centre in the lower level of the Okhotny Ryad complex serves up the kind of soulless, functional flavour of food that Westerners have come to expect from suburban shopping malls. But in Moscow it's a godsend. The centre comprises nine outlets: the French bakery Café de France; a Filippino joint called Laguna; a chicken-house called Rostik's; Zolotaya Ribka which offers Asian (for want of a better description) fare; Baskin Robbins; Pizza Solo Mio; Russkoye Bistro; a wonderful place entitled Stolovaya #14 (where 100g/4oz of any item on the menu costs only $2), and the Finnish fast-food joint, Carrols.

more vodka to flush the slithery little bugger down. However the speciality of the restaurant is 'Bull's Pride'. Yes, two gleaming broiled bull's testicles nicely garnished with greens and vegetables. A much better cure for male impotence than Viagra, or so they say in China.

Koreisky Dom

Korean House, Volgogradsky Prospekt 26 (270 9070/ 1300). Metro Volgogradsky Prospekt. **Open** 11am-midnight daily. **Average** $40. **Credit** JCB, MC, V.
This Korean restaurant is rather far from the city centre, but near enough to the metro to make it fairly easily accessible. European-style tables are separated by screens in the traditional Korean manner. Some of the more interesting items on the menu are *poulgogui* (finely cut beef marinated in special Korean sauce, roasted on a real fire) and fried bamboo with mushrooms or meat. There's also a small shop trading in Korean seasonings and souvenirs.

Lilly Wong

Hotel Intourist, Tverskaya Ulitsa 3/5 (956 8301/fax 956 8356). Metro Okhotny Ryad. **Open** noon-midnight daily. **Average** $60. **Credit** AmEx, MC, V **Map p278 C2**
The metal detector on the door gives the game away a bit. The Intourist remains a hooker and mafia stamping ground: this is their gourmet restaurant of choice. The service is mixed and the food overpriced, but it does the best Peking duck in Moscow and the rest of the menu is as good as a decent Chinese restaurant back home.

Pyat Spetsii

Five Spices, Pereulok Sivtsev Vrazhek 3/18, corner Gogolevsky Bulvar (203 1283). Metro Kropotkinskaya. **Open** noon until last customer leaves daily. **Average** $50. **Credit** AmEx, JCB, MC, V. **Map p280 A4/B4**
Five Spices is an Indian-run Chinese restaurant that leans towards the piquancy of the Sichuan style and favours thick spicy sauces. The portions are big (one main dish is almost enough for two) and tasty. The honey-glazed spare ribs are delicious and the king prawns in oyster sauce and the barbeque chicken in hot black bean sauce are both filling and succulent. The emphasis on gluttonous sauces and the hefty prices mean that this is the place to come to for a light snack.

Silla

Valery Bryusov Ship, Park Kultury, Krymskaya Naberezhnaya (956 6527). Metro Barrikadnaya. **Open** 10am until last customer leaves daily. **Average** $50. **Credit** AmEx, MC, V. **Map p280 B5/B6**
Opened in 1993, this was one of the first shots in the restaurant boom. It's located on a ship, moored near the Central House of Artists, and packed full of aquariums. Try the bamboo shoots or the pelmeni à la Korean, which are stuffed with beef, vegetables, noodles and soy cottage cheese. Other recommendations include the sweet and sour pork and the rib of beef.

Russian

Bochka

Barrel, Ulitsa 1905 Goda 2, opposite Mezhdunarodnaya Hotel (252 3041). Metro Ulitsa 1905 Goda. **Open** 24 hours daily. **Average** $45. **Credit** AmEx, MC, V.
The décor is a little overdone, all craggy rural bare brick and rough-hewn wooden beams, but the Russian cuisine with Caucasian overtones is simply superb. Try the excellent shashlik, served with a spicy sauce and a selection of vegetables, or the *golubtsy*, a blend of meat and rice wrapped up neatly in cabbage and served with *smetana* (sour cream). To finish, try the unbelievable *vareniki*, sweet pelmeni stuffed with cherries. The only turn-off here is the clientele, hideous New Russians with mobile phones glued to their ears.

Grilling up a storm at **Traktir Yolki Palki**: *fake cockerels, fake décor and the best affordable*

Khlestakov Traktir

3-ya Frunzenskaya Ulitsa 1 str 9 (257 2692). Metro Frunzenskaya. **Open** noon-midnight daily. **Average** $50. **Credit** AmEx, DC, JCB, MC, V.

A graceful stylisation of an eighteenth-century roadside tavern with hostesses in hoop skirts and canaries twittering in cages, Traktir is for those gourmets who are interested in Russian food beyond borsch and blini. Owned by Sergei Gazarov, director of the all-star Russian film *The Inspector General*, the eatery is trendy among the bohemian crowd. Its menu is humorously written and features dishes such as 'duck that didn't make it to the middle of the River Dneiper'. Another must-try is a beef loaf stuffed with liver and served with buckwheat. For drinks, order *medovukha*, a slightly alcoholic honey drink, or cranberry cider.

Kropotkinskaya 36

Ulitsa Prechistenka 36/21 (201 7500/203 8259/fax 200 3217). Metro Kropotkinskaya. **Open** noon-11pm daily. **Average** $55. **Credit** AmEx, DC, MC, V. **Map p280 A5/B5**

Opened back in the dark culinary days of 1987, this was the first private restaurant in the city. It consists of two floors: the ground floor, offering traditional Russian classics, and the basement, where there is a lighter, tavern-style approach. Start with caviar, then try mushrooms baked in sour cream followed by borsch with pirozhki. For the main course, there's veal in a pot, roast suckling pig or sturgeon and shrimp. One of the best places in town for real Russian food.

On Lomonosovsky

Lomonosovsky Prospekt 7/1 (132 0628/7563). Metro Profsoyuznaya. **Open** noon-midnight daily. **Average** $50. **Credit** MC, V.

Sports a fairly sumptuous interior, with everything adhering to the strict rules of high classicism, including furniture and tableware. A lot of the items on the menu must be ordered 24 hours before arrival, including suckling pig stuffed with chicken ($250) or sterlet on blocks of ice ($140). From the selection of simpler and faster food check out Russian jellied fish with sturgeon and the beef stroganoff. Fruit juice is free.

Razgulyai

Spartakovskaya Ulitsa 11 (267 7613). Metro Baumanskaya. **Open** noon-11.30pm daily. **Average** $50. **Credit** AmEx, DC, MC, V.

A restaurant consisting of three halls, one of which is decorated in the distinctive blue and white style of *Gzhel* ceramic folk art and another in the *khokhloma* red and gold style. The house speciality is Razgulyai beef, a fairly straightforward concoction of beef with potatoes and vegetables. Blini with red or black caviar are especially good. Drinks include traditional Russian tipples such as *kvas* and *medovukha*.

Rus

Ulitsa Arbat 12 (291 9626/241 9592). Metro Arbatskaya. **Open** noon-11pm daily. **Average** $42. **Credit** MC, V. **Map p280 A4/B4**

A spacious place with two halls, aquariums and a fireplace. Among the selection of cold cuts, the standouts include

Russian fare in town.

venison, a fish assortment with red and black caviar, and sturgeon, which comes in three varieties. Hot meals include *pokhlebka a la Suvorov*, a hotch-potch macaroni soup and *poltavskaya pokhlebka*, a variation on the same soup but containing galushki. Other fortifying liquids include *medovukha* or *klukovka*, a drink made from vodka and berries.

Samobranka

Marriott Grand Hotel, Tverskaya Ulitsa 26 (937 0000). Metro Pushkinskaya. **Open** 7am 11pm daily. **Average** $100. **Credit** AmEx, DC, MC, V. **Map p278 C2**
Offers a fine selection of Russian cuisine as well as more standard European fare such as onion soup, boiled salmon with mashed potatoes, chicken fillet in puff pastry and cutlets in mushroom sauce with mashed potatoes. The best items on the menu include the spring rolls and the pork chop. There's also a snack bar that charges an 'all you can eat' flat fee of $29.

Sidmoya Neba

Seventh Heaven, Ostankino TV tower, Ulitsa Akademika Koroleva 15 (282 2038). Metro VDNKh. **Open** 10am-11pm daily. **Average** $50. **Credit** AmEx, MC, V.
Located halfway up the gigantic Ostankino TV tower: you'll come here not for the fairly average Russian food but for the view. All the tables are positioned by windows, through which you'll see the whole of Moscow, laid out rather as it would be on a map. The restaurant revolves so you'll never get bored with the same view. Avoid on foggy days.

Traktir Yolki Palki

Ulitsa Bolshaya Dmitrovka 23 (200 0965). Metro Chakhovskaya. **Open** 11am 11pm daily. **Average** £16. **No credit cards. Map p278 C2**
Queues up to 20 minutes long can be the norm at Yolki Palki, which has carved out a niche as a dependable supplier of good, cheap Russian food. All restaurants in the chain offer a salad bar plus all the usual Russian fare. Farmyard décor and waiting staff kitted out in traditional gear complete the package. Fake cockerels teeter on fences, and the Tretyakovskaya branch on Klimentovsky has a live one squawking around its outdoor dining area. The name means 'Oh, My Goodness'. Quite.
Branches: Klimentovsky Pereulok 14 (953 9130); Ulitsa Bochkova 3A (215 2939); Ulitsa Bolshaya Gruzinskaya 50 (254 1604).

U Babushki

At Granny's, Ulitsa Bolshaya Ordynka 42 (230 2797). Metro Tretyakovskaya. **Open** noon 11pm daily. **Average** $60. **Credit** MC, V. **Map p281 D5**
For all those who crave home-made food, just like your granny used to make (or would have if she was Russian). U Babushki is small and consummately cosy (there are only five tables) and you'll instantly feel like you're on a visit to out-of-town relatives. Old photos abound, as do quietly ticking clocks, all of which combine to create an atmosphere tinged with intimacy and eeriness. Just as you might expect, the menu features home-made borscht, blini, *pirozhki* with mushrooms and pelmeni. Unlike a visit to your grandmother, however, this will cost you about $60 per person.

Selling your soul for caviar and blini at **Zamok Mephisto**. *See page 94.*

Tartar

Tatarstan

Sebastopol Hotel, Bolshaya Yushunskaya Ulitsa 1 (318 6600). Metro Kakhovskaya. **Open** noon-midnight daily. **Average** $30. **No credit cards.**

A restaurant devoted to the cuisine of the nomadic Mongol hordes who dominated Russia throughout the twelfth and thirteenth centuries. Tatar dishes are meaty – primarily beef and mutton, all prepared in a large dish. Try *tcheburek*, mashed potato wrapped in pastry, or *Tatar pelmeni*, which are smaller than regular Russian pelmeni and difficult to prepare, but extremely tasty.

Theme restaurants

The age of the *stolovaya*, the grubby cafeterias that existed in every public building in Soviet times, has now officially passed into history. These days, native and foreign diners alike are eagerly looking for ever-more funky and unconventional eating-out experiences. This has led to a boom in theme restaurants, where diners can not only find good food but also surrender themselves to the latest eccentric gimmick.

Beloye Solntse Pustyni

White Sun of the Desert, Neglinnaya Ulitsa 29/14 (209 7525/6015). Metro Tsvetnoi Bulvar. **Open** noon-midnight daily. **Average** $58. **No credit cards. Map p278 C2**

Based on the classic 1960s Soviet Western about a Red Army guard making his way home through Central Asia during the Russian Civil War, this restaurant features waitresses in Uzbek dresses and various scenes from the film mocked up around the place. The thing to order is a *dastarkhan*, or set dinner, which includes numerous visits

to a sumptuous salad bar, one Uzbek national dish (the best is the wonderful *langhman* soup), a plate of pilau and sorties to the dessert table.

Grand Opera

Hotel Budapest, Ulitsa Petrovskiye Linii 2/18 (923 9966/ 921 4044). Metro Kuznetsky Most. **Open** noon-midnight daily. **Average** $60 (not including show). **No credit cards. Map p278 C2**

This place is meant to recreate the ambience of Odessa in the 1920s but feels like a high-class speakeasy from a 1930s Hollywood movie. Visitors sit in ornate velvet boxes watching the legs of can-can dancers flicker up and down on stage while the big band toots its way through a nightly show starting at 8pm. The menu is an odd mix of Russian, Ukrainian, French and Jewish, reflecting the cuisine of old Odessa.

Raisky Dvor

Paradise Courtyard, Chistoprudny Bulvar 8 (928 0907). Metro Chistye Prudy. **Open** 11am-11pm daily. **Average** $60. **Credit** AmEx, DC, MC, V. **Map p279 E2**

A restaurant in the form of a caveat against the dangers of totalitarianism. The barnyard setting was inspired by George Orwell's *Animal Farm*, and features, on its walls, joyful, striding depictions of various four-legged characters from the book. Diners are treated to dishes with names like 'Pig's Squeal' and 'Horror of Humanity', which can be washed down from a drinks menu that has been dubbed 'Root Causes of the Revolution'.

Petrovich Club

Myasnitskaya Ulitsa 24/3 (923 0082). Metro Chistye Prudy. **Open** 1pm until last customer leaves daily. **Average** $30. **No credit cards. Map p278 D2/ p279 E2**

It had to happen – a Soviet-era theme restaurant. Vibrant retro tunes that most Russians know by heart provide the soundtrack, while authentic Soviet paraphernalia lines the walls. The menu is crammed with dishes named after old films, books, celebrities and communist slogans. Black caviar, for instance, goes by the (rather un-PC) name of 'Paul Robeson', the black American singer who was extremely popular in the Soviet Union.

Shinok

Ulitsa 1905 Goda 2 (255 0204). Metro Ulitsa 1905 Goda. **Open** 24 hours daily. **Average** $80. **Credit** AmEx, MC, V.

This is no ordinary restaurant; the place is decked out as a three-dimensional, nineteenth-century Russian pastoral scene, where a couple of chickens, a cockerel, a goat and a dog frolicking around you while you dine, to add to the 'authenticity'. There is also a real horse phlegmatically chewing away in a central courtyard, where a genuine *babushka* in traditional costume quietly sits knitting (God knows what they pay her, if anything). Try the *salo*, or salted fat, if you've got the stomach for it, or the dumplings with potatoes and mushrooms.

Eating & drinking by area

Tverskaya & around

Restaurants & Cafés Azteca p82; Delifrance p95; Donna Clara p95; Dzhonka p87; Fuji p80; Gambrinus p82; Le Gastronome p84; Hong-Kong p87; Kofeinya Aleksandriya p95; Konservatoriya p95; Lilly Wong p89; Monroe p95; Moscow Bombay p85; Patio Pasta p86; Pyat Spetsii p89; Samobranka p91; Soleil-Express p96; Starlite Diner p82; Talk of the Town II p86; Tandoor p86; TGI Fridays p83; Traktir Yolki Palki p91; TsDL p82; U Dyadi Gilyaya p82; U Lukomorya p95.
Pubs & Bars American Bar & Grill p100; BB King p100; Garazh p96; Mesto Vstrechi p97.

Teatralnaya, Manezhnaya Ploshchad & around

Restaurants & Cafés Arkadia p80; Beloye Solntse Chevignon p92; Grand Opera p92; Iberia p83; Konditerskaya p95; Manhattan p89; Maxim's p85; Il Pomodoro p86; Beloye Solntse Pustyni p92; San Carlo p86; Serebryanny Vek p81; Stelle del Pescatore p86.
Pubs & Bars Golodnaya Utka p100.

Kitai-Gorod

Restaurants & Cafés Elegance p83; Spago p86;
Pubs & Bars Armadillo p100.

Beyond Lubyanka

Restaurants & Cafés Amarcord p86; Coffee Bean p95; Johnny-Tolstyak p89; Maharaja p85; Nostalgie p85; Petrovich Club p92; Raisky Dvor p92; Tibet p94; Vinso Grand p85.
Pubs & Bars Papa John's p100; Chesterfield's p102; Country Bar p102; Rio p100; Whisky Bar Saigon p102.

Arbat & around

Restaurants & Cafés Le Chalet p84; Dinastiya p87; Khram Luny p87; Kropotkinskaya 36 p90; Praga p81; Rus p90; Tiflis p83.
Pubs & Bars Angara p98; Krizis Zhanra p96; Rosie O'Grady's p99; Shamrock Irish Bar p99; Sports Bar p100.

Zamoskvorechye

Restaurants & Cafés Dorian Gray p80; Silla p89; U Babushki p91.
Pubs & Bars Bedniye Lyudi p96; Canadian Moosehead Bar p102; Sally O'Brien's p99; Vermel p98.

Beyond the Garden Ring

North

Restaurants & Cafés Bulochnaya p95; Cah's p82; China Tang p86; Club T p84; From Dusk Till Dawn p84; Incognito p81; Kabanchik p83; Moosh p83; Navruz p95; Sidmoya Neka p01; Vegetarian Café p95;
Pubs & Bars California p100; Jack Rabbit Slim's p102.

West/North-west

Restaurants & Cafés Bochka p89; Mario p86; Planet Hollywood p82; Santa Fe p82; Shinok p93; Tsarskaya Okhota p82; Vitosha Nostalgia p94; Zamok Mephisto p94.
Pubs & Bars Baskerville p100; John Bull p98; Sixteen Tons p99; Taxman p97.

South-west

Restaurants & Cafés Aktyor p84; Guriya p83; Khlestakov Traktir p89; Ne Goryui! p83; Pirosmani p83; Tamerlan p86.
Pubs & Bars Bingo p99; Samba p100.

South

Restaurants & Cafés Amalteya p94; Darbar p85; On Lomonosovsky p90; Talk of the Town p86; Tatarstan p92.
Pubs & Bars Cactus Jack's p100; Pivnushka p99; Yama Bar p102.

South-east

Restaurants & Cafés Bakhor p95; Koreisky Dom p87; Sloboda p81.
Pubs & Bars American Bar & Grill p100; Horse & Hounds p98.

North-east

Restaurants & Cafés Razgulyai p90.

Zamok Mephisto

Mephisto's Castle, Shmitovsky Proyezd 10 (259 8113).
Metro Ulitsa 1905 Goda. **Open** noon-6am daily.
Average $40. **Credit** AmEx, V.

A restaurant disguised as a Gothic haunted house.
Vampires in tail-coats greet diners while a cook, looking like
a paler version of Alice Cooper, fries a hunk of meat on an
open fire underneath a bunch of skeletons dangling from
the ceiling. Quotations from Goethe's *Faust* are written on
the walls and an iguana stares at the diners from the mock
ruins of a castle. The founders of this subsoil hangout got
the idea after visiting the Dr Jekyll and Mr Hyde restaurant
in New York. Their creation, though, is far closer to Scooby
Doo than to Robert Louis Stevenson. The largely Russian-
flavoured menu contains items such as 'slightly spotty sea
perch' and 'dried meat from Mephisto's labs'. We suggest
sticking with the quail or the salmon.

Tibetan

Tibet

Ulitsa Pokrovka 19 (917 3985). Metro Chistye Prudy or
Kitai-Gorod. **Open** noon-midnight daily. **Average** $30.
Credit AmEx, DC, MC, V. **Map p279 E3/F2**

Set up by Tibetan refugees and decorated with pictures of
the Dalai Lama, Tibet is an oasis of calm in the high-octane
atmosphere of eating out in Moscow. Given the fact that
Tibet doesn't have much of a cuisine, the food is good, especially for the price. The menu is a mix of Chinese and Indian
styles, with highlights including the stir-fried pork. The
restaurant of choice for visiting vegetarians.

Turkish

Amalteya

Stremyanny Pereulok 28/1 (236 0256). Metro
Serpukhovskaya. **Open** 11am-midnight Tue-Sun.
Average $30. **Credit** MC, V.

Jiggling Russian belly dancers wobble in your face at
Moscow's most affordable Turkish restaurant. A vast array
of cheapo starters means you could go home full after the
first course. Don't. Save room for the crisply barbecued
shashlik and a deathly sweet baklava. Ask for Ziya, the
voluble Turkish manager, for a friendly and very attentive
welcome and make an evening trip for the Lebanese singer,
who – when she doesn't sing in English – has a voice worth
a thousand and one bad meals.

Vitosha Nostalgia

Khoroshevskoye Shosse 35/2 (195 4084/fax 195 4044).
Metro Polezhayevskaya. **Open** noon-midnight daily.
Average $55. **No credit cards**.

A great Turkish restaurant, which, from 9pm onwards,
features amazing belly dancers who will often dance on the
tables. Vitosha Nostalgia also plays host to various
musical acts, including a 20-piece orchestra fully outfitted
in scarlet uniforms. Ask the staff for a selection of starters,
which should include salads, yoghurts, beans and
aubergine – usually about two dishes for every diner. Make
sure that you get the Turkish bread that is actually made
on the premises. Then go for a selection of meats and
chicken with spices – it doesn't really matter which you
choose, as they're all good. Finish with baklava and
Turkish coffee.

Power-lunching

The eating habits of Russian leaders.

It is a little-known fact that throughout the October
Revolution, Lenin existed almost solely on English
canned meat donated by sympathetic overseas
socialists. So, for the subsequent 75 years of
Russian communism, Spam must shoulder a tiny
tin-sized portion of blame. When he wasn't storming the Winter Palace, however, Lenin liked to eat
regular Russian fare: soups and caviar (preferably
red). During a spell in internal exile he developed
a liking for Siberian pelmeni, stuffed with a special blend of three different kinds of meat. He was
also partial to a cut of ram now and again.

Stalin was much more of a gourmet. Feasting
with his henchmen could often go on for hours.
Unlike most of his countrymen, millions of
whom fell prey to the famine that resulted from
the Great Leader's forced collectivisation of
farmland, Stalin would regularly partake of
goose, quail and partridge. He also liked to
drink the most expensive brands of Cognac and
the finest Georgian wines and champagne. For
daily consumption, though, he often eschewed
the spicy cuisine of his homeland, Georgia, in
favour of good old borsch and shchi.

Khrushchev was famously backward when
it came to discerning eating. In the White
House, while dining with the US president,
he once tried to drink from the finger bowls,
the water in which had been coloured blue.
In China, when the Russian party was served
a local speciality called 'the dragon slaying the
tiger' in which the former was represented by a
snake and the latter by a roast cat Khrushchev
refused even to taste the dish, while his wife
simply burst into tears. He did, however, enjoy
his native Ukrainian cuisine, particularly
Ukrainian borsch with *galushki*.

Gorbachev was something of a culinary
ascetic, whose only vice was tea, English-style
with milk, which might explain why he
seemed to get along so well with Margaret
Thatcher. Yeltsin has a particularly strong
liking for potatoes, though he'll allegedly
eat anything as long as it's washed down
with copious quantities of vodka. Alcoholic
drinks for Mr Yeltsin should always be served
chilled and at an altitude of 30,000 feet en route
to Shannon Airport in Ireland.

Uzbek

Bakhor

Tovarishchesky Pereulok 12 (911 7181). Metro Marksistskaya or Taganskaya. **Open** noon until last customer leaves daily. **Average** $50. **Credit** MC, V. **Map p282 F5**

Decorations adorning Bakhor include an antique *dutar* (an Uzbek stringed instrument) that once belonged to some Uzbek noble, and a dagger donated by the president of Uzbekistan. Other embellishments include a mirror ceiling studded with shining stars and tablecloths splashed with the colours of the Uzbek flag: green and blue. Best on the menu is the Bakhor's speciality, 'Bouquet of Uzbekistan', a blend of tomatoes, peppers, aubergine, quince leaves, mutton, rice and spices. The pilau is good, too.

Navruz

Begovaya Ulitsa 36, corner Leningradsky Prospekt (945 0451). Metro Begovaya or Dinamo. **Open** noon-midnight daily. **Average** $40. **Credit** AmEx, MC, JCB, V.

Get ready for a feast of pilau: Tashkent pilau, made with mutton; Bukhara pilau, with chicken and served in layers; Fergana pilau, with a special kind of rice; and Samarkand pilau, made from mutton ribs. Before the meal, your hands will be washed with water poured from an eighteenth-century Uzbek jug.

Cafés

Bulochnaya

Renaissance Moscow Hotel, Olimpiisky Prospekt 18/1 (931 9000). Metro Prospekt Mira or Rizhskaya. **Open** 8am-9pm daily. **Credit** AmEx, DC, JCB, MC.

Expensive and stylish with friendly and efficient service. The coffee is great but unbelievably exorbitant at $4.50 a cup or $5.50 for a cappuccino. Also serves sandwiches, croissants, cakes, cookies, fruit and chocolate rolls.

Chevignon

Stoleshnikov Pereulok 14 (733 9205). Metro Okhotny Ryad. **Open** 24 hours daily. **Average** $30. **Credit** MC, V. **Map p278 C2**

A delightful but small French café that should be visited early in the morning while Moscow is still sleeping, just to sample a superlatively un-Russian breakfast of croissant con confiture.

Ooffce Bean

Ulitsa Pokrovka 18 (923 9793). Metro Chistye Prudy or Kitai-Gorod. **Open** 9am-8pm daily. **No credit cards. Map p279 E3/F2**

A real oasis: a little on the small side, but the coffee is delicious. The fact that there is a no smoking policy adds to its Frenchness and – considering its size and lack of air-conditioning – is probably a blessing in disguise. Coffee beans are also on sale at $3.50-$15 for 100g (4oz). Not cheap, but after a few months of bad supermarket coffee, expats gladly hand over their cash.

Delifrance

Triumfalnaya Ploshchad 4/31 (no phone). Metro Mayakovskaya. **Open** 9am-11pm daily. **No credit cards. Map p277 B1**

Decent French fast-food joint offering croissants, brioches with cheese, really good éclairs and sandwiches. You also get to share the toilets with Tverskaya prostitutes making themselves up on cold winter evenings. A new branch has recently opened on the Arbat.

Donna Clara

Malaya Bronnaya Ulitsa 21/13 (no phone). Metro Mayakovskaya. **Open** 10am-10pm daily. **No credit cards. Map p277 B2/B3**

A very friendly, relaxed place just a few yards away from Patriarshye Prudy. Lounge around at a bay-window table with a bottle of wine, any of the great selection of cakes and with the café cat sitting on your lap.

Kofeinya Aleksandriya

Tsvetnoi Bulvar 25, building 1 (299 7712). Metro Tsvetnoi Bulvar. **Open** 10am-11pm daily. **Credit** AmEx, JCB, MC, V. **Map p278 D1**

This moderately sized establishment is the best café and cake shop anywhere in the city. Everything is created with tender loving care right on the premises: cakes, pies, sherbets and terrific ice-cream. There are a dozen different kinds of coffee and many more varieties of tea. Our recommendation is 'Blend of Her Royal Highness', a combination of Darjeeling, Ceylon and Assam, which, they claim, was first prepared for Queen Victoria. A cut above your everyday PG-Tips.

Konditerskaya

Confectionery, Metropol Hotel, Teatralny Proyezd 1/4 (927 6066). Metro Teatralnaya, Okhotny Ryad or Ploshchad Revolutsii. **Open** noon-midnight daily. **Credit** AmEx, DC, MC, V. **Map p278 C3**

Tarts, flans, gateaux and puff pastry in an ultra-luxurious setting. Expensive.

Konservatoriya

Bolshaya Nikitskaya Ulitsa 13, in the Bolshoi Zal Conservatory (229 3833/0710). Metro Biblioteka Imeni Lenina. **Open** 11am-10pm daily. **No credit cards. Map p277 B3**

A simple, cheap and plain little place that is packed with students from the conservatory.

Monroe

Gallery Aktyor shopping mall, Tverskaya Ulitsa 16 (no phone). Metro Pushkinskaya or Tverskaya. **Open** noon-9pm daily. **No credit cards. Map p278 C2**

If you're weary from shopping in the mall and dying for a coffee and a cigarette, this is the place. Nice Black Forest gateau and fruit flans.

Soleil-Express

Sadovaya-Samotechnaya Ulitsa 24/27 (825 6474/725 6475). Metro Tsvetnoi Bulvar. **Open** 9am-10pm daily. **Credit** DC, JCB, MC, V. **Map p278 C1**

Nice place with a modest selection of desserts. Try the soleil express, a frambois gateau with grated nuts, raspberry, cream and delicate soufflé. After 9pm, all pastries go for a third of the original price.

U Lukomorya

Pushkinskaya Ploshchad (229 0003). Metro Pushkinskaya, Chekhovskaya or Tverskaya. **Open** 24 hours daily. **Credit** AmEx, MC, V. **Map p278 C2**

The handy location makes up for the fairly ordinary and pricey range of gateaux and flans.

Vegetarian Café

Yamskoye Polye Club, 3-ya Ulitsa Yamskogo Polya 14/16 (257 0490/1053). Metro Belorusskaya. **Open** noon-8pm daily. **No credit cards.**

Not a particularly wonderful place and miles out of the city centre, but if you're a vegetarian, you don't have that many options in Moscow. The salads are decent, as are vegetable soup, curry beans and soya meat steak. On the floor above is a New Age store, which sells all kinds of trinkets and esoteric literature.

Pubs & Bars

Pickle your fancy in the land that 12-step programmes avoid.

As the capital city of a country in which drinking is a religion, you might expect Moscow to have a raging bar scene. Yet, while the club scene really has taken off and evolved rapidly in the years since the collapse of the Soviet Union, the local bars have generally languished. Practically nothing at all has changed since the first wave of Western-style establishments opened over half a decade ago. The main problem is the lack of an indigenous bar culture, which perished as the country hauled itself from Tsarist-era dissolution towards a drab, functional and completely pub-free utopia. Of course, Russians are still serious drinkers; even Gorbachev's disastrous abstinence drive of the mid-1980s couldn't kill that. It's just that their dedication to the cause of alcohol is so complete that they are reluctant to waste time on such trivialities as ambience, tasteful décor, atmospheric music and comfy seats. Russians do most of their drinking at home or in the workplace. And when they do venture further, their preference is for places offering a more complete entertainment workout than the average pub has to offer.

Local businesses have not been helped by the large North American and European alcohol distributors, who have gained a near stranglehold on the market. The Irish are particular offenders and the Celtic 'Big Three' (Guinness, Kilkenny, Harp) are ubiquitous, with the Danish brand Tuborg also muscling in just about everywhere. In the Latin-flavoured establishments, you might make it as far as a Corona, Sol or Dos Equis but that's about it.

Rather than put any real effort into the design, most bar owners have simply opted to decorate their bars with marketing handouts, and the background music spectrum ranges from lowest-common-denominator techno to pop schlock such as *I Just Called to Say I Love You* and *The Lady in Red*. And to top it all, getting drunk in Moscow is likely to leave your wallet with a mighty hangover. In all but a small handful of Moscow bars, $6-$7 is the standard price for a half-litre (occasionally a full pint) of beer, while mixed drinks go for $7 and up. And don't expect the happy hours offered by many places to lessen the blow – 50 per cent off on a second drink is about the best you can hope for, and some bars even go as low as an insultingly trivial 5 or 10 per cent. Nevertheless, with many bars staying open well into the small hours

(usually 5 or 6am) and a few real gems hiding out there, it is possible to devote a thoroughly entertaining evening entirely to drink.

Leave the rental car behind, even if you're only having one. The drink driving limit is zero. It shouldn't be a hardship given the ease of flagging down a taxi at any hour of the day or night. Bars with live music typically charge $3-$8 for entry; on weekends, even some non-music bars adopt a cover charge in the same range. During the brief spring-summer season, impromptu beer gardens with plastic furniture pop up all over town, and many of the bars listed below have outdoor seating. Among the better bets are the Taganskaya branch of **American Bar & Grill**, **Chesterfield's** (both listed under **Prefab saloons**) and **California** (under **Meat markets**), with the latter two featuring barbecues.

Basement boozers

Bedniye Lyudi
Poor Folk, Chernigovsky Pereulok 6/11 (951 3342).
Metro Tretyakovskaya. **Open** 3pm-5am daily.
Admission $8.50 after 8.30pm Mon-Thur, Sun, after 8pm Fri, Sat; free before 8.30pm Sun-Thur, before 8pm Fri, Sat. **Credit** DC, JCB, MC, V.
Named after the Dostoyevsky novel, this was once the archetype for Moscow sub-culture cellar bars. But the crowds have fallen off thanks to its sullen doormen and inconsistent membership policy. Nevertheless, the atmosphere is cosy, and there are decent bands from time to time. At $3.50, the Irish coffee is one of the cheapest and most potent in town.

Garazh
Garage, Tverskaya Ulitsa 16/2, entrance on Pushkinskaya Ploshchad (209 1848). Metro Pushkinskaya. **Open** 24 hours daily. **Credit** MC, V. **Map p278 C2**
Superbly located new bar from the BB King team (*see below* **Prefab saloons**) that combines theme elements like giant stainless-steel monkey wrenches and furniture carved out of car and cycle chassis with a slightly yuppie-ish, but mostly laid-back, atmosphere. The draft beer selection is unusually extensive, the $4 Beavis and Butt-Head nachos are a cut above what you'd expect, and the smallish dance area attracts a lively student crowd at weekends. Claims to be members only, but with some haggling you ought to be able to weasel your way in without a card. English spoken.

Krizis Zhanra
Genre Crisis, Bolshoi Vlasyevsky Pereulok 4 (241 2940).
Metro Kropotkinskaya. **Open** 11am-11pm daily. **No credit cards. Map p280 A4**
This shadowy, atmospheric cellar bar has been packing in a student-heavy crowd for years now, and is perhaps the most unstuffy, laid-back place in the city. Daily live music (no cover charge) varies from jazz standards to alternative

rock; the background music (funk, hip hop, jazz) is great, too. Add to this cheap drinks, Czech beer on tap and good coffee. It's packed to bursting during live music hours (7-9.30pm), so afternoons and the hour just before closing tend to be the best times for a relaxing drink. Unfortunately, problems with the neighbours made it necessary to curtail the closing time.

Mesto Vstrechi

Meeting Point, Maly Gnezdnikovsky Pereulok 9/8 (229 2373). Metro Pushkinskaya. **Open** noon-5am daily. **Credit** AmEx, MC, V. **Map p278 C2**
The heavy wood and brick cellar interior is fairly typical, but the inexpensive, Russian-tinged bar food and Paulaner

beer on tap are big pluses. With music played at a reasonable volume and classic films being shown on the TVs near the two bars, your senses will definitely approve.

Taxman

Krymsky Val 6 (238 0864). Metro Oktyabrskoye Pole. **Open** noon-6am daily. **Admission** $4. **No credit cards. Map p280 B6**
Combining a tasteless, provincial-style interior that somehow manages to be quite endearing with fairly cheap drinks, this place often packs in an attractive mix of suburban students and bored representatives of the middle class looking for something more exciting out of life. The DJ is pretty crap, but the live acts are usually good.

The beer necessities

It may come as some surprise that Russia produces an extremely wide variety of beer – from lager to porter; from tasty to unpleasant. Prior to the reform era, beer (and *kvas, see page 98* **Old-school boozing**) was commonly dispensed from large metal cisterns directly on the street. The practice is now returning to a certain extent, with special beer kiosks reappearing throughout Moscow. The beer is unlabelled generic stuff and it's a bring-your-own-container job, but the price is always ridiculously low. Most Russian beers are not not pasteurised, so you'll frequently see a stamp somewhere on the label bearing the 'best-before' date. If you do have the misfortune to get a bottle that has gone bad, you'll probably be able to tell even without looking at the label – the taste of spoiled beer is easily distinguishable from even the bitterest Russian brew.

For boozers on a shoestring budget, the super-cheap Zhigulyovskoye, first brewed in Samara at the end of the nineteenth century and later synonymous with 'beer' in the Soviet Union, is also not a bad option. The brand has

been widely licensed, so the place of manufacture and recipe varies widely, as does the flavour. A still cheaper option is the bland, but inoffensive Ochakovskoye, which comes in budget-priced, two-litre bottles.

Baltika, the best Russian beer by far, is actually brewed in St Petersburg, but, as one of the few indigenous brews to appear in bars in keg form, is available all over Russia. There are nine types, each with individual sobriquets like Classic, Parnas and Porter, getting progressively stronger until you end up with No.9, which is rocket fuel and quite possibly a conspiracy to obliterate all sentient life forms. The first two are light, jovial, slightly anarchic little numbers, best drunk chilled. No.3 (ask for Troika) is the people's favourite, No.4 is its darker counterpart. No.5 is perhaps the best, but it comes in a smaller bottle, so penny-pinchers beware. No.6 and No.7 are the ones generally on tap in seedy billiard bars, while No.8 is something of a rarity. And, as already intimated, you don't need to drink much of No.9 to get drunk, which is just as well.

Old-school boozing

Although it seems at times as if Moscow has completely surrendered itself to Western-style drinks like tequila, whisky and rum, it is not yet too late to find a more traditional Russian drinking experience.

VODKA

Vodka (from the Russian for water, *voda*) is still the drink of choice for the majority of folk. As such, it's what you'll see people indulging in at home and on the street as well as in bars and restaurants. The range of brands (both domestic and foreign), packaging (everything from glass bottles to little plastic pouches) and flavours (infused with every herb, fruit or berry imaginable) is also extremely wide. Several of the better Russian brands (such as Stolichnaya Kristall) go down just as smoothly as expensive imports such as Absolut or Finlandia, but then again, there are certain occasions when you just need the unpleasant taste of Kubanskaya or even some still more dubious domestic brand.

SAMOGON

Samogon (the name means something like 'self-fire') is Russia's version of hooch or moonshine. In its raw state, it is simply home-brewed vodka made from the usual rye or barley malt, but, depending on what's available, potatoes, sugar beets or any potentially fermentable product might be used as the base. Not surprisingly, *samogon* tends to be most popular during government-enforced anti-alcohol campaigns, such as Gorbachev's ill-fated crusade of the late 1980s (at the time, people were even caught distilling jet fuel). The only chance you'll have to try raw, home-made *samogon* is if you are invited to the home or dacha of a Russian. Although the quality varies from superb to practically unpalatable, you won't want to miss out on this singular opportunity if you are privileged enough to be offered it.

Two particular types of *samogon* have managed to gain sufficient popularity to earn names of their own: *medovukha* and *khrenovukha* (flavoured with, respectively, honey and horseradish, from which their names are derived). Both have a thick consistency not unlike Greek ouzo and, as such, are less suited to consumption in mass quantities. *Khrenovukha* is an especially interesting concoction, combining a surprising degree of spiciness with an underlying flavour that can only be described as intense. These and other traditional beverages tend to be available at the various establishments specialising in old-style Russian cuisine, such as **Gvozdy** (Bolshaya Nikitskaya 19, Metro Arbatskaya; 290 3645).

KVAS

Kvas is a different kind of beverage altogether: a lightly carbonated, slightly alcoholic, tangy brew made from rye and barley malt, tasting something like a cross between beer and apple juice. It has been around in various forms for about 1,000 years, since the beginning of Russian civilisation. During Soviet times, *kvas* was dispensed primarily from large metal cisterns on the streets, but these days, an endless array of bottled brands is available at kiosks, shops and even at the innumerable Russkoye Bistro fast-food joints that dot central Moscow.

Vermel
Raushkaya Naberezhnaya 4 (959 3303). Metro Tretyakovskaya. **Open** noon-5am daily. **Admission** $5. **No credit cards. Map p281 D4**
An adult version of Krizis Zhanra (*see above*), managed by the same people. Despite its impressive location across the river from St Basil's and a good roster of live acts (usually on at 10pm) it's always been more boring than its younger cousin. Food is cheap and good, and the view as you leave is breathtaking.

The Brits

Horse & Hounds
Malaya Kommunisticheskaya Ulitsa 16/27 (912 6963). Metro Marksistskaya. **Open** noon-2am daily. **Credit** AmEx, MC, V. **Map p282 F4/F5**
This comfy British pub with pretty respectable food is popular with cigar smokers. The real attractions are the massive TV screens broadcasting live horse and dog racing via satellite and the on-site betting window.

John Bull
Kutuzovsky Prospekt 4 (243 5688). Metro Kievskaya. **Open** noon-1am Mon-Thur, Sun; noon-3am Fri, Sat. **Credit** AmEx, MC, V.
These franchised prefab 'British' pubs are all over central Moscow, but the Kievskaya location is generally the least bogus. Good beer selection and Chinese food from the take-away place next door.

Eurotrash

Angara
Ulitsa Novy Arbat 19 (203 6936/291 9079). Metro Arbatskaya. **Open** noon-2am Mon-Thur, Sun; noon-3am Fri, Sat; *restaurant* noon-midnight daily. **Credit** DC, MC, V. **Map p280 A4/B4**
This low-ceilinged German beer hall is lacking in atmosphere, but the agreeable and inexpensive house brew can make the trip worthwhile. A lame cover band has been known to stretch its rendition of *Hotel California* a long way

past the 10-minute barrier – a factor that has apparently helped this place evolve into a magnet (and a meat market) for the emerging Russian middle class. The downstairs lounge area is a good choice of venue for a quick drink if you're in the neighbourhood.

Pivnushka

Little Beer Place, Leninsky Prospekt 28 (952 5567). *Metro Leninsky Prospekt.* **Open** noon-11pm daily. **Credit** AmEx, MC, V.

Unusually for a Moscow bar, Pivnushka has actually had ample thought applied to its design. It is an exquisitely decorated, two-level German beer hall with a great selection of beers and delicious, imaginative Bavarian/ Austrian cuisine. The lower level has some huge round tables that can accommodate large groups; the upper overlooks it and makes for good people-watching.

Sixteen Tons

Ulitsa Presnensky Val 6 (253 5300). Metro Ulitsa 1905 Goda. **Open** noon-2am daily. **No credit cards.**

There's one extremely good reason to come here: the reasonably priced Belgian and home-brewed beer. With that consideration of quality beer in mind, it's just a shame that the atmosphere is a little too stuffy to do any serious drinking in and that the food is mediocre and overpriced. They've recently added a second level with live music (blues, folk, funk) at the weekends.

The Irish

Rosie O'Grady's

Ulitsa Znamenka 9/12 (203 9087). Metro Borovitskaya. **Open** noon-1am Mon-Thur, Sun; noon-5am Fri, Sat. **Credit** AmEx, DC, JCB, MC, V. **Map p280 B4**

The original Irish pub expatriate hangout. A management takeover by some gentlemen from the Caucasus (rumoured to be somewhat hostile) resulted in the removal of most of the Irish bar staff, which killed the atmosphere and drove off some of the foreigners – not always a bad thing. However, Rosie's is getting by on its old reputation. It's got a welcoming feel and they say they don't close until the last customer leaves. The décor, within the kitschy perimeters of the Irish pub genre, is impressive and the location just metres from the Kremlin doesn't hurt either. Live bands twice a week.

Sally O'Brien's

Ulitsa Bolshaya Polyanka 1 (330 0050). Metro Polyanka. **Open** noon until the last customer leaves. **No credit cards.** **Map p281 C5/C6**

Moscow's 'other' Irish pub has always been a bit more subdued than Rosie O'Grady's, but has picked up in recent months as its big sister falters. These days, it's probably the more vital of the two. The crowd of lawyers and accountants is split fairly evenly between Russians and foreigners, the music is better than average, but the food is mediocre.

Shamrock Irish Bar

Arbat Irish House, Ulitsa Novy Arbat 11 (291 7681). *Metro Arbatskaya.* **Open** 10.30am-midnight Mon-Thur, Sun; 10.30am-2am Fri, Sat. **No credit cards.** **Map p280 A4/B4**

Given the penchant of the Irish for shoe-horning formula pubs into the most cramped and unlikely places, this establishment in the Arbat Irish House supermarket could make a claim to being Moscow's most authentic Irish watering hole. Grim location aside, the first foreign pub to open in post-Perestroika Moscow has friendly staff and still manages to attract a respectable and often refreshingly lively crowd well into the microscopic hours of weekend nights.

Loosely Latin

Due perhaps to the large number of Soviet-era students from Latin America who have remained in Moscow and opened nightclubs, New Russians have fallen in love with Latin music and dancing. These days, mariachi bands in full black and red regalia are a common sight not just at Latin-style restaurants and bars, but at other establishments as well. Sometimes you even find them at such unlikely events as movie premières and fashion shows. **Azteca** (*see chapter* **Restaurants**) is probably one of the best Mexican restaurants in town, but there are also plenty of places where you can find a more active, full-on Latin experience.

Bingo

Izmailovskoye Shosse 71, Izmailovo Tourist Complex, Korpus Gamma, 2nd floor (166 3746). Metro Izmailovsky Park. **Open** noon-midnight Mon-Thur, Sun; noon-5am Fri, Sat. **Credit** MC, V.

This truly bizarre mish mash of Moscow flavours begins reasonably enough with a dancefloor that alternates between pop techno for the masses (which draws a crowd of under age rave kids) and Latin disco music (which draws a number of couples who look as if they've been mambo-ing since before they could walk). Things get weird at about 1am at weekends, when the music stops and everyone gets to play bingo (from which the place gets its name), with the prizes ranging from cellular phones to TVs. Then the music starts up again, until about 3 or 4am when the fenced-off centre area becomes the setting for an exotic-dance show that sometimes features a hideously flexible guy wearing a full-body costume that resembles two midgets joined at the head. Suffice it to say that this can be pretty disorienting after a full night of boozing. An all-round night of entertainment that includes just about everything except bowling, which you can nevertheless engage in elsewhere in the complex if you so desire.

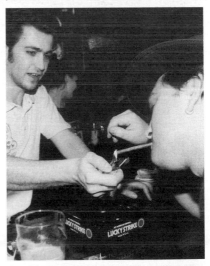

A traditional Irish fag break at **Rosie O'Grady's.**

Rio

*Taganskaya Ploshchad 86/1 (915 6031). Metro
Taganskaya.* **Open** noon-midnight Mon-Thur, Sun; noon-
6am Fri, Sat. **No credit cards. Map p282 F5**
The staff at this well-designed basement bar are all
highly trained in the art of Latin dancing and can ably lead
even the clumsiest customer in a spin around the floor. For
some unfortunate reason, Russians seem to like a strip show
to accompany their Latin dancing and it's no different here
– there are usually shows on weekend evenings, which 'add'
to the lively, party-time atmosphere. To make your trip
worthwhile, Rio also boasts some of the best Margaritas in
town, Cuban cuisine jam-packed with flavour, and one of
Moscow's only real happy hours (two for one on all drinks
from 5 to 7pm daily).

Samba

*Komsomolsky Prospekt 8 (246 0329). Metro
Park Kultury.* **Open** 7pm-5am Thur-Sun. **Map
p280 A6/B6**
One of the better medium-sized dance halls in town
featuring Latin music (when it's not playing techno). The
terrifyingly acrobatic regulars come from all over Moscow
to strut their stuff on the dancefloor, which makes for good
watching but can be somewhat intimidating if you're not a
pro yourself. Cheap drinks.

Meat markets

California

Leningradsky Prospekt 31/9 (212 7900). Metro Dinamo.
Open 10am-6am daily. **Credit** AmEx, MC, V.
Affectionately known as Cali's, this spacious bar/restaurant
housed in a former Imperial palace serves huge (1 litre) beers
and Margaritas, as well as terrific, inexpensive California-
style Mexican cuisine. Sadly, the music is the standard
Russian-style fizzy pop, and the alcohol content of the
Margaritas has been slowly dropping since the place opened.

Golodnaya Utka

*Hungry Duck, Pushechnaya Ulitsa 9/6 (923 6158).
Metro Kuznetsky Most.* **Open** noon-6am daily.
Admission $6-$12.50. **Credit** AmEx, MC, V. **Map
p278 D2**
Labelled the wildest bar in the East (or even the world)
by various Western media organs, this place is the
debauched stuff of Moscow legend. The Ladies' Nights on
Tuesday, Friday and Sunday give a whole new meaning
to the phrase 'meat market' (*see p146* **The horrors of
the Hungry Duck**). This is how it works: from 7 to 9pm
a women-only crowd is allowed to drink entirely free while
a mob of testosterone-charged males queues outside in
anticipation. Then at 9pm, when all the gals are nicely
bombed, the doors are thrown open to all. The purely
chemical reaction that follows is perhaps one of the most
bizarre and frightening sights in the whole of Russia. With
rampant bar-top dancing and a dangerously pumped
security force, this will be one of the first places to
disappear if liability insurance ever makes it to Moscow.

Papa John's

*Myasnitskaya Ulitsa 22 (755 9554). Metro
Turgenevskaya.* **Open** 6pm-6am daily. **Credit** MC, V.
Map p278 D2
This bar and grill, hidden away in the basement of
the Johnny Fat Boy pizza and burger joint packs in a
regular crowd of Russian teeny-boppers, African students
and expatriates of all stripes. It also attracts some of
the better live acts in town. Weekend specialities on the
dancefloor include wet T-shirt and banana-sucking con-
tests (specially laid on for gender studies students). Above-
average burgers, pizzas and other bar food are available
in the dining area.

Sports Bar

*Ulitsa Novy Arbat 10 (290 4311/4498). Metro
Arbatskaya.* **Open** noon-6am daily. **Credit** AmEx, DC,
JCB, MC, V. **Map p280 A4/B4**
Another bar that's been around since the beginning of
the reform era. Erratic management policies have led to it
falling in and out of favour more often than Yeltsin's
government. But it still packs a pretty good crowd
of novice foreigners as well as a bevy of junior thugs on
weekends. Despite the name, it's not the best place to go
looking for live TV sport.

Out of town

Baskerville

*Leningradskoye Shosse 55, Rechnoi Port Vokzal
(234 1790). Metro Rechnoi Vokzal.* **Open** noon-5am
daily. **Credit** MC, V.
Few Moscow bars are without at least one pool table, but
this place on the edge of town is one of the few comfortable
bars to specialise in billiards and offer a number of
professional-quality tables. The quasi-posh Russian food
is decent and the adjoining park makes for a nice stroll, but
it's a long way (about 30 minutes' drive) from the centre.

Prefab saloons

American Bar & Grill

*1-ya Tverskaya-Yamskaya Ulitsa 2/1 (251 7999). Metro
Mayakovskaya.* **Open** 24 hours daily. **Credit** AmEx, MC,
V. **Map p277 B2**
Cowboy-themed saloon that's packed with unadventurous
expats and Russian girls looking for foreign husbands.
The hearty food, including some good Tex-Mex breakfast
choices, makes it one of the better late-night joints in town.
The sister branch, which is much larger, with loads of
pool tables and more of a true New Russian atmosphere,
doesn't serve breakfast at all but the food tends to be
better. Its summertime patio grill is one of the best open-
air options in town.
Branch: *Ulitsa Zemlyanoi Val 59 (912 3615). Metro
Taganskaya.* **Open** noon-2am. **Credit** AmEx, MC, V.

Armadillo

Khrustalny Pereulok 1 (293 3553). Metro Kitai-Gorod.
Open 5pm-6am daily. **No credit cards. Map
p278 D3**
Enormous Tex-Mex bar with passable food, live music at
about 11pm on Fridays and Saturdays and a fabulous wealth
of pool tables. Popular with young adult Russians and some
youthful thuggish types who haven't yet ripped off enough
people to move on to more exclusive hangouts.

BB King

*Sadovaya-Samotechnaya Ulitsa 4/2 (299 8206). Metro
Tsvetnoi Bulvar.* **Open** noon-2am Mon-Thur, Sun; noon-
5am Fri, Sat. **Map p278 C1**
Good live music venue with friendly staff, a reasonably tasty
'soul food' menu and an undistinguished interior (*see
chapter* **Music: Rock, Roots & Jazz**).

Cactus Jack's

*Ulitsa Ordzhonikidze 13 (958 0866). Metro Leninsky
Prospekt.* **Open** noon-2am daily. **Credit** MC, V.
Wood-finish watering hole with picnic tables for furniture
that offers inexpensive beer, pizza and Tex-Mex free

*For that little bit of extra horsepower,
try the* **Sports Bar**.

darts. Decent music (if you like rock standards) and hearty atmosphere when there's a good-sized crowd. However, the location is a little out of the way and difficult to find, and the grey, depressing-looking building it's housed in does nothing to heighten the appeal.

Canadian Moosehead Bar

Ulitsa Bolshaya Polyanka 54 (230 7333). Metro Dobryninskaya. **Open** noon-5am daily. **Credit** AmEx, DC, MC, V. **Map p281 C5/C6**

There is nothing particularly Canadian about this place (there's often not even any Canadian beer), but the spacious, multi-room layout makes it a hit with expats and drab Russians. The happy hour on Wednesdays (6-8pm) is popular with foreign business types, but the burrito special is a much better reason to come that day. English-speaking live bands also gig here intermittently, playing rock, blues and country.

Chesterfield's

Ulitsa Zemlyanoi Val 26 (917 0150). Metro Kurskaya. **Open** 6pm-6am daily. **Admission** $6 after 8pm Tue-Sat. **Credit** MC, V. **Map p282 F4**

This red-brick wind-tunnel of a pub, created by the same guy who brought you the delightful Hungry Duck, has really caught on with the middle-class office-worker set. It boasts the longest bar in Moscow, they say. And a parade of unknown American blues and rock acts. Impoverished, munchies-suffering clubbers often come here for the all-you-can-eat $2 breakfast special that runs from 6 to 10am daily. On the minus side, the coffee is hideous, the service often poor and the food sometimes cold by the time it reaches you. The $6 cover charge at night entitles you to one free beer.

Country Bar

Ulitsa Pokrovka 50/2 (917 2882). Metro Chistye Prudy, Krasnye-Vorot or Kurskaya. **Open** 11am-midnight Mon-Wed, Sun; 11am-2am Thur-Sat. **Credit** AmEx, MC, V. **Map p279 E3/F2**

Conveniently located but nondescript place that features blues more often than true country. It recently added a strip show at weekends, lowering the tone. The real reason to go is for the cheap Ethiopian food on Sunday afternoons.

Jack Rabbit Slim's

Volokolamskoye Shosse 1 (158 8794). Metro Sokol. **Open** noon-5am daily. **No credit cards**.

About the only thing this cavernous saloon-type place has in common with the twist scene in *Pulp Fiction* is its name. On the other hand, it is probably the least pretentious of the Tarantino-derived bars in town. It has a regular crowd of not-terribly-hip emerging middle-class types and is occasionally visited by the many expats who live in the neighbourhood.

Whisky Bar Saigon

Sukharevskaya Ploshchad 16/18 (208 4638). Metro Sukharevskaya. **Open** 11am-midnight daily. **No credit cards**. **Map p278 D1**

A would-be post-Soviet kitsch theme bar from the same people as Armadillo (*see above*), but which falls a good measure short of wry or clever. The food is pretty bland, but the whisky selection is good (for Moscow). It seems destined to become popular with young Russian graduates who have just got their first real jobs. Watch out for the pricetags still dangling from their clothes.

Yama Bar

Ulitsa Novaya Bashilovka 11 (no phone). Metro Savyolovskaya. **Open** 10.30pm until last customer leaves daily. **No credit cards**.

A genuine biker bar located a few minutes beyond the city centre, complete with Confederate flags, fat biker chicks and the grimy-faced bearded guys who love them, and an imposing row of hogs on the pavement at the front. The bikers seem rather less threatening than their American counterparts: it's really quite a relaxing setting in which to enjoy a very cheap ($2) Czech or Russian beer.

Who said Canadians were boring? Shed your prejudices at the **Canadian Moosehead Bar.**

Shopping & Services

How to buy into Moscow's fledgling shopping scene.

Spiralling consumerism: the **Okhotny Ryad** *shopping centre. See page 105.*

When people marvel at the radical changes that have ripped through Moscow over the last decade, all their effusive awe, wide eyed bewilderment and woolly theorising can usually be broken down into one constituent element: shops.

Rampant consumerism in the capital is perhaps the most conspicuous result of the Russian revolution of the early 1990s. Lining Tverskaya Ulitsa there are now rows of stylish, often wildly expensive establishments, presided over by icy assistants who can count the dollars in your wallet with a single disparaging glance. Buried deep beneath Manezhnaya Ploshchad, right under the spot where tanks would once await their entrance to Red Square, there's the unwieldy **Okhotny Ryad** underground mall, the most high-profile property development of the post-Soviet period. Every underpass is infested with kiosks selling everything from

bootleg CDs to designer underwear to biscuits to French perfume. In all big malls, branches of multi-nationals such as Reebok, Benetton and Christian Dior proliferate. The mythical empty shelves and long, sullen queues of communism have largely disappeared. Dirty capitalism is now the defining spirit of the age.

Even though contemporary Moscow is a consumer paradise in comparison to what it once was – or to the rest of Russia – it's still a long way from being a fully developed, user-friendly consumer society. If you choose to shop *à la Russe*, you may have to contend with the remnants of the old system: surly clerks, jumbled opening hours and store layouts that make browsing almost impossible. Russian stores often have next to nothing in the windows and are regularly given imaginative, minimalist names such as House of Books, House of Toys,

All very natural at **Sadko Arkade**. *See p106.*

Shoes, Bedroom Furniture or Women's Clothes. The merchandise is often kept in glass cases or behind counters, so you have to squint and/or perform contortions to see the items or read the labels before asking to see something.

If you do find something you want to purchase, you will have to contend with one of the ogres of Russian shopping: the dreaded *kassa* system. This involves making a mental note of the price of your chosen item and the department where it is located, proceeding to the *kassa* (or cash desk), turning over all the information to the cashier, paying, obtaining a receipt and returning to the original department to claim your purchase. Make a mistake anywhere along the chain and you may have to start again. Need a shopping bag? You should have said so when you paid – back to the *kassa* to pay and get another receipt. For those without Russian language skills (though friendly sales staff will often help you along by writing out the prices and department numbers), the *kassa* experience can range from being a time-consuming pain in the neck to a hugely confusing nightmare.

If you want to shop Western-style, the challenges are of an altogether different nature: intimidating designer salons, bodyguarded shoppers, and, worst of all, extortionate prices. Pop along to the turn-of-the-century **Petrovsky Passazh** and you'll find Nina Ricci silk scarves for $195 and in Stephane Kélian, the most expensive shop in Moscow, a pair of red sling-backs for $500. A container of 20 Californian strawberries has been sighted in one city centre supermarket for $20. Tacky 20p Christmas cards at the **Sadko Arkade** have been known to go for $3. Ordinary shoe polish from a couple of Tverskaya establishments can set you back $10.

Even when money is no object, there's no guarantee you'll get what you want. Stocks are always scant, and while a shop may have the desired item, odds are it won't be in the right size or colour. People are generally not joking when they say that they *simply don't shop* in Moscow. For designerwear, fashion-conscious Russian kids go to Prague or Budapest, where everything is cheaper and more plentiful, and expats stock up on the likes of pesto sauce and underwear on visits home. That said, shopping in Moscow isn't all drudgery. Though overpriced, some of the mid-range places like Naf-Naf or Chevignon now offer decent casualwear, and supermarkets have revolutionised the lives of many foreigners here. Window-shopping in the more expensive joints – Tiffanys in Okhotny Ryad, for example – can be a lot of fun. If at any time you feel at all frustrated, plonk yourself down on the comfy couch of some swanky establishment, gaze at the overloaded shelves and think of what it must have been like in the bad old days.

SHOPPING STREETS

Wide, functional and hugely unattractive, Novy Arbat (Metro Arbatskaya or Smolenskaya) is lined with stores such as **Melodiya, Ecco, Mothercare, Moskovsky Dom Knigi**, Benetton and Kookai. These are interspersed with restaurants, cafés and Russian shops. Moscow's Irish community holds its St Patrick's Day parade here. Between Novy Arbat and Smolenskaya, the Arbat has been a pedestrian street since the Perestroika period of the late 1980s. It is one of Moscow's most historic and atmospheric streets; unfortunately, it's filled with grotty places to eat and stalls selling tacky souvenirs. Right in the centre of new consumer Moscow is Tverskaya Ulitsa, lined all the way from Belorusskaya station to Red Square with expensive hotels and shops. But despite the **Palace Hotel, Davidoff**, a **Jacques Dessange** hair salon and some designer shops, it's still sparsely populated and doesn't quite pass muster as a fancy shopping street. More pleasant and cosmopolitan is Ulitsa Kuznetsky Most (Metro Kuznetsky Most), which was a favoured haunt of writers and poets in the nineteenth century. Shops here tend to cater for New Russians and include Versace and Louvre.

One-stop shops

Malls & shopping centres

Frantsuzskiye Galerei

French Galleries, Vetoshny Pereulok 9 (no central phone). Metro Ploshchad Revolutsii. **Open** 10am-9pm daily. **Credit** varies. **Map p278 D3**

A relatively new shopping complex with a glass-ceilinged central atrium and polished floors, which, despite its name, comprises mostly pricey Italian shops. The café, located in the middle of a red, white and blue Eiffel Tower, serves delicious cakes.

Galleria Aktyor

Ulitsa Tverskaya 16 (935 7796). Metro Tverskaya, Pushkinskaya or Chekhovskaya. **Open** 10am-9pm daily. **Credit** varies. **Map p278 C2**

Hidden inside a building at the corner of Ulitsa Tverskaya and Strasnoi Bulvar at Pushkinskaya Square, the Galleria Aktyor is easy to pass by, since it's quite discreet. Its interior of black marble and chrome with a central waterfall gives the impression of a minimalist art deco interior in New York. The shops are the expensive kind with the odd exception, such as Naf Naf and Levi's. The complex is often deserted bar a few New Russian women on their daily shopping spree and the beefy security guys, who watch customers with a supercilious air.

GUM

Gosudarstvenny Univer Mag, Krasnaya Ploshchad (Red Square) 3 (929 3211/921 3171). Metro Okhotny Ryad or Ploshchad Revolutsii. **Open** 8.30am-8.30pm Mon-Sat, 11am-7pm Sun. **Credit** varies. **Map p278 D3**

Standing in Red Square can take your breath away. Going into GUM (State Department Store, as it became after the 1917 Revolution) will restore it. On the micro-level, it's big, busy and ordinary. But stand still and listen to the chirping birds and you can take in a long view of the spectacular glass ceilings, the railings and the central fountain. Built a century ago to replace old trader booths, GUM stands on one side of the square, opposite Lenin's Mausoleum. The first of its three floors is filled with Levi's, Clinique, Estée Lauder, Benetton, Nike, Galeries Lafayette and other foreign shops. The Lego store window displays are amazing – the constructions on display include a miniature St Basil's. There's also a good stationery shop, a wide selection of fur hats, a small hardware shop, several Russian snack bars and some foreign cafés.

Okhotny Ryad

Manezhnaya Ploshchad (737 8409). Metro Okhotny Ryad. **Open** 10am-10pm daily. **Credit** varies. **Map p278 C3**

This showy $350-million pet project of Moscow's ambitious Mayor Yuri Luzhkov, near the Kremlin, opened just before Moscow's 850th anniversary in September 1997. It looks like a tarted-up suburban shopping mall, with lots of columns, gold, brass and stained glass. But it's warm in winter, and over three storeys you can find furs, Cuban cigars, even a food court and familiar brands: Sisley, Benetton, Waterford, Geiger,

*Stand out from the crowd – a wild horde of matrioshki at **GUM**.*

*Do you have this one in pink? Choosing cosmetics in **TsUM**.*

Estée Lauder, Speedo and Guess. There's a theatrical shop, a fancy lingerie shop and a wildly expensive children's designer clothes store. Prices are not too bad, but there are still more people hanging out than handing over cash. The glass elevators are hugely popular, providing views of a central fountain and a stained-glass sun roof. And don't miss Novy Russky Mir (New Russian World; 737 8534). At first glance, the goods appear to be run-of-the-mill souvenirs, but the lacquer boxes have pictures of Jeeps or naked men in banyas with their mobile phones, and the wooden spoons carry the Versace logo.

Olympic Plaza

Prospekt Mira 33/1 (no central phone). Metro Prospekt Mira. **Open** 10am-9pm Mon-Fri, 10am-8pm Sat-Sun. **Credit** varies. **Map p278 D1**
Within the tinted-glass walls of this recently opened shopping complex shoppers will find mid-price establishments such as Glenfield, Disegni and Tom Klaim. An elaborate, test-tubular fountain in the middle of the staircase unites the three floors. The atmosphere is sleepy and the security men too numerous, but it's a good place to shop for cosmetics.

Petrovsky Passazh

Ulitsa Petrovka 10 (928 5047). Metro Okhotny Ryad or Kuznetsky Most. **Open** 10am-8pm Mon-Sat; 11am-6pm Sun. **Credit** varies. **Map p278 C2**
A quiet, upmarket arcade, which opened in 1903 and was recently restored by Turkish contractors. You'll find Kenzo, Cartier, and Godiva chocolates here; there's even a copy shop and the odd weird item, like a suit of armour for $6,000.

Sadko Arkade

Expocenter, Krasnogvardeisky Proyezd 1A (253 9592). Metro Ulitsa 1905 Goda. **Open** 10am-10pm daily. **Credit** AmEx, DC, JCB, MC, V.
A good 20-minute walk from the nearest metro stop, this fancy shopping mall is clearly not designed for the public transport crowd. Its motto is 'Moscow's first choice', but on many days you can hear your footsteps echo as you walk along the outdoor plaza (where, like so many places in Moscow, the tiles

are crumbling and the sidewalk cracking). The shops – and shoppers – are chic and fashionable. The prices are high: a $370 doll's bed, flip-flops for $42, strappy, heeled sandals for $320. At the cafés, you can find black-clad mobsters with crewcuts and bulging muscles smoking imported cigarettes and talking on mobile phones.

Department stores

British Home Stores (Bhs)

Ulitsa Novy Arbat 15 (202 3575). Metro Arbatskaya. **Open** 10am-9pm Mon-Sat; 10am-8pm Sun. **Credit** AmEx, DC, JCB, MC, V. **Map p277 A3/B3**
This two-storey branch of the British chain offers everything from children's clothing to household goods. Prices are higher than they would be in a Russian store, but if you don't speak Russian it's easier to buy your basics here.

TsUM

Ulitsa Petrovka 2 (292 1157). Metro Teatralnaya. **Open** 9am-8pm Mon-Sat; 10am-6pm Sun. **Credit** MC, V. **Map p278 C2**
At first glance TsUM just looks like another huge, ugly building, but it is considered by many – local experts even – to be a masterpiece of modernist architecture. Inside it's quite like a Western department store with many small sections over five floors selling clothing, cosmetics, wigs, coats, TVs, crockery, photographic equipment and underwear.

Markets

The Russian *rynok*, or market, is grass-roots capitalism in its purest form. Typically comprising a shabby collection of outdoor stalls that offer little protection from the elements, the *rynok* is where most Russians do their shopping. The most common *rynoks* sell fruit, vegetables, fish and meat, but there are also *rynoks* specialising in electronic and computer equipment, stationery, clothing, plumbing supplies, tobacco, pets and traditional Russian crafts. Some are seasonal: little glove and scarf markets sprout like mushrooms in the autumn and vanish within a month. *Rynoks* are popular for one very good reason: they're cheap. They can also be the most pleasant, interesting places to shop in Russia. What sets the *rynok* apart from most Russian shopping experiences is that people actually want to sell you something. Far from ignoring you, as many store clerks do, they'll holler at you as you stroll by and even smile if you appear likely to buy. If you have a common language, you're guaranteed a chat – unless it's too busy, as is invariably the case. Which brings us to the downside of rynoks: you're competing with some of the sharpest elbows – and tongues – in the known universe. A few other warnings: don't buy meat; it's not worth the risk. Ditto vodka or other hard liquor; the bottle may look legit, but chances are it's bootleg and possibly poisonous. If you buy fruit or vegetables, be sure to scrub or, better, peel them. If you buy any manufactured product, be aware that it's likely to be 'grey' market material at best, counterfeit at worst. If you buy CDs or videotapes, you can bet they're bootleg. And one last tip: watch your wallet.

Electronics

Bagrationovsky Rynok *Metro Bagrationovskaya.*
Open 9am-5pm Sat, Sun.
Located at the back of a food market is this rather chaotic electronics market, which is basically just a bunch of articulated lorries packed full of tellies and stereos. Prices are well below what you would find in regular shops, with occasional astonishing bargains. If you're having trouble finding it trace back to its origins the trail of people carrying 32in televisions. A much bigger electronics market is located at Mitino on Pyatnitskaya Shosse, but until the new Mitinskaya metro station opens the bus journey is prohibitively long.

Food

Cheremushkinsky Rynok *Lomonosovsky Prospekt 1/64 (134 0519). Metro Profsoyuznaya or Universitet.*
Open 7am-7pm daily.
This indoor-outdoor market, named after a flowering tree, is Moscow's best for fruit, vegetables, fish and meat from the former Soviet Union and beyond, as well as some neat Soviet-era signs in the indoor section. The sight of whole goat and lamb carcasses being hacked apart in the meat section might turn the most hardened carnivore into a vegetarian, but at least you're in the right place to begin your life as a herbivore.

Other big food *rynoks* (usually open 7/8am-6/7pm daily):
Danilovsky Mytnaya Ulitsa 74 (954 2602). Metro Tulskaya Leningradsky. **Aeroport Rynok** Chasovaya Ulitsa 11 (151 7871). Metro Aeroport. **Dorogomilovsky** Ulitsa Mozhaisky Val 10 (249 1331). Metro Kievskaya.

Pets

Ptichy Rynok *Bolshaya Kalitnikovskaya Ulitsa 42A (270 5010). Metro Marksistskaya, then bus N51 or trolleybus N16 or 63.* **Open** 9am-4pm daily.
In the days of Soviet price controls there were few private markets, but because breeding and selling pets did not constitute direct exploitation of people, this was an exception. Moscow's Ptichy market has been open since the 1930s. Many Muscovites hold it dear, and it's fun to wander through even if you're not buying. There are more animals at weekends.

Souvenirs

Izmailovsky Vernisazh *Izmailovsky Park (166 7875). Metro Izmailovsky Park.* **Open** 10am-5pm daily.
The vast outdoor market known as Izmailovsky is one of the wellsprings of post Soviet Russian capitalism. Once a small, outpost of Soviet entrepreneurs and artisans, it has become an bazaar where you can find everything from kitschy *matrioshka* dolls to truly beautiful linens and crafts. There are also Soviet military uniforms, posters, cameras, fur hats, wool sweaters, slippers, CDs, Christmas ornaments, toys, lacquerware, rugs, ceramics, books... you get the picture. Vendors are friendly, and many speak English. It can get crowded in summer and just before Christmas. Some people hate it, but everyone should go once. From the metro, follow the crowds past the Izmailovo Tourist Complex and the 'unofficial' market that's sprung up outside the gates. There's a 50¢ entry fee.

They certainly know how to pull in the crowds at **Cheremushkinsky Rynok.**

Children

There are small Russian children's shops all over Moscow, but **Detsky Mir** and **Dom Igrushki** are landmarks worth visiting. For children's books, check out **Anglia** and the **American Bookstore** (*see below* **Leisure & sport: Books**). Credit cards aren't widely accepted, so keep cash on hand.

Daniel
Kutuzovsky Prospekt 9 (243 2061). Metro Kievskaya. **Open** 11am-9pm daily. **Credit** AmEx, DC, JCB, MC, V.
Kids' shoes from the likes of Moschino for $75-$150. Very stylish boots with fake leopard fur or distressed leather, sandals in bright colours, and proper European lace-ups.

Detsky Mir
Children's World, Teatralny Proyezd 5 (927 2007). Metro Lubyanka. **Open** 9am-8pm Mon-Sat. **No credit cards. Map p278 C3/D3**
The largest toy shop in Russia, this behemoth near the former KGB headquarters is worth a visit. Like GUM, it's more of a mall than a single store, and, unfortunately, much of its space has been given over to unchildish ventures like women's clothing and household goods. It's still the best place in Moscow to find mass-produced Russian toys, which have the virtue of being extremely cheap, and the vice of frequently breaking. (Russians joke that this is intentional, to prepare Soviet children for the world of shabby consumer goods.) There are also plenty of imported toys, most notably on the ground-floor.

Dom Igrushki
House of Toys, Bolshaya Yakimanka Ulitsa 26 (238 0096). Metro Polyanka. **Open** 9am-8pm Mon-Sat. **No credit cards. Map p281 C5/C6**
Another hangover from Soviet times, Dom Igrushki is a one-floor version of Detsky Mir. It's usually not as crowded, often more manageable and always offers a wide variety of infant accessories and affordable toys.

Mothercare
Ulitsa Novy Arbat 15 (202 3575). Metro Arbatskaya. **Open** 10am-9pm Mon-Sat; 10am-8pm Sun. **Credit** AmEx, DC, JCB, MC, V. **Map p277 A3/B3**
A UK chain located within **Bhs** (*see above* **One-stop shops: Department stores**) with maternity wear, pushchairs, and lots of clothes for babies and children. Expect to pay quite a bit more than you would at the same shop in the UK.

Fashion

Where once a new style meant only different buttons on the same frumpy designs, now Moscow has the full range of clothes. Cheap and cheaply made clothes are sold at lots of neighbourhood *rynoks* and old-style shops; haute couture and labels abound; the mid-range is much harder to find.

Kuznetsky Most has Valentino, Fendi, Guerlain, Versace and Christian Lacroix boutiques, all within a short stroll from **TsUM**. At Kutuzovsky Prospekt 31, between the Ukraine Hotel and Pobedy Park, there is **Torgovy Dom Moskva**, which, despite its pedestrian name meaning Moscow Trade House, is a mini-mall for Chanel, Gucci and Dior.

Costume hire

Teatralny Salon
Bolshoi Afanasyevsky Pereulok 41 (203 1861). Metro Arbatskaya. **Open** 11am-8pm daily. **Credit** MC, V. **Map p280 B4**
A treasure trove for a whole range of outlandish customers: from actors looking for makeup to wild teenagers in search of a neon green wig. Also hats in different styles, dresses for hire and cool bags.

God, she is so embarrassing. Fun for all the family at **Detsky Mir.**

Laundry/dry-cleaning

Both places listed here have branches throughout the city and provide both dry-cleaning and laundry services.

Diana

Kutuzovsky Prospekt 22 (243 4280). Metro Kutuzovskaya. **Open** 10am-8pm Mon-Sat; 11am-5pm Sun. **Credit** MC, V.

California Cleaners

Maly Gnezdnikovsky Pereulok 12 (497 0011). Metro Pushkinshaya. **Open** 11am-8pm Mon-Fri; 11am-6pm Sun. **No credit cards. Map p277 B2, P278 C2**

Russian designers

Valentin Yudashkin

Kutuzovsky Prospekt 19 (785 1055). Metro Kutuzovskaya. **Open** 11am-8pm Mon Sat; 11am-6pm Sun. **Credit** MC, V. Yudashkin's clothes are sophisticated and sober; his vast shop is opulent and cool. Customers, of the chauffeur-driven cadre, can pick over dresses and skirts in luxurious fabrics and own-design jeans and leatherwear.

Vyacheslav Zaitsev

Zaitsev's House of Fashion, Prospekt Mira 21 (971 1122). Metro Prospekt Mira. **Open** 10am-7pm Mon-Sat. **No credit cards. Map p278 D1**
Zaitsev's, in a remote location on Prospekt Mira, has a surprisingly Soviet interior, giving the two halls the feeling of a museum or hotel restaurant. His collection consists of suits à la Coco Chanel in pastel colours, hats and bags

Second-hand

Dubl 3

Yasnogorskaya Ulitsa 13/1 (426 9811). Metro Yasenevo. **Open** 11am-8pm Mon Sat; 11am-7pm Sun. **No credit cards.**
This regular second-hand shop on the outskirts of town sells jeans, jackets, military clothes and bags

Second Hand

Ulitsa Kievskaya 20 (249 2934). Metro Studencheskaya. **Open** 10am-1pm, 2-8pm, Mon-Sat; 10am-1pm, 2-6pm, Sun. **No credit cards.**
This small, homely second-hand shop, which shares its premises with a 24-hour grocery store, is a good place to find bargains. Clothes are of varying degrees of quality, but if you rummage, there is cool stuff to be had.

Vtoroye Dykhanie

Second Breath, Ulitsa Pyatnitskaya 2 (951 3161). Metro Tretyakovskaya. **Open** 11am-8pm Mon-Fri; noon-8pm Sat. **No credit cards. Map p281 D5**
This small shop with an all-pink interior specialises in used haute couture clothes. Labels include Kenzo, Boss, Chanel and Escada. It's not a place for bargains, but if you are looking for something special, it's worth a visit.

Streetwear

Bulldog

Ulitsa Novy Arbat 22 (291 8750). Metro Arbatskaya. **Open** 10am-8pm daily. **No credit cards. Map p277 A3/B3**
A bit of a hangout for technokids, this shop offers Doc Martens and platform shoes. The choice of clothes is poor and if you aren't comfortable with darkness and loud music, it's probably not the place for you.
Branch: Okhotny Ryad, Manezhnaya Ploshchad (737 8409).

Cozmo

Smolenskaya Ulitsa 23/25 (241 1158). Metro Smolenskaya. **Open** noon-8pm Mon-Sat; noon-6pm Sun. **No credit cards. Map p280 A4**
One of the city's most extensive collections of clubwear. Inside it's more like a Soviet bank than a mecca for the avant garde, but the clothes could easily make a Londoner feel out of date.

Depeche Mode

Petrovsky Passazh, Ulitsa Petrovka 10 (no phone). Metro Teatralnaya. **Open** 10am-8pm Mon-Sat; 11am-6pm Sun. **No credit cards. Map p278 C2**
Hidden among the expensive shops in Petrovsky Passazh shopping mall is this friendly little store. Clothes with psychedelic patterns and cool shoes are offered at affordable prices.

Maska

Boyarsky Pereulok 2 (923 7643). Metro Krasnye Vorota. **Open** noon-8pm daily. **No credit cards. Map p279 E2**
The major streetwear shop in Moscow, Maska is a treasure trove for hip young Muscovites. Wigs and platforms with soles resembling roots are to be found here.

Quiksilver

Bolshaya Dorogomilovskaya Ulitsa 5 (931 9171). Metro Kievskaya. **Open** 10am-9pm daily. **Credit** MC, V. The atmosphere is far from the laid-back beaches of Australia, even if the shelves are surfboard-shaped. Trendy brands like Quiksilver are reasonably priced.

Fashion accessories

Jewellery

Moscow is full of jewellery shops, but the selection is ordinary and varies little from shop to shop.

Valerio

2nd floor, Okhotny Ryad, Manezhnaya Ploshchad (no phone). Metro Okhotny Ryad. **Open** 10am-10pm daily. **Credit** MC, V. **Map p278 C3**
Innovative designs in amber and silver, mostly large rings and heavy necklaces. Some items appear so unwieldy that they can't possibly have been designed for wearing.

Samotsvety

Ulitsa Novy Arbat 35 (241 0765). Metro Arbatskaya or Smolenskaya. **Open** 10am-8pm Mon-Sat; 11am-5pm Sun. **Credit** MC, V. **Map p277 A3/B3**
Possibly the largest jewellery shop in Moscow. Rings, watches and chains are sold from behind counters. Mostly gold and silver, but gemstones too, all at good prices.

Lingerie

Dikaya Orkhideya

Wild Orchid, Okhotny Ryad, Manezhnaya Ploshchad (209 2608). Metro Okhotny Ryad. **Open** 10am-10pm daily. **Credit** DC, JCB, MC, V. **Map p278 C3**
This is something of an experience: expensive, luxurious women's underwear in tacky colours under the hefty guard of security men, who may well ask you to wait outside if there are more than five customers.

Karstadt Fashion

GUM, Krasnaya Ploshchad (Red Square) 3 (no phone). Metro Okhotny Ryad or Ploshchad Revolutsii. **Open** 8.30am-8.30pm Mon-Sat; 11am-7pm Sun. **Credit** DC, JCB, MC, V. **Map p278 D3**
You wouldn't dream of buying outerwear from this German mini-department store, but the serve-yourself lingerie section is a relief from all the point-at-what-you-desire shops.

Bringing it all back home

Anywhere else in the world, it might be easy to resist the lure of the brightly painted wooden spoon, the brightly painted lacquer box and the brightly painted nesting doll. But if you come to Russia, chances are you won't leave the country without at least one of these garish folk-art items.

The most popular and emblematic of Russia's souvenirs is the ubiquitous *matrioshka*, in which each wooden doll splits open to reveal a smaller, similar doll hidden away inside. Invented in 1890 at the Children's Education Workshop in the Abramtsevo estate near Moscow, the *matrioshka* was inspired by similar Japanese nesting figurines. It wasn't until the 1980s that makers began to experiment with the form, risking arrest to produce dolls of various Soviet leaders, each nestling inside its successor. Expect to pay from $15 for a five-piecer, all the way to $150 for an intricate 16-piece set.

Next in the souvenir hierarchy come lacquer boxes, wooden containers decorated with various pastoral scenes, classified according to the Russian villages that produce them. The oldest tradition originates in the village of Fedoskino. Fedoskino boxes are easy to recognise: they're painted in translucent oil on a gold or mother-of-pearl base. The youngest tradition comes from Palekh, originally a centre of icon painting until the Bolsheviks flicked the switch in 1924. Palekh miniature boxes feature elaborate tableaux from Russian fairytales. Authentic lacquer boxes can cost anything between $30 and many thousands. Crude copies in Arbat shops and stalls go for much less, but remember: never buy at the asking price – it's usually double what you'll get with a little haggling.

In general, there should be no need to declare even the fancier *matrioshki* or lacquer boxes on your way out of the country.

Shoes

Ecco
Galleria Aktyor, Ulitsa Tverskaya 16 (935 7796). Metro Tverskaya, Pushkinskaya or Chekhovskaya. **Open** 10am-9pm daily. **Credit** AmEx, MC, V. **Map p278 C2**
Danish shoe chain selling sensible sandals, boots and shoes for all. Well-made, comfortable and reasonably stylish shoes come at about $100.

Econica
Ulitsa Arbat 17 (202 2923). Metro Arbatskaya. **Open** 10am-9pm Mon-Sat; 11am-7pm Sun. **Credit** DC, JCB, MC, V. **Map p280 A4/B4**
Shoes designed between gigs by Russia's top pop star, Alla Pugacheva. Hilarious to look at and awkward to walk in.

Na Nikolskoi
Nikolskaya Ulitsa 4/5 (298 0323). Metro Ploshchad Revolutsii. **Open** 10am-8.30pm Mon-Sat; 11am-7pm Sun. **No credit cards. Map p278 D3**
The shoe shop for teenagers: it stocks all the brand-names they love: Kickers, Caterpillar, Doc Martens and others.

Food & drink

For markets *see above* **One-stop shops: Markets**.

Bakeries

You can barely walk a block in this town without passing a *khleb* (bread) kiosk. The loaves are practically free: only the fanciest raisin breads approach $1, but most of the time you get what you pay for. You can get better, but only if you schlep around. Try the French breads at the **Irish House** (*see below* **Supermarkets**), and keep an eye out for the woman who sometimes sells delicious *khachipuri*

(Georgian cheese bread) from a table on Leninsky Prospekt, up the road from Dom Tkani. **Sadko Arkade** (*see above* **One-stop shops: Malls & shopping centres**) also sells good bread, as does **Yeliseyevsky** (*see below* **Supermarkets**).

Fillipov's
Tverskaya Ulitsa 10 (292 1427). Metro Pushkinskaya. **Open** 24 hours daily. **No credit cards. Map p278 C2**
The bakery of this general food store and delicatessen is legendary. The cream cakes are indeed delicious, but the black and white breads are pretty run of the mill (pardon the pun). There's a small deli section as well, where you can get good caviar. Don't forget to look up or you'll miss the wonderful white and gold ornamented stucco ceiling.

Caviar

The little black eggs of the sturgeon are the swankiest of swanky food, and Russians, too, eat it to celebrate and impress. Black if they can afford it, red (from salmon) if not. Also served is pink whitefish caviar. Pollution in the Caspian Sea, poaching and the black market have affected quality and price. Caviar sold on the street may be phoney, especially if you're pegged as a tourist. Always check the packing date and don't buy if six months have passed. Buy caviar in jars; look for tightly packed and intact eggs. It should smell of freshly caught fish.

As well as the shops listed below, check out **Fillipov's** (*see above* **Bakeries**), **Yeliseyevsky** and the **Irish House**, which will measure out the desired amount (for both *see below* **Supermarkets**). You could also try Palashevsky Fish Market (Sytinsky Tupik 3A; Metro Pushkinskaya) or Okean, a chain of seafood shops scattered around the city.

Dary Morya

Tverskaya Ulitsa 17 (229 5562). Metro Pushkinskaya.
Open 9am-9pm Mon-Fri; 10am-6pm Sat, Sun. **No credit
cards. Map p278 C2**
Rich selection of fresh fish and seafood. Red and black caviar
at prices from $30 to $50.

Dieta

Tverskaya Ulitsa 4 (292 0413). Metro Okhotny Ryad.
Open 8am-8pm Mon Fri; 8am-7pm Sat, Sun. **No credit
cards. Map p278 C2**
Red, black and pink caviar. Prices range from about $4 to $55.

Coffee & tea

Chai-Kofe

Myasnitskaya Ulitsa 19 (921 1634). Metro Chistye Prudy.
Open 8am-8pm Mon-Sat. **No credit cards. Map p278
D2, P279 E2**
The exotic pagodas of this historic Chinese-style building
help the Soviet style within, with old-fashioned counter
service. A great range of imported teas and some coffees.

Confectionery

Grand Candy

*Ground floor, Okhotny Ryad, Manezhnaya Ploshchad (no
phone). Metro Okhotny Ryad.* **Open** 10am-10pm daily.
No credit cards. Map p278 C3
One of Moscow's few pick 'n' mix shops, selling imported
candies for sucking and chewing but hardly any chocolate.
Don't even think about tasting before paying; the cashier is
watching.

Krasny Oktyabr

*Red October, Ulitsa Povarskaya 29 (no phone). Metro
Barrikadnaya.* **Open** 9am-1pm, 2-8pm, Mon-Sat. **No
credit cards. Map p277 A3/B3**
Generally coarser and more strongly flavoured than Western
brands, Red October chocolates come in many varieties. The
stout, fierce-looking women behind the counters will guide you
to the tastiest choices. Sadly, the elaborate packaging – colourful and wonderfully old-fashioned and including some paintings from the Tretyakov – may soon be history as Red October
seeks to be more like its foreign competitors.

Supermarkets

Not so long ago, the word 'supermarket' would have
drawn quizzical stares in Moscow. Aside from a
Western 'hard currency' store called Stockmann's,
nothing came remotely close. Now Stockmann's
accepts rubles and has plenty of competition.

Arbat Irish House

Ulitsa Novy Arbat 11 (291 7641). Metro Arbatskaya.
Open 10am-10pm Mon-Sat; 10am-9pm Sun. **Credit**
AmEx, MC, V. **Map p277 A3/B3**
Large central supermarket that sells everything you'd
expect – food, cleaning stuff, a few basic pieces of clothing.
Despite the unhelpful attitude of the saleswomen and the risk
of being squeezed out of the queue, the bread section is one
of the best in Moscow. The Irish House also houses the
Shamrock Bar (*see chapter* **Pubs & Bars**).

Eldorado

Ulitsa Bolshaya Polyanka 1/3 (230 3662) Metro Polyanka.
Open 24 hours daily **Credit** AmEx, V. **Map p281 C5/C6**
The place to go if you have a craving for jumbo shrimp,
German sausage or French pastries at 3am. Decent selections
of meat, seafood, fresh vegetables, wine. Everything is
imported, even the water.

Kalinka-Stockmann

Ulitsa Zatsepsky Val 4/8 (282 4558). Metro Paveletskaya.
Open 9am-midnight daily. **Credit** MC, V. **Map p282
E6, P279 F3**
The food outlet of an expanding Finnish shopping empire, this
was the first Western supermarket to open here, in 1989. It's
cramped, with prices that sometimes cause customers to laugh
out loud, but they know what they're doing. Good produce,
lots of British and American ingredients that are hard to find
elsewhere, a small selection of Indian food and mediocre bread.

Seventh Continent

*Ulitsa Bolshaya Lubyanka 12/1 (928 9527). Metro
Lubyanka.* **Open** 24 hours daily. **Credit** DC, MC, V. **Map
p278 D2**
There are several stores in this chain, of varying size and qual-
ity. At their best, they offer perhaps the finest selection of
imported and Russian foods. Try the one on Lubyanka first.
Branches: Ulitsa Serafimovicha 2; Ulitsa Okhotny Ryad 2;
Leninsky Prospekt 61/1.

Yeliseyevsky

*Tverskaya Ulitsa 14 (209 6304). Metro Pushkinskaya,
Chekhovskaya or Tverskaya.* **Open** 8am-9pm Mon-Sat;
10am-6pm Sun. **No credit cards. Map p278 C2**
Worth seeing for the architecture, if not the food. This pre-
Revolutionary shop was a showpiece during the Soviet era.
It has a good drinks section, where connoisseurs will find a
good selection of foreign wines and all kinds of beer.

Speciality food

Japro

Prospekt Mira 12 (207 7247). Metro Sukharevskaya.
Open 10am-10pm daily. **Credit** AmEx, DC, JCB, MC, V.
Map p279 D1
Premium-priced Japanese produce, meat, rice, canned and
prepared goods, tofu, wasabi and sauces. You can find bean-
sprouts and kumquats and a large saké selection. Japanese
products are upstairs; downstairs it's an upmarket grocery.

Mega Center Italy

*Ulitsa Akademika Pulyugina 10 (132 3233). Metro Novye
Cheremushki.* **Open** 9.30am-9pm Mon-Sat; 9.30am-7pm
Sun. **Credit** DC, MC, V.
OK, you won't exactly have to pinch yourself to remember
you're not in Rome, but this place does offer the biggest
selection of pasta in the city, not to mention a nice selection of Italian cheeses and meats. Many prices are in lire.

Nokturn

Ulitsa Sretenka 36/2 (207 1621). Metro Sukharevskaya.
Open 9am-9pm daily. **No credit cards. Map p278 D1**
A decent assortment of Indian food ingredients: rices,
curries, mixes and dried beans and spices.

Vodka

Vodka is one of the few commodities you won't have
to work to find in Moscow's shops. It's never out
of stock, available in all sizes and, following the
twisted logic of Russian capitalism, even the good
stuff can be as cheap as bottled water. In addition to
the prestige brands, Stolichnaya, Kristall and
(Russian) Smirnov, good stockists will carry some of
the better national regional makes, such as Flagman
from Kaliningrad or Altai from Siberia. And then
there are the various flavoured and herbal vodkas,
and the old-style, tawny vodkas, which are more like
brandy than the neutral-tasting spirit most know.

Yeliseyevsky – a supermarket sweep for the connoisseur. See page 111.

From the consumer standpoint, your main concern is poison vodka, which is made from industrial ethyl or methyl alcohol, and can kill. Bootleggers have become increasingly sophisticated, and it may be impossible to tell whether a bottle contains poison or the real thing. Basically, do not buy vodka from kiosks or street vendors, but from stores that seem reputable. Obviously, if there is anything even faintly weird about the look, taste or smell, or if the seal has been tampered with, don't drink it. In addition to the shops below, **Yeliseyevsky** (*see above* **Supermarkets**) has a good range of vodkas.

Armenia

Tverskoi Bulvar 17 (229 7021). Metro Pushkinskaya. **Open** 8am-midnight daily. **Credit** MC, V. **Map p278 B2**

The only thing Armenian among the groceries here is the paper-thin *lavash* (flat bread). It is on the booze shelves that customers will find the delicacies of the Caucasus. In addition to the wide choice of foreign wines, beers and vodkas, you can get a bottle of the Georgian wine Kindzmarauli, Armenian Cognac and brandy.

Davidoff

Tverskaya Ulitsa 23 (200 5700). Metro Mayakovskaya. **Open** 10am-10pm daily. **Credit** AmEx, DC, JCB MC, V. **Map p278 C2**

In this professional spirits and tobacco shop, expats buy bottles of their favourite French wine, and New Russian men, eager to seem cosmopolitan, choose Cuban cigars. The wine cellar offers bottles produced in California, South America, Europe, Moldova and Israel.

Kristall

GUM, Krasnaya Ploshchad (Red Square) 3 (no phone). Metro Okhotny Ryad or Ploshchad Revolutsii. **Open** 8.30am-8.30pm Mon-Sat; 11am-7pm Sun. **No credit cards. Map p278 D3**

This inviting, tiny shop fronted by a vodka-quaffing wooden bear is the outlet for vodka manufacturer Kristall. It's crammed full of the stuff, in forms ranging from vodka-filled *matrioshka* to speciality blends and bottles bearing an image of St Basil's or the face of Russia's No.1 film director, Nikita Mikhalkov.

Gifts & souvenirs

See also above **Malls & shopping centres** for **Novyrussky Mir** in Okhotny Ryad, and **Markets** for the souvenir *rynok* **Izmailovsky Vernisazh**.

Gzhel

Sadovaya-Samotechnaya Ulitsa 2 (299 2953). Metro Tsvetnoi Bulvar. **Open** 10am-7pm Mon-Sat. **Credit** MC, V. **Map p278 C1**

A bright, pleasant shop that specialises in Russia's famous blue-patterned Gzhel porcelain but also has a small selection of other crafts and souvenirs.

Ikonnaya Lavka

Nikolskaya Ulitsa 1 (298 3780/3788). Metro Ploshchad Revolutsii. **Open** 10am-2pm, 3-7pm, Mon-Fri; 10am-2pm, 3-6pm, Sat. **No credit cards. Map p278 D3**

This place is really a religious iconography shop, but the chalices, candlesticks, icons, silver and brass wouldn't look entirely out of place in most Russian houses.

Khudozhestvenny Salon

Okhotny Ryad, Manezhnaya Ploshchad (737 8409). Metro Okhotny Ryad. **Open** 10am-10pm daily. **Credit** varies. **Map p278 C3**

A good selection of well-made dolls, costumes, dishes and other crafts, but the prices can be twice those at Izmailovsky Vernisazh (*see above* **One-stop shops: Markets**).

La Casa de Cuba

1st floor, Okhotny Ryad, Manezhnaya Ploshchad (737 8409). Metro Okhotny Ryad. **Open** 10am-10pm daily. **Map p278 C3**

No Caribbean atmosphere, but you will find Cuban cigars here, as well as tobaccos from different countries, luxurious lighters and pipes.

Salon Moskovskogo Fonda Kultury

Moscow Culture Foundation Salon, Pyatnitskaya Ulitsa 16 (no phone). Metro Novokuznetskaya or Tretyakovskaya. **Open** 10am-8pm Mon-Sat. **No credit cards. Map p281 D5**

An intimate little shop that sells tasteful and authentic craft products such as Gzhel porcelain, *gorodets* (primitive paintings on wood) and *palekh* (black lacquered boxes and plates with exquisite paintings). The ground floor has a remarkable collection of nineteenth-century ephemera: bottles, barrels,

Buying in to the skin trade

Russia is the land that political correctness forgot – where Jewish jokes are not uncommon, feminists still risk getting burned at the stake and the phrase 'fun fur' means a Mongolian goatskin dyed in an unusually bright colour. In Russia's peltocracy, those who instead of fur opt for natural fibres or – horror of horrors – synthetic fabrics are viewed as abnormal, a lowly caste soon to be wiped out by the inexorable logic of the elements.

The most common type of fur hat you're likely to see on Moscow's streets is the chunky, traditional *ushanka*, a kind of furry air-raid shelter firmly anchored to the top of the head. Flaps can be lowered to cover the ears, but as this tends to look foolish, Russians generally leave them tied up while their ears burn in the cold. Women may favour the more feminine *eshimosha*, whose most prominent feature is a dainty little pom-pom up top. Coats can range from cheapo rabbit to sables costing as much as your average apartment. Fox is usually red or pale grey; polar fox is either pure white or artificially dyed; nutria, a type of otter, is the poor man's mink – longer, coarser and more glossy – and other options include reindeer, fox, wolf and the all-time favourites, mink and sable.

Though it is far less acceptable to wear fur in the West, hats at least remain a popular souvenir for tourists. Two good outlets are listed below.

Dublyonki
Leninsky Prospekt 6/7, enter via the courtyard (236 9923). Metro Oktyabrskaya. **Open** 24 hours daily.
This two-storey warehouse, packed full of coats and jackets, is a treasury for fur and suede lovers. The generic woman's suede coat with fur lining costs $1,150; a short leather jacket with fur lining is $450 and a man's coat $925.
Branch: Ulitsa Staroalekseyevskaya 21 (no phone).

Rosenberg & Lenhart
GUM, Krasnaya Ploshchad (Red Square) 3 (929 3211/921 3471). Metro Okhotny Ryad or Ploshchad Revolutsii. **Open** 8.30am-8.30pm Mon-Sat; 11am-7pm Sun. **Credit** DC, JCB, MC, V. **Map p278 D3**
Not the place to come for a whole coat unless you are seriously over-financed, but it has a great selection of fur hats.

dishes, lamps. There are also various turn-of-the-century bric-a-brac such as skates, appliances and home decorations. It's all authentic and in pretty good nick. Do ask about which items are allowed be taken out of the country without you having to pay duty (*see chapter* **Directory: Essential Information**).

Florists
Flowers are also for sale at most metro stations.

Elite Flora
Bolshaya Gruzinskaya Ulitsa 32 (254 3992). Metro Barrikadnaya. **Open** 9am-7pm Mon-Fri; 9am-5pm Sat-Sun. **Credit** MC, V. **Map p277 A1/A2**
One of the best flower shops in Moscow.

Tsvety
Kiosk between Komsomolsky Prospekt 31 & 33 (242 8729). Metro Frunzenskaya. **Open** 9am-8pm Mon-Fri; 10am-7pm Sat; 10am-4pm Sun. **No credit cards**. **Map p280 A6/B6**

Health & beauty

Opticians

Comec
Okhotny Ryad, Manezhnaya Ploshchad (737 8368/8369). Metro Okhotny Ryad. **Open** 10am-10pm daily. **Credit** AmEx, V. **Map p278 C3**
Contact lens specialists.

Karstadt Optics
GUM, Krasnaya Ploshchad (Red Square) 3 (no phone). Metro Okhotny Ryad or Ploshchad Revolutsii. **Open** 8.30am-8.30pm Mon-Sat; 11am-7pm Sun. **Credit** DC, JCB, MC, V. **Map p278 D3**

Salons

Alexander Todchuk
Tverskaya Ulitsa 31/4 (299 3602). Metro Mayakovskaya. **Open** 10am-10pm Mon-Sat; 10am-7pm Sun. **Credit** MC, V. **Map p278 C3**
The studio of this Russian hair designer is in the same building as the Tchaikovsky Concert Hall. Together with his colleague Alexei Karakulov, Todchuk creates hairstyles for Moscow's rich and hip. Prices start at $50.

Jacques Dessange
Lesnaya Ulitsa 10/16 (251 0212). Metro Belorusskaya. **Open** 8am-10pm Mon-Sat, 10am-10pm Sun. **Credit** DC, MC, V.
This expensive French beauty parlour draws its regulars from the higher levels of society. A visit can be an amazing experience. You may feel a bit out of it among the New Russian women chatting on their mobile phones while they have their hair streaked. All kinds of face and body treatments are offered. Haircuts cost about $70-$80.

Leisure & sports

Books

American Bookstore
Denezhny Pereulok 8/10 (241 4224). Metro Smolenskaya. **Open** 10am-3pm, 4pm-7pm, Mon-Sat. **Credit** MC, V. **Map p280 A4**
The latest bookstore to feature English books. Its advertisements in the local English newspapers claim 'Your search ends here' and the selection is extremely comprehensive.

Anglia British Bookshop

Khlebny Pereulok 2/3 (203 5802). Metro Novy Arbat or Arbatskaya. **Open** 10am-7pm Mon-Wed, Fri; 10am-8pm Thur; 10am-6pm Sat. **Credit** AmEx, MC, V. **Map p277 B3**

A pleasant, well-lit place with a surprisingly good selection of literature, non-fiction and reference books. It's especially good on books about Russia and children's books. Americans may find it a bit too British, and anyone is likely to be taken aback by the prices, which are steep. Anglia holds readings and other events.

Moskovsky Dom Knigi

Ulitsa Novy Arbat 8 (290 4507). Metro Arbatskaya. **Open** 10am-7.30pm, Mon-Fri; 10am-6.30pm Sat. **Credit** MC, V. **Map p277 A3/B3**

This was once Moscow's premier bookstore. It has a small English-language section of books and magazines as well as stalls selling albums, videos, computer games and inexpensive posters.

Shakespeare & Co

1-y Novokuznetsky Pereulok 5/7 (231 9360). Metro Paveletskaya. **Open** call for details. **Credit** MC, V. **Map p281 D6**

A cosy bookshop that's a branch of the famous Paris store, with crammed shelves, helpful staff, literary readings and good coffee. Shakespeare has a little of everything, including used books, and will do its best to order anything you can't find. The only drawback is that it only seems to open when the owner feels like it.

Zwemmer's

Ulista Kuznetsky Most 18 (924 2068/921 0035). Metro Kuznetsky Most. **Open** 10am-7pm Mon-Fri; 10am-6pm Sat. **Credit** AmEx, MC, V. **Map p278 C2/D2**

A small, popular English-language bookshop, with travel guides and a broad selection of Russian literature and history, plus bestsellers, cookbooks and a smattering of pretty much everything else.

Records, tapes & CDs

Melodiya

Ulitsa Novy Arbat 22 (291 1421). Metro Novy Arbat. **Open** 9am-8pm Mon-Sat. **Credit** MC, V. **Map p277 A3/B3**

Once the Tower Records of the Soviet Union, this modern, two-storey shop is still probably the biggest record store in Moscow, if you don't count the huge outdoor market held at Filovsky Park every weekend. There's a broad selection of classical music at low prices; the old Soviet classics are a bargain. It also has videotapes and video/computer games.
Branch: Leninsky Prospekt 148 (433 6622).

Soyuz

4th floor, TsUM, Ulitsa Petrovka 2 (292 1157). Metro Teatralnaya. **Open** 9am-8pm Mon-Sat; 10am-6pm Sun. **Credit** MC, V. **Map p278 C2**

Large, modern music store offering everything from classical music to children's records. Good selection of classic rock and independent labels. Also videotapes.

Maps

Slavyanka

Ulitsa Kuznetsky Most 9 (928 6109). Metro Kuznetsky Most. **Open** 10am-2pm, 3-7pm, Mon-Fri; 10am-2pm, 3-6pm, Sat. **Credit** MC, V. **Map p278 C2/D2**

Friendly, helpful staff and a good selection of maps of Moscow, the former Soviet Union and the rest of the world.

Sport

Kant

Nagornaya Ulitsa 2 (316 9577). Metro Nagornaya. **Open** 10am-8pm daily. **No credit cards.**

Many brands of skis, boots, poles and accessories, including some equipment a few seasons old at reduced prices – with a ski slope right outside.

Okhotnik, Rybolov, Turist

Hunter, Angler, Tourist, Leninsky Prospekt 44 (no phone). Metro Leninsky Prospekt. **Open** 10am-2pm, 3-7pm, Mon-Sat. **No credit cards.**

The name pretty much says it all. This is a typical Soviet-style shop carrying equipment for fishing, hunting (including guns) and diving, with a smattering of other odds and ends.

Olymp

Krasnopresnenskaya Naberezhnaya 23 (255 0592). Metro Ulitsa 1905 Goda. **Open** 10am-7pm Mon-Sat. **No credit cards.**

A large store with a good selection across each of its small departments for skiing, skating, fishing, soccer and tennis. Medals and trophies are also sold, and recently there was even a motorboat for $14,000.

TsUM

Ulitsa Petrovka 2 (292 1157). Metro Teatralnaya. **Open** 9am-8pm Mon-Sat; 10am-6pm Sun. **Credit** MC, V. **Map p278 C2**

The sport section is to be found on the second floor of the department store (*see above* **One-stop shops: Department stores**). It's one of the best sports shops in town, selling equipment for a wide range of activities, including a good selection of inline skates (from $85).

Travellers' needs

Leather goods & luggage

Robinzon

1st floor, Okhotny Ryad, Manezhnaya Ploshchad (no phone). Metro Okhotny Ryad. **Open** 10am-10pm daily. **Credit** AmEx, MC, V. **Map p278 C3**

All kinds of bags from the brand Robinzon. Also a good selection of Samsonite suitcases and stewardess bags at reasonable prices.

Texier

Frantsuzkiye Galerei, Vetoshny Pereulok 9 (725 4765). Metro Ploshchad Revolutsii. **Open** 10am-9pm daily. **Credit** AmEx, DC, JCB, MC. **Map p278 D3**

Stylish leather bags for men and women in arty designs both classic and modern. It also sells suitcases, flight baggage, belts and other leather accessories.

Photo processing

Moscow is full of kiosks and small shops offering developing, often located in or near metro stations.

Tekhsoyuz

1st floor, Okhotny Ryad, Manezhnaya Ploshchad (no phone). Metro Okhotny Ryad. **Open** 10am-10pm daily. **Credit** MC, V. **Map p278 C3**

Offers a one-hour developing service. A large selection of automatic cameras is also on sale, at pretty good prices, too.

Travel agents

See page 254 **Directory: Getting Around Moscow.**

Entertainment

Banyas

If you really want to go native, strip, dip – and whip – at one of Moscow's steam baths.

Imagine stripping naked in a room full of strangers, putting a starched sheet about the waist and making your way across a slippery, tiled floor towards an unmarked wooden door. Opening the door, you are hit in the face with a hot, humid blast of air smelling like a belch of swamp gas. A few steps beyond the door and you are in a poorly lit room, crowded with naked, sweating bodies, some sitting, some smeared with honey, a few occasionally speaking in hushed tones. Your eyes grow accustomed to the murk and it all begins to seem normal, until suddenly, the church-like quiet is broken by the rhythmic thwacking sound of tree branches hitting flesh. Flushed and sweating, you flee the dark, steamy room and follow others to a five-metre-square pool. A plunge into the achingly cold water leaves you breathless and wondering what madness possessed you ever to leave the well-trodden tourist trail.

With its homoerotic elements, extremes of hot and cold and a sometimes thuggish clientele, a trip to a public *banya* in Moscow is not for the timid, pregnant or those with a heart condition. But it is a sure-fire way to witness a truly Russian phenomenon, one that survived Communism and post-Soviet tumult.

First mention of the cult of the banya comes in Russia's earliest written record, the *Primary Chronicle*, with an account of the apostle Andrew's first trip to the Russian heartland and his inevitable encounter with the steam room.

'Wondrous to relate,' gushes St Andrew, 'I saw the land of the Slavs, and while I was among them, I noticed their wooden bathhouses. They warm them to extreme heat, then undress, and after anointing themselves with tallow, they take young reeds and lash their bodies. They actually lash themselves so violently that they barely escape alive. Then they drench themselves with cold water, and are thus revived. They think nothing of doing this every day, and actually inflict such voluntary torture upon themselves. They make of the act not a mere washing but a veritable torment.'

Early on in Russia's history, death by banya was apparently not such an uncommon occurrence. According to a well-known legend, in the wake of the slaying of the Kievan Prince Igor by rival tribesmen in AD945, his wife Olga exacted a cruel revenge by inviting a group of their finest warriors

Hanging out at **Sandunovskye Bani** *(p118).*

to take a banya and then torching the entire structure. She later became Russia's first saint.

The banya slowly developed into the hub of the world of Russian wheeling and dealing and remained so throughout Communist times, becoming a place where agreements were forged in steam and sweat and party advancement was assiduously mapped out between gruelling sessions. In Russia's current bout of 'wild capitalism', banyas continue to be venues for shady power-brokering and in some instances for scandal, as when former Minister of Justice Valentin Kovalyov was caught on video cavorting with naked women in a mafia-run banya. In another infamous criminal banya episode, the legendary wrestler-turned-mobster Otari Kvantrishvili was gunned down as he left the Bani na Presnye in 1994.

For most of us, however, Moscow's banya complexes are generally safe and wholesome. The banya is a place where fathers initiate sons, where female slaves to fashion are liberated and where everybody goes to rid themselves of the detritus of too much vodka, too much bad food and the psycho-bile of everyday life. The banya accomplishes what the Bolsheviks never did: it is the great equaliser, where the naked are set apart by little more than skin tone and tattoos.

BANYA KNOW-HOW

To reach banya Valhalla, there are a few basic steps to follow. As with the Russian language, if you make a humble, well-intentioned effort to experience a banya, Muscovites will meet you halfway and more. First, set aside a few hours and don't plan on performing any serious mental tasks afterwards. Save a few rubles by bringing a pair of flip-flops, a towel, a plain white sheet, soap and shampoo, although these can be hired at all the banyas listed here. Most banyas have cafés but you can bring your own snacks and drinks. Some people bring lager; purists take herbal tea. Salted fish called *vobla*, pistachios and pickled garlic are all effective ways to replenish lost salt without getting bloated. Bear in mind that it's only acceptable to eat food in the changing room where people rest between sessions. When, on their first visit to a Moscow banya, two young Swedish women started eating heads of smelly pickled garlic in the sanctuary of the steam room, they were scolded for fouling the air and told to leave.

The women's and men's sections of each banya are divided into four components. The dressing room is staffed by *banshchiki* (attendants), who safeguard valuables, rent linens and assign places. The shower room is for just that, as well as for soaking the bundles of twigs employed in the steam room. Shower at the beginning and end of a session.

The most exalted part of the banya is the *parilka* (steam room), which invariably has a tiled floor, wood panelling and dim lighting. The kind of heat its oven produces is what makes or breaks a banya. Temperatures rise up to 110°F (43°C) and humidity up to 90 per cent; a combination that sets the parilka apart from a Turkish or Finnish variant.

The key to success lies in striking a balance between the heat and humidity, where the air is moist enough to draw a quick sweat but dry enough to give a penetrating but not too painful warmth. This is where the master or mistress of steam is crucial. In most places, the patrons control the steam by deciding when to ladle water on the oven's rocks and how much oil to add.

Most parilkas are dominated by a wooden structure that looks like an out-of-place tree house, which allows patrons to sit or lie at different levels according to their heat tolerance.

After five to ten minutes in the parilka, the next stop is the dipping pool, which can be tropically warm or ice cold and is designed to accelerate the

cooling process so you can return to the parilka more quickly. Banyas without dipping pools are deemed inferior and are generally cheaper.

Two hours is the standard length of time for a banya session, long enough for six or eight parilka-pool cycles, depending on how often and long you choose to rest and snack. At the end, be sure to bid other patrons farewell with 'S lyogkim parom', loosely translatable as 'May the steam be with you'.

Astrakhanskye

Astrakhansky Pereulok 5/9 (280 4329). Metro Prospekt Mira. **Open** *8am-11pm Tue-Sun.* **Admission** *per 2-hour visit* $6.50. **No credit cards.**

Sticks & steam

Like any old and revered institution, the Russian banya has a good number of rituals attached to it. In the case of the banya, they are often pleasantly painful and sometimes humiliating.

At all the banyas listed here, vendors sell bundles of two-foot-long tree branches for between $1.50 and $2. Just ask for *venniki*. Birch is most common, but oak and pine are sometimes also available. Each kind of tree is supposed to have specific curative powers for heart, lungs or whatever – but we can't verify such theories here. In the shower room, fill a plastic tub with lukewarm water and soak your twigs for a few minutes while taking a shower. In the steam room, beat yourself to exfoliate dead skin, boost circulation or just to have something to do. When steam room space permits, it is particularly enjoyable to lie down on a towel and have a friend beat you. Like the overall banya experience, the idea with the twigs is to strike a balance between pleasure and pain, hence all the cathartic moaning that goes on. For some people, that means using the twigs as a brush for the sweat; for others it means emerging from the steam room with red welts.

While twigs are used by both men and women, men don't often subscribe to the second common banya ritual, which involves applying various edibles to the skin. This isn't recommended for the beginner, who might well end up a big sticky, smelly mess and miss out on the basic joys of the banya. People sit in the lower parts of the parilka smeared in salt (to draw out water), honey (for skin tone and cellulite removal), coffee grounds (as an exfoliant) or dairy products (wrinkle mitigation). Bring your own, as most banyas don't sell these extras

*Up a bit... right a bit... a wholesome naturist night at the **Varshavskye Bani**.*

Solid steam and kitschy but competent Soviet design make this a bargain for the admission fee, but the lack of a dipping pool is a serious drawback. Massages, available at almost all banyas, are a particularly good deal here.

Bani Na Presnye
Stolyarny Pereulok 7 (255 0115). Metro Ulitsa 1905 Goda. **Open** 8am-10pm Mon, Wed-Sun; 2-10pm Tue. **Admission** $13 Mon-Fri; $16 Sat, Sun. **Credit** AmEx, DC, MC, V.
A good place for beginners. As the last major Moscow banya built in Soviet times, it is modern and accessible. The overwhelming mood is friendly but serious, with everyone taking a turn at dispensing the steam. The women's side has a stricter regime, with mistresses of steam controlling patrons' movements in and out of the parilka and occasionally calling for silence with an indignant 'We are trying to rest here!'
Beauty salon. Gym. Hairdresser. Restaurant. Solarium.

Sandunovskye Bani
Neglinnaya Ulitsa 14 (925 4631). Metro Kuznetsky Most. **Open** 8am-10pm daily. **Admission** $16-$32. **No credit cards. Map p278 C2**
Moscow's oldest, fanciest and most famous banya. Aesthetically, no other place comes close. The curved, marble staircase and vaulted blue ceiling of the men's entrance give a sense of how the rich kept clean in the waning years of the Russian Empire. The main Gothic Room is just that, with dark wood panelling and finely carved benches and booths. Uniformed attendants take orders for snacks. The shower room is cavernous, bright and decorated with the kind of imitation Greek statues sold at Western garden centres. White-haired, pink-fleshed men often inhabit the plastic furniture flanking the statues, adding to the place's patrician air. The main dipping pool is huge, but the parilka can be disappointing. Prices vary according to the décor and size of pool.

Seleznovskye Bani
Seleznovskaya Ulitsa 15 (978 8491). Metro Seleznovskaya Ulitsa. **Open** 8am-10pm. **Admission** *per 2-hour visit* $10 Mon-Fri; $12 Sat, Sun women; $25 Mon-Fri; $30 Sat, Sun men. **No credit cards.**
For the serious, hardcore banya-goer this place can't be beat. People don't come here to socialise, but to milk every minute to maximum effect. The dipping pool is polar cold, hastening a return to the parilka. Prices for women are considerably lower because their section has not yet been renovated. Men's prices include a buffet of tea, fruit and biscuits.

Varshavskye Bani
Varshavskoye Shosse 34 (111 1545). Metro Nagatinskaya. **Open** 9am-9pm Mon-Fri; 8am-9pm Sat, Sun. **Admission** *per 2-hour visit* $6. **No credit cards.**
A bare-bones establishment that is functional but in need of a revamp. Both men's and women's parilkas are immense and tend to be more humid than hot. The price is hard to beat, but the dipping pool is murky and there is no café. Naked naturists gather in the women's section for mixed-gender sessions on Mondays and Wednesdays. The naturist crowd is mostly young and wholesome; single men are likely to be turned away, but couples and single women are welcome.

Vyatka Health Complex
4-ya Vyatsky Pereulok 10 (285 8672). Metro Savyolovskaya. **Open** 8am-10pm daily. **Admission** $6. **No credit cards.**
New management renovated this solid, neighbourhood banya and opened a café with an Armenian kitchen. Beer and kvas are often thrown on the oven's rocks instead of fragrant oils, giving the parilka a malty, yeasty smell. A Scientologist-run drug-rehabilitation programme is scheduled to open here, so be careful not to end up in the wrong section. The overall atmosphere is relaxed and unpretentious perhaps due to the dearth of gangsters – and the price.

Children

It might not be the world's prettiest city, but Moscow is more child-friendly than it appears.

Russians adore children. Almost to the point of obsession. They protect and dote on them, swaddling them in adoration and affection. They will shield them from wayward draughts, protect them from the horrors of cold drinks in winter and forbid them from doing anything as unruly and potentially unhygienic as playing or horsing around. Many older Russian women – the infamous and much-feared *babushka* horde – may even make it their business to ensure you do the same with yours, and won't hesitate to tell you if your child is underdressed, overdressed, too hot, too cold, eating something they really shouldn't, or not behaving themselves. Just grin and bear it. They mean well, and, regardless of how you may feel at that precise moment, beating them with a blunt object would certainly be viewed as an overreaction.

Despite this overbearing and somewhat dictatorial concern, Moscow doesn't appear, at first glance, to be a city that is particularly child-friendly. For a start, it's dirty, monotonously grey and frighteningly immense. The inhuman scale of the cityscape seems specifically designed to furnish kids with plenty of raw material for nightmares. Foreign parents, used to an array of clean, clinical, colourful and convenient diversions for their children, may find this a frustrating and even terrifying place. The children themselves, however, tend to be far less spooked by it all. They seem to barely notice the dirty, dilapidated conditions of their surroundings and are far more sensitive than adults to the sparkle and magic of the Russian experience. While their parents grapple with various preconceptions, kids can get stuck into the weird and downright exotic treats Moscow offers. While it will never compete with Disney World, there are some interesting and unusual theatres, two excellent circuses, grand, meandering rivers for cruising and an abundance of parks that provide plenty of fun in the sun.

SPORTS

Moscow is not overflowing with sporting facilities for children, but there are some child-friendly places. For full details of the city's swimming pools, ice rinks, bowling alleys and horseriding facilities, *see chapter* **Sport & Fitness**.

Practicalities

Be certain that you and your children are up to date with vaccinations against diphtheria, cholera, polio and measles. For adults, this usually means getting a booster shot (the tetanus-diphtheria vaccine) at least two weeks before travelling. Buy bottled water and use it for drinking, teeth-cleaning and making up baby formula.

MT Out, in Friday's *Moscow Times*, includes listings of children's activities, as does the *Moscow Tribune's* Wednesday entertainment section. *Vash Dosug* (Your Leisure), a weekly Russian-language listings mag, has a very good children's section.

Babysitting & childminding

There are no drop-in daycare centres, and the hotels do not have babysitting services. Young Russian couples use their parents and grandparents and most of Moscow's foreign residents hire full-time nannies. Temporary residents will find getting a sitter an almost impossible task. If you have any local friends or contacts, ask around: many nannies are willing to babysit for other people.

Eating out

Child-friendly restaurants are a completely foreign concept in Moscow. While things are improving with the influx of foreign investors and management philosophies, some popular restaurants, such as **Guriya**, turn parents away at the door. The Western idea of customer service is lacking, and high chairs, children's menus and crayons are almost unheard of. Desserts can be ridiculously expensive (sometimes as much as $10 for a slice of cake), so enjoy your meal and then get some ice-cream from another vendor (including Baskin Robbins) on the street. Needless to say, fast-food options (McDonald's, Pizza Hut, Kentucky Fried Chicken) are plentiful; children will also like **Planet Hollywood** and **TGI Fridays** (*see chapter* **Restaurants & Cafés**).

Shopping

Moscow has been slow on the uptake as far as child-specific shops are concerned, but there are three branches of UK chain Mothercare here, and department stores cater well for children. There

*Feathered friendship at the **Moscow Zoo**.*

are also small native children's stores all over Moscow. **Detsky Mir** (Children's World) and **Dom Igrushki** (House of Toys) are city landmarks worth visiting; for children's books, check out **Anglia** and the **American Bookstore** (for all *see chapter* **Shopping & Services**).

Entertainment

Animal attractions

Aquarium World

Mir Akvariuma, Novinsky Bulvar 22 (202 0906). Metro Barrikadnaya. **Open** 11am-7pm Mon, Wed-Sun. **Admission** $1; 50¢ schoolchildren; free under-6s. **Map p277 A3**
Watching fish is a great remedy for stress, and can also have a miraculously calming effect on overactive children. At Aquarium World you'll find 150 species of exotic, brightly coloured, spiky, weird and wonderful fish and mammals in well-kept aquaria.

Circus on Sparrow Hills (New Circus)

Tsirk Na Vorobyovykh Gorakh (Novy Tsirk), Prospekt Vernadskogo 7 (930 2815). Metro Universitet.
Performances 7pm Wed-Fri; 11.30am, 3pm, 7pm, Sat, Sun.
Russian circuses are renowned the world over and are never a disappointment. This new(-ish) circus has five interchangeable arenas. The acts change constantly, but guarantee a great time for very little money. Kids are transfixed by trapeze artists, very unusual acrobatic acts, animals and clowns.

Dolphin Circus

Delfinary, Dvorets Vodnogo Sporta, Mironovskaya Ulitsa 27 (369 7966). Metro Semyonovskaya. **Performances** 4pm, 6pm, Wed, Thur; noon, 2pm, 4pm, 6pm, Sat, Sun. **Admission** $4; free under-6s.

Performing Black Sea dolphins, North Sea sea lions and a polar white whale perform tricks that will enchant your children. While some adult visitors are saddened at seeing such animals in a swimming pool, children are blissfully oblivious of animal rights.

Moscow Zoo

Moscovsky Zoopark, Bolshaya Gruzinskaya Ulitsa 1 (254 4693). Metro Barrikadnaya or Krasnopresnenskaya.
Open *May-Sept* 9am-6pm, Tue-Sun. **Map p277 A1/A2**
Not as large as most major cities' zoos, the Moscow Zoo has been recently renovated and is worth a visit. Keep in mind that it's mobbed on public holidays and at weekends when the weather's fine. The only disappointment is the lack of shady spots and benches or places to rest.

Tsvetnoi Bulvar Circus

Tsirk Na Tsvetnom Bulvare (Stary Tsirk), Tsvetnoi Bulvar 13 (200 6889). Metro Tsvetnoi Bulvar.
Performances 7pm Mon, Wed-Fri; 3pm, 7pm, Sat, Sun. **Map p278 D1**
The 'old' circus is the smaller of the two, and produces fabulous shows that usually have a central theme. The costumes are intricate and colourful and the acts second to none. Like the new circus, the show includes a wide variety of acts, from clowns to animals to acrobatics.

Uncle Durov's Wonder Land

Teatr Zverei Imeni Durova, Ulitsa Durova 4 (971 3047).
Performances *big stage* 3pm Wed-Fri; noon, 3pm, 5.30pm, Sat, Sun; *small stage* 2pm Wed-Fri; 11am, 2pm, Sat, Sun.
A famous animal theatre, Uncle Durov's Wonder Land doesn't quite live up to its name. The building houses several small, intimate stages surrounded by uncomfortable seats. The ageing structure is filthy and smells like a barn. Nevertheless, small children genuinely enjoy the acts, which include elephants, cats, dogs, flamingoes, horses, tigers and more – though you might not. Give it a miss if any of your family have allergies to animals.

Yuri Kuklachyov Cat Theatre

Teatr Koshek Yuriya Kuklachyova, Kutuzovsky Prospekt 25 (249 2907). Metro Kutuzovskaya. **Performances** 4pm Fri; 11am, 2pm, 5pm, Sat, Sun. Closed in summer.
Most people think of cats as being independent creatures that always do exactly the opposite of whatever their owner wants. With that in mind, it's extraordinary to see them performing amazing tricks on command. Children will be riveted by Kulachyov's comic routines and well-trained cats.

Museums

Moscow's museums may not be quite up to scratch with those in Washington, DC, or London, but their style and variety are enough to occupy children of all ages and all fascinations. For the **Space Museum**, the **Darwin Museum**, the **Palaeontology Museum** and the **Polytechnical Museum** and the **Zoological Museum**, *see* chapter **Museums & Galleries**.

Antique Doll Museum

Muzei Unikalnykh Kukol, Ulitsa Malaya Dmitrovka 9 (299 2800). Metro Pushkinskaya or Chekhovskaya. **Open** 10am-6.30pm Tue-Sun. **Admission** free. **Map** p277 **B1, p278 C1/C2**
The museum's owner, Yulia Vishnevskaya, is a former theatre make-up specialist and has donated 250 dolls from her personal collection to the museum display. There are dolls dating back to the seventeenth century from France, England, Germany and Japan.

Armed Forces Museum

Muzei Vooruzhennykhsil, Ulitsa Sovetskoi Armii 2 (281 4877). Metro Tsvetnoi Bulvar, then trolleybus 13. **Open** 10am-5pm Wed-Sun. **Admission** $1; free under-7s. **Map** p278 D1
Planes, helicopters, rockets, tanks and an armoured train, up close – a big hit with the kids. Inside, the museum showcases the history of the Soviet army and fleet in the Civil War of 1918-22 and World War II, in 25 halls of weapons, photos, captured German standards, toy soldiers, military equipment and old Russian uniforms.

Theatre & puppetry

Moscow has many wonderful theatres specifically for children. Some of the exceptional ones include the Academic Youth Theatre, the Children's Musical Theatre, the Young Spectator Theatre and the Obraztsov Puppet Theatre. To find out what is currently showing, call the theatre, or consult one of the English newspapers. Performances, of course, are in Russian, and that includes the dialogue in puppet shows.

Academic Youth Theatre

Molodyozhny Akademichesky Teatr Rossii, Teatralnaya Ploshchad 2/7 (292 0069). Metro Teatralnaya. **Map** p278 C3
Founded in 1921, this theatre is the second oldest children's theatre in Russia. It originally only staged fairytales, but now performs many Russian classics, as well as Shakespeare and Mark Twain. The majority of its performances are for children between the ages of seven and 16.

Bat Cabaret Theatre

Letuchaya Mysh, Povarskaya Ulitsa 33 (290 2811). Metro Barrikadnaya. **Performances** 7pm, days vary. Call for more details. **Map** p277 A3/B3

This historical theatre employs a troupe of very talented actors and actresses who can sing, dance and bring the house down. Part of their repertoire includes *The Wonderful Trip*, especially for children. If it is playing, be sure not to miss it.

Children's Musical Theatre

Detsky Muzykalny Teatr, Prospekt Vernadskogo 5 (930 5177). Metro Universitet. **Performances** two per day, times vary. **Tickets** prices vary.
This theatre opened to educate children between the ages of ten and 16 about the art of acting. Before each play begins, the actors discuss it with the attending children. The theatre's repertoire includes *Peter and the Wolf*, *Winnie the Pooh*, *King Lear* and *The Magic Flute*.

Clown Theatre of Teresa Durova

Teatr Klounov Terezy Durovoi, Dom Kultury Zavoda Vladimira Ilicha, Pavlovskaya Ulitsa 6 (237 1689). Metro Tulskaya. **Open** Sat, Sun.
In addition to the regular performances of the clowns, performers teach the audience tricks during the intervals. The programme changes every three weeks.

Obraztsov Puppet Theatre

Teatr Kukol Obraztsova, Sadovaya-Samotechnaya Ulitsa 3 (299 5373). Metro Tsvetnoi Bulvar or Mayakovskaya. **Map** p278 C1
Without a doubt, the Obraztsov is the best puppet theatre in Moscow. The name of its founder, Sergei Obraztsov, is renowned worldwide. In existence since 1931, it now has a staff of more than 100 and a repertoire of over 40 plays. Whether or not your children understand Russian, they will truly enjoy this theatre. The building houses an interesting museum displaying hundreds of puppets and masks from about 50 countries. The Obraztsov also does performances for adults, so before going be certain the show is suitable. One of the first nudes on the Moscow stage was a puppet.

Young Spectator Theatre

Mamonovsky Pereulok 10 (299 5360/9917). Metro Tverskaya or Mayakovskaya. **Map** p277 B2
Dating back to 1927, this theatre differs from all others by the way the actors interact with the audiences. Sometimes they change places and encourage the spectators to perform. Best appreciated by children over ten.

Children's clubs

Harlequin Children's Club

Detsky Klub Arlekino, Verkhnyaya Radishchevskaya Ulitsa 19/3 (915 1107/1106). Metro Taganskaya. **Open** 1-7pm daily. **Age** 3-12s. **Credit** MC, V. **Map** p282 E5/F5
This slightly run down club next door to the Taganka Theatre will provide entertainment for children and ply them with fruit, drink, cake and other goodies. In summer, fees range from $5 to $9 per hour per child, depending on whether parents stay and if drinks and snacks are provided. Champagne and harder drinks are available for adults. There's a clown show, playrooms, computer games and a café.

Zebra Children's Club

Detsky Klub Zebra, Tallinskaya Ulitsa 14, Strogino (449 2990). Metro Tchukinskaya, then any tram towards Strogino. **Open** noon-4pm Sun.
Theatre and clown shows, toys and other amusements.

Limpopo

1-ya Vladimirskaya Ulitsa 10B (302 3302). Metro Shosse Entuziastov. **Open** 10am-8pm daily. **Admission** cover $4.25/2 hours supervised play. **Age** 1-8s.
An American entertainment centre located near the Prozhektor Palace of Culture. It has toys, games and other play equipment. Limpopo is also equipped to have birthday parties on the premises.

*Get high and wired at the **Circus on Sparrow Hills**. See page 120.*

Outdoor activities

In addition to beaches, river cruises and the zoo, Moscow has approximately 100 parks and gardens, offering daily activity. Even though Russian parents tend to be slightly neurotic about their children, keeping them 'healthy' does not preclude taking them out for walks in weather conditions that would prompt parents elsewhere to wrap them them up in blankets and tie them to the TV set. Perambulating is an artform in Moscow. Muscovites fully appreciate the opportunity to observe children at play, surveying the greenery and breathing fresh air. Nearly all the city's parks are great for cycling, rollerblading and skateboarding.

If you go for an open-air swim, the outlying lakes are preferable, followed by the river locations reached by hydrofoil, which aren't affected by Moscow's industrial waste. Swallowing water may cause mild stomach cramps, so young kids should only be allowed to wade. Everyone should shower as soon as possible to avoid 'swimmer's itch'.

Serebryanny Bor

Metro Polezhayevskaya, then trolleybus 20, 21, 65 (coming from town, leave the station via the staircase near the front carriage). **Open** 24 hours daily.
Pack your swimsuit, towels, buckets and spades and a picnic lunch and head for the public beach of Serebryanny Bor. A short bridge across to the island and you're immediately removed from the noise and bustle of the city into peace, quiet and the shade of huge pine trees. The island's main road leads to Moscow's most popular beach, but there are less crowded spots to be found off through the woods to the left, where you should find the island's main inlet, Bezdonnoye Ozero (Bottomless Lake). Cross the bridge and head left until you come to the river. In summer, take the kids for a ferry ride round the island or hire a boat or pedalo. A great retreat from the fast pace of sightseeing downtown, but keep in mind that there are stretches on the island for nudists and gays, and it can get crowded at weekends.

Tishkovo or Bukhta Radosti

Metro Rechnoi Vokzal.
The hydrofoils that ply the Moscow River are great for sightseeing or to travel to the woodland settings and sun-drenched coves of Tishkovo or Bukhta Radosti. To get to the jetty, go to Rechnoi Vokzal, cross Leningradskoye Shosse and walk through the station grounds. It's a wonderful boat ride, a great opportunity for a picnic lunch and plenty of sun and swimming. For details *see page 254* **Getting Around Moscow**.

Tsaritsyno

Metro Tsaritsyno or Orekhova (325 0922). **Open** 24 hours daily; *restaurant* noon-11pm daily; *stables* 9am-9pm daily.
Let your children explore these palace ruins, set beside lakes and woods at the Tsaritsyno public park (*see chapter* **Sightseeing**). There are rowing boats for hire, a restaurant by the water and stables behind it. The kids can hire a horse by the hour or go on a horse and cart ride. Close by is a wonderful playground with wooden boats, seesaws and swings. If the dirty water doesn't intimidate you, bathing in the lake is permitted.

Water Stadium

Vodny Stadion. Metro Vodny Stadion. **Open** 10am-10pm daily. **Admission** $1.50 adults; $1 children.
Walk east from the metro toward Leningradskoye Shosse, take the underpass and follow signs to the market and park entrance. With the market on your left, walk straight to the water, turn right at the concrete grandstand and before you is this attractive private beach set in a bend on the west bank of the Moscow River. It's a great spot for a family picnic; not only is it in a convenient location, but it has showers, changing rooms and kiosks.

Film

Crisis? What crisis? Russian cinema may be in transition, but don't write it off.

For almost a decade, one word has perfectly summed up every aspect of Russian film: crisis. The suspension in the early 1990s of state funding for Lenin's cherished 'greatest of the propaganda arts' and the almost total collapse of the country's distribution system led to an unprecedented and catastrophic drop in output. A global film-making nation that had once run a close third to Hollywood and Bollywood could now barely muster up a handful of titles every year. In 1996, the centenary of Russian cinema, a paltry 20 new films were made – most of them ad hoc junk cobbled together via various funding sources.

It was bad, but then something had to change. Despite its illustrious beginnings, Russian cinema had grown, during the Soviet period, into a massive and unwieldy industry, barely able to produce an Oscar nomination once a decade. But now the flood of pictures had slowed to an anaemic trickle, the Russians seem to have secured a permanent place on the Foreign Film nomination line-up. In 1997 and 1998, the Motion Picture Academy's top five included Sergei Bodrov's *Prisoner of the Mountains* and Pavel Chukhrai's excellent *The Thief*; in 1994, Nikita Mikhalkov had carried off the prize for his family tale of Stalinist duplicity, *Burnt by the Sun*. On the European festival circuit, where Russian films have traditionally enjoyed a good deal of success, the crisis barely made a dent.

But despite continuing government indifference to calls for emergency funding and even a for re-nationalisation of the distribution network, the Russian cinema industry has managed to gather new momentum. In 1997, recovering miraculously from the nadir of the previous year, the country released an impressive 50 films, some of them of an extremely high standard. Included in this crop was Ukrainian director Kira Muratova's compact masterpiece, *Three Stories*, a powerful and subtle comment on Russian contemporary life in which the impact of criminality on the central character is graphically illustrated. Another 1997 film, *Brat* (Brother), by director Alexei Balabanov, was also a grim portrait of criminality, this time of the squalid, mindless, reflex variety endemic in the mafia underworld. The first half of 1998 also produced a couple of brilliant pictures. *Strana Glukhikh* (Land of the Deaf), from director Valery Todorovsky, is a strikingly original story of a young woman's experiment in prostitution that

takes its inspiration from Dostoyevsky's *Crime and Punishment*, and the Oscar-nominated *The Thief* is a gripping, faultlessly professional piece that examines life on the fringes in post-war Stalinist Russia. 1998 should see the release of Oscar-winning director Nikita Mikhalkov's *The Barber of Siberia*, whose budget of $35 million makes it the most expensive film in the history of Russian cinema. More important than numbers or isolated examples is the general character of this sudden and unexpected upsurge. The majority of directors currently working are aged under 40 and eager to tackle contemporary subjects in unflinching and innovative ways. And while the basic financial situation is unchanged, rather than whining about lack of government spoon-feeding, the new generation has assiduously embraced the market, carefully balancing aesthetic with commercial concerns, just as film-makers have been doing in other countries throughout the twentieth century. In short, catastrophic collapse has led to the formation of a young, vibrant film culture, with tremendous potential to produce stunning work over the next few years.

CINEMA-GOING

Film buffs may find the choice of movies and cinemas in Moscow a bit disappointing. In Soviet times, the city had a huge variety of cinemas; these days many have either shut or been turned into offices and warehouses. Of those that have survived, a large proportion are now showing tawdry erotic and violent films, once forbidden on the Russian screen. Ticket prices have soared: if going to see a movie once cost less than a can of cola, now it can be as much as a meal at a restaurant. Nevertheless, there are a few places worth a visit, and plans to build more multi-screen cinemas within the next year should add variety at least.

US produced movies are the hottest (and generally the only) ticket here, so if you are keen to see the latest Hollywood product, this place is for you. But if you're after some funky independent or foreign offering, you may find Moscow a bit of a celluloid desert. Art-house or alternative films are a particularly endangered species. The best guide to what's on (in both Russian and English) is the *MT Out* section in each Friday's *Moscow Times*. For film festivals, *see chapter* **Moscow by Season**.

Russian rushes

Russia's place in the annals of cinematic history is ensured by the likes of Eisenstein and Tarkovsky, but what of the humbler efforts in the celluloid archives? Here's the definitive guide to the good, the bad and the extremely ugly of Russian film.

Battleship Potemkin (1925)
(Bronenosets Potyomkin). **Director** Sergei Eisenstein.
The story of the 1905 Kronstadt navy mutiny that sparked the Revolution. The most written-about film in history.

Oktyabr (1928)
Director Sergei Eisenstein.
Another constructivist-inspired classic with a hurtling angular narrative.

The Man with the Movie Camera (1929)
(Chelovek c Kinoapparatom). **Director** Dziga Vertov.
Surreal pseudo-documentary about the state of the Soviet State. It's a seminal work exploring modes of representation that still continues to influence.

My Grandmother (1929)
(Maya Babushka). **Director** Kote Mikaberidze.
Grotesque comedy poking fun at that traditional Russian ogre: bureaucracy.

Lenin in October (1937)
(Lenin v Oktyabr). **Director** Mikhail Romm.
Lenin storms the Winter Palace, that great event that led inexorably to the later glut of Lenin films.

Lenin in Paris (1938)
(Lenin v Parizhe). **Directors** Sergei Utkevich, Leonid Edlin.
Lenin in Paris, the Soviet film-maker's answer to Lassie and the Lone Ranger rolled into one, sets up school outside Paris to teach *les enfants* how to be good revolutionaries.

Poster for **The Man with the Movie Camera.**

Cinemas

American House of Cinema
Amerikansky Dom Kino, 2nd floor, Radisson Slavjanskaya Hotel, Berezhkovskaya Naberezhnaya 2 (941 8747). Metro Kievskaya. **Tickets** $8-$13. **No credit cards.**
This cinema is located in one of the most expensive hotels in Moscow. It's not a particularly pretty space, but there is an adjacent bar to lounge around in before the showing and enough capacity – 500 seats – to mean that tickets are generally available. From Monday to Thursday students and pensioners get half-price tickets. All films are in English with a simultaneous Russian translation via headphones.

Cinema Centre
Kinotsentr, Druzhinnikovskaya Ulitsa 15 (205 7306/255 9692). Metro Krasnopresnenskaya. **Tickets** $4-$11. **No credit cards.**
This theatre has one of the best selections of films in town. It usually shows around 15-20 a month, among them new European, US and Russian releases in the original language. There are two screens, one seating 750, the other 140, both equipped with digital Dolby. Though the overall design is gloomy and unfriendly, the auditoria are comfortable, and there's a café on the first floor and a bar on the second.

Cinema Museum
Muzei Kino, Druzhinnikovskaya Ulitsa 15 (255 9086). Metro Krasnopresnenskaya. **Tickets** $2-$3. **No credit cards.**
One of the cheapest and most democratic theatres in Moscow, this is the only place in the city to show old classic European and US films in their original language. There are seven cosy screens, each seating about 30 people, and a homey atmosphere, with people shoving in and sitting on straight-back chairs. Students, *babushki* and arty film-industry types make up the clientele. A must for buffs, but it's usually closed in July and August. Located in the same building as the Cinema Centre.

Dome Theatre
Pod Kupolom, Olimpiisky Prospekt 18/1 (931 9873). Metro Prospekt Mira. **Open** Thur-Sun. **Tickets** $8. **No credit cards.** **Map p278 D1**
Plenty of seats (300) and a Dolby Surround system; the only problem with this theatre is its location. Even though it's only ten minutes' walk from the metro, it's still quite hard to find. Leaving the metro, walk past the Olympic Stadium and then turn right towards the Olympic Penta hotel. The Dome is situated in a small house with a glassy roof right in front of the hotel. On Thursdays, women pay half price; on Fridays it's the same deal for students. A restaurant offers a 20 per cent discount to cinema-goers.

Alexander Nevsky (1938)

Director Sergei Eisenstein.
Nationalist epic, scored by Prokofiev and approved by Stalin. Laurence Olivier studied its stirring battle scenes for his still-definitive *Henry V*.

Ivan the Terrible (1944-46)

(Ivan Grozny). **Director** Sergei Eisenstein.
Incomplete trilogy (only the initial two thirds were ever finished) that offers, depending on your standpoint, a consciousness-raising tale or a camp essay about tyranny.

Ivan's Childhood (1962)

(Ivnovo Detstvo). **Director** Andrei Tarkovsky.
Eerie, glacial and grainy portrait of a child-spy in World War II. Tarkovsky's début showcases the poetic stillness that would characterise later films such as *Solaris* (1972).

Hamlet (1964)

Director Grigory Kozintsev.
No procrastination here: an unfeasibly blond Hamlet (period joke – Gertrude: 'Hamlet! What *have* you done to your hair?' Hamlet: 'I've had a rinse!') gets the positive hero treatment.

Andrei Rublev (1966)

Director Andrei Tarkovsky.
Mute fifteenth-century icon painter finds his voice. One of the best films ever made? Many think so.

War and Peace (1967)

(Voina i Mir) **Director** Sergei Bondarchuk.
Epic Tolstovian tale weighing in at an unbelievable 507 minutes in its Russian version. Watch it for its set scenes of ballrooms and battles. Spectacle apart, bring your lunch.

My Heart is in the Highlands (1967)

(B Gorakh Moye Serdste). **Director** Ruslan Hamdamov.
Poetic, lyrical film about a miniature metropolis

6th of July (1968)

(Shestova Yulye). **Director** Yulia Karasik.
Lenin struggles against his leftie foes, the Socialist Revolutionaries. Watch him triumph over false consciousness! Brimming with the optimism borne of historical inevitability.

White Sun in the Desert (1969)

(Beliya Solnitsa v Pustine). **Director** Vladimir Motyl.
Russian Western about one man's efforts to rescue a travelling harem. Brezhnev's favourite made-for-TV film.

The Colour of Pomegranates (1969)

(Nran Gouyne). **Director** Sergei Paradjanov.
Astonishingly beautiful film based on the life of the eighteenth-century Armenian poet Sayat Nova. The painterly images may seem obscure to western eyes, but this paean to Armenian culture caused problems for the Soviet censors.

Irony of Fate (1975)

(C Lyogkim Parom). **Director** Eldar Ryazanov.
Corny tale of a drunkard who knocks on the wrong door in the wrong city. Shows on Russian TV every New Year's Eve.

The Meeting Place Can't be Changed (1979)

(Mesto Vstrecha Izmenit Niyelza). **Director** Stanislav Govorukhin.
Russian spy movie featuring a shady organisation called the Black Cat. Russians settle round the samovar for this one.

Katia Ismailova (1994)

(Podmoskovnye Vechera). **Director** Valery Todorovsky.
Adapted from Leskov's 1864 novella, this crime of passion story comes over as Chekhov meets *Double Indemnity* or *The Postman Always Rings Twice*.

Of Freaks and Men (1998)

(Pro Urodov i Lyudi). **Director** Alexei Balabanov.
Stunner of a period piece about St Petersburg pornographers at the turn of the nineteenth century.

Illuzion

Kotelnicheskaya Naberezhnaya 1/15 (915 4353). Metro Taganskaya, then trolleybus 63. **Tickets** 90¢-$2. **No credit cards. Map** p282 E4/5
This is one of the oldest theatres in town and was once the most popular, but it lost most of its patrons during Perestroika and has since been completely renovated. It's located in one of the big Stalin skyscrapers (you'll know it when you see it, it looks like something out of *Batman*). There are 320 seats in the hall, which is equipped with Dolby. The majority of films shown are in Russian, but the 7pm show on Monday is a French-language film and the 7pm show on Wednesday is an English-language film, and German-language films are planned. There's a bar in the lobby.

Khanzhonkov's House

Dom Khanzhonkova (Moskva Movie Theatre), Triumfalnaya Ploshchad 1 (251 5860). Metro Mayakovskaya.
Tickets $1-$10. **No credit cards. Map** p277 B1
The main advantage of this theatre is its central location, close to Tverskaya Ulitsa and steps from a host of international restaurants. Unfortunately, that's probably its only advantage. The 550-seat auditorium is equipped with an old mono system, and there's no bar. Most films are Russian, and are shown in the original language. English-language shows are occasional. Students and pensioners pay half price.

Kodak Cinema World

Kodak-Kinomir, Nastasin Pereulok 2 (209 4359). Metro Pushkinskaya. **Tickets** $3-$15. **No credit cards. Map** p277 B2
The most popular theatre in town, teeming with crowds of America-philes. Loads of popcorn, Coke and latest Hollywood blockbusters are always available, along with souvenirs, soundtracks and videos (some in English). Seating 475 and Dolby-equipped, it's frequently the chosen venue for premières.

Pushkinsky Cinema

Pushkinskaya Ploshchad 2 (229 2111/7300). Metro Pushkinskaya, Chekhovskaya or Tverskaya. **Tickets** $5-$8. **No credit cards. Map** p278 C2
This theatre used to be the traditional venue for Soviet celebrations and festivals. These days, it's used for gala presentations of foreign and Russian blockbusters. After Perestroika, the Pushkin was repaired, renamed and turned into an entertainment complex. It has state-of-the-art equipment, including an acoustic ceiling, 38 speakers and a mobile stage. Also on the premises are a nightclub, casino and restaurant. The latest US releases are the usual fare, and if you're not happy with the selection, Kodak Cinema World is just around the corner. Occasional English-language shows.

A bluffer's guide to Russian film

Though the Lumière brothers gave the first Russian demonstration of cinematography, way back in 1896, Russian cinema didn't really get in gear until the mid-1920s, with the release of Eisenstein's *Battleship Potemkin*. Inspired by the constructivist movement in art, Eisenstein used the montage technique to edit together contrasting fragments in order to create a hurtling, angular narrative. *Potemkin* (1925) and *Oktyabr* (1928) elevated communist ideology to the realm of the sublime, and became world classics into the bargain. Eisenstein put down his unsurpassed technical brilliance to the shortage of film stock after the Revolution. It gave him time to theorise.

Another great director of this period was Dziga Vertov (the pseudonym of Dennis Kaufman), who made *The Man with the Movie Camera* (1929), a seminal work exploring modes of representation that still continues to influence. Experimentation was effectively stamped out, however, in the 1930s with the imposition of stultifying socialist realism, which bullied the

genre into empty, optimistic posturing. This period was also famous for its ludicrous Lenin and Stalin biopics.

Khrushchev's thaw in the 1950s and early 1960s brought with it a cinematic deluge of self-reflection, satire and experiment, all elements that fed the work of Andrei Tarkovsky, who received the Palme d'Or at Cannes in 1962 for his stunning début *Ivan's Childhood*, the story of a boy reconnaissance agent. He went on to make the extraordinary film *Andrei Rublev (below)*, based on the life of the fifteenth-century icon painter. Though finished in 1966, it was released only in 1971 after much international pressure.

Gorbachev's reforms of the mid-1980s ushered in Russian cinema's next notable phase. Perestroika film was distinguished by political exposé, sex and violence. Stock characters included prostitutes, killers, mafiosi and drug addicts. While this period produced no great figures or films, it was a necessary release of social and artistic pressure and a springboard for the (hopefully) bright future of Russian cinema.

Gay & Lesbian Moscow

Russia has finally decriminalised homosexuality, but Moscow is still far from gay-friendly.

The Nutcracker – Pyotr Ilich Tchaikovsky.

Here's a heartening statistic: in 1989, 33 per cent of Russians advocated that homosexuals should be 'exterminated'. By 1995, that number had fallen to a mere six per cent. No word on what the 27 per cent who changed their answer now advocate (Chinese water torture was thankfully not an option on the questionnaire), but it may be safe to assume that the live-and-let-live attitude that was prevalent in cosmopolitan Russia before the communists took over is taking hold once again.

The infamous Article 121 of the Russian constitution, which criminalised male homosexual acts (though, in classic Victorian manner, failed to mention lesbians) was only repealed in 1993 (the age of consent is 16), making Russia one of the last countries in the world to junk its outright ban. Since then, gay life has been sashaying quietly out of the closet. Gay clubs, many with drag shows, strippers and other such diversions, now draw not only crowds of gays, but hordes of young, straight Russians looking for a hip place to hang out. Being gay may not be quite fashionable (yet), but there is an openness that would have been unthinkable back in the USSR.

Beware, however: post-Soviet Russia is still far from a gay-friendly place. Even though Article 121 has been repealed, the laws are whatever police with machine guns decide they are. Gay clubs are still raided regularly by baton-wielding police thugs, allegedly searching for drugs, and customers have been known to receive quite brutal beatings. Gay celebrities still fear to acknowledge their sexuality in case it would be bad for business among the puritan babushka set. But the big news about gay life in Moscow is that there *is* such a thing. From clandestine meetings in parks and alleyways, Russian gays have moved on to less clandestine gay bars and cafés too. Feel free to get down and get friendly with a same-sex partner in the venues where gays hang out. It ain't Greenwich Village or even Soho's Old Compton Street, but it's a damn sight closer than it used to be.

Bars & pubs

Dary Morya

Maly Gnezdnikovsky Pereulok 9/8, behind Tverskaya Ulitsa 17 (229 7709). Metro Tverskaya. **Open** 10am-3am daily. **Admission** free. **No credit cards. Map** p278 C2

An almost obligatory stop for gay visitors to the capital: a friendly, comfortable café/bar just down the road from the Kremlin, in the middle of one of Moscow's prime shopping districts. The Dary Morya ('gifts of the sea'), so named because it's nestled in a quiet courtyard behind the voluminous Dary Morya seafood store on Tverskoi Bulvar, is the perfect place to stop off for a drink in the middle of a busy sightseeing day. Just go through the arch to the right of the Dary Morya store, then turn left and look for the Winston cigarettes sign. It's intimate (small, but not uncomfortable), with a bar at one end and a glowing fish tank at the other. Customers are mostly men, though women stop by too. The random musical instruments that adorn the walls add an incongruous touch to its quirky charm. The friendly staff cater to a mostly male clientele; it's one of very few places to be upfront about catering to gays.

Elf

Ulitsa Zemlyanoi Val 13/1 (917 2014). Metro Kurskaya. **Open** 11am-midnight daily. **Admission** free Mon-Thur; $4 Fri-Sun. **No credit cards. Map p282 F4**

Elf is a pretty apt name for this place, so tiny it feels like a miniature gay bar. The space, very small to begin with, has been divided into three rooms: the European café room, the disco mania room and the hunting lodge room. Trouble is, they're all so close together, you can hardly turn around in one without falling into another. The café room has the most unforced atmosphere: dainty tables dot the *faux*-parquet floor, and a bar seats three or four comfortably. The disco room has the requisite coloured lights, mirrors and dark walls, but is about the size of a postage stamp. The hunting lodge room borders on camp, with its fake fireplace, stone walls and clunky wooden booths. It's a classic case of trying to do too much with too little, and the management plans to add yet more: a billiard room in another part of the building. The Elf expands! Perhaps eventually to human size.

Clubs

Ask a random young Russian if there are any bars or clubs for gays in Moscow, and they will most likely know the correct answer: yes. But ask them how many there are, and they'll probably be off by more than half. There are at least two clubs here that everyone seems to know about: **Shans**, the cranky belle of the gay scene; and **Chameleon**, the young, brash upstart. Both are worth a look. But don't neglect the smaller, out-of-the way cafés and bars that may lack the same star power, but they have their own charm, nonetheless.

Chameleon

Ulitsa Presnensky Val 14 (253 6343/6346). Metro Ulitsa 1905 Goda. **Open** 10pm-8am Fri, Sat; $11 Thur, Sun; $8 Wed; $5 Tue (women only); free Mon, Tue (men only). **No credit cards.**

When Chance began to wane, Chameleon moved in to take its place. Buff, barely dressed go-go boys writhe in cages above the main dancefloor. A smaller room is packed with men stripped to the waist, flaunting immaculate musculature. Drag queens and strippers perform regular shows throughout the night. In general, this is the queer place to be. Get there quick, though, as fashions on the mercurial Moscow club scene can change overnight, and the place may be passé by the time you turn the page. Avoid the back room, which is populated with pickpockets and other assorted no-goodniks. The door differentials tell their own story: women are expected to pay or stay away.

Delfiny

Rakhmanovsky Pereulok 1/24 (200 5566). Metro Teatralnaya/Kuznetsky Most. **Open** midnight-4am Mon-Thur; 11pm-4.30am Fri-Sun. **Admission** $12; free before midnight Mon-Thur. **No credit cards. Map p278 C2**

Dominated by a designerish blue décor, Delfiny (or dolphins) is themed around maritime subjects and cobalt colours: suitable, seeing that 'goluboi' (light blue) means gay in Russian slang. Delfiny's main feature is its swimming pool, in which men (for women are strictly limited here) disport themselves after a spot of disco dancing. Towels and togs are available, but many people swim naked. The restaurant resembles a ship, offering optimistic views (a view of the Moroccan seaboard) and a food and drinks menu with nautically named items, brought to you by waiters in naval attire. A chill-out area, filled with Turkish couches and carpets, is less hectic and in the evenings, offers strip shows. The VIP room boasts souvenirs of pop-diva Alla Pugacheva and Versace-style paintings.

Dyke

Ploshchad Trubnaya 4 (208 4637/3341). Metro Tsvetnoi Bulvar. **Open** 6-11pm Sat, Sun. **Admission** $8. **No credit cards. Map p278 D1**

On Saturday nights, the Three Monkeys (*see below*) becomes Dyke, Moscow's premier lesbian night, run by über-dyke Zhenya Debryanskaya, a long-time gay activist. It has a cosy, welcoming feel, thanks not only to the décor, but also to the fact that all the women there seem to know each other. (How could that be?) The DJ plays a good mix of Euro, Russian and American dance and the girl-to-girl *frisson* keeps this institution alive and alluring.

Imperiya Kino

Ulitsa Povarskaya 33 (290 1923/fax 290 3922/4489). Metro Barrikadnaya. **Open** 11pm-6am Fri-Sun. **Admission** $6.50-$12. **No credit cards. Map p277 A3/B3**

Imperiya Kino is located in one of those Soviet-era Houses of Culture, which means it's got all the charm of a warehouse decorated with faded mosaics extolling the achievements of the five-year-plan wheat harvest. A few years ago, this place would have been on the top of your list of desirable party spots. Now it's somewhat passé, though the management is pinning all its hopes on a planned renovation. The transvestite/transsexual scene here is still unsurpassed in Moscow, however. Check out the fabulous Varvara, who performs every Friday night. The camp factor is through the roof.

Shans

Chance, Dom Kultury Serp I Molot, Goncharnaya Ulitsa 11/15 (298 6247). Metro Ploshchad Ilicha. **Open** 11pm-6am daily; *large dancefloor* Thur-Sun. **Admission** $8-$14 depending on night and gender. **No credit cards. Map p282 E4/E5**

Once the hippest, funkiest (gay or straight) venue in town, Chance has taken on a more wasted, jaded feel. Having suffered a few raids from the gentlemen at OMON (an aggressive Russian police agency), the club's patrons have understandably lost some of their enthusiasm. It's still fun to drop by, but it's not the 'must-see' kind of place it once was. Definitely worth a look is the famous merman show: in an aquarium along the back wall of the small dancefloor, near-naked, sculpted, young men swim around in a kind of erotic water ballet. The action on the dancefloor depends mostly on the DJ and the crowd. On the downside, the goons on the door aren't very polite about searching you and the club is less gay than previously, which is a little daunting for some, especially closeted gay Russians who don't want to run into workmates or acquaintances.

Three Monkeys

Ploshchad Trubnaya 4 (208 4637/3341). Metro Tsvetnoi Bulvar. **Open** 6pm-9am daily; *women's nights* 6-11pm Sat, Sun. **Admission** free with membership. **Map p278 D1**

Three Monkeys, which has always billed itself as a members-only establishment, has something of a country club feel. Back in the halcyon days of the Moscow scene, the club could afford to be picky about who it let in, but now a polite interrogation and the surrender of some basic information – as opposed to fabulous pecs and/or a briefcase full of rubles – will get you membership. Six guests can go in with one member. The club itself is quite comfortable and civilised: there's a pool table on the first floor, and upstairs there are lounge-about couches and a small dancefloor. The club itself is a little difficult to find – but look out for the little hunting shop with stuffed pheasants, lynxes and wolves in the window and you're almost there.

Russia's Pride and joy: the national colours fly alongside those of the international gay movement on National Flag Day.

Camping it up – Vaslav Nijinsky.

Cruising

Aleksandrovsky Sad A Soviet-era relic; this is the small garden just outside the Kremlin, where the Tomb of the Unknown Soldier and monuments to the city's World War II heroes are. Mayor Luzhkov's monstrous shopping plaza has made this a less discreet venue. Good for a nostalgic stroll, though.

Bolshoi Theatre People have always gathered in front of the Bolshoi – not just gays, but all manner of fringe elements in Soviet society. It was popular to the point of infamy when there weren't any gay bars or meeting places. Increasing tolerance has dimmed its status, however, and a recent refurbishment of the square has made it less intimate.

Ilinsky Park Not so much a park as a green strip of land between the two exits of Metro Kitai-Gorod. Look for the skateboarders, and wander up the strip, by the statue. A prime cruising spot (we're told), but look out for police on the prowl.

Prospekt Vernadskogo Dodgy, and probably best avoided; it's cruisy, but with a dangerous edge. Lots of reports of soldiers meandering around and people getting beaten up. You figure out the rest.

Serebryanny Bor Beach From Metro Shchukinskaya, walk down Novoshchukinskaya Ulitsa, and cross the bridge over the river. Turn left and walk down the peninsula for about 15 minutes. Eventually you'll come to a nude beach, and a little further on you'll find the gay beach. Alternatively go via metro to Polezhaevskaya and find a *marshrutny taksi* going in the direction of the peninsula.

Dom Zdorovya (Novoalekseyevskaya 25, Metro Alekseyevskaya). The 'House of Health' has a good *banya*. Russian gay men do not advise visiting a gay *banya* unless you're in the company of someone who has been there before. Or, at the very least, first time you go, stick to the idea of simply bathing with fellow *muzhiki*; no funny stuff, or you could find yourself in an unfunny situation.

HIV & AIDS

Russia is not exempt from HIV infection, so do as you would in any other place and play safe. If you don't bring your own condoms (and you're advised to do so), condoms ('prezervativy') are available in most Russian chemists, but avoid the local brands in favour of the better-known ones. Try Pridenet's website for general information. The following Moscow-based organisations can provide useful details:

AESOP Centre *PO Box 27, Moscow 121552 (141 8315).*

International Gay & Lesbian Human Rights Commission *Bolshevistskaya Ulitsa 21/15 (252 3316).*

Moscow Union of Lesbians *(152 1657).*

Pridenet http://www.pridenet.com/russia.html

The Rainbow Foundation *Malomoskovskaya Ulitsa 4 (489 2543).*

Publications

Lots of publications have come out in the last six or seven years, but not one seems to have much, if any, staying power. The most stable at the moment seems to be *1/10*, published by a Russian living in Prague. Go figure. Other titles to look for include *ARGO, Risk, Uranus* and *Partnyor(sha)*. These are the actual gay publications, published on shoestring budgets, available mostly through word of mouth. They won't be at your regular kiosk, although you might find them occasionally on the magazine tables in the metro between Pushkinskaya and Tverskaya stations.

Restaurants

Angelico's

Bolshoi Karetny Pereulok 6/1 (299 3696). Metro Tsvetnoi Bulvar. **Open** 11am-1am daily. **Credit** AmEx, DC, MC, V. **Map p278 C1**

A sophisticated setting in which gays with money can enjoy good Mediterranean cuisine. The dining area is elegant, tastefully done out with polished hardwood floors, a long bar with a brass rail, and fresh flowers on all the tables. Signed photos of Bolshoi dancers grace the entrance, including one from the incomparable Maya Plisetskaya. Angelico's is definitely gay-friendly, but the management seems unsure whether to make a real play for gay customers.

Branch: Rossini, Ducat Platsa, Ulitsa Gasheka 7 (785 0262).

Media

Where to find English-language news and listings, plus an overview of Moscow's buoyant media scene.

After years of a depressing lack of choice and reliable information, the Russian media has suddenly been blasted into an anarchic era of head-spinning proliferation and pluralism. Moscow is now saturated with mass communications, with new print titles that sprout up on the newsstands on a weekly basis and television channels that hit the market with a fanfare every year.

Communist stalwarts such as *Komsomolskaya Pravda*, now virtually a tabloid, as well as *Argumenti i Fakti* (Arguments and Facts) and the former union mouthpiece *Trud* have completely thrown off the shackles of party dogma and now cover everything from herbal cooking to sado-masochism. TV magazine and chat shows hungrily devour such formerly taboo subjects as drug addiction and, on the terrifically entertaining and coyly titled *Pro Eto* (About That) on NTV, the unfettered joys of sex in the ex-Soviet Union.

As far as printed magazines go, a plague of glossies has been visited on the capital: *Premiere*, *Cosmopolitan*, *Marie-Claire*, *Good Housekeeping*, *Playboy* and even *Men's Health*, as well as home-grown concoctions like the supremely trendy youth magazine *Ptyoch* and the contemporary culture mag *OM*. Even *Vogue* has been planning a Moscow edition. In short, the Russian media sector is booming, and despite the glut of new titles, market saturation still seems years away.

This mass-media revolution has not been without its troublesome side effects and distasteful, noxious by-products. In some cases, Russian media has liberated itself not only from the strait-jacket of state censorship but also from the strictures of good taste. Sensationalist TV crime documentaries and *911*-style emergency shows are little more than graphic roll-calls of brutal murders or hideous accidents complete with unflinching shots of mutilated dead bodies, and post-midnight TV is a riot of bouncing breasts and badly dubbed grunts.

Far more disturbing are the behind the scenes ownership struggles that have begun to distort Russian media catastrophically over the past few years. Russia's new oligarchs have been buying up cash-starved media outlets not only to make a fast buck but also for the indirect benefits of self-promotion, prestige and political influence. A gigantic swathe of the country's media holdings is controlled by just three moguls: ex-theatre director and banker Vladimir Gusinsky (NTV,

Sevodnya, *Itogi* and *Sem Dnei*), billionaire car dealer and oil magnate Boris Berezovsky (*ORT*, *Ogonyok* and *Nezavisimaya Gazeta*); and super-banker Vladimir Potanin (*Komsomolskaya Pravda*, *Expert* magazine and the *Russky Telegraph*.) Twisted links between media, commerce and politics have often dumped readers and listeners back to where they were in the communist control-freak heyday, poised somewhere between fact, fabrication and downright propaganda.

Print

Foreign publications

The English foreign language papers listed below are free and available at distribution points around the city, including all the main hotels and restaurants. All of them provide weekly listings, though the *Moscow Tribune*'s are by far the weakest. For comprehensiveness, go for the *Moscow Times* (culture on Friday, TV on Saturday) and for offbeat subcultural hilarity, choose the *Exile*, which covers clubs and music venues.

Imported newspapers are available mostly from hotel stores (those at the Radisson and Metropol are two good central examples) but always at exorbitant prices – usually between $2.50 and $4 for the UK and US dailies. Most papers reach Russia a day late but it is always good to check the date, particularly in smaller outlets, as they can sometimes be weeks old.

Note that Russian newspapers and magazines are printed in Cyrillic: even the TV schedules and sports results will be unintelligible to non-Russians.

The Exile

The *Exile* is a phenomenon that couldn't really happen anywhere else in the world: an American college fraternity paper intended for a wider readership. The articles, even the ones dressed up as serious features, are basically a series of sketches targeting everything from the IMF to Moscow's stable of foreign correspondents. Misogynist, defensive, puerile and often distasteful, the *Exile* is read by almost every English speaking resident of Moscow and is, arguably, the most exciting and definitely the most entertaining expat publication around. It comes out every other Wednesday.

The Moscow Times

Founded in 1992, the *Moscow Times* gradually built itself up from a twice-weekly, bite-size 16-page paper into a very respectable daily, offering impeccable news reporting, decent features and hefty sections dealing with business, lifestyle and culture. Its coverage of the Chechen war was probably its finest hour – unflinching, courageous and unrivalled elsewhere in the international press. However, with the arrival of editor Geoff Winestock in 1997, it seems to have lost its way a little. As emphasis has shifted almost entirely to business, everything else has been allowed to languish.

The Moscow Tribune

Always prefaced by the qualifier 'barely breathing', the *Tribune* is what you read if there are no copies of the *Moscow Times* left on the stand. It's primarily a collage of wire stories, with a few substandard in-house articles thrown in. The *Tribune* was planning to relaunch itself in September '98 as a daily once again – it had scaled down to just three times a week – and promised a beefed-up cultural listings section and such unheard of innovations as editorials.

The Moscow News

A straight translation of the Russian weekly that was once one of the powerhouses of Perestroika. Some of the political commentary is interesting in that it gives foreigners access to shades of Russian opinion normally closed to them. But the clunky style of translation makes the paper a difficult and often tedious read.

Newspapers

Argumenty i Fakty

Argumenty i Fakty is a relatively independent, private weekly newspaper owned by its editor Vladislav Starkov and staff rather than some banking or industrial group. It is extremely popular thanks to its 16 regional editions and it also publishes alternating theme issues such as *AiF*

Health or *AiF I'm Young*. Its circulation of 33 million has entered the *Guinness Book of World Records*.

Izvestiya

One of the country's oldest surviving publications, *Izvestiya* was once the flagship of Soviet propaganda, but has supported the economic reforms of the 1990s. *Izvestiya* kept its status as the national paper until 1996, when a fierce political battle over ownership split it in two, creating Russia's first colour daily, *Noviye Izvestiya* (*see below*). Since it started to receive financial backing from Russia's biggest oil company, LUKoil, old *Izvestiya*'s stories have been of meagre and more conservative content, and sales figures show a loss of readers' confidence.

Kommersant

Some of the most sober news coverage, along with profound observations on the Moscow power élite can be found in the respectable *Kommersant*. The must-read newspaper for financiers, it also has extended property, arts and sports sections and, more than any other Russian paper, keeps up with the standards of Western journalism.

Komsomolskaya Pravda

The main competition to *Moscow Komsomolets* (*see below*) is *Komsomolskaya Pravda*, Russia's third-largest newspaper. Formerly the organ of Komsomol (the Communist Youth League), it has drifted politically from the Neanderthal, communist left to slightly right of centre, no doubt due to the input of its powerful sponsors – Gazprom (the world's largest natural gas company and state gas monopoly), Uneximbank and the Moscow city government. It has great street sense, targeting mostly young people.

Bubble trouble

When the Mexican soap opera *The Rich Also Cry* first hit Russian screens in 1992, it was blamed for deserted city streets, low agricultural production and unmanageable surges in power usage. Starved of suds, a huge chunk of the Russian populace tuned in daily to this 249-part saga of Mariana, a poor, uneducated peasant girl who gets co-opted into a rich family and eventually makes good. The show's popularity was undiminished by such technical quirks as the use of one male actor to dub the entire cast into Russian.

After *The Rich Also Cry* had established that the Russian market had a voracious appetite for the sex, glamour and ultra-simplification of soap, it was inevitable that would follow: 'le déluge savonneux'. The US serial *Santa Barbara* became the other great foamy landmark of the era, followed by *Simply Maria*, *Neighbours*, *Dallas*, *Beverly Hills 90210* and *Melrose Place*, as well as a host of daytime offerings wallpapering the lesser-known channels. Most remarkable about the Russian incarnations of these serials is the unbelievable turnover, with an episode once a day instead of the original

weekly dose. On *Dallas*, for instance, Pam and Bobby can break up and get back together again (twice), JR get shot and Jock die all in the space of a couple of weeks.

The undeniable power of soap has even, on occasion, been harnessed by the government for its own ends. During the second round of the 1996 presidential elections, when it was feared that a low turnout would hurt Yeltsin's chances, ORT showed the three last episodes of popular soap *Tropicanka* to prevent voters from disappearing off to their dachas (which don't usually have TV sets) instead of casting their ballots. According to the statistics, the tactic appears to have worked. More recently, in an effort to persuade Russians to pay their taxes, RTR has been involved in the making of *Maroseika 12*, a soap that draws its characters from the country's tax police.

Even Tony Blair has got in on the act, making a cameo appearance during one of his visits to Russia on the radio soap *Dom 7, Podyezd 4* (House 7, Entrance 4). Apparently, he was so well received by the public that Russian TV offered him his own serial: *Wet Liberal Pseudo-Lefties Also Cry*.

Moscow Komsomolets

Without a doubt, the most widely read paper on the Moscow metro. Published in broadsheet format, but thoroughly tabloid, it specialises in sensational coverage of crime, show-biz scandals, gossip and other populist items. The investigations are often shallow and the reporting can be unreliable.

Nezavisimaya Gazeta

In the early 1990s, *Nezavisimaya Gazeta* (Independent Gazette) was a feast of newly found freedom of speech – until it turned to 'sponsorship' from oil and car magnate Boris Berezovsky at the expense of its editorial integrity. Nowadays it's filled with opinion-led pieces, and hard news is clearly not a priority.

Noviye Izvestiya

Noviye Izvestiya was Russia's first colour daily, founded by former *Izvestiya* editor Igor Golembiovsky as a result of a political battle over *Izvestiya* ownership. A few months after his sacking, Golembiovsky founded his own paper with financial support from Boris Berezovsky and 30 of the better *Izvestiya* writers, including the award-winning Otto Latsis.

Pravda

The once-mighty mouthpiece of the communist party has been one of the more conspicuous media casualties of the post-Soviet period. After a nasty editorial squabble, the paper split in two. The new incarnation, *Pravda-5*, is owned by Greeks, who are now facing a lawsuit filed by the old *Pravda* over the use of the name. The original *Pravda* is the more interesting and hard-hitting of the two in its often outrageous statements and its continuing loyalty to the communist party. *Pravda-5*, by comparison, is bland and meek.

Russky Telegraph

The paper has one brilliant journalist, Maxim Sokolov, who used to work at *Kommersant*, but otherwise it's an organ of the powerful and politically influential bank Uneximbank.

Segodnya

Segodnya was formed in the early 1990s by *Nezavisimaya Gazeta* journalists who left the paper, tired of fighting with tyrannical editor Vitaly Tretyakov. Among them were one of Russia's best political reporters, Sergei Parkhomenko, who now edits *Itogi* magazine, and Mikhail Berger, who is the current *Segodnya* editor. *Segodnya* used to be an upbeat, democratic paper but recently turned rather bland.

Weeklies

In recent years Moscow has seen an explosion of tabloid press feeding readers a staple diet of crime, sex, the occult and, as often as not, the plain ridiculous. This larger-than-life formula was pioneered by *Speed-Info*, a colourful potpourri of articles about human psychology and relationships, which is now Russia's fifth top-selling magazine. Other populist and sensationalist sheets include *I am a Bodyguard*, *Third Eye*, the *Terrifying Newspaper* and *Beyond the Law*. More enlightened weeklies include *Obshchaya Gazeta* and the fat *Literaturnaya Gazeta*, a journal of literary critique, prose and poetry owned by former Communist Youth League leader Mikhail Khodorkovsky, now of Bank Menatep.

Magazines

Created in co-operation with the US's *Newsweek*, *Itogi* provides deep and extensive coverage of politics and business, and its society section gives an insight into the lives of Russians. The two Soviet stalwarts, *Ogonyok* and *Rabotnitsa*, have traditionally targeted, and managed to keep, a middle-class, working readership. Putting quality above hard news and business, they've hired good writers and improved their design.

Broadcasting to the masses: Ostankino Tower

The best of Moscow's entertainment magazines used to be *Vechernyaya Moskva*, which was one of the first media casualties of the 1998 crisis and is now, sadly, no more. *Stolitsa* has sizeable listings for TV, theatre, film, concerts, restaurants and shopping, as do three pocket-sized nightlife guides, *Ne Spat!*, *Razgulyai* and *Dosug v Moskve*, available free in bars, clubs and restaurants.

Gone are the days when the so-called 'fat journals' were indispensable, witty and intelligent reads. Their Glasnost mission of publishing forbidden literature has exhausted itself. Readers are more interested in the glossy lifestyle and celeb magazines like *Litsa*, the local equivalent of *People* magazine.

Television

Channel-surfing in Moscow is limited to ten channels, though that's three times more than a few years ago. With all the major heavyweight advertisers here, Russia's TV stations are extremely commercial. New channels such as CTC, as well as a wave of local and cable broadcasting companies, are taking a significant bite out of the top networks' audiences.

For English-language TV schedules, see the *Moscow Times*'s Saturday listings, which include Russian TV and foreign cable and satellite but no Russian cable channels. Note that dubbing rather than subtitling is the norm for imported programmes and foreign films.

Terrestrial TV

The typical Russian daytime TV follows Western scheduling almost to a T: morning news, the first round of soap operas at 9am, children's films, vintage re-runs and game shows. Early evening is the domain of high-rated talk shows such as *Ya Sama* (Myself), women's chat on TV6, and quizzes. News broadcasts are at 6pm and on the hour every hour on different channels through to midnight, interspersed with films, music videos and chats with assorted weirdos. Closing the day are erotic shows.

ORT (Channel 1)

Soviet survivor ORT is still the acknowledged industry leader with such ratings hits as *Name That Tune* and *Field of Wonders*. It shows a stock of classic Soviet movies.

RTR (Channel 2)

As the only broadcaster that is entirely state-subsidised, RTR bears the burden of having to air unwatchable programmes on the workings of the Cabinet and, therefore, has the lowest ratings. However, it is due to become the base for an enormous state media holding.

Center TV (Channel 3)

New kid on the block is Center TV (Channel 3), started by Moscow city council in June 1997. This state-of-the-art, ambitious channel deserves a better news service than it has.

Kultura (Channel 5)

This new public channel is the only real alternative to all the commercial stuff that's churned out by the other stations. Its highbrow attitude means advert- and soap-opera-free coverage of cultural life in Moscow, the provinces and abroad, including uninterrupted theatre performances and classical music concerts. It shares airtime with entertainment and shopping channel TeleExpo.

NTV (Channel 4)

A daring 1993 start-up by the Most Group, NTV (Channel 4) is the only entirely private Russian network. Targeting the young and the wealthy, it features a trademark ironic style and specialises in hard-hitting news reporting as in the case of its no-nonsense coverage of the Chechen war. It also does a quality line in thrillers and foreign action dramas.

TV6 (Channel 6)

TV6, pioneer of commercial TV in Russia founded with the help of CNN's Ted Turner, has developed a niche as a light entertainment youth channel.

Cable TV & satellite

Moscow has four channels, which are included in the local cable circuit in some areas of Moscow but otherwise require a special antenna to be viewed. These will soon include a Russian version of MTV, set to replace the current jukebox channel BizTV. Foreign cable channels that can be received here include CNN, NBC Superchannel, BBC World, TNT, Eurosport, Discovery, Travel and Pro7.

The major Russian cable channels are NTV Plus Sports, NTV Plus Nashe Kino (classic Russian films), NTV Mir Kino (foreign films and TV series), an NTV children's channel called Detsky Mir, NTV Plus Music and NTV Nochnoi Kanal (soft porn after midnight).

Radio

Russia still pipes four state-owned radio stations directly in to every home that has a (free) receiver. It features ad-free public stations **Radio of Russia** (Channel 1), **Vozrozhdeniye** (Channel 2) and Soviet stalwarts **Mayak** and **Govorit Moskva** (sharing Channel 3). At the other end of the spectrum, there are all kinds of sounds and styles from Hare Krishna radio **Krishna Loka** (963 AM) to purely techno **Stantsiya** (106.8 FM). As in the West, most interesting talk and information radio can be found on the AM dial, with plenty of Russian-language and international news and interviews. Most music radios are on the FM waves.

Russian commercial radio is rigidly formatted and repetitive during the daytime. News bulletins are interspersed with sports and motor vehicle news, weather reports, reviews and other small-format newscasts. Call-in shows are ubiquitous and invariably boring, and ads dominate.

News & talk

Ekho Moskvy (73.82 AM or 91.0 FM) is the most popular and upbeat info radio. Radio of Russia (966.44 SW) is perhaps the most conservative station with a lot of info, interviews, programmes for children and teenagers and old Soviet archive recordings of poetry and radio. Otkrytoye Radio (102.5 FM) specialises in business news and press digests and is home for a new show by famous dissident Seva Novgorodtsev, who once broadcast programmes about rock music into the USSR from the London-based BBC Russian Service. Nadezhda (1044 AM or 104.2 FM), aimed at older adults, tends to broadcast in a larger format with extended interviews and feature stories.

International news

Nemetskaya Volna (693 MW) is German; the BBC World Service is English (1260 MW); RFI (1440 AM) is French.

Rock, pop & dance

Russkoye Radio (105.7 FM) plays unremarkable Russian pop and *devushka* music; Nikolai Fomenko, known for his comic stream-of-consciousness monologues, hosts *Good Morning, Vietnam!* on Wednesdays from 9am to 11am. Serebryany Dozhd (100.1 FM) is a more upbeat mix of international chart music. It's the home of *Gloomy Morning* with Alexander Gordon (7-11am Mon, Fri), whose style many compare to Howard Stern's. Maximum (103.7 FM) pumps out rock, independent and electronic music and is known for the *Runway* morning show (7-11am Mon-Fri) majoring on joke phone calls broadcast live. Evropa Plus (106.2 FM) broadcasts the usual mixture of contemporary music and features erotic call-ins with Zheni Shaden on weeknights, midnight to 3am. Stantsiya (106.8 FM) pounds out heavy techno, trip-hop, acid funk and experimental electronica, getting partygoers in the mood 24 hours a day.

Other music

Klassika (102.1 FM) offers a splendid mix of classical hits in all conceivable musical styles. Hit-FM (107.4 FM) is based on the same idea, but limited to pop and rock music. Nostalgie (100.5 FM) plays, well, the name speaks for itself. Romantic music from all eras, with a heavy emphasis on French songs. Retro (72.92 SW) is the most popular station with middle-aged and elderly taxi drivers, playing solely Soviet songs from the 1930s to the 1980s.

Music: Classical & Opera

When audiences complain that the loss of two urns from Rachmaninov Hall ruined its acoustics, you know serious listening is in order.

Moscow is one of the world's great centres for classical music. The audiences are critical and demanding but highly appreciative when a good performance takes place. While Muscovites are unable to pay more than a few dollars for tickets, they remain enthusiastic concert-goers. At the end of a concert, performers are regularly showered with flowers and gifts. The slow hand clap is the very highest honour that the public can accord the performer. An evening out at a performance in Moscow is certainly an experience not to be missed by any classical music lover visiting the city.

Despite this demand for classical music concerts, Moscow has surprisingly few halls. There are only three main concert halls, two of them housed in the **Moscow Tchaikovsky Conservatoire**. Smaller halls do exist, some in museums, which often stage excellent recitals or choir performances. The Orthodox Church does not allow instrumental music to be played within its walls, but both Catholic and Anglican churches have regular concerts that are well worth attending. During the summer, several palaces are also opened for concerts.

To this day, foreigners visiting the city and even Muscovites themselves are confused as to which orchestra is which. Moscow orchestral life has still to recover from the near-fatal blow it was struck in 1990 when pianist Mikhail Pletnev announced that he was founding an orchestra where the average salary would be 1,000 rubles, a large increase on the 200 rubles current at the time. Needless to say, musicians from every Moscow orchestra jumped ship to join the new orchestra. Overnight, two of the world's greatest conductors, Yevgeny Svetlanov and Gennady Rozhdestvensky, were left with orchestras that were mere shadows of their former selves. Where Pletnev got the money for this venture is still a well-kept secret. The orchestra claimed to be the first independent orchestra in the USSR and not to be state supported. Muscovites were unconvinced, especially since so many so-called 'private' ventures were founded with money taken from the state's coffers.

During the 1991 coup, Pletnev got further support from Boris Yeltsin. To the horror of musicians and public, the world-famous State Orchestra of the USSR (Svetlanov's orchestra) was abandoned by the new Russian state and Pletnev's orchestra was declared to be the **Russian National Orchestra**.

Svetlanov's orchestra ended up paying their own airfares to Japan for a tour because the daily allowances were so good there. Unsurprisingly, the new Russian state lost one of its most celebrated sons as Rozhdestvensky departed for a post in Stockholm while Svetlanov in principle remained but in practice conducted more abroad than at home.

These days, the stricken orchestras are fighting hard not only to survive but to create imaginative programming. Svetlanov's orchestra recently hosted concerts with German virtuoso conductor Kurt Mazur. Rozhdestvensky and Svetlanov sometimes come back to conduct their old orchestras. Rozhdestvensky's orchestra, now named the **Russian Capella**, is in the hands of his former pupil, Valery Polansky. Nevertheless, with musicians' salaries in these orchestras between $150 and $200 a month, it is a critical state of affairs. Surprisingly, the orchestras can still rally to present some fine performances. It is best to wait for performances with Rozhdestvensky and Svetlanov and other renowned guest conductors. Thankfully, these are now becoming more frequent.

Halls

Main halls

A few words of caution. Booking tickets over the telephone is not recommended. A personal visit to the box office is always the best option. Information given out on the phone can often bear no resemblance to the actual situation. Needless to say, credit card payment is still a thing of the future. Unless otherwise stated, performances in Moscow start at 7pm.

Bolshoi Zal Konservatorii

The Great Hall of the Moscow Tchaikovsky Conservatoire, Bolshaya Nikitskaya Ulitsa 13 (229 8183). Metro Pushkinskaya, Biblioteka Imeni Lenina or Okhotny Ryad. **Open** *box office* noon-7pm daily. **Map P277 B3**
Also occasionally referred to simply as the Moscow Tchaikovsky Conservatoire, which, in fact, contains two concert halls: the Bolshoi (Great Hall) and the Maly Zal (Small Hall, *see below*). Whatever name you know it by, there is no disputing that this is Moscow's main classical music venue. You can expect only the best here, and in its adjoining small hall, for the world reputation of the hall and its adjacent music school is immense.

Maly Zal

Small Hall of the Moscow Tchaikovsky Conservatoire, Bolshaya Nikitskaya Ulitsa 13 (229 8183). Metro Pushkinskaya, Biblioteka Imeni Lenina or Okhotny Ryad. **Open** *box office* noon-7pm daily. **Map P277 B3**
Moscow's main chamber music hall. The venue attracts performers of international calibre, as well as some younger ones aspiring to maestro status.

Tchaikovsky Hall

Koncertny Zal Chaikovskogo, Triumfalnaya Ploshchad 4/31 (information 299 3681/season tickets 3957/tickets 0378). Metro Mayakovskaya. **Open** *box office* noon-7pm daily. **Tickets** $4-$100. **Map P277 B1**
Not to be confused with the Great Hall in the Tchaikovsky Conservatoire (*see above*), this was built in 1940 and is the biggest of all the concert halls, seating over 1,600 people. Apart from orchestral concerts, it often presents organ recitals by Russia's much-loved Garry Groberg.

Other halls

Chaliapin Museum *Sadovo-Kudrinskaya Ulitsa 25-27 (252 2530). Metro Barrikadnaya.* **Map P277 A2**

The House of Composers *Bryusov Pereulok 8/10 (229 1365). Metro Pushkinskaya.* Modern music specialists. **Map P277 B3**

Glinka Hall & Museum of Musical Culture *Ulitsa Fadeyeva 4 (972 3237/250 4408). Metro Mayakovskaya.* **Tickets** $4-$8. **Map P277 B2** Chamber music-sized hall and instrument museum.

Lean years for fat ladies

How could anything, ever, go wrong at the Bolshoi? Its august history and its royal origins marked it out for lustrous success. While its splendid neo-classical building, built by architect Osip Bove and Alexander Mikhailov, was constructed between 1820 and 1824 (and rebuilt in 1856, following a fire), its foundations were laid 50 years earlier, in 1776, when Moscow's procurator, Prince Urusov, decided to give his family's collection of singing, dancing serfs a theatrical outlet. Since then, the Bolshoi (it means 'great theatre') set about establishing itself as a theatre and a company to be reckoned with. Chaliapin sang here and the opening night of Tchaikovsky's *Swan Lake* was danced here in 1877. International reputations were made – or lost – on its boards.

Unfortunately, in recent years, it has been the company itself that has been at the receiving end of bad times, finding itself – metaphorically, at least – in a flutter of dead swans' feathers. The reduction of massive state subsidies has left holes in its repertoire and, in some cases, the theatre's fabric. The Bolshoi's A-list cast is often touring the world in an attempt to bring in much-needed foreign funds, and visitors to the Moscow theatre should check they aren't shelling out to see a less than perfect cast. Desperate shame though this is, the Bolshoi has not done itself any favours through the backstage shenanigans. Top jobs have gone to candidates who have done little to revitalise the Bolshoi's fortunes (creative or pecuniary), with the effect that Muscovites – who are probably among the most musically literate of the world's civic populations – are less than impressed.

All this aside, the Bolshoi does still manage to turn out the occasional rare gem. And the 1998-2000 seasons promise some interesting productions, including Tchaikovsky's *Lady of Orleans*, Peter Ustinov's production of Prokofiev's *The Love for Three Oranges* and revivals of Pokrovsky's 1993 productions of Borodin's *Prince Igor* and Tchaikovsky's *Eugene Onegin*. Even better, it is rumoured that the former theatre director Lubimov will make a Bolshoi comeback with *Carmen* in 1999. Already Moscow is discussing who will be taking the lead.
● For listing, *see* **Opera companies**.

Slake your thirst for opera at the **Helikon Opera Theatre**.

Gnessin Concert Hall *Ulitsa Povarshaya 30/36 (290 6737). Metro Arbatskaya.* **Tickets** free-$5. **Map P277 A3** Recitals and student opera during Oct-May season.

Kremlin Palace *Ulitsa Vozdvizhenka 1 (929 7901/ 7990). Metro Biblioteka Imeni Lenina.* **Map P278 C3** Built for Party conferences, the Kremlin Palace has terrible acoustics, so avoid seeing the Bolshoi here.

Prechistenka Concert Hall *Ulitsa Prechistenka 32 (information 213 2719/hall 201 4524/3783). Metro Park Kultury or Kropotkinskaya.* **Tickets** $4. **Map P280 A5**

Rachmaninov Hall *Bolshaya Nikitskaya Ulitsa 11 (229 0294). Metro Pushkinskaya, Biblioteka Imeni Lenina or Okhotny Ryad.* **Map P277 B3** The student hall of the Moscow Conservatoire, its acoustics were ruined when two urns situated in its alcoves disappeared.

St Andrew's Anglican Church *Voznesensky Pereulok 8 (Tel/fax 201 7967). Metro Pushkinskaya.* **Tickets** $8-$10. **Map P277 B3** Ensemble XXI Moscow plays here.

Scriabin Museum *Bolshoi Nikolopeskovsky Pereulok 11 (241 1901). Metro Okhotny Ryad.* **Open** *museum* noon-7pm Wed, Fri; 10am-5pm Thur, Sat, Sun. **Closed** last Fri of the month. **Map P277 A3** The museum is in the house where the composer lived from 1912-15. There is a striking scarlet grand piano in the main hall.

Opera companies

Bolshoi Theatre
Teatralnaya Ploshchad 1 (292 9986). Metro Teatralnaya. **Closed** Mon. **Admission** $15-$300. **Map P278 C3** (*See p136* **Lean years for fat ladies**).

Helikon Opera Theatre
Bolshaya Nikitskaya Ulitsa 19 (290 0971/fax 291 1323). Metro Arbatskaya. **Box office** noon-5pm daily. **Map P277 B3**
Chamber opera ensemble using this tiny theatre, the company is more popular with the foreign community than with Muscovites. Still, its budget productions of operas such as *Aida* are enterprising, if not optimistic.

Novaya Opera
Taganskaya Ulitsa 40/42 (911 1440). Metro Taganskaya. **Map P282 F5**
Innovative productions of lesser known operas from this peripatetic company set up during Perestroika by Yevgeny Kolobov. Recent works — all praised to the hilt — have included operas from Verdi and Donizetti.

Stanislavsky & Nemirovich-Danchenko Musical Theatre
Bolshaya Dimitrovka Ulitsa 17 (229 8388). Metro Pushkinskaya or Chekhovskaya. **Map P278 C2**
Named after two theatrical giants, this company produces a reliably interesting repertoire with *Ernani*, *La Bohème*, *Tales of Tsar Sultan*, *Eugene Onegin*, *The Marriage of Figaro* and *Iolanthe* among recent works. Forthcoming attractions include those standards of European repertoire, *Carmen*, *Die Fledermaus* and *L' Elisir d'Amore*. Unfortunately, the hall will be closed between March and November 1999 for renovation.

Orchestras

Academic Orchestra of the Moscow Philharmonic
In residence at the Tchaikovsky Hall, this is the former orchestra of Kirill Kondrashin and Dmitri Kitayenko, known for many things: its classical and romantic repertoire; the best brass section in Moscow; and the antics of its leader, Yuri Simonov, who is best known for his unceremonious sacking technique. Wanting to cast off a lot of musicians before a tour to Hungary in Soviet times, he announced the news when the orchestra was already at the Moscow train station. To the horror of Simonov, many of the outraged musicians got off the train in solidarity with their colleagues. As the train pulled out, Simonov was last seen crying from the train, 'All communists come to me!' The 1998-99 season will see a series of concerts in memory of Kondrashin. Much awaited is the guest appearance of Latvian conductor Mariss Jansons, chief conductor of the Oslo and Pittsburgh Orchestras.

Chamber Orchestra of Russia

This is the former Moscow Chamber Orchestra, which came to world fame under Rudolf Barshai. Since then it was conducted by many eminent Russian violinists such as Bezrodny, Tretyakov and Korsakov. In the early 1990s in the midst of extreme financial hardship, the musicians appointed the American-Armenian pianist Constantin Orbelian as their director, who promptly lost most of the former members of this orchestra. It was a tragic end to what was one of the world's greatest ensembles. While rumour has it that Orbelian is about to leave for other pastures, it remains to be seen what will happen to the orchestra.

Ensemble XXI Moscow

This was the first independent (and international) chamber orchestra in the USSR and, later, Russia, when it was founded in 1988. Its chief conductor Lygia O'Riordan, is a former student of Gennady Rozhdestvensky. Its tenth anniversary season during 1998-99 kicks off with a revival of Nicolo's opera *Cendrillon* conducted by Richard Bonynge with an international cast of singers. Apart from the baroque, classical and romantic repertoire, the orchestra plays a great deal of twentieth-century music, rarely played in Russia.

Website: www.paqo.demon.co.uk/ensintr1.html

Great Radio Symphony Orchestra

Well-established orchestra that was conducted by Rozhdestvensky, until his departure for the BBC in the 1960s. Vladimir Fedoseyev, a Communist Party favourite, inherited the baton and continues to this day. Possessing many fine players, the Great Radio Symphony has nevertheless had its share of scandals. Huge rows broke out last season when guest conductor Valery Gergiev performed unrehearsed concerts of Shostakovich's Fifth Symphony. The nerve!

Kremlin Chamber Orchestra

Like the Russian National Orchestra and the Helikon Chamber Opera, this orchestra is mainly targeted at Moscow's foreign community. It was founded by the entrepreneur and former violinist Misha Rachlevsky to fulfil a recording contract. A huge marketing machine now backs up the KCO in Moscow's foreign community.

Musica Viva Orchestra

Conducted by cellist Alexander Rudin, this orchestra pulls in some interesting guest artists (*see below* **Festivals**), while the programming is characterised by its imaginative streaks. The only Moscow orchestra to concentrate on early music, the fact that it attracts Christopher Hogwood is testimony to the respect it has earned. Early Mozart symphonies and rare works of Schubert that otherwise would remain unplayed in Moscow are Musica Viva's sine qua non.

Russian Capella

Gennady Rozhdestvensky's former Orchestra of the Ministry of Culture. Chief conductor Valery Polyansky has delivered some very good performances of great choral masterpieces for choir and orchestra. In 1998-99, Rozhdestvensky conducted a riveting Shostakovich Fourth Symphony and the world première of Schnittke's Ninth Symphony with this orchestra.

Russian National Orchestra

Despite its huge marketing campaign, this orchestra, conducted by pianist Mikhail Pletnev, specialises in performances of a standard repertoire that leave much to be desired. A recent grant from the British Council led to a brief season of British music and there are occasional interesting appearances of guest conductors. But in general, RNO's decent musicians suffer from a lack of direction.

State Academic Orchestra

With Yevgeny Svetlanov making many appearances as chief conductor, this resident orchestra of the Bolshoi Zal of the Moscow Conservatoire is the one to keep an eye on. Svetlanov's orchestra has the secret of the Russian repertoire, playing with charm and abandon. Programmes include the Russian greats – Tchaikovsky, Rachmaninov and Prokofiev.

Virtuosi of Moscow

This famous chamber orchestra, under violin virtuoso Vladimir Spivakov, went into exile in Spain a decade ago, but is rumoured to be permanently returning to Moscow in 1998 with many new members. If so, it will make a welcome and exciting addition to Moscow's orchestral life.

Festivals

Check the local English press for details of dates and venues.

Annual Moscow Contemporary Music Festival

Information 290 5181.

Directed by Valery Gorokovskaya, this is an excellent and innovative festival that features top international performers and many premières of new repertoire. Usually taking place each spring, in 1999 it will be held in the autumn.

December Evenings Festival

Pushkin Museum of Fine Arts, Volkhonka Ulitsa 12-14 (203 7998/9578). Metro Kropotkinskaya. **Map P280 B4**

Founded by the late pianist Sviatoslav Richter, this is Moscow's most famous festival, and rightly so. International artists appear here against a backdrop of the Pushkin Museum's art. Its programmes always come highly recommended and tickets – as one might expect – are difficult to come by.

Festival of Symphonies & Serenades

Inaugurated by the Ensemble XXI Moscow, this city-based festival takes place in central Moscow courtyards during June and July.

Moscow Autumn Contemporary Music Festival

A boring festival that makes a virtue of works by third-rate local composers who rehashed classical and baroque forms in bad imitations of Schnittke. But there are some augurs of future change with brilliant and innovative young Moscow composers such as Vorotnikov and Stasov being featured next time round.

Musica Viva Festival

Held annually in the spring, this chamber music festival is run by the orchestra of the same name. Recent guest artists have included the high calibre of Christopher Hogwood and Alexei Lubimov.

Tchaikovsky Competition

Information 229 8183.

Held every four years since 1958, this is the world's big piano competition. Prestigious isn't even adequate to describe it. Let's just say that if you win this, then the world will be yours, all yours – until, that is, the next competition. Held every four years (the next is to held in 2002), the Tchaikovsky is for pianists, violinists, cellists and singers. In the piano section, winners have included the Louisiana-born Van Cliburn, numerous Russians, including Vladimir Ashkenazy and Boris Berezovsky (who now lives in north London and drives a taxi as his vehicle of choice), and British champions Peter Donohoe and Barry Douglas.

Music: Rock, Roots & Jazz

**Balalaika Abba bands, Red Army refuseniks and Eurovision mamas?
Ra, ra Rasputin!**

While Russians have always excelled in 'high culture', any attempt to pitch their efforts at a more lowly level has given them a reputation as the popular culture dunces of Europe. Russian pop music is crude and saccharine; local rock is a mixed bag that might occasionally be interesting, but a lot depends on understanding the lyrics. The jazz scene is essentially down to bland lounge-type combos; improvised music and good folk gigs are very few.

Even so, this situation may be on the brink of a transformation. One positive indicator is the meteoric rise of Mummi Troll, a Vladivostok band that has sparked a Beatlemania-like phenomenon. Their skinny, fey, intellectual singer, Ilya Lagutenko, has led to comparisons with Pulp, though musically the Trolls are more lightweight and poppy. Basically, they're just like a normal European pop group, and in Russia, that's a monumental achievement.

Other decent acts include Alyona Sviridova, a singer/songwriter often called the Russian answer to Alanis Morissette, although in both music and looks she's closer to Annie Lennox. Male vocalists include Leonid Agutin, a young Latin jazz singer; Valery Meladze, the romantic heart-throb, reminiscent of Bryan Ferry in smoochy mode; and Valery Sutkin, an ironic 1950s revivalist, the Russian cool cat. The only other worthwhile pop band is Lube, slightly controversial because of its trademark 'Soviet chic' gimmicks, which include Red Army uniforms, but nonetheless quite interesting. Any Spice Girls fans may try the Russian versions, namely Strelki (Little Arrows) and Blestyashchiye (the Glittering), as well as their boy band counterparts, Ivanushki International and Tête-à-Tête. A guy named Delphin is the new star of rap – and he's good. On the more exotic side is MD & C Pavlov, displaying a strange blend of Russian reggae and funk influences.

There are about 30 full-size concert halls in Moscow (a substantial decrease since Soviet times, as many have been converted into office spaces, showrooms or nightclubs) and more than 200 clubs and discos (compared to about a dozen ten years ago). Gigs start anywhere between 8pm and 2am and are always accompanied by discos, often with go-go dancers and strippers. Entrance fees are between $10 and $50, with women often enjoying (if that's the right word) a 50 per cent discount. For gig lists, consult the *Moscow Times*'s Friday what's-on supplement, *MT Out*. We have not listed the admission prices or concert times for venues where these vary significantly according to the act.

For nightclub venues such as **Bedniye Lyudi, Chetyre Komnaty, Kak By** and **MDM**, which also host live acts, *see chapter* **Nightlife**.

Alla 'Air Guitar' Pugacheva, Russia's finest.

Major venues

Central House of Artists

Ulitsa Krymsky Val 10/14 (238 9634/9821). Metro Park Kultury or Oktyabrskaya. **No credit cards. Map P280 B6, P281 C6**
This compact hall surrounded by galleries and antique shops is the place to go for contemporary and improvised music, serious jazz, world bands and acoustic acts – mostly local. Weekend gigs start early, between 6pm and 7pm.

DK Gorbunova

Novozavodskaya Ulitsa 27 (145 8531/8305). Metro Bagrationovskaya. **No credit cards.**
Nicknamed Gorbushka, this is one of the only true rock venues in Moscow. Out of the centre and slightly run-down, it's great for uproarious, no-holds-barred gigs. The Smashing Pumpkins, the Rollins Band and Nick Cave have played here.

Green Theatre

Ulitsa Krymsky Val 9 (237 1088/1089). Metro Park Kultury or Oktyabrskaya. **No credit cards. Map P280 B6, P281 C6**
Situated at the edge of Gorky Park, this is the only big open-air venue in Moscow. Due to the unpredictability of the weather, concerts are infrequent. Boy George and Paul Simon played here in the 1980s.

Kremlin Palace

The Kremlin (929 7990/7881). Metro Biblioteka Imeni Lenina or Aleksandrovsky Sad. **No credit cards. Map P281 C4**
A monstrous 1960s convention centre in the middle of the ancient Kremlin where everything (interiors, acoustics and atmosphere) completely sucks, but due to its capacity and location, it remains the city's most prestigious venue. Diana Ross, Tina Turner, David Bowie and Sting have all performed here.

Luzhniki Sports Arena

Luzhnetskaya Naberezhnaya 24 (201 0813/1440). Metro Sportivnaya. **No credit cards.**
An ice hockey stadium, occasionally hosting big name bands like Deep Purple and the Scorpions and others considered outré for the Kremlin.

Rossia Concert Hall

Ulitsa Varvarka 6 (298 5163/3614). Metro Kitai-Gorod. **No credit cards. Map P278 D3**
The fave venue of the big Russian stars and where Cliff Richard and Elton John made their Soviet débuts back in the 1970s, to be supplanted by the Prodigy in the 1990s.

Other venues

Beverly Hills

Kudrinsky Pereulok 1 (255 4228). Metro Barrikadnaya or Krasnopresnenskaya. **Open** 10pm-6am Thur-Sun; concerts 1am. **Admission** $25-$45. **Credit** AmEx, JCB, MC, V. **No credit cards. Map P277 A3**
Co-founded by Chuck Norris, the vertically challenged martial arts star of a zillion bad movies, this is a combination of disco, restaurant (open from noon) and casino, located betweeen the Moscow Zoo and US embassy.

Kristall

Marksistskaya Ulitsa 38 (912 3554). Metro Proletarskaya. **Open** 24 hours daily. **Credit** AmEx, DC, JCB, MC, V. **Map P282 F5/F6**
One of the latest additions to the posh club list, boasting a unique laser show and the largest casino capacity in Moscow.

Manhattan Express

Ulitsa Varvarka 6 (298 5354). Metro Kitai-Gorod. **Open** 7pm-6am Mon-Sat. **Admission** $20. **Credit** AmEx, JCB, MC, V. **Map P278 D3**
Conveniently located just outside Red Square in one of the wings of the Hotel Rossia, this spot has a casino and a very eclectic repertoire that includes fashion shows, talk shows and some interesting young bands besides the usual disco thing.

Mirage

Ulitsa Arbat 21 (291 1423). Metro Smolenskaya. **Open** 9pm-3am Mon-Thur; midnight-late Fri-Sun. **Admission** $15-$20. **Credit** AmEx, JCB, MC, V. **Map P280 A4/B4**
Luxurious disco with pretensions towards sophistication. Besides the usual Russian pop, it regularly holds live shows of Western soul and fusion acts like Shakatak and Tower of Power. Jazz takes priority Monday toThursday.

Svalka

Profsoyuznaya Ulitsa 27/1 (128 7823). Metro Profsoyuznaya. **Open** 6pm-6am daily. **Cover charge** $10 Fri, Sat; $5 Mon-Wed, Sun (incl 1 Mon, Tue, Sun). **No credit cards.**
Svalka means 'junkyard' and this is, as one might guess, a club primarily aimed at punk rockers, rockabilly and heavy metal kids. Mainstream acts also appear here.

Jazz, blues, folk & country

Moscow's home jazz scene is rather small and hardly entertaining, being represented mostly by bland, lounge-type combos. The names to watch out for are Igor Butman, the premier Russian sax player, and Tim Strong, a New York-based singer, currently working in Moscow. The blues scene is stronger if not quite sensational: acts like Crossroads, Alexei Belov Band, Masha Katz and Liga Blyuza play with authentic bluesy licks. Among the several country acts around, by far the best are Grassmaster, featuring a great banjo player, and Kukuruza. Although the only reggae club in Moscow is now gone, some bands remain, of which Jah Division, Ostrov and Olga Areyeva's Kovcheg are the best known. African music is represented by two good St Petersburg bands, Dva Samolyota and Markscheider Kunst. Folkies will be pleased by the healthy conglomeration of Irish and Celtic bands, although there are surprisingly few native Russian folk performers. Nevertheless, look out for Posledny Shans (Last Chance), an incredibly funny folk theatre ensemble that uses dozens of weird instruments and toys and has two impressive female singers who write beautiful, traditional songs.

The standard balalaika bands are considered completely kitsch and uncool, relegated to hotel floor shows and 'official' pop festivals. The only group of this kind that sometimes appears in clubs is called Belu Den, specialising in balalaika interpretations of classic Western pop tunes – everything from Abba to Deep Purple – resulting in a richly disorienting experience.

Slop pop

When Père Ubu's David Thomas visited Moscow to check out the music scene in 1992, he described Russian pop as 'probably the worst in the world'. A master of understatement, Thomas was just being kind to a phenomenon that exceeds all known limits of taste and, perhaps, of morality as well. Even when you take into account the transgressions of the Romans during an average end-of-empire orgy, Genghis Khan on a Mongolian battlefield or Imelda Marcos on a shoe-shopping spree, this is one of humanity's extreme extremes.

Some of Russian pop's worst crimes against taste must be laid at the feet of **Filippe Kirkorov**, the 193-centimetre (six foot four), bug-eyed son of a Bulgarian, who sounds like a cross between Engelbert Humperdinck, Michael Jackson and Bob Downe and, on stage at least, looks like a drag queen from *Priscilla, Queen of the Desert*. His almost freakish appearance doesn't seem to have any effect on his popularity; Russian female fans recently voted him the sexiest man in Russia. In 1997, Russian émigrés packed out Madison Square Gardens to hear him play, one of only two artists to sell out the venue – the other was Barbra Streisand and her tickets cost only a fifth of Filippe's whopping price of $250.

It seems only natural that the king of Russian pop should have a queen. **Alla Pugacheva**, Russia's favourite pop-diva, has been around since time began. A huge (in every sense) star of the Soviet era, she managed to survive the transitional period by staying as bad as she had ever been. Those who followed the Eurovision Song Contest in 1997, where audiences were convinced she was an elderly transvestite, will recall her vocal style: belting, throaty, laced with grimacing melodrama. In appearance, Pugacheva is almost as kitschy as Kirkorov: micro-skirts, macro-thighs, hair red and flaming. The two met when Kirkorov was a schoolboy seeking autographs. Alla decided to keep an eye on him to see how he would turn out, and in 1994 they married – he was 26, she 46 – in a marriage ceremony made in kitsch heaven.

Other flamboyant figures on the Russian pop scene include **Masha Rasputina**, a ghastly blonde singer dressed up in Ann Summers style porno lingerie; **Sergei Penkin**, whose heavy make-up and obsession with everything glittery makes Liberace look like Sid Vicious; and **Sergei Krylov**, blessed with a body twice the size of Barry White's, a falsetto voice and numerous strange hair ornaments balanced on his balding head.

No matter how fantastically awful their costumes, they are as nothing compared to the music. Russian mainstream pop hasn't changed since Soviet times. The dominant style may be described as ultra-banal Eurovision, with cheapo synth arrangements and moronic lyrics that usually feature the line 'Without you, I'll go out of my mind'. Although a new generation of performers has emerged, Russia remains a natural reservation of archaic pop vulgarity. Unlike other museums, this one you can explore free of charge and without leaving your hotel room: just turn on any TV channel.

For more detailed information concerning the Moscow International Jazz Festival, the Baltic-Russia Jazz Festival and the Celtic Music Festival, *see chapter* **Moscow by Season**. For bars that host the occasional, not regular, live gig, such as **Canadian Moosehead Bar** and **Vermel**, *see chapter* **Pubs & Bars**.

Arbat Blues Club

Filippovsky Pereulok 11 (291 1546). Metro Kropotkinskaya. **Open** 8.30pm-5.30am Fri, Sat. **Cover charge** $10. **No credit cards. Map P280 B4**
The Arbat is a reasonably priced blues club that usually delivers the goods pretty well. There's just one snag: it's closed during summer.

Art Café

Begovaya Ulitsa 5 (191 8320). Metro Begovaya. **Open** noon-midnight daily. **No credit cards.**
Tucked away discreetly inside the Vernisazh Theatre, is this upmarket French restaurant, which has a rota of different jazz combos that play on a daily basis.

BB King

Sadovaya-Samotechnaya Ulitsa 4/2 (299 8206). Metro Tsvetnoi Bulvar. **Open** noon-2am Mon-Thur, Sun; noon-5am Fri, Sat. **Admission** Thur, Sat after 8pm $9. **No credit cards. Map P278 C1**
Favoured hangout for post-gig jam sessions by Western rockers and still a decent live music venue. Autographs on the walls include BB King, Marc Almond and Michael Nyman.

Country Bar

Ulitsa Pokrovka 50/2 (917 2882). Metro Chistye Prudy, Krasnye Vorota or Kurskaya. **Open** 11am-midnight Mon-Wed, Sun; 11am-2am Thur Sat. **Admission** $9 for major concerts. **Credit** AmEx, MC, V. **Map P279 E3/F2**
Bands play Thursdays through to Saturdays from 9pm.

Gnezdo Glukharia

Bolshaya Nikitskaya Ulitsa 22 (291 9388). Metro Barrikadnaya or Krasnopresnenskaya. **Open** noon-11pm daily. **Admission** $3.50. **Credit** V. **Map P277 B3**
The club and concert spot of Moscow's singers and song-writers (or 'bards', as they call themselves).

Nightlife

Paint the town red? Nobody bats an eyelid with a backdrop as lewd and lurid as this.

Welcome to Moscow Babylon – the capital of excess, promiscuity, hedonism and weird, twisted stuff that even Quentin Tarantino couldn't invent. Where else in the world, for instance, could you witness a bar full of 800 sweaty, frenzied, half-naked women baying for five male strippers, while a Mongol horde of drunk, horny men riots outside for the doors to open? Or see ultranationalist politician Vladimir Zhirinovsky swilling vodka arm in arm with Chuck Norris in a subterranean casino done up to look like a Spanish village square? Or have an intense, drink-fuelled conversation in a grungy dive club run by punks and runaways with a loved-up, shaven-headed guy whose baby had recently been stolen by Satanists, causing his wife to throw herself out of a tenth-floor window? Strange tales from a strange time.

Moscow is speeding on a rush of scorching, incandescent energy, fuelled by a perverse mixture of desperate escapism, obscene wealth and the maximalist Russian soul. It isn't a 'party city' in the conventional sense – a hip Berlin clubber wouldn't find enough to amuse them here and a Prada-shod London barfly would be unimpressed by New Russians' 'sophistication'. Moscow's a hit and miss scene, veering from the embarrassingly cheesy to the painfully pretentious. If you are lucky enough to tap into the main nerve, however, to pin down Moscow's elusive *tusovki* (party animals) at their Bacchanalian best, it has an energy and a sheer, exuberant abandon unrivalled by more self-conscious (and maybe more self-respecting) Western capitals.

Whether it's pseudo-bohemian squat clubs of the **Trety Put** variety; seething, sweaty meat-markets like the **Hungry Duck** or **Bells**; fashionable discos that make you think you're in a George Michael video or giant techno barns like **MDM** and **Plasma**, mobbed with juiced-up, lobotomised ravers, Moscow – as the Intourist guides used to say – has 'something for everyone'. Clubbing in Moscow may be expensive and dangerous, but at least you won't forget it in a hurry. As Tolstoy observed, it is through our own suffering and witnessing the moral collapse of others that we become stronger people. You have been warned. Always call ahead or check local press before visiting nightlife venues.

For clubs such as **Chameleon** and **Shans**, which is known primarily as gay clubs but are really semi-straight, *see chapter* **Gay & Lesbian**.

Clubs

A-Club
Delegatskaya Ulitsa 1 (972 1132). Metro Mayakovskaya, Novoslobodskaya or Tsvetnoi Bulvar. **Call for details.** **Credit** DC, MC, V. **Map p278 C1**
Large, packed and flirting with the fringes of trendiness, the once-dead A-Club is reinventing itself as one of the regular Saturday-night pitstops for Moscow's aspiring beautiful people. The new managers gleaned from the legendary, but now sadly defunct, Ptyutch club, have assembled a relatively sophisticated crowd, and guest DJs from London have upped the music from the usual Muscovite Eurotrash techno to something approaching cool. There's a large dancefloor, three bars, cheap drinks and live music on Friday nights.

Angely
Angely, Tverskaya Ulitsa 29/2 (299 3690). Metro Tverskaya. **Open** 6pm-6am daily. **Admission** call for details. **Map p278 C2**
Black painted walls, psychedelic day-glo Indian murals and a suspended steel walkway make this one of the coolest-looking clubs in Moscow. There's even a dark cubby hole behind the dancefloor with an arty slide-projector show and deep, comfortable couches where you can ride out the nasty 5am crash. The problem with Angely is that its pretensions to super-trendiness mean nobody gets in – unless they are Kate Moss or a close friend of the owner, Timur Lanksy, who vets people personally at the door. Ergo, the crowd is beautiful, fashionable and virtually non-existent; perhaps it's just as well, considering the size of the dancefloor.

Bedniye Lyudi
Chernigovsky Pereulok 6/11 (951 3342). Metro Tretyakovskaya. **Open** 3pm-5am daily. **Admission** $4-$8. **Credit** DC, JCB, MC, V. **Map p281 D4/D5**
Once-arty blues cellar that has become yuppified beyond recognition. It's a mellow hangout with occasional good concerts, a cool brick interior and candlelight, though the introduction of middle-aged members of the 'emerging middle class' beloved of the *New York Times* has killed the atmosphere. Food is mediocre and drinks overpriced, but it's a good place to recharge your batteries between Trety Put and the Jazz Café. The rude doormen enforce a 'strict' members-only policy, or a cover charge of roughly $10.

Bell's
Ulitsa Bolshaya Polyanka 51A (959 3737). Metro Dobrininskaya. **Open** noon-3am Mon-Wed, Sun; noon-5am Thur; noon-6am Fri, Sat. **Admission** Fri, Sat after 8pm $4 men, $3 women; Mon-Thur free. **No credit cards.** **Map p281 C5/C6**
Bell's once came close to rivalling the legendary Hungry Duck (*see p146* **The horrors of the Hungry Duck**) for its heady mixture of drunken girls, sharkish men on the pull and music. Free entrance made it a hit with Moscow's check-out girls and the men who loved them – but the management decided the packed and noisy formula was working too well and decided to screw it up by introducing a cover charge and taking the place 'upmarket'. Expect an increase in the working girl and red blazer contingent.

Buchenwald

Ulitsa Novye Cheremushki 54A (no phone). Metro Novy Cheremushki. **Open** 11pm-5am Fri, Sat. **Admission** free. **No credit cards.**

Crazy name, crazy place. Underground bunker hangout of Moscow's upmarket skinheads and their arty, grungy friends. Despite the obnoxious name, the people are uncannily friendly and the atmosphere relaxed – once you get acclimatised. The toilet is decorated with public health warning posters depicting spectacularly virulent genital infections. Be careful where you sit and who you hit on – the vomit and unpredictable-violence factors run high. The drinks are kiosk-cheap and the music is the sort of breakbeat-industrial techno only enjoyed by people whacked on drugs the normal punter would never dream of. Not for the faint of heart – or epileptics, due to the non-stop high-wattage strobe on the dancefloor. It's technically free, but the doorman may try to tap you for $3.

Bulgakov

Bolshaya Sadovaya Ulitsa 10 (209 9914). Metro Mayakovskaya. **Open** 8pm-7am daily. **Admission** Mon-Thur, Sun $8 men. **Credit** MC, V. **Map** p277 A2/B1/B2

Trendy micro-club frequented by Mercedes-driving trendies and models who spend a lot of time exchanging air-kisses. It's very much the look-but-don't-touch scene; highly pretentious and not much fun, unless, of course, you also wear Versace and carry a Prada bag. The dancefloor is tiny, the music unremarkable and the doormen incredibly rude.

Cabana

Raushskaya Naberezhnaya 4 (239 3065). Metro Tretyakovskaya. **Open** noon-6am daily. **Admission** Mon-Thur $9; Fri $18 men, $9 women; Sat $27 men, $18 women. **Credit** AmEx, DC, MC, V. **Map** p281 D4

Wonderfully colourful design, friendly service, decent music and a great location in the centre of the Raushskaya Naberezhnaya strip make Cabana one of the staples of the Moscow scene. The place is well laid out, shifting from quiet hangout area to bar to dancefloor, so you can gear up your mood in the space of a two-minute cruise. There's also a great Brazilian restaurant tucked away at the side. Unfortunately, the clientele has gone downmarket recently, and the usually energetic, trendy crowd is slowly being replaced by shifty *biznesmeny* and whores. But the club's saving grace and energy powerhouse is the bunch of cool regulars who keep it hopping on Saturday nights.

Chetyre Komnaty

Four Rooms, Raushskaya Naberezhnaya 4/5 (239 3038). Metro Tretyakovskaya. **Open** 7pm-7am Thur-Sun. **Admission** $12 Fri, Sat. **Credit** AmEx, MC, V. **Map** p281 D4

There's a prize for anyone who can come up with a connection between this club and the Tarantino flick of the same name. After the rich trendies abandoned the place some time ago, there's nothing left but memories and a strange assortment of losers and aspiring B-list clubbers; not surprisingly, the members-only policy has slackened. It livens up when there's live music (10pm-midnight), but has lost its energy and atmosphere. Billiard tables are available.

Chudo Bar

Myasnitsky Proyezd 4 (925 4380). Metro Krasnye Vorota. **Open** 10pm-6am Mon-Fri; noon-6am Sat. **Admission** varies. **No credit cards. Map** p279 E2

Chudo Bar has a cool, LA-style interior with lots of pseudo-Pop Art and psychedelia on the walls, lots of curved surfaces and designer chairs. Non-stop animation plays on one wall while young day-glo club kids stoke up for a big night. DJs occasionally spin cool acid jazz and funk, but it's mostly the standard dance/house, though a cut above most places in town. Unfortunately, the Chudo is too small to be anything but a bar with loud music and aspirations to club status. Good warm-up for greater things.

From Dusk 'til Dawn

Ot Zakata Do Rassveta, Sredny Tishinsky Pereulok 5/7 (253 2323). Metro Belorusskaya. **Open** noon-midnight Mon-Wed, Sun; noon-6am Thur-Sat. **Admission** $10 Fri, Sat; free Mon-Fri. **Credit** AmEx, MC, V. **Map** p277 A1

Exuberantly cheesy, Mayan-themed restaurant/club with strip shows on Thursdays and live music on Fridays and Saturdays. It gets going on weekends (if you count overweight men in suits taking their shirts off), attracting an older crowd who come for dinner and a dance to standard pop fare. The food is excellent and the service friendly.

Gippopotam

Hippopotamus, Ulitsa Mantulinskaya 5/1, building 6 (256 2346). Metro Ulitsa 1905 Goda. **Open** 10pm-5am Wed-Sun. **Admission** $10-$20 men; free women. **Credit** AmEx, JCB, MC, V.

A packed meat-market, popular with an immigrant crowd of secretaries and students. Mercifully techno-free, with regular salsa nights and long, sweaty, slow-dance sessions where *produkty* shop girls grind their crotches against the Latin lovers of their dreams. Wednesdays have an all you can drink deal for $20 – take it as a challenge. Eccentric décor (on a man-eating reptile theme) and friendly service add to the atmosphere of wild, low-rent hedonism: bear in mind the deceptively low lighting before choosing a dance partner.

Jazz Café

Bolshaya Ordynka 27. Metro Tretyakovskaya. **Open** 2pm-1am Mon-Thur; noon-5am Fri-Sun. **Admission** free to members. **Map** p281 D5

How does it feel to be one of the beautiful people? Find out at Jazz Café – if they let you in. This club is the current headquarters of Moscow's international bright young things, gorgeous girls so beautiful you feel like shooting yourself just to get their attention and muscular men in thousand-dollar suits. The Thursday night parties are like being in a George Michael video, complete with the don't-touch-what-you-can't-afford stares and sylph-like models with heavy eye make-up and more attitude than the Million Man March. Things get wild after 3am, with spontaneous stripping and major-league seductions. The music's a superb mix of funky house, jungle and progressive, keeping the place hopping well into the morning. As you might expect, drinks are spectacularly expensive, as is membership – $1,000. Don't even bother turning up on spec. Only some heavy-duty advance blagging or coming with a member will open the gates.

Kak By

As If, Baumanskaya Ulitsa 50/12 (267 4504). Metro Baumanskaya. **Open** 6pm-midnight Mon-Thur, Sun; 6pm-6am Fri, Sat. **Admission** varies Fri, Sat; free Mon-Thur, Sun. **No credit cards.**

Relaxed, unpretentious hangout with graffitoed walls, occasional shows and live music. Good DJs spin a mix of house and pop for an arty, young clientele.

Liga

Ulitsa Ramenki 5 (932 0101). Metro Prospekt Vernadskogo. **Open** 7pm-6am Fri, Sat. **Admission** $7.50. **No credit cards.**

A dark, grungy, Soviet-style club, where some of Moscow's crustiest dirtheads pogo to some of the town's worst heavy metal bands. Cheap beer, a lousy sound system and a charming clientele add up to an authentic post-apocalyptic atmosphere. The crowd takes its music seriously – two years ago a singer was killed by being pulled off the stage by demanding music critics in the audience.

Luch

Ray, 5-y Monetchikovsky Pereulok 5, building 3 (951 9463). Metro Paveletskaya. **Open** 5pm-6am daily. **Admission** $8-$10. **Credit** DC, MC, V. **Map** p281 D6

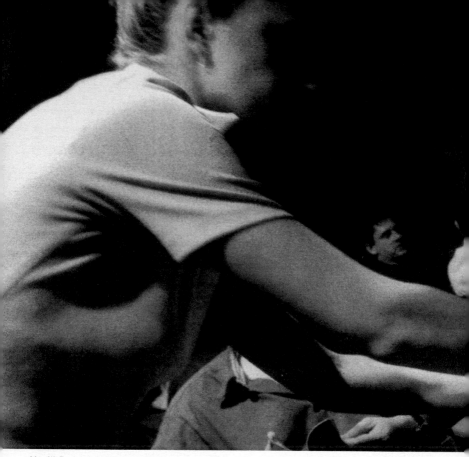

You'll find sylph-like, scintillatingly beautiful women and men with million-dollar pecs at the

A shadow of its famous predecessor, Ptyutch, the original crucible of Moscow's club scene, Luch survives on nostalgia and occasional flashes of the old brilliance. It's mainly a case of loud, thumping techno, blinding lights and teenies too skint to buy drugs dancing away and wondering why this is meant to be fun. Luch sometimes hosts fantastic bashes when the older generation of party animals revisits its old haunt – otherwise, Friday-night Love Parties attract decent DJs and an entertaining contingent of lycra-clad babes and kids in wraparound sunglasses.

Master

Pavlovskaya Ulitsa 6 (237 1742). Metro Serpukhovskaya. **Open** 11pm-6am Thur-Sun. **Admission** $10-$16 men; $7-$10 women. **No credit cards**.

Four doormen got sprayed with bullets here in 1988, apparently for being rude to a customer, but don't let that put you off; no one got caught in the crossfire, and the management has pepped up the service as a result. Another concrete techno-hangar, located in a former cinema. Very young, teeny-bopper crowd mixed with wannabe bandits (hence, presumably, the Kalashnikov unpleasantness). There are live strip acts (where else would you get strippers in a techno club?), occasional 'faces' parties, which attract the beau monde, and a cool chill-out room.

MDM

Moscow Palace of Youth, Komsomolsky Prospekt 28 (245 8423/8402/8427). Metro Frunzenskaya. **Open** 8pm-6am Fri, Sat. **Admission** $8-$10; concerts $5-$50. **No credit cards. Map p280 A6/B6**

Located in a huge Brezhnev-era building along with a disco, shops and offices, this is a giant techno barn of a venue. Huge expanses of concrete, endless corridors, rows of gyrating techno-geeks with lobotomised expressions, smoke and flashing lights give the place a vaguely sinister feel. It's also frequented by old rock and blues acts, including Chuck Berry, BB King and Uriah Heep.

Monte Carlo

Ulitsa Balchug 3/2 (232 9394). Metro Tretyakovskaya. **Open** 10pm-5am Mon-Fri; 10pm-8am Sat, Sun. **Admission** $25. **Credit** AmEx, DC, MC, V. **Map p281 D4**

As vulgar, flashy and tasteless as the real thing, Monte Carlo is popular with suits, babes and working girls. It can be hard to tell the pros from the talented amateurs and, while watching middle-aged American managers attempting to get down on the dancefloor is slightly depressing, watching them trying to hit on 19-year-old waifs can be amusing. On the whole, though, spoiled girls and desperate men don't make for a fun evening.

Jazz Café – but obviously not tonight. See page 143.

Night Flight

Nochnoi Polyot, Tverskaya Ulitsa 17 (229 4165). Metro Tverskaya. **Open** 9pm-5am daily. **Admission** $20. **Credit** AmEx, MC, V. **Map p278 C2**

There's an advertisement in Sheremetyevo Airport that says 'Night Flight – Do It Tonight', a slogan that combines poetic alliteration with Scandinavian frankness. This Swedish-run club has to be seen to be believed. The place is packed with drop-dead gorgeous women, pretty much every one of whom is for sale. Yes, Night Flight is Moscow's Whore Central, the respectable face of prostitution, a favourite for corporate entertainment and a great place to run into your boss or Russian girlfriend (as has actually happened to several people). On the plus side, the food is delicious, and the toilets are spotless.

Parizhkaya Zhizn

Paris Life, Ulitsa Karetny Ryad 3 (209 2076). Metro Mayakovskaya or Pushkinskaya. **Open** 1pm-7am daily. **Admission** free Mon-Thur, Sun; $15 Fri, Sat. **Credit** DC, MC, V. **Map p278 C1**

In fact, about as Parisian as a pork-fat sandwich. It tends to be frequented by moustachioed suburban electricians and their moustachioed girlfriends, who gyrate under the large model of the base of the Eiffel Tower that spans the dancefloor. The DJ has been known to play Duran Duran and Chris

de Burgh; you get the picture. Downstairs, though, it's a different story – there's a charming, candlelit cellar bar with a pianist accompanying the non-stop Charlie Chaplin films playing on the back wall. The food is pretty appalling, but it's a great place for a quiet drink.

Plasma

Ulitsa Novye Cheremushki 54A (128 7603). Metro Novye Cheremushki. **Open** 11pm-6am Fri-Sun. **Admission** $8-$13; Fri before 1am women free. **No credit cards.**

A teeny-bopper techno club in a disused cinema, complete with Dayglo murals and spaced-out schoolgirls with tiny backpacks. The techno is mind-numbingly loud, and some times you can see charmingly amateur 'techno dance' shows. There's a bar upstairs, which looks like it could be in one of the more unfashionable railway stations, where you're likely to be approached by teenage girls with bloodshot eyes asking for drugs money.
Website: www.aerodance.ru

Propaganda

Bolshoi Zlatoustinsky Pereulok 7 (924 5732). Metro Kitai-Gorod. **Open** noon-6am daily. **Admission** $5. **No credit cards. Map p278 D3**

This cool, brick-lined bar/club is popular with hip students, foreigners and non-lobotomised club kids and is one of the few genuinely relaxed, fun clubs in Moscow. Early in the evening it serves decent, cheap food, before clearing away the tables as people start dancing to a mix of funk, acid jazz and progressive house. Reasonably priced beer, a not-too-steep cover and excellent people-watching balconies make this a great place for a quiet, early evening drink.

Res Publica
Nikolskaya Ulitsa 17 (928 4692). Metro Lubyanka or Ploshchad Revolutsii. **Open** 6pm-6am daily. **Credit** MC. **Map p278 D3**
A recent addition to the Moscow club scene is this mini-rave club near Red Square, which stands a good chance of capturing aspiring trendies. The dancefloor's a bit small for the occasional famous DJs spinning jungle, house and funk, but usually the music is on the acceptable side of pop. There's a restaurant and a billiard room in the back, where you can escape from the music. When the place gets too hot, crowds spill out on to the car-free Nikolskaya Ulitsa, where junkies buy prescription drugs from babushki outside Lubyanka by day.

Svalka
Profsoyuzunnaya Ulitsa 27 (128 7823/120 5144). Metro Profsoyuzunnaya. **Open** 6pm-6am daily. **Admission** $5 Mon, Tue, Thur, Sun; $10 Fri, Sat; women free (Thur).
This attempt at designer-grunge in the boondocks of south Moscow is frequented by teenagers and aspiring bikers. Svalka (literally 'Rubbish Dump') is cheap, cheerful and unpretentious and the industrial-chic interior is cool; but on the flip-side, it's dull, the music is the usual techno trash and it's a schlep to get to.

Tabula Rasa
Berezhkovskaya Naberezhnaya 28 (240 9289). Metro Kievskaya. **Open** 7pm-6am daily. **Admission** Mon-Wed $8 men, $3 women; Thur, Sun $14 men, £7 women; Fri, Sat $16 men, $8 women. **Credit** DC, MC, V.
Just when you thought it was safe to go out in Moscow, you discover Tabula Rasa, lair of the killer nerds. If you thought Perestroika brought an end to this sad race, think again: they're all here, limp ponytails, leather pants and a penchant for art rock. Like Parizhkaya Zhizn, Tabula Rasa is the haunt of failed, early 1990s alternatives who've copped out and gone into marketing, making it about as tragically unhip as you can get, complete with Dire Straits.

Territoria
Tverskaya Ulitsa 5 (737 8865). Metro Okhotny Ryad. **Open** 1pm-late daily. **Admission** free. **Credit** DC, MC, V. **Map p278 C2**
A chic little lounge club just off Tverskaya (enter through the arch), frequented by trendy men in wraparound shades and goatees and hip rave chicks in minis. There's a tiny dancefloor complete with projector showing Disney wildlife movies and a small bar area with avant-garde-looking steel furniture. It's a good place to drop in to get up to speed before a heavy night of clubbing, with a friendly crowd and a relaxed atmosphere.

Titanic
Stadion Yunnykh Pionerov, Leningradsky Prospekt 31 (213 4581/fax 213 6095). Metro Dinamo. **Open** 11pm-7am Thur-Sun. **Admission** $25. **No credit cards.**
The club that launched 1,000 clichés, Titanic is the oft-proclaimed heart of the 'high octane' Moscow scene. It's in a bunker done up to look like the inside of a sinking ship (eerily appropriate, given current social unrest), where the rich, the beautiful and the heavily armed come to play. The car park looks like a Mercedes showroom and the girls look like they're fresh from a post-catwalk party. There's a steel gallery for observing the masses on the dance-floor and a New York lounge-style back room for kicking

The horrors of the Hungry Duck

The Hungry Duck is Moscow's *Apocalypse Now*, and evil genius Doug Steel is its Captain Kurtz. Steel's shrewd knowledge of the feral side of human nature has turned what was once a normal, respectable bar into a seething *bagno* of sin unprecedented since the Book of Revelation. To stay the distance through what they laughingly call 'Ladies' Night' at the Duck is to experience a baptism of fire and moral degradation like it took St John the Divine years to achieve. The basic formula is simple – get 800 young women into a bar for a dollar a head, feed them unlimited quantities of strong liquor, free, then get five male models to strip (and, in the process, also get them to undress and grope some of the customers), and finally, just as the sexual tension is so thick you could cut it with a knife, let in a horde of drunken, horny men. Perhaps the Duck triggers some rape and pillage folk memory buried deep in the Russian subconscious – but whatever it is, the ensuing scene is carnage. By 9pm on any given Ladies' Night a minimum of three women have to be carried out of the bar blind drunk; by the end of the evening there are at least two fights, a dozen injuries resulting in drunken girls falling off the bar and, by a conservative estimate, approximately 200 people who get laid.

It's not a place for the faint-hearted – or the sober. The stench of Slavic pheromones burns your nose, sweat drips from the ceiling, the floor is slippery with spilled beer and vomit and the toilets are awash with puke, unidentifiable body fluids and blood. Beware – spectacular, Wild West-style fights break out on a regular basis and picking someone up there will leave you feeling all empty and mixed up in the morning. Not to mention the high risks of sweaty, unprotected sex that could land you at the American Medical Centre's STD clinic, ever-popular with expatriate batchelors.

Golodnaya Utka
The Hungry Duck, Pushechnaya Ulitsa 9/6 (923 6158). Metro Kuznetsky Most. **Open** 6pm-6am daily. **Ladies' Night** Tue, Fri, Sun. **Admission** $1-$12.50. **Credit** AmEx, MC, V. **Map p278 D2**

back. Titanic throws regular parties and non-stop striptease marathons – admission to which is a mere $100. Beware of the security guards, the ones wearing ninja-style black fatigues and carrying billyclubs, and also of apparently unattended girls – their boyfriend's bodyguards may suffer a sense-of-humour failure.

Trety Put
Third Way, Pyatnitskaya Ulitsa 4 (951 8734). Metro Tretyakovskaya. **Open** 9pm-5am Thur-Sat. **Admission** $6. **No credit cards. Map p281 D5**
The last bastion of Moscow's squat club scene of the late 1980s and early 1990s, Trety Put is in a rambling apartment inhabited by the inimitable artist Boris Raskolnikov (yes, as in *Crime and Punishment*). There's a home-made bar, a chill-out room, where long-haired people wearing meaningful-message T-shirts play chess, a small stage-cum-dancefloor where 'underground' bands play and a TV room where shroomed-out bohos sprawl on couches. Relaxed, cheap and friendly, Trety Put is the perfect refuge from New Moscow's nauseating vulgarity and a great place to meet the capital's failed artists.

TsEKh
Workshop, Ulitsa Presnensky Val 14 (no phone). Metro Ulitsa 1905 Goda. **Open** 10pm-6am daily. **Admission** $10 men, free women. **No credit cards.**
A would-be rival to Titanic-located in a vast, disused factory, but without the beautiful people or the decadent atmosphere. The design is cool, but the jobsworth security minding the dancefloor and mind-scrambling techno played far too loud could give you brain damage. The DJ is mounted on a gantry crane, which travels up and down the dancefloor, but, despite all the gimmicks, the place is empty. Those ravers who do show up either dance like LSD-dosed lab rats or hover round the bar, sheltering from the music. A classic example of bad management turning a potentially cool club into a complete dump.

Up & Down
Zubovsky Bulvar 4 (201 5070/5291). Metro Park Kultury. **Open** 8pm-6am daily. **Admission** $10 (disco); $70 (bar/restaurant); free before 10pm. **Credit** AmEx, MC, V. **Map p280 A5/B5/B6**
One of the few places in town where you can see the real live Moscow banditi of legend at play in all their gold-chained, Rolex-toting glory. This is where the gangsters and their molls you read about in the papers hang out, complete with burly bodyguards, fat bellies and fistfuls of mobile phones. The trouble is, it'll cost you a few hundred dollars for the privilege. Up and Down is the most overpriced and overrated club in Moscow and, believe us, there's some stiff competition. The upstairs bar is tiny and the drinks stratospherically expensive. We saw one gang of partygoers guzzling down bottles of Dom Perignon at $1,400 a pop. They make sure you can settle the bill by forcing you to pay with a pre-paid drinks card.

Casinos

Moscow has more sleazy hustlers on the make, more contract killings, far more dirty money than Las Vegas – and almost as many casinos. Fast, easy wealth, combined with a very short life-expectancy among the people who make it, has led to a boom in excess on the gambling table. Any Western casino manager will tell you that the Russians are the worst gamblers in the world. They play to lose or win spectacularly, and since the former is generally easier, they go for that.

Even if you're not a gambler, Moscow's casinos are an unmissable zoo of New Russian excess. The casino is the habitat of Moscow's legendary banditi and mafiosi, who show up, true to form, in convoys of black Mercedes and Jeeps, surrounded by security guards. As a rule, the shorter the hair and the more expensive the silk shirt, the more careful you should be about spilling your drink in their vicinity, but they're usually pretty friendly. You'll see some of the most breathtakingly vulgar interiors ever created by the hand of man, clients straight out of the Central Casting 'baddy' book, and call-girls to kill for... many no doubt have. Look smart, be polite, don't crowd the tables and you'll fit in fine. Enjoy.

Beverly Hills
Kudrinskaya Ploshchad 1 (255 4228). Metro Barrikadnaya. **Open** 6.30pm-6am daily. **Admission** free. **Credit** DC, MC, V. **Map p277 A3**
American action-movie star Chuck Norris is a shareholder in this place, which tells you almost all you need to know. The underground restaurant is done up to look like a Spanish village plaza, complete with fake trees and fountains, and the black and chrome dancefloor next door looks like somewhere *The Kids from Fame!* would hang out, circa 1983. The clients aren't quite rich or scary-looking enough to excite the true connoisseur of Moscow phantasmagoria, but the food is good.

Golden Palace
3-ya Ulitsa Yamskogo Polya 15 (212 3909/3941). Metro Belorusskaya. **Admission** $10 men; free women. **Credit** MC, V.
Nero would have been proud. The Golden Palace is a spectacular monument to New Russian excess, with black-clad, shotgun-toting security and clients who look like extras from *Name of the Rose* costumed by Versace. The piranhas swim in fish tanks set in the floor and walls.

Karusel
1-ya Tverskaya-Yamskaya Ulitsa (251 6444). Metro Mayakovskaya. **Open** 10pm-6am daily. **Admission** $420 Fri, Sat; $250 Tue, Thur; $160 Mon, Sun. **Credit** DC, MC, V. **Map p277 B2**
Karusel's claim to fame is that it's the most expensive club in Moscow. Congratulations! Robocop security, non-stop strip shows and drinks that cost half of Russia's national debt. The downside is that it's full of clients who come because it's the most expensive club in town.

Metelitsa
Ulitsa Novy Arbat 21 (291 1423). Metro Arbatskaya. **Open** 8pm-5am daily. **Admission** $26 Mon-Thur; $35 Fri-Sun. **Credit** DC, MC, V. **Map p277 A3/B3**
Moscow's answer to Caesars Palace (sic), Metelitsa is bigger, brasher, more vulgar and more packed with dangerous, wealthy men than any other Moscow casino. On a Saturday night, the place looks like an upmarket version of the alien bar in *Star Wars*, with an outlandish cabaret upstairs, literally hundreds of prostitutes lining the bar and sweating, silk-shirted clients blowing millions of hard-earned dollars at the roulette tables.

Royale
Begovaya Ulitsa 22 (945 1963). Metro Begovaya. **Open** 10pm-5am daily. **Admission** $15 men, $10 women. **Credit** DC, MC, V.
A classy casino in the palatial Hippodrome, where the more discerning Moscow gamblers come to throw away their money. Chandeliers, stucco and velvet curtains give the place a pre-Revolutionary feel, which is spoiled by the Charlie Chaplin theme bar and cheesy disco downstairs.

Sport & Fitness

If you want to keep fit in Moscow, you'd better put your skates on.

Misha, the tubby brown bear that floated into Moscow for the 1980 Olympics, was brought out once again for summer 1998, when the world – well, the under-18 world at least – looked to Moscow for sporting excellence as the World Youth Games took over the city. And none too soon... Moscow sport had really been rooting through the dustbins over the previous few years: the great Soviet sporting machine sank into a deep funk. Players and athletes fled Russian sport to earn millions abroad, while stadia and facilities received little or no funding.

The money has finally started to come through, though. Luxurious gyms are opening, **Luzhniki Stadium** sparkles with a multimillion dollar facelift and one of the most popular papers in the country is a sports daily. It's nowhere near perfect; national team victories are far rarer than in Soviet days and many facilities are still archaic. But Russia will seemingly always churn out more world champs than most countries can dream of. If it ever had the facilities of the United States the rest of the world could just pack up and go home.

Catching the stars or just stretching your legs can be a struggle. Chaos is included in the admission price, but there's a depth of sports experience in Moscow found in few other cities in the world.

INFORMATION

The *Moscow Times* and the *Moscow Tribune* have daily sports sections; both try hard but leave many dissatisfied, as they squeeze in both European and North American sports. The *Moscow Times* has more in-depth coverage of Russian sports.

Watching international sport isn't easy in Moscow. Most bars have satellite dishes that only pick up Eurosport; others have the Russian satellite channel NTV+, which occasionally shows the cream of international sporting events, but for most major events, **Chesterfield's** (*see chapter* **Pubs & Bars**) is the only one that screens Sky Sports. Russian terrestial television usually has tape-delayed coverage of the NBA and NHL finals.

TICKETS

Don't even think about trying to pay with plastic. Tickets for all events are sold at the stadium on the day, for cash only. For more important matches they're sold a few days in advance. Touts occasionally appear when matches are sold out.

The sporting venues listed below accept credit cards only where stipulated.

Spectator Sports

Watching sport hasn't been a priority for Muscovites over the last few years, but things have been improving recently: more people are joining the hardcore support for football, ice hockey and basketball and there are early signs, although too few, that the clubs are now starting to appreciate the fans.

Arm-wrestling

International Golden Bear Tournament

Club MGU, Sparrow Hills Baseball Stadium (939 2431). Metro Universitet. **Open** 7-8.30pm Thur, Sat.

This world-class tournament has been going for eight years and takes place in February. And if you fancy trying a bit of bicep-bending yourself then this is one of the country's top training centres.

Athletics

Moscow is part of the European indoor and outdoor athletics circuit and hosts tournaments in January and August. Both regularly attract world class competitors, including the Olympic 100 metre champion Donovan Bailey and the world long-jump record holder Ivan Pedroso. There are also two annual marathons. The first is strictly for Muscovites and takes place in May, the second has an international field and takes place in September. Both events start and finish at Gorky Park. If you are interested in taking part in either, call 222 1425 for details.

CSKA Indoor Sports Arena
Leningradsky Prospekt 39A (213 2954). Metro Dinamo. **Admission** $1.50-$15.

Lokomotiv Stadium
Bolshaya Cherkizovskaya Ulitsa 125A (161 9385/9063). Metro Cherkizovskaya. **Admission** $3-$8.

Baseball

Beisbolny Stadion

Sparrow Hills Baseball Stadium (939 2431). Metro Universitet.

This Japanese-donated baseball stadium, located slap bang in the middle of the University, plays host to the Russian baseball league. The Russian national team is one of the best in Europe, and no slouch across the pond, either: a recent tour of the United States saw a local Moscow club come away with a highly respectable 0.500 record. The season runs from April to October.

Join the rollerblading majority – whether you're wearing wheels or not, you're likely to take

Basketball

Basketball ranks third after soccer and ice hockey in popularity, although there are signs that it is gaining fans due to NBA exposure.

CSKA

CSKA Sports Hall, Leningradsky Prospekt 39A (213 2954). Metro Dinamo. **Admission** $1.50-$15.
CSKA is pretty much the only decent basketball team Russia has got. Champions for the last seven years, they have reached the latter stages of the European Championship in two of the last three seasons. It often serves as a retirement home for NBA rejects. The women's team is also a powerful force with many players making the reverse journey to the WNBA. Season runs September to May.

Football

Russian football is at something of a low point at the moment: failure to qualify for the World Cup, increasing crowd trouble and heavy hints at corruption and criminal influence are all contributory factors. Having said that, crowd numbers are beginning to swell, money is trickling in through sponsorship and there is the possibility of a European trophy final coming to Moscow. Try to catch the CIS Cup, an indoor tournament between all the former Soviet republics held every January, which invariably pits arch Soviet rivals Spartak and Dinamo Kiev.

CSKA Moscow

CSKA Stadium, 3-ya Peschanaya Ulitsa 2 (157 5975). Metro Sokol. **Admission** $1.50-$6.50.
There are a number of CSKA teams in Moscow; this one is the army football team.

Dinamo Moscow

Dinamo Stadium, Leningradsky Prospekt 36 (212 2252). Metro Dinamo.
Historically the team of the militia. Dinamo fans reserve their special hatred for Spartak.

Luzhniki Stadium

Luzhnetskaya Naberezhnaya 24 (201 1164). Metro Sportivnaya.
Reopened last September after a $200-million high-class refit, then embarrassingly reclosed after two matches to have its pitch replaced. When it reopens the Luzhniki will continue to host national games, Torpedo home matches and purportedly a European final.

Minifootball

Universalny Sportivny Zal Druzhba (Druzhba sports hall), Naberezhnaya Luzhniki 24 (201 1164). Metro Sportivnaya. **Season** Sept-Apr. **Tickets** $1.
Not a bunch of stunted Muscovites with a marble: lots of skill, a smaller indoor pitch and a world-contending national team. They beat a Brazilian team in an international tournament in Moscow in 1997.

Spartak Moscow

Lokomotiv Stadium, Bolshaya Cherkizovskaya Ulitsa 125A (161 9385/9063). Metro Cherkizovskaya. **Admission** $3.50-$6.50.
Spartak is Russia's Manchester United, loved and hated in equal measures. They're successful at home, yet Champions League flops in Europe, and reached the semis of the 1998 UEFA Cup only to be blown away by Ronaldo and Inter Milan. Big games are currently played at Dinamo Stadium, but that may change when Luzhniki Stadium reopens.

Torpedo Moscow

Torpedo Stadium, Vostochnaya Ulitsa 4 (275 0745). Metro Avtozavodskaya. **Admission** $1.50-$6.50.
The team beloved of Moscow Mayor Luzhkov.

Horse racing

Hippodrome

Begovaya Ulitsa 4 (945 0437). Metro Begovaya. **Open** Sat, Sun. **Admission** $1.50. Minimum bet 20¢; maximum bet $175.
Moscow Hippodrome is over 150 years old and it shows. All its buildings are crumbling and shabby, and most of the punters are old enough to remember Khrushchev's trips down the track. The intentions of the management are to bring in the new-monied but they have got a long way to go. There's no show-jumping or flat racing at all, only harness racing

a fall on Moscow's inline-crazy streets.

(trotting) and troika races (three horses pulling a driver in a buggy) once a year. The betting system is extremely confusing; be warned.

If the standard of play isn't of NHL quality, the mayhem and violence are the same: blood on the ice is as exciting in Russia as in North America. The season runs from September to April. The Izvestia Cup pits the Russian national side against the best in Europe, Sweden, the Czech Republic and Finland. Only European-based players take part in this tournament. Call 912 5571 for details.

Ledovy Dvorets CSKA

CSKA Ice Palace, Leningradsky Prospekt 39A (213 7163). Metro Aeroport or Dinamo.
Formerly Russia's best, now split into two teams, cunningly called CSKA and HC (hockey club) CSKA. One's not that good and the other's worse. Provincial teams Torpedo Yaroslavl and AK Bars (Kazan), title-winners for the last two years, are top dogs now. Catch the CSKAs play each other for extra bad feeling on the ice.

Dvorets Sporta Luzhniki

Luzhniki Sports Palace, Luznetskaya Naberezhnaya 24 (201 1632). Metro Sportivnaya.
Home to Spartak – a good Moscow team.

Dvorets Sporta Krilya Sovietov

Krilya Sovietov Sports Palace, Ulitsa Tolbukhina 10/3 (448 8777). Train from Belorussky Station.
Home to Krylia Sovietov (Soviet Wings), one of Moscow's better teams.

Dvorets Sporta Sokolniki

Sokolniki Ice Palace, Ulitsa Sokolnichesky Val 1B (268 6958). Metro Sokolniki. Tickets $1-$10.

Dinamo Moscow

Dinamo Ice Palace, Leningradsky Prospekt 36 (221 3145). Metro Dinamo. Tickets $1.50-$10.
Moscow's best side, runners-up to Metallurg in the championship.

Kremlin Cup

Moscow Olympic Sports Centre, Olimpiisky Prospekt 16, Metro Prospekt Mira. Tickets $1.50-$40.
Building up into one of the top European tournaments, the Kremlin Cup has over $1 million in prize money and a regular shoal of top tennis stars. Yevgeny Kafelnikov always plays although teen star Anna Kournikova's money demands mean that she has yet to compete in Russia's biggest tennis event. The ladies' Kremlin Cup takes place in October, the men's in November.

Active Sports

If you want to be active in Moscow, it helps to strap something on your feet. Rollerblades in late spring and summer become skates and skis once the snow falls. Without attachments life is harder, except for those who can afford the new, deluxe gyms.

Moskovsky Klub Veloturizma

Moscow Bike Touring Club, Staraya Basmannaya Ulitsa 20-2 (267 4468). Metro Baumanskaya. **Meetings** 7-10pm Tue. **Yearly membership** $8; $4 over-65s; $1 students. **Map p279 F2**
A friendly cycling club that welcomes non-members. Organised group trips range from tours of the environs of Moscow to trips as far as Lake Baikal or the Kara Kum desert. Family trips and weekend tours are also organised; prices are negotiable.

Ballet

Moskovsky Klassichesky Balet (Moscow Classical Ballet), Neglinnaya Ulitsa 6 (924 1089). Metro Kuznetsky Most or Okhotny Ryad. **Lessons** beginners 6.30-8.30pm Tue; advanced 6.30-8.30pm Thur. **Cost** $10. **Map p278 C2**

Ballroom dancing

*Dom Kultury Militsii (Militia Cultural Centre),
Novoslobodskaya Ulitsa 45/3 (978 8046). Metro
Novoslobodskaya.* **Open** *Sept-May* times vary. **Lessons**
$2.50; monthly pass $8.
The witty instructor here leads the most donkey-like of
students through a respectable shuffle.

Salsa

*La Bamba, Molodyozhnaya Hotel, Dmitrovskoye Shosse 27
(977 4266). Metro Timiryazevskaya.* **Lessons** 10pm Fri;
disco 11pm. **Cost** free; a cover charge of $10 for men, $4 for
women may be payable.

Fitness centres

Besides the fitness centres listed below, most of
Moscow's luxury hotels, including the **Metropol**,
have their own gyms that are open to the public
for a single-use fee, as well as to hotel residents.
For details, *see chapter* **Accommodation**.

Gold's Gym

*Leningradsky Prospekt 31/30 (931 9616/9625).
Metro Dinamo.* **Open** 7am-11pm Mon-Fri; 9am-
10pm Sat, Sun. **Membership** $2,500 annual; $600
3-month; $895 6-month. **Credit** AmEx, DC, EC, JCB,
MC, V.
As well as all the usual facilities, this gym boasts a good
health food café with a juice bar.

International Studio Aerobic Workout

*Ulitsa Maksimova 11 (196 7352). Metro Oktyabrskoye
Polye.* **Open** 3-8pm Mon, Wed, Thur; 10am-9pm Tue, Fri;
5-8pm Sat; noon-4pm Sun. **Admission** $5 for 1 day; $33
for 8 visits.
Offers all types of aerobic exercise classes, from salsa to step,
plus aerobics for pregnant women.

Olimpiisky Sportivny Tsentr

*Olympic Sports Complex, Olimpiisky Prospekt 16 (288
1333). Metro Prospekt Mira.* **Open** 8am-9pm daily.
Rates vary for each activity.
The city's best public facility. There are classes for board
diving, scuba diving, water ballet, ice skating, hockey, aerobics, weight lifting, ballroom dancing, regular gymnastics
and rhythmic gymnastics as well as group and individual
swimming lessons. There are two 50m (164ft) swimming
pools as well as a diving pool with 25m (82ft) swimming lanes
roped off. Carried over from Soviet times is the rule that the
public must buy monthly passes for a designated time each
week. If you want more flexibility, buy a one-off pass.

World Class

*Prospekt Vernadskogo 101 (974 3200/3215). Metro
Prospekt Vernadskogo.* **Open** 7am-11pm Mon-Fri; 9am-
9pm Sat, Sun. **Annual membership** $3,000; $4,800 2
people. **Credit** MC, V.

Golf

When Brezhnev asked Armand Hammer what
was needed for Americans to invest in Russia, he
received the unexpected reply: a limousine and the
means to play golf. Since its arrival in 1989, golf is
slowly growing in popularity.

Moscow Country Club

*Nakhabino, Krasnogorsky District, Moscow Oblast (926
5928/fax 564 8896).* **Open** 7am-8pm daily. **Course** 18
holes. **Membership** $27,000, plus $1,750 a year; *corporate*
$108,000, plus $8,000 a year. **Credit** AmEx, DC, MC, V.
Host of the Russian Open, and described by a top European
golfing official as one of the ten best golf courses in Europe.
It is also equipped with a driving range, pool, sauna, tennis
courts, squash courts and a golf school for kids; unfortunately
it's members-only.

Cheating in high places

Russian sport has always been afflicted by inter-
ference from the power élite. Stalin's most
vicious henchman, Lavrenty Beria, a former professional football player in Georgia, was such a
fan of the team CSKA Moscow that he sent two
players from a rival team to the gulag to help his
team win. One referee who once sent Beria off is
said to have lived the rest of his life in fear.

Nikita Khrushchev, a keen and surprisingly
successful fisherman, had to get a helping hand
from below in the shape of KGB scubadivers
who were instructed to swim beneath his boat
and manually attach fish to his hook. And
Leonid Brezhnev was such a bad hunter that his
officials had to tie bears to the trees to give him
a chance of taking a kill home. Rabbits, by the
hundred, would also be released by bodyguards
hiding behind the trees.

Even today, the enthusiasm among Russia's
ruling class for 'assisted' sports has not

diminished much. In one notorious incident,
two helicopters, a fleet of Volga cars, professional hunters, bodyguards and agents of
the FSB were called upon to help former Prime
Minister Viktor Chernomyrdin hunt down a
mother bear and her two cubs. An entire section of a forest was cleared to make space for a
helicopter pad and a spanking new stretch of
road was built right up to the den, just so he
could plug the helpless bear, which dutifully
emerged from its den to confront Russia's
finest men in uniform.

Boris Yeltsin took a similarly easy route when
he went on a fishing holiday in the summer of
1997. The lake was specially stocked with more
than 10,000 extra fish to ensure Yeltsin a
successful day with the rod. And when Tsar
Boris plays tennis, his opponents are given helpful tips about the weaker elements of his game
– so that they can avoid them.

Moskovsky Golf-klub

Moscow Golf Club, Ulitsa Dovzhenko (147 8330/6444).
Course 9 holes. **Open** 8am-7pm daily. **Fees** $55 per
round; *membership* $1,500-$3,000 per year; *life membership*
$1,500 a year; *corporate membership* $2,000-$2,500 a year.
The first golf club in the Soviet Union. Non-members can
play (but you need to call in advance). Even Pele and Mike
Tyson turned up for the opening in 1988. The clubhouse also
has a fine Chinese restaurant.

Ice skating

Cold weather is one thing there's no shortage of in
Moscow and ice rinks, both indoor and out, are
another. The ideal temperature for outdoor skating
is -2°C to -8°C (18-30°F), when the ice is both fast
enough for skilled skaters and suitable for begin
ners. Outdoor rinks are closed during the summer.

Outdoor

Katok Stadiona Torpedo

*Torpedo Stadium Rink, Vostochnaya Ulitsa 4 (275
4586). Metro Avtozavodskaya.* **Open** 8am-10pm daily.
Admission $1.50. **Skate hire** $2.

Park Gorkogo

Gorky Park. Metro Oktyabrskaya or Park Kultury. **Open**
11am-10pm daily. **Admission** $1.50; *ice disco* $3. **Skate
hire** $1.50 per hour. **Map p280 DG**
No longer the place to leave your victim à la Martin Cruz Smith,
Gorky Park is packed with couples and four-year-olds who
make Tara Lipinsky look like the *babushka* selling cigarettes
at the metro. Can be hectic at weekends and in the evenings.

Sokolniki Park

10th Sports Pavilion (268 8277). Metro Sokolniki. **Open**
11am-9pm daily. **Admission** $3 per 2 hours. **Skate
hire** $3 per hour, plus $58 deposit (ID required).
Sokolniki's outdoor rink has the best skates for hire in the
city, offering almost new and comfortable ice skates.

Indoor

Katok Kristall

*Luzhniki Sports Complex, Luzhnetskaya Naberezhnaya
24 (201 1815). Metro Sportivnaya.* **Open** hours vary.
Admission $2.50. **Skate hire** $1.50-$2.50 per hour.
An indoor facility used by professional skaters, so the hours
when it is open to the public vary.

Lokomotiv Ice Palace

*Bolshaya Cherkizovskaya Ulitsa 125 (161 9385). Metro
Cherkizovskaya.* **Open** 11am-5pm daily. **Admission** $4.
No skate hire.
Eight metro stops from the city centre, the Lokomotiv Ice
Palace is a great indoor rink with fast ice.

Paintball

Paintland

*Dom Otdykha Shchokolovsky (126 0943/584 1495).
Metro Shchyolkovskaya.* **Rates** *gun, camouflage hire* $35;
paint pellets $120 for 2,500.
There are two sheds 'em up areas, one of which includes a
disused trolleybus to storm. The staff will fax a map of their
location to you, or pick up groups from a metro station. They
also offer table tennis, football and horse riding and there's
a café serving home-made Russian food.

Riding

Lessons are available for complete novices, as well
as advanced riders. Most stables provide all the
necessary equipment, but of course, it is preferable
to take your own riding hat.

Bitsa

*Balaklavsky Prospekt 33. Metro Chertanovskaya or
Kaluzhskaya.* **Open** 10am-9pm daily. **Lessons**
individual $20-$25; $15-$20 children; *group* $5-$8; $4.50-
$7 children.
A premier complex, Bitsa was built for the 1980 Moscow
Olympics and houses stables, a 12,000-seater showjumping
stadium, indoor riding hall, gym, swimming pool and a rifle
range. Classes are held once or twice a week.

Hippodrome

*Moscow Hippodrome, Begovaya Ulitsa 22/1 (945 2052).
Metro Begovaya or Dinamo.* **Lessons** $6 per hour; $3 per
hour 12-16-year-olds; *obligatory safety course* Sat, Sun
$1.50.
Associated with Moscow's racetrack, this riding school was
opened more than 30 years ago and its arena is the largest in
Europe. Riders aged ten and older are welcome to train here;
there are 30 minute introductory lessons for novices

Sokoros

*Sokolniki Park, Poperechny Prosek 11 (268 5942). Metro
Sokolniki.* **Lessons** *individual* $24 for 45 minutes; *group*
$12 for 45 minutes.
This parkland setting offers trail rides in the quiet forest as
well as indoor lessons.

Unikum

Call for details (249 1134). **Lessons** $3 per hour
beginners; $5 per hour advanced.
Lidia Ospinnikova runs Unikum, a retirement home for
horses from the Hippodrome, the circus and the mounted
police. She keeps the refuge running by offering weekend
lessons. For information on how to get there and lesson
times, call Lidia Ospinnikova in the evenings on 249 1134.

Rollerblading (inline skating)

No self-respecting teen bothers walking in
Moscow; the city's awash with rollerbladers. The
most popular places are Poklonnaya Gora, Gorky
Park, Sparrow Hills, VVTs (VDNKh), Alexander
Gardens and Dinamo. Follow the river from Gorky
Park to Moscow State University and watch the
more experienced bladers take the death-defying
steps leading to the Stalin skyscraper. The steps
of the Lenin statue at Oktyabrskaya are a top spot
for spins and crashes.

Detsky Mir

*Teatralny Proyezd 5 (927 2007). Metro Lubyanka or
Kuznetsky Most.* **Open** 9am-8pm Mon-Sat. **Map p278
C3/D3**
The sports department of 'Kids' World' is on the ground
floor and offers a varied selection of high-quality
rollerblades ($82-$250), while the shop next door has the
cheaper Chinese variety ($50-$90).

Kant Sports Club

Nagornaya Ulitsa 2 (213 3325). Metro Nagornaya.
Open 9am-6pm. **Rates** depend on age and size of group.
Kant offers rollerblading lessons in the summer for kids, and
adults if you ask nicely.

Scuba diving

Akvanet
Olimpiisky Prospekt 18 (288 5645). Metro Prospekt Mira.
Open 10am-6pm daily. **Rates** $330 for PADI course.
Founded three years ago, Akvanet is the first and biggest dive-club in Moscow providing PADI courses. The course takes two weekends.

Krokodil
Olimpiisky Prospekt 2 (437 4800/437 4765). Metro Yugo-Zapadnaya. **Open** 11am-9pm Mon-Sat. **Open** $270 for PADI course, payable in rubles only.

Skiing

Cross-country
Within Moscow cross-country skiers head for any of the city's parks: Izmailovsky (Metro Izmailovskaya), Serebryanny Bor (Metro Polezhayevskaya) and Bitsevsky (Metro Cherta-novskaya) usually have decent tracks. You can also try Timiryazevsky Park (Metro Timiryazevskaya) but you have to go at a quiet time to avoid hitting any strolling *babushki*.

Outside Moscow try Usovo, a small dacha town, just south of the Moskva River, west of the city. The slopes are easy-going and there are plenty of options for different length out-ings. Trains leave Belorussky station once an hour, at about half past the hour, and the journey takes about half an hour.

Nekrasovskaya is great for a quiet day in the woods. Take the train from Savyolovsky station but be aware that not all trains stop at Nekrasovskaya. The journey takes about 40 minutes. Get off from the last wagon of the train, cross the tracks, head left along them until you have passed the village and put on your skis. Go west (to the right) into the woods for 6km (3.75 miles) until you see Nerskoye Lake ahead. You can either turn round here or head northeast (right). After 6km, you cross a road; after another 4km (2.5 miles) in a north-east-ern direction you reach Trudovaya station, where you can catch a train back.

Downhill
The Krylatskoye slopes (Metro Krylatskoye) are the most popular; the rather rickety ski lift costs barely a dollar. Otherwise Sparrow Hills offers a great view on the way down and two ski jumps. Ten minutes' walk south from Nagornaya metro station is a nice steep hill, and there are several good slopes with lifts near Tsaritsyno Palace (Metro Tsaritsyno). Although primarily a children's ski school, **Kant Sports Club** (*see above* **Rollerblading**) has eight skiing and snow-boarding instructors who also work with adults. The club has its own artificial slope, a 40m- (131ft-) high ice climb, and a 4.5km (3-mile) cross-country lighted trail.

Swimming

Going swimming can be a battle in Russia: most pools require a *spravka* (a certificate to verify that you are free of any contagious skin diseases). Some have doctors on site who will issue one for a small fee. Some pools also insist on caps. The pools offer one- to three-month passes or a one-off fee. Some monthly passes are limited to specific days or times, while a one-off ticket often only allows you to swim for a certain length of time, usually 45 minutes.

Bassein Centralnogo Sportivnogo Kluba Voyenno-Morskogo Flota
Russian Navy Central Sport Club Pool, Leningradskoye Shosse 25A (150 5560). Metro Voikovskaya. **Open** 8am-

8.30pm Mon-Sat; 9am-7pm Sun. **Admission** $5 for 45 minutes; $27 3-month pass.

Dom Plavania
Olympic Nautical Sports Centre, Ulitsa Ibragimova 30 (369 0649/4803). Metro Semyenovskaya. **Admission** $10 per visit (incl use of all facilities).

Fili Pool
2-ya Filyovskaya Ulitsa 18A (148 3046). Metro Bagrationovskaya. **Open** 7am-10pm Mon-Sat; 8am-8pm Sun. **Admission** $4 for 45 minutes; $25 3-month pass.

Olympic Sports Complex
Olimpiisky Prospekt 2 (288 1333/8333). Metro Prospekt Mira. **Open** 7am-9pm daily. **Rate** $5 for 45 minutes.
The Olympic pools are down the road from the main sports centre, *see above* **Fitness centres**.

Serebryanny Bor
Metro Polezhayevskaya, then trolley bus 21 or any bus heading west.
Thousands flock here to bathe in the often dubious-looking Moskva River.

Tschaika
Turchaninov Pereulok 1/3 (246 1344). Metro Park Kultury. **Open** 7am-10pm daily. **Admission** $8; $3 with a combination ticket. **Map p280 B5**

Tennis

Not surprisingly, there aren't any municipal courts for this most bourgeois of sports, but the success of Yevgeny Kafelnikov and Anna Kournikova has made it popular. Mayor Yuri Luzhkov also plays a mean game, as Yeltsin did at one time – he once partnered Steffi Graf in an exhibition game.

Dvorets Tennisa CSKA
CSKA Tennis Palace, Leningradsky Prospekt 39A (213 6547). Metro Dinamo. **Open** 7am-11pm daily. **Rates** $12 per hour; *grass courts* $15 per hour.

Dvorets Detskogo Sporta
Children Sports Palace, Rabochaya Ulitsa 63. Metro Ploshchad Ilyicha. **Open** 7am-11pm daily. **Rates** $25 per hour.

Korty Sportcomplexa Chaika
Chaika Tennis Courts, Korobeinikov Pereulok 1/2 (202 0474). Metro Park Kultury. **Open** 7am-11pm daily. **Rates** $30-$50 per hour. **Map p280 B5**

Tenpin bowling

Despite being horribly expensive, bowling (or *kegel-bahn*, the Germn name it is known by) is starting to spread here.

Eurobowl
Izmailovo Hotel, Izmailovskoye Shosse 71 (166 7418). Metro Izmailovsky Park. **Open** noon-6am daily. **Cost** $20 per hour until 7pm Mon-Fri; $32 per hour after 7pm Mon-Thur; $46 after 7pm Fri, Sat, Sun.

Setun Kegelbahn
Ulitsa Tolbukhina 10A (448 7186). Metro Kuntsevskaya, then bus 16 or 45. **Open** 6pm-2am Mon-Fri; 2pm-2am Sat, Sun. **Cost** $30 per hour Mon-Thur; $45 per hour Fri $50 Sat, Sun; $1 shoe hire. **Credit** DC, MC, V.

Theatre & Dance

Its classic heritage is undisputed – now Moscow's contemporary performing arts are making their own mark.

Theatre

Moscow boasts over 150 theatres. Add to this impressive total the national and international theatre festivals that attract luminaries from all over the globe and you can begin to understand the tradition that caused the first Soviet cultural commissar Anatoly Lunacharsky to call Moscow a theatrical mecca. Home-grown theatre here is extremely diverse, from the stiff and desperately staid to the weird and decidedly wonderful. The Russian capital on the cusp of the twenty-first century is a study in contrasts and the terrain of its theatre world is no different. That is especially true on the battlefield pitting the old against the new. Almost every established venue is run by someone who came to prominence in or around the 1960s. For those who like their theatre traditional and familiar that is a boon. Yet for those who like an edge of risk, there are plenty of other playhouses to haunt.

Tsentr Debyut (the Debut Centre; *see below*), a laboratory designed to launch new playwrights, directors and actors, appeared in 1996 as a backlash to the heavy weight of conservatism. While it isn't yet turning out cutting-edge work, it is absorbed in a noble enterprise: taking chances.

And then there is Pyotr Fomenko. Another of those respected directors who has been around since the 1960s, he sealed his place in history by hooking up with some kids specifically, his 1993 graduation class at the Russian Academy of Theatre Arts, around whom he formed the popular **Fomenko Studio** (*see below*). This talented troupe has had hits and misses, but its energy and style make it one of the hippest and most promising in town. Watch for the opening of the Studio's new stage on Kutuzovsky Prospekt, expected during the 1998-9 season.

Plays remain in repertory for several years and often up to a decade or more (one production has been on since 1902), so most of those detailed here will still be running for the life of this guide.

There are no Western musicals in Moscow and no English-language theatre, with the exception of productions of both Russian and American works by a student theatre company, the American Studio at Moscow Art School. These run from March to May: for more information consult the listings papers detailed below. The most accessible works for non-Russian speakers are those by Valery Fokin, which use minimal language. He currently has shows in rep at **MTYuZ**, the **Satirikon** and the **Tabakov Theatre** (*see below*). Note that the puppet theatres are not dumb shows and in fact are quite language-dependent.

TICKETS & INFORMATION

For information in English, consult the *Moscow Times*'s *MT Out* section or the *Moscow Tribune*'s calendar (*see chapter* Media). *MT* also publishes a Stage Page on Thursdays.

Tickets are available at theatre box offices, and at over 60 ticket booths throughout the city, usually in or near metro stations. The selection at the booths is limited, but they sometimes have tickets to shows that are sold out at box offices. If you just arrived in town and there's a great show tonight, go to the theatre: tickets may be released for sale at the last minute, or chances are that someone may be selling a spare outside the theatre.

Chekhov MKhAT

Moscow Art Theatre, Kamergersky Pereulok 3 (229 8760). Metro Okhotny Ryad. Tickets $1.50-$8.50. **Map p278 C2**
Not to be confused with the Gorky Moscow Art Theatre, which broke away in 1987, the Chekhov may be the most famous playhouse in the world. Founded 100 years ago by Konstantin Stanislavsky and Vladimir Nemirovich-Danchenko, it recently enjoyed a high-profile centenary celebration – but nothing can disguise the fact that this theatre is currently in crisis. Such classics as Chekhov's *Three Sisters*, Gogol's *The Marriage* and Griboyedov's *Woe From Wit* are wearily conventional; Nelson and Gelman's *The Birthday Party* is livelier, and we have yet to see what will come of Nikolai Yevreinov's *The Main Thing*, to be staged in winter 1998.

Fomenko Studio

Fomenko office, Ulitsa Arbat 35, room 369 (information 248 9162). Metro Smolenskaya or Arbatskaya. Tickets $1-$9. **Map p280 A4/B4**
This talented troupe has had hits and misses, but its energy and style make it one of the hippest and most promising in town. Since it does not yet have its own stage, the studio performs at different venues.

Lenkom Theatre

*Ulitsa Malaya Dmitrovka 6 (299 0708). Metro
Chekhovskaya or Pushkinskaya.* **Tickets** $3-$9. **Map
p277 B1, p278 C1/2**

The ageing Lenkom holds its audience by resting on its lau-
rels. Artistic director Mark Zakharov made his name in the
1970s, imitating the Broadway musical, and all his recent
shows – Beaumarchais's *The Marriage of Figaro*, Gorin and
Kallosh's *King's Games* and *Barbarian and Heretic*, based on
Dostoyevsky's *The Gambler* – have been flashy boomers, with
just enough substance to keep the faithful happy. More challenging is Alexander Galin's *Sorry*, staged by renowned film
director Gleb Panfilov and starring the great Inna Churikova.

Maly Theatre

*Teatralnaya Ploshchad 1/6 (923 2621/924 4083). Metro
Teatralnaya.* **Tickets** $1-$4. **Map p278 C3**

The Maly was founded in 1824, and some wiseacres say it's
showing its age. They may be right: the old-fashioned productions of predominantly nineteenth-century plays can look
pretty musty. However, there are a few fine actors here,
among whom Vasily Bochkaryov especially shines. See him
in AK Tolstoy's historical chronicle *Tsar Boris* or Fridrikh
Gorenshtein's contemporary historical play *Tsar Pyotr and
Alexei*. The posh, stately interiors of both the main stage and
the affiliate are a sight to behold.
Affiliate venue: Bolshaya Ordynka 69 (237 3181/4472).

Mossoviet Theatre

*Bolshaya Sadovaya Ulitsa 16 (299 3377/2573).
Metro Mayakovskaya.* **Tickets** $1.50-$9. **Map p277
A2/B1/B2**

The 1,200-seat main auditorium at this venue offers popular
comedies and pseudo-musicals, while the 150-seater, Beneath
the Roof, tends to host more adventurous outings. Up there,
a camp version of Molière's *School For Wives* and a fine modern take on *My Poor Marat*, Alexei Arbuzov's tale of a
ménage à trois among teenagers during World War II, are
especially noteworthy.

MTYuZ

*Young Spectator Theatre, Mamonovsky Pereulok 10 (299
5360). Metro Pushkinskaya or Tverskaya.* **Tickets** $2-
$9. **Map p277 B2**

Don't let the name fool you. Since Genrietta Yanovskaya
debuted as chief director with a powerful version of
Bulgakov's *The Heart of a Dog* in 1987, this venue has
become a seat of innovation. That is thanks both to
Yanovskaya, whose eclectic 1997 production of Ostrovsky's
The Storm pulled down a bevy of awards, and to her husband Kama Ginkas, whose powerful small-stage productions
of *KI From 'Crime'* and *The Execution of the Decembrists*
are among the shows that have earned him a reputation as
one of Europe's top directors. Ginkas's unorthodox handling
of Pushkin's *The Golden Cockerel* opens in autumn 1998, as

Five shows, five stars

A truism today is that no one Moscow theatre
guarantees quality, but any venue may put out a
brilliant show at any moment. Following are five
regularly staged shows that exemplify the best
in the city's extraordinary creative potential.

Fomenko Studio

The Magnificent Cuckold by Fernand Crommelynck.
In this spellbinding tale of a loving husband whose wild
jealousy drives his wife to promiscuity, director Pyotr
Fomenko wraps everyone and everything in a shimmering veil of evocative, sensory effects that, like fine
spices, highlight every aspect of the compelling drama.
Fomenko's shows are famous for their remarkable deli-
cacy and subtlety, and this is one of his best.

Satirikon Theatre

The Metamorphosis, adapted from Franz Kafka.
Valery Fokin creates total-environment experiences, and
here he has built a box that spectators enter and share
with Gregor Samsa (*pictured below*), who, one horrible

morning, awakens as an insect. The stage, the front half
of which lowers almost out of sight and the back half of
which disappears behind a screen when lit from the front,
is a place of fantastic goings-on, not the least of which is
Konstantin Raikin's brilliant performance of the clerk-
turned-bug.

KI From 'Crime', adapted by Daniil Gink from
Fyodor Dostoyevsky's *Crime and Punishment*.
One of the stars of the so-called Russian Season at
Avignon in 1997, this stunning production by Kama
Ginkas is capable of leaving audiences racked by
sobs. A strictly structured, and yet highly improvisa-
tional piece, it presents the story of Katerina Ivanovna,
the widow of the drunken clerk Marmeladov, but it
strikes at nothing less than our innermost thoughts on
life and death.

Vakhtangov Theatre

Tanya-Tanya by Olga Mukhina.
Staged at the Vakhtangov (Arbat 26, 241 1679, Metro
Smolenskaya) by Andrei Prikhodko with help from Pyotr
Fomenko, this is a dazzling example of contemporary
Russian drama. Funny, moving and always insightful, it
presents an assembly of star-crossed lovers who seem to
soar weightlessly in a heady atmosphere of heightened
passions. Hearts are broken inexorably and irreversibly
as people dance and kiss, and champagne flows. Apart
from this, the Vakhtangov has done little else of great
innovative merit.

Young Spectator Theatre

Amphitryon by Molière.
This outrageous look at the gods wreaking havoc on
mortals is arguably the finest example of Vladimir
Mirzoyev's borderline bizarre style. Weird behaviour,
striking visual puns and an atmosphere so thick you can
cut it – all tinted with a light eroticism – are the director's
trademarks, and here he serves them up in spades.

does Valery Fokin's dual French-Russian production of Chekhov's early dramatic jest *Tatyana Repina* The latter had its world première at Avignon in summer 1998, starring French actress Consuelo de Haviland with a Russian cast.

Satirikon

Sheremetyevskaya Ulitsa 8 (289 7844). Metro Rizhskaya, then trolleybus 18 or 42. Tickets $5-$10.
In the 11 years since he took over the reins, the director and star actor Konstantin Raikin has made the Satirikon into a mean theatre machine. Brilliant shows directed by visitors (Valery Fokin's *The Metamorphosis* and Pyotr Fomenko's *The Magnificent Cuckold*) share the programme with Raikin's own spirited shows, most notably *Romeo and Juliet*. A certain highlight of the 1998-9 season will be Raikin starring in *Hamlet*, under the guidance of the great Georgian director Robert Sturua.

School of Dramatic Art

Povarskaya Ulitsa 20 (290 4796/291 4457). Metro Arbatskaya or Barrikadnaya. Tickets $1.50-$8. Map p279 E3/F2
This is the hermetic laboratory created by world-renowned director Anatoly Vasilyev in 1987. With the exception of the religious musical production of *The Lamentations of Jeremiah* and, in 1998, Alexander Pushkin's *Don Juan* or *The Stone Guest and Other Verses*, Vasilyev seldom allows the public to see what he is up to. Occasional showings of experimental studies can be crashed with perseverance and manipulation of contacts, but the rewards may be scanty: detractors of Vasilyev's latest work talk of his attempt to create an interminably talky 'radio-theatre'.

Sovremennik

Chistoprudny Bulvar 19A (921 6473). Metro Turgenevskaya or Chistye Prudy. Tickets 50¢-$10. Map p279 E2
Russian for 'contemporary', Sovremennik was founded in 1957 and was one of the most influential venues in the 1960s. Today, under the guidance of Galina Volchek, it churns out comfortable, well-attended classics and contemporary plays. One of the most popular Russian playwrights in the 1990s, Nikolai Kolyada, has several plays running here, including the formulaic comedies *Murlin Murlo* and *We Are Riding, Riding, Riding*. The Sovremennik's tours to Broadway with *Three Sisters* (1996) and *The Cherry Orchard* (1997) may have excited some Americans, but in Moscow these shows are no longer anything special.

Stanislavsky Drama Theatre

Tverskaya Ulitsa 23 (299 7224). Metro Pushkinskaya or Tverskaya. Tickets $1-$10. Map p278 C2
One of Moscow's more troubled venues in the 1980s and early 1990s, the Stanislavsky is now the principal home of Vladimir Mirzoev, a strikingly original director whom critics and fans either love or hate. His strange, atmospheric productions of Gogol's *The Inspector General*, which he retitled *Khlestakov*, and Alexei Kazantsev's *That, This Other World*, are, indeed, other-worldly. Mirzoev is currently preparing three different productions of *Twelfth Night* – with all-male, all-female and mixed casts respectively – the first of which is scheduled to open in November 1998.

Tabakov Theatre

Ulitsa Chaplygina 1A (928 9685). Metro Turgenevskaya or Chistye Prudy. Tickets $1.50-$25. Map p279 E2
This 11-year-old, 100-seat venue, founded by the popular actor Oleg Tabakov, has taken a page from the Lenkom book: find out what the audience wants and give it to them in buckets. The formula has worked, because a repertory of fluffy comedies spiced with a few cloying dramas has made a ticket to the Tabakov almost as rare as a lily in winter. Far above the average is Valery Fokin's compelling and unorthodox exploration of art and insanity in *Another Van Gogh*.

Tolstoy's Tsar Boris *at the* **Maly Theatre** *(p156).*

Taganka Theatre

Ulitsa Zemlyanoi Val 76 (915 1217/1015). Metro Taganskaya. Tickets $1.50-$10. Map p278 F4
Yury Lyubimov founded this world-famous theatre in 1964 and has since survived exile in the 1980s and the break-up of the house into two warring factions in the 1990s. At over 80 years old, some past glories, such as Mikhail Bulgakov's *The Master and Margarita*, still have that Lyubimov touch – broad, cutting social statements that appeal directly to the spectators even if they are a bit ragged. The best of Lyubimov's recent shows include Euripides' *Medea* and a dramatisation of Dostoyevsky's *The Brothers Karamazov*, which opened on the director's 80th birthday in September 1997. Lyubimov's next show, set to open in December 1998, will be *The Cabin*, a dramatisation of Alexander Solzhenitsyn's *The First Circle*.

Teatr na Pokrovke

Ulitsa Pokrovka 50 (917 0263). Metro Kurskaya or Kitai-Gorod. Tickets $4-$15. Map p279 E3/F2
Founded in 1990 by Sergei Artsibashev, this 100-seat theatre has achieved international recognition. Artsibashev excels at creating modern interpretations of the classics. His low-key, almost cinematic style of direction has thrown new light on such familiar titles as *Three Sisters*, Turgenev's *A Month in the Country*, Ostrovsky's *Talents And Admirers*, Gogol's *The Marriage* and *The Inspector General* and, in 1998, *Hamlet*.

Tsentr Debyut

The Debut Centre, Dom Aktyora, Ulitsa Arbat 35 (248 9106). Metro Smolenskaya or Arbatskaya. Tickets $1.50-$6. Map p280 A4/B4
Located across from the Vakhtangov Theatre and entered via Kaloshin Pereulok is the home of Moscow's cutting-edge theatre. The company's inaugural show, Garold Strelkov's production of Yelena Gremina's *The Sakhalin Wife* – about Siberian convicts awaiting the arrival of Anton Chekhov in 1890, remains the best so far. But every production here features a programme full of names who may be the next decade's history-makers.

Obraztsov Puppet Theatre

Sadovaya-Samotechnaya Ulitsa 3 (299 3310). Metro Tsvetnoi Bulvar. **Map p278 C1**
This is one of the oldest and most prestigious puppet theatres in the world. Now located in a venue that opened in 1970, it was originally founded by the late Sergei Obraztsov in 1931. While the peak of its popularity has now passed, it remains a highly respected house. Many of Obraztsov's own productions, such as *The Divine Comedy* and *An Unusual Concert*, remain in repertory. They once were innovative for their injection of adult themes and satire into an artform traditionally considered the realm of children's entertainment.

Shadow Theatre

Oktyabrskaya Ulitsa 5, between Ploshchad Suvorov and Trifonovskaya Ulitsa (281 1516/3590). Metro Novoslobodskaya.
This family theatre run by Ilya Epelbaum and Maya Krasnopolskaya offers exquisite puppet theatre on a miniature scale. Such unusual shows as *The Tour* (of the Lilikan Grand Royal Theatre in Russia) – a delightful enactment of a performance by an opera troupe whose actors are so tiny they tour with their own elaborate opera house – and *Tchaikovsky's Swan Lake: the Opera* have brought them success not only in Russia, but on frequent tours throughout Europe, Canada, the US and Japan.

Dance

Traditionally, the highlight of a journey to Moscow was an evening at the ballet. But Russia's dominance as a dance power is on the wane. Many of the country's best dancers and teachers have departed for better opportunities abroad. A painful transition in artistic leadership at the Bolshoi has yet to yield vibrant direction. Still, the Bolshoi name carries magic, even if the dancing doesn't always live up to it. Visitors may soon find the splendid old theatre closed, however, as part of a multi-million renovation that could take as long as a decade. During the renovation, performances will be given at an auxiliary theatre being constructed nearby.

The other major ballet theatre in Moscow is the Stanislavsky (not to be confused with the drama theatre of the same name). While it has generally been considered the number two Moscow company, at times the dancing is better here than at the Bolshoi. Moscow has a number of other smaller ballet troupes offering programmes of lesser quality. Modern dance, which was anathema to Soviet cultural authorities, has yet to flourish in the new Russia. Experimentation has begun with a handful of modern companies around the country, but with few exceptions the results are so far disappointing. Occasionally foreign artists or artists from elsewhere in Russia guest in Moscow. One Russian company not to be missed is St Petersburg's Boris Eifman troupe, best described as neo-classical, with heavy emphasis on dramatic presentation. Among its most powerful productions are *Tchaikovsky*, based on the life of the composer, and *Red Giselle*, based on the tragic life of the dancer Olga Spessivtseva. Meanwhile, folk dancing has maintained its respected place on the Russian dance scene, with three major companies.

Bolshoi Theatre

Teatralnaya Ploshchad 1 (292 3491/0050). Box office located in a separate building just west of theatre. Metro Teatralnaya. **Open** *box office* noon-3pm, 4-7pm, Tue-Sun. **Tickets** 50¢-$15 (rubles only). **Map p278 C3**
If it's Tuesday it must be *Giselle*. This is the place for the classics. A new work is occasionally premièred, but it is often simply an update of an old classic. This is, incidentally, the only place in town where you can see a full-length *La Bayadère*. The ballerinas reigning at the Bolshoi today display little of the style and artistry of their predecessors. Some of the male dancers are noteworthy: Andrei Uvarov, Sergei Filin and especially Nikolai Tsiskaridze, a dancer with both exquisite technique and a rare dramatic power. It is almost impossible to get good tickets through the box office, due to the Bolshoi's convoluted system of distribution. If you're staying in a big hotel, chances are that the reception provides a booking service for the Bolshoi; alternatively, try EPS ticket service at the Metropol Hotel, but expect to pay $85 for a seat in the front stalls. You may want to take your chances with the scalpers, who specialise in tickets for the Bolshoi over and above those for any other theatre – understandably so, since tourists always seem willing to pay over the odds for them.

Stanislavsky & Nemirovich-Danchenko Musical Theatre

Ulitsa Bolshaya Dmitrovka 17 (229 2835/299 8388). Metro Chekhovskaya. **Open** *box office* 11.30am-3pm, 4-7pm, Mon, Wed-Sun. **Tickets** $1.50-$6.50 (rubles only). **Map p278 C2**
Not to be confused with the Stanislavsky Theatre, this venue's full name is the Teatr Imeni Stanislavskogo i Nemirovicha-Danchenko. Obiously it hasn't got the name-recognition of the Bolshoi, but it currently boasts Moscow's best ballerina, Tatiana Chernobrovkina. She and the company are at their best in *Les Sylphides* (or *Chopiniana* in Russian), *Don Quixote* and *Le Corsaire*. Among the new

The **Stanislavsky**'s Inspector General *(p157)*.

ballets, *Illusory Ball*, a piece for five couples to the music of Chopin, shines. Conversely, the campy *Taming of the Shrew* and just plain inane *Othello* are to be avoided.

Kremlin Palace

Box office Ulitsa Vozdvizhenka 1 (917 2336/information 929 7901/7900). Metro Aleksandrovsky Sad or Biblioteka Imena Lenina. **Open** box office noon-2pm, 3-7pm, Mon-Wed, Fri-Sun. **Tickets** $1.50-$12 (rubles only). **Map p277 B3, p278 C3**

When the box office is closed, there is a recorded message to tell you (in Russian only) the current repertoire with dates and performance times. There are three main companies that have the privilege of performing in the beautiful setting of the Kremlin Palace:

Moscow Classical Ballet Once an incubator of new talent and new ideas, Moscow Classical Ballet has seen better days. The productions are low-budget and the dancing uneven, although a few of the soloists sometimes can be inspiring.

Kremlin Palace Ballet The talents of former Bolshoi star-turned-coach Yekaterina Maksimova notwithstanding, this is a second-string classical troupe, with a *Swan Lake* that is particularly embarrassing. The company, founded in 1990, often dances its version of *Cinderella*.

The Russian Ballet Founded in 1981 and directed by former Bolshoi principal Vyacheslav Gordeyev, the Russian Ballet performs his versions of the classics as well as his new choreography with mixed results.

Modern

Consult the local papers – the *Moscow Tribune*, the *Moscow Times* (cultural listings on Friday) and the *Exile* all publish listings information – to find out where these itinerant companies are performing during your stay.

Comedy in cabaret

In Soviet times, it was easy to be funny: you mocked the system's foibles and failures, took the piss out of the Homo Sovieticus and made ample use of hints and metaphors. These days, it's just as easy: the system's just as askew as it ever was and new stereotypes have moved in to replace the old models. Today popular jokes, or *anekdoty*, poke fun at the obnoxious New Russians: 'Nice tie,' says one New Russian to another. 'How much was it?' '$200,' comes the answer. 'You idiot.' The first guy is genuinely shocked. 'You could've got the exact same one for $400 just around the corner!'

In fact, the only difficult thing about Russian humour, even for foreigners with a good command of Russian, is understanding it. Jokes in Russia still make use of literary references and require at least basic knowledge of gloomy Soviet realities as well as Odessa Jewish folklore. The reaction of most Westerners to a Russian joke is less likely to be a laugh than: 'Ah, yes,' or 'Oh, really?' However, the Russian funny bone is slowly Westernising. Slapstick has generally replaced satire. And the sitcom has arrived. A Russia-made offering, *Café Strawberry*, on TV Center at 5.54pm daily, is a totally apolitical (and absolutely unfunny) comedy of errors that features a very liberal use of canned laughter.

In addition to the venues listed below, **Central Station** (Bolshaya Tatarskaya Ulitsa 16/2, 959 4643, Metro Novokuznetskaya) and **Chameleon** (Ulitsa Presnensky Val 14, 253 6343, Metro Ulitsa 1905 Goda) are gay clubs that often feature drag queen shows and musical revues with male impersonators of Russian pop divas.

Grand Opera Restaurant

Belgrad Hotel, Ulitsa Petrovskiye Linii 2/10 (923 9966). Metro Kuznetsky Most. **Map p278 C2**

The only venue in Moscow where you can sip drinks and eat while actors on the stage try to make you laugh. Cabaret-style performances with a straw-hatted big band and Odessa Jewish flavour.

Estrada Theatre

Bersenevskaya Naberezhnaya 20/2 (230 0444). Metro Biblioteka Imeni Lenina or Aleksandrovsky Sad. **Map p281 C4/C5**

With Gennady Khazanov as an artistic director, the best Russian stand-up comics perform here. Also puts on variety shows.

Tereza Durova Clowning Theatre

DK Zavoda Ilicha, Pavlovskaya Ulitsa 6 (237 1689). Metro Serpukhovskaya.

Buffoonery shows based on *Commedia dell'Arte* for children and adults, with music, dance and acrobatics.

MGU Student Theatre

(939 3701/203 6612). No permanent location.

The MGU occasionally plays at the Moscow University Cultural Centre on Sparrow Hills and at the Central House of Writers (Bolshaya Nikitskaya Ulitsa 53). Most of its work involves amateur student actors attempting to recreate the traditions of pre-Revolutionary artistic cabaret, resulting in boisterous, colourful collections of unrelated musical parodies and sketches.

Old Moscow Circus

Tsvetnoi Bulvar (200 0668). Metro Tsvetnoi Bulvar. **Map p278 D1**

Russian circus is not so much for the kids as it is for the adults. Besides the goofy clowns, there are Valentin Gneushev's erotic, music hall-type shows featuring girl dancers in sparkling tight bodices and pink feathers.

Operetta Theatre

Bolshaya Dmitrovka Ulitsa 6 (292 2345). Metro Teatralnaya. **Map p278 C2**

Light-hearted, old-world version of the American musical by classic composers such as Strauss and Offenbach.

Companies

Alla Sigalova Independent Troupe

Because of financial troubles, Sigalova's troupe has no home theatre and is rarely seen these days, but dance enthusiasts will find her eclectic hybrid modern dance and drama productions intriguing. Performances are primarily at the Tchaikovsky Concert Hall.

Beryozka

This lovely troupe, whose name means 'little birch tree', specialises in Slavic folk dances. Watch the women as they glide in a floating walk.

Moiseyev

The most lavish of the three top folk dance companies, the internationally renowned Moiseyev troupe performs dances from around the world. Often on tour, the company is a must-see if it's in town.

Moscow Chamber (Kamerny) Ballet

Moscow Chamber Ballet is a small, experimental group perhaps most associated with a piece called *Theatre in the Time of Nero and Seneca*, a portrait of a corrupt, decaying society in which Nero's chief of secret police goes around popping balloons between murders. Its occasional performances take place at the Pushkin Theatre.

Piatnitsky

The Piatnitsky folk choir traces its beginnings from before the Revolution. Later the dance ensemble was added, and the singers and dancers make for a fine, colourful evening's entertainment.

Venues

Pushkin Drama Theatre

Tverskoi Bulvar 23 (203 8582). Metro Tverskaya or Pushkinskaya. **Map p277 B2**
Hosts performances by the Moscow Chamber Ballet.

Tchaikovsky Concert Hall

Koncertny Zal Chaikovskogo, Triumfalnaya Ploshchad 4/31 (299 0378/3681). Metro Mayakovskaya. **Open** box office noon-3pm, 4-7pm, daily. **Tickets** $1.50-$30 (rubles only). **Map p277 B1**
With an auditorium that seats 1,600, this is the biggest of all the concert halls.

Theatre of Operetta

Ulitsa Bolshaya Dmitrovka 6 (292 6377/1237). Metro Chekhovskaya. **Open** box office noon-performance, usually 7pm, daily. **Map p278 C2**

Ballroom

Ballroom dancing is remarkably popular in Russia. As with any other art or sport here, the training starts early and in earnest. You'd be surprised how well six-year-olds can perform a cha-cha. Moscow hosts various ballroom-dancing competitions, and venues include the Kremlin Palace and the CSKA and Luzhniki stadia (*see* chapter **Sport & Fitness**).

Ten names to drop at the ballet

The tale is still told of the Bolshoi ballerina who took a flying leap and missed. Performing the role of Kitri in *Don Quixote*, Olga Lepeshinskaya, popular in the 1940s and 1950s, was running into a jump towards her partner's arms. She missed, landing in the orchestra pit instead. Some say a musician broke her fall; others say she landed on a drum. Whatever happened, the game dancer was quickly up on her feet, up on a chair and back on stage, hardly missing a beat.

The greatest legends are former stars Marina Semyonova and Galina Ulanova. Semyonova, still coaching at the Bolshoi at age 90, was known for her poignant performances in *Swan Lake* and *La Bayadère*. Ulanova became a heroine for a suffering people during the dark decades of the 1930s and '40s. Both intelligentsia and common folk identified with her unaffected portrayals of vulnerable but courageous characters, particularly Odette, Giselle and Juliet. Russian soldiers in World War II often carried Ulanova's picture with them. At the ballerina's funeral in March 1998, thousands of fans turned out to pay their last respects, although the dancer had left the stage almost 40 years earlier.

With the sunset of Ulanova's dancing career came the rise of Maya Plisetskaya, a red-haired, green-eyed spitfire who recently penned a vituperative autobiography. Born in 1925, Plisetskaya, who set the standard for generations of Odettes, Kitris and Carmens, cannot seem to let go of the limelight. She still dances occasionally in Moscow, bringing to mind the words of Yury Grigorovich, who ruled the Bolshoi for 30 years as artistic director. Asked if it were possible for ballerinas of a certain age to dance, the acerbic balletmaster reportedly replied that while it is possible to dance, it is impossible to watch.

The loveliest ballerina legs at the Bolshoi belonged to Yekaterina Maximova, wife of the current artistic director, Vladimir Vasiliyev, himself one of the greatest dancers ever to have taken the Bolshoi stage. Vasiliyev was part of a pleiad of male dancers in their prime in the 1960s and '70s, including Mikhail Lavrovsky and Maris Liepa.

If you really want to impress someone with your ballet knowledge, drop the name that most Muscovites have long since forgotten – Yekaterina Sankovskaya (1816-78), the first Moscow ballerina.

Trips Out of Moscow

Trips Out of Moscow

From artists' colonies to medieval towns via landmarks of history and politics, Russia can be easily sampled from its capital.

Locals find that regular trips out of Moscow are an absolute necessity for the sake of health, sanity and bank balance. In fact, getting out of the city is not just an activity but a social phenomenon. Every weekend most residents decamp to their dacha, a suburban country house usually bereft of any communications whatsoever. For poor folk and visitors, Moscow offers many day-trip and overnight possibilities, though they're fewer and less obvious than in St Petersburg and usually require chugging around on rickety *elektrichka* trains or bouncing up and down in uncomfortable buses.

The main destinations fall into three principal categories: ecclesiastical, literary and Soviet nostalgia. Though you may be church-saturated after a few days of Moscow, trips to **Sergiyev Posad** and **New Jerusalem** are still an exciting option. **Peredelkino** is densely populated with the ghosts of some of Russia's greatest writers, notably Boris Pasternak. **Abramtsevo**, too, was an artistic and literary powerhouse – and the inspiration for Chekhov's *The Cherry Orchard*. And then for Lenin freaks there's **Gorki Leninskiye**, with its fabulously laid-out museum, which was renovated just before the USSR went down and has been recently restocked with unwanted Lenin relics from all over Moscow.

If you are dependent on public transport, the suburban train system is usually more efficient than the regular bus service, and tickets are uniformly cheap (local journeys 50¢-$3). However, some destinations are served by improved long-distance buses; details are given where relevant. For more information and for details of tour companies running out-of-town excursions *see chapter* **Directory: Getting Around Moscow**. For a map covering the area, *see page 276*. Phone numbers are given as dialled from Moscow, including the long-distance prefix (8). Drop this and the area code if you are calling locally.

When visiting churches and monasteries, behave with respect. Women should cover their heads and wear skirts rather than trousers, and neither sex should wear shorts. You can usually go in during services but try to be unobtrusive.

Day Trips

Sergiyev Posad

Visiting Russia without going to see Sergiyev Posad is like ignoring the Pyramids on a trip to Egypt. Simply put, this is the most beautiful example of Russian monastery architecture in the country. Located 60 kilometres (38 miles) to the north-east of Moscow, Sergiyev Posad's greatest treasure is the **Trinity Monastery of St Sergei** (Troitse-Sergiyeva Lavra), founded in 1340. The original wooden monastery was sacked and burned down by Tartars in 1408, but less than a decade later the exquisite sandstone **Trinity Cathedral** (Troitsky Sobor) had risen from the ashes. Much of the decoration was undertaken by the famous icon painter Andrey Rublyov, who created many of his greatest masterpieces here, including the Icon of Holy Trinity, now in the Tretyakov Gallery, though you'll find a later copy here in the iconostasis. An entire three rows of the Sergiyev Posad iconostasis, however, are the genuine article, painted by Rublyov, his friend Daniil Chyorny (Daniil the Black) and their artel. The cathedral also contains the tomb of the monastery's founder, St Sergei, whose relics are the most esteemed in the Russian Orthodoxy and attract thousands of pilgrims every year.

The architectural highlight of the monastery is the five-domed, sixteenth-century **Cathedral of the Assumption** (Uspensky Sobor), which would be the spitting image of the Cathedral of the Assumption in the Moscow Kremlin were it not for the golden stars decorating its elegant domes. Inside, you'll find the tomb of controversial Tsar Boris Godunov. Its gorgeous blue belfry, built in the mid-eighteenth century, sports delicate little arches that let the blue sky come shining through.

Also of interest on the site is the graceful, Gothic-flavoured **Church of the Holy Spirit**

The dreaming domes of the **Cathedral of Assumption** *in the Trinity Monastery of St Sergei.*

(Dukhovskaya Tserkov), which was built in 1746, and the monastery's surrounding walls, whose **Duck Tower** (Utichya Bashnya) is decorated with a bronze duck.

At the time of its closure in the nineteenth century, the monastery's treasury (*riznitsa*) was stocked with the finest examples of Russian and foreign art. Even after the devastation wreaked by the Soviets, the **museum** that replaced it (located in chambers on the other side from the entrance gates) boasts an outstanding collection of icon painting and applied arts.

Russia's main seminary is located in the **Tsar's Chambers**. To assist future priests in finding a church-approved wife, the monastery also houses a special institute for young women, where they study the fine art of marital responsibility. This exercise in ecclesiastical matchmaking is only partially successful, as male students constantly complain that the girls on offer are dim, unattractive or loafers who couldn't think of anything else to do with their lives. The seminary building also contains another museum of icons, as well as various church treasures and relics collected in the twentieth century. Unfortunately, this isn't open to the public, though students of Russian history or theology can arrange a visit via the excursion bureau. Many of the guides speak good English. Call 8-254 45356 or 45721.

Contacts

Monastery
Open morning service–evening service (approx 7am–8/9pm) daily. **Admission** free.

Museum
Open 10am–5.30pm; days vary. **Admission** $15 approx. The various elements of the museum are open on different days. Your best chance of catching most things open is to avoid Mondays altogether, along with the first Tuesday and last Wednesday and Friday of the month.

Getting there

By train
Trains for Sergiyev Posad leave from Yaroslavsky Vokzal every hour or more frequently. Note that the town used to be known as Zagorsk, and still is on some timetables.

By bus
Buses leave from Yaroslavsky Vokzal every half an hour from 7am to 5pm daily. They are generally faster than the train, except on Sunday evenings, when you will encounter traffic jams.

New Jerusalem

New Jerusalem (Novy Iyerusalim) ranks among the more bizarre sights in the vicinity of Moscow – a complete re-creation of the temples and shrines of the Holy Land built among the woods and pastures of central Russia.

The idea was the brainchild of Patriarch Nikon (the same guy who was responsible for the schism in the Orthodox Church in the eighteenth century), who was irritated by the fact that the Holy Land was, at the time, controlled by Muslims and inaccessible to pilgrims. He chose an area around the picturesque Istra river valley and re-christened its geographical features with names lifted from the Bible. Now, just 60 kilometres (38 miles) northwest of Moscow, there's a little hillock called Mount Sion, a clutch of buildings known as Capernaum and a river that goes by the name of Jordan. The principal structure of the monastery compound, the **Cathedral of Resurrection** (Voskresensky Sobor), is intended to resemble Jerusalem's Church of the Holy Sepulchre.

Although the monastery was founded in 1656, work on the various structures went on for over a century, with constant interruptions. In 1723 the cupola of the cathedral collapsed under its own weight and it wasn't until 20 years later that the famous Italian architect Rastrelli was finally commissioned to complete it. The result was the unusual (for Russia, at least) rotunda with its rows of windows and a set of adjacent churches whose cupolas rise from subterranean basements just like their counterparts in Jerusalem. The most noteworthy of these is the **Church of St Konstantin and Helena**, entered through the door on the right of the entrance to the Cathedral of the Resurrection. After the Revolution, a group of enthusiasts led by a Jewish accountant created a museum of the history of the region here, and by the beginning of World War II it housed a huge collection of relics from the monastery and other buildings in the area.

Most of the monastery was destroyed by the Nazis in 1941, during the short spell when their armies penetrated right to Moscow's city limits. During their stay, it became a Gestapo headquarters; on their departure soldiers blew up most of the monastery buildings, including the main cathedral. Most of the treasures of the monastery, hidden in secret underground passages, were lost in the explosion. What you now see is the result of a process of reconstruction that has been going on for the last 50 years.

The cathedral is still closed to visitors most of the time, though you can arrange to view it through the excursion bureau at the entrance to the monastery. The former Patriarchal Chambers and the monks' dining room at the rear end of the monastery host a museum displaying religious and historical relics from the monastery and the surrounding areas as well as an interesting collection of porcelain.

If you leave the monastery from the back, on your right you'll find a spring, whose water is believed to have healing properties. In front of you, you'll see several wooden buildings: a chapel, a peasant's house, a windmill and others, all relocated from adjacent villages and now forming a museum of wooden architecture. If you walk across the bridge on your left, you will come to the Hermitage, which

Borodino *'s bulbous battle memorial marks Russia's Waterloo. See page 167.*

looks more like a banquet hall than an ascetic's cave. Its architect received three roubles for his work – just about enough for a can of Coke these days.

Contacts

Monastery
560 3643. **Open** *10am-5pm Tue-Sun. Closed last Friday of month.* **Admission** *free.* **Exhibition admission** *$6.50. Guided tours in English for groups of ten and over (details 8 331 11375).*

Getting there

By train & bus
The nearest stations are Istra and Novoiyerusalimskaya: trains leave every hour or more frequently from Rizhsky Vokzal and take one hour 20 minutes. From either station, take bus 44 to the museum. Alternatively, go by bus from Moscow. It leaves from Tushinskaya metro and goes to Istra and Novoiyerusalimskaya stations.

Zvenigorod

Welcome to Zvenigorod, otherwise known as Russian Switzerland, a picturesque series of slopes that boasts some stunning examples of Russian architecture as well as excellent little nooks and crannies for swimming, sunbathing, camping and hiking.

About 50 kilometres (21 miles) west of Moscow, Zvenigorod is a typical satellite town with shabby houses and several small kiosks. It's difficult to believe that it once rivalled the capital in the struggle to control the territories of Russia. Its main attractions are the **Monastery of St Savva at the Guard Post** (Savvino-Storozhevsky) and the **Cathedral of the Assumption** (Uspensky Sobor), which lies 1.5 kilometres (just over a mile) to the west of the town on the site of the former Kremlin.

The Cathedral of the Assumption is one of the oldest buildings in the Moscow region, dating back to the fourteenth century. The frescoes inside are believed to have been created by the artel (or studio) of Andrey Rublyov. The Monastery of St Savva, with its Cathedral of Christmas (Rozhdestvensky Sobor), completed in 1404, is another architectural masterpiece. Since the monastery was chiefly used as a country residence for the royal family, a large part of it is taken up with royal chambers for the Tsar and Tsarina. If you have the stamina to make it to the top, the bell tower located on the left of the entrance gate affords a terrific view of the surrounding countryside. While you're up there, keep an eye out for the red-brick villas of the nouveau riche that are replacing the traditional wooden houses.

You can walk down the valley slope from the monastery and have an excellent time lazing in the sun on the bank of the river, where it can be pleasant to swim (though be careful of the strong current). The Moscow River at this spot is also popular with amateur canoeists preparing for more challenging trips to Karelia or the Altai.

Contacts

Monastery of St Savva
Excursion bureau 592 9464. **Open** 10am-5pm Tue-Sun. **Admission** $1.50-$3.50.

Cathedral of the Assumption
Open 7am-5pm daily. **Admission** free.

Getting there

By train
Trains leave from Belorussky Vokzal about every hour; the journey takes an hour and a half. From the station take a No.23 or 51 bus to both cathedral and monastery.

Gorki Leninskiye

The collapse of the Soviet Union swept away, almost overnight, the once ubiquitous cult of Lenin. But for those feeling nostalgic, or looking for insights into the nation's former devotion, there's nothing like a trip to Gorki Leninskiye, the small village about 30 kilometres (21 miles) southeast of Moscow where the father of the Revolution spent his last incapacitated days. There are two parts to the Gorki Leninskiye experience: the monstrous late '80s **Lenin Museum**, built to commemorate the 70th anniversary of the Revolution, and, a little further down the road, the **Gorki Leninskiye Estate**, where the ginger-bearded dictator whiled away his final years.

Though the hulking, grotty-looking museum may, at first sight, seem a bit of a turn-off, it's worth a quick visit. Be sure to have the museum personnel demonstrate the ultra high-tech, remote-control three-dimensional display cases.

Once you've had enough of this, head on down to the estate. Once the property of Lidiya Morozova, the wife of Savva Morozov, an industrialist and arts patron, it was appropriated by the Bolsheviks shortly after the Revolution. It was chosen as the place for Lenin to recuperate after being shot in 1918 and again after his first stroke in May 1922. You'll be struck by Lenin's Spartan tastes in furnishing, which the guides always cite as proof of his proletarian hero credentials. There are some clues, though, that this man was the leader of the Soviet empire, particularly the special phone lines installed so he could communicate directly with the Kremlin.

In 1995, a decision to renovate Lenin's apartment in the Kremlin meant that the furnishings were moved out to the estate, where a replica of the apartment was created. These are scheduled to be moved back as soon as the renovation has been completed, but three years later it was becoming increasingly obvious that these Lenin relics won't be going anywhere any time soon. One of the highlights is a statuette of a monkey intently pondering a human skull it holds in its hands, a gift to Lenin from the future US oil magnate Armand Hammer. Also not to be missed is Lenin's Bentley in the garage off to the side of the main building. The car was specially fitted out by the manufacturer with skids in place of the front wheels so it could be operated in the snow. Lenin died at the Gorki Leninskiye in January 1924.

Contacts

The Lenin Museum/The Gorki Leninskiye Estate
548 9309. **Open** 10am-4pm Wed-Mon. Closed last Mon of the month. **Admission** $3; $2 students and under-17s.

Getting there

By bus
There are no trains to Gorki Leninskiye. Take bus No.439, which leaves every half-hour from Domodedovskaya metro.

Borodino

If you're fan of Napoleon, a Tolstoy aficionado or simply get a kick out of visiting rolling green fields where lots of men ran around and killed each other, then Borodino, about 115 kilometres (75 miles) west of the city by train, is a must.

History buffs will remember Borodino as the major battle of Napoleon's 1812 campaign in Russia. Although the French technically won the day (they killed more of the opposition), and went on to capture the abandoned city of Moscow, the Russians eventually triumphed with just a little help from the Russian winter, which froze the French armies into submission on the long road back to Paris.

The **battlefield** itself is intermittently marked with small obelisks dedicated to the fallen units of both sides. In some areas you can see groups of bunkers, some dating from 1812 and others from 1941-5, when the Germans followed in Napoleon's footsteps. After you've toured around a little, you can get an overview of the site from the miniature battlefield in **Borodino Museum**, just opposite the giant obelisk honouring the dead. The museum also houses a collection of the uniforms of the period and has the field cot that Napoleon slept on.

Also worth a look is **Borodino Convent**, which was built by the widow of a Russian nobleman who died at Borodino. She came out to the battlefield to search for her husband's body and ended up building the convent on the spot. It's open to visitors (7am-5pm daily), as long as they dress and behave respectfully.

Contacts

Borodino Museum

8-238 51057/51546.
Open 10am-5pm Tue-Sun. Closed last Fri of month.
Admission $3; $1.50 students, under-17s.
Tours of museum, convent and battlefield in Russian; occasionally in English for large groups.

Getting there

By train

Trains leave from Belorussky Vokzal every hour for Borodino station (the stop after Mozhaisk). Take the train either for Borodino or for Gagarin. The journey takes about two hours.

Abramtsevo

Abramtsevo first became a centre of culture in the mid-nineteenth century, when Slavophile writer Sergei Aksakov began to entertain his circle of literary and intellectual friends – among them Gogol and Turgenev – at his home here. The main house so impressed Chekhov, another visitor, that it became the model for the manor in *The Cherry Orchard*, his play about the twilight years of the declining Russian aristocracy.

A wealthy railway tycoon and active patron of the arts, Savva Mamontov, bought the estate in 1870 and built it up into one of Russia's most high-profile artists' colonies, frequented by Repin, Valentin Serov and Mikhail Vrubel as well as Konstantin Stanislavsky. Two of the most famous works actually produced here are Nesterov's painting *Young Sergy* (now housed in the Tretyakov Gallery) and Serov's *Girl With Peaches*, which is in Mamontov's house (and on many huge boxes of chocolates available from the surrounding kiosks). It was also at Abramtsevo that the first-ever *matrioshka* (nesting doll) was created in 1890, thus spawning countless generations of kitschy Russian souvenirs.

The Abramtsevo colony also made an important contribution to the modern era of Russian architecture. Among these early experiments is the pretty 'church not made by hand' (*nerukotvoreniye*), which features an iconostasis by Repin, and a wooden *teremok* (bathhouse) in and which the artist Ivan Ropet combined the traditional log

Relight my fire... a babushka keeps the flame in one of **Abramtsevo***'s dachas. See page 168.*

structure with more daring, asymmetrical forms. The strangest building on the grounds is the 'hut on chicken legs' in the park – a house built for the children of the artists to play in that featured in the Russian fairytale *Baba Yaga the Witch*.

Spread out over several acres in the birch woods are more than a dozen dachas belonging to the various cultural figures who stayed here, many of them filled with sketches, books, photos and examples of their one-time occupants' work. An afternoon can be pleasantly spent strolling under the trees or picnicking in the grass, popping in and out of each house.

Contacts

Abramtsevo
8-254 32470.
Open 10am-5pm Wed-Sun. Closed last Fri of month. **Admission** 80¢; 50¢ students, under-17s. Main exhibition included in admission; supplementary exhibitions 20¢.
Guided tours in English Sat, Sun $11.

Getting there

By train
Abramtsevo is a few kilometres south of Sergiyev Posad, to the north-east of Moscow. Trains leave from Yaroslavsky Vokzal approximately every hour. Take trains for Sergiyev Posad or Aleksandrov but check that they stop at Abramtsevo – not all do.

Peredelkino

The village of Peredelkino, which is located 20 kilometres (12 miles) south-west of Moscow, dates back to 1646, when it was originally part of the estate of the Kolychev family, who were in service at the Tsar's court. After the Revolution, the Writer's Union took it over and converted it into a colony where the best-known Soviet writers could enjoy their privileges in peace and tranquillity. Isaak Babel was given a dacha here in 1938, a year before he was arrested and later shot. But by far the most famous of Peredelkino's former residents is Boris Pasternak, whose dacha at Ulitsa Pavlenko 3 was opened in 1990 as the **Pasternak House Museum**.

About 15 minutes' walk from the station, the wooden dacha is much like any other, though rather bigger. Everything inside is just as it was in Pasternak's day. Walking through the house, you will be shown the plain iron bed where he died and the room where he finished *Doctor Zhivago*. There are various of his sketches on the wall and bookshelves of the works of his favourite authors – well worth a browse. The *babushki* keepers of the flame will recount numerous stories from Pasternak's life, their favourite being how he was awarded the Nobel Prize for Literature in 1958 but was forced by Soviet authorities to turn it down.

A visit to the house is the work of an afternoon. To make the most of the trip, you should also pay a visit to the writer's grave in the cemetery of the small fifteenth-century church (located up the hill from the train station). A de rigueur site of pilgrimage for arty Russians in Soviet times, the cemetery is still a favourite picnic stopover for day trippers, who sit by Pasternak's grave munching sandwiches and mulling the meaning of life.

Contacts

Pasternak House Museum
Ulitsa Pavlenko 3 (934 5175). **Open** 10am-4pm Thur-Sun. **Admission** 80¢.
Guided tours in English (free).

Getting there

By train
Peredelkino is a 20-minute ride on the Kaluga II *elektrichka* line that runs from Kievsky Vokzal. Just as easy would be to take a taxi along Kutuzovsky Prospekt, for about $10-$15.

Arkhangelskoye

Arkhangelskoye estate, located 30 kilometres (19 miles) west of Moscow, was once home to one of Russia's richest men, Prince Nikolai Yusupov, a famous *bon vivant* who dabbled in science and was a friend of Voltaire, Beaumarchais and Diderot. It still has a certain run-down grandeur, even though the **palace** seems to be undergoing eternal restorations and is consequently currently not open to the public. Partly because of its state of dishevelment, the architecturally naive have been known to go and stare in mistaken awe at the grand Stalinist Military Convalescence Home, which is also located on the estate.

Originally built in 1780 for Prince Nikolai Golitsyn, the palace came into Yusupov's possession in 1809. Despite the inconveniences caused by the rampages of Napoleon's troops, a serf riot and a fire, Yusupov's architects produced a delightful, ornate, yellow stuccoed building, the main aim of which was 'for joy, and not for profit'. Visitors to the estate, who included Pushkin, Herzen and a number of other famous writers, were regularly treated to performances by Yusupov's serf theatre, whose dancers were said to strip naked.

Many of Yusupov's treasures – a vast art collection, including paintings by Tiepolo and Van Dyck – are still on the premises: frustrating, since the nearest you can get to them is a walk around the rubbish-strewn courtyard. There is no realistic date in sight for a reopening.

The **estate** is vast, though, and a delight to wander around in. From the palace, head down two terraces that are guarded by a series of busts and urns, which, for much of the year, are protected from the cold by little wooden huts. At the end of the terrace the grand convalescence home looms up. Just to the left it a map marks out a series of walks for its residents with strict and rather bizarre instructions on how they should be conducted: 60 to 120 steps per minute for spells of between six and 50 minutes.

These walks or your own ramblings will take you past the **serf theatre**, which was opened in 1818 during a visit by Tsar Alexander I and still houses many spectacular theatre sets and a stage curtain by the Italian theatre designer Pietro Gonzaga, who visited the estate in 1792. Unfortunately, the theatre is also closed. Nearby, you'll find the Yusupov family mausoleum, which was built by architect Roman Klein but never used because of the rude interruption of the Revolution.

Next is the charming **Church of the Archangel Michael**, after which the estate was named. The attendant *babushka* at the adjacent graveyard warns people to take care lest they sink into the ageing and unstable graves. It is said that the white stone grave beside the church is that of a Yusupov daughter who threw herself from a cliff after being refused permission to marry her beloved. Near the church is the unusual **Bridge of the Ravine**, a pseudo-Gothic wooden structure built over an archway.

Contacts

Arkhangelskoye

561 9456. **Open** 10am-5pm Wed-Sun
Admission $1; 50¢ students, under-17s.
Occasional tours in English.

Getting there

By metro & bus

The estate is about 22 kilometres (13 miles) from the centre of Moscow. Take the metro to Tushinskaya and then get the No.549 bus. The journey takes about 30 minutes and buses appear at roughly five past, half past and a quarter to each hour. Buses stop just outside the entrance to the estate.

Overnighters

Yasnaya Polyana

Yasnaya Polyana – Leo Tolstoy's lush, sprawling estate 240 kilometres (125 miles) south of Moscow – is one of Russia's most famous literary landmarks. Translated as 'Clear Glade', it consists of endearingly unkempt grounds, sections of which are marked with little green signs displaying fragments of Tolstoy's prose or poetry inspired by that location, and two museums, the **Tolstoy House Museum** and the **Tolstoy Literary Museum**.

The house, originally just one wing of a larger structure, is a modest two-storey building preserved just as it was in the years before the writer's death in 1910. The father of 13 children with his wife Sofia, Tolstoy maintained a warm, practical and entirely unpretentious home. The tour guides are adept at picking out quirky details – the miniature stool the nearsighted writer used while working on *Anna Karenina* and *War and Peace* so that he could squint in comfort and the bedside dumbbells he used for morning calisthenics.

From Tolstoy's house, it's a short walk along a dirt track to his unmarked grave in a grassy clearing fenced off by cherry trees. The grave itself is little more than a raised rectangular earthen mound under a large beech tree that is always strewn with freshly cut flowers. Visiting the grave is traditional for newly-weds, with an average of 20 couples and their wedding parties – tipsy and in high heels – making the trip from the main road to the grave each weekend.

To reach Yasnaya Polyana from Moscow, you will need to go through **Tula**, a city with a population of 500,000 people and a number of rather strange museums. Opened in 1996, the **Pryaniki Museum** (open Sept-June 9am-5pm Tue-Sat) is a one-room facility devoted entirely to the jam-filled spice cakes invented in Tula. Located at the back of the pryaniki store at Ulitsa Oktyabrskaya 45A, it houses a permanent collection of 300 dark brown, flat pryaniki, some a century old, recounting the history of these chewy cakes throughout the Tsarist and communist periods.

One thing that goes well with pryaniki is tea, so a visit to the **Museum of the Samovar** (open 10am-5pm Tue-Sat; closed last Wed of month) is a natural follow-up. Located just outside the Kremlin walls in a grey building with a classical portico, the museum's three halls display a multitude of samovars, all made locally. Less cosily, Tula is known for its guns, and a selection is on display at the **Museum of Arms** (open 10am-4.45pm Wed-Sun), located somewhat cynically in the Cathedral of the Epiphany in the Kremlin.

Contacts

Yasnaya Polyana House Museum & Estate

8-0872 339 832. **Open** *house* 11am-3pm, *estate* 10.30am-4.30pm, Wed-Sun. Closed last Wed of month.
Admission $3; $2.50 students, under-17s.
Russian-language tours.

Getting there

By train

Fast trains bound for the Crimea and stopping in Tula depart frequently from Kursky Vokzal. One-way tickets are $28. For those making a one-day excursion, the daily 7.37am train that takes three hours to reach Tula is recommended.

By bus

The Tula bus, which leaves from outside Komsomolskaya metro, takes about four hours. From 6am to 10pm the service operates in both directions about every 30 minutes.

From Tula to Yasnaya Polyana

Yasnaya Polyana is a 20-minute, 30¢ bus ride from Tula's bus station, on the corner of Prospekt Lenina and Ulitsa 9-go Maya. Take bus 114, which runs all day, in theory every six minutes, and ask the conductor to tell you where to get off. The entrance to the estate is about 15 minutes' walk west from the bus stop.

Accommodation

Tula's accommodation is not impressive. Your best bet is the **Hotel Moskva** (8-0872 200 341), situated next to the train station, which offers double rooms for about $40. It's decidedly dodgy, but far better than the only other possibility, the **Hotel Tula** by the bus station, which is definitely not recommended. The Moskva rarely answers its phone, so just show up. If you don't fancy it, get up early and do the trip in a day.

Vladimir

Vladimir is visited primarily as a staging post en route to Suzdal (*see below*), 35 kilometres (22 miles) away, and is included here for that reason. However, though unlovely, it does have some interest of its own. In fact, were it not for the Mongols, who devastated Vladimir in 1238, this guide could well be the *Time Out Guide to Vladimir*, while Moscow would only have been given a brief description in the Trips Out of Town chapter. Founded in 1108, 40 years before Moscow, the town quickly grew into a flourishing cultural centre dotted with magnificent churches and cathedrals. The scale of construction work is illustrated by the fact that during a terrible fire in 1183 a total of 32 churches were burned to the ground, twice as many as now remain standing.

These days, Vladimir, 180 kilometres (112 miles) to the east of Moscow, comes across as provincial and run-down – a little Soviet town with one main street and lots of shabby apartment blocks. However, it is still possible to root out some magnificent examples of old Russian architecture and art. Most of the main sights are located on Ulitsa 3-go Internatsionala behind the impressive **Golden Gates** (Zolotye Vorota), built in 1164 and restored during the reign of Catherine the Great. The gatehouse now hosts an exhibition devoted to the military history of Vladimir. On the incline of the Klyazma river valley, you'll find the **Assumption Cathedral** (Uspensky Sobor; open 7am-5pm daily), which still amazes with its ravishing simplicity. Built between 1158 and 1160, (and reconstructed in the late 1180s after fire damage) its exterior is decorated with majestic stone carvings, while inside are gleaming frescoes painted in 1408 by Andrey Rublyov and Daniil Chyorny.

Further along, at the edge of the valley, is the **Cathedral of St Dmitry**, famous for its beautiful stone carving – fantastic birds and strange animals with decidedly pagan overtones. Unfortunately, you probably won't get a chance to see the wonderful twelfth-century Byzantine-style frescoes inside, as the cathedral is usually locked. Adjacent to the church is the **Historical Museum** (Ulitsa 3-go Internatsionala 64).

Vladimir has one more place of historic interest: the **Central Prison**, where many famous Revolutionaries were held, in chains. After the Revolution, and particularly during Stalin's purges, it was occupied by the next generation of political prisoners – Germans, Britons, Americans and citizens of Central European states who happened to be in the wrong place at the wrong time. Among the most notable prisoners were the Swedish diplomat Raul Vallenberg, who saved hundreds of Jews in Hungary, and a US military pilot whose reconnaissance plane was shot down by a Soviet missile. The prison is located at the end of Ulitsa 3-go Internatsionala. Go there at your own risk: although you are not likely to be locked up for taking illicit photos – as one American student was in the 1960s – unpleasant brushes with the militia cannot be ruled out.

One excursion worth making from Vladimir is to possibly the most beautiful church in Russia, the **Church of Intercession on the Nerl** (Pokrova na Nerli), a two-kilometre (1.2-mile) riverside walk from the village of Bogolyubovo, 10 kilometres (6 miles) east of Vladimir. The simple, geometrical harmony of its construction, the lovely carving on its exterior walls and the splendid waterside location all make the church one of Russia's greatest architectural treasures. Its opening hours are subject to the whim of its keepers, who live in the house behind. To get here, catch a bus from Vladimir's central bus station (in front of the train station), towards Penkino or Kameshnovo, or take a taxi.

Getting there

By train

There are numerous inter-city trains daily between Moscow and Nizhny Novgorod (Gorki on old timetables), which stop at Vladimir. Trains leave from Kursky Vokzal; a one-way ticket costs $20.

By bus

Frequent services leave from Central Bus Station.

Accommodation

There is little reason to spend the night in Vladimir, but if you get happen to miss the last train out, try the **Hotel Vladimir** (Ulitsa 3-go Internatsionala 74; 8-0922 343 042), where double rooms are $50, or the **Hotel Zolotoye Koltso** (Ulitsa Chaikovskogo 27; 8-0922 248 807), where singles are $20 and doubles $30.

The gingerbread-house architecture of Suzdal.

Suzdal

Located some 35 kilometres (22 miles) north of Vladimir, Suzdal is a perfect example of how Russia might have looked if the Communists hadn't ripped out the heart of its architectural heritage. Though some districts are a little shabby, the town is dotted with beautiful monasteries and churches, most of which are wholly intact, giving the place a majestic fairytale ambience.

The oldest buildings are located in the Kremlin. Among the most remarkable is the **Nativity of the Virgin** cathedral (Rozhdestvensky Sobor), built in 1225 and rebuilt in 1528. Also interesting are the beautifully decorated **Archbishop's Chambers**, in which you'll find a good collection of icons. On the other side of the Kamenka River, there's a **museum of wooden architecture**, where churches and peasant huts taken from adjacent villages have been plonked down in a field. From the Kremlin, walk up Ulitsa Lenina through Krasnaya Ploshchad (Red Square) to the north of the city. To the left of Ulitsa Lenina are the impressive **Pokrovsky** and **Spaso-Yefimvevsky** monasteries. The first served as a prison for many noblewomen, the most famous being the wife of Ivan the Terrible, the daughter of Tsar Boris Godunov and the first wife of Peter the Great. Also worth a visit are two monasteries located right by Red Square: the **Rizopolozhensky** monastery and the **Aleksandrovsky** convent. The latter is believed to have been created by Alexander Nevsky for widows of warriors who died in his battles against the Germans and Swedes.

It makes sense to spend at least a whole day in Suzdal, preferably in winter when it is at its most attractive. Strolling from one monastery to another, you'll also come across multitudes of adorable little churches and wooden houses. Suzdal is relatively tourist-friendly and has a **Main Tourist Complex** and several hotels and restaurants, some of which are located right inside monastery premises.

Contacts

Main Tourist Complex

Glavny Turistsky Komplex, Ulitsa Korovniky (8-09231 21530/fax 20666). English spoken.

Getting there

By bus

Suzdal has no train station. There is one daily bus from Moscow's Central Bus Station in the morning (hours vary, as the bus usually leaves once it is full). It is probably better to take the train or one of the relatively frequent buses to Vladimir (*see above*), then take a bus to Suzdal from the central bus station there (outside the train station). They go about every half an hour.

Accommodation

The best and most atmospheric accommodation option is to stay in the wooden *izbi* (cabins) in the **Intercession Convent** (Pokrovsky Monastyr) on Pokrovskaya Ulitsa, which are clean and great fun but rather pricey at $78 for a single and $90 for a double. Alternatively, try the Soviet-style concrete comforts of the **Glavny Turistsky Komplex** or GTK (*see above* **Contacts**), where singles are $30 and doubles $45. Both the Convent and the GTK hotel can be reached at 8-09231 20908; the convent also has a separate booking line on 8-09231 20889.

St Petersburg

Introduction

St Petersburg is not a city. It's an idea set in stone, a vast public artwork, a devastatingly beautiful neoclassical stage set lining the banks of the river Neva. Built on the whim of a tyrant on a stretch of inhospitable marshland, it was never intended to be anything more or less than a symbol. Peter the Great wanted to create a 'Window on the West' that would prove, both at home and abroad, that Russia was a great power and cultural force. Italian architects were shipped in en masse to dress the new capital in the latest fashions from Rome or Venice and, over the course of just a couple of centuries, they dutifully assembled the most elaborate window display the world has ever known. Against this synthetic backdrop, many of the main episodes of Russian history have been played out. And even today, when its own history appears to be over and its façades are crumbling, St Petersburg continues to infuse its population and its visitors with an air of intoxicating unreality.

The best way to appreciate the uniqueness of St Petersburg is to travel here via any Russian city – it doesn't matter which, but Moscow fits the bill quite nicely. Cities in Russia are naturally conspiratorial places, medieval warrens of low-slung, squinting, shack-like constructions and squiggly roads, and the bleak urban development projects of the communist era have done little to dispel this. Give yourself a few days and then jump on a plane or a train bound for St Petersburg. The impact is instantaneous. Suddenly, Russia cracks open into wide, stately boulevards, gently flowing waterways, manicured parks and what seems like an eternity of colonnaded palaces. It's the obscene abundance that is most striking. St Petersburg drips with municipal jewellery: massive church domes, ornate porticos, friezes and riots of statuary. You don't even have to bother trekking along to the better-known landmarks. Just position yourself at any decent vantage point in the centre, or at any spot along the Fontanka or Neva embankments, and the views are simply breathtaking. Beauty is everywhere in St Petersburg. Come in June or early July, when the illustrious White Nights have begun to kick in, and the effect is even greater. For a whole month, the sun dips below the horizon for just a few short hours a day and the endless evenings recline lazily across the rooftops. After midnight, the buildings dissolve into a pale, white glare. It is at these times that the stage set gets the lighting effects it deserves.

It seems only natural that St Petersburg should also be the venue for a thriving, vibrant cultural scene. Dubbed Russia's 'cultural capital', it nightly plays host to some of the best opera and classical ballet on the planet. There are more museums per square mile here than in any other city, culminating in the Hermitage, whose staggeringly immense collection rivals that of the Prado or the Louvre. It still sends a shiver down the spine to think how many great names these streets have nurtured: Pushkin, Gogol, Dostoyevsky, Tchaikovsky, Mussorgsky, Borodin, Shostakovich, Prokofiev, Malevich, Blok, Akhmatova.

In the sphere of contemporary culture, the city has the dubious honour of being the birthplace of Russian rock 'n' roll, a genre that sometimes has the same effect on the Western ear as a cheese-grater. Its run-down, *fin-de-siècle* ambience and rich pool of 'borrowed' classical styles continue to fuel a lively and irreverent visual arts scene. St Petersburg, among other things, is a postmodernist's wet dream.

Dwarfed by their surroundings, the city's inhabitants can occasionally seem like bit players; extras in some worthy period costume drama. But when the sun is shining, they can also take to the blazing catwalk of Nevsky Prospekt and flaunt it like a bunch of craven supermodels. People here are often accused (by other Russians) of being somehow un-Russian. It's an accusation they only half-heartedly refute, primarily because it's true. You don't have to be particularly observant to notice, in the stripped-down summer crowds, a relaxed, almost Scandinavian self-assurance.

Yet St Petersburg is at something of a low ebb at the moment. Politically and economically, it is completely in the shadow of Moscow. With every passing day, it looks and feels more provincial. Ranked as the tenth most expensive travel destination in the world – well ahead of London or New York – it has managed to slip down the investment scale to the point where it is now the beneficiary of less foreign capital than a non-entity like Nizhny Novgorod. Crime and corruption are rampant, as was demonstrated by the very public assassination in 1997 of vice-governor Mikhail Manevich.

But St Petersburg has survived numerous hardships in the past: floods, recurring revolutions, war, Stalin's purges and the inconceivable agony of the Leningrad Blockade. It's unlikely to balk at the prospect of just a few more minor inconveniences. St Petersburg is just biding its time before the curtain rises on the next phase of its rich and always eventful history. Buildings can be neglected and roadways left to rot. But you can't destroy the ideal of a great and glorious city.

History

From boggy beginnings, through the reign of the Romanovs, revolution, Bolshevism and several wars – St Petersburg had to grow up fast.

The history of St Petersburg gets under way, on 16 May 1703, with a nice, juicy morsel of legend. This was the day when Peter the Great is supposed to have hacked up two sods of peat from a grubby bog recently captured from the Swedes, laid them crosswise and proclaimed, 'The city will lie here.' Afterwards, with characteristic gusto, he apparently grabbed a shovel and began to dig the foundations for what would become one of the city's first buildings, the Peter and Paul Fortress.

Actually, Peter wasn't even there when the city was founded, and the peat-cleaving proceedings were overseen by his sidekick, Menshikov. But the myth slots in nicely beside all the other myths that collectively make up the life and reign of one of Russia's greatest Tsars. Born in 1672, Peter grew up to be monstrously tall (over six ft seven inches) and stubborn, mercurial and often cruel by temperament. His hatred of all things Russian, the arcane traditions as well as the chaos and the filth, is often traced back to his bawdy teenage adventures in the Nemetskaya Sloboda (Foreigner's Colony) in Moscow. His Westernising impulse blossomed during the so-called Grand Embassy of 1696, when he travelled incognito through the Low Countries and all the way to England, where he learned shipbuiding in the less than imperial location of Deptford. The reforms he would later implement had a wacky, eccentric edge to them. As well as shoe-horning the aristocracy into European fashions, he ordered all members of the urban male population to shave off their beards, subjecting defaulters to a special Beard Tax. Many who complied apparently continued to carry their beards with them for safekeeping in their pockets.

In 1712, Peter moved the capital of Russia from Moscow to St Petersburg and that is where it and the royal court would remain until the revolution of 1917. The creation of St Petersburg was the centrepiece of Peter's Western-inspired projects. In October 1714, to speed things up, the Tsar banned the use of brick and stone as construction materials anywhere else in the Russian Empire. He also rounded up hordes of slave labourers, many of whom fell victim to insanitary living and unsafe working conditions. 'Petersburg is founded on tears and corpses,' commented the official court historian. But by the time of his death on 8 February 1725, Peter had achieved the impossible: a great city had risen from the marsh.

Pinhead Peter by Mikhail Shemyakin.

THE RAUCOUS REIGN OF ELIZABETH

After Peter came a dizzying succession of rulers, none of whom made much of a mark either on the city of St Petersburg or on the Russian psyche. It was left to the blonde, vivacious and, according to Pushkin, 'voluptuous' Elizabeth, daughter of Peter the Great, who took the throne in 1741 in a palace coup, to move the city on to the next stage of its development. Elizabeth was intelligent and wilful but uneducated and practically illiterate. Blessed with an almost total disinterest in the tedious business of ruling Russia, she treated the new city as a playground for her exuberant, baroque tastes and, with the help of her favourite architect, Bartolomeo Rastrelli, transformed St Petersburg into a landscape of stucco tassels, undulating surfaces and bold, Mediterranean colours (*see chapter* **Architecture**). She also transformed the dour court of Anna Ivanovna into one of the most lavish in Europe, bankrupting the country in the process. But Elizabeth's reign was not only characterised by gaiety and hedonism; to her credit, she ended the interminable war with Sweden and founded both Moscow University and the Academy of the Arts in St Petersburg.

CATHERINE THE GREAT

It is pleasingly ironic that one of the greatest rulers of the Romanov era was nether a Romanov nor a Russian. Catherine took the throne from her weak, moody and fickle husband, Peter III, in time-honoured Russian fashion with a palace coup, aided by court guards whom she plied with gifts and champagne. She was born Sophie Fredericke Auguste von Anhalt-Zerbst, in Stettin, Poland on 2 May 1729, the daughter of a minor German prince. When she married Grand Duke Peter, she did everything possible to accommodate herself to the Russian people, changing her name to Yekaterina and converting to the Orthodox religion, though she never quite managed to lose her strong German accent. Famous for her romantic escapades, Catherine lavished attention and presents on her lovers. St Petersburg's Marble Palace, one of the most opulent buildings in the city, was a present to Grigory Orlov. But Catherine's greatest love and

devotion was Count Grigory Potemkin, the mastermind of the Potemkin villages. These were sham peasant settlements, complete with scrubbed and smiling villagers, developed to convince Catherine, during her tour of the Crimea in 1787, that she was ruler of a gleaming rural wonderland. He was well rewarded for this deceit. While Catherine spent a total of 92.5 million rubles on all of her lovers combined, she spent 50 million on Potemkin alone. During Catherine's reign, Russia greatly expanded its territories to encompass three partitions of Poland and the addition of the Crimea, after two victories over the Turks. The character of St Petersburg altered radically, too, as neo-classicism was adopted – a more severe style that would dominate to the middle of the nineteenth century.

FROM PAUL TO ALEXANDER I

The reign of Catherine's son, Paul I, is a strange interlude in Russian Imperial history. A naturally neurotic and irascible individual, whose hatred of his mother was equalled only by his love of all things military, he alienated almost everyone with his attempts to regiment society along Prussian lines, his ban on travel abroad and his outbursts of rage (which also led to rumours that he was insane). When he ascended to the throne, he tried to protect himself by building a fortified castle – his only

1917: what really happened

The history books are more or less unanimous in their version of events, but the repercussions and anecdotal evidence are often more telling...

● Talk about writing things down for posterity: Tsar Nicholas's diary entry for 26 February 1917, when the Revolution was at its peak, read: 'At ten o'clock I went to Mass. The reports were on time. There were many people at breakfast, including all the foreigners. Wrote to Alix and went for a walk near the chapel by the Bobrisky road. The weather was fine and frosty. After tea I read and talked with Senator Tregubov until dinner. Played dominoes in the evening.'

● When the moment came to raise a red lantern on the flagpole of the Peter and Paul Fortress, a signal for the storming of the Winter Palace to begin on the night of 24 October, no red lantern could be found. One of the Bolshevik commanders went in search of the necessary item, got lost in the dark and fell into a bog. When he finally returned, the lantern he appropriated was found to have a couple of drawbacks: it could not be attached to the flagpole and it wasn't red.

● When the *Aurora* battleship fired its blank shell over St Petersburg, the infamous Women's

Shock Battalion of Death, part of the defending group inside the Winter Palace, became hysterical and had to be locked in the cellar for their own safety.

● The greatest threat to Bolshevik discipline in the days following the October Revolution was the discovery, inside the Winter Palace, of a gigantic wine cellar. Commanders tried in vain to seal off the cellar. They then attempted to pump the wine reservoir into the street, but soldiers drank it from the gutter.

● According to a local St Petersburg legend, an aristocrat who was stripped of his wealth in the wake of the Revolution went to work at the Kunstkammer, Peter the Great's collection of freaks and oddities. There, it is claimed that he cracked open the canisters containing the two-headed babies, drained out the spirit and sold it on the street to unsuspecting punters.

● As the post-Revolutionary expectations of the people sky-rocketed, there was a rash of industrial unrest throughout Russia. Waiters protested against tipping, a practice they claimed was degrading. Prostitutes staged a nationwide strike, complaining of unsocial hours.

The Peter and Paul Fortress, scene of blundering chaos on the night of 24th October 1917.

architectural contribution to St Petersburg – on the site of his birth. In March 1801, he was murdered in his bedroom by conspirators who strangled him and then beat in his skull with a paperweight.

When the sentimental and sensitive Alexander heard about his father's murder, his first reaction was to burst into tears. 'Stop playing the child and go rule,' barked one of the conspirators. Alexander did as he was told and was the first male ruler to break the decade-barrier since Peter the Great. Throughout his reign, Alexander shrank from the task with which he had been confronted and dreamed of withdrawing to a cottage in the countryside somewhere in Germany. While his rule promised a great deal in the area of civil liberties and an established rule of law in the country, it soon became obvious that he was more interested in military evangelism and in organising society along military lines than in real reform, and the knell of rebellion began to sound in the distance. The highpoint in his reign was, of course, the victory over Napoleon in the war of 1812, known in Russia as the Patriotic War. But the subsequent march into Paris sowed the seeds for the Decembrist Uprising. For the first time, ordinary Russians (and among them most of the Decembrists) could see how their European neighbours lived.

THE DECEMBRIST UPRISING

It was during the reign of Nicholas I, however, that the situation really exploded, and his tenure was, in many ways, simply a protracted epilogue to the Decembrist Uprising. The uprising was masterminded by two major insurrectionary groups: the Southern Society, which hoped to establish a republic, and the Northern Society, which wanted a constitutional monarchy. Together they planned to assassinate Alexander I, but were thwarted by his timely natural death in 1825. During the constitutional wrangling that followed, they seized the opportunity to stage a coup and on 14 December 1825 confronted loyal Tsarist troops on St Petersburg's Senate Square (now Ploshchad Dekabristov, or Decembrists' Square). For much of the day, both sides nervously faced each other, neither daring to shoot. To end the stand-off, Nicholas ordered his men to open fire and, at the cost of several hundred lives, the whole farcical affair ended. Nicholas was to live in the shadow of this event and he kept a copy of the Decembrists' manifesto for the rest of his reign, consulting it frequently. Ironically, the rebellion compelled him to create a police state to rival that of his father, Paul. Nicholas's reign succeeded in bringing the country to an orderly standstill, in which the relationship between the ruling classes and the serfs deteriorated and grievances festered. In February 1855, Nicholas caught the flu and died within a few days.

THE TSAR LIBERATOR

The reign of Alexander II is best known for his liberation of the serfs in 1861, as well as the creation of local government bodies and the introduction of a jury system. Alexander's brand of Glasnost introduced a more or less independent press, which led to the flowering of publications – some of a relatively radical nature – and universities that, in theory, threw open their doors to all classes.

Alexander's reforms, however, raised expectations they singularly failed to fulfil and simply exacerbated social tensions in the country: the intelligentsia were condescending towards him and the radicals wanted more. Serfs who chose to stay on the land found themselves tied into a payment process lasting 49 years, during which they were not allowed to sell their property. They were still tried in special courts and given only a limited voice in local government. Those who moved to Russia's bulging cities filled the teeming new slums. The impact of the liberation of the serfs on St Petersburg was enormous. A deluge of freed serfs gushed into the city in an attempt to earn a living, swelling the population to almost half a million (making it the fourth largest city in Europe, after London, Paris and Constantinople). The industrial boom that was just beginning to get under way soaked up much of this influx, but many were forced to resort to prostitution, begging and theft. With a cordon of sooty, ugly factories laagered along the outskirts and littered with seething tenements, St Petersburg had become the living nightmare described by Dostoyevsky in *Crime and Punishment*.

Nothing that Alexander could do, it seemed, could ease growing social tensions. On 4 April 1866, a nihilist named Dmitry Karakozov attempted to assassinate Alexander as he strolled in the Summer Garden, and in 1878, the revolutionary Vera Zasulich shot and wounded the governor of St Petersburg, a crime of which she was actually acquitted (another consequence of Alexander's law reforms). Then, on 1 March 1881, when Alexander was returning from a military parade along the banks of Yekaterininsky Kanal (Catherine Canal), a member of the terrorist group People's Will (Narodnaya Volya) tossed a bomb under his carriage, injuring two guardsmen. Miraculously unharmed, Alexander leaped from the wreckage of his carriage, but was confronted by another terrorist. A second explosion left him mortally wounded. He was brought to the palace, but died shortly afterwards. Ironically, on his desk was a draft of promised sweeping constitutional reforms, which he had been planning to sign that day.

The assassination of Alexander II was disastrous both for Russia and for the course of reform. Alexander III reacted to the assassination of his father with a wave of repressive measures, which included rolling back all the reforms of the previous decades. Immediately, a state of emergency was declared, and a police regime was instantly reinstated, a situation that existed in some parts of the country right up to the Revolution.

THE 1905 REVOLUTION

The reign of Nicholas II, Russia's last Tsar, began fairly inauspiciously. At his coronation in 1894, the crowd suddenly surged forward, crushing 1,400 to death and injuring 600. Apparently, this tragic incident was caused by a rumour that the free beer and sausages were running out. Nicholas would later trace all of his misfortunes back to this moment.

From the onset, Nicholas – a childish, ineffectual, intransigent and deeply conservative man, simply didn't have the skills to rule a gigantic, fractious country. Signs of discontent were evident as early as 1899, when police brutally suppressed student demonstrations. Dissent grew even louder after Russia's defeat in 1904 in its territorial war against Japan, and on 9 January 1905, Tsarist troops panicked and opened fire on a demonstration as it made its way to the Winter Palace to petition the Tsar for workers' rights. Two hundred were killed and 800 wounded. Immediately, Bloody Sunday, as it became known, sparked off strikes and demonstrations of an increasingly violent and aggressive character all over the country. Nicholas pulled the Tsarist state back from the abyss by agreeing to a reform programme – contained in what was called the October Manifesto – which introduced a host of civil liberties, a cabinet government and a democratically elected assembly, the Duma. However, the jubilation on the streets of St Petersburg and Moscow was short-lived as, over the next decade, Nicholas slowly clawed back the concessions he had so reluctantly made. This period also coincided with Nicholas's association with the 'holy man' Rasputin, who was credited with alleviating the suffering of the Tsar's haemophiliac son, Alexei. The rumours swirling around Rasputin and his murder by the Yusupov brothers helped drag Nicholas's reputation to an all-time low. Throughout Nicholas's reign, Russia continued to grow as an industrial power, with an annual growth rate of nine per cent. More than ever before, St Petersburg became a city of factories and industrial workers, and consequently, a city of revolutionaries.

WAR, REVOLUTION & NAME CHANGES

Nicholas's war with Germany in 1914 proved to be a disastrous misadventure. Russia's war machine was a rusting, decrepit, spluttering vehicle that carried millions merrily to their deaths. At the infamous Battle of Tannenberg the Germans killed or wounded 70,000 Russians and took 100,000 prisoner, at the cost of only 15,000 casualties. Absolute chaos on the Front combined with a population stricken with general wartime deprivations to produce a combustible situation. In August 1914, the Germanic-sounding Sankt Peterburg had been peremptorily renamed Petrograd, the first of this century's name changes. This newly christened city provided the spark that ignited the Revolution, when, on the bitterly cold morning of 23 February, a mob of workers advanced on the city centre demanding bread. After a failed police attempt to damp the uprising by force, the mob was joined by mutinous soldiers from regiments stationed in the Mars Field, and the writing was on the wall for Nicholas: he was forced to abdicate on 1 March. Together with the rest of the Imperial family Nicholas was placed under house arrest and then executed by the Bolsheviks in the eastern city of Yekaterinburg on 17 July 1918.

At this point, power was handed over to a curious alliance of the Petrograd Soviet, a workers and soldiers collective, and the Duma to form what became known as the Provisional Government. This compromise alliance, along with the new body's refusal to take Russia out of the war, led to further discontent and ultimately to the Bolshevik coup, allowing Lenin to build up support among the people with promises of land and peace. After a period of disarray and panic from the new government, the Bolsheviks successfully stormed the Winter Palace on 24 October and took power. The new regime took up residence in the Smolny Institute for Girls until March 1918, when Lenin fled to Moscow, fearing a German attack. He also took the capitaldom with him, a move that had more impact on St Petersburg than anything the Germans could have mustered: within two years, the defrocked St Petersburg had been decimated, and its population had shrunk by 65 per cent to 799,000.

LENINGRAD & THE BLOCKADE

After Lenin's death in 1924, St Petersburg was rechristened Leningrad and would remain so for 70 years, though inhabitants continued to refer to it simply as 'Piter', just as they do today. In the Stalinist years, the old Tsarist capital and the birthplace of the hated intelligentsia, fell under the tyrant's paranoid suspicion. In an attempt to stamp out dissent, the city was subjected to many of the excesses of industrialisation and, after the assassination of Leningrad Party Chief Sergei Kirov, the 'murder of the century' which Stalin himself probably carried out, it fell victim to the worst ravages of the purges.

Then came the darkest hour in the history of Peter's city, the Leningrad Blockade. From September 8 1941 to January 27 1944, just a few days short of the 900 days now enshrined in legend, Nazi troops attempted to strangle the city, cutting off all supplies and submitting it to constant shelling. Approximately a third of the population died, half of them from hunger. Even the city's miraculous survival was resented by Stalin, who unleashed another purge here in the late '40s. It took until 1960 for the city to reach the population levels it enjoyed in the 1930s.

Post-war Leningrad was a fairly bleak and provincial place. It wasn't until Gorbachev's Perestroika that it began once again to realise its potential. Under the auspices of its liberal mayor,

Anatoly Sobchak, the city led the way in the area of commercial joint ventures and privatisation. In 1991, the city came out resolutely against the coup-plotters. Though Moscow threatened to send in tanks, and a group of volunteers gathered to defend City Hall, the whole thing fizzled out before there could be bloodshed. Later that year, a referendum was held proposing to resurrect the Tsarist-era name of St Petersburg.

Then, in July 1998, the remains of Nicholas II, the last Tsar, were laid to rest along with his family in the Peter and Paul Cathedral. 'Today is a historic day for Russia,' proclaimed President Yeltsin at the ceremony. 'By burying the remains of these murdered innocents, we are atoning for the sins of our forefathers. Burying the victims of the Yekaterinburg tragedy is an act of human justice, a symbol of unification in Russia, and redemption of our guilt.' The turbulent history of this extraordinary city had finally come full circle.

ST PETERSBURG TODAY

As St Petersburg approaches its tercentenary in 2003, its architectural heritage is fast becoming a public menace. Away from the centre, the city disintegrates into dirt, decay and lunar-surface roads, strewn with potholes cavernous enough to swallow up an entire fleet of Ladas. Every winter's freeze and thaw brings down chunks of stucco from the crumbling façades, occasionally splitting open pedestrians in the process. Many central apartment blocks haven't seen major repairs since the nineteenth century and are poised on the brink of dereliction.

So, what is being done to protect a city that was once a contender for the world's great wonders and which UNESCO designated a Site of World Heritage? The answer is brutally simple: not much.

In the euphoria that followed the collapse of the USSR, there was optimistic talk of transforming the city into a free-trade zone, even of moving the capital back from Moscow, in an attempt to wipe away 75 years of communism. None of this came to pass, and as Moscow experienced an unprecedented boom, St Petersburg languished, both politically and economically. The city now receives less foreign investment than the surrounding Leningrad district, which while a few years ago was not enlightened enough to dump its Soviet name now offers substantial tax breaks to businesses and is regarded as one of the most economically progressive regions in the country.

The reasons behind St Petersburg's failure to thrive are stark: it suffers from debilitating delusions of grandeur, with officials prattling incessantly about the 'Cultural Capital', while investors just want to get down to pertinent issues of tax laws and shareholders' rights.

The Lenin Express: the train that brought the great man home in 1917.

Without a single, all powerful guiding force, like Moscow's Mayor Luzhkov, the city's largely corrupt bureaucracy is out of control, smothering businesses with entreaties for personal gain disguised as arcane fire or water regulations. Good intentions, such as a recent plan to turn over derelict buildings to private companies for development, get lost in red tape. Organised crime is as endemic here as it is in Moscow, but without the balancing factor of substantial profit margins. Finally, and probably fatally, the total centralisation of power in Moscow and its ruthless determination to guard its dominant position have meant that St Petersburg, historically its closest rival, is being pushed further and further into the shadows.

An improvement on the present situation seems unlikely under current Governor Vladimir Yakovlev, who ousted the high-profile reformer Anatoly Sobchak in the first ever democratic transfer of power in Russia's history. During his first two years in power, he has proved grey, unimaginative and mired down in petty political infighting. Even if he had the will, Yakovlev simply doesn't have the mandate (he slipped in on a two per cent margin) to bring about the radical overhaul that would get the city back on its feet.

However, while the prognosis is bleak, it is not entirely without hope. With gubernatorial elections coming up again in 2000, St Petersburg may well flex its democratic muscles once more, perhaps installing the dynamic and untainted leadership it desperately needs.

Architecture

St Petersburg's fanciful architecture is a three-dimensional catalogue of its monarchs' whims.

Yum, yum, the bubblegum domes of the **Church of the Saviour on the Blood.** *See page 183.*

It's difficult to imagine a more radical solution to defining the future of a country's architecture than the crazed moment of inspiration that became St Petersburg. Not even Europe's most brilliant urban planners, from Sir Christopher Wren, with his dreams of a concentric London, all the way to Baron Haussmann, author of the wide, tidy boulevards of Paris, have ever dared to venture this far. The marsh where Peter the Great chose to build his shining new city from scratch was a spotlessly clean slate, a canvas so blank it could hang in the Tate, the architectural equivalent of absolute zero. Here, the patriarchal domes and the squat fortifications of Moscow could be entirely obliterated from the collective memory. In their place, the resourceful Tsar was completely free to implant the foreign styles he had discovered and admired during his European travels. At the time, the project seemed like demented folly, but in retrospect, Peter could not have chosen a more symbolic site for the brick and stucco embodiment of his new, improved, thoroughly westernised Russia.

Up to the middle of the nineteenth century the history of St Petersburg architecture is the chronicle of its monarchs' tastes. While the city may seem, at first

glance, to be a neo-classical whole, it embodies a spectrum of styles reflecting the dominant aesthetic dogma of the time: from baroque to neo-classicism in its various shades through to neo-Renaissance, eclecticism and finally the *style moderne*, Russia's variant of art nouveau. What really gives St Petersburg its unity is not the decoration on the façades but superb planning, an impeccable sense of municipal theatre that ushers the 'spectator' from one ensemble to the next and the height restrictions that have kept the city in line for centuries.

● More information on buildings picked out in **bold** is given elsewhere in the Guide; see **Index**.

THE PETRINE ERA

Even though relatively few buildings have survived from the Petrine era, the modern metropolis probably bears the stamp of its founder more boldly than that of any ruler that followed. Peter was a meticulous planner and approached every task with scientific precision, regardless of whether he was constructing a ship or a building. Even when the city was no more than a scattered frontier outpost, he had already, in 1706, established the Office of City Affairs to co-ordinate construction according to

*The **Winter Palace** on the Bolshaya Neva.*

clearly laid-out rules and regulations. Later, he commissioned the French architect Le Blond to come up with a street plan, the result of which looks amazingly like a computer chip. Eventually, Peter settled for a pattern of concentric avenues converging at the Admiralty, in a design inspired by the gardens of Versailles. While later rulers came up with their own ideas – the most famous of which is Nicholas I's decree that no secular building could exceed the height of the cornice of the Winter Palace – they all took their cue from Peter.

While foreign architects had been imported into Russia before, most notably to build the 'archetypally Russian' Kremlin in Moscow, Peter began to bring them in on an unprecedented scale. In 1703, he ordered the Russian ambassador to Denmark to round up a flock of architects and ship them over en masse. The first batch included Swiss-Italian fortification engineer Domenico Trezzini, who promptly built the **Peter and Paul Fortress** and its famous, though ugly, cathedral, as well as Peter's **Summer Palace** residence and the impressive **Menshikov Palace** on the Vasilyevsky bank of the Neva. All of these were constructed in a curious, outdated, Dutch-tinted baroque style that became known as Petrine baroque. Because of a shortage of materials, the earliest buildings were built of wood and painted to look like brick. Later, Peter would move on to brick, stuccoed to look like carving – the predominant style of St Petersburg today.

ELIZABETHAN ROCOCO

After the devastating fires and architectural idiosyncrasy of Anna Ivanovna's reign, it was left to Peter's daughter Elizabeth, who ascended to the throne in 1741, to propel the city on to its next phase. Elizabeth was an unabashed sensualist and presided over one of the most lavish courts in Europe. Her sumptuous tastes were complemented perfectly by the talents of her favourite architect Bartolomeo Rastrelli, the son of the Florentine sculptor who made Peter's death mask. Between them, Elizabeth and Rastrelli concocted the fabulous, frothy and wildly opulent Russian rococo style, a kind of decadent turbo-baroque that was applied to many of the city's most famous buildings, including the **Catherine Palace** in Tsarskoye Selo, the **Great Palace** at Peterhof (which was remodelled to bring

it in line with the tastes of the new monarch), **Smolny Cathedral** and, of course, Rastrelli's masterpiece, the **Winter Palace**, one of the last buildings in the world to be built in the late baroque style. In general, the Rastrellian style is characterised by a plastic energy, vast scale and a copious use of pilasters, statuary and other decorative baubles. He also had a fetish for vibrant, Mediterranean colours: pale pistachio to azure, gold to orange.

CLASSIC CATHERINE

Despite the vigour, sensuality and voracity with which she approached her eventful love life, Catherine the Great, on her ascension to the throne, almost immediately brought a cool reserve to the architecture of St Petersburg, moving it into the neo-classical groove that it would travel along for a century. The next great monarch to exert architectural influence on the capital admitted that she felt an 'instinctive nausea' for the tastes and antics of Elizabeth. She dispensed with Rastrelli almost immediately and later began ripping out some of his interiors from the Catherine Palace in Tsarskoye Selo. A self-proclaimed daughter of European Enlightenment, Catherine was really just following fashion, which meant baroque was passé practically everywhere else in the world.

The fruits of Catherine's neo-classical conversion include the magnificent **Marble Palace** on the corner of Marsovo Pole, a present from the Tsarina to her lover Count Gregory Orlov, the man who shared responsibility for the murder of her husband Peter III. Constructed from grey and green Siberian marbles and designed by Antonio Rinaldi, the palace is one of the very few buildings in the city clad in stone. Later on, Catherine commissioned the Russian architect Ivan Starov to build the **Cathedral of the Trinity** in the Alexander Nevsky Lavra and the magnificent Tauride Palace, intended for the most enduring and resourceful of Catherine's lovers, Gregory Potemkin. The result of all this neo-classical building activity gave the city a much more imperious and formal appearance.

THE EMPIRE STYLE

After a brief interlude, during which the insane Tsar Paul I tried, in time-honoured fashion, to wipe out his mother Catherine's architectural legacy – the Tauride Palace, for instance, was turned over to the regiments of the Guard and its Great Hall

became a stable – normality was restored when Paul was murdered just weeks after moving into his only architectural achievement: the 'impregnable' Mikhailovksy Castle (now the **Engineer's Castle**), designed to protect him from danger.

The succession to the throne of Paul's son, Alexander, signalled the beginning of a new, even more puritanical era of St Petersburg classicism. This might have been dull had it not coincided with the rise of some of St Petersburg's most talented architects. The former serf Andrei Voronikhin built the stunning **Kazan Cathedral**, inspired by St Peter's in Rome but embellished with colonnades, which embrace Nevsky like a neo-classical crustacean. Andreyan Zakharov built the golden spired Admiralty. And then came Carlo Rossi, the masterbuilder who was to leave the greatest mark on the city since Rastrelli. Rossi was an architect and urban planner whose talents bordered on genius. He created or gave facelifts to no fewer than 13 squares and 12 streets in the centre of St Petersburg and, as an architect, is responsible for four major ensembles. One of Rossi's greatest talents was his natural sense of the theatrical. Set into his greatest creation, the **General Staff Building** facing the Winter Palace, is a triumphal arch that funnels spectators down a strange little 'duct' street leading from Nevsky Prospekt, so that they get an optimum view of the Winter Palace. It is perhaps the greatest compliment ever paid by one major architect to another.

THE RISE OF ECLECTICISM

And then: the long, slow trudge downhill. Surprisingly, the decline begins with what is still considered one of St Petersburg's finest landmarks, **St Isaac's Cathedral**. Though impressive, this is just an amalgam of classical motifs on a monumental scale. Despite being credited to Auguste de Montferrand, it was designed almost by committee. Entirely lacking the inbuilt grace of classicism, it is closer in spirit to Konstantin Ton's Church of Christ the Saviour in Moscow than anything in St Petersburg. This was the opening shot of the eclectic upsurge.

By the 1840s, Alexander's rigorous laws governing the style of buildings were abrogated and, with the rise of a wealthy merchant class, individuality became much more important than conformity. Commercial buildings employed new materials and made new demands both in the area of finances and

aesthetics. This led to experiments with neo-Gothic, neo-Renaissance and neo-baroque, often with overtones of Egypt or Islam. This path would ultimately lead to the gigantic, clashing neo-Byzantine style of the **Church of the Saviour on the Blood**, which, though gruesomely impressive, could not be more garishly out of tune with the architectural milieu of the city.

THE MODERN AGE

St Petersburg may seem like a city that has escaped the ravages of the modern age, but tucked away, even on its main thoroughfares, are quite a few buildings that belong indisputably to the twentieth century. Most of these were built in the first years of this century in the Russian variant of art nouveau – the *style moderne*. Striking examples include the Fabergé building on Bolshaya Morskaya Ulitsa, with its pseudo-Gothic touches, and the lavish **Yeliseyevsky** store on Nevsky Prospekt. Also notable is the Singer building, now the main city bookstore (**Dom Knigi**), with its bulbous tower and glass panelled façades.

After the Revolution, the loss of its status as the Russian capital meant that St Petersburg largely escaped the ravages and rewards that characterised the utopian, experimental architecture of the 1920s, though you will find a few constructivist buildings on the outskirts of the city, such as the Moscow Narva House of Soviets, which now houses a nightclub, and the Apartment House of the Leningrad Soviet on the Petrograd side of the city.

In the Stalinist era, a bizarre plan was formulated to shift the centre away from Nevsky Prospekt and Palace Square and south to the grand avenue of Moskovsky Prospekt (the road most people know from dashes to and from the airport), where we now find the bloated totalitarian proportions of the House of Soviets. The scheme thankfully came to nothing, because of the outbreak of war and tacit resistance from city authorities.

Since the demise of communism, there has been little new building in St Petersburg and almost nothing at all in the centre, owing partly to the depressed economy and partly to the regulations that have protected the metropolis since the time of Peter the Great. Architecturally, the city of St Petersburg is stuck in a spectacular timewarp, a nineteenth-century city-museum of some of the greatest eras of Russian architecture.

Literary St Petersburg

St Petersburg proved fertile soil for Russia's first literary flowering. These are the landmarks that inspired it.

The literary boom experienced by St Petersburg in the nineteenth century is one of the most startling cultural phenomena of the modern age. Up to this point, 'Russia' and 'Literature' were two words that sat together rather uncomfortably in the same sentence. Before the tenth century, the written form of the Russian language didn't even exist. Until the literary debut in the 1820s of Alexander Pushkin, the poet credited with casting the die of the Russian literary lexicon, the country had produced no writers of note whatsoever. And then came Pushkin, Dostoyevsky, Nikolai Gogol, as well as lesser-known figures like the fablist Ivan Krylov and the playwright Alexander Griboyedov – all writers who defined the so-called Golden Age of Russian literature. In the space of a lifetime, the Russian nation had become the world's greatest literary late-starter.

While **Alexander Pushkin** is not all that widely known in the West, primarily because his spare, tight, rhythmic verse does not lend itself to translation, he is a towering literary landmark in Russia. Everyone from octogenarians to schoolchildren can recite his verse by heart and works like *Eugene Onegin*, the prose poem *The Queen of Spades* (both of which Tchaikovksy adapted into opera) and *Ruslan and Ludmila* have all been co-opted into the Russian psyche. One of Pushkin's most famous long poems, *The Bronze Horseman*, set during the great flood of 1824, confronts that moment when Peter the Great decided to found the city. Its opening lines are perhaps the most famous in Russian literature: 'On the shore of empty waves/He stood, filled with great thoughts, and stared out.'

Most of the famous Pushkin sights in the city have strong associations with the poet's fatal duel in 1837 with the French cavalry officer D'Anthes, whom he accused of having an affair with his beautiful and flighty wife Natalya Goncherova. Pushkin awaited his 'second' for the duel in what has now become an abysmal tourist trap, the Literaturnoye Café at Nevsky Prospekt 18, then the Wolff et Beranger Café, a well-known haunt also frequented by the young, still unknown Dostoyevsky.

The actual duel took place on the banks of Chornaya Rechka (Black River), which can now be reached via the metro station of the same name. On the banks of the river, a large red obelisk marks the spot where Pushkin was fatally wounded. Afterwards, Pushkin was conveyed to his house on the Moika Canal (now the main Pushkin museum in the city) where he lay dying for two days as the entire city came to pay respects, directing carriage-drivers with the simple words: 'To Pushkin'.

The aspiring writer **Nikolai Gogol**, who hailed from the tiny Ukrainian backwater of Nezhim, moved to the capital in 1828, just before his collection of short stories of Ukrainian life, *Evenings on a Farm Near Dikanka,* made him an instant celebrity. Almost from the moment he arrived in St Petersburg, Gogol hated the place, as much for the pettiness of its social hierarchies as for its artificial architecture: 'O, don't trust that Nevsky Prospekt!' he wrote in his short story named after that street. 'It's all deceit, all dreams, it's all not what it seems.' Gogol's most famous works include *The Government Inspector*, the novel *Dead Souls* and the short story *The Nose*. During his eight years in the city, Gogol moped about in various lodgings, the last of which was at Malaya Morskaya 17. One essential stopover for Gogol fans, however, is the monument to Major Kovalyov's Nose. Basically, it's a nose sticking out of the wall at Vozhnesensky Prospekt 36.

Dostoyevsky's attitude to St Petersburg, where he moved from Moscow at the age of 15, was just as equivocal as Gogol's. He regarded the city's magnificent architecture as the palest mishmash imaginable of Western and retro styles. 'Here's the characterless church architecture of the last century,' he wrote, casting a critical eye across the city's panorama. 'There's a pathetic copy of the Romanesque style of the turn of the century, and there's the Renaissance.' In *Crime and Punishment*, he writes: 'This city is for the half mad... There are few more grim, harsh and strange influences on a man's soul than in Petersburg.' However, this neurotic, dislocated landscape was the perfect backdrop for the febrile action of his greatest masterpieces: *The Idiot, The Brothers Karamazov* and, of course, *Crime and Punishment*, which could not have been set in any other city.

Many of the sights most associated with Dostoyevsky are in the region of Sennaya Ploshchad (Haymarket), which has not lost any of its chaotic ambience since Dostoyevsky's time. It was here that Raskolnikov, the hero of *Crime and Punishment*, knelt to kiss the stinking mud and ask forgiveness. Just down the embankment, located in a crook of the canal, Stolyarny Pereulok is widely accepted to be the site of Raskolnikov's own dwelling place, either at the corner of Grazhdanky Prospekt or No.9, though the public has capriciously voted for No.19 by splashing its staircase with adoring graffiti. A little further still down the canal brings us to Kanal Griboyedov 104, the house where Raskolnikov murdered the old pawnbroker Alyona Ivanovna.

As the Golden Age of Russian literature passed away with the death of Dostoyevsky in 1881, St Petersburg was readying itself to usher in the Silver Age, spearheaded by symbolist poet **Alexander Blok**. The 'unbearably, unbelievably handsome' poet won hordes of devoted female admirers – some of whom followed him around collecting his cigarette butts as keepsakes – with works such as his collection *Verses About a Beautiful Lady* and his poem *The Unknown Woman*. The latter was so widely known that prostitutes on Nevsky Prospekt would rope in punters with the line: 'I'm the Unknown Woman. Would you like to get to know me?'

The two Blok highlights in the city are the building where the poet spent his childhood at Petrogradskaya Naberezhnaya 44, in the more industrial sector of the Petrograd Side region, and Blok's last home, Ulitsa Dekabristov 57, now the Blok Museum. Here you can find the desk where he wrote all of his work, including the famous collection *The Twelve*.

Anna Akhmatova is widely regarded as the muse of St Petersburg and, for her courage during the Stalinist purges, its patron saint as well. Her first volumes of romantic verse, *Evening* and *The Rosary* (1912 and 1914 respectively), were instant popular and critical successes. Akhmatova's post-revolutionary martyrdom began with the arrest and shooting of her ex-husband, the poet Nikolai Gumilyov, and then, in the 1930s, with the imprisonment of her son, Lev. Indirectly, however, the red terror inspired some of Akhmatova's most important and memorable work, *Requiem* and *Poem Without a Hero*. 'In the terrible years of the Yezhov terror,' she wrote in the preface to *Requiem* – which was entitled *Instead of a Preface* – 'I spent 17 months waiting in line outside the prison in Leningrad. One day, somebody in the crowd identified me and asked in a whisper. "Can you describe this?" And I said: "I can."'

Akhmatova inhabited a number of addresses along the Fontanka Naberezhnaya: Nos.2, 18 and 34, which is now the main Anna Akhmatova museum. From 1962 until her death in 1966, she lived mostly in her dacha in the region of Komorova.

Vladimir Nabokov, author of the infamous and still headline-grabbing *Lolita*, was born in 1899 in St Petersburg, where his father was a leading politician in the Kadet Party. His brilliant memoir *Speak, Memory* describes life in the upper middle-class family home, just down the road from Fabergé's famous jewellery shop: 'We drift past the show windows of Fabergé,' he recounts in one episode about a spring carriage ride, 'whose mineral monstrosities, jewelled troikas poised on marble ostrich eggs and the like, highly appreciated by the Imperial family, were emblems of grotesque garishness to ours.' Carriage rides ended with the Revolution, however, which forced the family to emigrate to Berlin.

Nabokov attended the Teneshev school at Ulitsa Mokhovaya 33, whose previous alumni also included the poet Osip Mandelstam. The family house, now a museum, is in Ulitsa Bolshaya Morskaya 47.

Nobel Prize-winning poet **Joseph Brodsky**'s life in Leningrad was characterised chiefly by confrontation with the authorities, leading inexorably to incarceration in a mental asylum, an 18-month spell in a prison camp and exile in 1972. The transcript of Brodsky's trial in 1964 for 'malicious parasitism', or the cardinal Soviet sin of being jobless, became an instant Samizdat classic. 'And who recognised that you are a poet? Who listed you among poets? …Did you study this?' Brodsky's reply was sanguine, stoic and somewhat bewildered: 'I think that it's…from God.' Brodsky was forced to emigrate in 1972. His work in translation includes *A Part of Speech* and *To Urania*.

The apartment building where Brodsky lived, which is described as a 'room and a half' in his book of essays *Less Than One*, still stands on Liteiny Prospekt 24. The Brodsky family lived in flat 28. This curious pseudo-Moorish building, known as the Muruzi House after its first aristocratic owner, was home also to the symbolist poetess Zinaida Gippius and, later, to Gorky's publishing house, World Literature.

Harsh, grim, strange... it's Dostoyevsky.

White Nights

Long days and non-existent nights make a midsummer night's dream of St Petersburg.

All through the spring and into early summer, the days stretch themselves quietly in anticipation of what's to come. Then, in early June, the last sad, redundant street lamps are finally extinguished and evening suddenly takes an acrobatic leap into the small hours and dawn and sunset merge to banish darkness from St Petersburg. For three sparkling weeks, the wide, deserted streets of the city blaze right through the night with a fine, powdery light. Cathedrals shimmer under gleaming halos. And the bridges on the River Neva, which have remained clasped shut throughout the icy, unnavigable winter, yawn magnificently into a boundless, sparkling sky.

While the nights may also be white in other parts of the world, St Petersburg is the sole possessor of *the* White Nights, which run officially from 11 June to 2 July. Perched up there, on the same latitude as Oslo and Helsinki, and just a squeak below Anchorage and Reykjavik, the city enjoys a deluge of daylight hours.

Leavened by an influx of visitors from all over the world, St Petersburgers take this opportunity to show off their flair for raucous social activity. The party – which, in other circumstances, would probably only continue until dawn – never ends.

Weirdly enough, it seems to have taken the population of St Petersburg over a century after the founding of the city to take any notice at all of these long, languorous, marathon summer days. It wasn't until Pushkin drew attention to 'the transparent twilight of dreamy nights, the moonless glow' in his 1833 poem *The Bronze Horseman* that the White Nights took their first step towards superstardom. Back then, the White Nights afforded a good opportunity to get the hell out of the city, as the aristocracy clambered to escape the dust and the stifling heat in lush, suburban summer residences. Dostoyevsky describes this flight of the nobility in his novella *White Nights*, depicting the city during this period as a sad, stark, depressing shell. 'Everything was moving to the country in whole caravans, it seemed that St Petersburg itself was threatened with becoming a desert.'

By the second half of the century, the White Nights were gaining notoriety as a time of unbridled deviance and debauchery. In a city already top-heavy with bachelors, the frenzied male population now swelled with poverty-stricken counts and affluent merchants' sons, who were steadily

turning St Petersburg into a mecca for prostitution and dalliance. Every evening during the White Nights, beginning around five o'clock, a procession of carriages would gather on the way to the islands to the north of the city. Here, profligate young men would display their female trophies: belly-dancers, voluptuous French actresses, high-class tarts and other curiosities from the demi-monde. They would gather at a single point overlooking the Baltic Sea and then disperse to various exotic spots, one of which was the aptly christened Garden of Joy (Sad Razvlichenei). This debauched ritual continued up until the Revolution, when the puritan, killjoy communists put an end not only to these various immoral practices but also to the 'class enemies' carrying them out.

The modern era of the St Petersburg White Nights only came about after Lenin, faced by the advancing German troops, fled to Moscow in 1918, taking the capitaldom with him. As the city withered and died, the White Nights came to be regarded as a great, immutable climatic asset. This was the one thing that the communists couldn't stick in a boxcar and pack off on a train to Moscow. The White Nights would always, indisputably, belong to St Petersburg. The whole event has now acquired an inevitable commercial tinge as hotels seek to pack their various establishments to capacity and tour operators brush the rust off their old buses. The population of baseball caps in St Petersburg during the month of June soars to ridiculous heights, dispersing again only towards the end of August. Nevertheless, the charm of the city remains largely intact throughout the White Nights, and there is always plenty to do.

A plague of festivals is visited on the city: the main ones are listed below, but there are multitudes of minor rivals. Past festival luminaries have included Joe Cocker, Sheryl Crow and Pavarotti. On occasion, the budget has only stretched as far as Terence Trent D'Arby and Steve Vai, but the weather is usually so glorious that the most garish booking blunders can be overlooked.

White Nights festivals

Other ad hoc festivals spring up throughout White Nights; sometimes the *St Petersburg Times* catches them in time. If you read Russian, keep an eye on the local press. Otherwise, follow the crowds.

A napping Neptune misses all the fun of the endless daylight nights.

Festival of Festivals

Information *Avrora Cinema, Nevsky Prospekt 60 (315 5254).*

A prime chance to catch movies that will never, ever grace the city's blockbuster-clogged cinemas again. The line-up often comprises stuff (Loach, Egoyan, Polanski) that would barely quicken the pulse in a regular European city, but here it's enough to send cinema-goers into a frenzy.

International Kharms Festival

Information *Anna Akhmatova Museum, Naberezhnaya Reki Fontanki 34 (272 2211).* **Venues** Anna Akhmatova Museum; Engineer's Palace; Peter & Paul Fortress.

Daniil Kharms, St Petersburg's own home-grown Dadaist, has achieved cult status throughout Russia due in equal measure to the quirky insouciance of his prose and his gruesome end at the hands of the communists. Festival events involve actors faffing about on stilts or in bumble-bee costumes.

White Nights Pop Festival

Information *Festival Information Office (279 1439).*

The non-appearance in 1996 of David Bowie dealt a blow to this festival from which it has never fully recovered. While continuing to use the rubric White Nights to organise one-off concerts, the festival organisers no longer have the will, but keep promising to deliver the goods 'next year'. In June 1998, they were responsible for the appearance of Julio Iglesias and Ringo Starr; who knows what the future holds: Rainbow, perhaps… maybe even Smokie?

Stars of the White Nights Festival

Information & tickets *Mariinsky Theatre, Teatralnaya Ploshchad 1 (114 4344) & Shostakovich Philharmonic Great Hall, Mikhailovskaya Ulitsa 2 (311 7333).* **Dates** Last week in June.

A showcase for St Petersburg's two major classical music institutions: the Mariinsky Theatre of Opera and Ballet and the St Petersburg Philharmonia. Mostly comprising their current repertoires, the proceedings are buoyed up by premières of new works and the occasional guest soloist or conductor.

White Nights Swing Jazz Festival

Information & tickets *Jazz Philharmonic Hall, Zagorodny Prospekt (164 8565).* **Dates** 3 days-1 week mid-June.

Run by St Petersburg's main jazz haunt, this festival brings together a rag-bag of musicians from all over Europe and, on occasion, the US. Even if you've never heard of anyone on the roster (as is likely), the festival is fun and positively drenched in the White Nights spirit.

American Music Festival

Information *Shostakovich Philharmonic Great Hall, Mikhaylovskaya Ulitsa 2 (311 7333).*

This series of concerts embraces American music from jazz to musicals, spirituals and classical. Featured guests in 1998 included the veteran American baritone William Warfield, who performed Jerome Kern's 'Old Man River' on July 4.

Palaces of St Petersburg International Chamber Music Festival

Information *113 3208.*

In mid-June a wide range of chamber music, from American spirituals to Rossini, resounds through 19 of St Petersburg's former aristocratic palaces, the Peter and Paul Fortress and the *Avrora* cruiser. Soloists and singers are often borrowed from the Mariinsky and the Bolshoi, which makes the standard as high and the ambience rich.

Solntsevorot (Solstice)

Information *Baltiisky Dom International Festival Centre (233 1302/232 0961).*

Solstice celebrations include this smorgasbord of theatre and general romping over a number of days at the height of mid-summer. Events include street performances by European troupes and drama mini-festivals in various venues.

Carnival

Information *466 0460.*

Just a tiny hint of Rio de Janeiro invades St Petersburg at the end of June with a costume parade through the centre of town.

Sightseeing

St Petersburg is an easily navigated nirvana for architecture addicts and culture vultures.

Column for column and cupola for cupola, this city boasts a higher concentration of architectural splendour right in its historic centre than any other on the planet. Strolling along Nevsky Prospekt is a little like strapping yourself into a virtual reality headset – cathedrals rear up at every corner, palaces jostle for attention on every square and colonnaded ensembles lay themselves out ingenuously along streets and canals waiting to be zapped with your point 'n' shoot.

Not only are St Petersburg's landmarks compactly grouped, they occupy the flat terrain of reclaimed marshland. This makes sightseeing here more effortless, enjoyable and unaerobic than in any other city. For those who want to experience one of the world's most astonishingly beautiful cities but can't be bothered with the trekking and the slogging, this is the place to be. All you are asked to do is loiter around and keep your eyes open. St Petersburg does the rest.

● Unless otherwise stated, sights listed do not accept credit cards as payment. Those marked in **bold** are covered in more detail elsewhere in the Guide: refer to the index.

Palace Square

No other stretch of cobbles in the world played such an influential and gory role in a country's tumultuous history. It was right here on Palace Square (Dvortsovaya Ploshchad), on what would later become known as Bloody Sunday, that jittery Tsarist troops mowed down a group of peaceful peasant and worker demonstrators – an atrocity that sparked off the 1905 Revolution. Just over a decade later, the square became the platform that launched the Bolshevik regime, as Lenin's troops poured across, en route to the **Winter Palace** (Zimny Dvorets, *see below*), where the Provisional Government was gasping its last. During the

A dome of your own: **St Isaac's Cathedral**. *See page 193.*

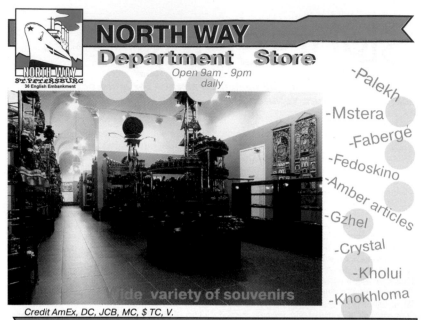

attempted coup of 1991, Mayor Sobchak addressed a crowd of 250,000 here in the country's biggest pro-Yeltsin demonstration. The tanks Moscow threatened to send in thankfully never arrived.

Yet, despite its violent past, the square itself seems to have few concerns other than harmony and equilibrium. The handiwork of generations of the city's finest architects, it began life in earnest only when Rastrelli built the Winter Palace between 1754 and '62. Even then, it was still an undefined tract of land trapped between the palace and the Moika River. The true author of Palace Square is Carlo Rossi, who enclosed it with the majestic ellipse of the **General Staff Building** (Glavny Shtab), which at that time had the longest façade in Europe. But the real stroke of genius is the passageway (a continuation of Bolshaya Morskaya Ulitsa) that leads through a succession of arches from Nevsky Prospekt to position you on the perfect spot to fully appreciate the magnificence of the ensemble. This is still the best way to approach the square. Right in front, the outline of the Alexander Column (Aleksandrovskaya Kolonna) lines up your sights on the Winter Palace. It was commissioned from the architect August Ricard de Montferrand to commemorate the victory over Napoleon in 1812 and, at a height of 47.5 metres (156 feet), it is the highest triumphal column in the world. The 600-ton granite monolith took a team of 400 workers two years to quarry. It is fastened to the pedestal by nothing more than Newton's laws of gravity.

Surrendering to the momentum of the square, you will now find yourself being sucked into the frothy confection of the Winter Palace. Once a fiery red – the 'enormous Crimson Sun' described in Andrei Bely's novel *Petersburg* – it is now a cool sea-green, slashed by a lattice of pilasters. Its huge size really makes a mockery of the buoyant, flighty ethic of baroque, but somehow Rastrelli carries it off. This is probably the last important baroque construction ever built in Europe.

Top 10 sights

1) The Winter Palace
2) St Isaac's
3) Kazan Cathedral
4) Peter and Paul Fortress
5) The Church of the Saviour on the Blood
6) Field of Mars
7) Summer Garden and Palace
8) Mikhailovsky Palace
9) Theatre Square
10) Vasilevsky Island's Strelka

At this point turn around to take a proper look at the General Staff Building. While it lacks the frills of the Winter Palace, it impresses with its classical discipline. The occasional volley of ornamentation – such as Victory in his chariot over the main arch – is impeccably timed: this is one of the most tactful, conscientious buildings in the world.

No longer a hotbed of conflict and revolution, modern Palace Square is most likely to resonate to the sounds of summer pop concerts, festivals and jaunty weekend rollerbladers, though it is still possible to find elderly communists hanging around or using it as a soapbox from which to sound off about late wages, low pensions and the Zionist conspiracy.

Winter Palace

Dvortsovaya Naberezhnaya 34 (311 3465/3420/tour bookings 311 8416). Metro Gostiny Dvor or Nevsky Prospekt. **Open** 10.30am-6pm Tue-Sun (last admission 5pm); tours by arrangement. **Admission** $10; free students, under-17s. **Credit** MC, V. **Map p287 C4/D4**
With more than 700 rooms, 2,000 windows and 250 external columns, the Winter Palace is the most wildly ambitious building in a city packed full of ambitious buildings. Empress Elizabeth thought that the structure could be thrown up in a couple of years; her pet architect Bartolomeo

*Here, Fido: frolicking on the **Field of Mars**. See page 197.*

The **Admiralty:** *a popular spot with aspiring athletes.*

Rastrelli delivered the finished article in eight. Originally allotted just 859,555 rubles for construction, the budget became increasingly more bloated, hiking the final figure up to 2.5 million rubles. To finance this massive overrun, Elizabeth was forced to open a network of beer halls and to hike up taxes on alcohol and salt, pushing the populace to the limit in the pursuit of her own capricious, decorative aims. The finished building is a strange, dissatisfying concoction. Just take a look at the top row of pillars that appears to be crushing the significantly shorter bottom row. Baroque excess on this scale can only amount to one thing: too much. It is probably these faults, combined with moments of great poise, daring and audacity, that make the Winter Palace the embodiment of Russian autocracy.

Since 1918, the Winter Palace has been in the hands of the **Hermitage Museum** (*see p204*), but even given the added

distractions of Picasso and Matisse, the original state rooms are among the most riveting in the building. Highlights include the Malachite Room, where the Provisional Government met during its last days and the White Dining Room, where ministers were arrested by the Bolsheviks. *Café. Guided tours and information in English. Shop.*

Admiralty to St Isaac's Square

From Palace Square there are two contrasting ways to approach the next of St Petersburg's great landmarks, the **Admiralty** (Admiralteistvo). If you proceed along the embankment, past the riverside bar and the water taxis vying for customers, you will also get a good view of Velten's granite embankments along the Neva, as integral a part of the city as the palaces. Alternatively, make your way through the shady Admiralty Garden (Admiralteysky Sad) on the left of this expansive, vibrant, ochre-yellow building. Originally built as a shipyard in 1704, to a design that Peter ran up himself, the current incarnation of the Admiralty is courtesy of Andreyan Zakharov, who produced this strictly neo-classical structure between 1806 and 1823. Though conceived on a mind-boggling scale with a main façade 407 metres (1,336 feet) long, the building is the essence of classical simplicity. Its most prominent feature is the 72-metre (236-foot) high spire, from which central point the city's main thoroughfares radiate.

Whether you approach from the embankment or from Alexander Garden, you will eventually arrive at Ploshchad Dekabristov, scene of the Decembrist Uprising in 1825 and site of St Petersburg's most famous public monument, the **Bronze Horseman**, Etienne Falconet's equestrian statue of Peter the Great (*see below*). On the west side of the square is another Rossi creation, the Building of the Synod and Senate, which like the General Staff Building features an ingenious arch. Through the archway, you'll find the **Senate Bar**, and the **Crocodile**, a funky little croc-theme eatery.

Then onward to **St Isaac's Cathedral** (*see below*), whose stupendous gilt dome bulges its way into the city skyline like a gilt protuberance. Straight ahead, on the other side of Isaakiyevskaya Ploshchad is the neo-classical Mariinsky Palace, built by Andrey Shtakenshneider in 1839-40 for the Grand Duchess Maria. It now houses the city government. The square itself sports an impressive equestrian statue of Maria's father, Tsar Nicholas I. Turning right along Naberezhnaya Reki Moiki, some parts of which are undergoing interminable repairs, you'll find the **Idiot** café, the city's most relaxed hangout, and a block further on the **Yusupov** mansion, where Rasputin was murdered. Round the corner, to the right, is Theatre Square (Teatralnaya Ploshchad), home to the **Mariinsky** theatre, the famous **Conservatory** music school and the **Shamrock** Irish pub. From here, you'll see the aquamarine rococo **Cathedral of the Trinity**, one of the few churches in Russia that remained open throughout the communist era.

Bronze Horseman

Commissioned by Catherine the Great from the Parisian sculptor Etienne Falconet, this statue of Peter the Great was the inspiration for Pushkin's poem of the same name, and takes a more prominent place in the history of literature than of art. It took Falconet four years to cast, the delay being mainly due to a terrible artistic block he experienced in trying to capture Peter's face. In the end, it was cobbled together in an evening by his assistant Maria Callot. Almost as important as the statue is the plinth by Georg Velten, which holds Peter suspended between the earth and the air.

St Isaac's Cathedral

Isaakiyevskaya Ploshchad 1 (315 9732). Metro Gostiny Dvor or Nevsky Prospekt. **Open** 11am-6pm Mon, Tue, Thur-Sun; tours by arrangement. **Admission** $8; $4 students, under-17s. **Map p287 C5**

The history of the present incarnation of St Isaac's began in 1818, when an unknown veteran of the Napoleonic War sent Nicholas I an album of sketched designs for a new cathedral in various styles from Gothic to Chinese. Unexpectedly, the Tsar liked the proposals and Auguste Ricard de Montferrand suddenly found himself at the helm of one of Russia's most ambitious building projects. The whole thing took 40 years and almost as many design revisions. This is another story of extraordinary statistics: 100kg (220lb) of gold coated the central cupola; 70 workers died from inhaling mercury vapour during gilding; 150 murals painted by 22 artists; 60 mosaics in the iconostasis; one hectare (2.47 acres) of floorspace; 16 years to decorate the interior alone. While the exterior impresses only because of its immense size, the frescoes and mosaics inside are superlative. Montferrand was destined never to see them: he died, bitter and disappointed, a month after the structural walls were finished. For a terrific view of the city, you can buy a ticket for the 'colonnade' (until 5pm), which allows you to walk around the outside of the dome. In a throwback to communism, cameras are still forbidden, lest you photograph 'restricted' areas of the city.
Bookshop. Information in English.

Nevsky Prospekt

St Petersburg's central artery was one of three main thoroughfares (the other two were Voznesensky and Gorokhovaya) that Peter the Great marked out on a map by placing one end of a ruler at the Admiralty spire and then slashing away with his pencil into the marshy hinterland. A band of peasants, soldiers, convicts, captured Swedes and Tartars, many of whom were forced to excavate dirt with their clothing due to lack of tools, were conscripted to make the Tsar's scrawl a reality. Nevsky Prospekt's first incarnation, Bolshoi Perspektivny Prospekt (Grand Perspective Street), was little more than a cutting in the forest. Later the road would be paved and extended to the **Alexander Nevsky Monastery** (Aleksandra Nevsky Lavra). Though it was now 4.5 kilometres (5.25 miles) long – the longest avenue in the city – Nevsky would have to wait until the late nineteenth century before it finally established itself as the commercial backbone of the city, a status it has maintained to this day.

The first stretch of the street, travelling east from the Admiralty and Palace Square, features its two oldest buildings, dating from the 1760s, the houses of Safonov (No.8) and Weimer (No.10). Further down, on a pillar of the school at No.14, a stencilled legend reads, 'Citizens, in the event of shelling, this side of the street is the most dangerous', preserved for posterity as a memorial of the Blockade. This section of Nevsky Prospekt culminates a little further on in the **Literaturnoye Café**, a bland tourist trap serving unremarkable food that was once the site of the Wolff et Beranger Café, where Pushkin met his second on the day of his fatal duel.

At the corner of Moika Kanal is Rastrelli's **Stroganov Palace**, built for one of the great

aristocratic families. Fairly restrained for Rastrelli, but still one of his greatest buildings, it has been appropriated by the **Russian Museum**. Across the canal is the ultra-luxurious **Taleon Club** in the mansion of the Yeliseyev brothers, among St Petersburg's richest nineteenth-century mechants.

The next portion of Nevsky is almost wholly given over to capitalist pursuits. On the right side you'll find the **English Fashion House**, located in the classically tinged, modernist Mertens building with its glazed arches, and **British Home Stores** in the claustrophobic new Nevsky 25 shopping complex. On the left is the **Minutka** sandwich joint, which is locked in a high-profile dispute with its one-time partner Subway. Then comes Bolshaya Konyushennaya Ulitsa on the left, home to many hi fi shops as well as Dom Leningradskoi Torgovli, an untidy, Soviet-style shopping arcade, followed by Malaya Konyushennaya Ulitsa, which was paved in 1997, making it St Petersburg's first pedestrianised street, though the lack of shops along its length makes for rather bleak strolling. Between the two streets, behind a summer street café, is the Lutheran Church, which was converted into a swimming pool during communist times, with a diving board supplanting the altar.

At this point Nevsky fans out to accommodate the **Kazan Cathedral** (*see below*), whose colonnades clasp the avenue like neo-classical tentacles. Across the road is the art nouveau Singer building, built for the Singer sewing machine company. It's a granite-faced masterpiece, whose most striking feature is a bulbous spire surmounted by two female figures supporting a globe bearing the Singer logo. The glass-panelled mini-tower, now clad in wooden boarding to prevent it falling down, could be illuminated as a built-in structural advert. The building now houses the sprawling, shopper-unfriendly **Dom Knigi**, the city's biggest bookstore. At this point, you can't really fail to notice the effusion of domes known as the **Church of the Saviour on the Blood** (Khram Spasa Na Krovi, *see below*)

Continuing down Nevsky Prospekt from the Catherine Canal past the **Nike** sportswear shop and **Chevignon** brings you to the **Grand Hotel Europe**, one of the plushest in the city. Looking through the window into the half-deserted wasteland of the hotel bar, **Sadko**, it's difficult to imagine its glory days in the early 1990s, when it was perhaps the only decent bar in the city and packed full of foreigners and prostitutes.

The road on which the Grand Hotel Europe stands, Mikhailovskaya Ulitsa, leads to one of St Petersburg's most striking ensembles, Mikhailovsky Ploshchad, usually known by its

Soviet name, Ploshchad Iskusstv (Arts Square). Designed by Rossi to be experienced as a whole, it includes the magnificent **Mikhailovsky Palace**, recently renovated back to its gleaming nineteenth-century health, the **Maly Theatre of Opera and Ballet** and the **Philharmonia**, opposite the hotel. The stern, neo-classical **Ethnography Museum** is a little further down Inzhenernaya Ulitsa. This surfeit of architectural beauty is presided over by none other than Alexander Pushkin, whose statue stands in the pretty central park, striking a curious 'Pass the scalpel, Nurse' pose.

A little further along Nevsky Prospekt to the right is **Gostiny Dvor**, the biggest department store in the city. With each arched and pilastered ochre façade almost a kilometre long, shopping here is a little like cross-country walking, though the visual effect of so much classical uniformity, courtesy of Vallin de la Mothe, is not unimpressive. The arcade to the right is St Petersburg's most famous gay cruising strip. Just across Nevsky Prospekt from Gostiny Dvor is the **Passezh** shopping arcade, home to St Petersburg's only half-decent city centre super-market. A little further along on the right is the finest *style moderne* building in the city, the **Yeliseyevsky** store, which went under the imaginative title of Gastronom No.1 in Soviet times. On the façade are campy statues representing trade and industry, though you'll probably find the gilt tracery of the interior far more alluring.

Crossing Nevsky Prospekt again brings you to one of its finest features, Ostrovskogo Ploshchad, a square designed by Rossi. Here stands the wheat-coloured, neo-classical bulk of the **Aleksandrinsky Theatre**, built between 1823 and 1832 as the centrepiece, with the **Russian National Library** to the right and the gardens of the **Anichkov Palace** to the left, one of whose pavilions is now a Gianni Versace showroom. In the centre of the square a chubby, maternal statue of Catherine the Great towers over her various minions and lovers, who sit at her feet.

Surrounding the famous theatre, which hosted premières of Gogol's *The Government Inspector* in 1836 and Chekhov's *The Seagull* in 1896, is the **Theatre Museum** and the **Varganova Ballet School**, whose alumni include Pavlova, Nijinsky, Nureyev and Baryshnikov. Behind is the perfectly proportioned Rossi Street.

Next on Nevsky is the Anichkov Palace itself. Built in 1741 by Rastrelli, when this stretch of the main street was still an empty wasteland, it fell into the hands of Catherine the Great's favourite, Gregory Potemkin, three decades later. Potemkin sold it twice, only for Catherine to buy it back on each occasion and re-donate it to him.

Across the Anichkov Bridge, with its four equestrian statues, is the chalky, crimson, neo-rococo **Beloselsky-Belozersky Palace**, built

---

Light reading, weighty columns: the **Kazan Cathedral**. *See page 196.*

in 1800. Dripping with ornamentation both within and without, it now hosts a tacky Russian folk show featuring a balalaika orchestra, with instruments ranging from the microscopic to bungalow-sized. Just past Carroll's Finnish fast-food emporium is the intersection with Vladimirskaya Ulitsa to the right (towards the Kuznechny Rynok) and Liteiny Prospekt to the left (towards the **Borey Art Gallery**, **Anna Akhmatova Museum** and the **Theatre on Liteiny**).

Past the five-star **Nevsky Palace Hotel**, whose concrete underground car park is so heavy that it has dragged the two buildings on either side to their deaths, you come first to Ulitsa Marata and then to Pushkinskaya Ulitsa, the contemporary art nerve centre of the city. Though the legendary Pushkinskaya 10 squat has lost its battle with property developers, the artists' colony has been offered pristine new premises. However, it's going to take a lot of 'redecoration' to mimic the grotty, decaying, putrid Pushkinskaya that Petersburgers all knew and loved.

At this point, Nevsky blossoms into the wide open expanse of Ploshchad Vosstaniya. A hoarding proclaiming 'Leningrad – Hero City' on top of the **Oktyabrskaya Hotel** competes for attention with a pixilated billboard flashing Marlboro ads. The square is dominated by Moskovksy train station, the second to be built in the city. At this point Nevsky Prospekt becomes Old Nevsky (Stary Nevsky), a more subdued and in many ways more stylish shopping street that exits the square to the west on the final leg of the road's four-and-a-half-kilometre (three-mile) trip to **Alexander Nevsky Monastery**.

Church of the Saviour on the Blood

Naberezhnaya Kanala Griboyedova 2A (314 4053 /315 1636). Metro Gostiny Dvor or Nevsky Prospekt. **Open** 11am-6pm daily. **Admission** $16; $11 students, under-17s; free under-12s. **Map p287 D4**
Commissioned by Alexander III to commemorate the death of his father the Tsar Liberator Alexander II, the Church of the Saviour on the Blood is one of the most incongruous sights on St Petersburg's skyline. Initially, all the designs submitted for the church were deemed 'not Russian enough': eventually it was constructed in an amalgam of Russian themes, superficially based on St Basil's in Moscow, between 1887 and 1907. In order to site the altar right on the point where Alexander was murdered, the church juts slightly into the Catherine Canal, giving it a strange, dislocated appearance. The church was reopened in 1997 after a post-Revolutionary hiatus of 60 years, during which it was used as a museum, a morgue and finally as a warehouse for theatre props; it was even slated for destruction at one point. The mosaics, which have just undergone a 20-year renovation, look almost too new and give a powerful impression of what the church must have been like when it was built.

Kazan Cathedral

Kazanskaya Ploshchad 2 (311 0495). Metro Gostiny Dvor or Nevsky Prospekt. **Open** 11am-5pm Mon, Tue, Thur-Sun. **Admission** $3; $1.50 students, under-17s. **Map p287 D5**

Modelled on St Peter's in Rome, Kazan Cathedral is St Petersburg's finest example of pure, cold, austere neo-classicism. Built between 1801 and 1811 by Andrey Voronikhin, formerly one of Count Stroganov's serfs, the cathedral was originally envisaged with another set of colonnades facing in the other direction, but the Napoleonic War scuppered these plans. The Kazan Cathedral has suffered immeasurably since the Revolution. First, the famous Lady of Kazan icon was removed and mysteriously vanished en route to Moscow only to miraculously show up in New York; then, in 1922, its 9,636kg (1,400lb) silver altar was cut into pieces and moulded into silver bullion. Finally, the obnoxious Museum of Religion and Atheism, now the **Museum of Religion**, was established in the church building, which set out to discredit religious belief with pictures of nuns and priests engaging in sex acts and an exhibit on the Spanish Inquisition featuring a cauldron with a pair of legs jutting out. The museum was radically toned down and discreetly tidied away into one corner when the cathedral was returned to the Church in 1991.

Alexander Nevsky Monastery

Founded by Peter the Great in 1710 to celebrate his victory over the Swedes, the **Alexander Nevsky Monastery** (Alexandra Nevsky Lavra) takes its name from that other great Swede-slayer subsequently awarded a sainthood for his pains. In 1797, the monastery was given *Lavra* status, elevating it to one of the country's élite ecclesiastic establishments. In 1918, it was shut down by the Bolsheviks and later turned into the Museum of City Sculpture. The monastery is located at the end of Stary Nevsky, opposite the concrete purgatory of the **Hotel Moskva**. While it's free to enter the grounds, you'll have to pay about $1.50 to go in to the Tikhvin Cemetery, located on the right just after you enter. Here you'll find the graves of Dostoyevsky, Mussorgsky, Borodin and Tchaikovsky. On the left is the Lazarus Cemetery, which offers a far less impressive selection of the famous dead: the architects Rossi, Quarenghi, Voronikhin and Starov. Deeper into the monastery, to the left, is the baroque **Church of the Annunciation**, and then the heart of the ensemble: the **Cathedral of the Trinity** (1790), built by Russian architect Ivan Starov. At the back of the monastery is the **Nicholas Cemetery**, which boasts no real stars but is an unmitigated joy to explore.

Cathedral of the Trinity

Nevsky Prospekt 179/2 (274 2635/tour bookings 277 1716). Metro Ploshchad Aleksandra Nevskogo. **Open** 10am-6pm Mon-Wed, Fri-Sun; tours by arrangement. **Admission** $2; $1 students. **Map p289 G6**
Built on the site of an older cathedral by Tressini that was in danger of falling down, the Cathedral of the Trinity is another example of the stark simplicity of the classicism of Catherine the Great. One of the few major churches in St Petersburg to completely break with the orthodox multi-domed plan, the interior is pretty much based on the Latin cross and is divided into naves by bulky pylons. Always packed with worshippers, the cathedral is worth exploring not only for the marble iconostasis and for Quarenghi's frescoes but for the heady atmosphere of ritual and devotion. *Guided tours in English.*

Towards the Field of Mars & the Summer Garden

Slinking away from the north-west corner of Palace Square is Millionnaya Ulitsa (Millionaires' Street). Home to the foreigners' colony in the first half of the eighteenth century, the street may have been named in honour of the burgeoning population of rich Germans from the Baltic provinces, who prospered during the Europhile reign of Peter the Great, even though the Russian aristocracy who later flooded in to snap up the fashionable riverfront property were far wealthier.

The first building you encounter on Millionnaya is the New Hermitage, erected between 1839 and 1852 to house the expanding Imperial art collection. The ten caryatid figures of Atlantis supporting the portico are almost comically over-opulent. After this, you cross the first bridge and carry on along the palace-laden length of the street to the **Marble Palace**, Millionnaya's best-known feature. This neo-classical box was one of the very few stone buildings in the city when it was constructed, faced with lilac marble from Karelia and the Urals and with even more extravagant use of marble for the interiors. The palace was a present from Catherine the Great to her lover Count Gregory Orlov and now houses the contemporary collection of the **Russian Museum**. The **Field of Mars** opposite began its life as a bog, later rising to become a parade ground for the nearby Pavlovsky regiment. In 1919, a memorial was added, dedicated to those who died in the Revolutionary struggle, and the park acquired its present appearance. It is still traditional for couples married here to clamber over the shrubbery here to be photographed beside the eternal flame. Across the Lebyazhya Kanavka is the famous Summer Garden, a favourite haunt of Alexander Pushkin. The garden dates back to early 1704, almost to the foundation of the city, and is the finest St Petersburg offers in the way of a ruminative or romantic stroll.

Right at the corner of the Summer Garden is the **Summer Palace** (*see below*), the oldest stone building in the city, constructed in the classic Petrine baroque style between 1710 and 1714. Other buildings in the Summer Garden include the Tea House, now an exhibition hall and souvenir shop, and the Coffee House, where you can buy rubbery schnitzel. Across from the main gates of the Summer Garden is the ill-fated **Engineer's Castle** (formerly known as Mikhailovsky Castle), where Paul I was murdered by conspirators just 40 days after he moved in. The castle is now part of the Russian Museum and a gay club roosts in one of its alcoves.

Engineer's Castle

Sadovaya Ulitsa 2 (210 4173). Metro Gostiny Dvor or Nevsky Prospekt. **Open** 10am-6pm Mon, Wed-Sun (last ticket 5pm). **Admission** $8; $4 students. **Map p289 E4**
The construction of the Engineer's Castle (also known as the Mikhailovsky Castle because it incorporated a church

devoted to St Michael) was intended as a way for Paul I to wipe his slate clean. In order to facilitate its construction, he tore down the wooden summer palace built by Rastrelli for Elizabeth I, the site of his birth. He also chose the architect that his mother Catherine the Great had mistreated and ignored: Vasily Bazhenov. But Bazhenov, now sick and old, wriggled out of the commission after supplying initial drawings and the job fell to Vincenzo Brenna. The idiosyncratic result, built between 1797 and 1800, is unique among buildings of the period: it has four contrasting façades following entirely different design principles. Such was the unbalanced Tsar's rush to take up residence that the masonry did not have time to dry out properly. A hot-plate device used to speed up the process caused the rooms to be blanketed in fog. After he was murdered, the rest of the royal family abandoned the castle and allowed it to fall into decay, leading Pushkin to write: '...sleeping in the fog-enveloped/Deserted tyrant's monument/Discarded palace given to the past'. *Shop. Guided tours and information in English.*

Summer Palace

Naberezhnaya Kutuzova 2 (314 0374). Metro Gostiny Dvor or Nevsky Prospekt. **Open** 10.30am-5pm Tue. **Admission** $3.20 foreigners; *group tour* (in Russian) $50 for 15 people. **Map p288 E3**
Built in 1710-14, Peter the Great's modest two-storey Summer Palace residence was one of the first stone buildings in St Petersburg and, by establishing the now ubiquitous brick-faced-with-stucco formula, was the model for almost everything that came afterwards. Both the exterior (plain ochre walls with mythological medallions by Andreas Schluter) and interior (small rooms, Dutch tiles and modest, almost bourgeois decorations) are remarkable for their simplicity. One room is set aside for Peter's lathes and other contraptions, including a huge device to measure wind speed, temperature and air pressure. The palace was the first building in the city to have running water, thanks to a system that was rigged up to the Summer Garden fountains. In the Summer Garden are pavilions where you can buy books and souvenirs.

Petrogradskaya, the Peter & Paul Fortress

The Petrogradskaya Storona (or Petrograd Side), the largest of four islands located in the Neva delta to the north of the city, is the historic birthplace of the city. This was where the peat-slicing incident took place (*see chapter* **History**), where the first buildings were erected and where Peter himself lived (in a cramped log cabin that is still preserved) through much of the early phase of St Petersburg's development. Even ten years into the grand experiment, the city was little more than a frontier outpost strewn across these northern islands. Only with the completion of the **Peter and Paul Cathedral** (*see below*) in 1733 and of the stone fortifications seven years later would it finally lose its ephemeral character. But Petrogradskaya would have to wait almost another two centuries before it really began to boom. With the building of the first permanent bridge to the island between 1897 and 1903 came a huge influx of wealthy traders, all hoping to spend their money on contemporary, stylish and modern housing. For this reason, Petrogradskaya is an explosion of the *style moderne*, with its main street, Kamennoostrovsky Prospekt, boasting some truly bizarre examples –

pseudo-Russian and pseudo-Gothic undulating façades unlike anything else in the city.

While there is now a wide choice of access points to Petrogradskaya, you are most likely to plump for the first to be built, the Trinity Bridge (Troitsky Most), which spans the Neva right by the Field of Mars. Once you have touched down on Petrogradskaya, it might be a good idea to take a detour down Petrovskaya Naberezhnaya to take in the contrasting joys of **Peter the Great's Isba** or log cabin (*see below*), with its minute rooms, glinting mica windows and unconvincing log-painted brickwork. A little further along is that Soviet relic the cruiser **Avrora** (*see below*), which sounded the opening shot in the Bolshevik coup.

However, the main attraction on Petrogradskaya remains the low-lying ramparts of the Peter and Paul Fortress, which is entered via a wooden foot-bridge and the Ivan Gate. In the *kassa* to the right, you can buy an all-in-one ticket to visit the museums and the cathedral for about $5. This entitles you to visit the rather incongruous **Museum of Gas Propulsion** around the corner, which will tell you more than you ever wanted to know about booster rockets, as well as all the museums further inside the fortifications (though it won't get you into the **Museum of Human Oddities**, a freak show in a tent featuring a wax model of Lolo Ferrari beside a woman with two heads). Down to the left, in the direction of the Neva, is the **Austeria** restaurant and bar. Continuing through Trezzini's miniature triumphal arch, St Peter's Gate, brings you into the inner sanctum of the fortifications, an area shaped like a hexagon with six protruding bastions, five of which bear the names of Peter's associates (Menshikov, Naryshkin et al), the final one (Gosudar, meaning 'sovereign') being reserved for Peter himself. Walking deeper into the compound, you'll come across the Engineer's and the Commandant's Houses to the left, both now part of the **Museum of the City**, with Mikhail Shemyakin's pinhead statue of Peter the Great sitting between. To the right is the baroque Peter and Paul Cathedral, the final resting place of the post-Petrine Tsars. Continue bearing right when you hit the courtyard and you'll come to the infamous Trubetskoi Bastion, once the interrogation HQ of the Tsarist police and later on of the Bolsheviks, which is now the Prison Museum.

Behind the fortress, just along the rampart known as the Kronwerk and facing the armaments of the **Artillery Museum**, you can take a 15-minute helicopter trip around town for $35. Afterwards, if you want to see animal misery on an unprecedented scale, pop along to the squalid St Petersburg's Zoo, which is also located on the Kronwerk to the left.

Leaving the fortress and heading down Kamennoostrovsky Prospekt brings you past the Hare Krishna Café Troitsky Most and into the heart of Petrogradskaya. Here is a plethora of shops and restaurants that tend to be a little cheaper than those in the centre. For good examples of *style moderne*, catch the apartment building spanning Nos.13, 16 and 20 and the weird, medieval house with towers at Bolshoi Prospekt 75. Continue all the way down Kamennoostrovsky to come to the Kirov Islands, three globules of land, on which is a beautiful, seemingly infinite network of parks.

Avrora
Petrogradskaya Naberezhnaya 2 (230 8440). Metro Ploshchad Lenina. **Open** 10.30am-4pm Tue-Thur, Sat, Sun. **Admission** free; *guided tour* $3.50, $1.50 students. **Map p288 E2**
One of St Petersburg's very few free attractions, the *Avrora* invites visitors on board to view the gun that fired the blank shot that started the Bolshevik coup. It now bears a brass plaque of congratulation for 'ushering in a new age of socialism'. More interesting than the commie memorabilia is the fact that this is a working nineteenth-century cruiser, which took part in the Russo-Japanese War of 1904-5. Cabins are done out just as they would have been a century ago. *Guided tours in English.*

Isba of Peter the Great
Petrovskaya Naberezhnaya 6 (232 4576). Metro Gorkovskaya. **Open** 10am-5pm Mon, Wed-Sun; tours by arrangement. Closed last Mon of month. **Admission** $2.50; $1.20 students. **Map p286 D2**
The miniature log cabin where Peter the Great lived during the construction of the Peter and Paul Fortress has now been encased in a red-brick sarcophagus and preserved for posterity. You can't enter the cabin itself but peering through the mica windows is enough to make you wonder how the six-foot-seven (two-metre) Tsar could possibly have squeezed himself into these extremely spartan matchbox-sized rooms. *Guided tours and information in English.*

Peter & Paul Cathedral
Peter & Paul Fortress, Petropavlovskaya Krepost 3 (232 9454). Metro Gorkovskaya. **Open** 11am-7pm Mon, Tue, Thur-Sun; tours by arrangement. Closed last Tue of month. **Admission** $3; free 6-7pm. **Map p286 C3/D3**
The most striking characteristic of the Peter and Paul Cathedral is its thin sliver of a spire that Peter had stipulated to Trezzini should be taller than the Ivan the Great Bell Tower in Moscow, at that time the tallest structure in Russia. This led to an emphasis on height and volume rather than grace and the huge tower seems divorced from the modestly proportioned church. Inside the church, the décor is truly horrible, with roof and pillar painted to imitate marble but turning out the colour of used chewing gum. Strewn all around are the sarcophagi of the post-Petrine Tsars, the latest addition being Nicholas II, laid to rest in an antechamber at the back in July 1998.

Vasilyevsky Island

According to Peter the Great's original conception of St Petersburg, the entire city was to have been compressed on to this modestly sized island, a clump of land that appears to have been inserted into the mouth of the Neva delta like a stopper. It was an insane, impractical idea, not only because the island, then still a century away from having a permanent stone bridge, would have been completely isolated during the spring thaw and the autumn freeze but also because of inevitable over-crowding and slicing winds. Peter decreed that his nobles build houses here, but most fled the island after just a few months, abandoning their half-built palaces and transforming Peter's ideal metropolis into a ghost town. It's on the tip of the island closest to the mainland – the little wedge of land known as the Strelka (spit) – that Peter's challenge seems to have been taken up anew, and here that you'll discover the most interesting features of the island. Crossing Dvortsovy Most from Palace Square you are immediately struck by the **Kunstkammer**, whose stately baroque outline is spoiled by a sheath of wooden hoarding around its polygonal tower and globe. When completed in 1734, this was Russia's first public museum, purpose-built to house Peter's collection of pickled freaks. In a special chamber upstairs, the museum now displays jars containing babies with two heads, withered limbs and shrunken torsos. According to well-placed sources, the cream of the collection is hidden away in storage and includes a collection of the biggest sexual organs in the land, all lopped off and preserved in spirit.

At the very end of the Strelka are two eccentric-looking rostral columns, whose outgrowths take the form of the prows of ships in imitation of the Roman custom of displaying battle trophies. These were installed to complement the imposing, temple-like Stock Exchange behind, now the **Naval Museum**. While the ensemble is impressive from a distance, up close it comes across as an empty exercise in immensity and columns. Venturing along Universitetskaya Naberezhnaya past the Kunstkammer takes you first to the Academy of the Arts, behind which are two good restaurants: the **Old Customs House**, whose clientele scatter Mercs all down the street, and **Academe**, also frequented by a nouveau riche set with a little less money but more youth.

After this, past the seated statue of Lomonosov, you'll come across the Twelve Colleges, located perpendicular to the river. Built between 1722 and 1742 to house the ministries of state set up by Peter, this simple, charming façade spans almost 400 metres (1,312 feet), is now occupied by the university. Recent renovations have added a decent bar and a good international bookshop.

A little further down the embankment is the **Menshikov Palace** (*see below*), the baroque mansion of Peter's 'favourite', Alexander Menshikov, which is far bigger and grander than anything the Tsar ever considered building for himself. This was where many of Peter's legendary, orgiastic 'assemblies' took place. Two sphinxes adorn the embankment outside the Academy of the Arts. They were carved out of synite in the thirteenth century BC and brought to Russia in 1832. Much of the rest of Vasilyevsky Island is just tatty, and the regular division of its roads into parallel lines

(a throwback to Peter's plan) seems dull and boring. It's very unlikely that you will ever need to venture beyond the Strelka, unless, of course, you are staying at the **Hotelship Peterhof**, moored on the island's northern embankment.

Menshikov Palace

Universitetskaya Naberezhnaya 15 (213 1112). Metro Vasileostrovskaya. **Open** 10.30am-4.30pm Tue-Sun; tours by arrangement only. **Admission** $5; $1 students. **Map** p287 B4

The friendship of Peter the Great and Alexander Menshikov went back to boyhood, when the latter had been a stable boy and later a street pie-seller. Speculation is rife that the two were lovers – they certainly shared concubines; Peter the Great's second wife Catherine was a Menshikov cast-off. This palace was built in classic Petrine baroque style, but on a greater scale than any other in the city, even those of the Tsar himself. Peter often borrowed it to receive guests and ambassadors. During the reign of Peter II, Menshikov fell from grace and was banished to Siberia. The palace is now part of the Hermitage Museum.
Café. Guided tours in English.

Smolny & around

A fair distance east from the centre of the city lies **Smolny Cathedral** (*see below*), casting its graceful, highly ornamented shadow down the length of Suvorovsky Prospekt. Its name literally translates as 'Tar' Cathedral after the tar yard that operated nearby at the beginning of the eighteenth century, and it is the main landmark of the eastern part of the city. Framing its soaring, dynamic form are the buildings of the adjacent convent. Nearby is the former Smolny Institute for Young Ladies of Noble Birth, best known as the place where Lenin plotted his coup in 1917. On Stavropolskaya Ulitsa is the Kikin Palata, another example of Petrine baroque, dating from 1714, though restored after bomb damage during World War II. Turning down Shpalernaya Ulitsa brings you to the Tavrichesky Palace, commissioned by Catherine the Great's lover and minister Gregory Potemkin (open by appointment only). Behind is the Tavrichesky Garden, featuring a sad, rusty but endearing Soviet playground.

Smolny Convent Cathedral

Ploshchad Rastrelli 3/1 (271 9182). Metro Chernyshevskaya. **Open** 11am-5pm Mon-Wed, Fri-Sun. **Admission** $3.50; $1 students. **Credit** MC, V.
Yet another of St Petersburg's buildings has sprung from the imagination of that master of flounce and froth, Bartolomeo Rastrelli. Much of the building work was finished after Rastrelli's death, meaning that much of the intended ornamentation was never completed and the planned bell tower was never even begun. Another amendment was the curious compressing of the cupolas, which now seem crushed up against the central dome. However, the cathedral remains hugely impressive, more augmented than diminished by its faults. Inside, the ravages and revolutions have left it entirely without décor and painted completely white, like an ecclesiastic operating theatre. A stairway to the right leads up to the roof and the second best view of the city (the best being St Isaac's Cathedral).
Shop.

Museums & Galleries

They may live in the shadow of the Hermitage, but St Petersburg's museums are a cornucopia of esoterica.

St Petersburg has a bewildering array of museums. The Soviet practice of calling everything a museum if it couldn't justifiably be bulldozed but didn't really have a place in the new world order has artificially padded out the grand total of around 60. Even if you subtract imposters like the Kazan Cathedral or the **Church of the Saviour on the Blood** (*see chapter* **Sightseeing**), there is still an intimidatingly large amount left over after you've seen the big ones: the **Hermitage** (*see page 204*) and the **Russian Museum**. However, the city's second-tier museums repay a small amount of extra effort with such wild and wonderful sights as jars of two-headed babies, prehistoric mammoths, copulating priests and nuns and Pavlov's slavering dog.

NB None of the museums listed accepts credit cards.

Art

Russian Museum

Inzhenernaya Ulitsa 4 (314 3448). Metro Gostiny Dvor or Nevsky Prospekt. **Open** 10am-6pm Mon; 10am-5pm Wed-Sun. **Admission** $8. **Map p287 D4**

The Russian Museum suffers an unenviable fate among Western tourists. They visit only if they have time after visiting the Hermitage and as a result tend to have gallery fatigue by the time they get there. This is patently unfair, as the Russian Museum is not only more manageable than the Hermitage (you don't need a global positioning system to find your way out), but also offers one of the best collections of Russian art in the world.

The Mikhailovsky Palace, where the majority of the exhibits are housed, was built between 1819 and 1823 by Carlo Rossi. It was turned into a museum in 1898, when it was decided to give the Russian paintings in the Hermitage a home of their own. The original palace now exhibits Russian painting and sculpture up to 1900 while a neo-classical annexe houses the museum's twentieth-century collection. Climb the spectacular ceremonial staircase in the main building and turn left to follow the chronological route, which begins with a couple of rooms of icons. Although visually striking, their unequivocal religious intent is undermined by the rather clinical, secular settting.

The opposite is true of the next rooms you come to, which exhibit ceremonial portraits and history paintings from the seventeenth and eighteenth centuries. Here, vast scenes of high drama and portraits of pompous aristocrats come into their own, hung in beautiful Imperial interiors with spectacular views over the Summer Gardens. Don't miss Karl Briullov's breathtaking version of the *Last Day of Pompeii*, the first Russian painting to acquire pan-European fame. On the ground floor, nineteenth-century artists turn their attention to contemporary society, at first with Aleksei Vanetsianov's paintings of peasants, who evidently had plenty of time to pose in carefully ironed smocks and elaborate headgear. Later, gritty reality takes over, culminating in *Barge Haulers on the Volga* by Ilya Repin, a vast scene of convicts pulling a river cargo that has become a landmark of Russian art. The Benois wing offers a welcome change, with works such as Valentin Serov's *Portrait of Ida Rubenstein*, in which the naked ballerina proudly brandishes the most angular knees and elbows in art history. Since 1991, the Russian Museum has also acquired the **Marble Palace** (Millionnaya Ulitsa 5; 312 9196), where contemporary exhibitions are held, the **Stroganov Palace** (Nevsky Prospekt 17; 311 8238) and the **Engineer's Castle** (Sadovaya Ulitsa 2; 210 4173).

Academy of Arts

Universitetskaya Naberezhnaya 17 (213 6496). Metro Vasileostrovskaya. **Open** 11am-6pm Wed-Sun. **Admission** $5; $2.50 under-17s. **Map p287 C4**

Here you'll be treated to three centuries of work by the Academy's student prize-winners and teachers. Much of it is clearly technical exercises with scant regard for taste: Professor Frolov's liver-ripping plaster sculpture *Prometheus*, for example, or the entire twentieth-century section, which is full of statues of happy, muscular workers and oils of grinning Red Army soldiers as hordes of student artists followed the dictates of socialist realism in an effort to graduate.

History

Museum of the Blockade of Leningrad

Solyanoi Pereulok 9 (273 7647/tour bookings 275 7208). Metro Chernyshevskaya. **Open** 10am-5pm Mon, Tue, Thur-Sun. Closed last Thur of month. **Admission** $2.50. **Map p288 E3**

A large exhibition hall full of militaristic memorabilia from the 900-day Siege of Leningrad, when the city survived through sheer will and by cooking up bags, cats, and anything else they could get their hands on. Some of the most moving exhibits include the black and white photographs of soldiers at the Front and dead bodies in the snow. Some displays, though, are dire, particularly the uniformed mannequins arranged around a hideous painting of the struggling proletariat.

Russian Political History Museum

Ulitsa Kuibysheva 2/4 (233 7048/7052). Metro Gorkovskaya. **Open** 10am-6pm Mon-Wed, Fri-Sun. **Admission** $6.40; $1.50 under-17s. **Map p286 D2**

Once a temple to the Communist Party, this is one of the few museums to have been comprehensively updated, and now has a lightly anti-Soviet feel. While it still contains lots of

Revolution memorabilia – souvenirs such as printing presses, subversive propaganda, banners and revolvers, from the heady days when Revolutionaries were Revolutionaries rather than bureaucrats – it also displays documents pertaining to the fall of communism, such as photographs of Boris Yeltsin standing on a tank outside the White House, and the giddy manifestos of new political parties.

St Petersburg History Museum

Peter & Paul Fortress, Petropavlovskaya Krepost 3 (238 4511). Metro Gorkovskaya. **Open** 10am-5pm Mon, 11am-4pm Tue, Thur-Sun. Closed last Tue of month. **Admission** $3; $1.50 students. **Map p286 D3**
The Peter and Paul Fortress houses a number of exhibition spaces, all of which fall under the auspices of the St Petersburg History Museum. In the **Engineer's Building**, an exhibition called Old Petersburg presents the visitor with a colourful mishmash of objects illustrating pre-Revolution St Petersburg (note the shop signs that once forested Nevsky Prospekt and the wonderful, early, German-made typewriters, telephones and sewing machines). The most interesting room is devoted to original designs of buildings by Giacomo Quarenghi. Nearby in the **Commandant's House**, you'll find an exhibition entitled the History of St Petersburg. Further along, in the **Trubetskoi Bastion** in the fortress's southern corner, is the **Prison Museum**. Built in 1872 (previously, prisoners were housed nearby in the so-called Secret House), the prison of the Trubetskoi Bastion contained 69 cells and two unheated punishment cells. Conditions here were so calculatedly terrible (total isolation, absolute silence, numbing cold, mind-shattering inactivity) that some found suicide preferable. English tours available.

Anna Akhmatova Museum

Naberezhnaya Reki Fontanki 34 (272 2211). Metro Gostiny Dvor or Nevsky Prospekt. **Open** 10.30am-5.30pm Tue-Sun. Closed last Wed of month. **Admission** $2. **Map p289 E4**
Generally speaking, literary museums are only for hardened devotees of the author or poet in question. Akhmatova's shrine is an exception, perhaps because the events of her life are still fresh in the memory and because the people she associated with, among them other poets of the Silver Age, the period of intense artistic flowering immediately before the Revolution, are also famous. She lived in only one of the rooms of the museum and wasn't very proud of it since it contained few books for fear they might incriminate her. Some items can really thrill or chill, such as Osip Mandelshtam's gulag certificate.

Blok Museum

Ulitsa Dekabristov 57 (113 8633). Metro Sadovaya or Sennaya Ploshchad. **Open** 11am-5pm Mon, Thur-Sun; 11am-4pm Tue. **Admission** $2. **Map p287 B6**
The poet Alexander Blok lived here with his wife, Lyubov Mendeleyeva (the actress and daughter of the famous scientist), in apartment No.21 on the fourth floor. The apartment remains much as it was in Blok's day. Two floors below, in apartment No.23 (where Blok's mother lived), is displayed photographs and other material relating to the Silver Age. A separate room contains the poet's death mask.

Dostoyevsky Museum

Kuznechny Pereulok 5/2 (164 6950). Metro Dostoyevskaya. **Open** 11am-5.30pm Tue-Sun. Closed last Wed of month. **Admission** $2.60. **Map p289 E6**
This museum, housed in the great man's flat, where he saw out his last days, is generally disappointing. Shiny and well-kept, it will appeal primarily to lovers of old books. Also displayed is the printed announcement of Dostoyevsky's death sentence (commuted) and Siberian exile (enforced), as well as a rusting pair of genuine prison-camp leg-irons.

Pushkin Museum

Naberezhnaya Reki Moiki 12 (314 0006). Metro Nevsky Prospekt or Gostiny Dvor. **Open** 11am-5pm Mon, Wed-Sun. Closed last Fri of month. **Admission** $2.50. **Map p287 D4**
Pushkin has always been a difficult figure for foreigners to understand (his poetry does not translate well), and this museum does not, at first sight, do much to explain the Pushkin phenomenon. The rather formal first rooms could have belonged to any moderately well-off Russian nobleman of the time. It is only when you reach Pushkin's study at the back of the house that the museum begins to prove itself. Here you'll find his extensive library of over 4,000 books, his collection of dandyish canes and the divan upon which he died on 29 January 1837, three days after returning from a duel against the Frenchman D'Anthes.

Theatre Museum

Ploshchad Ostrovskogo 6A (311 5243). Metro Nevsky Prospekt or Gostiny Dvor. **Open** 11am-6pm Mon, Thur-Sun; 1-7pm Wed. **Admission** $3.20. **Map p289 E5**
Only really interesting when something related to Meyerhold, Fokine or Diaghilev crops up: otherwise the museum's full of busts of playwrights and yellowing posters or fading photographs of once-famous actresses, which all begin to merge into one before very long. Ask the attendants to open the ballet room, which is the most compelling part of the museum, possessing, for example, the garish costumes from the first production of *Sleeping Beauty*.

Artillery Museum

Aleksandrovsky Park 7 (238 4704/232 0296). Metro Gorkovskaya. **Open** 10am-6pm Wed-Sun. **Admission** $4. **Map p286 D2**
There's a definite pro-Soviet tinge to this array of weaponry dedicated to the art of shredding the enemy from a safe distance. The best rooms are the smallest, such as those concerning the Napoleonic Wars or devoted to antiquated radio technology. There is a separate exhibition of small arms – the infamous Kalashnikov and some ornate pistols.

Naval Museum

Birzhevaya Ploshchad 4 (218 2502). Metro Vasileostrovskaya. **Open** 10.30am-4.35pm Wed-Sun. **Admission** $3.20. **Map p286 C3**
The first room of the museum is devoted to early Russian maritime history and is full of large reconstructed ships, log-books, anchors, compasses, insignia and short histories of the development of the Imperial fleet. After that, a series of smaller rooms charts the progress of the navy into a formidable defender of the Soviet Union against the NATO aggressor. What looks like a big green column as you mount the stairs is in fact a ballistic missile.

Arctic & Antarctic Museum

Ulitsa Marata 24A (311 2549). Metro Dostoyevskaya. **Open** 10am-5pm Wed-Sun. **Admission** $2. **Map p289 F6**
The Arctic section on the ground floor is much larger than the Antarctic section above. While neither is exactly stuffed full of gripping relics, the museum does all it can to convey what it must be like to be very alone and hideously cold short of sending you to live in Arkhangelsk. The emphasis is on polar exploration, flora and fauna, and the cramped and primitive conditions that Russian polar pioneers had to endure. Some exhibits are tentatively labelled in English, including the surgical tools one explorer used to operate on himself.

Kunstkammer

Universitetskaya Naberezhnaya 3 (218 0712/1412).
Metro Vasileostrovskaya. **Open** 11am-4.30pm Mon-Wed,
Fri-Sun. **Admission** $2.40; $1.60 under-17s.
Map p287 C4

Russia's first museum, officially opened in 1728, the
Kunstkammer hosts hordes of crouching, snarling primitives
or bare-breasted women indulging in occupations like hunting or basket-weaving under the glare of stone idols and buffalo skulls. The main section gives you a good idea of the
Imperial attitude to ethnography, and to the savage peoples
whose clothes, tools and weapons were tirelessly sought after
by Tsarist explorers – for example, the flaking Eskimo wet-
suits (which look totally inappropriate for freezing climates),
and the thousands of carefully labelled arrowheads and
spears. Closer to home are such gems as the Women and
Magic exhibit, which deals with the black arts in Russian peasant life. A separate ticket will get you into Peter the Great's
infamous 'babies in jars' exhibit, officially known as the
Anatomical Rarities Exhibition. Included in the ticket price is
admission to the Lomonosov Museum, located on the top floor
of the main building (not inside the tower).

Museum of Ethnography

Inzhenernaya Ulitsa 4A (219 1174). Metro Nevsky
Prospekt or Gostiny Dvor. **Open** 11am-4pm Tue; 11am-
6pm Wed-Sun; tours by arrangement. **Admission** $3.50;
$1.50 students. **Map p289 E4**

This is the place to be if you want a glimpse of traditional
Russia or of the ways of life of the 150 different peoples that
made up the old Soviet Union. Founded in 1934, the museum
contains material illustrating the cultures of the cattle-graz-
ing Ossetians, the fish-catching Kalmyks and the Slavs of the
Ukraine and Belorussia, with elaborate mock-ups of traditional log-houses crammed full of authentic household items.
Café. Information in English. Shop. Tours in English.

Zoological Museum

Universitetskaya Naberezhnaya 1 (218 0112). Metro
Vasileostrovskaya. **Open** 11am-5pm Mon-Thur, Sat, Sun
Admission $1.20. **Map p287 C4**

One of the oldest and largest collections of its kind, the
Zoological Museum (founded in 1832) contains stuffed exam
ples of every animal that you might ever wish not to meet in
the home, farmyard, sea, jungle or prehistoric forest.
Skulking around in the atmospherically dim rooms are
authentic mammoths (pulled out of the Siberian permafrost
in 1903) and a submarine-size blue whale – not to mention
various anonymous cats and chickens, and Peter the Great's
anaconda, his dog Titan and horse Lizetta.

Religious

Museum of Religion

Kazan Cathedral, Kazanskaya Ploshchad 2 (311 0495).
Metro Nevsky Prospekt or Gostiny Dvor. **Open** 12.30-5pm
Mon, Tue, Thur, Fri; 11am-5pm Sat; noon-5pm Sun.
Admission $3. **Map p287 D5**

Opened in 1932 in Nevksy Prospekt's main cathedral, what
used to be the Museum of Religion and Atheism (founded in
1932) still carries echoes of the Communist Party line on religion. Many of the exhibits (blood-curdling images of hell,
torturous-looking instruments of religious asceticism, pictures of nuns and monks copulating) were obviously originally selected to do for religion what the Museum of Hygiene
does for alcohol and sex. That said, the museum now offers
an interesting review of the colourful history of Christianity

*Thrills, chills and pillars at the **Arctic &***
***Antarctic Museum.** See p201.*

in Russia, and its collection of more than 5,000 icons dating
from the fifteenth to the twentieth centuries is a winner.
Expect a major reorganisation when the museum moves to
larger premises on Pochtamtskaya Ulitsa in 1999.

Science, technology & medicine

Bread Museum

Ligovsky Prospekt 73 (164 1110). Metro Ligovsky
Prospekt. **Open** 10am-5pm Tue-Sat. **Admission** $1.30.
Map p289 F5

One of the 13 museums in the world dedicated to bread
begins with early variants on millstones and ends with high-
tech German vacuum-packers. Also on display are examples
of the different types of flour used in bread baking.

Gas-Dynamics Laboratory Museum

Ioannovsky Ravelin, Peter & Paul Fortress (238 4664/
4540). Metro Gorkovskaya. **Open** 11am-5pm Mon; 11am-
4pm Tue-Sun. Closed last Tue of month. **Admission** $3;
$1.50 students. **Map p286 D3**

In the Peter and Paul Fortress, near the Ivan Gate, you can find
the improbably placed (and unalluringly named) Gas-
Dynamics Laboratory Museum, which once housed the original Soviet rocket-engineering programme in the 1930s and now
tells the story of Russian space travel. There are lots of boring
cross-sections of booster rockets, as well as segments of a
Soyuz space capsule.

Museum of Hygiene

Italianskaya Ulitsa 25 (210 8508). Metro Gostiny Dvor or
Nevsky Prospekt. **Open** 10am-6pm Mon-Fri. **Admission**
30¢. **Map p289 F5**

Set up in the 1920s, the euphemistically named Museum of
Hygiene is a kind of Soviet horror house of disease. Garish,
badly painted plaster or rubber models of various sensitive
parts of the human body demonstrate the perils of, for
instance, opening a bottle of vodka or entering into sexual
relations with another human being. Come here to wonder
at curiosities such as a nineteenth-century dentist's chair and
Pavlov's actual dog.

Commercial galleries

Borey Art Gallery

Liteiny Prospekt 58 (273 3693/272 8098). Metro Liteiny
Prospekt. **Open** noon-8pm Tue-Sat. **Admission** free.
Map p289 E5

Snug little gallery on Liteiny Prospekt. Past exhibitions have
ranged from photos by David Byrne to chaotic assemblages
from one of the city's best-known art factions, the Mitki.

The Manezh

Konnogvardeisky Bulvar 2 (312 8156). Metro Nevsky
Prospekt or Gostiny Dvor. **Open** 11am-6pm daily.
Admission from 70¢, depending on exhibition.
Map p287 C5

Expansive venue located in the former barracks of the Horse
Guards, which was given a concrete refit in the 1980s. Wide
range of art exhibitions, including an annual St Petersburg
contemporary showcase.
Café.

Pushkinskaya 10

Pushkinskaya Ulitsa 10, main entrance via Ligovsky
Prospekt 53 (164 5371). Metro Mayakovskaya or
Ploshchad Vosstaniya. **Open** call for details.
Map p289 F5

An artists' complex with no fixed opening times and no
admission charges. The complex contains a number of individual galleries including Gallery 21 (164 5263) and Gallery
103 (164 5353).

The Hermitage

With a history that's passed into legend and 25 Rembrandts to call its own, the Hermitage is one of the world's great art museums.

There are more myths and legends surrounding the Hermitage than any other museum in the world. The extraordinary thing is that the majority of them are true. It contains so many works of art that it would take you nearly a decade just to glance at each one. Its staff ate restorers' glue and boiled shoes to make soup in order to survive the Siege of Leningrad and hid priceless impressionist and post-impressionist paintings for half a century after World War II, despite international efforts to find them. And, most recently, its director appeared on national television walking through the museum in his overcoat to publicise its perilous financial state, which means that one of the world's greatest cultural institutions is not even heated properly. It is, therefore, with a certain amount of awe that you enter this intriguing building. You will immediately lose your bearings. You will also understand why there was a Russian revolution, for if ever there was a museum designed to showcase the indecent opulence of the Tsarist regime, this was it.

The origins of the Hermitage date back to the time of Peter the Great, who was the first of the Russian rulers to begin to buy art on a large scale. It was marine paintings by Dutch artists that captivated him – his growing obsession with all things nautical attracted him to finicky images of ships at sea. Peter also bought Rembrandt's *Farewell of David and Jonathan*, which remains one of the highlights of the Hermitage's Dutch collection.

However, despite his forays into the art world, Peter was more concerned with collecting the bottled anatomical freaks and pickled Siamese twins now housed in the Kunstkammer (*see chapter* **Museums & Galleries**), which is not particularly surprising – we are, after all, talking about a man who enjoyed practising amateur dentistry. It wasn't until Catherine the Great came to power that the Imperial art collection began to acquire international importance.

German by birth and education, Catherine was painfully conscious that she had no legitimate claim to the Russian throne, and her reign was characterised by frenetic activity to justify her position. Culture played a major role in this, and Russia witnessed a boom in the arts toward the end of the eighteenth century.

Catherine not only commissioned new works, but also cheekily bought entire collections from under the noses of other European governments. Her first major artistic venture was to purchase a collection of 225 paintings, which Friedrich II of Prussia had intended to buy but was forced to relinquish after the damaging effects of the Seven Years' War. Delighted both to snub Friedrich II and to boast of the healthy state of the Russian treasury, Catherine shipped the paintings to St Petersburg in 1764, marking the foundation of the Hermitage art gallery.

A frenzy of commissions and acquisitions ensued and Catherine's predatory patronage soon began to attract attention. When, in 1770, she acquired the collection of Pierre Crozat, which included Giorgione's *Judith*, Titian's *Danäe* and Raphael's *Holy Family*, there was a public outcry in France. Nine years later, the acquisition of the collection of Robert Walpole caused the British parliament to make desperate but fruitless last-minute attempts to keep the collection in England. Indeed, so great was British outrage at the sale that Russia refused to lend any Walpole paintings to British exhibitions until the late twentieth century, for fear they would be sequestered.

Thanks to Catherine's voracious patronage, the Hermitage was established as an art gallery of international importance by the 1770s and she decided to commission a new building attached to the Winter Palace to house it. Catherine called her new building the Hermitage, as it was a place to which she could retreat from the hustle of court life. Later, further extensions were added. Just to ensure widespread confusion generations later, these were named the Old Hermitage and the New Hermitage, the latter built by German architect Leo von Klenze in the middle of the nineteenth century.

Now the term Hermitage is used to describe the entire complex of buildings, from the original Winter Palace opposite the Admiralty, to the Hermitage Theatre at the far end of the embankment façade. The buildings are all interconnected and you walk vacantly from one to the next, barely noticing the transition as another acre of art come into view.

Young Woman with an Earring: One of the Hermitage's vast cache of Rembrandts.

The most important thing to do in the Hermitage is to decide what you want to see. With something approaching three million exhibits in 400 halls and a 20-kilometre (12.5 mile) walk ahead if you decide to visit them all, choices obviously have to be made. Remember, it is a museum of superlatives at every step. The malachite vase by the Council Staircase is the largest in the world. The paintings by Picasso and Matisse on the top floor were some of the most influential in the modern art movement. The Gonzaga cameo is one of the greatest treasures of antiquity. And, at the other end of the spectrum, the museum brews St Petersburg's worst coffee. Whatever route you choose, you will see incomparable riches, so decide what you most want to experience and then stick to the plan.

The majority of the collection is housed in the Winter Palace, a building that not only hosted some of the most extravagant functions ever held by Russian Tsars but was also the focus for the Revolution that toppled them. The State Rooms on the first floor are best reached via the ceremonial Jordan Staircase on the river façade of the building. Soon you find yourself blinking at mile after mile of glittering gilt, obscene amounts of marble and (for those wearing slippery soles) temptingly well-polished parquet floors. The drama of the history associated with so many of these halls is intense. It was, for example, in the White Dining Room in the northern wing that Kerensky's Provisional Government was arrested by the Bolsheviks, who stopped the clock on the mantelpiece at the moment when the Provisional Government was dissolved. Nearby, the beautiful circular rotunda with its covered dome was where the museum's future director, Boris Piotrovsky, met with a fellow curator by night during World War II to exchange knowledge that both believed might be lost to humanity if they should starve to death in the siege. More chillingly, the Hermitage library is situated directly over an old mortuary.

It should be mentioned at this point that the fate of the Hermitage during World War II provides some of the most heroic episodes in museum history. Hitler invaded Russia on 22 June 1941 and nine days later half a million of the Hermitage's exhibits were sent by train to Sverdlovsk (now Ekatrinburg) in Siberia. This was arguably the most efficient cultural evacuation in history and demanded enormous physical and mental effort: the curators packed the items round the clock, frequently developing nosebleeds as they were stooping for such long stretches of time. They would lie down for a few minutes to stem the flow, and then rush back to the boxes. Later, with most of the museum's treasures hidden in Siberia, curators would still take guided tours around the building, describing what usually hung on the bare walls to maintain morale. Even during the Siege of

The lavish **Winter Palace**.

Leningrad, the nadir of the Hermitage's history, the staff didn't lose their fighting spirit: birthdays of curators were still celebrated, on one occasion with a bottle of 100 per cent proof eau de cologne, donated by the director to help wash down some frozen breadcrumbs that his brother had brought back from the Front. Hearing such stories, you begin to appreciate why Russia is so reluctant to return the 'Trophy Art', which the Red Army removed from Germany during and after the war. The question of the restitution of the Trophy Art became the fiercest cultural dispute of the 1990s, and remains unresolved.

Moving on to the collection itself, the enfilade of rooms running perpendicular to the river, starting at the carriages on display in the Field Marshall's Hall, is unmissable. Be sure to read the small print: Peter the Great's Throne Room, for example, was not built until a century after his death. The 1812 Gallery, however, really is what it's cracked up to be – an extraordinary collection of portraits of all the Russian military leaders who fought in the campaign against Napoleon. The portraits are the work of George Dawe, the most famous English artist in Russia. The fact that British tourists have never heard of him never ceases to disappoint their tour guides. Dawe's portraits are hung floor to ceiling, with blank spaces when he didn't know what a particular general looked like. The 1812 Gallery was one of the rooms damaged in the fire of 1837, when the building suffered enormously, but the priceless contents were saved by devoted members of staff.

Leaving the State Rooms, you are faced with a bewildering array of options. You could go back down to the ground floor to see the Classical and Egyptian Antiquities, passing (and not stopping at) the disastrous café. This section of the museum also houses the monumental Kolyvan Vase, which would crash through the floor if it was placed on any higher level. The Kolyvan Vase, an elliptical jasper bowl over five metres (five yards) long and three metres wide, took 11 and a half years to make and 154 horses to pull to the port at Barnaul for embarkation to St Petersburg. The journey to Barnaul had to take place during winter, as it was feared the bridges might collapse under the weight of the vase: instead it was hauled across frozen rivers. When it arrived in St Petersburg, it was housed in temporary structures until the walls of the new Hermitage were literally built around it.

Despite the attraction of seeing something as ludicrously immovable as the Kolyvan Vase, by now the pull of the paintings will be proving irresistible. For a chronological route (though it will take you years unless you skip the odd decade), make your way to the Pavilion Hall on the first floor, where you can see the Hermitage's most tasteless exhibit – the Peacock Clock, which was given to Catherine the Great by her lover Potemkin. The clock, a vast three-dimensional affair in a large glass case, tells the time in a completely incomprehensible fashion by various mechanised means including – get this – a rotating mushroom. Moving swiftly on, you will reach the Renaissance wing, straight ahead, or the Dutch wing, on your right.

After some time spent in these two wings, you really begin to appreciate the strengths of the Hermitage collection. The building itself is so large that the museum's two paintings by Leonardo da Vinci, the *Benois Madonna* and the *Madonna Litta*, are exhibited in a spectacular hall all of their own. Elsewhere, no fewer than 25 paintings by Rembrandt are on show – about 20 more than in the average national gallery. These include one of Rembrandt's most famous works, *Danäe*, which was severely damaged after a disenchanted nationalist from the Baltic states threw acid at it in 1985. Dramatic photographs taken after the event show the image disappearing off the canvas in murky streams of paint. The Hermitage immediately embarked on the most ambitious painting restoration project ever; the results were revealed in 1997 in an exhibition that included photographs documenting every stage of the restoration. The painting may no longer be a bona fide Rembrandt but it does confirm that, even without modern Western technology, the Hermitage's restoration department remains one of the best in the world.

Just when you thought that you no longer had the capacity to be amazed, the second and final floor of the Hermitage takes away any breath you may have left. It is here that the outstanding impressionist and post-impressionist paintings collected by Sergei Shchukin and Ivan Morozov are on display. Other museums have two or three paintings by either Matisse or Picasso. The Hermitage has two or three rooms of paintings by Matisse and Picasso. Originally thought decadent and morally subversive by the Soviets, they were only put on display after international pressure to do so, and even then, were hung on the second floor, in the former quarters of the ladies in waiting, in the hope that nobody would actually find them. They remain in the most inaccessible part of the building, reached via an undistinguished staircase that is not even lit properly.

Shchukin and Morozov were two Moscow merchants whose family fortunes came from the textile industry. Both began to buy modern art on a large scale in the early years of the twentieth century, and they were soon commissioning vast works to decorate their mansions from the most innovative contemporary French artists. Their passion for patronage rivalled that of any of the more established aristocratic families. As the famous opera singer Fedor Chaliapin said, 'I have never encountered anything equal to the lavishness of the Russian merchant. I do not believe Europeans could have any idea of its scale.'

The most famous of all the Shchukin and Morozov acquisitions was Shchukin's purchase of two huge canvases from Matisse: *Music* and *Dance* in a transaction that has now become legendary. Shchukin commissioned the two works in early 1909, but soon got cold feet as he had three young girls staying and no longer felt that he could flank his stairway with enormous canvases of naked men. He asked Matisse to paint clothed girls instead. The painter refused and, after several months, much public controversy, and extensive vacillations on the part of Shchukin, the two panels were sent to Moscow as originally planned. Shchukin continued to agonise about the prominent nudity of the flautist and decided to paint out the hapless musician's private parts with his own hand. When, a few months later, Matisse came to Moscow to help rehang the panels, he apparently examined the changes, shrugged and declared, 'It doesn't change anything.' One wonders whether the flautist would agree.

The Hermitage

Dvortsovaya Naberezhnaya 34 (311 3420/3465). Metro Nevsky Prospekt or Gostiny Dvor. **Open** 10.30am-5pm Tue-Sun (last admission 4pm). **Admission** $10; group discounts; under-16s and students free. **No credit cards. Map p287 C4/D4**
Bureau de change. Café. Shops. Tours by arrangement.

THE ACTIVE ISSUE NO.172   model naomi campbell photographer elfie semotan january/february 1998

£2.50 US $6.75

9 770262 357037

i-Deas,fashion,clubs,music,people

steady...

Subscribe now to i-D to receive 12 issues
full of the latest i-Deas, fashion, clubs, music and people.

Entertainment

St Petersburg is known as the culture capital of Russia – with good reason.

The *St Petersburg Times* publishes a listings supplement on Fridays that gives details, in English, of the city's entertainment events.

Ballet

St Petersburg is undoubtedly the world's classical ballet capital, with a tradition dating back to the 1750s. Many of the great ballets were created here by the Frenchman Marius Petipa, and the city was once home to such legendary figures as Anna Pavlova and Vaclav Nijinsky. It was also in St Petersburg that George Balanchine began his career, which flourished when he emigrated to the US. Although the recent political changes have brought financial stress to artistic institutions, the ballet here remains world-class. And with the current stable of superb young dancers at the Mariinsky, St Petersburg's ballet star is unlikely to wane in the foreseeable future.

Companies

Eifman Company
The city's only contemporary troupe, which recently celebrated its 20th anniversary, has an enormous following in St Petersburg and abroad. It applies a rather superficial modern gloss to classical ballet styles, with a focus on Russian themes. The troupe's April 1998 première at City Center, New York, received top reviews. 'The world has been waiting for its next great choreographer,' gushed the reviewer. 'He is Boris Eifman.'

Valery Mikhailovsky Male Ballet
Classical ballet spoofed in a witty and intelligent manner: men sporting tutus, pointe shoes and all.

Mariinsky Ballet
The Mariinsky Ballet (known abroad as the Kirov) is the most eminent classical ballet company in the world. Recently, a clutch of new faces have also made it one of the youngest. The sheer talent of Diana Vishneva, Svetlana Zakharova and Yuliana Lopatkina is stunning audiences from New York to London, while the outstanding charm and innate musicality of Altynai Asylmuratova continues to delight. The male stars include Farukh Ruzimatov, an eccentric mover with flamenco fire, and Igor Zelensky, a wunderkind with the potential to rival Russia's balletic greats.

Venues

Many of the city's major venues host classical music and opera performances as well as ballet.

For the Mussorgsky Theatre, the Rimsky-Korsakov Conservatory Theatre, the Mariinsky Theatre and the Hermitage Theatre, *see below* **Music: Classical & Opera**.

Oktyabrsky Concert Hall
Ligovsky Prospekt 6 (275 1275/1273). Metro Ploshchad Vosstaniya. **Open** 11am-8pm performance days only **Performances** 7pm. Tickets $2.50-$250. **No credit cards. Map p289 F4/5/6**
St Petersburg's largest dance venue, the new Oktyabrsky Hall hosts performances by the Boris Eifman Company and Valery Mikhailovsky Male Ballet, as well as touring companies such as New York's Eliza Monte Dance. The plain yet attractive modern theatre and comfortable non-obstructed viewing – the rows of seating are sufficiently inclined – make for enjoyable dance watching.

Heavy dub

A common practice in St Petersburg cinemas, which has thankfully died out in Moscow, is simultaneous dubbing. Astonishingly, this involves someone at the back of the cinema growling a live translation into a microphone while the film is running. Due to the translator being dispossessed of the mental processes required for simultaneous interpretation, the Russian translation comes just after the screen dialogue. The overall result: wickedly awful translations, no concessions to the finer dramatic points and a complete lack of differentiation between male and female voices.

GREAT FILM MOMENTS RUINED BY SIMULTANEOUS DUBBING
1. Greta Garbo's death scene in *Camille*.
2. The scene in *Broadway Danny Rose* in which Woody Allen and Mia Farrow try to take refuge from gangsters in a warehouse storing floats for the Macy's Day Parade.
3. Practically all of *Grease*, particularly the songs.
4. *Casablanca*'s famous 'Play it, Sam' scene.
5. Michael Palin's dialogue in *A Fish Called Wanda*.
6. The climax of *Tootsie*.
7. Most of *Some Like it Hot*.

*Hey, it's tutu time. The Kirov Ballet takes to the stage of the **Mariinsky Theatre** for another*

Children

PRACTICALITIES

The only restaurants with baby seats are in major hotels and fast-food establishments, with rare exceptions. Baby-changing areas are non-existent. Baby food and formula and other necessities such as nappies and bottles are readily available in shops and pharmacies (*apteki*) throughout the city; they are marked with a green cross.

BABYSITTERS

The St Petersburg International Women's Club keeps a nanny register – call Michelle Dobbins, the co-ordinator, on 301 3136. Your hotel may also provide a babysitting service.

Entertainment

St Petersburg's parks and playgrounds can be spartan and/or furnished with old equipment. Among the best is the Alexander Garden near the Admiralty, a large park with a good playground, sandpit and sledging ramp, and the Mariinsky Gardens near Mariinsky Palace, which has a rather shabby playground but a great sandpit.

Palace Square is a reliably relaxed place to take the kids. This is where toy manufacturers, confectioners and athletic equipment companies hold carnival-type launches, usually in the summer. Several vendors offer horse-drawn cart rides – about $5 for a jaunt round the square. Older children enjoy inline skating here; the smooth granite slabs and the ramp beneath the entrance to the Winter Palace make for a wonderful practice run. The Neva Embankment is another good, cost-free place to take kids in central St Petersburg. There are boats and barges to ogle and monuments and statuary to clamber on. With no one to bark 'don't touch', kids can even climb up the Palace Bridge lions for a photo. There are pony rides along here, too, usually from Admiralty Embankment.

Central Circus

Naberezhnaya Reki Fontanki 3 (210 4390). Metro Nevsky Prospekt. **Open** Sept-May daily; performance times vary. **Tickets** $1-$2. **No credit cards. Map p289 E4**
This is a true daredevil one-ring show, complete with tigers riding motorbikes, illusionists and trapeze artists.

Children's Ethnographic Centre in the Ethnographic Museum

Inzhenernaya Ulitsa 4/1 (210 4715). Metro Gostiny Dvor. **Open** 10am-5pm Tue-Sun. Closed Mon, last Fri in month. **Admission** $1; 50¢ children. **No credit cards. Map p289 E4**
Instructors teach children handicrafts such as pottery, weaving and printmaking on Saturday and Sunday, from 11am to 5pm. Afterwards, explore the museum's collection of Russian folk art and décor.

soaring night of pointes, pirouettes and pas-de-deux. See page 216.

Leningrad Zoological Park

Aleksandrovsky Park, Kronversky Prospekt entrance (232 3145). Metro Gorkovskaya. **Open** *summer* 10am-6pm. **Admission** $1.50; 80¢ children; free under 2s. **No credit cards. Map p286 C2**

An elderly collection featuring interesting Siberian species. The human wildlife outside the enclosures, throwing sweets at the animals and selling rides on sad-looking camels, is more engaging, but annoying with it.

Museums

Of the places detailed in the **Museums** chapter (*see page 200*), the best for children are the **Arctic & Antarctic Museum** (gruesome auto-surgery), the **Kunstkammer** (but avoid the disturbing foetuses) and the **Zoological Museum** (40,000 stuffed species and those famous mammoths).

Transport Museum

Sadovaya Ulitsa 50 (315 1476). Metro Sadovaya or Sennaya Ploshchad. **Open** 11am-5.30pm Mon-Thur, Sun. **Admission** 60¢; 30¢ children. **Map p287 C6**

Wax Museum

Beloselsky-Belozersky Palace, Nevsky Prospekt 41 (315 5636). Metro Nevsky Prospekt. **Open** 11am-6.30pm daily. **Admission** $2.40 per exhibition. **Map p287 D5**

Shopping

The best place to shop for children's clothing, shoes and toys is the **House of Leningrad**

Trade (DLT, *see chapter* **Shopping**). While most toys on display are Western and expensive, poke behind counters and you'll find a selection of locally produced wooden games, dolls and model cars. For an excellent and functional souvenir, buy a pair of woollen *valenki*: thick, warm boiled-wool boots with rubber bottoms that Russians claim contributed to their World War II victory (because their feet stayed warm during the Blockade). Here, they come in children's sizes and colours, and cost only about $10.

Theatres

There are dozens of children's theatres scattered throughout the city, and many theatres stage morning performances for kids; unfortunately, most close for summer. A selection of the best children's theatres are listed below. None accepts credit cards. Note that the puppet theatres are not dumb shows.

Bolshoi Puppet Theatre *Ulitsa Nekrasova 10 (273 6672). Metro Chernyshevskaya.* **Tickets** $1-$1.50. **Map p289 F4**

Children's Philharmonic *Ulitsa Dumskaya 1-3 (219 4175). Metro Gostiny Dvor.* **Performances** noon, 3pm, Sat, Sun. **Tickets** $1-$2.40. **Map p287 D5**
Concerts, puppet shows and plays for babies to teens. The venue is a bit dingy but enthusiastic. Professional performances are well attended by Russian families.

Marionette Puppet Theatre *Nevsky Prospekt 52 (311 1900). Metro Nevsky Prospekt.* **Tickets** $1-$1.50. **Map p287 D5**

Puppet Story Theatre *Moskovsky Prospekt 121 (298 2263). Metro Moskovskiye Vorota.* **Performances** Mon-Fri, Sun; call for times. **Tickets** $1-$2. **Map p287 D6**
Well-done, creative and funny marionette performances, including Russian variants of classical fairytales.

Zazerkalye Children's Theatre *Ulitsa Rubensteina 13 (112 5135). Metro Dostoyevskaya or Vladimirskaya.* **Tickets** $1-$1.50. **Map p289 E5**

Banyas

As one St Petersburg masseur and *banya* guru put it, you go to the banya to 'talk, forget about life, get things off your chest or simply to listen to other people. But many people come for the *kaif*, the 'high' that the banya can bring. When you hear the music begin deep inside, you know that the banya has worked its magic.'

There are around 70 public bathhouses in St Petersburg, of varying prices and standards. Most of those listed in the *Yellow Pages* are good, and many have a separate, 'luxury' floor that is cleaner and quieter but can cost up to $35. There will always be a market for the standard version, where a session of approximately two hours costs between $1.50 and $5. The banyas listed here have facilities for men and women.

Banya 24
Laboratornaya Ulitsa 9 (540 5821). Metro Ploshchad Lenina. **Open** 8am-10pm Mon, Tue, Fri-Sun. **Admission** 70¢ per hour; luxury $5 for 90 mins.
Some like it hot, some like it really hot, and some like it at Banya 24. There are men-only and women-only days, so check first. Banya 24 is next door to the horrible Gigant Hall; you'll pass the Kristy Prison on the way.

Banya 45
Pereulok Makarenko 12 (114 3447). Metro Sennaya Ploshchad or Sadovaya. **Open** 9am-9.30pm Wed-Sun. **Admission** $1 for 90 mins; luxury $6.50 for 2 hours (men only).
Wood-heated banya with an unusual cold plunge pool. Rumour has it that the fun really begins after closing time.

Nevskiye Bani
Ulitsa Marata 5-7 (311 1400). Metro Mayakovskaya. **Open** 8am-10pm Thur-Sun. **Admission** $2.40 for 90 mins. **Map p289 E5/6**
A huge, grey temple to sweat. It's not the cleanest banya in the city, but it's central and has plenty of room.

Yamskiye Bani
Ulitsa Dostoyevskogo 9 (312 5836). Metro Dostoyevskaya. **Open** 9am-9pm Wed-Sun. **Admission** $1-$1.50 for 90 mins. **Map p289 E6**
Excellent; friendly in a gruff sort of way, Yamskiye has cubicles for privacy and the consumption of edibles.

Znamenko Banya
Ulitsa Znamenskaya 8 (427 7377). Metro Baltiiskaya, then train to Peterhof. **Open** 9am-11pm daily. **Admission** $3.20 per hour.
This banya is so far from the centre of town that even the

staff don't know the address, though they'll gladly tell you how to get there. Highly recommended, especially for private bookings. Phone ahead to find out the men's and women's days. The $3.20 price is for the bog-standard 'communal' banya; it can cost anything up to $35 for the luxury version.

Film

As a location, St Petersburg has more to offer than Moscow, with the result that several films have been shot here in recent years, including the James Bond flick *GoldenEye* and the 1997 Hollywood remake of *Anna Karenina*. It used to be cheap to make films in the city's Lenfilm studio, where sections of Sue Potter's *Orlando* were made, but not any more. Only one of Lenfilm's 12 lots is currently devoted to film-making – the rest are rented out for parties or used as furniture salesrooms.

Unless there's a real blockbuster on release, cinemas tend to have two evening screenings. All venues listed have slightly run-down bars selling Soviet-style snacks and instant coffee, with the exception of Kristall Palace, whose café-bar is somewhat plusher. All cinemas have a no smoking policy, and none accepts credit cards.

Avrora
Nevsky Prospekt 60 (315 5254). Metro Gostiny Dvor. **Tickets** $1.50-$5. **Map p289 E5**
Named after the battleship that started the Bolshevik Revolution, this cinema is another little hunk of the Soviet legacy. Its large, unreconstructed auditorium combines ugliness with lack of comfort. In an attempt to turn the place into a mulitplex, films are sometimes shown in the café, but the sound is poor and employees are constantly shuffling about.

Barrikada
Nevsky Prospekt 15 (312 5235). Metro Nevsky Prospekt. **Admission** $1.60-$5. **Map p287 D4/5**
Also housing a rather natty billiard club, this characterless barn of a cinema often champions relatively unusual work (for St Petersburg) such as Lynch or Bergman but compensates for this with mountains of dross.

The Kolezei
Nevsky Prospekt 100 (272 8775). Metro Mayakovskaya. **Tickets** $1.60-$3. **Map p289 F5**
A truly gigantic place, more of an amphitheatre than a cinema, the Kolezei (Coliseum) can seat about 3,000 people. But the only time it ever does these days is during morning meetings for various St Petersburg mystics when thousands of old women show up hoping for a cure for arthritis.

Kristall Palace
Nevsky Prospekt 72 (272 2382). Metro Mayakovskaya. **Tickets** $3-$15. **Map p289 E5**
Formerly the hideous Soviet Oktyabr cinema, this is now St Petersburg's only modern joint, showing mostly block-busters. Ticket prices can be as high as $15, depending on the film. Morning showings cost less, around $5.

Leningrad
Potemkinskaya Ulitsa 4 (272 6513). Metro Chernyshevskaya. **Tickets** $1-$5. **Map p288 F3**
A little off the beaten track, by the Botanical Gardens, this is a huge cinema that is practically always empty.

Molodyozhny

Ulitsa Sadovaya 12 (311 0045). Metro Gostiny Dvor.
Tickets $1.30-$3. **Map p289 E5**
A two-cinema complex that sometimes presents interesting mini-festivals based around the work of a single actor or director (Pierre Richard, Alain Delon, Von Sternberg.) Like so many in St Petersburg the cinema itself is run down, squalid and the seats are uncomfortable.

Spartak

Ulitsa Saltykova-Shchedrina 8 (273 7913). Metro Chernyshevskaya. **Tickets** $1-$5. **Map p288 F3, p289 F4**
St Petersburg's only art-house repertory cinema is located in an old church. The films are good, ranging from Cocteau to Alfred Hitchcock, though the prints often look as if they have been around the world twice and then chewed by a domestic animal. Some films are pirate videos projected on a tiny screen. The automatic volume control turns up the silence so loud that it sounds like a blast of white noise.

Gay & Lesbian

In Soviet times, the Philharmonia and the Mariinsky Theatre were the two big meeting places for gay men and women. It was the high arts that did it for us back then. Now, there is a (relative) proliferation of gay clubs and plenty of gay parties. The law that criminalised homosexual activity has been repealed. Gay power is now taking its rightful place once again in the city of Peter the Great (who was, incidentally, bisexual). Blue (the Russian version of pink in this context) is increasingly the colour of the cultural capital.

ADVICE & INFORMATION

The St Petersburg Gay & Lesbian Association, Kriliya (Wings), is the city's oldest lesbian and gay organisation. It can provide advice, help and up-to-date information on gay services in the city, including accommodation, and some of the staff speak English. Call 312 3180 or e-mail krilija@ilga.org.

Clubs

69

2-ya Krasnoarmeiskaya Ulitsa 6 (259 5163). Metro Tekhnologichesky Institut. **Open** 10pm-6am Tue-Sun.
Performances 2am. **Admission** varies; up to $7 men; $15 women.
The city's premier gay venue – a tastefully decorated, subdued place that advertises itself on street level with full-length images of sailors that recall Fassbinder's *Kirill*. The clientele consists mostly of gay men but there are also lesbians, a bevy of trendy fag-hags and straight male party animals. Up a mysterious-looking spiral staircase is a dark room (which, incidentally, is off-limits to women), the first of its kind in Russia.

Cabare Club

The Sailors' Club, Ploshchad Truda 5 (312 0934). Metro Gostiny Dvor. **Open** 10pm-6am Fri, Sat. **Performances** 2am. **Admission** 10pm-midnight free; after midnight $5.
Map p287 B5
It is nicely symbolic that this club is situated in the city government's sailing club, a big old building housing sailors'

barracks. It's a tastefully done, spacious place, though the DJs are over-fond of Russian pop and Eurodance. A young, progressive crowd.

Jungle

Ulitsa Blokhina 8 (238 8033). Metro Gorkovskaya. **Open** midnight-6am Fri, Sat. **Admission** $3.50-$6. **Map p286 B2/C2**
A disco for gays and lesbians. Pop, commercial house, Eurodance, Russian dance music.

Vodelei

Aquarius, Inzhenernaya Ulitsa 8 (219 2895). Metro Gostiny Dvor. **Open** 9pm-6am daily. **Admission** up to $2.50. **Map p287 D4, p289 E4**
Nicely located in a portal of the Mikhailovsky Castle, Vodely tries to create an atmosphere of Imperial luxury. However, the grandeur is skin-deep and decidedly plastic (particularly the flowers on the wooden trellis that makes up the Venetian-style courtyard).

Cruising

Historically, the central parks were the best places to meet those 'with that special gaze'. It's pretty much the same today, but keep your wits about you: robberies are not uncommon.

Gostiny Dvor under the colonnade along Porinnaya Liniya.
The best-known cruising area in town. Busiest 10pm-midnight.

Yekaterininsky Sad *Nevsky Prospekt.* **Map p289 E5**
An all-day, all-night cruising spot, at its busiest from 9pm to midnight.

Yamskive Bani *Ulitsa Dostoyevskogo 9 (312 5836). Metro Dostoyevskaya.* **Open** 9am-9pm Wed-Sun. **Admission** $1-$1.50 for 90 mins. **Map p289 E6**
These public baths aren't an official gay venue. Cruising used to happen on the second floor but due to renovation has now moved to the ground. Straight men go just to bathe but are tolerant. Not a particularly clean place, but fun.

Lesbian St Petersburg

There's not much, but lesbians often also hang out in predominantly male places such as **Jungle** or **69** (*see above*).

Cafe Kapris *Ulitsa Krzhizhanovskogo 1/3 (584 0950). Metro Ulitsa Dybenko.*
Lesbian parties are held here from 6 to 10pm on Sundays. It's a bit of a hike from the city centre, though.

Grechniki *Naberezhnaya Kanala Griboyedova 28 (219 4291). Metro Gostiny Dvor or Nevsky Prospekt.* **Open** 7pm-6am Wed, Thur; 7pm-7am Fri, Sat; 7-11pm Sun. **Admission** $10 Fri, Sat; $3.20 men, free women, Wed, Thur, Sun. **Credit** MC, V. **Map p287 D4**
Lesbian evenings are Fridays from 7 to 11pm. *See also below* **Clubs**.

Media

Foreign-language papers

Neva News

Neva News is an occasional newspaper that has been around as long as the various incarnations of the *St*

Boys are go: the vinyl delights of the 69 club. See page 213.

Petersburg Times and resolutely refuses to die. The English articles are all poor translations and the newsprint looks as if it has been produced by pressing half a potato against some toilet roll.

Pulse

This egregious colour lifestyle magazine comes out every month in both Russian and English editions.

St Petersburg Times

Formerly the hilarious, crime-obsessed *St Petersburg Press*. The 1996 takeover of the paper by Moscow's Independent Media – publishers of the *Moscow Times* – has brought improvements, notably in the design and local news and business reporting. But it still lacks any decent feature writing, and is often either pompous or monumentally dull. It appears on Tuesdays and Fridays; on Fridays it includes a what's on listings supplement.

Television & radio

Channel 5

The city's main TV station underwent a radical upheaval recently when Boris Yeltsin stripped it of its national broadcasting rights and turned it into a completely regional station. The shockwaves have resulted in a small number of improvements, but in general there are still too many filmed ballet performances, poetry readings and extended and extremely dull interviews with cultural figures.

Of the local radio stations, currently the most popular is Europa Plus (100.5FM), which transmits a diet of Western rock and pop music. Then comes Radio Baltica (104.8FM), a Russian pop music channel.

Music: Classical & Opera

St Petersburg resonates nightly to the sounds of the multitude of composers that it has produced over the last three centuries: Tchaikovsky, Borodin, Rimsky-Korsakov, Shostakovich and Prokofiev, to mention just the stellar names. The city's rich musical heritage is reflected in the devotion of its audiences; attending classical concerts is a tradition that is kept very much alive in this city, an activity as fashionable and as sexy as cinema.

Because tickets – for orchestral music, at least – are still relatively cheap by Western standards, regular concertgoing is a good way of stretching your budget.

TICKETS

Tickets are available directly from theatres, via the swankier hotels and from the network of Teatr kiosks dotted across town. You can also get *abonimenty*, which are batches of tickets to about ten concerts on a loose theme, be it chamber music, Mahler symphonies or simply concerts at a single venue. There are a number of different *abonimenty* to choose from every season; not only are they excellent value for money, but they also save you from having to queue for more popular concerts (if you've been canny in your choice of *aboniment*).

Opera venues

Hermitage Theatre
Dvortsovaya Naberezhnaya 34 (311 3465/1920). Metro Gostiny Dvor or Nevsky Prospekt. **Open** *box office* 10.30am-5pm Tue-Sun. **Tickets** $10-$50. **Map p286 D3, p287 C4**
This beautiful, intimate theatre was formerly the private court theatre of the Winter Palace. Mariinsky soloists regularly perform gala concerts from a classical repertoire. During the summer season performances are almost daily. Tickets are not numbered, so come early.

Mussorgsky Theatre of Opera & Ballet
Ploshchad Iskusstv 1 (219 1978/1346). Metro Gostiny Dvor or Nevsky Prospekt. **Open** *box office* 11am-3pm, 4-7pm, Mon, Wed-Sun. **Performances** 7pm Mon, Wed-Sun. **Tickets** $7.50-$24. **Map p287 D4**
People tend to resort to the city's second opera house when the Mariinsky is booked out. Productions here vary greatly in quality; go for something Russian, like *Khovanshchina*; anything else can be either passable or excruciating. There is an interesting museum on the second floor, where you can see the designs for the first productions of Shostakovich's *The Nose* and Prokofiev's *War and Peace*.

Rimsky-Korsakov Conservatory Theatre of Opera & Ballet
Teatralnaya Ploshchad 3 (312 2519/311 6265). Metro Sadovaya or Sennaya Ploshchad. **Tickets** $1-$5. **No credit cards. Map p287 C6**
A wide repertoire of primarily Russian works featuring final-year students from the Conservatory, meaning that the standard is generally high, but the productions themselves are fairly spare and most haven't changed for decades.

Orchestral venues

Cappella
Naberezhnaya Reki Moiki 20 (314 1159/1048). Metro Nevsky Prospekt or Gostiny Dvor. **Open** noon-7pm daily. Closed public holidays. **Performances** 7pm. **Tickets** $2.40. **No credit cards. Map p287 D4**
The Rector of the Conservatory, Vladislav Chernushenko, and his son Alexander bring students to these excellent surroundings in the form of the State Cappella Orchestra. It's full of raw talent but lacks the guidance and inspiration that could turn it into an orchestra rather than simply a bunch of players.

Glinka Philharmonic Chamber Hall
Nevsky Prospekt 30 (312 4585). Metro Mayakovskaya. **Open** 11am-8pm daily. **Performances** 7pm. **Tickets** $13-$16; $1 children. **No credit cards. Map p289 F5**
The venue for solo and chamber recitals, usually of extremely high quality. Internationally renowned artists who perform at the Shostakovich Philharmonic Hall (*see below*) usually play here first, not least because the acoustic is much more suitable.

Shostakovich Philharmonic Hall
Mikhailovsky Ulitsa 2 (311 7333). Metro Gostiny Dvor or Nevsky Prospekt. **Open** *box office* 9.30am-10pm daily. **Performances** 7pm. **Tickets** $16-$48. **No credit cards. Map p287 D4/5**
Home to the St Petersburg Philharmonic Orchestra, not to be confused with the second, 'understudy' orchestra, the St Petersburg Academic Philharmonic Orchestra. The St Petersburg Philharmonic is capable of turning in some good performances, but it largely depends on who is waving the stick: when Yury Termikanov or Mariss Jansons are in town, the hall is usually packed. For lovers of Strauss waltzes and other popular stuff, an orchestra called Klassika is a regular feature worth looking out for.

Music: Rock, Roots & Jazz

While Moscow may spawn the kitsch, the glitz and the glam of pop, St Petersburg is Russia's undisputed rock capital. This is intelligentsia rock, where the words are just as important as the tune. St Petersburg's rock history of the past two decades revolves around Boris Grebenshchikov, the man behind the most important Russian rock band ever, Akvarium. Its only other landmark was Kino, formed by Viktor Tsoi, a punk turned New Romantic. Because Tsoi's songs were easy to play on the guitar, Kino's repertoire was adopted by young buskers all over Russia. Since his death in a car crash in 1990, Tsoi's tomb in a local cemetery has become a shrine for fans.

Venues

While they may have the capacity, St Petersburg's music venues can't boast of quality sound. For **Oktyabrsky Concert Hall**, which is primarily a dance venue, but has hosted concerts by Elton John (1979) and Nick Cave (1998), *see above* **Ballet**.

SKK
Sport & Concert Complex, Prospekt Yuriya Gagarina 8 (264 1710). Metro Park Pobedy. **Open** 10am-7pm daily; concert times vary. **Tickets** $5-$16 dance party, $5-$65 concerts. **No credit cards.**

Yublielny Sports Palace
Prospekt Dobrolyubova 18 (119 5614). Metro Sportivnaya. **Open** 10am-7pm daily; concert times vary. **Tickets** $5-$16 dance party; $5-$65 concerts. **No credit cards. Map p286 B3**
A huge reinforced concrete bowl in the Petrograd region, whose most memorable visitors were UB40 and Motorhead.

Lensoveta Palace of Culture
Kamennoostrovsky Prospekt 42 (346 0441). Metro Petrogradskaya. **Open** noon-6pm daily; concerts 7pm, 11pm. **Tickets** 7pm $1-$40, 11pm $5-$40 depending on the band. **No credit cards. Map p286 C1**
The most famous concert here was by Rage Against the Machine. The place is infamous for its aggressive guards.

Rock clubs

City Club
Korpus Apraksin Dvor 13, 2nd floor, Ulitsa Sadovaya 28-30 (110 4316). Metro Gostiny Dvor or Nevsky Prospekt. **Open** 8-11pm Mon-Thur, Sun; 8pm-5am Fri, Sat. **Admission** $1.60-$3.20. **No credit cards. Map p287 D5**
Spacious, comfortable and surprisingly civilised, not only for live gigs, but as a club as well. The sound system is good, there are two bars, a pool room (bigger than in most St Petersburg clubs) and real fireplaces. The only drawback is that the current temporary entrance is via Money Honey Saloon (*see below*), so you have to pay twice to get in.

Dobrolyot
Kamennoostrovsky Prospekt 42, room 423 (325 2505). Metro Petrogradskaya. **Open** times vary, Thur. Call for

The Mariinsky Theatre

The Mariinsky ranks second only to the Hermitage in the glittering hierarchy of St Petersburg's cultural landmarks. Established in 1860, the theatre has nurtured some of the great names of Russian classical music and opera: Tchaikovksy, Rimsky-Korsakov, Shostakovich and Prokofiev all premièred many of their major works here. Under the direction of Marius Petipa, a French choreographer who came to Petersburg at the age of 29 in 1847, the theatre also became one of the world's great ballet superpowers. Ballet standards such as *Sleeping Beauty*, *Swan Lake*, *Giselle* and *The Nutcracker*, even in the incarnations we see them today, all derive from the genius of Petipa. The Mariinsky has played an important role in literature, too: a studio apartment used as a literary meeting place by Blok, Akhmatova and others at the beginning of the century nestled under its rafters.

After the Revolution, the Bolsheviks considered closing the theatre down, but instead chose to open its doors to the proletarian masses, a move that resulted in much talking, sniggering and, contemporary accounts reveal, even belching during performances. In 1935, the theatre was renamed after Sergei Kirov, the St Petersburg party chief whom Stalin is purported to have had murdered. It was under this name that it gained fame in the West, primarily for its technically mind-blowing classical ballet productions. Since the arrival of Valery Gergiev as principal conductor in 1989, however, the focus has switched to opera again, and now that Gergiev (recently appointed guest conductor at the New York Met) is steadily heading for classical music superstardom in the West, it looks like a new golden age of Mariinsky opera has arrived.

Without exception, the operas are musically faultless, but production values generally gravitate towards the conventional, in the nineteenth-century sense of the word. Expect flapping foliage and canvas brickwork. Also, skip anything Italian – they're by far and away the worst productions. The ballets are always impeccable, though they, too, are conventional. Tickets cost between $20 and $50 for foreigners – many times the price for locals. Those who try to buy from Russians on the street will be sent by canny ticket-tearing *babushkas* to the box office to pay the wallet-crunching discrepancy in price. *See also above* **Ballet**.

Mariinsky Theatre

Teatralnaya Ploshchad 1 (114 4344). Metro Sennaya Ploshchad or Sadovaya. **Open** 11am-2pm, 3-7pm, Tue-Sun. **Performances** matinées 11.30am; evening 6.30pm. **Tickets** $20-$50; from $8 children. **No credit cards. Map p287 C6**

details. **Admission** up to $5. **No credit cards. Map p286 C1**
A smallish place that holds semi-acoustic concerts every Thursday. Call for details.

Jam

Dachny Prospekt 9. Metro Prospekt Veteranov. **Concerts** 6pm. **Admission** up to $5. **No credit cards.**
A rock club in the outskirts that hosts mainly second-rate local acts at irregular intervals. The beer's cheap.

Money Honey Saloon

Apraksin Dvor 14 (110 4316). Metro Gostiny Dvor. **Open** 7.30-11.30pm Mon-Thur; 7.30pm-5am Fri-Sun. **Admission** $1.60-$3.20. **No credit cards. Map p287 D5**
What began as a fetid little rockabilly shack has grown into a vast, vaulted rockabilly emporium, decorated with wagon wheels, cowboy boots and saddles.

Poligon

Lesnoi Prospekt 65/5 (245 2720). Metro Lesnaya. **Open** 6-11pm for concerts. **Admission** $3.20-$6.50. **No credit cards. Map p288 E1**
The fourth location for this rock club for Russian metalheads, punks and followers of all things thrash, doom and death. A grimy place noted for its fearless, sometimes fatal, stage-diving.

Jazz venues

Jazz Club Na Maloi Monetnoi

Malaya Monetnaya Ulitsa 3B (232 3137). Metro Gorkovskaya. **Open** 7-10pm Fri-Sun. **Admission** $5. **No credit cards. Map p286 D1/2**
New jazz club featuring a wide range of styles, with manager Sergei Khilko's St Petersburg Jazz Band as the virtuoso house act. Backyard gigs – barbecue and all – in summer.

Jazz Philharmonic Hall

Zagorodny Prospekt 27 (164 8565). Metro Vladimirskaya. **Open** 7-11pm daily. **Admission** $3.20-$10. **No credit cards. Map p289 E6**
Staid jazz venue organised by local jazz patriarch David Goloshchokin, who fills most of the bill. A bar, a restaurant and a mostly respectable, well-dressed crowd. Mainstream and Dixieland fill the auditorium.

JFC Jazz Club

Shpalernaya Ulitsa 33 (272 9850). Metro Chernyshevskaya. **Open** 7-10pm daily. **Admission** $1.60-$5. **No credit cards. Map p288 F3**
Less formal jazz venue. All styles up to avant garde and improv, with occasional classic and folk concerts. A jazz crowd, including some expats.

Kvadrat Jazz Club

Ulitsa Pravdy 10 (no phone). Metro Vladimirskaya. **Open** 8-11pm Tue. **Admission** $1.60. **No credit cards. Map p289 E6**
A small venue where mostly young musicians play. Performances are followed by jam sessions; musicians and students fill most of the chairs.

Manhattan

Naberezhnaya Reki Fontanki 90 (113 1945). Metro Sennaya Ploshchad. **Open** 6pm-5am daily. **Admission** $3.20. **No credit cards. Map p287 D6**
Established as a stomping ground for the city's intelligentsia, Kotyol (the Boiler), as it is also known, has now relaxed its membership policy and made a dash for youngish professionals, allowing them to simply buy membership on the door for around $20 (guests of a member go free). Live gigs

are mainly rock, blues and jazz. Food is basic but reasonably priced and there's a pool room as well.

R&B

Blues Billiard
LDM, Ulitsa Professora Popova 48 (234 4448). Metro Petrogradskaya. **Open** midnight-6am daily. **Admission** free. **No credit cards**.
A real blues venue, with billiard tables, whose repertoire is supervised by 'Russia's Jimi Hendrix', Alexander Lyapin, the former Akvarium guitarist.

Nightlife

In the mid-'90s, St Petersburg enjoyed a phase of being the cool and anarchic place to party. The city's wealth of gutted premises were transformed overnight into grungy dens peopled by funky neo-phyte clubbers with such a clumsy, enthusiastic adherence to fashion that they had a certain edge of originality. Combined with a dash of Russian assurance that everything could be sacrificed to the greater good of partying, and you got a frontier clubbing scene shot through with dirt, danger and an almost unbearable pitch of unrefined energy.

In 1996, it all began to come unstuck. The TaMtAm, the city's first real club, was shut down, sacrificed in the interests of property development, and the property market and ownership squabbles devoured such favourites as the Art Clinic and the Tunnel Club. In June 1998, Fish Fabrique was forced to move, bringing the final curtain down on the golden era of St Petersburg clubbing.

The new generation of clubs, such as the multi-million dollar techno-hangar **PORT**, have failed to arouse much enthusiasm and many remain desert-ed on a Friday night. Strip joints increasingly define the scene, but it is possible to capture a few nostalgic echoes of the past in such hangouts as **Moloko**, the **Griboyedov** and, hopefully, the all-new **Fish Fabrique**, which is due to relocate to new premises at Ulitsa Pushkinskaya 10.

Clubs

Apart from the clubs listed, a second tier of haunts lurks in St Petersburg. With names like Candyman, Continent and Hollywood Nites, they are generally tacky and laced with prostitutes. For clubs that also operate as rock venues, such as **Manhattan**, **City Club**, **Money Honey Saloon** and **Poligon**, *see above* **Music: Rock, Roots & Jazz**.

Grechniki
Sinners, Kanal Griboyedova 28 (219 4291). Metro Nevsky Prospekt. **Open** 11pm-6am Wed, Thur, Sun; 7pm-6am Fri, Sat. **Admission** *women* $10 Fri, Sat; free Wed, Thur, Sun; *men* $10 Fri, Sat; $3.20 Wed, Thur, Sun. **Credit** MC, V. **Map p287 D4**
Grechniki is primarily known for its art-house strip show on

Friday nights, with in-your-face costumes from designer Tatyana Petrova. The club itself is rather sad, with curious Flintstones rubble-effect décor, but the upstairs pool room is a good party venue.

Griboyedov
Ulitsa Voronezhskaya 2A (164 4355). Metro Ligovsky Prospekt. **Open** 5pm-6am Mon, Wed-Sun. **Admission** $6.50 Fri, Sat; $5 Mon, Thur, Sun; free before 8pm. **No credit cards**.
A clone of the now-defunct Tunnel Club, the Griboyedov pos-sesses much of the same exotic nuclear bomb-shelter chic. Unfortunately, this shelter is rather cramped, with an airless pillbox of a dancefloor and an angular bar, often cluttered with poseurs gleaming eerily under the UV. The music – pro-gressive house and techno – is a consolation.

Mama
Malaya Monetnaya Ulitsa 3B (232 3137). Metro Gorkovskaya. **Open** 11.55pm-6am Fri, Sat. **Admission** $5. **Map p286 D1/2**
A slick place with cool, minimalist décor from the Tunnel Club folk. Aimed at teens, it's packed with the city's wealth-iest, most fashion-conscious youth. If you're over 17, expect stares. Unlike lesser teen hangouts, there's almost no pick-up scene, just a lot of dancing, mostly to house and techno.

Metro
Ligovsky Prospekt 174 (166 0204). Metro Ligovsky Prospekt. **Open** 10pm-6am daily. **Admission** $5 Mon-Thur; $7.20 before midnight, $10 after midnight, Fri-Sun. **No credit cards. Map p289 F6**
Teeny-bopper club complex catering to every taste, with a techno dancefloor upstairs and a bigger Eurodance space on the ground floor. The industrial accoutrements and graffiti-adorned walls give it a 1980s feel, but it's still one of the few clubs that is regularly packed with real live clubbers.

Moloko
Perekupnoi Pereulok 12 (274 9467). Metro Ploshchad Aleksandra Nevskogo or Ploshchad Vosstaniya. **Open** 7-11.25pm Thur-Sat. **Admission** $2.50-$3.20 Fri, Sat; $1.60 Thur. **Map p289 G5/6**
Depending on the band and on who has bothered to turn up to watch, Moloko can seem like either a dull, dusty base-ment theatre (which is what it is) or an underground tem-ple to the vitality of live music. The pressure-cooker ambience, accentuated by low ceiling and miniscule stage, means that a whole arena-ful of live energy is compressed into an area the size of an average living room. The bar, rem-iniscent of a shared kitchen, makes the studenty crowd feel right at home.

Monroe
Kanal Griboyedova 8 (312 1331/311 3060). Metro Nevsky Prospekt. **Open** 1-11pm daily. **Admission** $4 after 5pm; free before 5pm. **Map p287 D4**
A bizarre place that combines a tepid pick-up scene with a back room crammed with booths showing soft porn. More porn plays on screens by the dancefloor, where dorky Russians try to shake their way out of leather trousers and minis while foreigners watch. Due to licensing problems, the club closes at 11pm, just as it should be getting started.

PORT
Pereulok Antonenko 2 (314 2609). Metro Nevsky Prospekt or Sennaya Ploshchad. **Open** 10pm-6am Wed-Sun. **Admission** $2.40-$14.50. **No credit cards. Map p287 C5**
This $3 million superclub, which opened in late 1997, was supposed to blow the St Petersburg club scene away. It didn't. The gigantic dancefloor, sizeable chill-out room and numerous bars serve only to emphasise that it is almost always empty.

All together now... undergrad merriment at the **Moloko**.

Strip joints

With the arrival of **Golden Dolls** in May 1998, complete with its 3-D breasts and bums emerging from the walls, the strip club attained a new profile in the city. They're all very similar – out rageous admission charges, meaty gals and the obligatory fireman's pole – except for **Hali Gali**, which aims for an artier feel in the style of a Berlin cabaret.

Golden Dolls
Nevsky Prospekt 60 (110 5570). Metro Gostiny Dvor.
Open 10pm-6am daily. **Admission** $130. **Credit** AmEx, DC, JCB, MC, V. **Map p289 E5**

Hali Gali
Lanskoye Shosse 15 (246 3827). Metro Pionerskaya.
Open 4pm-6am daily. **Admission** $20-$25 men; $13-$16 women. **Credit** AmEx, MC, V.

Luna
Voznesensky Prospekt 46 (310 1616). Metro Sadovaya or Sennaya. **Open** noon-4am daily. **Admission** $19-$32. **Credit** AmEx, DC, JCB, MC, V. **Map p287 C6**

Casinos

There's a dress code at all of St Petersburg's casinos, which boils down to no casual wear or trainers; suit and tie desirable, evening dress preferable.

Premier Casino
Nevsky Prospekt 47 (315 7893). Metro Mayakovskaya.
Open noon-9am daily. **Credit** MC, V.
Map p289 E5

Taleon Club
Naberezhnaya Reki Moiki 59 (315 7645/312 5357).
Metro Gostiny Dvor. **Open** 2pm-6am daily. **Credit** AmEx, MC, V. **Map p287 D4**

Venice Casino Club
Ulitsa Korablestroiteley 21 (366 1660). Metro Primorskaya. **Open** 6pm-5am daily. **No credit cards.**

Theatre

The Maly Drama Theatre apart, St Petersburg's theatre is only for buffs and PhD students with eccentric areas of specialisation. Dusty classics abound and production values are stuck in a nineteenth century groove. Occasionally, interesting productions do crop up, usually at the **Theatre on Liteiny** or the **Priyut Komedianta**. These, along with the very occasional foreign tours and the impressive Baltic House Festival in early autumn, keep the tiny flame flickering. There is next to nothing by way of English-language productions, although the occasional West End musical does appear, as in the case of *Hair* and *Jesus Christ Superstar*, but once again, these are produced in Russian. It is best to book in advance. We have yet to find a theatre in the city that accepts plastic of any variety and only the Theatre on Liteiny has wheelchair access.

Akimov Comedy Theatre
Nevsky Prospekt 56 (312 4555). Metro Nevsky Prospekt.
Performances 7pm Tue-Sun. **Tickets** $2.60-$6.50.
Map p289 E5

*Testing, testing... getting the sound right at **PORT**. See page 218.*

This is the place to be if you have a perverse inclination towards staid Russian comedies. The directors generally go for cheap laughs at the expense of any textual subtlety, and the actors ham it up for all they are worth.

Alexandrinsky Theatre
Ploshchad Ostrovskogo 2 (315 4464). Metro Nevsky Prospekt. **Performances** 7.30pm or 8.30pm, Mon, Thur-Sun. **Tickets** $3.50-$25. **Map p289 C5**
A temple to Russian drama, with four venues and nearly 40 plays in its pocket (most by Alexander Ostrovsky). Things have gone downhill since the legendary director Vsevolod Meyerhold directed some of his more ground-breaking productions here, including Blok's *The Fair Show Booth*, premièred just as the 1917 Revolution was cranking up.

Bolshoi Drama Theatre
Naberezhnaya Reki Fontanki 65 (310 0401). Metro Nevsky Prospekt. **Performances** **Tickets** $1-$4. **Map p287 C5/D4/6, p288 E3, p289 E4/5**
It's the *grande dame* of St Petersburg theatre, but the Bolshoi Drama Theatre's reputation has suffered over the last decade, with good reason: many of its productions are guaranteed to cure even the most chronic insomniac. Nonetheless, its company still includes some of the best actors in Russia.

Komissarshevskaya Drama Theatre
Italianskaya Ulitsa 19 (315 5355). Metro Gostiny Dvor. **Performances** 7pm Mon, Wed-Sun. **Tickets** $1-$4. **Map p287 D4, p289 E4/5**
The house policy here is to be as intense as possible, weighing down every gesture and textual nuance with a deep significance it doesn't necessarily contain. Sometimes it works surprisingly well, sometimes not.

Maly Drama Theatre
Ulitsa Rubinshteina 18 (113 2078). Metro Vladimirskaya. **Tickets** $1.70-$5. **Map p289 E5**

Since Lev Dodin took over the Maly in 1983, he's transformed this provincial troupe into one of the world's leading companies. Dodin's productions were immediate hits with Western critics and have earned him fistfuls of awards, including an Olivier Award. The Maly can be a total washout for contemporary works, but when they are good, they're scintillating.

Molodyozhny Theatre
Naberezhnaya Reki Fontanki 114 (316 6870). Metro Tekhnologichesky Institut. **Performances** times and prices vary; call for details. **Map p289 E4/5**
The home of sharp-witted director Semyon Spivak, who is at his best with unusual, quirky plays. Look out for Vladimir Tumanov's 'contemporary' approach to *Twelfth Night*, which has the actors chanting 'William, William Shakespeare' to the tune of Queen's 'We Will, We Will Rock You'.

Priyut Komedianta
Comedian's Refuge, Malaya Morskaya 16 (Ulitsa Gogolya) (312 5352). Metro Vladimirskaya. **Performances** 7pm Tue-Sun. **Tickets** $2-$5. **Map p287 C5**
One of the more interesting theatres in the city, where 90 per cent of plays are overseen by the red-hot directorial whizz-kid Yury Tomoshevsky. Work ranges from monologues to full-blooded, very decent stuff. It is due to move to a plusher venue next to Sadovaya metro in late 1998.

Theatre on Liteiny
Liteiny Prospekt 51 (273 5335). Metro Vladimirskaya. **Performances** times and prices vary; call for details. **Map p289 E4**
The winner of the coveted Critics' Prize in the 1998 Golden Mask Awards for Eugene O' Neill's *Moon for the Misbegotten*, the Theatre on Liteiny employs some of the city's finest actors. The repertoire is surprisingly diverse – Shakespeare can be found rubbing shoulders with almost everyone, from Goldoni and Tolstoy to David Henry Hwang.

Accommodation

Rooms in St Petersburg are either pricey or the pits... whichever you go for, you pay for it.

Since St Petersburg rediscovered the joys of foreign investment (circa 1991), the city has been poised on the brink of a luxury hotel explosion. But while a steady trickle of funding has nurtured some top-class establishments, the anticipated boom has stubbornly refused to materialise.

The most potent symbol of these frustrated hopes is the Clarion North Crown, a projected $97-million four-star complex that ran out of funding just as the bathroom fittings were being installed and that is now a derelict, ghost hotel gathering tumbleweeds in the heart of the Petrogradskaya region. The **Oktyabrskaya**, a dingy, unkempt dive that enjoys a stellar location in the centre of the city, has probably hosted more investment rumours than guests over recent years, but has resolutely managed to scupper every deal. The bid for the 2004 Olympics was to solve all of the city's infrastructure ills – accommodation included – in a single swoop. If only St Petersburg could have made it on to the shortlist.

With Intercontinental, Hilton and Sir Rocco Forte all hovering at the moment, the city is probably closer to the brink than ever before. But even if the floodgates open and the cash finally does come gushing in, the planned developments are unlikely to address St Petersburg's most glaring accommodation problem: an almost total lack of mid-range establishments.

If you are staying in one of the low-end establishments, in bed and breakfast accommodation or in a private apartment, note that the local authorities shut off the hot water supply for a month in summer for maintenance. If you can't do without your morning shower, then ring ahead to check.

Deluxe

Angleterre

Bolshaya Morskaya Ulitsa 39 (210 5757/fax 210 5059 /e-mail business@astoria.spb.ru). Metro Gostiny Dvor. **Rates** *single* $200-$220; *double* $240-$260; *suite* $280-$700; *continental breakfast* $15; *buffet breakfast* $20. **Credit** AmEx, DC, MC, V. **Map p287 C5**
Sister to the Astoria (whose facilities it shares), the Angleterre has 193 comfortable rooms with stunning views of St Isaac's Cathedral. Much of the hotel's notoriety was bestowed on it by the imagist poet Sergei Yesenin, who hanged himself here in 1925, in the room where he had stayed some years earlier with his wife, Isadora Duncan. In a melodramatic final flourish, he left a poem written in his own blood, proclaiming, 'To die is not new – but neither is it new to be alive'. Subsequent renovations will have destroyed any evidence to support speculations that Yesenin was murdered.
Hotel services *Bars. Beauty salon. Business services. Car park. Casino. Currency exchange (24 hrs). Dry cleaning. Fitness facilities. Hairdresser. International payphone. Laundry. Lift. Limo hire. Newspaper kiosk. Nightclub. Non-smoking rooms. Restaurants.* **Room services** *Hairdryer. Minibar. Radio. Room service (24 hrs). Safe. TV. Phone.*

Astoria

Bolshaya Morskaya Ulitsa 39 (210 5757/fax 210 5059 /e-mail business@astoria.spb.ru). Metro Gostiny Dvor. **Rates** *single* $250-$280; *double* $290-$320; *suite* $325-$835; *breakfast* $15-$20.* **Credit** AmEx, DC, MC, V. **Map p287 C5**

Monstrous monoliths

Vast, nightmarish buildings, drab décor and sullen, narcoleptic service: yes, the Soviet Hotel offered all this and more. Guests of the USSR were treated much like the general populace – they went without water for as long as a month in summer, dared not utter the words 'room service', and ate unfeasible amounts of cabbage. While communism may have been dumped on the scrapheap of history, the monstrous hotels it spawned are still here, barely alive, and dotted across St Petersburg. So, no matter what the guy at the travel agency says, these are the monoliths to avoid.

Sputnik – Offers more shades of beige than you ever thought existed. 24-hour traffic noise laid on for free.

Sovietskaya – A fantastically ugly little joint, which features in the writings of George Orwell.

Oktyabrskaya – If you can put up with nicotine-flavoured pillows and hungry throngs of cheap prostitutes, it might just be worth it for the location.

Kievskaya – The highlight is the minimalist communal bathroom: a single shower-head sticking out of the wall. There are good views of the Obvodny Canal too.

Vyborgskaya – Known as 'purgatory' among the Swedish tour group set. A good place to watch waitresses playing cards.

An imposing Imperial establishment built during the last pre-revolutionary throes of neo-classicism, the Astoria is light and airy inside, with majestic chandeliers and acres of white marble, with 240 rooms in tasteful pastel and white, many enjoying excellent views of St Isaac's Cathedral or the Mariinsky Palace. It has a touch more class than the city's other five-star places, and a dash of Russian authenticity. And there's the illustrious company too: such diverse historical figures as Maggie Thatcher, Chuck Norris and Lenin all stayed here.
Hotel services *Bars. Beauty salon. Business services. Car park. Currency exchange (24 hrs). Dry cleaning. Fitness facilities. Hairdresser. Laundry. Lift. Limo hire. Newspaper kiosk. Nightclub. Non-smoking rooms. Restaurants.* **Room services** *Hairdryer. Minibar. Radio. Room service (24 hrs). Safe. Satellite TV. Telephone. Website: www.spb.astoria.*

Grand Hotel Europe

Mikhailovskaya Ulitsa 1/7 (329 6000/fax 329 6676/ e-mail: res@ghe.spb.ru). Metro Nevsky Prospekt or Gostiny Dvor. **Rates** *single* $280-$310; *double* $320-$350; *suite* $370-$2,250; *breakfast* $24. **Credit** AmEx, DC, MC, V. **Map p287 D4/5**
Built in the last quarter of the nineteenth century, the Europe was upgraded to its current state of marble-clad sumptuousness by a Swedish-Russian joint venture in the late 1980s. Gargantuan bathrooms are the most striking feature of its 300 elegant rooms, with the more exclusive suites – like the one Clinton used during his 1996 visit – featuring his-and-hers sinks and cavernous bathtubs on gilt legs. Other presidential guests have included Nixon, Carter, Kohl and Chirac.
Hotel services *Bars. Beauty salon. Business services. Currency exchange (24 hrs). Dry cleaning. Fitness facilities. Hairdresser. Limo hire. Lounge. Restaurants.* **Room services** *Air-conditioning. Hairdryer. Minibar. Modem. Room service (24 hrs). Safe. Telephone. TV. Website:www.grandhotel-europe.com*

Nevsky Palace Hotel

Nevsky Prospekt 57 (275 2001/fax 301 7323/7524). Metro Mayakovskaya. **Rates** *single/double* $275; *suite* $325-$1,525; *breakfast* $20. **Credit** AmEx, DC, MC, V. **Map p289 E5**
Situated in the heart of the city, the Nevsky Palace is a modern hotel in the shell of a nineteenth-century mansion. A little less swish and a touch more functional than its two rivals, it still offers everything the business set could hope to expect.
Hotel services *Babysitting. Bar/café. Business services. Currency exchange (24 hrs). Fast postal service. Fitness facilities. Hairdresser. Restaurants. Shop.* **Room services** *Air-conditioning. Hairdryer. Minibar. Room service (24 hrs). Telephone. TV. Website: www.ittsheraton.com*

Expensive

Hotelship Peterhof

Naberezhnaya Makarova, nr Tuchkov Bridge (325 8888/fax 325 8889). Metro Vasileostrovskaya. **Rates** (incl breakfast) *single* $75-$170; *double* $60-$140. **Credit** AmEx, DC, MC, V. **Map p286 B3**
A modern Swiss hotel enjoying the unusual location of a moored cruise ship on Vasilyevsky Island. As on a working liner, there's barely room to swing a cat in the rooms, and the bathrooms are tiny, but comfortable and light. Unfortunately, the view from deck is not the riverside panorama you might expect, but largely a grotty dockside. The Svir restaurant (*see page 229*) is pleasant enough, especially if you like live piano.
Hotel services *Bar. Business services. Car park. Conference rooms. Fitness facilities. Hairdresser. Hotel bus. Laundry. Nightclub. Reading room. Restaurants. Safe. Shop. Travel agent.* **Room services** *Air-conditioning. Minibar (deluxe only). Radio. Telephone. TV.*

St Petersburg

Pirogovskaya Naberezhnaya 5/2 (542 9411/8149/ fax 248 8002/542 9064/e-mail: postmaster@spbhotel. spb.su). Metro Gorkovskaya or Ploshchad Lenina. **Rates** (incl breakfast) *single* $77-$100; *double* $97-$120; *suite* $160-$210.* **Credit** AmEx, DC, MC, V. **Map p288 E2**
Something of a 1970s eyesore this; directly opposite the *Avrora* cruiser but with the disadvantage of being on an extremely busy road. Some of the 300 rooms are a little dowdy and the bathrooms tend to be on the small side, but there are good views to be had across the Neva river.
Hotel services *Bar. Booking service. Business services. Car park. Clothing repairs. Currency exchange (24 hrs). Dry cleaning. Hairdresser. Lift. Post office. Restaurant. Safe. Sauna. Shop. Restaurants.* **Room services** *Radio. Telephone. TV. Website: www.spb. hotelspb*

Pribaltiskaya

Ulitsa Korablestroitely 14 (356 4135/fax 356 6094). Metro Primorskaya. **Rates** (incl breakfast) *single* $140; *double* $160; *suite* $230-$340. **Credit** AmEx DC, MC, V.
This enormous, imposing building on the Gulf of Finland would be better if the same concept of size were applied to its 1,200 rooms. It's well equipped (there's a chemist, bowling, billiards and a nightclub), but its size and location make it pretty bleak. Recent guests include the head of the Russian Orthodox Church, Patriarch Alexy II.
Hotel services *Babysitting. Bars. Business services. Car park. Conference rooms. Dry cleaning. Garage. Fitness facilities. Hairdresser. Lift. Lounge. Newspaper kiosk. Non-smoking rooms. Restaurants. Safe. Taxi hire.* **Room services** *Air-conditioning. Minibar. Room service (24 hrs). Telephone. Satellite TV. Voice mail.*

Pulkovskaya

Ploshchad Pobedy 1 (123 5122/fax 264 6396). Metro Moskovskaya. **Rates** (incl breakfast) *single* $146; *double* $165; *suite* $242. **Credit** AmEx, DC, MC, V.
An ugly building near the airport that, like the Pribaltiskaya, disproves the theory that big is beautiful. Its 523 rooms are shoddy, but overlook the amazing Victory Monument, with its thickly built Soviet figurines.
Hotel services *Bars. Booking service. Business services. Cafés. Car park. Chemist. Conference hall. Currency exchange (24 hrs). Fitness facilities. Hairdresser. Laundry. Lift. Nightclubs. Restaurants. Shop. Taxi service.* **Room services** *Air-conditioning. Hairdryer. Room service. Telephone. TV.*

Moderate

Mercury

Tavricheskaya Ulitsa 39 (275 8745/fax 276 1977). Metro Chernyshevskaya. **Rates** *single* $58; *double* $68; *suite* $73-$106. **No credit cards**. **Map p288 G3**
Sweet little 1950s hotel down the road from Smolny Cathedral. Small, ordinary rooms have leather sofas and tear-at-the-touch Soviet sheets, but their views of the Tauride Palace compensate. Gorby dropped by a couple of times. Note that there's no sign on the front door. Rates given include breakfast.
Hotel services *Bar. Fax. Laundry. Restaurant.* **Room services** *Air-conditioning (some). Fridge. Room service. Telephone. TV.*

Moskva

Ploshchad Alexandra Nevskogo 2 (274 4001/fax 274 2130). Metro Ploshchad Alexandra Nevskogo. **Rates** (incl breakfast) *single* $82; *double* $104-$114; *suite* $162-$234. **Credit** AmEx, DC, MC, V. **Map p289 G6**
A dark, cavernous 1970s monolith with seedy billiard rooms and awful food. Some of the 750 rooms have views of the Alexander Nevsky monastery, but peaceful gazing can be harshly interrupted by the flow of traffic below.

Clear the decks – it's lunchtime at the **Hotelship Peterhof**.

Hotel services *Bars. Cafés. Car park. Conference facilities. Dry cleaning. Fax. Lift. Lounge. Restaurants. Safe. Souvenir shop. Taxi hire.* **Room services** *Radio. Room service (24 hrs). Telephone. TV.*

Okhtinskaya Victoria

Bolsheokhtinsky Prospekt 4 (227 4438/3767/8602/fax 227 2618/2514). Metro Novocherkasskaya. **Rates** (incl breakfast) *single* $87; *double* $100; *suite* $175. **Credit** AmEx, DC, V.

Plush Russian-French hotel, many of whose 350 rooms offer great views of Smolny Cathedral. Rooms come in flowery pastels; surprisingly, for a hotel this size, there are no baths, only showers. Take a cab: public transport here is tricky.
Hotel services *Bars. Booking service. Café. Car park. Conference facilities. Currency exchange (24 hrs). Fax. Hairdresser. Lift. Lounge. Newspaper kiosk. Restaurant. Safe. Sauna. Shop.* **Room services** *Air-conditioning. Minibar. Radio. Room service (24 hrs). Telephone. TV/VCR.*

Rus

Artilleriiskaya Ulitsa 1 (273 4683/fax 279 3600). Metro Chernyshevskaya. **Rates** *singles* $60; *doubles* $70; *suites* $99-110; *breakfast* $4. **Credit** AmEx, JCB, MC, V.
Map p289 E4
A plain, modern Soviet hotel whose staff vary between chirpily helpful and Brezhnev-era don't-cares. As you might expect in a modern hotel, the 164 rooms are pretty ordinary, but have strange, crunchy floors, suggesting there's still bubble-wrap beneath the carpet. En suite bathrooms are minute.
Hotel services *Bars. Car park. Mobile phone hire. Chemist. Conference facilities. Currency exchange. Dentist. Fitness facilities. Hairdresser. Newspaper kiosk. Restaurant. Shop.* **Room services** *Fridge. Radio. Room service. Telephone. TV/VCR.*

Sovietskaya

Lermontovsky Prospekt 43/1 (329 0150/0186/fax 329 0188/e-mail: sovot@pop.convey.ru). Metro Baltiiskaya. **Rates** (incl breakfast) *single* $52; *double* $76; *suite* $126. **Credit** AmEx, MC, V. **Map p287 B6**
A 1960s dump comprising three blocks – the Rizhsky, the Fontanka and the Lermontovsky – of 1,018 rooms. Unless you pay extra, rooms are basic and low on comfort.

Hotel services *Bar. Business services. Café. Cash machine. Chemist. Currency exchange. Fitness facilities. Hairdresser. Lift. Newspaper kiosk. Restaurants. Safe. Shop. Taxi hire. Travel agent.* **Room services** *Hairdryer (deluxe only). Minibar (deluxe only). Radio. Telephone. TV. Website. www.sovietskaya.hotel.service.ru*

Sputnik

Ulitsa Morisa Toreza 36 (552 5632/fax 552 8084). Metro Pionerskaya. **Rates** (incl breakfast) *single* $44; *double* $58; *suite* $88-$8. **Credit** AmEx, JCB, MC, V.
Cheesy cacti, black leather sofas and a row of slot machines adorn the reception lounge of this 1960s monstrosity. Beige lino-floored corridors lead to clean rooms, furnished with dark blue carpet and gawdily covered narrow beds. If these don't deprive you of sleep, the cars outside will.
Hotel services *Bar. Booking service. Car park. Conference hall. Fax. Hairdresser. Laundry. Lift. Limo hire. Restaurant. Safe.* **Room services** *Radio. Room service (24 hrs). Telephone. TV.*

Cheap

Dvorets Molodyozhi

Ulitsa Professora Popova 47 (234 3278/5341/fax 234 9818). Metro Petrogradskaya. **Rates** *single* $19-$32; *double* $30-$48. **Credit** MC, V.
Triffid-like plants in the ground-floor Winter Garden disturb rather than cheer. Rooms are on the small, uncomfortable side, but at least there's plenty to do if you can't sleep: billiards, golf course, disco, 24-hour bars blaring bad techno...
Hotel services *Bars. Car park. Club. Concert hall. Fax. Fitness facilities. Hairdresser. International payphone. Laundry. Lift. Restaurant. Shop.* **Room services** *Room service (24 hrs). Telephone. TV (demi-luxe only).*

Kievskaya

Dnepropetrovskaya Ulitsa 49 (166 0456/5398/fax 166 8250). Metro Ligovsky Prospekt, then bus 14, trolleybus 42. **Rates** *single* $16-$25; *double* $23-$47; *breakfast* $5. **No credit cards.**
15 minutes' walk from the nearest metro, this 'hotel' is housed in a miserable 1960s building in a miserable location

Sheraton
Nevskij Palace
H O T E L
ST. PETERSBURG

ST. PETERSBURG'S PREFERRED ADDRESS

Location: In the city centre, in the main business and shopping district. All major cultural and historical attractions are nearby, 1 km from Moscow railway station, 17 km from Pulkovo II International airport.

Accommodation: 285 guest rooms including 2 Presidential suites, 29 suites and 110 non-smoking rooms.

Satellite/cable TV, IDD telephone, air-conditioning, minibar, hair-drier, deposit safes in the rooms.

Dinning: 4 restaurants featuring Russian, International, Italian and Austrian cuisine; Cafe Vienna with Viennese-style pastries and desserts, 24-hour Room Service.

Meeting facilities: 6 function rooms for meetings and banquets accommodating up to 200 persons.

Business Centre: Fully equipped for today's business traveller.

Fitness Centre: The right place to relax.

NEVSKY PROSPECT 57, ST. PETERSBURG 191025, RUSSIA
PHONE: +7-812-275 2001, FAX: +7-812-301 7323

next to the Obvodny Canal. Ugly red carpets are mucky and threadbare and only some of the matchbox-sized rooms have en suite bathrooms.
Hotel services *Bar. Ironing rooms. Lift. Newspaper kiosk. Post office. Restaurant.* **Room services** *Fridge. Room service. Telephone. TV.*

Oktyabrskaya

Ligovsky Prospekt 43-45 (277 7281/fax 315 7501). Metro Ploshchad Vosstaniya. **Rates** (incl breakfast) *single* $12-$30; *double* $15-$43; *suite* $20-$45. **Credit** MC, V. **Map p289 F5**
Dingy, dismal lair next to Moscow Station on Nevsky Prospekt. The entrance opens directly on to the street, inviting anyone who cares into its filthy interior. Rooms (all 750 of them) are decorated in sleazy dark red with dim lights and peeling wallpaper in the manner of a cheap, let's say, massage parlour.
Hotel services *Cash machine. Currency exchange. Conference hall. Fax. Hairdresser.* **Room services** *Fridge. Room service. Radio. Telephone (some, local lines only). TV.*

Vyborgskaya

Torzhkovskaya Ulitsa 3 (246 9194/9141/fax 246 8187). Metro Chyornaya Rechka. **Rates** (incl breakfast) *single* $13-23; *double* $23-$39; *suite* $25-$52. **No credit cards.**
An unlikely recent guest of this half-dead Soviet-era hotel, was Vladimir Mashkov, star of the award-winning Russian film, *The Thief*. There's very little else to entice you to stay here: the 400 rooms are depressing, with few home comforts.
Hotel services *Bar. Café. Car park. Conference hall. Currency exchange. Hairdresser. Lift. Lounge. Safe. Taxi service.* **Room services** *Room service. Telephone. TV.*

Hostels

There's no competition for the Russian-American International Hostel, only minutes' walk from Nevsky Prospekt. The others may be central, but aren't half as clean or efficient. On the ground floor, there is also a branch of Sindbad Travel, a budget youth and student travel agency, which can be contacted at the address below. Its website is full of useful information for shoestring travellers.
Sindbad Travel PO Box 8, SF-53501 Lappeenranta, Finland (e-mail sindbad@ryh.spb.su).
Website: www.spb.su/ryh/sindbad.html

Bolshoi Teatr Kukol

Ulitsa Nekrasova 12 (273 3996/272 3055). Metro Chernyshevskaya. **Rates** *single* $13-$15; *double* $19-$23; *suite* $24-$29. **No credit cards. Map p289 E4**
Turn into the Sluzhebny Vkhod (trade entrance), left of the Puppet Theatre just off Liteiny Prospekt, go upstairs to the fourth floor and turn left through an unmarked door to the office of this tiny hostel. The elderly lady, sitting at a desk with her samovar and TzV, will help you get installed and add up your bill on an abacus.
Hostel services *Lounge.* **Room services** *Fridge. Radio. Telephone (some).*

Herzen University Hostel

Kazanskaya Ulitsa 6 (314 7472/fax 314 7659). Metro Nevsky Prospekt. **Rates** *single* $8-$29; *double* $12-$49. **No credit cards. Map p287 D5**
Mostly for Herzen students, but accepts foreigners too – that's if you can get past the door, unhelpful reception staff. Plain, warm rooms with delightful Soviet white ruched curtains. Excellently located, however. Book in advance.
Hostel services *Bar/café. Conference hall. International payphone. Lift. Lounge. Safe. Snack kiosk.* **Room services** *Fridge. Radio. Telephone.*

Hostel Holiday

Ulitsa Mikhailova 1 (327 1070/fax 542 7364/e-mail: postmaster@hostelling.spb.su). Metro Ploshchad Lenina. **Rates** (incl breakfast) *all rooms* $22. **Credit** MC, V. **Map p288 F2**
Five-storey hostel on the Neva embankment next to the notorious Kresty Prison, but otherwise a good location. Rooms sleep two to six and their narrow beds aren't made any more comfortable by army-surplus-style blankets. Good views across the river, though.
Hostel services *Café (9am-9pm). E-mail. Fax. Kitchen. Laundry. Safe. Telephone.*

St Petersburg International Hostel

3-ya Sovetskaya Ulitsa 28 (329 8018/fax 329 8019/ e-mail: ryh@ryh.spb.su). Metro Ploshchad Vosstaniya. **Rates** (incl breakfast) *2-5 persons* $19. **No credit cards. Map p289 F4**
Cheerful hostel run along Western lines, with clean rooms, new furniture and helpful staff. There are no bathrooms, but a shower room. Book in advance as there are only 14 rooms. From London, book ahead at the YHA Travel Store, 14C Southampton Street, London WC2 (0171 836 1036).
Hostel services *Booking service. E-mail. Fax. International payphone. Library. Luggage storage. Shop. Website: www.spb.su/ryh*

Camping

Olgino Motel-Camping

Primorskoye Shosse 59, Dom 18 (238 3671). Metro Chyornaya Rechka, then bus 110 or 210 (35 mins). **Rates** Motel (incl breakfast): *single* $40; *double* $50; *deluxe* $65 Camping (June-mid-Sept) *per person per 24 hrs* $7; *car parking* $2; *breakfast* $5. **No credit cards.**
Camping facilities are open during the summer months only but the 50-room motel is open all year round. You can go horseriding too for $18 an hour.
Services *Bar. Restaurant. Safe. Sauna.* **Motel room services** *Shower. Telephone. TV.*

Retur Motel-Camping

Primorskoye Shosse 202, Dom 29 (237 7533/fax 273 9783). Metro Chyornaya Rechka, then bus 110 or 210 (25 mins). **Services** *Pool. Sauna.*

Longer stays

Renting

There's a critical difference between finding a flat on a corporate pay packet and finding one on a shoestring. For the former, Western-run agencies advertise apartments costing thousands in the back of the *St Petersburg Times*. Try Pulford (325 6277), Atlantic (325 2500) or Henry Chichester (325 9005). Those without corporate cushioning should have a look at the classifieds in the *St Petersburg Times* or Russian daily *Iz Ruk V Ruki* (hand to hand). Buy it early in the day to catch the bargains.

Staying with a family

The **Travellers' Guest House**, based in Moscow, arranges stays with families, usually in the centre, for about $26 per night, including breakfast and supper. Stays can be as brief as a night, or as long as several months. Call Katya Alexeyeva in St Petersburg on 233 6803, or the Travellers' Guest House in Moscow on 095 971 4059/e-mail: tgh@glas. apc.org. Payment is in advance, by Visa or MasterCard. Alternatively try the **St Petersburg Host Family Association** (279 5198/fax 275 1992).

Eating & Drinking

St Petersburg's restaurants vary wildly between the uneatable and the unbeatable. If you've got the dosh, go posh.

Restaurants

Even taking into account the privations of the communist years, it seems astounding that St Petersburg, a city of almost five million people, is now served by only a couple of hundred restaurants. And barely a fraction of this total would meet the standards of even the most lackadaisical gourmet. Sullen, grudging service is the order of the day in the low to mid-range, and even in some of the more expensive establishments. Quality can be erratic, as new places open with a fanfare but soon afterwards find themselves slipping into the stodgy, slovenly mire.

All this aside, however, the city harbours a small number of really superb restaurants, for those willing to pay or persevere. And over the last three years, menus have grown exponentially more imaginative and ethnically diverse. It's now possible to find terrific sushi, tapas and tandoori chicken as well as such Russian staples as caviar and sirloin steak of bear, all within a few blocks of the centre. Sumptuous, Tsarist-era eateries like the **Taleon Club** and the **Dvorianskoye Gnezdho** would grace any restaurant scene in any city in the world. And while the choice is still tiny, particularly for those dining without the safety net of a five-star expense account, new places are opening at such a frantic rate that the culinary horrors of St Petersburg's recent past may soon finally be laid to rest.

● The average price listed is based on the cost of a three-course meal (starter, main course and dessert), not including drinks. For an explanation of Russian menu items, *see box page 81*. Staff in most of these restaurants will be able to understand English.

American

California Grill
Nevsky Prospekt 176 (274 2422). Metro Ploshchad Alexander Nevskogo. **Open** 24 hours daily. **Average** $36. **Credit** AmEx, DC, MC, JCB, V. **Map p289 G6**.
Gaudy and loud, the Grill has particularly awful West Coast beach bum murals splashed across the walls. Still, the burgers are very decent and it's the only place in town where you'll find passable Tex-Mex food. Avoid the salad bar, which is well stocked with poorly preserved cabbage.

Caucasian

Kavkaz
Ulitsa Stakhanovtsev 5 (221 4309). Metro Novocherkasskaya. **Open** noon-midnight daily. **Average** $50. **Credit** MC, V. **Map p289 H6**
Main dishes at Kavkaz (Caucasus) are generally a cut above Pirosmani (*see below*), though more expensive. After gorging on the usual melted cheese starters, try the Lyula kebabs, the marinated meat basturma or the rather splendid shashlik. The wine list features good, moderately priced Georgian selections. The service, however, is unpolished and the restaurant is quite a trek from the town centre. *Tables outdoors (summer).*

Pirosmani
Bolshoi Prospekt 14 (235 4666). Metro Petrogradskaya. **Open** noon-midnight daily. **Average** $25. **No credit cards. Map p286 B2/C1/2**
Booking is a necessity here, especially if you've got your eye on the table moored in the centre of the miniature indoor lake. There's no need to venture much beyond the starters, in particular the superlative khachipuri or suluguni cheese specialities and the dolma (vine leaves stuffed with meat and rice), for the main courses are lacklustre by comparison.

Chinese

Aquarium
Kamenoostrovsky Prospekt 10 (237 0647). Metro Gorkovskaya. **Open** noon-11.30pm daily. **Average** $16. **Credit** AmEx, V. **Map p286 D2/3**
A good sight less exorbitant than Chopsticks (*see below*), but worse all round. Too many of the dishes are smothered in a thick, tasteless cornflour-like sauce. The desserts are pitiful. The décor is dominated by a king-size aquarium.

Chopsticks
Grand Hotel Europe, Mikhailovskaya Ulitsa 1/7 (329 6000). Metro Gostiny Dvor. **Open** noon-11pm daily. **Average** $50. **Credit** AmEx, DC, MC, V. **Map p287 D4/5**
This may be one of the world's most expensive Chinese restaurants. But the expense is probably worth it if you're in St Petersburg with an insatiable craving for Szechuan chicken, hot and sour soup or ton yung gung, all of which are absolutely top rank. Try the lychee or the fried bananas for dessert if you've any cash left over.

Eclectic/European

Academe
Birzhevoi Proyezd 2 (327 8949). Metro Vasileostrovskaya. **Open** noon-5am daily. **Average** $60. **Credit** AmEx, DC, MC, V. **Map p287 C4**
Loaded with gun-toters, but an elegant, beautifully appointed restaurant on university premises. From wood-oven pizza (not that great) to caviar (good) and pasta (even better), the food is eclectic and light – a rarity in St Petersburg.

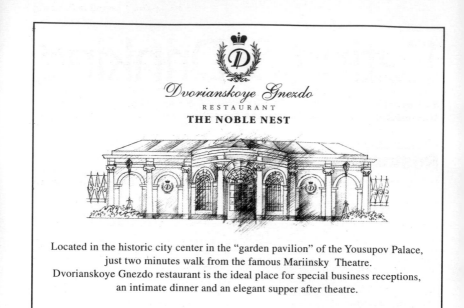

Camelot

Nevsky Prospekt 22-24, entrance on Bolshaya Konyushennaya Ulitsa (325 9906). Metro Nevsky Prospekt. **Open** noon-midnight daily. **Average** $38. **Credit** MC, V. **Map p278 D4**
Everything you'd expect from a medieval theme restaurant is on the menu here: a model of King Arthur on his throne, Gothic furniture, waiters in medieval costumes and vaulted ceilings. The food is an interesting mix from all over Europe, with some Russian dishes thrown in for good measure.

Bistro Le Cite

Naberezhnaya Reki Moiki 20 (314 1037). Metro Nevsky Prospekt. **Open** 11am-midnight daily. **Average** $16. **Credit** AmEx, MC, V. **Map p287 D4**
Stylish café-style place decorated in muted greys, which is almost more suited for coffee than it is for a full-scale meal. The food is French via New York and a little above average. Service can occasionally be astonishingly brusque.

Old Customs House

Tamozhenny Pereulok 1 (327 8980). Metro Nevsky Prospekt. **Open** 1pm-3am daily. **Average** $50. **Credit** MC, V. **Map p287 C4**
Located in a Tsarist-style customs house with more than a whiff of theme park about it. The prefab elegance couldn't be more to the taste of the clientele: a who's who of local mafia that lines the road outside with Mercs. The menu is pretty special; it features a generous caviar sampler and some fabulous fish dishes.

9vir

Hotelship Peterhof, Naberezhnaya Makarova 1 (325 8888). Metro Vasileostrovskaya. **Open** noon-11pm daily. **Average** $23. **Credit** AmEx, DC, MC, V. **Map p286 B3**
Svir goes one better than all the other maritime-theme places: it is actually on a ship. Festivals of various cuisines are often hosted on board, but festivities or not, it serves great seafood at moderate prices.

Senat Bar

Galernaya Ulitsa 1 (314 9253). Metro Nevsky Prospekt. **Open** 11am-5am daily. **Average** $40. **Credit** AmEx, MC, V. **Map p287 B5/C5**
A stylish basement place that's popular both as a restaurant and a bar, though regarding the food merely as an alcohol sop would be doing it a disservice. Senat got its 15 minutes of fame when Bill Clinton dropped in for a meal during a visit to St Petersburg a couple of years ago, but it's more usually frequented by a business crowd. The menu lists standards of European cuisine along with several traditional Russian items. The fresh fish dishes are invariably a good choice.

French

Bistro Le Français

Galernaya Ulitsa 20 (315 2465). Metro Nevsky Prospekt. **Open** 11am-1am daily. **Average** $35. **Credit** AmEx, DC, JCB, MC, V **Map p287 B5/C5**
Considered to be the only authentic French restaurant in town, Bistro Le Français is very popular with upmarket Russians and the expatriate crowd. It serves traditional French cuisine but adapts it to a number of local Russian ingredients – which makes for some great seafood, particularly salmon, sturgeon, pike-perch and crayfish. Pretty good food for the price.
English spoken. Vegetarian meals.

Le Chandeleur

Bolshaya Konyushennaya Ulitsa 1 (314 8380). Metro Nevsky Prospekt. **Open** 10am-midnight daily. **Average** $8. **Credit** MC, V. **Map p287 D4**
A crêperie with blini overtones that features a wide range of fillings from vegetarian, through seafood, to die-hard cholesterol-packed Russian, loaded down with sour cream and meat. The salads are way above the St Petersburg average, particularly the Niçoise.

Affordable eats

It ain't cheap to eat out in St Petersburg, and the quality doesn't always merit the price. If you're going to get average food, it makes sense to get it for average prices. If you're light on *nalichnive* (cash), forget about your credit card, bring a Russian dictionary and a lot of patience, ignore the occasional cat chasing its unsavoury prey and sample these atmospheric options.

The Crocodile

Galernaya Ulitsa 18 (314 9437). Metro Sennaya Ploshchad. **Open** 1-11pm Mon-Thur, Sun; 1pm-2am Fri, Sat. **Average** $13. **Map p287 B5/C5**
The funky croc-motif décor and the relaxed throng of fashionable diners make this one of the more interesting places in town for an informal meal. The vegetarian and pasta choices are to be recommended.

La Cucaracha

Naberezhnaya Reki Fontanki 39 (110 4006). Metro Gostiny Dvor. **Open** noon-1am Mon-Thur, Sun; noon-5am Fri, Sat. **Average** $16. **No credit cards. Map p289 E5**

The name says it all. Abysmal is probably a good way to describe the faux-Mex food, especially considering the owners are Latin American. Crisps instead of tortilla chips and runny lime-coloured gunk pretending to be guacamole.

Idiot

Naberezhnaya Reki Moiki 82 (315 1675). Metro Sennaya. **Open** noon-midnight daily. **Average** $10. **No credit cards. Map p287 C5**
A vaulted warren furnished with period junk, the Idiot, named after the Dostoyevsky novel, is best for just hanging out over a beer or coffee with other foreigners and a sprinkling of arty Russians. The vegetarian food has its moments, the blini, pelmeni and the borscht are good, but steer clear of any of the soy concoctions which suffer from a lack of imagination.

Salt & Pepper

Ploshchad Aleksandra Nevskogo 2 (274 3001, ext 2172). Metro Ploshchad Aleksandra Nevsky. **Open** noon-midnight daily. **Average** $23. **Credit** AmEx, DC, MC, V. **Map p289 G6**
On the second floor of the awful Hotel Moskva, Salt & Pepper is a real treat. The food can be bland, but always good, and served in a dimly lit, friendly atmosphere.

Haute cuisine

Dvorianskoye Gnezhdo
Ulitsa Dekabristov 21 (312 3205). Metro Sadovaya. **Open** noon-midnight daily. **Average** $65. **Credit** AmEx, DC, JCB, MC, V. **Map p287 B6/C5/6**
Located in the tea house of the opulent Yusupov Mansion, a stone's throw from the spot where the Yusupov brothers led the cabal responsible for poisoning and shooting Rasputin, the Dvorlandkoye Gnezhdo (noble nest) is an unsurpassable culinary adventure. Whizzkid Dutch chef Marcel Frantzen serves up traditional Russian standards such as pelmeni, normally filled with pedestrian pork or beef, but now concealing such delights as goose liver, fried quail and crayfish. Try anything you fancy – there's barely ever a weak link in the constantly changing menu, which incorporates elements of Chinese, Indian, Asian and European cuisine.

Podvorie
Filtrovskoye Shosse 16, Pushkin (465 1499). No public transport. **Open** noon-1am daily. **Average** $30. **Credit** AmEx, DC, MC, V.
Located in a wooden cottage or *isba* on the road from Tsarskoe Selo to Pavlovsk, this is another all-round experience restaurant. Its proprietor, Serguey Gutsait, has come up with the perfect balance of atmosphere and excellent dishes including some wonderful soups (the green soup, made with sorrel, is especially good), fresh caviar, great pickled mushrooms and other delicacies, and the usual Russian (but this time high-quality) fare. Highly recommended – but you'll need a taxi.

Taleon Club
Naberezhnaya Reki Moiki 59, corner Nevsky Prospekt (315 7645). Metro Gostiny Dvor. **Open** noon-6am daily. **Average** $100. **Credit** AmEx, DC, JCB, MC, V. **Map p287 D4/5**
Located in the beautifully renovated mansion of the Yeliseyev brothers (nineteenth-century merchants), the Taleon features a café downstairs, a sauna and health club, a casino on the top floor and a restaurant. Be warned: it's hugely expensive. The extensive wine list is particularly financially draining – and beware the $300 glass of Cognac. The menu ranges from traditional Russian to nouvelle cuisine and the fish dishes are especially delicious. *See also p244* **Floorshows** for the Taleon's entertainment.

Indian

Swagat
Bolshoi Prospekt 91 (217 4428). Metro Petrogradskaya. **Open** noon-11pm daily. **Average** $22. **Credit** AmEx, DC, JCB, MC, V. **Map p286 B2/C1/2**
Since it opened in late 1997, Swagat has remained the second choice for Indian food, and not only because of its somewhat out-of-the-way location. On the whole, the food is not great and even the once-generous portions have gradually shrunk. One consolation is the service, which is both personal and friendly.

Tandoor
Voznesensky Prospekt 2 (312 3886). Metro Sadovaya. **Open** noon-11pm daily. **Average** $16. **Credit** AmEx, DC, JCB, MC, V. **Map p287 C6**
Calcutta-born Swapan Biswas, the chef at St Petersburg's first Indian restaurant, tones down the spices to cater to Russian tastes, but nevertheless reliably manages to produce dishes that are consistently good and authentic. Try the tandoori chicken or the dhal or just submit to the set thali menu. Avoid the salads, which are dull and often served only with sour cream.

Italian

Milano
Karavannaya Ulitsa 8 (314 7348). Metro Nevsky Prospekt. **Open** noon-midnight daily. **Average** $35. **Credit** AmEx, DC, MC, V. **Map p289 E4**
A beautiful space, immersed in cool, pastel colours. The food, however, is a little lacking in spark. Salads are substantial and the puttanesca sauce (a spicy blend of caper, olive and garlic) and the salmon drenched in orange sauce are wonderful. To round off, ask the waiter about their large grappa selection.

La Strada
Bolshaya Konyushennaya Ulitsa 27 (312 4700). Metro Gostiny Dvor. **Open** noon-midnight daily. **Average** $18. **No credit cards. Map 287 D4**
The décor here is designed to imitate a street scene – a kind of inside-out sidewalk café – but don't let that put you off. The wood-oven pizzas are great, particularly the quattro stagioni, and the vegetarian lasagne is also delicious.

Landskrona
Nevsky Palace Hotel, Nevsky Prospekt 57 (275 2001). Metro Mayakovskaya. **Open** 12.30pm-midnight daily. **Average** $47; *set lunch* $29 Mon-Fri. **Credit** AmEx, DC, MC, V. **Map p289 E5/F5**
On the top floor of the Nevsky Palace Hotel, the Landskrona affords a terrific view of the city skyline. Be prepared to pay three times regional Italian prices for a familiar line-up of Italian cuisine, all nicely prepared and presented.

Rossi's
Grand Hotel Europe, Mikhailovskaya Ulitsa 1/7 (329 6000). Metro Gostiny Dvor. **Open** noon-11pm daily. **Average** $50. **Credit** AmEx, DC, MC, V. **Map p287 D4/5**
Pasta primavera is superb here, as is the pasta marinara, and the salads come big and fresh. But the endless *Godfather* soundtrack playing as background music, when combined with the metal detector and security guards, makes for a rather sinister atmosphere.

Japanese

Fujijama
Kamenoostrovsky Prospekt 54 (327 5285). Metro Gorkovskaya. **Open** noon-11pm Sun-Thur; noon-1am Fri, Sat. **Average** $29. **Credit** MC, V. **Map p286 D2**
Fujijama serves decent sushi and other Japanese food at – best of all – decent prices. There are intimate, private rooms, and various seating arrangements (including on the floor).

Sakura
Naberezhnaya Kanala Griboyedova 12 (315 9474). Metro Nevsky Prospekt. **Open** noon-11pm daily. **Average** $60. **Credit** MC, V. **Map p287 D4**
A maze of *shoji*-screened rooms simmering in an appropriately hushed atmosphere. The sushi here is fresh and delicious – and breathtakingly expensive. Try the speciality seafood and meat soups, which come with instructions for at-table preparation.

Russian

Adamant
Naberezhnaya Reki Moiki 72 (311 5575). Metro Gostiny Dvor. **Open** 1pm-midnight daily. **Average** $34. **Credit** V. **Map p287 C5/D4/5**
A garish, gilded labyrinth, lined with second-rate modern art and brutalist piping, the Adamant has been tailor-built

*Huffing and puffing at the **Taleon Club** cigar room. See page 230.*

for the wealthy and tasteless. But despite the queasy, self-conscious 'New Russian' ambience, the food is terrific. The seafood is best, particularly the sturgeon, prepared in a choice of three ways.

The Admiralty

Nevsky Palace Hotel, Nevsky Prospekt 57 (275 2001). Metro Mayakovskaya. **Open** 5-11pm daily. **Average** $40. **Credit** AmEx, MC, V. **Map p289 F5/6**
Maritime, shmaritime. Dining or drinking out in St Petersburg is enough to make you never want to see another bottled boat ever again. But this is rather tasteful with acres of burgundy leather upholstery. Diners are welcomed with a shot of vodka. The menu is conventional but uniformly good: pelmeni, chicken kiev, beef stroganoff, golubtsy, shashlik and soups like bortsch and ukha (fish broth). For dessert don't miss the grassky cake – meringue with plums marinated in red wine.

Austeria

Ioannovsky Ravelin, Peter & Paul Fortress (238 4262). Metro Gorkovskaya. **Open** noon-midnight daily. **Average** $48. **Credit** AmEx, DC, MC, V. **Map p286 C3/D3**
Named after one of Peter the Great's ships and with a great location in an old officers' meeting hall within the Peter and Paul fortress, Austeria offers quite a lot in the way of ambience, but, unfortunately, somewhat less in terms of food, which doesn't quite measure up to its ship-shape context. The sturgeon shashlik on pasta is one of the better choices, but the fried fish and meat dishes are languorous and bulky and should be avoided.

The Caviar Bar

Grand Hotel Europe, Mikhailovskaya Ulitsa 1/7 (329 6000). Metro Gostiny Dvor. **Open** 5-11pm daily. **Average** $60. **Credit** AmEx, DC, MC, V. **Map p287 D4/5**

Before the Revolution this caviar bar was a well-known aristocratic hangout. Revived a couple of years ago, it still retains that intoxicating, grainy, elitist air. Try the Kamchatka crab, the sturgeon and salmon mousse or the Siberian style dumplings with a champagne sauce. And, of course, the caviar, a selection of both black and red served with blinis and sour cream.

Count Suvorov

Ulitsa Lomonosova 6 (315 4328/314 6301). Metro Gostiny Dvor. **Open** 2pm-1am daily. **Average** $80. **Credit** AmEx, DC, JCB, MC, V. **Map p287 D5, p289 E6**
There's a rather Soviet flavour to the décor here – fussy pseudo-porcelain and other fake-luxury trappings – but a definite Russian flavour to the food. Try the bear filet or the deer carpaccio for that authentic fresh-off-the-hunt taste. Animal conservationists or those who prefer their meat less real can stick to the extensive selection of salads. The wine list contains a good selection of champagnes at whopping prices as well as the Chateau 'Peter I' exceptionelle, a snip at $1,200.

Evropa

Europe Restaurant, Grand Hotel Europe, Mikhailovskaya Ulitsa 1/7 (329 6000). Metro Nevsky Prospekt. **Breakfast served** 7-10.30am; **dinner served** 7-11pm, daily. **Average** $85. **Credit** AmEx, MC, V. **Map p287 D4/5**
What was a distinguished restaurant a couple of years ago seems to have become an afterthought (unless you are staying at the Grand Hotel Europe). The cuisine is sauce-oriented, and the sauces tend to be overcomplex. All ingredients are first class, however, as is the service.

1913

Voznesensky Prospekt 13/2 (315 5148). Metro Sennaya Ploshchad. **Open** noon-4am daily. **Average** $32. **Credit** MC, V. **Map p287 C6**

Well-located near the Mariinsky Theatre and the Astoria Hotel, 1913 is the Russian restaurant of choice for many locals and expatriates, so evening booking is a necessity. Great blini, pelmeni and caviar abound.

Restaurant St Petersburg

Naberezhnaya Kanala Griboyedova 5 (314 4947). Metro Gostiny Dvor. **Open** noon-1am daily. **Average** $50. **Credit** AmEx, DC, MC, V. **Map p287 D4**
Chef Ilya Lazerson aims to combine a lightness of touch with traditional Russian cuisine – and succeeds. The beef stroganoff is a treat, and the seafood is wonderfully fresh. Try the sturgeon or the marinated salmon, flavoured with juniper and saffron.

Staroye Café

Naberezhnaya Reki Fontanki 108, corner Moskovsky Prospekt (316 5111). Metro Sennaya Ploshchad or Sadovaya. **Open** noon-11pm daily. **Average** $15. **No credit cards. Map p287 D6**
A microscopic little nook, suffused with dingy, pitchy atmosphere and adorned with designer knick-knacks, bare brick and gaping cracks. The traditional Russian food doesn't quite match up to the cosy surroundings.

Spanish

Sevilla

Malaya Morskaya Ulitsa 7 (315 5371). Metro Gostiny Dvor. **Open** noon-11pm. **Average** $30. **No credit cards. Map p287 C5**
The only Spanish restaurant in town, Sevilla has a menu that aspires to be authentic. It's occasionally let down, particularly by the tapas, in which some of the ingredients appear to be of the canned variety. However, the gazpacho and the paella are usually good and the wine list contains some great Spanish bottles.
Occasional flamenco performances.

Pubs & Bars

Liverpool Bar

Ulitsa Mayakovskogo 16 (279 2054). Metro Mayakovskaya. **Open** 11am-2am Mon-Thur; 11am-4am Fri-Sun. **Map p289 F4/5**
A theme bar that pipes early Beatles into your brain through every sensory duct. Despite the relatively tasteful, woody décor, you'll soon be crying out for the Breeders' version of *Happiness is a Warm Gun.*

Molly's Irish Bar

Ulitsa Rubenshteina 36 (319 9768). Metro Vladimirskaya or Dostoyevskaya. **Open** noon-midnight Mon-Thur; noon-3am Fri, Sat; noon-1am Sun. **Map p289 E5**
Overpriced Guinness is served to you in a seething, lathery, unsettled mass (could there be any greater Irish Bar sin?). Still, the bar is lively and popular.

New Holland Bar

Ploshchad Truda 3 (314 6240). Metro Nevsky Prospekt. **Open** 11.30am-11.30pm daily. **Map p287 B5**
A cute, welcoming little watering hole based around a schizophrenic nautical theme (there's a poster of a knickerless rollerblader scratching her arse among the bottled ships). The relaxed young local crowd, a smattering of foreign students and the cheap (if basic) grub make this the best Russian-style pub in the city.

Rose Pub

Liteiny Prospekt 14 (275 3554). Metro Chernishevskaya. **Open** 11am-5am. **Admission** $4 men, $2 women. **Map p289 E4, p288 E3**
Dismal Finnish cellar bar frequented by hoods, sad guys sitting alone and young women hoping to earn a little extra money on the side.

Sadko's

*Grand Hotel Europe, Mikhailovskaya Ulitsa 1/7
(329 6000). Metro Gostiny Dvor.* **Open** noon-1am daily.
Map p287 D4/5
Once the only place where you could drink in relatively hos-
pitable surroundings, now a ghost pub, frequented only by
disoriented guests of the adjacent Grand Hotel Europe.

The Shamrock

*Ulitsa Dekabristov 27 (219 4625). Metro
Sennaya Ploshchad.* **Open** noon-2am daily. **Map**
p287 B5/C5/6
Cut into cosy snugs and laced with all the usual emeraldy
bric-à-brac, the Shamrock is one of the best pubs in the city.
It sports some nice eccentric touches like the backroom
devoted to opera and ballet (it's just across the road from the
Mariinsky Theatre), as well as hosting surprisingly decent
Irish music at the weekends.

Tribunal Bar

*Ulitsa Dekabristov 1 (311 1690). Metro Gostiny
Dvor.* **Open** 4pm-3am Mon-Thur; 7pm-3.30am Fri,
Sat. **Admission** $10 men, $2 women. **Map p287**
B5/C5/6
Kitschy, overdone touches include religious icons and a
model of Marilyn with her dress aflutter over a grating. The
rowdy, crass clientele sums up this cavernous place nicely.

Tinkoff

Kazanskaya Ulitsa 7 (314 8485). Metro Nevsky Prospekt.
Open 11am-5am daily. **Credit** MC, V. **Map p287**
C5/D5
The city's first microbrewery is a funky, minimalist joint
that that looks as if it was transplanted from London's Soho.
Great beer, fashionable clientele and cheap pizzas give it an
edge on every other pub in St Petersburg.

Tschaika Bar

*Naberezhnaya Kanala Griboyedova 14 (312 4631). Metro
Nevsky Prospekt.* **Open** 11am-3am. **Credit** AmEx, MC,
V. **Map p287 D4**
Popular with prostitutes and Finns sporting haircuts like
Limahl from Kajagoogoo, the Tschaika isn't recommended
unless you're really stuck, or one of the above.
Meals served.

Zapravka

Bolshoi Prospekt 28 (235 2816). Metro Petrogradskaya.
Open noon-2am daily. **No cedit cards. Map p286**
D2/C1/2.
A cosy little bohemian hangout cluttered with designer junk.
One of the best, cheapest and most relaxing places in town.

Cafés & bistros

Bahlsen – Le Café

*Nevsky Prospekt 142 (271 2811). Metro Ploshchad
Vosstaniya.* **Open** 1pm-1am daily. **Average** $30. **Credit**
AmEx, DC, MC, V. **Map p289 F5/G6**
A kind of supercafé with bar and restaurant attached. The
tasteless interior décor is offset by the relatively clean out-
door veranda and the superior cakes from Germany.

Captain Nemo

Prospekt Kima 28 (350 3966). Metro Primorskaya.
Open 11am-10pm. **Average** $16. **No credit cards**.
This weird, metallic, sub-aqueous, nautical themed café
proves almost intriguing – all that's missing is the periscope.

Orient

Bolshaya Morskaya Ulitsa 25 (311 9733). **Open** 24
hours daily. **Average** $8. **Credit** MC, V. **Map p287**
C5/D5

Floorshows

The floorshow, a basic essential of the Soviet
restaurant experience, is dying a long and
painfully slow death in St Petersburg. An
evening out is not quite complete, it seems,
unless a young nubile Russian is waving her
glands under your nose, or the chorus from
Swan Lake are clacking by on points. Some
shows are diverting; others uproariously bad.
Here are the stand-outs:

The Valhall

*Nevsky Prospekt 22-24 (311 0024). Metro Nevsky
Prospekt (Malaya Konushennaya Ulitsa exit).* **Open**
9am-5am Mon-Thur, Sun; 9am-5am Fri, Sat. **Average**
$30; *set lunch* $12 noon-6pm daily. **Map 287 D5**
Watch out at 1.30am for the scrawny stripper in the
fold-out jacuzzi French-kissing a rubber snake. The
perfect complement to any meal.

The St Petersburg

*Naberezhnaya Kanala Griboyedova 5 (314 4947).
Metro Gostiny Dvor.* **Open** noon-1am daily.
Average $50. **Credit** AmEx, DC, EC, MC, V.
Map 207 D4
A testosterone-charged Peter the Great is surrounded
nightly by a bevy of scantily dressed showgirls. For
the tourists, you know.

The Taleon

*Naberezhnaya Reki Moiku 59 (312 5373). Metro
Gostiny Dvor.* **Open** noon-6am daily. **Average**
$100. **Credit** AmEx, DC, MC, V. **Map p287 D5**
During its Red And Black parties on the last Friday of
every month (by invitation only), the club hosts a glam-
rock circus performer juggling a baby alligator whose
jaws are clamped shut with sellotape.

An unremarkable, Western-standard café, which offers the
usual selection of Russian salads and pouffed-up cakes. The
great thing about it is that it's always open.

Sever

*Nevsky Prospekt 22-24 (315 9017). Metro Nevsky
Prospekt.* **Open** 10am-9pm daily. **Average** $6. **No
credit cards. Map p287 D4/5**
One section of Sever is a huge (and rather wasteful) marble
barn, where Russian-style pastries are sold; the other half is
a tasteful little café where you can watch life on the Nevsky
passing you by.

Tetris Internet Café

*Ulitsa Chernyakhovskogo 33 (164 1877). Metro Ligovsky
Prospekt.* **Open** 9am-9pm Mon-Fri, 1-9pm Sat, Sun.
Cost *per hour* 10am-1pm $4, 1-9pm $8. **Map p289 F8**
A boffin's compu-chamber with en suite café (good beans).

Zhyli-Bhyli

*Sadovaya Ulitsa 14/52, corner Nevsky Prospekt (314
6230). Metro Gostiny Dvor.* **Open** 24 hours daily.
Average $6. **No credit cards. Map p289 E4**
Zhili-Buili (once upon a time) is a quaint place adjacent to a
puppet theatre on Nevsky Prospekt – an almost too convenient location. The line-up of cakes is very inviting and there
are unnervingly huge pottery insects lurking around.

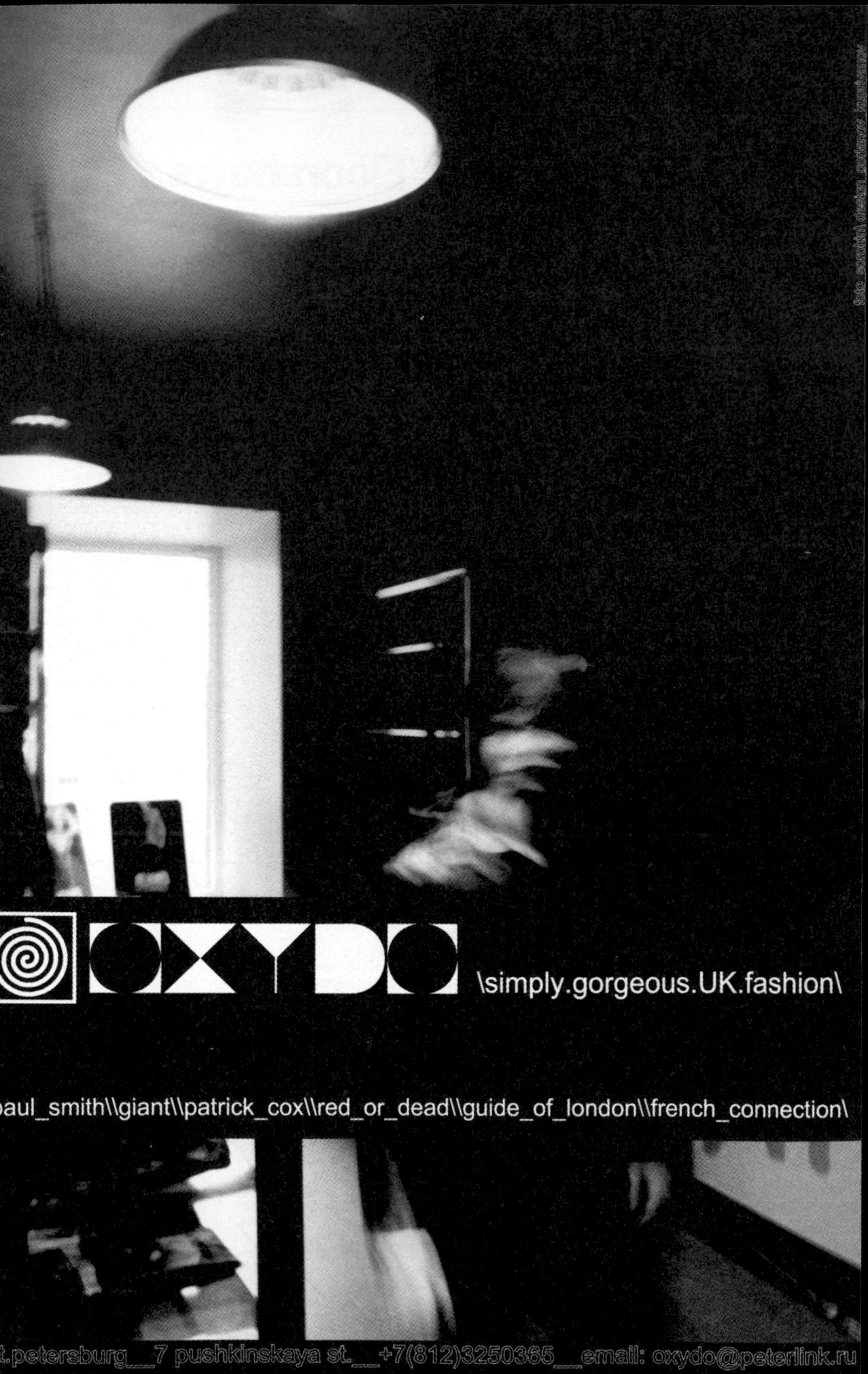

OXYDO
\simply.gorgeous.UK.fashion\
paul_smith\\giant\\patrick_cox\\red_or_dead\\guide_of_london\\french_connection\
t.petersburg__7 pushkinskaya st.__+7(812)3250365__email: oxydo@peterlink.ru

Shopping & Services

Poised between Western and Soviet-style shopping, St Petersburg has unique purchase power.

Though it may no longer be necessary for locals to make shopping forays to Helsinki to find the basic designer necessities, St Petersburg is far from a shopping paradise. Shops tend to be small and stocks even smaller, so that while it is relatively easy to find good stuff out there, it's much more tricky finding it in the size or colour you want. Many shopfronts still give hardly any indication of what lies inside. This is the town, as temporary resident Brian Eno once remarked, 'where the shops have no name'. Many of the city's stores are just international chain imports, but some are home-grown gems.

A host of new shops can now be found lining the more upscale areas, transforming Nevsky Prospekt, Kamennoostrovsky Prospekt and Liteiny Prospekt back into the vibrant commercial areas they were before the Revolution.

Minimalist chic – **Tatyana Parfionova**, *p236.*

One-stop shopping

Department stores

Bolshoi Gostiny Dvor
Nevsky Prospekt 35 (314 9986/fax 314 9881). Metro Gostiny Dvor or Nevsky Prospekt. **Open** 10am-9pm daily. **Credit** MC, V. **Map p287 D5**
The biggest and oldest department store in the city. Originally an open air market, Gostiny Dvor retains many of the characteristics of a bazaar. The layout is sprawling, with rectangular arcades broken up into stall-like segments around a gigantic courtyard. The shops vary enormously, from gaudy stands offering cheap Chinese toys and pet food to quality clothing and sports shops. Finding anything can involve walking miles, often to no purpose. After a long period of restoration, the section facing Nevsky Prospekt opened in 1998, offering a clutch of new designer fashion shops tailored to the tastes of the New Rich.

Dom Leningradskoi Torgovli
Bolshaya Konyushennaya Ulitsa 21-23 (219 9502/315 2192). Metro Gostiny Dvor or Nevsky Prospekt. **Open** 10am-9pm Mon-Sat; 11am-8pm Sun. **No credit cards.** **Map p287 D4**
Known locally as DLT, this chaotic department store has about it the typically Soviet feel of a lack of central planning. The unruly roster of concessions includes lots of no-name places selling shoes, lingerie, TVs and sportswear. One of the highlights is a small Doc Marten's store on the first floor.

Passazh
Nevsky Prospekt 48 (311 7084/fax 311 1426). Metro Gostiny Dvor. **Open** 10am-9pm daily. **Credit** MC, V. **Map p289 E5**
Built in neo-Renaissance style in the mid-nineteenth century to cater for the shopping predilections of the growing upper-middle classes, the Passazh was known in pre-Revolutionary times for its luxury establishments. These days, it's a fairly untidy affair, cluttered with junky stalls. Not much use for anything other than picking up soap powder, cosmetics and cheap antique knick-knacks.

Markets

Apraksin Dvor
Sadovaya Ulitsa. Metro Gostiny Dvor or Nevsky Prospekt. **Open** (approx) 9am-6pm daily. **Map p289 E4**
A taste of Bangkok in the heart of St Petersburg, Apraxin Dvor is a squalid, anarchic labyrinth of stands, kiosks and grubby hut-like shops. You can pick up a limited range of stuff from cheap (and probably bootleg) vodka to pirate GameBoy cartridges to grotty Chinese-made clothes. Worth a look, even if there's nothing here you'd ever want to buy.

Kuznechny Rynok
Kuznechny Prospekt (312 4161). Metro Vladimirskaya. **Open** (approx) 8am-6pm daily. **Map p289 E6/F6**
This market is one of the main reasons why St Petersburg survived communism – when the shelves in the regular shops were empty, you could always find something in this little enclave of raw, fresh capitalism. It sells mostly fruit and vegetables, but also devotes a large section to the joys of *smetana* (Russian sour cream) and honey.

Veshchevoi Rinok

Ulitsa Marshala Kozakova. Metro Avtovo, then special market bus from across the street. **Open** (approx) 9am-6pm Sat, Sun.

This is St Petersburg's pirate compact disc mecca (both audio and CD-Rom). Collections of software that should cost thousands of dollars are crammed on to a single CD going for about five. Most of the stalls sell identical stuff, so don't waste your time going around to them all. The market also sells hi-fi equipment and some cheap clothes.

Fashion
Clubwear

Renegade

Naberezhnaya Reki Fontanki 50 (312 8086). Metro Gostiny Dvor or Nevsky Prospekt. **Open** noon-8pm daily. **No credit cards. Map p289 E4/5**

This funky bunker on Fontanka stocks a small but cutting-edge range of T-shirts and day-glo jackets. Also the best footwear line-up in town: Shelly's, Doc Marten's, Grinders.

Designer

Gianni Versace

Nevsky Prospekt 39 (310 9711). Metro Gostiny Dvor or Nevsky Prospekt. **Open** 11am-8pm Mon-Sat. **Credit** AmEx, JCB, MC, V. **Map p289 E5**

Probably the most luxurious shop in St Petersburg, based in one of Carlo Rossi's pavilions in the Anichkov Palace (*see p189*, **Sightseeing**). The crisp, classical lines of Versace's *Dolce Vita* style are perfectly set off by the bold classicism of the surroundings. All very New Russian.

Oxydo

Pushkinskaya Ulitsa 7 (325 0365). Metro Mayakovskaya. **Open** 11am-8pm daily. **Credit** MC, V. **Map p289 C5**

Not just a shop that sells fashion, but a fashion force in itself, where you'll encounter the trendiest faces in the city. One room is devoted to funky glasses (Ray Ban, Oxydo), including designer swimming goggles, all suspended on gunmetal racks. The second room is full of Red or Dead, French Connection, Helmut Lang and Patrick Cox.

Tatyana Parfionova

Nevsky Prospekt 51 (113 3669/fax 113 1917). Metro Mayakovskaya. **Open** noon-8pm daily. **Credit** MC. **Map p289 E5**

A terrific boutique from one of Russia's best and best-known designers. The interior, designed by local artists, is both restful and innovative. Clothes range from party stuff to classical businesswear for women, all immaculately made.

Vanity Boutique

Nevsky Palace Hotel, Nevsky Prospekt 57 (325 1077). Metro Mayakovskaya. **Open** 11am-9pm daily. **Credit** MC, V. **Map p289 F5**

This plain, no-frills establishment was the first designer boutique in St Petersburg, and created quite a splash when it opened back in 1993. Now that there is competition, it's lost its sparkle. The designer selection includes Paul Smith, MaxMara, Calvin Klein, Fendi, Alberta Feretti and Moschino.

Furs

Lena

Nevsky Prospekt 50 (311 7169/fax 312 3234). Metro Gostiny Dvor or Nevsky Prospekt. **Open** 10am-9pm daily. **Credit** MC, V. **Map p289 E5**

Rather staid and Soviet store selling conventional furs for

the frumpy monied set. Also stocks slightly more stylish numbers from the Italian fur companies Mazzi and Karuma.

Capital Palace

Nevsky Prospekt 57 (275 4372). Metro Mayakovskaya. **Open** 11am-9pm daily. **Credit** MC, V. **Map p289 F5**

Astonishingly beautiful and unspeakably decadent (or just unspeakable) furs, some at mind-blowing prices. Yves Saint Laurent sables and astrakhans from Turkmenistan go as high as $25,000. Also sells Cartier watches and accessories and Mont Blanc pens.

Mid-range

Chevignon

Nevsky Prospekt 32-34 (219 4434). Metro Gostiny Dvor or Nevsky Prospekt. **Open** 10am-10pm Mon-Sat; 11am-9pm Sun. **No credit cards. Map p287 D5**

Sporty, young casualwear for men, with a smattering of the same for women. Good selection of leather jackets. Everything is fairly expensive.

English Fashion House

Nevsky Prospekt 21 (312 5307/fax 312 2526). Metro Gostiny Dvor or Nevsky Prospekt. **Open** 11am-9pm daily. **Credit** MC, V. **Map p287 D4/5**

An expansive place known in Soviet times as the House of Fashion. The clothes are generally by second-rate English designers with a few talented, up-and-coming Russians thrown in, such as Yulia Bunakova.

Fashion accessories
Footwear

Charles Jourdain

Nevsky Prospekt 156 (277 1063). Metro Gostiny Dvor or Nevsky Prospekt. **Open** 11am-7pm daily. **Credit** AmEx, MC, V. **Map p289 G6**

Sleek little shop selling designer footwear by Charles Jourdain from about $150, and from Karl Lagerfeld and Montana from $300.

Salon Po Remonto Obuvi

Ulitsa Furmanova 25/6 (273 1802). Metro Chernyshevskaya. **Open** 9am-2pm, 3pm-9pm, daily. **Credit** MC, V. **Map p288 E3**

One of the few shoe-repair joints here that isn't just a guy in a kiosk on the corner. The results are variable – they might do a decent job, or they might totally destroy your shoes.

Jewellery

Ananov

Hotel Europe, Mikhailovskaya Ulitsa 1/7 (329 6577/fax 329 6578). Metro Gostiny Dvor or Nevsky Prospekt. **Open** 10am-1pm, 2-7pm, Mon-Sat. **Credit** AmEx, MC, V. **Map p287 D4/5**

A complete rip-off of Fabergé. You can get replicas of Fabergé's famous surprise eggs, which here contain precious gem representations of the Church of the Saviour on the Blood (from $25,000), plus smaller egg-shaped perfume bottles and Fabergé's gold and jade flowers in rock-crystal vases. Carl Fabergé must be spinning like a lathe in his grave.

Iakhont

Bolshaya Morskaya Ulitsa 24 (314 6447/enquiries 314 4235). Metro Gostiny Dvor or Nevsky Prospekt. **Open** 10am-7pm Mon-Sat; 11am-6pm Sun. **Credit** MC, V. **Map p287 C5/D5**

Based in the building that once housed Carl Fabergé's factory, Iakhont is one of the biggest jewellery stores in the city. A typical Soviet place offering a mishmash of wares from classic diamond rings to cheap trinkets.

Food & drink

Gallery de Vin

Isaakiyevskaya Ploshchad 13 (315 4731). Metro Gostiny Dvor or Nevsky Prospekt. **Open** 2-8pm Mon-Sat. **Credit** DC, JCB, MC, V. **Map p287 C5**
An unsurpassable selection of about 250 different French wines, champagne and Cognac. Unsurpassable prices, too.

Kalinka Stockman

Finlyandsky Prospekt 1 (542 2297). Metro Ploshchad Lenina. **Open** 9am-10pm daily. **Credit** AmEx, MC, V. Clean, clinical Scandinavian produce at ridiculous prices. Some foreigners – the very rich variety – won't shop anywhere else.

Supermarket

Nevsky Prospekt 48 (321 4701). Metro Gostiny Dvor or Nevsky Prospekt. **Open** 10am-9pm Mon-Sat, 11am-9pm Sun. **Credit** DC, MC, V. **Map p289 E5**
As this is the only large supermarket vaguely close to the centre of town, you really pay for the luxury of aisles and checkouts. Keep away from the frozen stuff, which is often expensive and none too pleasant.

Vendi English Bakery

Grechesky Prospekt 25 (275 6440). Metro Mayakovskaya. **Open** 10am-10pm daily. **No credit cards. Map p289 F4/5**
Simply great bread, pastries, cakes and sweets. You won't do better anywhere else in the city.

Yeliseyevsky

Nevsky Prospekt 56 (311 9323/fax 312 1865). Metro Gostiny Dvor or Nevsky Prospekt. **Open** 9am-9pm Mon-Fri; 10am-9pm Sat; 11am-8pm Sat. **No credit cards. Map p289 E5**

Better known for its lacy gold décor than anything in the display cases, Yeliseyevsky's is located in one of the most spectacular *style moderne* buildings in the city. In the room to the left is fruit, wine, spirits and cheese; to the right, it's predominantly fish, including a good selection of caviar.

Gifts & souvenirs

Antiques

Tertsia

Triad, Italianskaya Ulitsa 5 (110 5568). Metro Gostiny Dvor or Nevsky Prospekt. **Open** 11am-7pm daily. **Credit** MC, V. **Map p287 B4, p289 E5**
Cluttered two-room junket of antiques, including Soviet memorabilia such as Lenin busts, social realist posters and postcards. Also amazing stuff, such as huge Chinese urns from the time of Mao Tse Tung, a snip at about $20,000.

Flowers

Natali

Nevsky Palace Hotel, Nevsky Prospekt 57 (275 2001). Metro Mayakovskaya. **Open** 10am-10pm daily. **Credit** DC, JCB, MC, V. **Map p289 E5**
A glass kiosk by the hotel entrance, Natali offers the usual selection of roses, carnations and so on. But it also sells pretty souvenirs and ornamental wreaths made from dried flowers and a nice selection of dinky flower pots.

Souvenirs

Art Shop

Floshchad Iskusstv 1 (219 1962). Metro Nevsky Prospekt. **Open** 10am-8pm daily. **Credit** MC, V. **Map p287 D4**
There are more *matrioshkas* (hollow dolls) here than you ever thought existed, in all of their incarnations. Giant and ornate will cost up to $70, though you can get a simple eight-piece nesting doll for about $15.

Shopping in Style Moderne – the glittering **Yeliseyevsky** *food store.*

North Way

*Ploshchad Truda 2 (312 2062/fax 312 2278). Metro
Gostiny Dvor or Nevsky Prospekt.* **Open** 9am-9pm daily.
Credit AmEx, MC, V. **Map p287 B5**
A souvenir megastore selling everything from *matrioshkas*
to Russian woollens to caviar to speciality vodkas to amber
necklaces to Soviet military trinkets. There is also an unsurpassable range of traditional lacquer boxes at prices ranging from $30 to $3,000. If you buy, you get a free drink.
Tourists may think this is heaven and never want to leave.

Suvenirnaya Yarmarka

*Souvenir Market, Kanal Griboyedova, between
Konyushennaya Ploshchad & Naberezhnaya Reki Moiki.*
Open 10am-6pm daily. **No credit cards**. **Map p287 D4**
Plenty of military watches, Red Army uniforms and hip flasks,
leavened with a healthy measure of *matrioshkas*. Never pay
what they ask, particularly if you only speak English.

Health & beauty

Opticians

Instrumentarium

*Nevsky Prospekt 60 (311 3262). Metro Gostiny Dvor or
Nevsky Prospekt.* **Open** 10am-8pm Mon-Sat; 11am-5pm
Sun. **Credit** V. **Map p289 E5**
Good selection of frames by Boss, Armani, YSL, Paloma
Picasso, Charmant, Marc O'Polo and Ray Ban. Standard lens-
es are kept in stock, as is contact lens paraphernalia.
Branch: Sredny Prospekt 70 (321 9989).

Salons

Carita

*Suvorovsky Prospekt 48/2 (271 9830/fax 327 3795).
Metro Ploshchad Vosstaniya.* **Open** 9am-8pm daily.
Credit AmEx, MC, V. **Map p289 F5/G4**
Slick, luxurious salon providing a wide range of beauty treatments in a pleasant, efficient atmosphere. Part of a worldwide chain. A straightforward men's haircut will set you
back about $40; women's prices start at $50.

Nevsky Palace Hairdressers

*Nevsky Palace Hotel, Nevsky Prospekt 57 (275 3524).
Metro Mayakovskaya.* **Open** 10am-9pm daily. **Credit**
AmEx, JCB, MC, V. **Map p289 E5**
Aims for a nouveau riche set by offering a range of styles
from super-chic to average via well-crafted glam. Stylists
and receptionists are all as carefully turned out as the clients.
Prices range from $43 for a simple men's short back and
sides to about $70 for women.

Leisure

Books

Dom Knigi

*Nevsky Prospekt 28 (219 6402/fax 311 9895). Metro
Gostiny Dvor or Nevsky Prospekt.* **Open** 9am-8pm Mon-
Sat; 10am-7pm Sun. **No credit cards**. **Map p287 D5**
St Petersburg's biggest bookstore, located in an art nouveau
building that was once the headquarters of the Singer sewing
machine empire in Russia. The books are all in Russian and
the layout is unreconstructedly Soviet, though there is a new
western-style department on the second floor.

Staraya Kniga

*Nevsky Prospekt 18 (312 6676). Metro Gostiny Dvor or
Nevsky Prospekt.* **Open** 10am-2pm, 3-8pm, daily. **Credit**
MC. **Map p287 C4/D4**

Large antiquarian bookshop, with one room devoted to old
Russian books and one to foreign tomes, where you can find
obscure gems: nineteenth-century French compilations on
the theme of love or first edition George Bernard Shaw
plays. Also a good selection of old maps, posters, prints
and stamps.

Electronics

Noteboutique

*Nevsky Prospekt 184 (274 1720/327 0321). Metro
Ploshchad Aleksandra Nevskogo.* **Open** 10am-9pm daily.
Credit MC, V. **Map p289 G6**
Billing itself as selling computer haute couture, this tiny
basement shop stocks flash notebooks as well as flat-screen
monitors and micro-desktops.

Music

Music Shok

*Ulitsa Vosstaniya 13 (277 3178). Metro Ploshchad
Vosstaniya.* **Open** 11am-11pm daily. **Credit** MC, V. **Map
p289 F4/5**
For years, Music Shok was one of the only places where you
could get real CDs (as opposed to Bulgarian bootlegs). While
it still takes far too long for new releases to filter on to the
shelves here, it still has the widest choice.

Travellers' needs

Laundry & dry cleaning

Beloruchka

*Mokhovaya Ulitsa 31B (272 8982). Metro
Chernyshevskaya.* **Open** 9am-8pm Mon-Fri; 10am-6pm
Sat, Sun. **No credit cards**. **Map p288 E3, p289 E4**
Features efficient English equipment for washing and dry
cleaning. Specialises in cleaning designer brands that else-
where could come out of the process looking like a dishrag.

Photographic

Express Peter the Great

*Bolshaya Morskaya Ulitsa 32 (110 6403). Metro Gostiny
Dvor or Nevsky Prospekt.* **Open** 9am-8pm daily. **No
credit cards**. **Map p287 C5/D5**
Develops not only your average snaps (in an hour or more)
but also processes slides. Other branches do professional
black and white developing and printing and sell developing requisites.
Branches: Malaya Konyushennaya Ulitsa 7 (110 6497);
Nevsky Prospekt 107 (275 3968); 64 Bolshoi Prospekt (232
9080); Prospekt Chernyshevskogo 17 (279 5233).

Sivma

*Ulitsa Koli Tomchaka 28 (298 6547). Metro Moskovskiye
Vorota.* **Open** 24 hours daily. **No credit cards**.
You can pick up a 'point and shoot' in most developing
places, but this is the best all-round camera store in the city,
with a full range of professional gear.

Printing, photocopy, fax

Alpha Graphics

*Nevsky Prospekt 25 (258 7500/fax 326 2551). Metro
Gostiny Dvor or Nevsky Prospekt.* **Open** 9am-9pm Mon-
Fri; 10am-6pm Sat. **Credit** AmEx, DC, JCB, MC, V. **Map
p287 D4/5**
Nicely renovated place with inexpensive services, particularly compared to the unbelievable prices charged in hotels
for photocopying.

Trips Out of St Petersburg

Royal residences and ancient citadels – St Petersburg's satellites are a history lover's heaven.

St Petersburg is a day-tripper's paradise. The Russian Imperial family's lust for quality leisure-time has left grand palaces scattered all over the outskirts of the city. Not a single one of these is less than spectacular, whether you want to stay indoors and gawk at the mouldings or just wander around the landscaped parks. And in winter, for your added tripping pleasure, huge ice slides form the grounds of some palaces, notably **Pavlovsk** and **Tsarskoye Selo**, giving a day out a raw edge of refreshing, headlong danger.

Further afield, St Petersburg is within fairly easy reach of the medieval towns Pskov and Novgorod. But perhaps the most fascinating of St Petersburg's out-of-town sights is **Kizhi Island**, an extraordinary enclave of traditional wooden architecture.

Details of stations, both bus and train, and of tour companies running out-of-town excursions are given in the **Getting Around St Petersburg** section of the **Directory**. For a map covering the area, *see page 285*. Note that the last admission to most palaces is an hour before closing time. Phone numbers are given as dialled from St Petersburg, including the long-distance prefix (8). Drop this and the area code if you are calling locally.

Peterhof

If you take only one trip out of St Petersburg, this has got to be the one. Known as either Petrodvorets (which translates as Peter's Palace) or Peterhof (which means Peter's Court in German and is pronounced 'Petergof' in Russian), depending on whether you prefer the Tsarist alternative to which it reverted in 1992, Peter the Great's summer residence began life as an observation point from which the Tsar could monitor construction at the Kronstadt Fortress some 10 kilometres (6 miles) to the north. Later it was upgraded to the status of a palace, with the help of the architect Jean-Baptiste Alexandre Le Blond.

By 1721, the famous fountains were already in place and the parks (both upper and lower) had been laid out. Later, Elizabeth II took an interest in Peterhof and commissioned Rastrelli to expand the Great Palace, producing much of what we see today. The last phase of Peterhof's construction took place after World War II, when most of the palaces and parks were wantonly destroyed by the Nazis. Only after an extensive and prolonged restoration was it reopened to the public.

If you come by hydrofoil, which is by far the most convenient and enjoyable means of travelling here, the first main feature you'll come across is the **Grand Cascade**, now gushing and spurting again after a six-year bout of restoration. In the centre is a glittering, golden statue of Samson tearing open a lion's jaws surrounded by three cascades, 64 fountains and 37 statues, all of which Tsar Peter helped to design and build.

The grounds also contain two other cascades – the Chequerboard cascade to the east (left when approaching the main palace) and the Golden Hill cascade to the west. Look out also for trick fountains that squirt water, triggered by hidden switches, at passers-by.

At the western end of the grounds, set behind a rectangular pond, is the **Marly Palace**, which served as Peter's guesthouse. The **Hermitage**, which is just to the east of Marly on the seafront and surrounded by a tiny moat, was designed to offer a little seclusion and isolation when members of the royal family were in a reflective mood. On the western side of the grounds is the Dutch-style **Monplaisir Palace**, which Peter designed himself and which is famous for hosting his wild, drunken and debauched 'assemblies'. To the left of the Monplaisir is the **Catherine Wing** (1747-54), which gets its name from the short period that Catherine the Great spent here during the reign of her husband, Peter III.

In the centre of the grounds is the **Great Palace**. The raised pediment that makes the building so striking when approaching from the shore dates back to Le Blond's first early eighteenth-century efforts. The rococo flourishes come courtesy of Rastrelli, who was commis-

Letting the train take the strain.

Contacts

Great Palace
420 0073. **Open** 10.30am-6pm Tue-Sun; *Grottoes* 11am-5pm summer only. Closed last Tue of month. **Admission** $8.50; $4 students, under-17s. **No credit cards.** *Guided tours by arrangment. Information in English.*

Marly
Open *summer* 10.30am-6pm Tue-Sun; *winter* 10.30am-6pm Sat, Sun. **Admission** $3; $1.50 students.

Hermitage
Open *summer* 10.30am-6pm Tue-Sun; *winter* 10.30am-6pm Sat, Sun. **Admission** $3; $1.50 students.

Monplaisir
Open *summer* 10.30am-6pm Tue-Sun; *winter* 10.30am-6pm Sat, Sun. **Admission** $6; $3 students.

Catherine Wing
Open *winter* 10.30am-6pm Sat, Sun; *summer* 10.30am-6pm Mon-Wed, Fri-Sun. **Admission** $3, $1.50 students.

Gardens
Open 9am-7pm daily. **Admission** *Lower Park* $4; $2 students, under-17s; *Upper Park* free. Fountains work 11am-5pm Mon-Fri; 11am-6pm Sat, Sun.

Getting there

By train
Take an *elektrichka* (suburban train) from Baltiisky Vokzal (Baltic Station) in the direction of Peterhof-Oranienbaum, get off at Novy Peterhof and take a bus (348, 350, 351, 352, 353, 356) to the Upper Park. Keep in mind that Russians pronounce 'Petergof' with a harsh 'r' and 'g'. Trains run every 30-40 minutes; journey time is 35 minutes.

By bus
You can get to the parks of Peterhof by taking a yellow double-decker bus from Baltic Station. These depart from the square in front of the station about every quarter of an hour, upon filling up. A 30-minute, $1 ride takes you to the gates of the Upper Park.

By hydrofoil
The easiest but most expensive option. Hydrofoils depart from Hermitage Pier (311 9506) every 10-15 minutes from 10am to 3pm daily and arrive at the Lower Park's Grand Cascade 40 minutes later. The fare one-way is $6.50; $3.50 students, under-17s.

Pavlovsk

In 1777, Catherine the Great gave this tract of land on the Slavyanka River to her son Paul (Pavel in Russian, hence Pavlovsk) to celebrate the birth of his son, the future emperor Alexander I. Catherine commissioned her favourite architect, the Scot Charles Cameron, to build a palace that mimicked the style of a Roman temple. Vincenzo Brenna later added wings to encircle the courtyard. In January 1944, the Great Palace was burned to the ground by German troops and the current incarnation is the result of 26 years of restoration.

The collection of classical statues housed here is the second largest in Russia, after that of the Hermitage. Some are over 2,000 years old. The more interesting rooms include **Paul's Military Hall**, where the crazy emperor indulged his love

sioned in 1745 to tart up the basic baroque structure with pilasters, rusticated quoins and various frilly touches. Inside, you'll find the restored interiors of some 20 rooms, including Peter's oak-lined study, the Crown Room, with its original Chinese silk wall hangings, Chesma Hall, dedicated to the victory over the Turks in 1770 and decorated with maritime paintings, and the Chinese Study with its amazing wooden floor mosaic, created in the 1760s when chinoiserie was all the rage. The Picture Hall, which is also known as the 'Room of Fashions and Graces', located at the heart of the palace, features 368 paintings of young girls from the court of Elizabeth, painted by Pietro Rotari.

It is also possible to roam around the **Grottoes**, a labyrinthine network of underground chambers, arches and pipes built to supply the fountains with water from nearby lakes.

of military paraphernalia, the **Throne Room** and the **Hall of Maltese Knights of St John**, of whom Paul was Grand Master.

The **park** is a delight, particularly in winter when residents of St Petersburg come here to ski, toboggan and slide on the ice. It also contains many pretty pavilions, the Colonnade of Apollo, the Temple of Friendship, a mausoleum and a circle of white birches known as the 'Great Star'. Also of interest is the area known as the **Old Woods**, where 12 bronze statues of the muses are arranged in a star around their protector, Apollo. You can rent a boat at the boat station for $2 per hour (plus $6.50 or an official document as deposit). Other seasonal attractions include horse riding, tennis courts in summer and Finnish sledges in winter. Classical music concerts are occasionally held in the Grand Palace's concert hall and the Rose Pavilion.

Contacts

Great Palace
Bolshoi Dvorets (470 2155/tours 470 6536).
Open 10am-6pm Mon-Thur, Sat, Sun. Closed Fri, 1st Mon of month. **Admission** $7; $3.50 students, under-17s.
No credit cards.
Guided tours $8.50. Information in English.

Pavlovsk Park
Open 24 hours daily. **Admission** *May-Oct* 10am-6pm 80¢.

Getting there

By train
Pavlovsk is 29km (18 miles) south of St Petersburg, one stop after Pushkin on the same *elektrichka* line from Vitebsky Vokzal. The ticket booth is the grey cement kiosk to the right of the station itself. The journey takes 35 minutes. The entrance to the park is just opposite the platform; the palace is a 15-minute walk away, or take bus 370, 493 or 383A.

Tsarskoye Selo

Originally the summer residence of Peter the Great's favourite, Alexander Menshikov, Tsarskoye Selo (Tsar's Village) became the principal out-of-town stomping ground of the royal family and the aristocracy throughout much of the Tsarist period. After the Revolution, the estate and village became the site of a children's sanatorium and were renamed Detskoye Selo (Children's Village).

In 1937, they inherited the name of Russia's greatest poet, Pushkin, who studied at the high school there. The post-Soviet era has done little to alleviate this name-changing confusion: the estate has reverted to its original name and the town is officially called Detskoye Selo once again, though the local population refers to both simply as Pushkin.

The centrepiece of the park and palace area is the exquisite baroque **Catherine Palace**, which was completed by Rastrelli between 1752 and 1756 and served as the main Imperial residence for a century and a half. The Nazis used it as a barracks for a time before looting and blowing it up as they retreated. Among the priceless works of art still missing are the priceless wall panels from the famous Amber Room (Yantarnaya Komnata), which historians are still desperately searching for at the bottom of various Lithuanian mineshafts where the Nazis purportedly stashed them. Meanwhile, a re-creation of the Amber Room is being constructed at its original location and, though work is barely half-finished, you will still get a vague idea of how it originally looked.

Only a quarter of the palace is open to the public, though from the photographs displayed around the rooms showing the destruction wrought by the German troops, it's obvious that you're lucky to get to see even that much.

Adjacent to the palace is **Catherine Park**, its regular French walkways lined with carefully manicured shrubbery and pretty statues. Around the Great Pond are the Grotto and the blue and white Hermitage, built by Rastrelli. The building resembling a minaret on the opposite side of the pond was once a Turkish baths. The Egyptian Pyramid marks the spot where Catherine buried some of her favourite dogs, including one that went by the unusual name of Sir Tom Anderson. Further along the lakeside path is the attractive Marble Bridge – a copy of the Palladian Bridge in Wilton, England.

The yellow and white **Alexander Palace** (not open to the public), was built by Quarenghi between 1792 and 1796. It was favoured by Tsar Nicholas II and his family and was their main residence from 1904 onwards. The long green paths of the surrounding Alexander Park lead you further into the woods to the unrestored but still fascinating Gothic Chapel, built in 1827, the Arsenal, the Chinese Village (part of which has now become a residential compound for rich foreigners), the Chinese Puppet Theatre and the Fyodorovski Gorodok, or Fyodor's Town – a miniature copy of a Russian fortress that once served as a barracks for the Tsar's bodyguards.

Contacts

Catherine Palace
466 6674/465 5308. **Open** 10am-5pm Mon, Wed-Sun. Closed last Mon of month. **Admission** $7; $3.50 students, under-17s. **No credit cards.**

Catherine Park
Open 10am-6.30pm daily. **Admission** *summer* $2; $1 students, under-17s; *winter* free.

Alexander Park
Admission free. **Open** 24 hours daily.

Getting there

Train

See above **Pavlosk**: Pushkin is the stop before. From the station, take bus 370, 371, 378 or ask for directions for a pleasant 20-minute walk. Bus 370 also runs to Pavlovsk, 4km (2.5 miles) south.

Novgorod

Novgorod, meaning 'New City', is actually one of Russia's oldest cities. Founded in AD859, it was once a haven of democracy and enlightenment, with all major decisions taken by an elected body known as the *Veche*. In the early part of the next millennium, the Novgorod republic stretched from the Gulf of Finland to the Urals and served as a shield against western invaders. Later it became the hub of the mighty medieval union of trading towns known as the Hanseatic League. These days, Novgorod is a quiet escape from the bustle of St Petersburg and, like Pskov, is a haven of superb and largely intact medieval architecture. It's 160 kilometers (100 miles) south of St Petersburg, so it's probably best to spend a night there.

The **Novgorod Kremlin**, also called Detinets (an ancient Russian word for fortress), houses most of Novgorod's main points of interest, including various museums and Sofiisky Sobor (St Sofia's Cathedral, built 1045-50), the only functioning church in the Kremlin – you can attend a service or just pop in (admission is free and it's open 8am-8pm daily). Amazing frescoes cover the interior walls of this five-domed white cathedral. Behind it stands the separate bell tower, with the 26-ton 'Holiday Bell' lying on the ground outside.

Many of the other churches in the Kremlin and on the riverside are undergoing restoration, so accessibility may be erratic. Worth checking out also is the monument dedicated to '1,000 years of Russia' (1862), which portrays Russia's most prominent historical figures in bronze around a huge orb symbolising the power and glory of the country.

A $1.50 boat ride from a pier just outside the Kremlin will bring you up the Volkhov River to Lake Ilmyen and eventually to the **Yuriev Monastery** (1119), one of the oldest in Russia. It's open from 10am to 6pm daily and admission is $2.50.

Contacts

Novgorod Kremlin
8-81622 73770.

Getting there

By train

Two trains a day leave Vitebsky Vokzal at 8.31am and 5.35pm, arriving in Novgorod at 1pm and 9pm respectively.

Single tickets cost about $5; the ticket booth is the grey cement kiosk to the right of the station. Return trains leave Novgorod at 7.35am and 6.45pm.

By bus

Buses leave Central Bus Station (Autovokzal) 2 once an hour. The journey takes four hours and costs $4.50 for a single ticket. To ensure a seat, buy tickets a couple of hours in advance.

Accommodation

A good option is the hotel **Rosa Vetrov** (Rose of the Winds, Novo-Luchanskaya Ulitsa 27A; 8-81622 72033), seven minutes' walk from the train station. From the station walk straight ahead until you come to a cinema, turn left and walk past a photography shop. A double room costs about $20. The hotel **Volkhov** (Frolovskaya Ulitsa 24; 8-81622 74221/fax 8-81622 31707) is a centrally located Soviet-type hotel with double rooms at $20-$50, including breakfast.

Where to eat

For breakfast or lunch, nothing in Novgorod beats **Blinok** (Lyudogorskaya Ulitsa 10; open 8am-8pm daily), which specialises in pancakes at bargain prices. Located inside Novgorod Kremlin, right of the main entrance, is **Detinets**, a great setting for a good dinner of Russian cuisine for a maximum $10 per head.

Pskov

Sleepy, provincial Pskov is 260 kilometres (175 miles) south-west of St Petersburg and again requires an overnight stay. Dating from the sixth century, it is best explored on foot. You should be able to hit all the sights in an afternoon. Check out the golden-domed **Trinity Cathedral** (originally erected in 957 but rebuilt four times), which is located right in the centre of the Pskov Kremlin in the area known as the Krom, or Fortress. The church has no strict opening hours; mornings are usually a sure bet. In medieval times, local governors were inaugurated here and town meetings held within the hallowed walls. When Ivan the Terrible once visited, a holy man predicted his later brutal excesses.

Also worth visiting are the many small churches outside the Kremlin, among them the Church of St Nicholas on the Dry Land (on Sovetskaya Ulitsa), topped with impressive wooden domes.

Getting there

By train

Trains depart from Varshavsky Vokzal six times a day after 1.45pm and take between four and a half and six hours to get to Pskov. Tickets cost $23-$25; buy them in advance. Pskov's station is a ten-minute walk from the town centre; all local buses go there.

Gushing gilt – the unmissable **Grand Cascade** *at Peterhof. See page 239.*

Accommodation

The Soviet-era **Hotel Oktyabrskaya** (Oktyabrsky Prospekt 36; 8-8112 721299) offers singles at $30 and doubles at $50, while the more sedate and cosy **Hotel Rizhskaya** (Rizhsky Prospekt 25; 8-8112 462223) has rooms at $35 for a single and $60 for a double.

Where to eat

The **Medved** (Bear) bistro serves up decent, inexpensive Russian fare; try its *solyanka* (mixed meat soup). Coming from the Krom, it's just past the Pedagogical Institute (a huge building fronted by a statue of Lenin), on the right.

Kizhi Island

Kizhi is one of the true wonders of the former Soviet Union. It's a small, unspoiled island on the western end of Lake Onega that not only hosts Russia's most impressive collection of wooden architecture, but is also a sanctuary of unsurpassable natural beauty. It's certainly no day trip – you have to take a hydrofoil from Petrozavodsk, which is 350 kilometres (219 miles) north-east of St Petersburg – but it is well worth the effort.

As the hydrofoil approaches the island, you'll get your first glimpse of the 22-domed **Church of the Transfiguration**, which, much like Moscow's St Basil's, has a mirage-like quality as it soars above the green fields. Built in 1714 entirely of pine logs and aspen shingles that shimmer in the sunshine like silver, the church is both an object of great beauty and an engineering marvel. The delicate wooden carvings on its exterior add to the fairytale quality.

Unfortunately, at the moment you won't be able to explore the interior of the church, as it's closed pending restoration, but its near-neighbour, the **Church of the Intercession** (built in 1764), is open and houses a collection of icons dating from the seventeenth to the nineteenth centuries. It is worth dawdling here for a few minutes and trying to imagine what it must have been like for the illiterate farmers who spent hours each Sunday contemplating these icons, some of which offer vivid depictions of what unrepentant peasants might find if they ended up in hell.

From the southern end of the island, where the main buildings are located, to the northern end is a pleasant three-kilometre (two-mile) trek through fields and past a small graveyard. Here, the 50 or so residents of the island (the whole of which is classified as a museum) live a Truman Burbank-style life in restored buildings that bear signs proclaiming 'poor peasant dwelling' and 'wealthy peasant dwelling'.

In all, it takes two or three hours to poke around the island and see all the wooden buildings. Afterwards, there are plenty of places along the lakeshore and in the fields to have a picnic or sunbathe. By the boat landing is a modest café and several kiosks selling *matrioshka* dolls, birch bark items and postcards.

Given the latitude on which Kizhi sits – it's 921 kilometres (575 miles) north of Moscow – visits are only viable during the ice-free months (May-Oct). Perhaps the best time to go is around the summer solstice, when the sun never sets and the locals say people are at their most cheerful.

Hydrofoils to Kizhi depart from Petrozavodsk. The capital of the north-western Russian republic of Karelia, it's a tidy, surprisingly un-Soviet city offering enough to keep a traveller busy for at least a day if not more.

Contacts

Museum of Wooden Architecture
Open 8am-3.30pm daily. **Admission** $9.

Getting there

By train to Petrozavodsk
There are four trains a day from Moskovsky Vokzal to Petrozavodsk, starting at about 2.30pm. The journey takes about eight hours and it's definitely best to take an overnight train (couchettes $30 single; $50 double; information 162 3334).

By hydrofoil to Kizhi
Petrozavodsk's passenger port is at the end of Prospekt Karla Marksa. As there is no accommodation on Kizhi, it is best to get a morning hydrofoil to give yourself more time there, although this can be problematic. Morning boats only leave if a group of 20 or more have pre-booked: this is almost always the case at weekends but cannot be guaranteed during the week. To find out what's happening, call 8-8142 561 374.

An afternoon boat leaves every day at 1pm, but will give you only an hour or so to explore the island before the return boat leaves – not nearly enough time. Return tickets for the 66-kilometre (41-mile) journey cost $20. The boats have a snack bar.

Accommodation

There is no accommodation in Kizhi, so you will probably have to stay overnight in Petrozavodsk. For location and view, the **Hotel Karelia** (Naberezhnaya Gyullinga 2; 8-8142 558897) can't be beaten. It's close to the lakefront and a five-minute walk from the hydrofoil terminal. A double room (including breakfast) costs about $35-$40; be sure to request a room with a view of the lake when booking.

Other hotel options include the **Hotel Fregat** on the lakeshore at Onezhskaya Naberezhnaya 1 (8-8142 561770), where doubles go for $84, or the **Hotel Severnaya** in the heart of Petrozavodsk at Prospekt Lenina 21 (8-8142 771258), where newly renovated doubles are $85.

Eating & drinking

Petrozavodsk has plenty of cafés, including a **Ben and Jerry's** outlet at Krasnaya Ulitsa 8. For the local, equally inexpensive variant, there's **Café Morozhenoye** at Ulitsa Kirova 12. For something more substantial, try the **Petrovsky Restaurant**, located in a cellar at Ulitsa Andropova 1 (8-81427 70992). Two people can eat and drink to excess here for under $25.

Directory

Directory

The definitive database for travellers to Moscow and St Petersburg.

Essential Information

Phone numbers for Moscow and St Petersburg locations are given as dialled from within that city, ie, without an area code. If dialling from outside the city, you will need to preface them with 095 for Moscow, 812 for St Petersburg.

Emergencies

In case of crisis, contact your country's embassy (*see below* **Embassies**), or dial the English-language Crisis Line in Moscow (244 3449), which can help with serious problems both practical and psychological. Leave your number with the operator and a counsellor will call you back.

Emergency numbers
01 Fire
02 Police
03 Ambulance (but *see below* **Health** for emergency numbers of private clinics)

Age limits

The age of consent for straight and gay sex is 16. The usual age limit to drink in bars is 18.

Attitude/etiquette

In the street, on the metro or in formal conversations on the telephone, Russians (and Muscovites in particular) can seem extremely brusque. Western concepts of personal space generally don't apply and you can expect to be regularly jostled. There are no accepted 'right of way' rules when meeting at junctions or in

doorways: it's basically a dash to get through first. And when ringing up for information, it's quite normal for the person at the other end to bark a response and hang up.

Dealing with officialdom is even more tricky. A lot of the time, the police, Customs officials or ticket sellers causing you hassle or delays will be doing no more than indulging their fetish for power and paperwork. In the case of the police or traffic police, however, there may be occasions when a little more than just patience is called for. If your discussions reach an impasse or if a problem goes unsolved for an unusually long time, you might offer to pay a 'small fine' (*malinky shtraf*) of $10 or $20. Don't pull the money out of a huge wad of bills unless you want to end up giving it all away. Sometimes police may just ask you for money or go through your wallet and take it. This usually ends up being less time-consuming but more expensive.

Once you have worked your way into their affections, however, Russians will be effusive and practically smother you with attention. When invited to parties or family gatherings, bring along a small present or a bouquet (which superstition dictates must be made up of an odd number of flowers). Most Russians dress in their Sunday best for the theatre or opera, but a certain amount of informality is tolerated in foreigners.

Banks & money

The currency in Russia is the ruble, usually abbreviated to R or RR (in Cyrillic P or PP). One ruble comprises 100 *kopeyek* (kopeks), back on the scene thanks to a recent devaluation that cut three zeros from the value of Russian notes.

Rubles come as notes in denominations of 10, 50, 100 and 500, each in a different colour and bearing a picture of a different Russian city, and as 1, 2 and 5 ruble coins. Coins are easily distinguishable: the bigger the coin, the higher its value. In addition to the 5, 2 and 1 ruble, there are 50, 10, 5 and 1 kopek coins. Before the financial meltdown of August 1998, inflation had been holding steady at about 12 per cent, with the ruble hovering at around six to the dollar. By press time, the rate was fluctuating around 15, with some predicting that it would fall to 30 to the dollar before the end of 1998. Unless this situation changes, convert your dollars into rubles in small batches of $50-$100.

CASH

There are hundreds of exchange offices in both Moscow and St Petersburg: you'll find them on the street, at hotels, shopping centres, transport terminals and post offices and, of course, in banks. As rates vary slightly you should shop around from place to place. US dollars and Deutschmarks are universally exchanged and many city centre offices will change most Western European currencies. In order to change money you will need to show your passport. Many central exchange offices are open late and some function around the clock.

There are exchange offices at both Moscow and St Petersburg airports. Rates there are considerably worse than in the city, so only change enough money for your immediate needs. In Moscow's Sheremetyevo 2 Airport the exchange office is in the departure hall on the second floor. Next to it is a cash machine changing US$ and major European currencies.

Banks are numerous with branches in many hotels. Banking hours are usually 9am to 6pm Monday to Friday and sometimes later; in St Petersburg, some may open later and close for lunch.

Between 1995 and mid-1998, the black market for currency exchange had largely disappeared. The recent financial crisis may, however, cause it to return – as we went to press in October 1998, the Russian banking system was paralysed, making cash withdrawals from ATMs and the purchase of travellers' cheques inside the country unreliable and sometimes impossible. This meant that all spending money had to be carried into the country in cash dollars. Check with your travel agent, in case this situation changes again. Whatever happens, always beware of con artists offering a good exchange deal: they just want to swap your money for a wad of fake and old notes.

The crisis has had less of an impact on credit card purchases and most establishments and all hotels still accept major cards.

Currently you are required by Russian law to make all cash payments in rubles, and the dollar economy has largely disappeared, but that, too, may be making a comeback for larger transactions.

Useful banks – Moscow

The economic crisis of August 1998 took a huge toll on Russia's banking system. Most Bank, which we have listed below, is now part of a larger conglomeration called Rosbank, though the numbers and addresses given still stand. Alfa Bank, which managed to stay open throughout the crisis with functioning ATMs, is now one of the most reliable.

Alfa Bank

Arbat 4/1 (230 3696). Metro Arbatskaya. **Open** 8.30am-7.30pm Mon-Sat; 8.30am-3pm Sun. **Map p280 A4/B4**

MOST Bank

Novy Arbat 36 (290 8206). Metro Arbatskaya. **Open** 9.30am-3pm, 4.30-7.30pm, Mon-Fri; 9.30am-2.30pm Sat. **Map p277 A3/B3**

Useful banks – St Petersburg

Baltiisky Bank

Muchnoi Pereulok 2 (326 9112). Metro Sennaya Ploshchad. **Open** 9.30am-1pm, 2-6pm, Mon-Fri. *Furshtatskaya 40 (273 4681). Metro Chernyshevskaya.* **Open** 9.30am-1pm, 2-6pm, Mon-Fri. **Map P287 D5**

MOST Bank

Nevsky Prospekt 27/29 (312 2865). Metro Nevsky Prospekt. **Open** 9.30am-7.30pm Mon-Fri. **Map p287 C4/D4/5**

TRAVELLERS' CHEQUES

We recommend using American Express travellers' cheques (in dollar denominations). It's the best-known brand, has offices in Moscow and St Petersburg and is the only company to offer in-town refunds. Travellers' cheques can be changed in the offices of all major banks, but not normally at currency exchange offices. You will always need to show your passport; some places also want to see the proof of purchase (the slip you're supposed to keep separately) and passport. The commission charge will be between 1.5 and 3 per cent. In general, travellers' cheques can be used as payment only in the major hotels. To report lost cheques, call your domestic helpline: (0)1273 696 933 in the UK, 910 333 3211 in the US.

Moscow

American Express

Sadovaya-Kudrinskaya Ulitsa 21A (955 9001). Metro Mayakovskaya. **Open** 9am-5.30pm Mon-Fri; 9am-1pm Sat. **Map p277 A2** Travellers' cheques cashed through a concessionary bank, plus travel advice and card-holder service centre.

St Petersburg

American Express

Grand Hotel Europe, Mikhailovskaya Ulitsa 1/7 (329 6060). Metro Gostiny Dvor or Nevsky Prospekt. **Open** 9am-5pm Mon-Fri; 9am-1pm Sat. **Map p287 D4/5**

CREDIT/CASH CARDS

Credit cards are widely accepted in restaurants, hotels, upmarket boutiques and supermarkets, but few ordinary shops. The most widely accepted cards are Visa and MasterCard. Many places also accept Diners Club, JCB and, increasingly, American Express.

Cash machines (*bankomaty*) are located at central metro stations, hotels, in bank offices and other public locations. If your bank or credit card bears a logo such as Cirrus, Plus or Maestro that matches the graphic on the machine, you will be able to withdraw cash using your usual PIN.

Report lost or stolen cards to your bank at home or to the United card service in Moscow at Grafsky Pereulok 10/12 (216 6849), which deals with most cards with the exception of American Express (call your domestic helpline: *see above* for numbers).

MONEY TRANSFER

Cash transfers can be made through Western Union. Call its office on 119 8250 in Moscow or 312 4342 in St Petersburg to find the closest accredited bank.

Climate

Moscow is renowned – even celebrated – for its cold, icy winters, but it's less well known that summers can be very warm. Either way, you can't count on anything for long. Year-round, temperatures can be unstable.

Average winter temperatures are between -8°C and -12°C (17°F and 10°F), but in the last few years the cold has been particularly bitter. The records were last broken on December 14 1997 when the thermometer plunged to -27.3°C (-18°F) – the coldest Decemeber day in Moscow since 1882. The coldest months are usually January and February, but because they're often sunny, too they're more pleasant than the slushy, windy weeks on either side. If you visit during winter, bring (or buy) weatherproof clothes: thermal underwear, a hat and waterproof footwear with a good tread on the sole. Other good times to come are between May and early June, and September and October.

Between June and August it's hot, sticky and dusty, with the occasional rainstorm, and the locals retire to their country dachas. Temperatures rise to an average of between 12°C (53°F) and 21°C (70°), but June 1998 saw the records broken again with the mercury climbing to 34.7°C (95°F).

St Petersburg's proximity to the sea brings some benefits but just as many disadvantages. In statistical terms, the climate is less severe than in Moscow, with the temperature for January averaging -7.9°C (17°F) and for July 17.7°C (64°F). But strong winds and high humidity can make the cold more severe and the summers hazy and rainy. St Petersburg becomes a mosquito breeding ground in summer: bring plenty of repellent.

Crime

Media reports overstate the level of crime in Moscow, which is no less safe than any city with a population of around ten million. The infamous mafia has more serious business to take care of than targeting foreign tourists. Pickpocketing does happen – you should be careful in crowded places, especially at train stations – but it is not endemic. The main dangers for tourists are drunken aggression from xenophobic locals, con artists, aggression from skinheads towards non-whites, and 'gypsy' children who combine in a crowd to attack your pockets (less common than previously).

In St Petersburg, the crime rate is generally lower than in the capital and some of the problems above are unknown. However, don't let the relaxed atmosphere lull you into a false sense of security. Stay alert, particularly in the usual crime hotspots – train stations and other crowded areas.

Customs & immigration

On flights to Russia you will be given two declaration forms. The first asks for details of money and goods you are bringing in. Fill it in, have it stamped at Customs and keep it

carefully. When you leave, you are required to fill in the second form, detailing the goods you are taking out. Officials will then take both forms from you. If you fail to present them you may be searched or face a fine. However, the documentation is largely a formality, at least in terms of bringing money in and out. If you lose your first form, tell officials that you came in through the green channel (for people bringing in less than $50). The process is similar – though normally more Kafka-esque – if you arrive by train, but vastly more complicated if you arrive by car (not recommended).

You are permitted to bring in anything you need for personal use, but large and therefore saleable quantities of goods are suspect. You are allowed to import one litre of strong liquor or wine and 250 cigarettes (this may rise to 1,000). Don't even think about bringing drugs in – the penalties are severe.

Going through immigration shouldn't be a problem if your visa is in order – you don't need to show any extra documentation. However, be prepared to queue, especially at Moscow. You may also be given a tax notice informing you that you will be liable to Russian taxes on worldwide earnings if you stay in the country for more than 168 days in any one year.

There are restrictions on the export of icons, antiques and objets d'art. If you have bought anything that may fall into these categories, have it assessed at the Russian Ministry of Culture (Neglinnaya 8/10, office 29 in Moscow; Malaya Morskaya 17 in St Petersburg), where you will pay up to 100 per cent of the purchase price for a certificate allowing you to take the items out of the country. 'Antiques' can include items produced as recently as 1970, though most casual flea market purchases will be exempt.

Disabled travellers

Moscow is an inconvenient place for disabled travellers. The metro is not accessible for people in wheelchairs, and bus and trams are accessible only with help. However, most major hotels are disabled-friendly and, as a legacy of the 1980 Olympic Games, there are wheelchair-accessible underpasses throughout Leninsky Prospekt.

In St Petersburg, the disabled get an even rougher deal, with only one (the Grand Hotel Europe) of the top three hotels offering facilities. The only disabled toilets or ramps around are at McDonald's.

Electricity

Standard voltage is 220V. Sockets require a plug with two round pins. Most new sockets are the standard European (not UK) size; old ones are slightly smaller. Adaptors are available from most hardware shops and markets for about a dollar. Appliances of a different voltage need a transformer, also widely available. The electricity supply is stable and cheap.

Embassies

Moscow

Australia
Kropotkinsky Pereulok 13 (956 6070). Metro Kropotkinskaya. **Map p280 A5/B5**

Canada
Starokonyushenny Pereulok 23 (956 6666). Metro Kropotkinskaya. **Map p280 B4**

Ireland
Grokholsky Pereulok 5 (742 0907). Metro Prospekt Mira.

New Zealand
Povarskaya Ulitsa 14 (956 3579). Metro Barrikadnaya. **Map p277 A3/B3**

South Africa
Bolshoi Strochenovsky Pereulok 22/25 (230 6869). Metro Serpukhovskaya.

United Kingdom

Sofiiskaya Naberezhnaya 14.
Entrance from Bolotnaya Ploshchad
(956 7200). Metro Oktyabrskaya
then trolleybus 7, 33, 62. **Map**
p281 C4

USA

Novinsky Bulvar 19 (252 2451).
Metro Barrikadnaya. **Map p277**
A3

St Petersburg

Several countries have
consulates in St Petersburg.
Nationals of countries whose
consulates are not listed below
should contact their Moscow
embassy (*see above*).

Canada

Malodetskoselsky Prospekt 32 (345
8442), Metro Tekhnologichesky
Institut.

South Africa

Naberezhnaya Reki Moika 11 (325
6363). Metro Gostiny Dvor or Nevsky
Prospekt. **Map p287 C5/D4/5**

United Kingdom

Ploshchad Proletarskoi Diktatury 5
(325 0036). Metro Ploshchad
Vosstaniya. **Map p288 G3**
Also represents Ireland.

United States

Furshtadtskaya Ulitsa 15 (274
8568) Metro Chernyeshevskaya.
Map p278 E3/F3

All visitors to Russia should
take out comprehensive
medical insurance with high
limits from a reputable
company. Westerners living
here seldom use Russian
medical facilities: they go to foreign-run health centres for
everything from an ingrown
toenail to the morning-after pill,
and visitors are recommended
to do the same. The Russian
ambulance emergency call-out
number is 03, but it's better to
use the emergency service of
the clinics listed – the same
goes for presenting yourself at
an emergency room.

You may be asked to pay up
front for treatment – not cheap
if you need to be flown out.
Keep those credit limits high.

Don't drink water from the
tap. Mineral water is available
from every supermarket and
street kiosk. St Petersburg tap
water is infected with *Giardia
lamblia*, a very nasty bug that
affects the digestive tract. Don't
even clean your teeth with it.

Vaccinations against
diptheria, tetanus and hepatitis
A and B are advised for
travellers to Russia.

Moscow

American Medical Centre

1-y Tverskoi-Yamskoi Pereulok
10 (956 3366). Metro
Mayakovskaya. **Open** by
appointment 8am-8pm daily;
emergency room 24 hours daily.
Credit AmEx, JCB, MC, V. **Map**
p277 B2

European Medical Centre

2-y Tverskoi-Yamskoi Pereulok 10
(251 6099). Metro Mayakovskaya.
Open 24 hours daily. **Credit** AmEx,
MC, V. **Map p277 B2**

Mediclub Moscow

Michurinsky Prospekt 56 (931 5018).
Metro Universitet. **Open** 9am-8pm
Mon-Thur; 9am-6pm Fri. **Credit** MC,
V.
Canadian-run. Emergency services
are available only to clinic members.

St Petersburg

American Medical Center

Serpukhovskaya Ulitsa 10 (326
1730). Metro Tekhnologichesky
Institut. **Open** 8.30am-6pm
Mon-Fri; 10am-4pm Sat; ambulance
24 hours daily. **Credit** AmEx, DC,
JCB, V.

Avelanche

Izmailovsky Prospekt 14 (112 6512).
Metro Baltiiskaya. **Open** 24 hours
daily. **Credit** MC, JCB, V.

PHARMACIES

Pharmacies (*apteki* in Russian) are
ubiquitous and marked with a green
neon cross. Each area of a city has a
designated 24-hour pharmacy. In
Moscow, the one at Nikolskaya
Ulitsa 19/21 (923 2633; metro
Lubyanka) is the best-located for
tourists; in St Petersburg it's Petro-
Farm, Nevsky Prospekt 22 (311
2004; metro Nevsky Prospekt or
Gostiny Dvor; night entrance via the
arch at Bolshaya Konyushennaya
Ulitsa 14). Non-prescription
medicines are sold in special kiosks
at major metro stations.

Russia uses a clunky five-
pronged telephone connection
plug. You can get UK/Russian
adaptors from UK electronics
shops (such as TeleAdapt in
London; 0181 233 3000) but the
easiest approach is to buy an
(American) Bell lead for your
modem (if it hasn't got one
already) and connect it directly
to a Russian telephone plug,
available at electronics kiosks.
This should allow you to access
from most places, including
hotel rooms that have not been
hardwired. Where to dial in is
more problematic. Due to
widespread credit card fraud,
Compuserve and America
Online have both closed down
their Russian gateways, and
many of the international
providers still operating will
give you nothing but a 24-hour
busy signal and a headache.
Short of opening a temporary
local account, all you can do is
make long-distance calls to
access points in other European
countries to pick up your mail.

If you do open a local
account, one of the better
companies is Matrix (967
8152/support@ matrix.ru).
However, getting and keeping a
line is a nightmare and capacity
low. For Net operations of all
kinds, it's best to wait until the
dead of night, when the lines
have cooled down.

In St Petersburg, where the
phone system is not so
overloaded, getting and
keeping a connection is far easier; almost as hassle-free as in a
regular European city. A local
provider to try is Nevalink (310
5442/e-mail info@nevalink.ru).

ACCESS POINTS

Moscow

Chevignon Internet Café

Baza 14, Stoleshnikov Pereulok 14
(733 9205). Metro Teatralnaya.
Open 24 hours daily. **Credit** MC, V.
Map p278 C2
On the second floor of a clothing
store, this café is popular with

teenagers, and has drinks and music along with computers for use for a reasonable fee.

MicroAge
Leningradsky Prospekt 53 (258 7585). Metro Aeroport. **Open** 10am-8pm Mon-Fri; 10am-6pm Sat. **Credit** AmEx, DC, MC, V.
A busy spot where you may have to wait in line. There are also computers and printers for word processing use.

St Petersburg

Tetris
Ulitsa Chernyakhovskogo 33 (164 4877). Metro Ligovsky Prospekt. **Open** 10am-9pm Mon-Fri; 1-9pm Sat, Sun. **Rates** $4 per hour 10am-1pm; $8 per hour 1-9pm. **Credit** MC, V. **Map p289 F6**
The first ever Net café in Russia is basically a boffin's computer cabin with a tiny café en suite. Located strategically beside one of the city's modern telephone exchanges, but a little out of the way for all other practical purposes.

Nevalink Public Access
Naberezhnaya Kanal Griboyedova 24, in the Central Ticket Agency (168 6734/info@ nevalink.ru). Metro Gostiny Dvor or Nevsky Prospekt. **Open** 8am-midnight daily. **No credit cards. Map p287 D4**
Ploshchad Vosstaniya 2, in Moskovsky railway station (277 2517/info@nevalink.ru). Metro Ploshchad Vosstaniya. **Open** 8am-midnight daily. **No credit cards. Map p289 F5**
The most convenient way to pick up e-mail and surf the Net if you find yourself laptopless in St Petersburg. Ten minutes' web access costs about $1.60, an hour is around $7. E-mail access costs just under 80¢ for ten minutes.

WEBSITES

www.russiatoday.com
A news service with a constant flow of stories updated throughout the day.

www.city.ru
A practical guide to cities throughout Russia including St Petersburg and Moscow.

www.russia-travel.com
A tourist guide to Russia giving accommodation and travel information.

www.infoservices.com
The traveller's *Yellow Pages* online: contacts of all kinds plus background info on Moscow and St Petersburg. Useful seating plans for theatres and auditoria.

www.mbtg.net
The cyberspace location of the *Moscow Business Telephone Guide* has useful contacts for various Moscow businesses – from photo-processing to pizza delivery to translators – plus good maps, weather reports and an art and culure tour. In English, and regularly updated.

www.moscowtimes.ru
The *Moscow Times*'s site, in English, includes electronic versions of the paper (archive included – free on a two-week trial basis, then $40 for six weeks) and its listings wing, *MT Out.*

www.moscowcity.com
The website of the Moscow City Tourist Office. A well-designed site with good historical background on the city and architectural info.

www.times.spb.ru
The website of the *St Petersburg Times*, one of the first newspapers in the world to be simultaneously published on the web. Local and Russian news plus cultural listings.

www.guide.spb.ru
The definitive web guide to St Petersburg.

Libraries (English language)

Moscow

All-Russian Library of Foreign Literature
Biblioteka Inostrannoi Literatury, Nikoloyamskaya Ulitsa 1 (915 3669). Metro Taganskaya. **Map p282 E4/F4**
As well as its own resources, the Rudomino contains American, French, Japanese cultural centres and the British Council each with their own libraries and resource centres.

St Petersburg

Galitzine Library
Biblioteka Golitsyna, Naberezhnaya Reki Fontanki 46 (311 1333). Metro Gostiny Dvor or Nevsky Prospekt. **Map p289 E5**
By far the best, most comfortable and most comprehensive English-language library in the city.

Lost property

Moscow

Lost documents 200 9957
Lost on the metro 222 2085
Lost on the bus, trolleybus or tram 923 8753

St Petersburg

Lost documents 278 3690
Lost on the metro 259 7111
Lost on the bus, trolleybus or tram 278 3690

Opening times

Typical opening hours are from 10am to 7pm with a lunch break between 1 and 2pm or 2 and 3pm. Many shops open later. You can often find 24-hour shops and kiosks near metro stations. Most shops and services operate on Saturdays and frequently on Sundays as well. Office hours are usually 9am to 6 or 7pm Monday to Friday, but they vary considerably. The occasional museum or library may close for August.

Police (militsia)

Though recent efforts by the Moscow city government to raise police morale have had a slight effect on their street manner – shifting them from the 'among the rudest in the world' to the 'quite rude' category – Russian police in general are still largely inefficient, quite corrupt and, for dark-skinned races, potentially a far greater threat than criminals. They aren't too much use at tracking down petty thieves or stolen goods. If you are the victim of a minor crime, there's not a lot of point in reporting it other than for insurance reasons unless you want to use up a lot of time and frustration. If the crime is serious, contact your embassy and ask them to help you deal with the police.

St Petersburg police have been getting bad press for targetting foreigners, beating them up and stealing their money. Hopefully, the outcry will put an end to its widespread practice. Another recent development is the revival of the Tsarist era *Gorodovye*, who are once again patrolling Nevsky Prospekt in their red peaked caps. They are supposed to be competent in a variety of European languages in order to help out foreigners, but their linguistic performance to date has been rather patchy.

The emergency police number is 02. To report a crime in Moscow call 200 8924, in St Petersburg 311 1851.

STREET CHECK & DETAINMENT

The *militsia* may stop you on the street for a passport check, especially if you look African, Asian or Caucasian (Mediterrannean/Arabic in appearance). Keep your passport and visa with you at all times (it's wise to keep a photocopy separately) and ensure that you have the appropriate visa and registration stamps. However, Western tourists are seldom targetted as most checks are directed against illegal immigrants or Russians without residents' permits.

Possession of drugs – even soft drugs – is illegal and can have serious consequences. If you are detained for any crime, insist on calling your embassy and try (politely) to avoid talking to the police until a representative arrives. If you feel you have been unfairly treated by police, contact the Moscow Helsinki Group (206 8507) or the Russian Foundation on Protection of Rights and Law (928 4728).

Post

Russian post is slow and not very reliable. It takes about a week for a letter to get from Moscow to London and about two weeks in the other direction. Packages are sometimes lost or arrive open with some of the contents missing (usually thanks to Customs). If the address is in Latin rather than Cyrillic script, the letter will probably arrive but may take longer. You can send letters from any post office or the blue postboxes on the street. However, for reliability it's best to use the locations listed below.

Ask for a *mezhdunarodny* (international) envelope. If it doesn't have AVIA clearly marked, ask staff for an airmail stamp. If you are sending a

package indicate precisely what it contains on the envelope, if possible in Russian. Don't send money.

For courier services *see below* **Business in Moscow**.

Moscow

Central Telegraph

Tsentralny Telegraf, Tverskaya Ulitsa 7 (245 2853). Metro Okhotny Ryad. Open *post* 8am-10pm, *phone* 24 hours, daily. **No credit cards.** Map p278 C2

Moskovsky Pochtamp

Myasnitskaya Ulitsa 26 (928 6311). Metro Chistye Prudy. Open 8am-8pm Mon-Fri; 8am-7pm Sat; 9am-7pm Sun. **No credit cards.** Map p278 D2, 279 E2

St Petersburg

Commercial Postal Services

Grand Hotel Europe, Mikhailovskaya Ulitsa 1/7 (329 6000). Metro Gostiny Dvor or Nevsky Prospekt. Open 24 hours daily. **No credit cards.** Map p287 D4/5

For a small charge (about $1.60 for a regular letter) the telecommunications booth (located to the left as you enter and down the corridor) will ferry your letters to the ultra-reliable Finnish postal system

West Post

Nevsky Prospekt 86 (275 0784/272 7896). Metro Mayakovskaya. Open 9.30am-8pm Mon-Fri; noon-6pm Sat, Sun. **Credit** MC, V. Map p289 G6 Delivers letters to the Finnish postal system and offers courier services.

Religion

Russian Orthodox churches usually hold Sunday services at 7.30am and 5 or 5.30pm

Moscow

St Andrew's Anglican Church

Voznesensky Pereulok 8 (245 3837). Metro Arbatskaya or Pushkinskaya. Services 10am Sun. Map p277 B3, 278 C2

Central Church of Evangelists/Baptists

Maly Tryokhsvyatsky Pereulok (917 5167). Metro Chistye Prudy, then any tram to end of Pokrovsky Bulvar. Services 10am, 5pm, Sun. Map p279 E3

St Ludovic's Catholic Church

Ulitsa Malaya Lubyanka (925 2034). Metro Lubyanka. Services English 8am; French 10.30am; Russian 11.30am, 5pm, 6.30pm; Polish 6.30pm, Sun. Map p278 D2

Lutheran Church of Peter & Paul

Starosadsky Pereulok 7 (924 5820). Metro Kitai-Gorod. Services German 10.30am, Russian 12.30pm, Sun. Map p279 E3

Main Mosque

Vypolzov Pereulok 7 (281 3866). Metro Prospekt Mira.

Moscow Choral Synagogue

Bolshoi Spasoglinishchevsky Pereulok 10 (923 9697). Metro Kitai-Gorod. Map p278 D3, 279 E3

Russian Orthodox Church

Headquarters, Danilovsky Val 22 (955 6749). Metro Tulskaya. The central administrative office; no services.

St Petersburg

Buddhist Monastery

Primorsky Prospekt 91 (239 0341). Metro Chyornaya Rechka. Open 9am-6pm daily. Services 9am, 5pm, daily.

St Catherine's Roman Catholic Church

Nevsky Prospekt 32/34 (311 5795). Metro Gostiny Dvor or Nevsky Prospekt. Services English-languge mass 9.30am Sun. Map p287 C4/D4/5

Choral Synagogue

Lermontovsky Prospekt 2 (114 0078). Metro Baltiiskaya. Open 11am-5pm daily. Map p287 B6

International Baptist Church

Karavannaya Ulitsa 12 (525 7733). Metro Gostiny Dvor or Nevsky Prospekt. Services 7.30pm Wed; 11am Sun. Map p289 E4

Mosque

Kronverksky Prospekt 7 (233 9819). Metro Gorkovskaya. Open 10am-4pm daily. Map p286 C2/3/D2

Orthodox Church of Vladimirsky Icon

Vladimirskaya Ploshchad 20 (112 4424). Metro Vladimirskaya. Open 9am-7pm Mon-Sat; 7am-7pm Sun. Map p289 E5

Directory

Smoking

Smoking is widespread in Russia, public spaces included. If you were hoping for a no-smoking room in a hotel or a no-smoking area in a restaurant, you can pretty much forget it. And most taxi drivers light up without so much as a 'May I?'. Most international cigarette brands are available, though the locally produced versions are of poorer quality.

Telephones

Rooms at all but the most basic hotels now have a telephone, but you may have to pay a sizeable cash deposit to have it activated, even if you are paying by credit card. Call charges are, of course, inflated.

INTERNATIONAL/ LONG DISTANCE

All Russian phone numbers consist of an area code (between three and five digits) and a number (usually five or six digits). The international access code for Russia is 7; the area code for Moscow is 095 and for St Petersburg 812. Note that some of the larger hotels and establishments use a different satellite code. Theoretically, you can get through on the usual code as well; if you have problems call the international operator.

Making calls out of Russia, you use the prefix 810 (wait for an uninterrupted tone after dialling the 8 before going on to the 10) followed by the usual country code (UK 44; New Zealand 64; Australia 61; Germany 49; Japan 81; USA and Canada 1). For long-distance calls within Russia preface the area code and number with 8, again waiting for the tone.

The simplest way of making international calls is to use your home phone company's calling card. Odds are the link will be better, too. Find out the Russian access number before you visit. British Telecom's is 810 800 110 1044; AT&T's is 810 800 497 7211. As far as we know there is no way of making reverse-charge (collect) calls out of Russia.

PUBLIC PHONES

There are two types of public phone in Moscow: old grey ones that take brown tokens and new blue ones that take plastic cards. Both tokens and cards are available from metro station cash offices. The old phones are for local calls only. Drop the token in once you hear the call answered.

The new card phones are more sophisticated. You can request dialling instructions in English by pressing the L button and then choosing English from the menu. When your call is answered, you need to press the button with a phone receiver sign. Card phones in bars and restaurants are not compatible with the street phones. You will need to buy a card from the bartender.

In St Petersburg, most public phones are now modern cardphones. You can buy the cards at kiosks where they are displayed in the window and at metro stations. The old token phones use the same token you use for the metro.

You can save money on international calls by calling from a phone office, such as Central Telegraph (*see above* **Post**) in Moscow or the 24-hour daily Mezhdunarodny Mezhdugorodny Telefon, Bolshaya Morskaya Ulitsa 3/5 (314 0140/311 4963; metro Nevsky Prospekt or Gostiny Dvor) in St Petersburg.

INFORMATION

There are *Yellow Pages* to both Moscow and St Petersburg. Listings are in Cyrillic, but there's an English index. If there isn't one in your hotel room, ask at the front desk. In Moscow, the English-language *Moscow Business Telephone Guide* is available at hotels.

Time

Moscow and St Petersburg are three hours ahead of GMT. Between spring and autumn, clocks go forward an hour.

Tipping

In Soviet times tips (*chayeviye*, from *chai*, the Russian for tea) were prohibited – but not very strictly. Nowadays tipping is not uncommon, but exercise caution: some people are offended if they are given money for what they intended as a courtesy. Often a small gift from your home country is better appreciated.

Restaurants are the only place where tipping is the norm. Leave the waiting staff about ten per cent if you are satisfied with their service. In some restaurants the service charge may be included in the bill. In most other cases tipping is optional. It is not usual to tip taxi drivers or doctors, but we would suggest rewarding your interpreter or guide.

Tourist information

Like all forms of information in Russia, tourist info is difficult to come by and often inadequate. The old monopoly, Intourist, which once handled every tourist activity in the country, is languishing in the Soviet past. Its offices in Moscow still display posters inviting people to come to Leningrad, a city that hasn't existed for over eight years, and its staff are virtually useless. A free tourist phone information service (247 0740/ 290 2011/242 0745) is useful and more or less English-speaking, but gives lots of wrong and obsolete information.

The situation in St Petersburg is even worse. If you're looking for tourist info in the city, you'll have to hope that your hotel is enlightened enough to provide it.

Intourist

Milyutinsky Pereulok 13, Moscow (923 8575). Metro Chistye Prudy. **Open** 10am-6pm Mon-Fri. **Credit** AmEx, MC, V. **Map p278 D2**

Visas & registration

Russia's convoluted visa system has gone basically unchanged since the great paper-pushing days of the Soviet Union. Back then, it was designed to track the movements not only of tourists and visitors but also of their host Russians (hence the ridiculous 'invitation' from a Russian individual or organisation, which is still required). Now it's just a money-spinner for the various agencies involved.

HOW TO APPLY

If you come to Moscow on an organised package, your tour operator should sort out your visa for you – a good reason to consider this option. Getting your own visa is generally a tortuous and time-consuming process.

Russian visas fall into a number of different categories. The most common is the single-entry visa, lasting up to three months. Multi-entry visas, more difficult and expensive to obtain, last up to a year. Tourist visas, which are cheaper but may take a little longer to process, are usually issued for less than a month; business visas can last up to a year and be processed within days if you are willing to pay the substantial sums involved. Depending on the type of visa and how quickly you want it, it will cost from $15 to $200.

For all visas, the application process has some immutable constants. First you must obtain an invitation to visit Russia, either from an individual or an organisation, or most usefully for tourists – the hotel where you have booked a room (most but not all hotels will do this). Being invited by a regular Russian is the most time-consuming option and will involve a delay of up to a month as your Russian friend applies to the local OVIR (visas and registration) office in Russia for an *izveshcheniye* or permission form that you must have in your possession before you can join the queue outside your local Russian embassy. Quicker and infinitely preferable is to find an organisation (a business or educational institution you may be visiting) that can just fax you an invitation letter. The organisation must be registered with the Ministry of Foreign Affairs (MID) and, according to regulations, must arrange for the Ministry to telex authorisation of the invitation

to the embassy where you intend to apply. If you have no contacts in Russia, then there are a number of commercial companies, such as IRO Travel (234 6553) and Andrews Consulting (737 3372) in Moscow and International Hostel (329 8018; tourist visas only) in St Petersburg, that will provide you with an invitation for a fee.

Once you have your invitation, you can move on to the next phase: the vigil outside (or inside, if you're lucky) your Russian embassy. Some will require travellers staying longer than three months to take an AIDS test, others won't bother; prices and regulations also vary. To find all this out, call ahead or, if you're in the US, access the Washington Russian embassy's website at www.russianembassy.org. In general, you will be expected to present your invitation, the number of your telex from MID, your passport, three passport photos and an application form. You can also post your application, though you should be prepared for a two- or three-week wait. Alternatively, you could pay a commercial visa service to do the queueing for you: try DJV in the UK (0171 916 7101) or Travel Document Systems Incorporated in the US (1-800 874 5100).

Once you have finally made it to Russia, you are supposed to register your visa within three working days of arrival. If you are staying in a hotel, this will usually be done automatically. If not, the person or organisation that invited you must go along to the local OVIR to register the visa for you. Commercial visa services (*see above*) will register the visa for free. However, if you fail to do this, as far as we know the worst you can face is a $6 fine.

Ireland

186 Orwell Road, Dublin 6 (3531 492 2048).

UK

5 Kensington Palace Gardens, London W8 4QS (0171 229 8027). There's also a Russian consulate in Edinburgh.

US

2641 Tunlaw Road, NW Washington, DC 20007 (202 939 8907/8913). Russia also has consulates in New York, San Francisco and Seattle.

Women travellers

You are unlikely to be harassed on the street. However, particularly in Moscow, the figures for sexual assault are relatively high, so try to avoid being alone at night away from central areas. Try not to get into conversation with drunks and don't take the front seat in the taxi if you're alone.

Tampons and contraceptives are widely available in pharmacies and supermarkets.

Working in Russia

Officially you cannot work if you are on a short-term or student visa.

Phone hell

There are two primary ways of attaining limitless reserves of patience, Zen restraint and boundless self-discipline. The first is to spend 16 years of self-deprivation in a Tibetan monastery. The second, and by far the more difficult, option is a week's worth of exposure to the Russian telephone system. Only the most unburdened, enlightened individual can hope to tolerate the unruly whines, squeals and crackles that inhabit this prehistoric network, the constant redialling and the furry connections that break down with capricious regularity. Inter-city calling can sometimes take up to 20 attempts, most of them ending in a rude bleeping sound or a hissing limbo. And sending a single fax can often take many excruciating hours.

Since the relaxation of the communist regime's paranoid grip on communications, the unwieldy Russian phone system has undergone a drive towards modernisation. Foreign investment has meant the installation of optical lines and digital switching stations, but these are punctuated along the network by mechanical relics, some of which have been around since the Revolution. Mechanical exchanges, last seen in the West in the 1960s, consist of banks of clicking switches, where each connection is made via a series of rods, gears, tripswitches and springs. Naturally, there is plenty of scope here for error, and wrong numbers are a daily, if not hourly, occurrence – even if the end you're calling from is high-tech.

Getting Around Moscow

TO & FROM THE AIRPORT

Moscow's main international airport, Sheremetyevo 2 (578 7518/7816/2372/8087), is 30 kilometres (19 miles) north-west of town along the St Petersburg road. Sheremetyevo 1, located across the common landing strip, serves domestic flights. Getting into town from here is problematic – there's a dearth of information on buses, taxi fares are high and there's no metro station (confusingly, the metro called Aeroport is somewhere else entirely). Taxi drivers will pester you at the exit, asking up to $60 for the 40-minute trip to the centre. You can usually bargain this down to $30-$45, especially if it's quiet. You could also hire a non-official taxi from the booths on the first floor for around $50. The best way to get a cheap ride is to head for the departure hall on the second floor and pick up a car that has just dropped passengers off. This way you should be able to get to the centre for $20.

If you're on a budget, bus is far cheaper, though hard to manage with luggage. We don't recommend it on a first visit. There are several express services to the city (most go to the nearest metro station, Rechnoi Vokzal, at the top of the green line) but it can be hard to track one down. You may be lucky and find a bus with an Aeroflot sign leaving right from the exit; if not, go out and head for the left side of the road going down from the second floor of the terminal. On your left is a parking zone, then shortly after, a bus stop for both express and ordinary buses. All express buses go to Rechnoi Vokzal metro.

A few international flights, particularly charters, use other airports. Sheremetyevo 1 is connected by the same bus services as its sister terminal. Vnukovo and Domodedovo are served by regular and express buses going to Yugo-Zapadnaya (bottom of the red line) and Domodevoskaya (bottom of the green line) metros respectively.

RAIL

Most of Moscow's main train stations (*see below* **Leaving Town**) have adjoining metros. Taxis wait outside the entrances, ready to charge you a higher than average price.

Though Moscow can be an intimidating and chaotic city, most of its famous sights are concentrated right in the centre, all within walking distance of each other. Most visitors won't have the desire or the time to stray beyond the Kremlin, Red Square, Teatralnaya, Lubyanka, the Arbat and the lower end of Tverskaya Ulitsa, all of which are extremely easy to locate and negotiate. Beyond these central areas the city disintegrates into confusion and greyness. Visiting friends in the suburbs will always present problems: get very clear instructions or try to take a Russian along and avoid lone evening visits: streetlighting is poor in residential areas.

During your visit, Cyrillic script will probably be the greatest obstacle you will encounter. The incomprehensible squiggles used on road signs, metro maps and shopfronts contribute greatly to the foreign and forbidding feel of the place. We have used an English transliteration on our street maps at the back of the book but given the Cyrillic form of important streets in the street index on page 271.

Finding your way around the extensive metro system is initially hard to master (*see*

below for tips), but once you get used to it, you will find it the best way of reaching locations beyond walking distance.

Mayor Luzhkov has some big ideas for improving Moscow's transport. Already in place is the European-standard ring road, and on the drawing board are plans for a monorail line to link the Sheremetyevo airports with the 'Moscow City' business area; an 'underground tram' along major streets such as Novy Arbat and Tverskaya Ulitsa; a circular railway connecting metro stations outside the ring line; and a VIP business airport.

ADDRESSES

Generally, Russian addresses are given thus: Tverskaya Ulitsa 24. Even numbers run up one side of the street; odd numbers the other. Navigation is easier if you recognise the various Russian words for street, square, and so on. They can come before or after the actual name.

street - ulitsa
УЛИЦА
square - ploshchad
ПЛОЩАДЬ
lane - pereulok
ПЕРЕУЛОК
passage - proyezd
ПРОЕЗД
avenue - prospekt
ПРОСПЕКТ
boulevard - bulvar
БУЛЬВАР
embankment - naberezhnaya
НАБЕРЕЖНАЯ

Street numbering is notoriously cryptic, and you will inevitably have trouble finding an address. Some street numbers have a slash in – Tverskaya Ulitsa 16/2, for example. This can mean one of three things.
● Most commonly, it refers to buildings that are on a corner. In this case they take a number for each street, the first number

usually being the principal street. Thus Tverskaya Ulitsa 16/2 might mean that the building is on the corner of Tverskaya Ulitsa and, say, Leontyevsky Pereulok, next to Tverskaya Ulitsa 14 and Leontyevsky Pereulok 4.

● If there are two consecutive odd or even numbers in ascending order, it may mean that a single building takes up two street numbers.

● Where complexes of buildings (usually residential or commercial) are set back from the road, they share a common street number. The principal building bears this number, sometimes alone (eg Tverskaya Ulitsa 16), sometimes followed by a slash and '1' (eg Tverskaya Ulitsa 16/1). Subordinate buildings have the same street number followed by their own *korpus* (in residential areas) or *stroyeniye* (in city centres) number. If the main building takes only the street number, the first subordinate building will be /1; if the main building is /1, the first subordinate building will be /2. The slash is used primarily in postal addresses: on the buildings themselves the addresses are written out – eg 16 kor 1 or 16 str 1.

In general, locate the first number in the address and take it from there.

Some streets have a number as well as a name, for example 1-ya Brestskaya Ulitsa and 2-ya Ulitsa. This is sometimes written as 1-y or 1-ogo.

Public transport

Moscow has an integrated public transport system comprising metro (subway), bus, trolleybus and tram. Visitors are best advised to stick to the highly efficient metro: surface transport is less reliable and harder to negociate. A monthly pass for the whole system is available at metro stations for about $30.

METRO

See map page 283.

Apart from being a sightseeing must, the Moscow metro is also the most efficient transport in the city. It's fast and reliable and services are frequent. The only drawback is that it can be crowded at peak hours. The metro comprises a circular ('ring') line and nine radial lines. Lines are most commonly distinguished by their colours on the metro map, although they also have both names and numbers. Metro stations are marked with a big orange letter M; metro maps are posted at most entrances and near ticket offices.

To pay for a single trip (35¢ adults and children) between any two stations on the network you buy a green plastic token (*zheton*) from a booth on the way in, though these are set to be replaced by magnetic tickets. You can also buy tickets valid for ten, 20 or 60 trips, or for one month (only the last two are a saving).

To enter the system, put the token or ticket into the appropriate slot in an entry gate. The machine will retain tokens and eject multiple-use passes for you to reclaim. Enter only after the light changes from red to green; otherwise a metal bar will block your way rather firmly.

A central platform accesses both directions of travel. Signs bearing a list of stops served and an arrow point you to the appropriate side. Almost no Latin script is used in the signage, so you'll need to refer to a metro map labelled in both Cyrillic and Latin (there's one on p283).

Train carriages have both metro maps and, above the doors, diagrams of the line you are on, the only place that gives names of stations in Latin script. When the train gets into a station, the station name is often obscured, so you should count your stops and listen carefully to the recorded announcements. These tell you which station you're pulling in to and, as the train pulls out, what the next stop is. They're in Russian yes, but quite clear, so you should be able to make out the station name. You are expected to offer your seat to the elderly, pregnant women and women with small children.

Lines may either intersect at a single station or, more commonly, at nearby stations linked by stairs or underground walkways. Transfer signs show a stick figure on a flight of stairs. They are colour-coded to indicate the line they are directing you to and list the stations on it. The metro opens at 5.30am daily. At 1am all escalators stop (you can walk up and down) and the last trains leave from the start of the line, passing through the city centre at around 1.20am.

BUS, TROLLEYBUS, TRAM

These are mainly used for short hops to metro stations. Most operate every five to 30 minutes between 5am and 1.30am daily. There are no night buses. Stops (mostly transparent booths) are marked with yellow boards featuring letter A for buses and a white board with letter T for trolleys and trams. The board also gives timetable information and occasionally even a schedule, which will not necessarily be adhered to but will at least give you an idea of whether to expect a bus in the reasonable future.

Getting to grips with surface transport is difficult without advice from locals. City-wide route diagrams are posted at some stops, but different operators run bus and trolleybus services in different areas and inside the vehicles only routes run by the same operator are displayed.

You can pay cash (about 40¢ adults and children) when you board, but it's cheaper to buy tickets in advance from metro ticket offices and booths (35¢). When you board, you have to manually punch your ticket in a device that makes a combination of holes in it. Be sure that your ticket is punched properly or a ticket inspector may claim that you punched it in a different bus.

Ticket inspectors are common and universally hated for their rudeness, but the fine for riding without a ticket is a mere £4. Check an inspector's ID and make sure you get a receipt: there are fakes out there.

Though in general tourists should stick to the metro where possible, overground routes do, of course, offer the advantage of showing you the city. The best routes for sightseeing are the Б trolley, which runs around the Garden Ring, trolley 2, which runs from Kutuzovsky Prospekt via Novy Arbat and Okhotny Ryad to Kitai-Gorod metro, and trolley 1, which goes through the 'old Moscow' district of Zamoskvareche, around the Kremlin and along Tverskaya Ulitsa. Routes with historical and literary associations include trams A (Annushka) and 39. It was an A tram that decapitated the fictional Berlioz in Bulgakov's *Master and Margarita*, though the route no longer passes Patriarch's Ponds, where the action of the novel takes place. Tram 39 is known as the lovers' tram, since it is the city's longest tram route. Starting from the university, in an hour and a half it makes a trip that takes only 15 minutes by metro – an excuse for lovers to spend longer in each other's company. The No.39 is mentioned in numerous songs and poems. There is also a line plied by restaurant trams. Catch them near Chistye Prudy: there's no fixed schedule but you'll usually find one waiting there.

On foot

Walking around Moscow would be pleasant were it not for two factors: cars and air pollution. Cars never stop for pedestrians, even at pedestrian crossings, and often go at dangerously high speeds. If you see one coming towards you, run. Also beware of street lights, which are known for switching straight from green to red when you are still in the middle of the road.

Moscow's cars are not known for clean exhaust systems, and walking along busy or jammed roads takes its toll on the lungs. Near the Garden Ring airborne pollution exceeds acceptable European levels by a factor of ten or more, though local legislation may soon change this.

Walking is harder in winter. Though few people visit at the coldest times, in late autumn and early spring slippy, slushy pavements are a hazard, as are falling icicles.

Taxi

Cab driving, or 'bombing', is the quickest route to raising the money to pay for a car, so in Moscow a taxi means any car that stops if you stretch out your arm. In the centre several will answer your hail within milliseconds. The vehicle you have stopped may be just an ordinary Lada or Moskvich, a black Volga that belongs to a government organisation, or, more and more often now, a proper yellow taxi with a green light on when it's empty. It could be also be something completely unexpected like a police car, an oil tanker or an ambassadorial limousine.

Whatever kind of car it is, your technique should be basically the same. Before you get in, tell the driver your destination and agree a price (check he has change – *sdacha* – if you need it). This holds true even for proper taxis with meters – drivers never use them. If you are going somewhere off the beaten track be prepared to give basic directions or point out your destination on the map. Licensed cab drivers will probably know the city best as its geography is part of their training.

Taking a lift from a non-licensed driver in Moscow is generally safe, but take the following precautions:
● Never get into a car that already has passengers.
● Lone women should sit in the back.
● Accept rides only in cars with a Moscow number plate (they should have '77' or '99' in the right corner).
● If you want to keep the fare down, never hail a taxi from the front of theatres or nightclubs – walk a little way first.

Generally, a trip from the centre to outer districts will cost anything between $5 and $8.50. A trip within the city centre should not cost more than $6. As there's no public transport between 1 and 5am a taxi becomes the sole means of getting home late at night.

Driving in Moscow

Unless you're a sucker for punishment or are used to driving in Rome or Paris, you're probably better sticking to the metro or, for trips out of town, bus or train. The rules of the road take some getting used to – traffic coming from the right has right of way and left turns are only allowed where indicated – and the drink-driving limit is zero.

Traffic jams are endemic: on weekdays, especially during rush hours (9-11am and 5-7pm) main arteries such as Tverskaya Ulitsa, Leninsky Prospekt and the Garden and Boulevard Rings are very slow moving as is the road to the airport. Many drivers, especially urban jeepsters, ignore signs, streetlights and other cars. And you will have to deal with the notorious traffic police (formerly the GAI, now the GIBDD). They're supposed to be less bolshy these days, but you should still be prepared to be stopped for allegedly breaking some minor rule and told to pay a fine (which will probably go straight into the inspector's pocket). If you do want the use of a private car, we suggest you hire one with a driver. Ask your concierge or look in the *Moscow Times* classifieds under 'Drivers' or 'Translators', some of whom can be hired together with their cars. City Limousine (960 1000) does the same thing in a limo.

Though it's easy to get lost in side streets, the radial road system is relatively straightforward. You need to know the three main circle roads: the outer MKAD, the intermediate Garden Ring and the inner Boulevard Ring. Among the most important radial roads are Leninsky Prospekt; Tverskaya Ulitsa and Ulitsa Novy Arbat, which become Leningradsky Prospekt and Kutuzovsky Prospekt respectively as they leave the centre. Note that the semicircle of roads around the Kremlin is one-way northbound.

PETROL STATIONS

Nearly all petrol stations in the city work 24 hours, unless they run out of petrol in which case they close temporarily. Most of them are on main roads outside the city centre.

PARKING

Parking is hard to find. The only parking meters are on Tverskaya Ulitsa: elsewhere, look out for uniformed ticket sellers. The good news is that clamping has recently been ruled illegal.

CAR HIRE COMPANIES

Car rental is not cheap: Hertz quoted us $950 for a mid-size for a week in spring. Technically, you only need your home country's driving licence, but UK citizens should also show an international licence as it has picture ID. You need to be 21 or over (25 for some cars) with a major credit card.

Eurodollar
Bolshaya Kommunisticheskaya Ulitsa (298 6146). Metro Taganskaya.
Credit AmEx, DC, JCB, MC, V. **Map p282 F5**
Also has a booth in Sheremetyevo 1.

Hertz
Arrivals hall, Sheremetyevo 2 Airport (578 5646). **Credit** AmEx, DC, JCB, MC, V.

Guided tours

Since the vast majority of tourists come to Moscow on package tours, there are few tour agencies. You can usually book tours and personal guides at the major hotels and business centres (expensive); independent travellers could also consider less traditional options such as calling people listed in the 'Translation' section of the *Moscow Times* classifieds, who are often happy to show you the city, or asking round students at reputable language schools such as the MSU Faculty of Foreign Languages (Lomonosovsky Pereulok 31/1; metro Universitet, then trolley 34 to Ploshchad Indiry Gandi.

The most popular tour agency is Patriarshy Dom, which offers excellent programmes including a wide range of traditional itineraries in Moscow and beyond as well as thematic tours on architecture, literature and theatre and visits to the museum of the former KGB and the Space Flight Control Centre, both otherwise inaccessible. Intourist also offers various tours (*see above* **Tourist information**) in and outside Moscow, including boat tours, none of them cheap; new agency Astur-Inform also has a wide range of itineraries local and national.

An excellent way to see the Moscow region from off the beaten track is to go on a weekend trip with the Hikers, Walkers and Nature Lovers group, comprised of both expats and Russians, which advertises in the Lifestyle section of the *Moscow Times* on Wednesdays. For bike tours *see chapter* **Sport & Fitness**.

Astur-Inform
Komsomolskaya Ploshchad 3/9, behind Tsentralnoye Zheleznodorozhnoye Agentsvo on the right of Leningradsky Vokzal (975 2175/3824). Metro Komsomolskaya. **Open** 9am-6pm Mon-Fri; weekend hours vary. **No credit cards. Map p279 F1**

Patriarshy Dom Tours
Vspolny Pereulok 6 (926 5680). Metro Barrikadnaya or Mayakovskaya. **Open** 9am-6pm Mon-Fri. **No credit cards. Map p277 A2**

River Cruises
Kievsky Vokzal, nr Radisson Hotel (157 0451). Metro Kievskaya. **Open** mid-Apr mid Sept. **Departs** *Kievsky Vokzal* 11.30am, 2.30pm, 5.30pm, Mon-Fri; every half hour Sat, Sun. **Tickets** Mon-Fri $2.50; $1.75 children; Sat, Sun $4; $2.50 children. **No credit cards.**
Boats run from Kievsky down to the Proletarskaya area of town and Novospassky Monastery, stopping along the way, and passing various Moscow landmarks. The view of the Kremlin from the river is exceptional; you'll also see Gorky Park, the new sports arena and Moscow University. The same company runs tours on the Volga River, to St Petersburg and elsewhere on Russia's rivers and canals. Call 458 9163/9624 for info.

Leaving town

Note that a dual pricing system for Russians and non-Russians (who usually pay more) has been operating on airlines and inter-city trains. However, following a test case, this may be on its way out: most airlines have abandoned the practice, although it persists on trains.

TRAVEL AGENTS

Andrews Consulting
Novaya Ploshchad 10, 5th floor (258 5198). Metro Lubyanka. **Open** 10am-6pm Mon-Fri. **Credit** AmEx, MC, V. **Map p278 D3**

IRO Travel
Komsomolsky Prospekt 13 (234 6555). Metro Park Kultury. **Open** 10am-6pm Mon-Fri; 11am-3pm Sat. **Credit** AmEx, MC, V. **Map p280 A6/B6**

Star/STA-Russia
Bolshaya Pereyaslavskaya Ulitsa 50, 10th floor (797 9555). Metro Prospekt Mira. **Open** 10am-6pm Mon-Fri. **No credit cards.**
Student/young people's specialist.

RAIL
Suburban trains are called *elektrichki*; tickets are sold at the station often from dedicated ticket desks. *Elektrichki* are ancient (many have wooden seats), often crowded and chug slowly through the suburbs. Note that few trains run between 10am and noon.

Long-distance trains tend to be all-sleeper owing to the distances covered, only on the St Petersburg line are there seats. As a rule they are fast and reasonably comfortable, though toilets can be quite dirty. Tickets can be bought at stations and are also bookable at all major hotels and RZhD (Russian railway) agents around the city. Tickets for international trains are not sold at stations: book through an agent.

Agentsvo
Leningradsky Prospekt 1 (262 0604/ 945 0807). Metro Belorusskaya. **Open** 8am-8pm daily. **No credit cards.**
International tickets.

Central Railway Agency
Tsentralnoye Zheleznodorozhnoye Agentsvo, Komsomolskaya Ploshchad 5 (266 8333). Metro Komsomolskaya. **Open** 7am-8pm Mon-Fri; 7am-5pm Sat, Sun. **No credit cards. Map p279 F1.**
All tickets sold, including some international. Bookings can be made by phone; tickets are delivered to your address (pay in cash).

Main-line stations

Belorussky Vokzal
Ploshchad Tverskoi Zastavy 7 (251 6093). Metro Belorusskaya. **Map p277 1A**
For Belarus, Poland, Lithuania, Western Europe.

Kazansky Vokzal
Komsomolskaya Ploshchad 2 (264 6409). Metro Komsomolskaya. **Map p279 F1**
For Volga, the Urals, Siberia, Central Asia.

Kievsky Vokzal
Ploshchad Kievskogo Vokzala 1 (240 0415). Metro Kievskaya.
For the Ukraine, Moldova, Hungary, Slovakia, Romania, the Balkans, Italy.

Kursky Vokzal
Zemlyanoi Val 29 (924 5762). Metro Kurskaya. **Map p279 F3**

For southern Russia, the Caucasus, eastern Ukraine.

Leningradsky Vokzal
Komsomolskaya Ploshchad 3 (262 9143). Metro Komsomolskaya. **Map p279 F1**
For St Petersburg, Estonia, Finland.

Paveletsky Vokzal
Paveletskaya Ploshchad 1 (235 6807). Metro Paveletskaya. **Map p282 E6**
For southern Volga, Central Asia, the Caucasus.

Rizhsky Vokzal
Ploshchad Rizhskogo Vokzala (971 1588). Metro Rizhskaya.
For destinations to Latvia.

Savyolovsky Vokzal
Ploshchad Savyolovskogo Vokzala (285 9005). Metro Savyolovskaya.
For the northern Volga.

Yaroslavsky Vokzal
Komsomolskaya Ploshchad 5 (921 5914). Metro Komsomolskaya. **Map p279 F1**
For the northern Urals, Siberia, the Far East, Mongolia, China.

AIRLINES

Aeroflot no longer has a monopoly. Several companies are now competing on major domestic routes, so you can search around for a better price and plane type. On international destinations, too, Aeroflot is rivaled by a number of respected foreign and Russian companies. A travel agent will know the best deals.

Air France 234 3377
British Airways 258 2492
Lufthansa 975 2501
Delta Airlines 578 2939/258 1288
Aeroflot domestic 155 0922/155 5003
international 156 8019/155 5045
Transaero 241 7676

Numbers given are also good for flight information/confirmation.

LONG-DISTANCE BUSES

A network of long-distance buses is springing up to rival the slow and often cramped suburban trains. The system is embryonic: generally journeys are faster than the train and more comfortable, but timetables are erratic. They're convenient for tourists as all they need to do is take a seat rather than queue at a ticket window. These buses often leave from outside the train station that serves the same destination.

A number of travel companies operate bus routes to Europe, particularly to Germany and Poland. Try Ost-West (Maly Znamensky Pereulok 7/10; 203 0104) or look for people distributing leaflets with bus schedules and prices near the German consulate at Leninsky Prospekt 95A.

Central Bus Station
Shcholkovskoye Shosse 75. Metro Shchyolkovskaya.

HITCHHIKING

Hitching used to be common in Soviet times, but people now consider it quite dangerous. Drivers do stop, but some will ask for payment. However, it is perfectly possible and never dull – you can end up getting rides in not just cars but barges, helicopters and military aircraft.

Between Moscow & St Petersburg

The journey between Moscow and St Petersburg has the potential to be your most pleasant Russian transport experience. The overnight trains are generally clean, relatively comfortable and, if you opt for one of the famous rust-coloured overnight 'Red Arrow' trains, have an added edge of romance and adventure.

The 650-kilometre (406-mile) rail trip usually takes around eight and a half hours, though some trains take longer. Once a week, leaving from Moscow on Thurdays at 12.22pm and from St Petersburg on Fridays at 12.15pm, there is a high-speed train that manages the journey in about five hours. Most overnight trains leave between 11pm and midnight. Later trains at 1am and 2am, which may cost less than half the usual price, should be avoided as they are very grubby and without security. Tickets for the journey are available from the Intourist ticket office in Leningradsky Vokzal in Moscow (which is located up a flight of stairs to your right as you stand in the main hall facing the platforms) and in Moskovsky Vokzal in St Petersburg (the Intourist office is in an annexe on the right as you enter the main hall). You can also get tickets at the Central Railway Agencies in both cities or at many travel agents (for a commission). Though prices tend to bounce up and down considerably, a one-way ticket on a regular express overnight train will cost around $45 one way in a four-person compartment and $70 for a two-person. On Red Arrows the cost will be $50 and $90. Returns cost double these amounts. Don't forget that on many trains you will be asked to pay between $2 and $3 for bedding.

Flying between the two cities is much less fun and means coming into contact with their domestic airports, both of which are hideous and largely bereft of signposting of any kind. The journey takes about 50 minutes. There are two airline choices: Aeroflot ($83 one way, $170 return), which has numerous flights every day, and the far superior Transaero ($95 one way, $190 return), which offers only two flights on weekdays, one in the morning and one in the evening, and one at weekends. Tickets for both are available from the airlines' respective offices or from a ticket office at the airport. Brace yourself for Russian air travel quirks such as people using their mobile phones during take-off and landing. Intercity buses also travel between Moscow and St Petersburg and cost around $40 one way. The journey is extremely uncomfortable and not recommended.

Getting Around St Petersburg

TO & FROM THE AIRPORT

Just as in Moscow, St Petersburg's two main airports, confusingly, go by the same name, with Pulkova 2 (104 3444) servicing international flights and Pulkova 1 (104 3822), located a few kilometres away across the main runway, covering only the domestic routes.

Getting into town from the international Pulkova 2 involves negotiating with taxi drivers all wanting to charge exorbitant rates. The asking price will be around $40 for the 40-minute journey, though you may beat them down to $25 or $30. Public transport, which means getting the No.13 bus (every 20 minutes 6am-midnight) and then transferring to the metro at Moskovskaya station, is not a good option if you're new to town or have a lot of baggage. But you might want to get the bus for 15¢ plus 15¢ for each item of luggage) or one of the fleet of minibuses (50¢) and then catch a much cheaper cab (about $5) at the metro.

If you're coming from Moscow and landing at the domestic airport, Pulkova 1, cabs will be marginally cheaper, though may still hike up the price when they see you're a foreigner. Getting to the metro involves taking bus No.39 (15¢ plus 15¢ for each item of luggage; every 20 minutes 6am-midnight) or a minibus (50¢).

RAIL

Most likely, you'll be arriving from Moscow at Moscovsky Vokzal, which is located right in the centre of the city. The cabs by the station will be overpriced but you can easily walk to Nevsky Prospekt to pick up a more reasonable one. All main rail stations are adjacent to metros.

Getting around St Petersburg is a breeze after the sprawl of Moscow. Practically everything you'll want to see is concentrated in a few square kilometres around Palace Square, across the river on Petrogradskaya or along Nevsky Prospekt.

The layout of St Petersburg's streets is more rational than in Moscow, and map-reading is relatively straightforward. In the centre, many of the street names are written in Latin letters as well as in Cyrillic, thanks to a street-sponsoring scheme initiated some years ago (the signs also bear corporate logos leading to lapses in taste such as 'Nevsky Prospekt, sponsored by Coca-Cola'). The names of streets all follow the Moscow pattern, though you are much less likely to encounter the confusing drop or slash (/) in street numbers as many of St Petersburg's original buildings are still standing and have not been replaced by larger buildings on the site of numerous older ones.

From April to November, the bridges across the Neva open at night to accommodate river traffic, which blocks road traffic between the centre and the north and eastern suburbs. Most bridges are impassable between about 2am and 5am daily, though some close briefly to let cars through; most taxi drivers know the schedules.

The transport system in St Petersburg comprises metro, trolleybuses, buses and trams. The metro is clean and efficient but limited; surface transport is more useful than in Moscow, and easier to negotiate, though tatty and often overcrowded.

METRO

See **map** *page 290.*
St Petersburg's metro can't compete with Moscow's, but it's fast, efficient and relatively clean. There are only four lines, so large tracts of the city, even in the centre, can be far from a station. Also, a section of the line 1 tunnel has collapsed between Ploshchad Muzhestva and Devyatkino; a bus shuttle takes over. A single fare is about 25¢. You buy a metal token (which doubles as a telephone token) from the ticket offices in the lobby of each station. Tickets for 50 and 25 trips are also sold. A monthly pass costs $20 with discounts for students and children. Most stations have the old barrier system where metal jaws can chew off your legs if the token gets stuck in the slot. The metro opens at 5.30am daily and last trains leave at 12.35am (up to 1am from the city centre).

BUS, TROLLEY & TRAM

St Petersburg's overland network is easier to negotiate than Moscow's, though it is just as tatty and, on main routes, even more overcrowded. Every route has conductors who will sell you a ticket for 15¢. The most useful trolleybus routes are Nos.1, 5, 7, 10, 19 and 22, which run the length of Nevsky Prospekt between the Malaya Morskaya and Ploshchad Vosstaniya, with Nos.1 and 22 continuing to the Aleksander Nevsky Lavra. Trams 2 and 54 go down Sadovaya Ulitsa and across Troitsky Most to the Peter and Paul Fortress, offering spectacular views from the bridge.

In St Petersburg, your feet are by far the best mode of transport. The centre is compact and most of the major sights are within walking distance of each other. St Petersburg suffers from similar pollution problems as Moscow, compounded by winds that can whip up choking dust storms in summer. Drivers are aggressive and you should always move sharpish when you see a car coming. Beware of dodgy-looking manhole covers, which can give way underfoot. In winter take care on slippery pathways and look out for falling ice, a St Petersburg speciality.

Directory

Taxi

In 1997, St Petersburg had the bright idea of outlawing 'gypsy' cabs and legitimising the taxi industry. A squad of plainclothes police was supposedly dispatched to roam the streets hailing cabs and slapping enormous fines on unlicensed drivers. The whole operation was a fiasco: on most main streets it is only marginally harder to flag down a private car now than it ever was. Fares are approximately $1.70 for any trip in the city centre and no more than $5 for relatively long journeys to the suburbs. All of the precautions listed for Moscow apply.

Driving in St Petersburg

St Petersburg offers no self-drive car rental companies, so even if you wanted some rough-terrain fun on its pockmarked roads, it's not possible unless you've driven a car here from Moscow. If you need a chauffeured car, hotel concierges have a regular roster of drivers, or try the classified ads in the *St Petersburg Times*.

CAR & DRIVER HIRE

Interavto-Hertz
Perekupnoi Pereulok 4 (277 4032). Metro Moskovskiye Vorota or Ploshchad Aleksandra Nevskogo. **Open** 8am-5pm Mon-Fri. **Rates** $30 per hour. **No credit cards. Map** 289 G5/6

Transservice
Hotel Sovietskaya, Lermontovsky Prospekt 43/1 (274 3588 9am-6pm daily/965 5500 24 hours). Metro Vitebsky Vokzal. **Open** 24 hours daily. **Rates** $6-$16 per hour. **No credit cards. Map p287 B6**

Tours & river cruises

The main terminal for river tours of St Petersburg is on the north bank of the Fontanka beside the Anichkov Bridge. The easiest way to get on a tour is just to go there and stand in

line. All of St Petersburg's waterways are also infested with smaller river taxis, which offer cut-price and more intimate and personalised tours. Sindbad Travel (*see below* **Travel agents**) organises daily walking tours including its famous rooftop tour, which will bring you over some of the most prestigious roofs in the city.

Ost West Kontactservice
Ulitsa Mayakovskogo 7 (327 3416/ 279 7045). Metro Mayakovskaya. **Open** 10am-6pm Mon-Fri; noon-6pm Sat. **Credit** MC, V. **Map p289 F4/5**
A tourist company that can organise river tours for individuals and parties small and large. Also walking tours of the city, literary tours and tours of the outlying palaces.

Leaving town

TRAVEL AGENTS

Okdail
Ligovsky Prospekt 43/45 (272 671). Metro Ploshchad Vosstanniya. **Open** 10am-5.30pm Mon-Fri. **No credit cards. Map p289 F4/5**

Sindbad Travel
3-ya Sovetskaya Ulitsa 28 (327 8384/329 8018). Metro Ploshchad Vosstaniya. **Open** 9.30am-5.30pm Mon-Fri. **Credit** MC, V. **Map p289 F5/G5**

RAIL

Tickets for St Petersburg suburban trains, or *elektrichki*, can be bought in stations. The system is cheap but slow. You've also got to work around a hole in the schedule between about 10am and noon, when no trains run.

For inter-city and international trains, foreigners are still obliged to buy tickets at the station's Intourist window. Often these offices are a little away from the main drag, such as in Moskovsky Vokzal, where the Intourist *kassa* is located in a small annexe to the right as you enter the main hall. International tickets generally cost the same for both Russians and foreigners (except the journey to Helsinki); tickets for journeys within Russia are usually sold to foreigners at slightly inflated prices. At the spanking new ticket office in the Finlyandsky Vokzal, you can book tickets for departures from any of the other stations as well as buy return tickets, a relatively recent Russian innovation. Far more convenient, however, is the central ticket office on Naberezhnaya Kanala

Griboyedova, just off Nevsky Prospekt, which also offers tickets to all destinations and takes credit cards. All ticket offices work from 6.30am until the last train of the day has departed, which can be as late as 2am.

Central Railway Agency
Naberezhnaya Kanala Griboyedova 24 (162 4455). Metro Nevsky Prospekt. **Open** 8am-8pm daily. **Credit** MC, V. **Map 287 D4**

General Railway Enquiries
168 0111.
24-hour train information – but in Russian and a billed service. Try asking your hotel concierge to call.

Main-line stations

Baltiisky Vokzal
Naberezhnaya Obvodnogo 120 (168 2259). Metro Baltiiskaya.
For Peterhof, Lomonosov, Gatchina, Strelna.

Finlyandsky Vokzal
Prospekt Lenina 6 (168 7687). Metro Ploshchad Lenina. **Map p288 F2**
For Vyborg, Helsinki.

Moskovsky Vokzal
Ploshchad Vosstanya 2 (168 4597). Metro Ploshchad Vosstaniya. **Map p289 F5**
For Moscow, the south of Russia.

Varshavsky Vokzal
Naberezhnaya Obvodnogo Kanala 118 (168 2690). Metro Baltiiskaya.
For Gatchina, Baltic states, Poland, Western Europe.

Vitebsky Vokzal
Zagorodny Prospekt 52 (168 5703). Metro Pushkinskaya.
For Pushkin, Pavlovsk, Minsk, Kiev, Poland.

AIRLINES
Aeroflot
277 2565.
Air France
325 8252.
British Airways
329 2565.
Finnair
315 9736.
Lufthansa
314 5917.
Transaero
279 1974.

LONG-DISTANCE BUSES
Not generally recommended: buses will be old and rickety. There are no regular routes from St Petersburg to international destinations, with the exception of Helsinki.

Bus station
Naberezhnaya Obvodnogo Kanala 36 (166 5777). Metro Ligovsky Prospekt.

Business in Moscow

Business infrastructure in Moscow is far ahead of anywhere else in Russia – hardly surprising for a city with a tenth of this vast country's GDP and an income per capita about four times the national average. Most business services are now available in Moscow at prices comparable to other international cities. This is not to say that operating in Moscow is easy: 'If you're not having problems, you're not trading,' as one British businessman put it. The difficulties are more bureaucratic than underworld-related, though precautions are advisable: information security is obviously a priority in a country with strong espionage traditions.

The bureaucratic problems vary from arcane specifications for imports to being sent from pillar to post by officials with ill-defined spheres of responsibility (a problem for everybody). The best solution for foreign business travellers is to work through local intermediaries who know the ropes: we have included several in the listings below.

Simply finding the organisations you need to visit can be frustrating. Even the head offices of big corporations (car trading giant Logovaz, or oil company Sibneft) prefer to give no visible signs of their presence. Smaller companies are often concealed in the bowels of huge ex-Soviet institutional buildings. Always get precise instructions, preferably with landmarks, and allow plenty of time for negotiating the traffic.

Business dealings in Moscow sometimes suffer from what one lawyer (and Monty Python fan) calls the 'You stay here and guard him' syndrome' – inexplicable communications failures that happen even when the language barrier is fully surmounted. The problem may be rooted in the Soviet habit of not calling a spade a spade. It helps to be absolutely clear about what you want. If you are not understood at first, it is perfectly acceptable (and even expected) to raise your voice and omit polite qualifiers.

Banks

Very few foreign banks, and none from the UK or US, offer retail services, but the larger branches of Russian banks offer most essential facilities. For addresses *see above* **Essential Information: Banks & money**. If you require retail services from a non-Russian bank, try Bank Austria on Dolgorukovskaya Ulitsa (965 3000).

Business centres/secretarial services

Most of the big hotels have business centres with a choice of do-it-yourself or secretarial support. They are open to non-residents.

Aerostar Hotel

Leningradsky Prospekt 37/9 (213 9000). Metro Aeroport. **Open** 24 hours daily. **Credit** AmEx, DC, JCB, V.
Photocopying, typing, translation and interpreting services, plus computer time by the hour.

Marriott Grand Hotel

Tverskaya Ulitsa 26 (935 8500). Metro Mayakovskaya. **Open** 8am-11pm Mon-Fri; 8am-9pm Sat, Sun. **Credit** AmEx, DC, MC, V. **Map** p278 C2
Photocopying, binding, typing and computing.

Sheraton Palace Hotel

Tverskaya-Yamskaya Ulitsa 19 (931 9700). Metro Belorusskaya. **Open** 7am-11pm Mon-Fri, 9am-5.30pm Sat, Sun. **Credit** AmEx, DC, MC, V. **Map** p277 B2
Photocopying, typing, computing, translation and interpreting, all at good prices.

Business consultants

The Big Six accounting firms also act as consultants, lawyers and tax specialists.

Arthur Andersen

Kosmodamianskaya Naberezhnaya 52/2 (755 9700). Metro Paveletskaya. **Open** 9am-6pm Mon-Fri. **Map** p282 E5

Coopers & Lybrand

Nikitsky Pereulok 5 (232 5511). Metro Okhotny Ryad. **Open** 9am-6pm Mon-Fri. **Map** p278 C3

Deloitte & Touche

Mokhovaya Ulitsa 8 (956 5000). Metro Okhotny Ryad. **Open** 9am-6pm Mon-Fri. **Map** p278 C3

Ernst & Young

Podsosensky Pereulok 20/12 (705 9292). Metro Kurskaya. **Open** 9am-6pm Mon-Fri. **Map** p279 F3

KPMG

Staraya Basmannaya Ulitsa 38/2, building 1 (937 4477). Metro Baumanskaya. **Open** 9am-6pm Mon-Fri. **Map** p279 F2

Price Waterhouse

Nikoloyamskaya Ulitsa 13 (967 6000). Metro Taganskaya. **Open** 9am-6pm Mon-Fri. **Map** p282 F4/F4

Communications

Beeline

Lesnoryadsky Pereulok 18 (747 9964). Metro Krasnoselskaya. **Open** call for details. **Credit** MC, V.
This mobile phone operator sets you up with a handset for a returnable deposit of $170-$385 plus call deposits of $360 for Moscow-area coverage or $600 for long-distance and international. Connection costs $36, rental $3.60 a day and local calls 42-59¢ depending on time of day.

Comstar

1-ya Tverskaya-Yamskaya Ulitsa 39/5 (956 0000). Metro Mayakovskaya. **Open** 8.30am-5.30pm Mon-Thur; 8.30am-4.30pm Fri. **Credit** AmEx, DC, MC, V. **Map** p277 D2
This commercial phone company has its own cables and beats the creaky state network on every front efficiency, speed of installation – except price. If you're setting up an office, come straight here.

Conference venues

Many of the big hotels offer facilities for business conferences. For Moscow's exhibition centres, *see chapter* **Museums & Galleries**.

Cosmos Hotel

Prospekt Mira 150 (215 6791). Metro VDNKh. **Open** 9am-6pm Mon-Fri.
Prices per day: less than 12 people $100; 20-30 people $160; 60 people $215; 1,000 people $1,530.

Radisson Slavyanskaya Hotel

Berezhkovskaya Naberezhnaya 2 (941 8020). Metro Kievskaya. **Open** 9am-6pm Mon-Fri.
Prices per day: boardroom $150; halls $720-$4,200. Charges for room and hall rental are waived if the delegates eat lunch (minimum $22 per person).

Couriers

It's best to stick with the big boys – smaller companies can take several days. FedEx promises next-day delivery to the US on packages submitted in the morning (two days to the

UK). In the other direction, it's three days from the US, two from the UK. Keep a note of your tracking number.

Federal Express
Aviatsionny Pereulok 8/17 (234 3400). Metro Aeroport. **Open** 8am-8pm daily. **Credit** MC, V.
Documents up to 500g (just over 1lb) cost $38 to Europe and the US. Call for a pick-up. English spoken.

TNT
Baltiisky Trety Pereulok 3 (931 9640). Metro Sokol. **Open** 9am-6pm daily. **Credit** AmEx, DC, JCB, MC, V.
Documents up to 500g cost $41 to Europe, $48 to the US.

Import & export

Russian Customs have a reputation for bureaucracy and corruption, but there is no getting round them.

Moscow Customs
Novaya Basmannaya Ulitsa 23/1 (267 8925). Metro Kurskaya. **Open** 9am-1pm, 2-6pm, Mon-Fri. **Map p279 F1**

Russian Logistics Service
Kutuzovsky Proyezd 8 (785 1109). Metro Kutuzovskaya. **Open** 9am-6pm Mon-Fri. **Credit** MC, V.
The Logistics Service will carry out all Customs clearance procedures for importers in return for a fee equal to about 10 per cent of Customs costs.

Lawyers

Most major UK and US law firms have offices in Moscow.

Allen & Overy
Dmitrovsky Pereulok 9 (258 3111). Metro Teatralnaya. **Open** 9am-6pm Mon-Fri. **Map p278 C2**

Baker & McKenzie
Bolshoi Strochenovsky Pereulok 22/25 (230 6036). Metro Serpukhovskaya. **Open** 9am-6pm Mon-Fri.

Clifford Chance
Sadovaya-Samotechnaya Ulitsa 24/27 (258 5050). Metro Tsvetnoi Bulvar. **Open** 9am-6pm Mon-Fri. **Map p278 C1**

Eckstein & Partners
Ulitsa Pokrovka 42/5 (916 4500). Metro Kitai-Gorod. **Open** 9am-6pm Mon-Fri. **Map p279 E3/F2**

Norton Rose
Bolshoi Sukharevsky Pereulok 26 (244 3639). Metro Sukharevskaya. **Open** 9am-6pm Mon-Fri. **Map p278 D1**

Office equipment

Bely Veter Kompyterny Mir
Bolshoi Cherkassky Pereulok 2/10 (928 7392/924 5372). Metro Lubyanka. **Open** 9am-9pm daily. **Credit** AmEx, MC, V. **Map p278 D3**
One of several locations. Well stocked with computers, printers and other equipment.

Partiya
Ulitsa Solyanka 1 (928 3939). Metro Kitai-Gorod. **Open** 9am-7pm daily. **Credit** MC, V. **Map p279 E3, p282 E4**
Computers, faxes, copiers and other office equipment. Lots of branches.

Printing/copying

Alpha Graphics
Leningradsky Prospekt 53 (258 7500). Metro Aeroport. Kosmodamianskaya Naberezhnaya 52/1 (961 2100). Metro Paveletskaya. **Map p282 E5**
Both **Open** 9am-9pm Mon-Fri; 9am-6pm Sat. **Credit** AmEx, DC, JCB, MC, V.
Printing bureau. Instant one-sided business cards are $24 per 100; A4 colour brochures $1,300 per 2,000. Tax is added to the prices.

Copy General
Bolshoi Zlatoustinsky Pereulok 7 (928 7859). Metro Lubyanka. **Open** 24 hours daily. **No credit cards.** **Map p278 D3**
The flagship branch of a new chain of competitively priced document centres. There's another branch at Novinsky Bulvar 12, opposite the US embassy, open 7am to 10pm daily.

Registration

It is possible to register a new company over the counter at the State Registration Chamber of the Ministry of Economy of the Russian Federation if you have the right documentation. After submitting your application, you have a month to furnish the requisite approvals. But it's not very straightforward – you need things like tax authority and foreigners are best advised to work through lawyers or business consultants.

State Registration Chamber
Smolensky Bulvar 3/5, Moscow 119835 (246 8649/3486/tel & fax for information & consulting centre 247 1639). Metro Smolenskaya. **Open** 10am-noon, 2-4pm, Mon-Fri. **Map p280 A5**

The Russian Legal Company
Ulitsa Bolshaya Pochtovaya 7 (Novosti Publishing House building), Office 511 (755 7765/265 5609. Ask for Oleg Vol, who speaks English). Metro Baumanskaya. **Open** 9am-6pm Mon-Fri.
Prices: $350 for registration of companies that also have Russian shareholder(s); $790 for registration of wholly foreign-owned companies; $1,090 for registration of Russian subsidiaries; $4,240 for registration of a representative office (includes $2,650 tax).

Tax

State Tax Inspectorate for Moscow
Ulitsa Ilyinka 13 (206 0430). Metro Kitai-Gorod. **Open** 10am-1pm, 2-6pm, Mon-Fri. **Map p278 D3**

Deloitte & Touche
See above **Business consultants.**
D&T's tax department (ask for Kevin Norville) offers advice and information on all aspects of paying tax in Russia, with the first consultation free.

Translation/interpreting

It is very hard to find native English or US translators in Moscow, so expect occasional lack of clarity and grammar in Russian-English translation.

Aerostar Hotel
See above **Business centres & secretarial services.**
Translation is $20 per page; interpreting $35 an hour.

Marriott Grand Hotel
See above **Business centres & secretarial services.**
Translation is $20 per page for general text, $23 for business text, $27 for technical text; interpreting is $25 per hour for sightseeing, $30 per hour for business and $50 for specialist subjects.

Translation & Information Bureau
Maly Kislovsky Pereulok 3 (374 7603). Metro Arbatskaya. **Open** 9am-6pm Mon-Fri. **Credit** MC, V. **Map p277 B3**
Translation into Russian costs $8-$12 per page; translation from Russian $10-$15 per page. Interpreting ranges from $100 to $600 a day depending on factors including whether it's simultaneous or not.

The Russian Language

More and more Russians are beginning to speak English, especially the young, but it still can't be guaranteed even on the tourist scene. In larger hotels front desk staff should be reasonably fluent, but not necessarily the switchboard operator: your calls may well go astray (it may help if you learn to pronounce your room number in Russian and pass it on to any potential callers).

Russians do not tend to understand Latin script, so if you need to ask directions it will not usually help to point at the transliterated addresses given in this book.

Learning Russian can take a lifetime, but communicating with a few basic phrases is within the tourist's grasp (given a patient listener). In general, transliterations are pronounced as they are written with a few exceptions, notably 'g', which is sometimes pronounced as 'v' (for example in 'ogo' at the end of most words).

THE CYRILLIC ALPHABET

А а - like 'a' in 'car'
Б б - like 'b' in 'bike'
В в - like 'v' in 'van'
Г г - like 'g' in 'gut'
Д д - like 'd' in 'done'
Е е - like 'ye' in 'yellow' at the beginning of a word, after vowels and after ъ and ь; after consonants like 'e' in 'letter'
Ё ё - like 'yo' in 'yolk' at the beginning of a word, after vowels and after ъ and ь, like 'u' in 'burn' after consonants
Ж ж - like 's' in leisure
З з - like 'z' in 'zoo'
И и - like 'i' in little
Й й - like 'y' in 'pay'
К к - like 'k' in 'key'
Л л - like 'l' in 'lion'
М м - like 'm' in ' mother'
Н н - like 'n' in 'nose'
О о - like 'o' in 'portrait' when stressed; like 'o' in 'pot' when unstressed
П п - like 'p' in 'pig'
Р р - a slightly rolled 'r'
С с - like 's' in 'sea'
Т т - like 't' in 'ten'
У у - like 'oo' in 'pool'
Ф ф - like 'f' in 'fan'
Х х - like 'ch' in Bach
Ц ц - like 'ts' in 'pets'
Ч ч - like 'ch' in 'chew'
Ш ш - like 'sh' in 'shelter'
Щ щ - like 'ss' in 'issue'
Ъ ъ - 'hard sign'. Not pronounced
Ы ы - between 'i' in 'list' and 'oo' in 'pool'
Ь ь - 'soft sign'. Not pronounced
Э э - like 'e' in 'bet'
Ю ю - like 'u' in 'tulip'
Я я - like 'ya' in yam

CYRILLIC WORDS
way out - (vykhod)
ВЫХОД

way in - (vkhod)
ВХОД

transfer on metro - (perekhod)
ПЕРЕХОД

toilet/restroom - (toilet) ТУАЛЕТ

men's toilet - (mushskoi toilet)
МЛЖСКОЙ ТУАЛЕТ

ladies' toilet - (zhensky toilet)
ЖЕНСКИЙ ТУАЛЕТ

USEFUL PHRASES
These phrases are given phonetically.

hello - **zdrastvui**tye; hi - pree'**vyet**
good morning - **dobray oot**ra
good evening - **dobry vech**er
Madam - Gospa**zha** (officals only)
Mister - Gospa**deen** (officials only)
I - ya; you - tee/vwee, she - ana, we - mwee; they - anee
yes - da; no - nyet
OK - khora**show**, **lad**na
How's it going? - kak dye**la**
please - pa**zhal**sta
thanks - spa**si**ba
thanks very much - bol**shya** spasiba
you're welcome - **nay**, za schto
sorry - prost**it**ye
Do you speak English - Vwee gavar**it**ye pa-**An**gleesky
I don't understand (Russian) - Ya ne poney**mai**yoo (pa-**Roo**ssky)
Speak more slowly, please - pa-**med**dlinye, pazhalsta.

Getting around
Where is? - Gdye na**khod**itsa?
ticket - bil**yet**
subway - met**ro**
bus - av**to**bus
trolleybus - trol**yey**bus
tram - tram**vai**
(bus) stop - asta**nov**ka (avtobusa)
station - **stant**seeya (metro, bus),
vak**zal**le (main train stations)
How can I get to...? - Kak ya ma**gu** dobrat**sya** doe...?
When is... leaving? - Kag**da**... otpravl**ie**yatsa
post office - **poech**ta
left - na-**lay**va
right - na-**pra**va
straight ahead - **pri**yama
opposite - na-**pro**tyev

Sightseeing
museum - mu**zay**
exhibition - vi**stav**ka
church - **tser**kov
monastery - monas**teer**

Accommodation
room for one/two persons - **kom**nata na ad**na**vo chela**ve**ka/na dvoikh chela**vek**
full - nyet myest
bed - kra**vat**
double bed - dvu**spal**naya kra**vat**
single bed - adna**spal**naya kra**vat**

with bath/shower - s**van**ny/s**dush**em
elevator - lift
toilet - **toy**let

Shopping
Have you got...? - U vas yest...?
How much does it cost? - **Skol**ka **ay**ta **stoy**it?
open - ot**kree**ta
closed - za**kree**ta

Eating out
waiter - afit**sant**
waitress - afit**san**ka
Please can we have the bill? - Schot, pa**zhal**sta?
bottled water - mineralnaya va**da**
salt - sol
pepper - **per**ets

Numbers
0 - nul	1 - a**deen**
2 - dva	3 - tree
4 - ch**teery**	5 - pyat
6 - schest	7 - syem
8 - vo**syem**	9 - **dye**vat
10 - **dye**sat	
11 - a**deen**adtsat	
12 - dve**nadt**sat	
13 - tri**nadt**sat	
14 - che**teer**nadtsat	
15 - pit**nadt**sat	
16 - schesh**nadt**sat	
17 - sim**nadt**sat	
18 - vosyem**nadt**sat	
19 - divit**nadt**sat	
20 - dva**adt**sat	
21 - dva**adt**sat a**deen**	
22 - dva**adt**sat dva	
30 - **treedt**sat	
40 - **sor**uck	
50 - pit**des**at	
60 - schest**des**yat	
70 - **syem**desat	
80 - **vos**yemdesat	
90 - **div**vynosta	
100 - sto	
1,000 - **tee**secha	
1,000,000 - mill**yon**	
1,000,000,000 - mill**vard**	

Days, months, seasons
Sunday - voskre**sen**ye
Monday - ponede**l**nik
Tuesday - vtornik
Wednesday - sreda
Thursday - chit**veerk**
Friday - **pyat**nitsa
Saturday - subbota
January - Yanvar
February - Fev**ral**
March - Mart
April - Aprel
May - My
June - **Iyune**
July - **Iyul**
August - **Av**gust
September - Sent**yabr**
October - Oktyabr
November - Noiyabr
December - Dekabr

Further Reading

Literature

Akhmatova, Anna
The Poem without a Hero
An unsurpassed poetic record of the suffering of Russians during Stalin's reign.

Blok, Alexander
Verses about the Beautiful Lady; The Scythians; The Twelve
Searing, often melancholic symbolist poetry.

Bulgakov, Mikhail
The Master and Margarita
One of the best-known, best-loved modern Russian novels, in which the devil arrives in Moscow and sets himself up in a downtown apartment.

Brodsky, Joseph
Less Than One
Brodsky's unsurpassed collection of essays.

Chekhov, Anton
Short stories
Though best known for his plays, Chekhov wrote mountains of uproarious short stories satirising Russia's social stereotypes.

Dombrovsky, Yury
The Faculty of Useless Knowledge
A neglected masterpiece of Russian literature, centring around the theft of archaeological gold in Kazakhstan.

Dostoyevsky, Fyodor
Crime and Punishment
One of the great landmarks of world literature and culture, the story of a squirmy neurotic who murders an old woman in an effort to achieve existential greatness.

Dostoyevsky, Fyodor
The Idiot
Psychotic masterpiece about an epileptic *idiot savant*.

Gogol, Nikolai
Dead Souls
A conman buys up the documents of dead serfs to transform himself, on paper, into a rich aristocrat. Pitch-black comedy.

Pasternak, Boris
Doctor Zhivago
Pasternak's panorama of Russian life set at the time of the 1917 Revolution.

Pelevin, Victor
Chapayev and the Void
Russia's new literary wünderkind shines a new light on the great Soviet civil war hero.

Pushkin, Alexander
The Queen of Spades
A hapless, lovelorn gambler tries to extract a winning formula from an old countess.

Solzhenitsyn, Alexander
One Day in the Life of Ivan Denisovich
Grim portrait of survival in a Stalinist camp.

Tolstoy, Leo
War and Peace
An epic as wide, long and expansive as Russia itself that centres around Napoleon's invasion of 1812.

Popular fiction

Cruz Smith, Martin
Gorky Park
Popular but involving detective novel set in Cold War Moscow.

Forsyth, Frederick
Icon
A megalomaniac military figure (not unlike ex-General Alexander Lebed) takes over Russia with dire, page-flipping consequences.

Harris, Robert
Archangel
A compulsive what-if thriller predicated on the events surrounding Stalin's death.

Womack, Jack
Let's Put the Future Behind Us
Supremely trashy thriller about gangland Moscow.

Yureseyev, Benedict
Moscow Stations
A stupendous work about heavy drinking and public transport in the 1970s.

Philosophy

Bakhtin, Mikhail
The Problem of Dostoyevsky's Poetics; The Creative Art of François Rabelais
The superstar of Russian philosophy puts forward his theories of 'carnival' and the 'grotesque body'.

History & biography

Figes, Orlando
A People's Tragedy – The Russian Revolution 1891-1924
Hugely detailed, sometimes tedious.

Gall, Carlotta, and de Waal, Thomas
A Small Victorious War
Terrific chronicle of Yeltsin's Chechen misadventure.

Hosking, Geoffrey
Russia: People and Empire 1552-1917
Traces Russia's turbulent history back to the conflict between nationhood and empire.

Pipes, Richard
The Russian Revolution 1899-1919
The definitive work on the subject.

Radzinsky, Edvard
Stalin
Chatty biography of a tyrant that draws on new archive material.

Reed, John
Ten Days That Shook the World
A classic analysis of the 1917 Revolution. The book of *Reds*.

Service, Robert
A History of Twentieth-Century Russia
Sometimes simplistic but informative.

Volkov, Solomon
St Petersburg – A Cultural History
Brilliant anecdotal history covering every aspect of the city's culture.

Memoir/travel

Bennett, Vanora
Crying Wolf
Mostly about Chechnya but a good take on life in Russia in the early '90s.

Copetas, Craig
Bear Hunting With the Politburo
He wrote the book about doing business in Russia

Montaigne, Fenn
Hooked
One man travels around Russia fly-fishing and finding out what makes contemporary Russians tick.

Nabokov, Vladimir
Speak, Memory
One of the best memoirs ever written, much of it set in St Petersburg.

Remnick, David
Lenin's Tomb
The seminal work of New Russian journalese, which barely a decade on seems dated.

Young, James
Moscow Mule
In which ex-Velvet Underground pianist Young explores 1990s Moscow from the bottom up.

Art & architecture

Berton, Kathleen
Moscow: An Architectural History
A bright, anecdotal survey.

Brumfield, William Craft
A History of Russian Architecture
Authoritative and inclusive, if dry.

Gray, Camilla
The Russian Experiment in Art, 1863-1922
A concise slice of Russian art history, dealing with its most fruitful period.

Index

Advertisers' Index

Street Index

To maps pages 277-289.

Streets are ordered according to their name, with the definer – such as street (ulitsa) or avenue (prospekt) – following. If there is no comma (eg Bogoslavsky Per), the word order is as given; if there is a comma (eg Balchug, Ul), the definer in fact precedes the street name – in this case, Ulitsa Balchug.

Many Russian street names also have a descriptive element, such as Maly/Malaya (small) and Bolshoi/Bolshaya (big), which varies depending on the grammatical context. Such streets have been listed alphabetically even if the first word is the adjective rather than the street name. Thus Bolshoi Levshinsky Pereulok is listed under B and Maly Levshinsky Pereulok under M. We have abbreviated road definers as follows.

Most (bridge) · Most
Ulitsa (street) · Ul
Ploshchad (square) · Pl
Pereulok (lane) · Per
Proyezd (passage) · Pr
Prospekt (avenue) · Prosp
Bulvar (boulevard) · Bul
Naberezhnaya (embankment) · Nab

Moscow

Akademika Sakharova, Prosp · P279 E1/2/F1
Arbat, Ul · P280 A4/B4
Arbatsky Per · P277 B3
Arbatskaya Pl · see Pl Arbatskiye Vorota
Arbatskiye Vorota, Ploshchad (Arbatskaya Ploshchad) · P280 B4
Aristarkhovsky Per · P282 F4
Arkhangelsky Per · P279 E2
Armyansky Per · P279 E2/3
Ashcheulov Per · P278 D2
1 Babyegorodsky Per · P281 C5/6
Bakhrushina, Ul · P281 D6, P282 E6
Balchug, Ul · P281 D4
Barashevsky Per · P279 E3/F3
Barrikadnaya Ul · P277 A2/3
1 Basmanny Per · P279 F1
Basmanny Per · P279 F1
Basmanny Tupik · P279 F2
Bernikovskaya Nab · P282 E4/F4
Bersenevskaya Nab · P281 C4/5
Blagoveshchensky Per · P277 B2
Bogoslavsky Per · P277 B2
Bogoyavlensky Per · P278 D3
Bolotnaya Nab · P281 C4/5
Bolshaya Dromnaya Ul · P277 B2
Bolshaya Dmitrovka, Per · P278 C2/3
Bolshaya Gruzinskaya Ul · P277 A1/2
Bolshaya Kommunisticheskaya Ul · P282 F5
Bolshaya Lubyanka, Ul · P278 D2
Bolshaya Molchanovka, Ul · P277 A3/B3
Bolshaya Nikitskaya Ul · P277 B3
Bolshaya Ordynka, Ul · P281 D5
Bolshaya Polyanka, Ul · P281 C5/6
Bolshaya Sadovaya Ul · P277 A1/B1/2
Bolshaya Tatarskaya Ul · P281 D5
Bolshaya Yakimanka, Ul · P281 C5/6
Bolshiye Kamenshchiki, Ul · P282 F5/6

Bolshaya Dmitrovka, Ulitsa P278 C2
Bolshoi Afanasyevsky Per · P280 B4
Bolshoi Cherkassky Per · P278 D3
Bolshoi Devyatinsky Per · P277 A3
Bolshoi Drovyanoi Per · P282 F4
Bolshoi Fakelny Per · P282 F5
Bolshoi Golovin Per · P278 D1
Bolshoi Kamenny Most P281 C4
Bolshoi Karetny Per · P278 C1
Bolshoi Kazenny Per · P279 F3
Bolshoi Kharitonyevsky Per · P279 E2/F2
Bolshoi Kiselny Per · P278 D2
Bolshoi Kislovsky Per · P277 B3, P278 C3
Bolshoi Kozikhinsky Per · P277 B2
Bolshoi Kozlovsky Per · P279 E2
Bolshoi Krasnokholmsky Most P282 E6
Bolshoi Levshinsky Per · P280 A5
Bolshoi Moskvoretsky Most P281 D4
Bolshoi Ovchinnikovsky Per · P281 D5
Bolshoi Patriarshy Per · P277 B2
Bolshoi Poluyaroslavsky Per · P282 F4
Bolshoi Sergiyevsky Per · P278 D1
Bolshoi Spasoglinishchevsky Per · P278 D3, P279 E3
Bolshaya Spasskaya Ul · P279 E1
Bolshoi Sukharevsky Per · P278 D1
Bolshoi Tatarsky Per · P281 D6, P282 E6
Bolshoi Tishinsky Per · P277 A1
Bolshoi Tolmachevsky Pereulok · P281 C6-D6
Bolshoi Ustinsky Most P282 E4
Bolshoi Vatin Per · P282 E4
Bolshoi Vlasyevsky Pereulok · P280 A4
Bolshoi Zlatoustinsky Per · P278 D3
Bolshoi Znamesky Per · P280 B4
Borisoglebovsky Per · P277 A2
Boyarsky Per · P279 E2/F2
1 Brestskaya Ul · P277 A1/B1
2 Brestskaya Ul · P277 A1/B1
Bryusov Per · P277 B3, P278 C3
Burdenko, Ul · P280 A5
Butikovsky Per · P280 B5
Chaplygina, Ul · P279 E2
Chayanova, Ul · P277 B1
Chernigovsky Pereulok · P281 D4/D5
Chistoprudny Bul · P279 E2
Chisty Per · P280 A5/B5
Chugunny Most P281 D4
Dayev Per · P279 E1
Degtyarny Per · P277 B2
Delegatskaya Ul · P278 C1
Denezhny Per · P280 A4
Devichyego Polya, Pr · P280 A5
Dinamovskaya Ul · P282 F6
Dmitrovsky Per · P278 C2
Dokuchayev Per · P279 E1
Dolgorukovskaya Ul · P277 B2
Durasovsky Per · P279 F3
Elektrichesky Per · P277 A1
Fadeyeva, Ul · P277 B2
Filippovsky Per · P280 B4
Frunzenskaya Nab · P280 A6/B6
Furkasovsky Per · P278 D1
Furmanny Per · P279 E2/F2
Gagarinsky Per · P280 A4/B4
Gasheka Yaroslava, Ul · P277 A1/B1
Gazetny Per · P278 C3
Georgiyevsky Per · P278 C3
Gilyarovskogo, Ul · P278 D1
Glinishchevsky Per · P278 C2
Gogolevsky Bul · P280 B4
3 Golutvinsky Per · P281 C5
Goncharnaya Nab · P282 E5
Goncharnaya Ul · P282 E4/5
1 Goncharny Per · P282 E5/F5
Goncharny Pr · P282 E5/F5
Granatny Per · P277 A2/B3
Gruzinsky Per · P277 A1
Gruzinsky Val, Ul · P277 A1

Gusyatnikov Per · P279 E2
Ilyinka, Ul · P278 D3
Internatsionalnaya Ul · P282 E4
Ipatyevsky Per · P278 D3
Kadashevskaya Nab · P281 C5/D4
1 Kadashevsky Per · P281 D6
Kalanchevskaya Ul · P279 F1
Kaloshin Per · P280 B4
Kamergersky Per · P278 C2
Karetny Ryad, Ul · P278 C1
Kazakova, Ul · P279 F2
1 Kazachy Per · P281 C6/D6
Khilkov Per · P280 B5
Khlebny Per · P277 B3
Khokhlovsky Per · P279 E3
Khrustalny Per · P278 D3
1 Khvostov Per · P281 C6
Kitaigorodsky Pr P281 D4
Klimashkina, Ul · P277 A1
Klimentovsky Per · P281 D6
1 Kolobovsky Per · P278 C1
2 Kolobovsky Per · P278 C1
Kolokolnikov Per · P278 D2
Kolpachny Per · P279 E3
Kolymazhny Per · P280 B4
Kompozitorskaya Ul · P280 A4
Komsomolskaya Pl · P279 F1
Komsomolsky Prosp · P280 A6/B6
Konyushkovskaya Ul · P277 A2/3
1 Koptelsky Per · P279 E1
Korobeinikov Per · P280 B5
Korovy Val, Ulitsa · P281 C6
Kosmodamianskaya Nab · P282 E5
Kostomarovskaya Nab · P282 F4
Kostyansky Per · P279 E1/2
1 Kotelnichesky Per · P282 E4
3 Kotelnichesky Per · P282 E4/5
Kotelnicheskaya Nab · P282 E4/5
Kozhevnicheskaya Ul · P282 E6
Kozitsky Per · P278 C2
Krupivensky Per · P277 A2
Krasina, Per · P277 A1
Krasina, Ul · P277 A1/2
Krasnaya Pl (Red Square) · P278 D3
Krasnokholmskaya Nab · P282 E6/F6
Krasnoproletarskaya Ul · P278 C1
Krasnoprudnaya Ul · P279 F1
Krasnye Vorota, Pl · P279 F1
Kremlevskaya Nab · P281 C4/D4
Krivoarbatsky Per · P280 A4
Krivokolenny Per · P278 D1, P279 E2
Kropotkinsky Per · P280 A5/B5
3 Krutitsky Per · P282 F6
Krylenko, Ul · P280 B5
Krymskaya Nab · P280 B5/6
Krymsky Most P280 B6
Krymsky Val, Ul · P280 B6, P281 C6
Kursovoi Per · P280 B5
Kuznetsky Most, Ul · P278 C2/D2
Lavrov Per · P282 F6
Lavrushinsky Per · P281 C5
Lenivka, Ul · P281 C4
Leontyevsky Per · P277 B2/3, P278 C2
Likhov Per · P278 C1
Lubyanskaya Pl · P278 D3
Lubyansky Prosp · P278 D3
Lukov Per · P278 D1
Lva Tolstogo, Ul · P280 A5/6
Lyalin Per · P279 F3
Malaya Bronnaya Ul · P277 B2/3
Malaya Dmitrovka, Ul · P278 B1, P278 C1/2
Malaya Kommunisticheskaya Ul · P282 F4/5
Malaya Lubyanka, Ul · P278 D2
Malaya Molchanovka, Ul · P277 B3
Malaya Nikitskaya Ul · P277 A2/3/B3
Malaya Ordynka, Ul · P281 D5/6
Malaya Polyanka, Ul · P281 C5/6
Maliye Kamenshchiki, Ul · P282 F5/6

Moscow (МОСКВА)

St Petersburg

St Petersburg (САНКТ ПЕТЕРБУРГ)

Maps

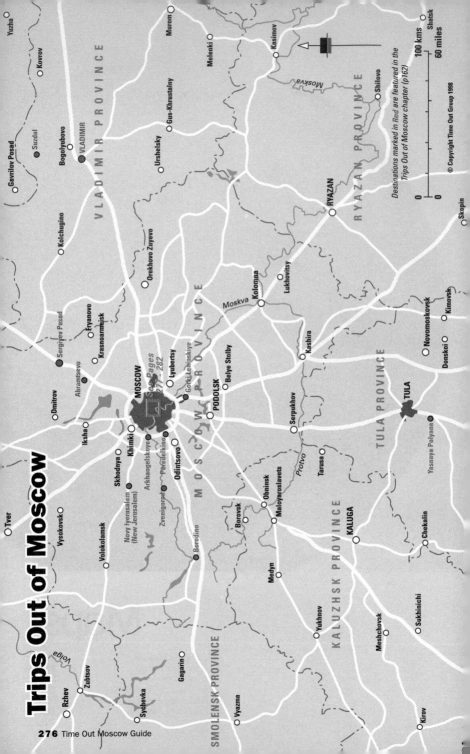

Trips out of Moscow

Destinations marked in Red are featured in the
Trips Out of Moscow chapter (p162)

100 kms
60 miles

VLADIMIR PROVINCE

RYAZAN PROVINCE

MOSCOW PROVINCE

TULA PROVINCE

KALUZHSK PROVINCE

SMOLENSK PROVINCE

Yuzha
Kovrov
Murom
Shatsk
Kasimov
Shilovo
Moskva
Suzdal
Bogolyubovo
VLADIMIR
Melenki
Gavrilov Posad
Gus-Khrustalny
Urshelsky
Skopin
RYAZAN
Kolchugino
Orekhovo Zuyevo
Sergiyev Posad
Fryanovo
Krasnoarmejsk
Kolomna
Lukhovitsy
Novomoskovsk
Kimovsk
Abramtsevo
Lyubertsy
Gorki Leninskiye
See pages
277 282
Kashira
Donskoi
Dmitrov
MOSCOW
Belye Stolby
Iksha
Khimki
PODOLSK
Serpukhov
TULA
Skhodnya
Arkhangelskoye
Peredelkino
Odintsovo
Protvo
Tarusa
Yasnaya Polyana
Tver
Vysokovsk
Novy Iyerusalem
(New Jerusalem)
Zvenigorod
Obninsk
Maloyaroslavets
Volokolamsk
Borovsk
KALUGA
Chekalin
Borodino
Medyn
Sukhinichi
Meshchovsk
Yukhnov
Volga
Rzhev
Zubtsov
Gagarin
Kirov
Sychevka
Vyazma

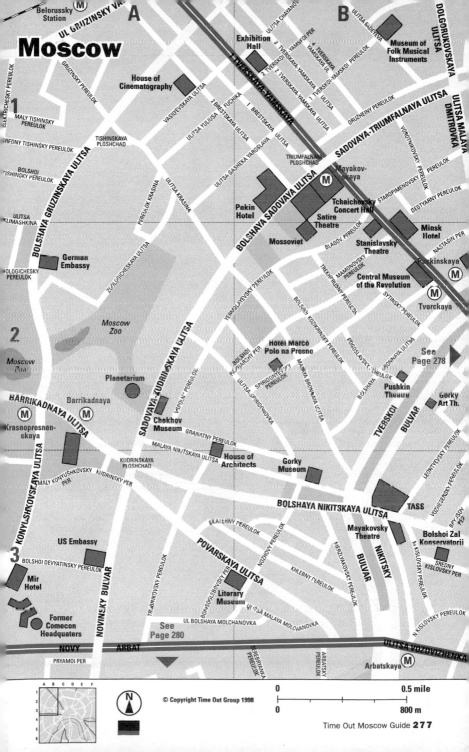

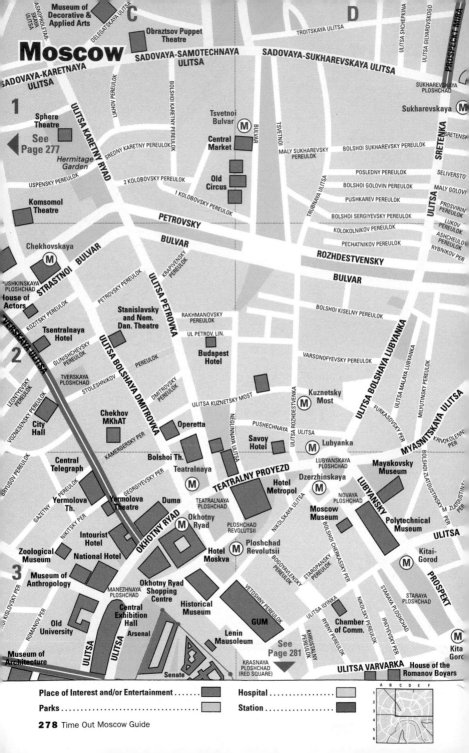

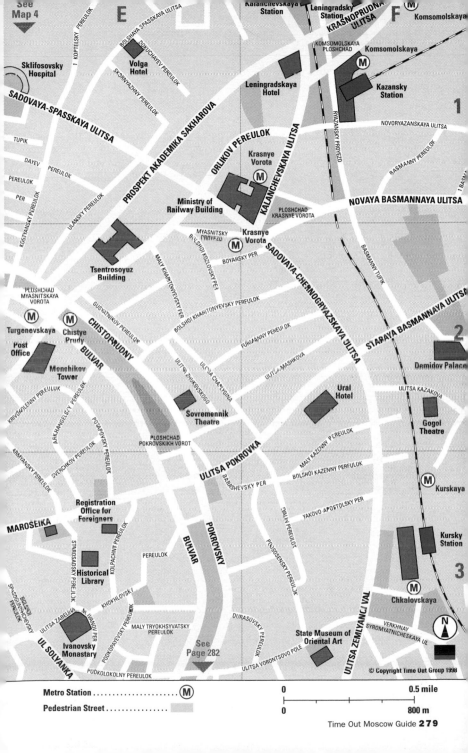

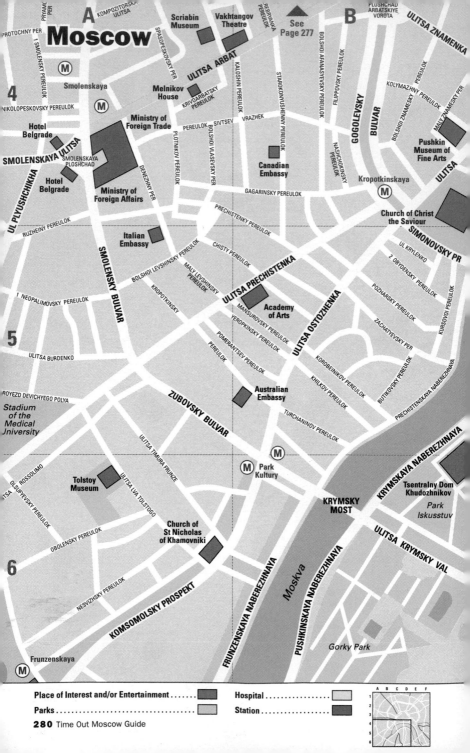

Moscow

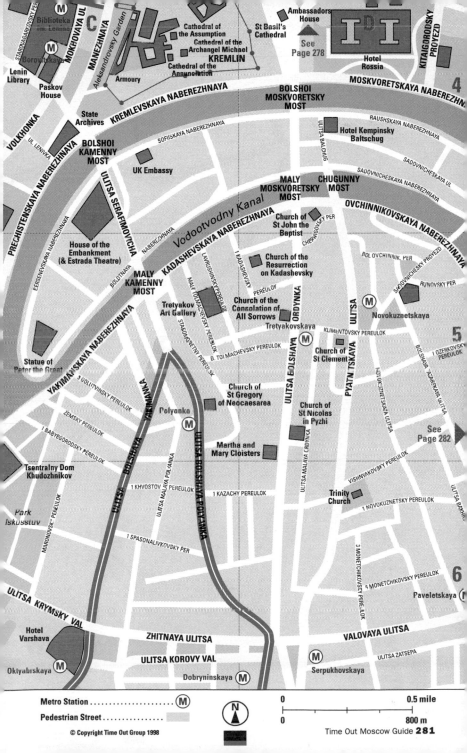

STARO AGARINSKY PER

B Biblioteka
im. Lenina

MOKHOVAYA UL

Borovitskaya

Lenin
Library

Paskov
House

VOLKHONKA

UL LENIVKA

State
Archives

BOLSHOI
KAMENNY
MOST

UK Embassy

ULITSA SERAFIMOVICHA

House of the
Embankment
(& Estrada Theatre)

MALY
KAMENNY
MOST

Statue of
Peter the Great

YAKIMANSKAYA NABEREZHNAYA

Tsentralny Dom
Khudozhnikov

Park
Iskusstv

Hotel
Varshava

Oktyabrskaya

ULITSA KRYMSKY VAL

C

MANEZHNAYA

Aleksandrovsky Garden

Armoury

Cathedral of
the Assumption

Cathedral of the
Archangel Michael
KREMLIN

Cathedral of the
Annunciation

St Basil's
Cathedral

Ambassadors
House

See
Page 278

Hotel
Rossia

KITAIGORODSKY PROYEZD

4

MOSKVORETSKAYA NABEREZHN

BOLSHOI
MOSKVORETSKY
MOST

KREMLEVSKAYA NABEREZHNAYA

SOFIISKAYA NABEREZHNAYA

PRECHISTENSKAYA NABEREZHNAYA

YEFIMOVSKAYA NABEREZHNAYA

NABEREZHNAYA

BOLOTNAYA

RAUSHSKAYA NABEREZHNAYA

ULITSA BALCHUG

Hotel Kempinsky
Baltschug

SADOVNICHESKAYA UL

MALY
MOSKVORETSKY
MOST

CHUGUNNY
MOST

SADOVNICHESKAYA NABEREZHNAYA

OVCHINNIKOVSKAYA NABEREZHNAYA

Vodootvodny Kanal

KADASHEVSKAYA NABEREZHNAYA

Church of
St John the
Baptist

CHERNIGOVSKY PER

Church of the
Resurrection
on Kadashevsky

1 KADASHEVSKY

PEREULOK

BOL OVCHINNIK. PER

SADOVNICHESKY PROYEZD

RUNOVSKY PER

LAVRUSHINSKY PEREULOK

MALY TOLMACHEVSKY PEREULOK

Tretyakov
Art Gallery

STAROMONETNY PEREULOK

Church of the
Consolation of
All Sorrows

Tretyakovskaya

B. TOLMACHEVSKY PEREULOK

ULITSA BOLSHAYA ORDYNKA

KLIMENTOVSKY PEREULOK

Church of
St Clement

PYATNITSKAYA ULITSA

Novokuznetskaya

NOVOKUZNETSKAYA ULITSA

BOLSHAYA TATARSKAYA ULITSA

1 OZERKOVSKY
PEREULOK

5

3 GOLUTVINSKY PEREULOK

ZEMSKY PEREULOK

1 BABYEGORODSKY PEREULOK

ULITSA BOLSHAYA POLYANKA

ULITSA BOLSHAYA POLYANKA

Polyanka

ULITSA MALAYA POLYANKA

Church of
St Gregory
of Neocaesarea

Martha and
Mary Cloisters

Church of
St Nicolas
in Pyzhi

ULITSA MALAYA ORDYNKA

See
Page 282

MARONINSKY PEREULOK

1 KHVOSTOV PEREULOK

1 KAZACHY PEREULOK

VISHNYAKOVSKY PEREULOK

Trinity
Church

1 NOVOKUZNETSKY PEREULOK

ULITSA BAKHR

1 SPASONALIVKOVSKY PER

3 MONETCHIKOVSKY PEREULOK

5 MONETCHIKOVSKY PEREULOK

Paveletskaya

6

ZHITNAYA ULITSA

ULITSA KOROVY VAL

Dobryninskaya

VALOVAYA ULITSA

Serpukhovskaya

ULITSA ZATSEPA

Metro Station . . . . M

Pedestrian Street . . . .

© Copyright Time Out Group 1998

N

0   0.5 mile

0   800 m

Time Out Moscow Guide **281**

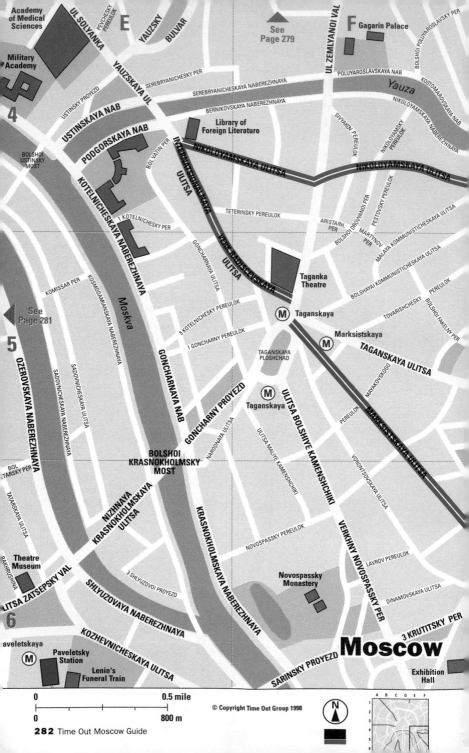

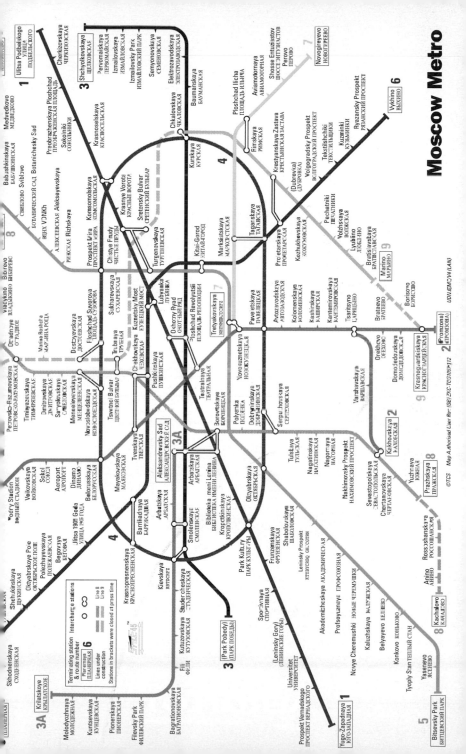

Moscow Metro

Welcome to Russia!

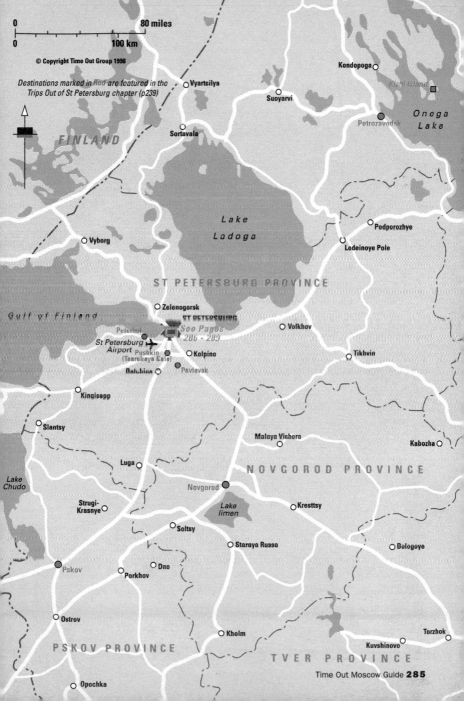

Trips Out of St Petersburg

Destinations marked in *Red* are featured in the
Trips Out of St Petersburg chapter (p239)

0
80 miles

0
100 km

FINLAND

Vyartsilya

Kondopoga

Kizhi Island

Suoyarvi

Petrozavodsk

Sortavala

O n e g a
Lake

Vyborg

Lake
Ladoga

Podporozhye

Lodeinoye Pole

ST PETERSBURG PROVINCE

Gulf of Finland

Zelenogorsk

ST PETERSBURG
*See Pages
286 - 289*

Volkhov

Peterhof

St Petersburg
Airport

Pushkin
(Tsarskoye Selo)

Kolpino

Tikhvin

Gatchina

Pavlovsk

Kingisepp

Slantsy

Malaya Vichera

Kabozha

Luga

N O V G O R O D   P R O V I N C E

Lake
Chudo

Novgorod

Strugi-
Krasnye

Lake
Ilmen

Kresttsy

Soltsy

Staraya Russa

Bologoye

Pskov

Dno

Porkhov

Torzhok

Ostrov

Kholm

Kuvshinovo

P S K O V   P R O V I N C E

T V E R   P R O V I N C E

Opochka

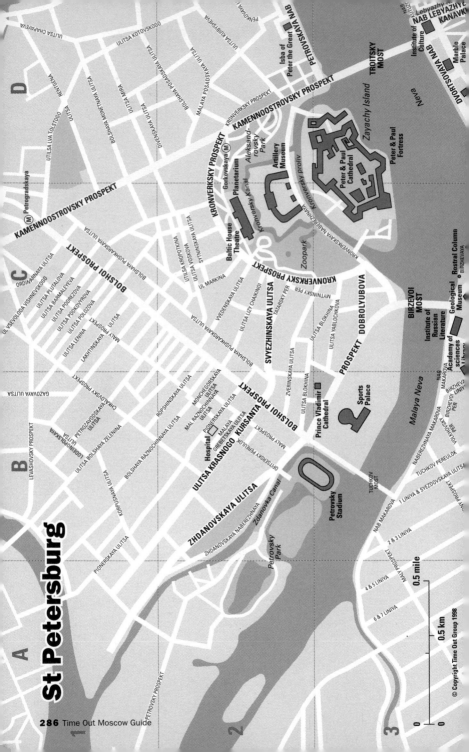

St Petersburg

Peter & Paul Fortress

Peter & Paul Cathedral

Zayachy Island

Artillery Museum

Aleksandrovsky Park

Planetarium

Gorkovskaya Ⓜ

Baltic House Theatre

Zoopark

KRONVERKSKY PROSPEKT

KAMENNOOSTROVSKY PROSPEKT

Petrogradskaya Ⓜ

KAMENNOOSTROVSKY PROSPEKT

BOLSHOI PROSPEKT

SVYEZHINSKAYA ULITSA

PROSPEKT DOBROLYUBOVA

Sports Palace

Prince Vladimir Cathedral

Institute of Russian Literature

Academy of Sciences

Geological Museum

Rostral Column

BIRZEVOI MOST

Institute of Culture

Marble Palace

DVORTSOVAYA NAB

TROITSKY MOST

Isba of Peter the Great

PETROVSKAYA NAB

NAB LEBYAZHY

KANAVK

Neva

Malaya Neva

Petrovsky Stadium

Petrovsky Park

ULITSA KRASNOGO KURSANTA

ZHDANOVSKAYA ULITSA

BOLSHOI PROSPEKT

Hospital

Zdarovka Canal

© Copyright Time Out Group 1998

0.5 km

0.5 mile

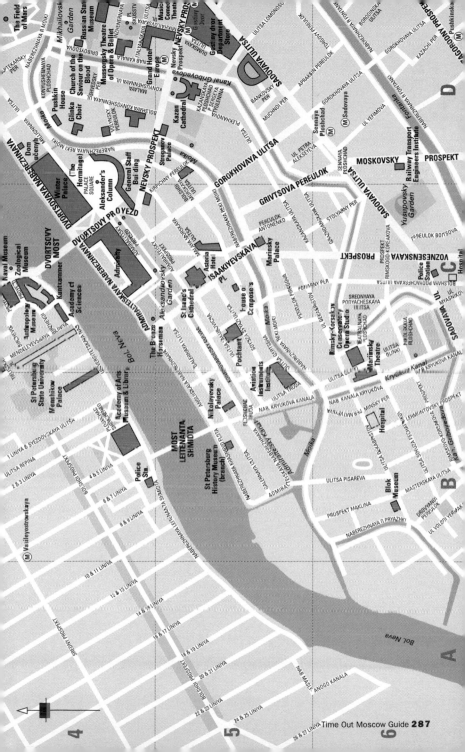

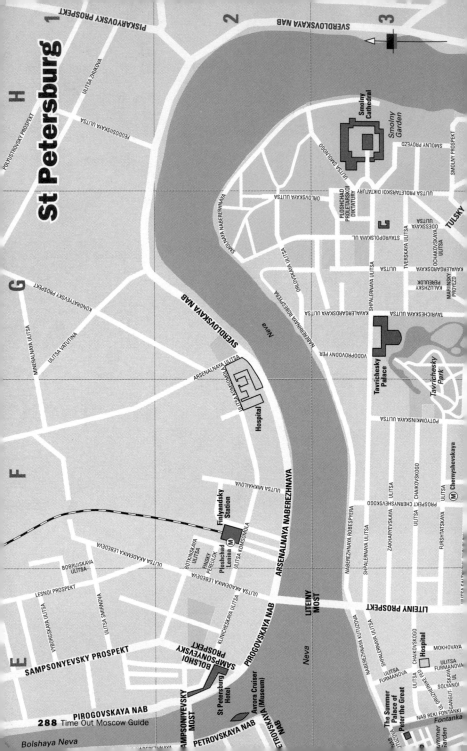

St Petersburg

St Petersburg Metro

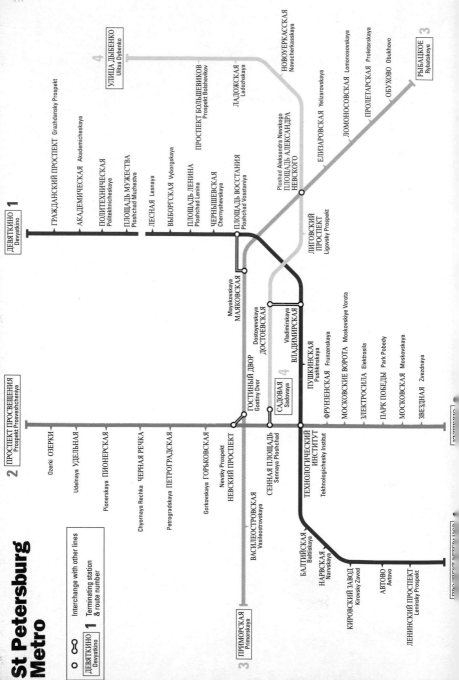